GW01325896

AT THE HEART OF THE REAL

AT THE HEART
OF THE REAL

PHILOSOPHICAL ESSAYS IN
HONOUR OF THE MOST REVEREND
DESMOND CONNELL
ARCHBISHOP OF DUBLIN

edited by

FRAN O'ROURKE

IRISH ACADEMIC PRESS

This book was typeset by
Seton Music Graphics Ltd, Bantry,
for Irish Academic Press Ltd,
Kill Lane, Blackrock, Co. Dublin, Ireland.

© Irish Academic Press
and individual contributors 1992

ISBN 0–7165–2464–3

A catalogue record for this book is
available from the British Library.

Frontispiece: photograph by Lafayette Photography Ltd, Dublin

Printed in Great Britain by
Billing & Sons Ltd, Worcester

HAEC AUTEM DILIGENTER COLLECTA
VIRO ILLUSTRISSIMO
LUSTRA TREDECIM NATO
NOVAM VITAM INCIPIENTI
SODALES AMICIQUE
OFFERUNT

ACKNOWLEDGEMENTS

This volume is published with generous financial assistance from

Church and General Insurance plc
The Faculty of Arts, University College Dublin
The National University of Ireland

Contents

UNDERSTANDING OF THE PHYSICAL WORLD
DERMOT MORAN
University College Dublin

———————— *St Thomas Aquinas* ————————

———————— *Philosophy of Religion* ————————

Preface

The vocabulary of the philosophical community has been enriched by a variety of words borrowed from the German language. One thinks readily, for example, of *Weltanschauung, Lebenswelt, Zeitgeist* or, of recent currency, the more brooding term *Angst*. Of happier association is the joyous term describing the volume present to hand: *Festschrift* literally means 'festive writing'—in fact a garland of writings. It is a celebratory and collective gift which befits a circle of philosophers who wish to honour a colleague in a special way. With the present volume the authors honour in a festive manner the Most Reverend Desmond Connell, Archbishop of Dublin. They express their admiration and affection for a distinguished friend—former teacher, colleague, indeed in two cases a former student.

The significance of the title will not be lost on anyone even slightly familiar with the philosophical interests of the former Professor of Metaphysics at University College Dublin. The essays published here, which deal with a broad diversity of themes, are concerned with central and fundamental aspects of the real and can be easily situated within the treasured tradition of the *philosophia perennis*. They are presented to Archbishop Connell to mark his sixty-fifth birthday. That is the occasion when a philosophy professor is normally rewarded with a life of leisure as the crowning of his labours. Dr Connell's life has taken a different course. We wish him well in his present office and, in due course, *otium cum dignitate*.

The publication of this *Festschrift* has been possible only through the co-operation of many individuals. I express my appreciation firstly to the contributors, for the promptness with which they responded to the invitation and the patience with which they accepted my suggestions and queries. Dr Patrick Masterson, President of University College Dublin, showed personal interest in the project from the beginning and encouraged the enterprise throughout. Professor Dermot Moran, Head of the Department of Philosophy and Editor of *Philosophical Studies*, showed his support in many practical ways. Ms Ann O'Dwyer, Secretary of the Department of Philosophy, was always willing to assist in any way possible. For their valuable advice and assistance, I express my warm thanks to Dr Hans Klieneberger and to Reverend Dr Patrick H. Daly.

I am very pleased to acknowledge with thanks the kindness of Mr John A. Burgess of Lafayette Photography Ltd. for permission to reproduce the portrait, and to Mr Tony Kenny of Keystrokes Ltd. for his expertise in the preparation of the frontispiece. The Dublin City and County Librarian kindly gave permission to reproduce the title page of Michael Moore's rare book *De Existentia Dei* from the Dublin Corporation Gilbert Library. I owe a great debt of gratitude to Michael Adams of Irish Academic Press who with enthusiasm and endless patience saw the volume through, from its genesis to completion. Warm thanks also to the typesetters, who put much care and dedication into its production.

Finally, on behalf of all concerned, I express most sincere and grateful thanks to the sponsors whose generous subventions have made publication of the *Festschrift* not only a possibility but, more importantly, an actual reality.

Fran O'Rourke

Desmond Connell

Desmond Connell was born on 24 March 1926. His father, John Bernard Connell, a native of Moycullen, Co. Galway, was a civil servant who was a member of the Irish delegation to the Ottawa Conference of 1932. He was later appointed by Sean Lemass as Vice-Chairman and subsequently as Managing Director of the fledgling Irish Sugar Company. His mother (née Mary Lacy), who was on duty as a telephonist in the GPO on Easter Monday 1916, was escorted to safety by The O'Rahilly when the building was taken over.

His early education was at St Peter's Primary School, Phibsboro; later he went on to Belvedere preparatory and secondary schools. In September 1943 he entered Holy Cross College, Clonliffe, and began his studies at University College Dublin. In 1946 he graduated in philosophy with First Class Honours and was awarded a post-graduate scholarship. The following year he gained a Master of Arts degree with a thesis on St Augustine and Malebranche, also with First Class Honours. In 1948 he was awarded the Travelling Studentship in Philosophy by the National University of Ireland. Meanwhile he began his study of Theology at Maynooth; among his fellow students were two other future Archbishops of Dublin, Dermot Ryan and Kevin McNamara. He led the BD class in 1950 and was ordained to the priesthood on 19 May 1951. The next two years were spent at the Institut Supérieur de Philosophie in Louvain. Here he continued his research into the writings of Malebranche under the direction of Professor Joseph Dopp. He was awarded the PhD degree *avec la plus grande distinction* for his dissertation 'The Passivity of the Understanding in Malebranche'.

In 1953 he returned to University College Dublin as Assistant Lecturer in the Department of Metaphysics under Monsignor John Horgan. During those years in Earlsfort Terrace, not even the largest theatre could accommodate the classes in philosophy and duplication of lectures was necessary. In 1961 Dr Connell was appointed to the position of College Lecturer. A close colleague from the sixties was Dr Patrick Masterson, a former student of his, later to become Registrar and President of University College Dublin. On the retirement of Professor Horgan, Dr Connell was appointed to the chair of General Metaphysics in 1972. This was shortly after the move of the Arts Faculty to the new campus at Belfield. It was a period of change and development within the University, with many new ideas circulating regarding society and education. Dr Connell contributed much to debate and discussions at this time.

Despite his generous dedication during those years to the onerous teaching and administrative tasks within the Department, Dr Connell also successfully pursued his research interests and in 1967 published his major work *The Vision in God—Malebranche's Scholastic Sources*, which is recognized internationally as an authoritative study on that philosopher. A substantial series of significant articles, produced with consistent regularity during the ensuing years, completed the body of written work for which Professor Connell was awarded the degree of DLitt by the National University of Ireland in 1981.

Professor Connell directed the research of numerous postgraduate students. He took a keen and active interest in the programme of the MPhil in Medieval Studies. He examined for Queen's University Belfast and the University of Leuven. As a member of the Faculty of Arts he served on many of its sub-committees, dealing with such matters as entry standards, the evening degree, and extension of Faculty membership. He was a founder Director of the Central Applications Office. In 1984 he was elected Dean of the Faculty of Philosophy and Sociology, an office which he held until his resignation from the College.

For thirty-five years, Desmond Connell's life was centred in University College Dublin. It could indeed be said that his vocation was also that of academic. Conscientious and hard-working, he was dedicated to his students, his teaching, research and administrative duties. Throughout his long teaching career he lectured on a wide variety of areas: history of philosophy, aesthetics, epistemology, cosmology and philosophy of religion among others. His reflection in latter years crystallized in a major course in Ontology, delivered to second year undergraduates. Students will recall how Professor Connell's lectures in the Philosophy of Being were not merely a detached theoretical exercise, but an occasion for renewed personal reflection upon the wondrous dimensions of everyday experience. Not only the mind but also the heart was brought into play in the quest for what is fundamental in the real. No one will deny the difficulty of this fundamental study—philosophy itself at its most general. Professor Connell's enthusiasm, however, together with his brilliance of insight and clarity of expression, was equal to this challenge; to the student who persevered it was an enlightening and rewarding experience. Professor Connell was perhaps at his most eloquent when he brought the principles of metaphysics to bear on his discussion of the profound mystery of the person. The categories of Aristotle and Aquinas were enlivened by a keen insight nurtured through lived appreciation, and clarified by the positive insights of phenomenology and existentialism. Grounded firmly within the tradition, he was open to the developments of recent thinking and took delight in discussing points of difference with his younger and sometimes more venturesome colleagues.

This appreciation of the individual person was concretely displayed, moreover, in his practical concern for those around him. For thirty-five years he was chaplain to the sisters of the enclosed Carmelite Order in Blackrock. At University College Dublin, his students over the years and both his academic and non-academic colleagues always found him courteous and approachable, unhurried and generous with his time, ready to give advice and encouragement. He was a deeply thoughtful person with a genuine spirituality. He had a very good sense of humour and was delightful in conversation, especially when it turned to his favourite topics, history and music.

Professor Connell's nomination in January 1988 as Archbishop of Dublin and Primate of Ireland came as no surprise to those who knew him. While giving a postgraduate lecture on Leibniz in his room in Belfield, he received a call from the Papal Nuncio; when asked if he would accept the office, he complied in the same spirit of generous dedication and service to which he was accustomed—summed up in the words which he chose as his motto: *secundum verbum tuum.* From the relative privacy of a philosophy professor, he was thrust overnight into the public arena as he became the focus of national and international media attention. The best picture of the Arch-bishop-elect was perhaps given by his students who spoke warmly about their professor, emphasizing his friendliness, openness and generosity; how he was always available to them and knew them by first name.

Dr Connell was consecrated Archbishop of Dublin, the 49th successor to St Laurence O'Toole, on 6 March 1988, at a ceremony attended by some two thousand of the more than one million faithful to whom he had become pastor. Archbishop Connell quickly won the affection of the people of Dublin, to whom, we confidently hope, he will continue to devote himself for many years.

Select Bibliography of Desmond Connell

'La passivité de l'entendement selon Malebranche', *Revue Philosophique de Louvain* 53 (1955), 542–65.

'Gassendi and the Genesis of Malebranche's Philosophy', *Proceedings of the XIIth International Congress of Philosophy* [1958], Vol. 12 (Florence, 1961), 109–13.

'The Thomistic Origin of Malebranche's Ontologism', *Irish Theological Quarterly* 34 (1967), 207–19.

The Vision in God—Malebranche's Scholastic Sources (Louvain-Paris, 1967).

'Professor Dewart and Dogmatic Development I: Consciousness and Truth', *Irish Theological Quarterly* 34 (1967), 309–28.

'Professor Dewart and Dogmatic Development II: Socio-Historical Consciousness', *Irish Theological Quarterly* 35 (1968), 33–57.

'Professor Dewart and Dogmatic Development III: Consciousness and Dogmatic Truth', *Irish Theological Quarterly* 35 (1968), 117–40.

'Father Lonergan and the Idea of Being', *Irish Theological Quarterly* 37 (1970), 118–30.

'Malebranche's Vision in God in *Méditations Chrétiennes*, I–IV', *Irish Theological Quarterly* 38 (1971), 116–29.

'Saint Bonaventure and the Ontologist Tradition', *S. Bonaventura 1274–1974*, II, (Grottaferrata, 1973), 289–308.

'Malebranche et la Scolastique', *Études Philosophiques* (1974), 449–62.

'Substance and Subject', *Philosophical Studies* 26 (n.d.), 7–25.

'St Thomas on Reflection and Judgment', *Irish Theological Quarterly* 45 (1978), 234–47.

'Cureau de la Chambre, Source de Malebranche', *Recherches sur le XVIIème Siècle*, II, (Éditions du C.N.R.S., Paris, 1978), 158–72.

'Substance and the Interiority of Being', *Neue Zeitschrift für Systematische Theologie und Religionsphilosphie* 25 (1983), 68–85.

'Existence and Judgment', *Philosophical Studies* 30 (1984), 127–43.

'L'idea di Teologia in John Henry Newman', *J. H. Newman*, ed. Massimo Marcocchi (Milan, 1991), 103–39.

Tabula Gratulatoria

Bo Almquist
Maria Baghramian
Maura Belton
Bruce Bradley, SJ
Eileen Brennan
Gay Brennan
P.V. Briscoe
Katherine Buggle
Sean Burke, PP
Úna B. Burke
Timothy J. Butler
Andreas Buttimer
Věra Čapková
Professor Patricia Casey
Dr Eoin G. Cassidy
F.F. Centore
Yasuo Chisaka
Dr John E. Chisholm, CSSp
Sean Clancy
Peter J. Clarke
Joe Cogan
Grainne de Verdon Cooney
Professor Art Cosgrove
Stephen Costello
William Cotter
Ann Jo Coughlan
Elizabeth P. Crowe
Professor Denis Crowley
Martin G. Cunningham
Pearse Cusack, OCSO
Cardinal Cahal B. Daly
Donal Daly, SVD
Dr Patrick H. Daly
Ersilia Davidson
Henry Devlin, PP
Thérèse Day
Charlie Doherty
Revd Kevin Doran
Dr Michael A. P. Dore

Bishop Joseph Duffy
Michael Dunne
Ricca Edmondson
Caroline Farey
Bishop Anthony J. Farquhar
Noel J. Fitzpatrick
Bishop Thomas Flynn
Mel Fox
Canon John Fraser
Thomas Gilroy, PP
Ronan Grimshaw, CSSp
M. Denise Harford
Michael G. Harrington
Bishop Michael A. Harty
Bonaventure F. Hayes, OFM
Dr John Hayes
Catherine Henry
Greg Holupchinski
Teresa Iglesias
Erwin Jaumann
Gavan Jennings
Eileen Kane
Sean P. Kealy, CSSp
Dr John J. Kelly
Rose Kelly
John Kennedy
Roddy Kernan
Michael Kirby
Hans Klieneberger
Yvette Kunz-Ramsay
Sean Landers
Dr Dermot Lane
Msgr Míceál Ledwith
A. Lehane, CSSp
Paul Lennon, OCarm
David Leonard
Joseph Long
Patrick Lynch
Tim Lynch

Cardinal Owen McCann
Donal McCarthy, SCA
Eunice McCarthy
Professor Donal McCartney
Ciarán McGlynn
J.I. McGuire
Adrian McKenna
Bishop Francis J. MacKiernan
Brian McLaughlin, CSSp
Msgr James Ardle MacMahon
Ernan McMullin
Jean de Madre
Professor F.X. Martin, OSA
Thomas P. Martin
Terry Meagher
Professor Patrick N. Meenan
Tom Miniter
Collins Montgomery
Maria Morgan
Canon Vincent Morris, DD, PP
Patrick Muldoon, PP
Thomas Murphy
Bishop Donal Murray
Josephine Newman
Próinséas Ní Chatháin
A.J. Nichol
Dr Thomas Norris
The Nugent Family
Gerard O'Brien
Ruari and Kathleen O Brolchain
Professor Breandán Ó Buachalla
Nicholas O'Byrne
Dr Noreen O'Carroll
Loretto O'Connell
Brian O'Connor
Oliver O'Connor
Revd E.F. O'Doherty
D.K. O'Donovan
Sr Jo. O'Donovan
Ann O'Dwyer
An t-Ollamh Pádraig Ó Fiannachta
Paul O'Grady
Dr Brenda O'Hanrahan
Diarmuid M. O'Hegarty
Andy O'Mahony

Bishop Dermot O'Mahony
Seán P. Ó Mathúna
John O'Meara
Clare O'Reilly
Revd Martin O'Shea
Bishop Diarmaid Ó Súilleabháin
Ivo O'Sullivan
Jennifer Petrie
Jean-Michel Picard
James Randles, PP
Dr Geo Rogmans
J.H. Desmond Ryan
Bishop Laurence Ryan
Msgr Gerard Sheehy
Dr Richard Sherry, PP
Anngret Simms
Patricia Spillane
Paula Tarrant
James B. Thomson
Colm Tobin
Dr Tilla Vulhopp
Bishop Eamonn Walsh
Professor Noel Walsh
Conor Ward
Cornelius Williams, OP
Professor Markus Wörner

INSTITUTIONS

Queen's University Belfast
Franciscan Study Centre, Canterbury
Niles College Library, Chicago
Dublin Diocesan Library
Milltown Institute of Theology and
    Philosophy, Dublin
Library, University College Dublin
Royal Irish Academy
Katholieke Universiteit te Leuven
Université Catholique de Louvain
Insitut des Études Augustiniennes, Paris
St Louis University
Library, St Mary's Priory, Tallaght
Library, St Patrick's College, Thurles
Library, St Jerome's College, Waterloo
Library, Pius XII Seminary, Queensland

Two Apologies of the World

Plotinus and Aquinas

GÉRARD VERBEKE

For some, the existence of the world does not pose a problem: it is simply there and that is all; no explanation is needed or is possible. From the earliest ages, however, philosophers have sought to explain why and how the world exists. One such account is that of Plotinus; another is that of Aquinas.

In 245 Plotinus began teaching in Rome: he was forty years of age; prior to that he had studied philosophy for eleven years with Ammonius Saccas at Alexandria. Born and educated at Lycopolis, he came to Alexandria at the age of twenty-eight; after some disappointing contacts with other teachers, he finally discovered the master he was seeking.[1] Plotinus was very eager to learn; in order to get a better knowledge of Indian and Persian wisdom he took part in a military expedition of the emperor Gordian III. This enterprise however had an unexpected outcome: the emperor was killed and the army routed; Plotinus did not return to Egypt, but went to Rome.[2] He thus settled at the centre of the empire and started a school of philosophy. From the viewpoint of higher education in our own time, the master was poorly qualified: he could not rely on any important series of publications; up until then he had not published anything; moreover his attempt to study Indian and Persian philosophy on the ground had failed. In fact he was the disciple of a single master, Ammonius Saccas, a philosopher of his own country.[3]

Despite these obstacles the new philosophical school was quite successful: Plotinus delivered his lectures in Greek and from the beginning he founded

---

1 According to his own testimony Plotinus was rather disappointed by the philosophy teachers he met at Alexandria: when he attended their lectures he was discouraged and saddened. Apparently what he wanted was a philosophy which would be a support for his own life. Thanks to the help of a friend he was able to meet Ammonius: this encounter was decisive, Ammonius was the man he had been looking for (Porphyry, *Vita Plotini*, 3, 6-13).

2 Plotinus first settled at Antioch, where already in the first century AD an important Christian community had developed. After a short stay at Antioch, Plotinus came to Rome (*Vita*, 3, 13-24).

3 During the first ten years of his teaching in Rome, Plotinus did not compose any written work. Together with Origen and Herennius he had promised not to divulge the teaching of Ammonius; yet his two former co-disciples did not hold to their promise, and so Plotinus also came to start lecturing. His message was that of Ammonius: it was like an initiation into a secret religious mystery. After ten years of oral teaching, at the age of fifty-five, Plotinus decided to write down his message (*Vita*, 3, 24-35).

his teaching on the authentic hellenic tradition, mainly on Plato.[4] He had a fair number of students and among them some mature people who fulfilled influential functions in Roman society. In his biography of Plotinus, Porphyry reports that at this time a great number of sectarian Christians who had been trained in ancient philosophy deceived other people with the help of all kinds of writings to which they referred. They wanted to proceed beyond Plato because in their view the latter had never penetrated to the deepest core of intelligible substance; according to them the thought of Plato needed to be completed.[5] Plotinus repeatedly referred to them in his lectures and criticized their opinions: the influence of these doctrines had spread even into the school of Plotinus; some of his students were stubbornly attached to these theories and could possibly contaminate his most faithful followers.[6] At the age of fifty, a very significant date from a Platonic perspective, Plotinus started to write: the first topic he expounds is beauty.[7] The choice of this topic is to be interpreted in the light of Gnostic pessimism as it was propagated in Rome, even among the friends of Plotinus. The master endeavours to show that it is possible, starting from sensible reality, to attain step by step to the highest degree of perfection, not only to the level of true being, but even beyond.[8] According to the author corporeal beauty is an image, a vestige or a shadow of a higher pattern (I 6, 8, 7); this conception is truly Platonic: in the opinion of the Greek master there is between the transcendent Forms and sensible things a relation of resemblance ($\mu\dot{\iota}\mu\eta\sigma\iota\varsigma$), of communion ($\kappa o\iota\nu\omega\nu\dot{\iota}\alpha$) and of participation ($\mu\dot{\epsilon}\theta\epsilon\xi\iota\varsigma$). This relationship is the ground of the ascending movement described by Plotinus: if no similarity or kinship existed between the lower world and the higher degrees of perfection, man could not start from sensible things and grasp immaterial principles. And yet there is quite a distance between the lower and the higher levels: in Plotinus' view it is only possible to contemplate the immaterial world by becoming more or less similar to this immutable reality; contemplation is not only a matter of theoretical understanding, but also of moral behaviour.[9] Anyhow, knowledge requires some similarity between

4 Plotinus' knowledge of Greek was not perfect: he made some mistakes in lectures as well as in his written texts (*Vita*, 13, 1-5; 19, 19-24).
5 *Vita*, 16, 1-9.
6 II 9, 10, 1-14. Plotinus does not understand the attitude of some school members: they profess a quite different doctrine from that of the master and yet wish to remain within the school community.
7 *Vita*, 4, 22.
8 I 6, 9, 40: Goodness is beyond beauty; it is the source and principle of whatever is beautiful. In Plato's view also the Idea of the Good represents the highest level of perfection (see V 5, 13, 31-38).
9 Wanting to lift himself to the contemplation of higher levels of perfection, man ought to become unified (I 6, 9, 17), since the highest principle is totally uncompounded and simple. The eye also should become similar to the object it endeavours to contemplate: only a beautiful soul is able to contemplate beauty (I 6, 9, 29).

the knower and his object, and when higher objects are concerned, a similarity between the point of departure and the reality that is contemplated. Now, to consider the material world as a valuable starting point with a view to contemplating perfect beauty, and even perfect goodness, is quite opposed to Gnostic teaching. In this first writing the author already shows that his views are radically at variance with cosmic pessimism.[10]

Plotinus waited till 263 before formally criticizing the Gnostic doctrines and he explains why.[11] As a matter of fact he himself felt in an awkward position: some members of his school had already been influenced by Gnostic doctrines before they attended his lectures.[12] Amazingly they remained in the school without discarding their former conviction. Plotinus calls them friends and avoids offending them. Yet he is very astonished that, being members of the school and attending his lectures, they still cling to their former opinions; he respects them although they are in his view too self-confident (II 9, 10, 11): he wonders, however, whether they personally agree with the theories they profess or rather endeavour to make their opinions more acceptable (II 9, 10, 5-7). The master does not attempt to persuade them: that seems to be hopeless, since they constantly and recklessly tear to pieces the teaching of Plato (II 9, 10, 12-14). Plotinus wants above all to protect his faithful followers against these erroneous and harmful theories (II 9, 10, 7-11). Obviously he does not intend to examine the various sects and groups of Gnostics, he rather prefers to consider the heart of the matter and to investigate critically what he believes to be the core of this religious trend.[13]

What is the origin of the material world? This question is fundamental with respect to our topic. The answer of the Gnostics may be summarized as

10   The beauty of the sensible world is a starting point for all those who want to attain to the contemplation of true reality. Plotinus is quite conscious of the ambiguous character of sensible beauty: its contemplation may help man to lift himself to the intuition of higher levels of perfection, but if people cling to the material world, they will never reach this superior knowledge. In this sense Plotinus asks us to detach ourselves from sensible reality and to fly to our dear homeland (I 6, 8, 16-27).

11   In the edition of Porphyry, the treatise of Plotinus against the Gnostics has been divided into four separate writings: III 8, V 8, V 5 and II 9. They have been put together by V. Cilento, *Plotino, Paideia antignostica* (Firenze, 1971). They have also been grouped in: *Plotins Schriften*, übersetzt von Richard Harder. Neubearbeitung mit griechischem Lesetext und Anmerkungen fortgeführt von Rudolf Beutler und Willy Theiler, Band III, a. Text und Übersetzung (Hamburg, 1964).

12   II 9, 10, 3-5. Hans Jonas (*Gnosis und spätantiker Geist*, 1934) believes that Plotinus himself actually belongs to the Gnostics; this viewpoint however has been generally rejected (Cf. G. Widengren, 'Les origines du gnosticisme et l'histoire des religions', in: *Le origini dello Gnosticismo* (Leiden, 1967), p. 41.

13   II 9, 10, 14-17. Who are the Gnostics of Plotinus? This question has been asked several times: according to H.-C. Puech and V. Cilento, when Plotinus opposes the Gnostics, he at once criticizes Numenius of Apamea. We know that Plotinus in his lectures used the commentaries of Numenius as a starting point and that he has been accused of plagiarizing this author (*Vita*, Chapters 14 and 17).

follows: the world was not created by God, but by some lower and evil
power; it is not the work of an almighty divine Creator: hence the universe
is basically evil.[14] This theory is carefully analysed by Plotinus: as he fundamentally disagrees with the position of the Gnostics, he concentrates his
attention on their notion of creation.[15] Who is the creator of the world and
what exactly is creation?

In Plotinus' view the material world never came to be and will never pass
away, it is everlasting (II 9, 7, 1–2). The three highest principles or hypostases
are involved in the creation of the cosmos and this making is essentially
contemplation: the world is the result of an everlasting contemplation. Let
us examine more closely what this viewpoint means. Plotinus repeatedly
excludes the possibility of a deliberation leading to the making of the cosmos;
in other words the Creator did not take the decision of producing the material
world after a process of reflection, in which he takes into consideration
various factors connected with a possible choice.[16] In this hypothesis the
world would be the result of a free option on the part of the maker who is
believed to have pondered over the matter. This view is decidedly dismissed
by Plotinus: it would inevitably imply some imperfection in the creative
cause. If the Creator deliberates whether or not he will proceed to the
making of the cosmos, it means that he was in a state of uncertainty and
hesitation.[17] In the course of life man has constantly to face new situations
which may be very complicated and include several aspects which he did
not meet previously: being conscious of the possible consequences of his
behaviour, he will carefully reflect on what he is going to do before taking a
decision. Humans live in a temporal evolution, they are changing all the
time and the future is mostly unpredictable. This condition however could
not be applied to the higher hypostases which are at the origin of the cosmos:
the One is characterized by an immediate self-consciousness without any

14 According to Plotinus the Gnostics maintain that the creation of the world was the result
    of an inclination of the soul toward matter: this propensity represents a kind of
    degradation; hence the cosmos is regarded as an evil production. This view is confirmed
    by the fact that it includes many things that are unpleasant (II 9, 4, 1–6; 22–24).
15 According to V. Cilento the conflict between Plotinus and the Gnostics is one of two
    worlds proceeding from the same Platonic roots: 'E l'urto tra due mondi sorti dalla stessa
    radice platonica; o, forse, addirittura l'urto tra la grecità e l'oriente, cioè tra due tipi di
    Contemplazione, l'una dialettica e viva, l'altra immota e addormentata come i suoi
    templi millenari' (Ibid., p. 17).
16 V 8, 7, 40: The creation of the world is not the conclusion of a kind of practical
    syllogism; the act of creation is prior to any logical consequence or reflection; V 8, 12,
    20–22; II 9, 4, 15; II 9, 8, 20.
17 Dealing with the notion of creation, V. Cilento writes: 'Creazione—in un senso tutto
    proprio, greco e plotiniano, il quale non ha che fare con la creazione cristiana—e
    Contemplazione sono un unico concetto duale; o, se vogliamo, c'è perfetta equazione
    tra θεωρία e ποίησις, mentre non possiamo parlare di equivalenza tra contemplazione e
    azione' (Ibid., p. 127). Action (πρᾶξις) is put on a much lower level, since it is also
    oriented toward contemplation (III 8, 4, 31–32; 6, 1–4).

kind of temporal evolution or any duality. As to the Intellect, it represents an immutable intuition of all perfect forms present in it. Then comes Universal Soul in which Nature is included: this principle stems from the two higher hypostases and is characterized by discursive reasoning, passing from one rational form to another. Including all seminal reasons, Universal Soul never happens to be in a state of uncertainty or ignorance.[18] As far as the highest hypostases are concerned, Plotinus dismisses every kind of a deliberative process, since it would imply imperfection in the creative principle.

Moreover, if the making of the material world is the outcome of a deliberation, it did not always exist; it came to be and will pass away. In this perspective the sensible cosmos is not an everlasting reality, it is not a permanent manifestation of the beauty and perfection of its creative principle.[19] Plotinus could not agree with this view: he deeply wants to be faithful to the ancient hellenic tradition.[20] The making of the World Soul, as it is described in the *Timaeus* of Plato, should not be understood as a temporal beginning, but as an everlasting process: the demiurge produces the cosmos as a permanent image of immutable patterns.[21] As for Aristotle, he formally maintains the material world to be always there: in his opinion it is absurd to claim that movement or time could ever start; such opinion is incoherent since the so called beginning always implies a previous movement and time.[22] According to Epicurus there are many worlds: they come to be and pass away, but this process is always going on. In the Stoic view there is only one world: it begins and comes to an end, but the cyclical development is permanent. Plotinus does not want to drop this valuable ancient tradition. Yet there is a much deeper ground for his philosophical option: creation coincides with contemplation; it is not comparable to some contingent event, something that

18   G. Verbeke, 'Pourquoi "trois" hypostases principales chez Plotin?' in: *Recherches d'Islamologie. Recueil d'articles offert à Georges C. Anawati et Louis Gardet par leurs collègues et amis* (Louvain, 1978), pp. 359-79.

19   In Plotinus' view the intelligible pattern of the world is always there. Those who maintain that whereas the world came to be and will pass away, the pattern is everlasting, are wrong; they seemingly believe that the cosmos was created after a deliberation of the maker (V 8, 12, 20-22).

20   The Gnostics are not faithful to the ancient hellenic culture: their doctrine is full of empty words and of newly invented theories that do not conform to traditional Greek thought (II 9, 6, 5-10). Cf. V. Cilento, Ibid., p. 230: 'Il dogma dell'eterna esistenza del mondo e della sua incorruttibilità è la tesi che, alla fine dell'antico, taglia in modo netto l'ellenismo tenacemente difeso dei neoplatonici e le forme invadenti di religioni escatologiche.'

21   In Plotinus'view it makes no sense to ask why the world was produced: this question may be reduced to wondering why there is a soul and why the demiurge is creating. The question implies that the world began, whereas it always exists; moreover it presupposes the demiurge to have become the cause of his work after some change or modification (II 9, 8, 1-5).

22   G. Verbeke, 'La structure logique de la preuve du Premier Moteur chez Aristote', *Revue philosophique de Louvain* 46 (1948), 137-60.

happens but could also not occur. It constitutes the very heart of reality at all levels. If creation is identical with contemplation, it makes no sense to wonder whether it ever began or will some day end.[23] Contemplation is present everywhere and always, from the highest Principle to the lowest, namely Nature. The One is characterized by an immediate self-contemplation; as to Nature, it produces the sensible world through rational forms operating in matter.[24]

But how could contemplation be creative? Is not contemplation the intuition of an existing reality? In Plotinus' view contemplation is not a merely passive knowledge of a given perfection; it is at once a dynamic act involving willing and love, and in this sense it is able to produce an image of what is contemplated.[25] Let us take the highest principle: it contemplates its own perfection and creates the second hypostasis. The One is beyond being; it represents the supreme degree of simplicity. Yet it is not beyond consciousness and willing, it is act and as such is penetrated by a dynamic energy; willing its own perfection, it creates as it were a new instance of that perfection, not however on the same level, but on a lower one. Thus contemplation is creative because it is permeated by volitional activity.[26] Of course one may object that what is produced is on a lower level than the perfection which is contemplated: in this sense there seems to be a constant degradation of reality. So contemplation seemingly leads to gradually lower degrees of perfection. In Plotinus' view this objection may easily be refuted. If the cosmos were basically evil, the objection would deserve careful consideration but the master is convinced that it is full of beauty and harmony.[27] As we already mentioned, the contemplation of the material world not only allows man to enjoy its beauty, but it gives him the capacity to raise himself to the intuition of the highest perfection.[28] It must be

---

23   III 8, 7, 1-15. According to Plotinus, being coincides with contemplation and contemplation is identical with creation (Cf. V. Cilento, Ibid., p. 140).

24   III 8, 3, 18-20. Nature itself is born from contemplation and what is coming to be is the result of Nature's silent contemplation (III 8, 4, 5: τὸ γενόμενόν ἐστι θέαμα ἐμὸν σιωπησάσης).

25   III 8, 3, 20-23: in Plotinus' view creation (ποίησις) coincides with contemplation. In this context the author makes a clear distinction between ποίησις and πρᾶξις: the latter activity is not identical with contemplation, it intends to achieve something external. A comparison is made with geometricians: they draw their figures according as they contemplate (III 8, 4, 8); in this way contemplation is productive.

26   VI 8, 16, 36-40; VI 8, 16, 22-24; VI 8, 18, 48-50; VI 8, 21, 29-33; VI 8, 13, 5-11; VI 8, 21, 7-16.

27   II 9, 8, 15-16. According to Plotinus the sensible world is the visible and beautiful statue of the intelligible gods. In the intelligible cosmos being and beauty are identical (V 8, 9, 36-37).

28   Living in this sensible world, it is possible to possess wisdom and to behave in conformity with the intelligible patterns (II 9, 8, 43-46). Anyhow the intelligible level could not be the lowest in the structure of reality, since it is permeated by a marvellous power: hence it is necessarily productive (II 9, 8, 24-29).

acknowledged that a great distance separates the perfection of the One and that of material things: yet the latter also are valuable and are not deprived of harmony. How could man ever reach the contemplation of the superior world, if he could not start from the perception of sensible beings? Sensible reality constantly discloses the marvellous perfection of the supreme hypostases.[29]

Yet a new difficulty may be formulated here: are there not many people who cling to the material cosmos and do not go beyond it? Seemingly they live in a world of shadows and do not even realize that they are looking at images. This consideration hardly bothers Plotinus: he does not appreciate the great mass of ordinary people; in his view they are manual workers and they have to provide the means of subsistence for cultivated individuals (II 9, 9, 10-11). In this respect also Plotinus continues an ancient tradition: Plato disqualified trading and Aristotle underestimated manual labour. Nevertheless there has been an important social change thanks to the Stoic teaching on human equality and the repudiation of slavery. Posidonius was concerned with the bad working conditions of slaves in the mines of Spain.[30] The idea of human equality is not present in the work of Plotinus: if the majority of people cling to the material world, this does not worry him, provided that at least a select group of educated people are able to use sensible reality as a starting point for the disclosure of higher perfections. True, contemplation produces lower levels of reality, but these lower beings are not evil; they are an image of something more perfect and they allow man to ascend to the intuition of the supreme principles.[31] During the five years of his stay with Plotinus, Porphyry found his master in ecstasy four times, in a mystical union with the One.

But why is contemplation of higher hypostases a privilege of only a small group of educated individuals? As has already been emphasized, contemplation is not a merely theoretical knowledge, it always requires a kind of similarity between the subject that contemplates and the object. An individual could only transcend the material world and attain to the intuition of a more perfect reality if he has become similar to it: thanks to moral behaviour, he will gradually free himself from the fascination of corporeal beauty and proceed beyond it. Through a persevering process of purification, he will strengthen his true self and make it more and more similar to spiritual reality. Contemplation of the highest principles could only be achieved by moral individuals.[32]

---

29 In Plotinus' view God is present in the cosmos (II 9, 16, 24); the world will never be abandoned by the divine Creator (II 9, 16, 29); all the lower beauties stem from a higher original pattern (II 9, 17, 25-26). Artistic activity also is never a mere imitation of sensible reality, it springs from the contemplation of intelligible exemplars; Phidias created his famous statue of Zeus without looking at a sensible model (V 8, 1, 38-40).

30 *Stoa und Stoiker*, eingeleitet und übertragen von Max Pohlenz, Zürich, 1950, p. 266.

31 If one endeavours to evaluate the world correctly, one should not confine oneself to the consideration of a particular part only, but look at it as a whole (II 9, 9, 74-75).

32 Wishing to contemplate beauty, man has to bring the beautiful into himself and to look at it within himself (V 8, 10, 39-42); it is impossible to contemplate beauty from without: to be in beauty, is to grasp the beautiful within oneself (V 8, 11, 19-21).

At this stage of our analysis we may already conclude that creation is not the result of a deliberative process; it is linked to contemplation, is even identical with it. This intuition however is not merely theoretical or passive, it is penetrated by a volitional dynamism and so it produces an image of what is contemplated.[33] Existing from always the world constantly manifests the perfection of its maker. In this perspective the teaching of the gnostics regarding the origin of the world makes no sense: it would be the result of a moral decline, of a propensity of the soul toward matter. In Plotinus' view one should rather acknowledge that creation was made possible because the soul did not decline toward matter (II 9, 4, 6-7). This reply fully corresponds to the doctrine of Plotinus: how could an inclination to matter produce something? If creation is contemplation, it will be quite the opposite that occurs; contemplating the rational forms, the soul will produce an image of these in the material world and thus even the cosmos will participate in beauty and harmony. Plotinus stresses the fact that Universal Soul should not be put on the same level as individual souls which are often captivated by corporeal beauty. Universal Soul is not in the same condition: it really governs and dominates sensible reality; it is not threatened by decline, nor is it fascinated by corporeal things (II 9, 7, 27-30).

If creation is not the result of a deliberative process, is it a necessary emanation? The answer of Plotinus is certainly positive, although some qualifications are to be introduced. Necessity may be understood as a constraint imposed from without: in this sense the Creator would exert his activity under the compelling pressure of another power. This kind of necessity ought to be excluded: the three supreme hypostases represent the highest level of perfection and could not be dependent upon something else in exercising their activity.[34] On the other hand the emanation of some lower degrees of perfection, for example the material world, is not the result of a blind necessity, an unconscious fatalistic production. Some people wonder why the cosmos is created: in Plotinus' view this question makes no sense; it is like asking why there is Universal Soul (II 9, 8, 1-2). As a matter of fact if Universal Soul exists and includes all rational forms, it will produce the sensible world. If somebody asks why it proceeds to the creation of lower beings, he seemingly supposes creation to be the outcome of a deliberation. Universal Soul necessarily produces the material cosmos: yet this necessity is not blind, it is a conscious making; it is not a *praxis*, but a *poiesis*. In Plotinus' view, *praxis* is an activity of a lower level: in this respect the vocabulary of our author is different from the terminology used by Aristotle. According to

33   In Plotinus' view the creating principle is always more perfect than what is produced (V 8, 1, 30; III 8, 9, 42); the cosmos is a shadow and an image of the Intellect (III 8, 11, 29).

34   VI 8, 20, 12-19; 31-36; VI 8, 21, 29-33. The One represents the highest level of freedom: yet it is not a freedom of choice, which would be an imperfection (VI, 8, 21, 3-7; VI, 8, 7, 36-37).

the latter, *poiesis* is an activity that intends to produce something, whereas *praxis* refers to responsible human conduct in which the good ought to be pursued for its own sake.[35] It has already been explained that in Plotinus' view creation is identical with contemplation, the highest intellectual activity; it has been stressed however that this contemplation is pervaded by a volitional dynamism. But if creation coincides with contemplation, how could this act be called necessary? The answer of Plotinus to this question would be that contemplation, although it is necessary, is at once spontaneous: it corresponds to the very nature of the creative principles.[36] Immediate self-consciousness belongs to the supreme perfection of the first principle: it knows and wills itself in an act that excludes any composition or duality (V 5, 13, 31-38). The second hypostasis constantly contemplates the fullness of all intelligible objects that are not separated from each other; at this level everything is present in everything (V 8, 4, 4-11). As for Universal Soul, it encompasses all rational forms and contemplates them, passing from one *logos* to another. Through Nature, which is not an independent hypostasis but is involved in Universal Soul, the material world is shaped: its beauty and harmony proceed from the forms that are implanted in it and make it conform to intelligible reality.[37]

In the light of all these considerations we may conclude that within the framework of Plotinus' philosophy Gnostic pessimism ought to be categorically dismissed: the maker of the world is not evil, since creation proceeds from the highest and most perfect principles; the world itself could not be evil since it is produced as a result of contemplation, a spontaneous but necessary activity of the creative powers. The world is a shadow, an image of the patterns that are contemplated. Human existence also could not be evil: man has the capacity to promote his moral behaviour, to make himself more and more similar to the spiritual world and to lift himself to the contemplation of the highest levels of perfection. In this ascending movement everybody starts from the beauty and harmony of the sensible world: thanks to this image, man is able to discover the original model. The material world is a starting point that allows man to attain to the contemplation of true being and even to what is beyond being. So within the perspective of Plotinus' metaphysics, Gnostic theories could not be accepted: they are totally incompatible with the author's philosophical interpretation of reality.[38]

---

35 Aristotle, *Eth. Nic.*, VI, 5, 1140b7.
36 V 8, 7, 12-16. According to Plotinus everything strives to contemplation since the highest principles always implement this activity: all beings tend to the ultimate ground of their existence (III 8, 7, 15-18).
37 In Plotinus' view Nature is a *logos*, a seminal reason (III 8, 2, 28-30). Nature creates everything and yet remains within itself: so it is contemplation (III 8, 3, 2-3).
38 With respect to Plotinus' attitude V. Cilento writes: 'In conclusione, Plotino non è solo antignostico e anticristiano ma altresì antiermetico e lontano da quei misteri di soteriologia ellenistica in cui culto come quello isiaco descritto da Apuleio consisteva nel far discendere la divinità in un certo tempo e in certo luogo' (Ibid., p. 211).

Aquinas lived ten centuries after Plotinus. During that period the western world had deeply changed: the Roman empire had collapsed, new peoples had immigrated into western Europe, christianity had considerably expanded, many monasteries had been founded and from the beginning of the thirteenth century universities were erected as centres of learning and higher education. Part of Aquinas' education was achieved at Paris university where he later lectured for some years.[39] Aquinas was not familiar with the writings of Plotinus: as early as the fourth century these had been translated into Latin by Marius Victorinus and had influenced the thought of St. Augustine. Apparently this Latin version had been lost; in any case there is no trace of it in Aquinas, who is however acquainted with some writings of other Neoplatonic philosophers. Among the latter Pseudo-Dionysius plays an important part: from the beginning of the ninth century this author was already known in the West and his work was translated several times into Latin.[40] Aquinas wrote a penetrating commentary on the *De divinis nominibus*. He also studied the *Liber de causis*: for a long time this treatise was believed to be a work of Aristotle. Thanks to the Latin translation of Proclus' *Elementatio theologica* undertaken by William of Moerbeke, Aquinas was able to uncover the true identity of the work.[41] As far as Pseudo-Dionysius is concerned Aquinas was quite aware of the Platonic character of his thought.[42] So without knowing the treatises of Plotinus, Aquinas was not ignorant concerning the teaching of at least some representatives of the Neoplatonic school.

At the time of Aquinas an important renewal of philosophical thought began as a result of Latin translations of Aristotle's writings: these versions were elaborated from Greek as well as from Arabic. Until the twelfth century only Aristotle's logic was known in the West, thanks to the translations and commentaries of Boethius. In Aristotle's view logic is not properly a part of

39 Aquinas probably arrived in Paris about the autumn of 1252; he composed his commentary on the *Libri Sententiarum* of Peter Lombard between 1253 and 1256; at the beginning of 1256 he receives the *licencia docendi*; the *Quaestiones disputatae de Veritate* date back to the period 1256-1259. At the end of 1259 or the beginning of 1260 Aquinas leaves Paris and goes to Italy. In 1268 (possibly about November 20) he leaves Viterbo and comes to Paris, where he continues to lecture until 1272 (F. Van Steenberghen, *La philosophie au XIIIe siècle*, Louvain-Paris, 1966, pp. 307-14).

40 Works of Pseudo-Dionysius were translated from Greek into Latin by Hilduinus, Scottus Eriugena, Joannes Sarracenus and Robertus Grosseteste.

41 *In librum de causis expositio*, ed. C. Pera, (Roma-Torino, 1955), Prooemium, n. 9: Et in graeco quidem invenitur sic traditus *liber Proculi platonici continens CCXI propositiones*, qui intitulatur '*Elementatio Theologica*'. In arabico vero invenitur hic liber qui apud latinos '*de Causis*' dicitur quem constat de arabico esse translatum et in graeco penitus non haberi. Unde videtur ab aliquo Philosophorum arabum ex praedicto libro Proculi excerptus, praesertim quia omnia quae in hoc libro continentur, multo plenius et diffusius continentur in illo.

42 *In librum beati Dionysii de divinis nominibus expositio*, ed. C. Pera, (Roma-Torino, 1950), Prooemium: Haec igitur Platonicorum ratio fidei non consonat nec veritati, quantum ad hoc quod continet de speciebus naturalibus separatis, sed quantum ad id quod dicebant de primo rerum Principio, verissima est eorum opinio et fidei christianae consona.

philosophy; it is regarded as an indispensable means to build a scientific system. Yet the logical treatises dealing mainly with language and scientific knowledge were very influential: they initiated a new way of thinking, mainly concerned with a rational explanation of sensible reality.[43] In the first half of the twelfth century James of Venice started translating some other works of the Stagirite; several scholars pursued the same project until the end of the thirteenth century, when all the works of Aristotle as well as some Greek commentaries were available in Latin. These writings are not only related to the various branches of philosophy (metaphysics, physics, psychology, ethics, politics); they also include the whole area of sciences: the study of plants, animals, inanimate beings, heavenly bodies. The work presents a real scientific encyclopedia which entered the Christian West and offered a coherent interpretation of the universe and of human life. It was a decisive challenge for western Europe.

Aquinas, like many of his contemporaries, was confronted with this invasion of new ideas. During the early centuries of our era, Christian intellectuals had already been constrained to settle their attitude toward Greek philosophy: they generally agreed to appeal to Plato for the interpretation of their faith, but they dismissed Aristotle. The latter was regarded as a typically pagan author whose teaching could not be reconciled with christian doctrine. One of the reasons was that the Greek master did not accept divine creation: in his view the world exists from always and was never created. As to the highest principle, it is considered to be Pure Act: it does not know the cosmos, it only grasps its own perfection; so it is not concerned with the world, not even with human beings.[44] These latter are moral animals by nature: they are able to attain some degree of happiness through ethical behaviour, but there is no life after death. The human soul is not immortal.[45]

Within the context of Aristotle's philosophy, of Neoplatonic theories and Christian theology, Aquinas is brought to examine carefully the notion of creation. Some Christians, Philoponus for example, had tried to prove through

---

43 In Aristotle's view scientific thought ought to clarify reality. The author is not satisfied with merely collecting facts that have been observed: something more is required. In order to clarify the observed facts, one has to explain why they occur; a fact is more understandable if its cause has been revealed. A further distinction may be made between immediate causes and the ultimate cause, but in any case the pattern of scientific knowledge is related to the uncovering of causes: this disclosure makes reality more intelligible.

44 Divine providence is an important issue in Christian doctrine; the same teaching is present also in Stoic philosophy, although the metaphysical context is different. In his strictly philosophical theory Aristotle had to discard divine providence, because the topic is incompatible with the interpretation of Divine Substance as Pure Act. On the other hand Aristotle also takes into account pre-philosophical opinions and beliefs; from this viewpoint he is inclined to accept some kind of providence.

45 According to the *De anima* of Aristotle, the human soul could only continue to exist after death if it is able to exert some activity without being linked to the body (I, 1, 403a10-12). But in Aristotle's view there is no psychic activity that is totally independent of the bodily organism, not even intellectual knowledge.

philosophical arguments, that the world could not have existed always.[46] In this respect Aquinas is more critical; according to him rational arguments are unable to demonstrate that the cosmos is not everlasting.[47] One of these arguments states that the maker must always be prior to the work he produces: with respect to the universe, it means that the divine creator exists before the world; hence the cosmos must have a beginning (*CG*, 2, 38, 1136). Aquinas agrees provided the productive activity under consideration be a movement or a change: in this case the product comes to be at the end of the process. But if the making is instantaneous, nothing prevents the product from being simultaneous with the maker.[48]

Creation is not an ordinary production, comparable to the making of an artefact: in creation there is no pre-existing matter; what is created is made from nothing (*ex nihilo*). So in this case being arises after non-being (*CG*, 2, 38, 1137). According to Aquinas creation from nothing does not mean that being starts after non-being; it simply means that the divine Creator does not proceed like an ordinary craftsman, he does not make the cosmos out of something.[49] From this argument no conclusion can be drawn concerning the beginning of the world.

However if the cosmos has always existed, an infinite number of days and sun rotations has already taken place, whereas according to Aristotle an infinite in act is impossible (*CG*, 2, 38, 1138). Aquinas criticizes also this argument: the number of past days is not an infinite in act, because these days do not exist simultaneously, but successively. The only conclusion to be drawn is that there would not be a first day: consequently nobody could ever traverse the past number of days.[50]

---

46 One of the works of Philoponus is entitled: *De aeternitate mundi contra Proclum* (ed. H. Rabe, Leipzig, 1899). In his commentary on Aristotle's *Physics*, based on the teaching of Ammonius, he also criticized the eternity of the world, referring to the Stagirite's theory concerning the impossibility of an infinite in act.

47 In his *Scriptum super libros Sententiarum* (II, 1, 1, 5), a work that dates back to 1253-1257, Aquinas already took a firm stand with respect to the eternity of the world and he always remained faithful to his initial viewpoint. Nevertheless there is some hesitation in his argument: 'Sometimes he rejects every infinite in act, whether simultaneous or in succession. Sometimes he rejects only the infinite in simultaneous act. And sometimes he admits the possibility of an infinite simultaneously in act' (cf. F. Van Steenberghen, *Thomas Aquinas and Radical Aristotelianism* (Washington D.C., 1980), pp. 18-19).

48 *Contra Gentiles* 2, 38, 1143: In his autem quae in instanti agunt, hoc non est necesse; *De aeternitate mundi*, ed. J. Perrier, c. 4 (p. 56): Ergo non repugnat intellectui si ponatur causa producens effectum suum subito non praecedere duratione causatum suum.

49 *Contra Gentiles* 2, 38, 1144: Ei autem quod est *ex aliquo aliquid fieri*, contradictorium quod oportet dare si hoc non datur, est *non ex aliquo fieri*; *De aeternitate mundi*, c. 6 (p. 57): Unde patet quod secundum hanc expositionem non ponitur aliquis ordo ejus quod factum est ad nihil, quasi oportuerit illud quod factum est nihil fuisse et postmodum aliquid esse.

50 *Contra Gentiles* 2, 38, 1145: Nam infinitum, etsi non sit simul in actu, potest tamen esse in successione: quia sic quodlibet infinitum acceptum finitum est.

Some people claim that it is quite impossible to add something to an infinite: if the number of past days is infinite, it will be impossible that new days be added. So the evolution of the universe must inevitably stop (*CG*, 2, 38, 1139). Aquinas replies that it is possible to add something to an infinite in so far as it presents a finite aspect: looking at the evolution of time from the present, the past may be infinite (if time never started), but the present instant is a frontier or a limit: in this respect time is finite and new days may be added to it.[51]

If the world exists without beginning, there will be an infinite series of efficient causes: wanting to explain a phenomenon, one will have to go back from one cause to another and will never reach a first principle; the series will continue indefinitely and the phenomenon under consideration will never be adequately clarified (*CG*, 2, 38, 1140). Aquinas specifies that this argument is correct if the causes in question act at once: a stick could only move something if it is itself moved by someone. But there are other cases in which the causes do not act simultaneously: if a man generates a child, his action does not depend upon the simultaneous activity of his own father. In this case the causes involved do not act at once: so there is no objection against the fact that in such cases the series of efficient causes is infinite.[52]

Finally there is the question of immortal souls: if the cosmos is eternal and human souls are immortal, there must be an infinite number of immortal souls (*CG*, 2, 38, 1141). Aquinas acknowledges that this objection is the most difficult. In his answer he draws attention to the fact that not everybody accepts the immortality of human soul; moreover some people believe that not the soul but only the mind is immortal. According to others there is a constant transmigration of a limited number of souls, which move from one body to another. Finally some think that an infinite in act is possible in the case of things which are not ordered: an orderly arrangement or disposition always implies a limit or a frontier; in this view things which are not incorporated into a harmonious arrangement may be infinite in number.[53] At the end of this critical investigation Aquinas concludes that it is more in agreement with divine goodness that the world does not exist from eternity, but had a beginning. When making the cosmos the creator intended to manifest his goodness; this aim will be more adequately achieved if the universe has a beginning.[54]

---

51 *Contra Gentiles* 2, 38, 1146. Aquinas considers this argument to be weak: Nam nihil prohibet infinito ex ea parte additionem fieri qua est finitum.

52 *Contra Gentiles* 2, 38, 1147: Quia causas agentes in infinitum procedere est impossibile, secundum philosophos, in causis simul agentibus: quia oporteret effectum dependere ex actionibus infinitis simul existentibus.

53 *Contra Gentiles* 2, 38, 1148: Quidam vero pro inconvenienti non habent quod sint aliqua infinita actu in his quae ordinem non habent.

54 *Contra Gentiles* 2, 38, 1148: Hoc igitur convenientissimum fuit divinae bonitati, ut rebus creatis principium durationis daret.

So Aquinas is convinced that the arguments put forward to demonstrate that the world is not everlasting are not stringent. In his view there is no contradiction between being created and existing eternally, neither from the viewpoint of what is produced nor from that of the maker. If the creation of the universe is not a movement, and the creating principle exists from always, it is quite possible that the world has no beginning. An eternal cause may always create.[55]

Aquinas does not side with those who endeavour to refute Aristotle and to prove through philosophical arguments that the universe could not exist eternally.[56] That does not mean, however, that he agrees with Aristotle and that he accepts his reasoning about the eternity of the world. In Aquinas' view, Aristotle's arguments also are not convincing: it is not true that any movement implies a previous one or that any time refers to a preceding one. In his opinion there could be a beginning of movement through an act that is not a movement, as there could be a beginning of time through an act that is not temporal: this act is divine creation.[57] From a philosophical viewpoint Aristotle's argument is not conclusive. What then? The question of the eternity of the world could not be resolved through philosophical reasoning; yet Christians know, thanks to divine revelation, that the universe had a beginning.[58] This conclusion is generally drawn from the first sentence of the Bible, although different interpretations of the expression '*in principio*' have been suggested.[59]

With respect to creation, Aquinas maintains that there is only one creative principle: any kind of metaphysical dualism is repudiated. The author does not deny the presence of some evil in the world: in this context he refers to the Manichaeans who claim that there are two supreme causes, one of which is good and the other evil; in this latter category are placed corruptible beings, in contrast to the incorruptible, as well as the Old Testament in contrast to the

55 *De Potentia* 3, 14: Si autem accipiamus possibile dictum secundum potentiam *activam*, tunc in Deo non deest potentia ab aeterno essentiam aliam a se producendi.
56 In his *De aeternitate mundi*, c. 10, (p. 59) Aquinas refers to John Damascene and Hugh of Saint-Victor: both authors declare that nothing created can be co-eternal with God; he calls their arguments *debile fulcimentum*. Seemingly Aquinas has been deeply impressed by the fact that many outstanding philosophers maintained the world to be eternal.
57 *In octo libros Physicorum* VIII, 2, 987: Sunt enim huiusmodi rationes efficaces ad proban-dum quod motus non inceperit per viam naturae, sicut ab aliquibus ponebatur: sed quod non inceperit quasi rebus de novo productis a primo rerum principio, ut fides nostra ponit, hoc iis rationibus probari non potest.
58 Aquinas does not agree with some of his contemporaries who claim Aristotle does not intend to prove that the world always existed; in their opinion he only wishes to expound some arguments *pro et contra* without coming to a definitive conclusion. Aquinas firmly dismisses this view: *quod ex ipso modo procedendi frivolum apparet* (*In octo libros Physicorum* VIII, 2, 986).
59 Cf. G. Verbeke, 'The Bible's First Sentence in Gregory of Nyssa's View', in: *A Straight Path, Studies in Medieval Philosophy and Culture. Essays in Honor of Arthur Hyman* (Washington D.C., 1988), pp. 230-43. 'According to Gregory the first words of the Bible (ἐν ἀρχῇ) have no temporal meaning. They refer to the simultaneous production of all beings' (p. 240).

New (*De Pot.*, 3, 6). Whatever is concretely regarded as evil, the question remains whether the same principle could be the source of what is good and of what is bad. Could divine goodness produce a world in which evil is constantly present? This issue had already troubled St Augustine, who at one period of his life sided with Manichaeism.[60] Aquinas strongly opposes metaphysical dualism: in his view all things in the universe possess a common character, namely being; they all participate in being, the source and principle of all perfection. Things are perfect in so far as they take part in being: being is the perfection of all perfections, the act of all acts, it coincides with goodness.[61] So all things in the universe are basically good: they are perfect and good in so far as they are. They are imperfect inasmuch as they are not, in so far as something is lacking or deficient: evil is characterized as nonbeing, absence of being. All beings in so far as they are being, refer to the same principle as their origin. It is impossible to imagine a second cause that would be the source of evil: a cause can only be active in so far as it is, and to this extent it is perfect since it partakes in being. It makes no sense to affirm that a cause characterized by the absence of being is the source of whatever is imperfect in the universe: this cause will be inactive to the degree that it lacks being.[62] Finally all things in the universe, also things that are corruptible, corporeal and imperfect, contribute to achieve one single harmonious whole. True, various things do not belong to the same level of perfection, but they all are integrated into the same orderly totality.[63] Aquinas even acknowledges that the majority of humans are evil and yet he persists in maintaining the origin of the world to be divine goodness. Humans are gifted with freedom: if their moral behaviour is culpable, it is because of their yielding to irrational impulses.[64] The Stoics also

---

60   Cf. *Confessiones* IV, i, 1: For nine years Augustine clung to Manichaeism—from the age of 19 to 28.

61   *De Potentia* 3, 6: unde oportet quod omnium istorum sit unum principium, quod est omnibus causa essendi. Esse autem, in quantum huiusmodi, bonum est. Aquinas frequently insists on this exceptional character of being: God is not beyond being, as the Neoplatonists maintained, nor is he a particular being (*ens*), but he is *esse subsistens* (*Qu. disp. De anima* 6, ad 2). *ST*, I, 4, 1, ad 3: Ad tertium dicendum quod ipsum esse est perfectissimum omnium: comparatur enim ad omnia ut actus. Nihil enim habet actualitatem, nisi inquantum est: unde ipsum esse est actualitas omnium rerum, et etiam ipsarum formarum; I, 5, 1; I, 7, 1; I, 8, 1. This concept of being is very important with respect to the notion of creation.

62   *De Potentia* 3, 6: Secundum vero quod actu est unumquodque, bonum est, quia secundum hoc habet perfectionem et entitatem, in qua ratio boni consistit.

63   *De Potentia* 3, 6: Oportet ergo omnia ista diversa in aliquod unum primum principium reducere a quo in unum ordinantur.

64   *De Potentia* 3, 6, ad 5: Et quia plures sequuntur sensus quam rationem, ideo plures inveniuntur mali in hominibus quam boni. Moral evil is a consequence of man's freedom: that was already the doctrine of St. Augustine in his *De libero arbitrio* (I, 13, 29: Ex quo conficitur ut quisquis recte honesteque vult vivere, si id se velle prae fugacibus bonis velit, assequatur tantam rem tanta facilitate, ut nihil aliud ei quam ipsum velle sit habere quod voluit). Aquinas adopts the same viewpoint; freedom is an exceptional privilege, but many people are dominated by their passions and emotions. Some Stoic influence probably penetrated into Aquinas' appreciation of moral life.

stressed the world as a masterpiece of divine Reason and yet they believed that only very few humans reach the ideal of wisdom: the overwhelming majority belong to the category of those who are called insane or foolish.

So there is only one creative principle; it is the origin of whatever exists, the source of all perfection in every being: at each moment of its existence a finite being is totally dependent upon the divine cause producing it. In the light of these analyses, it is quite clear that creation is not a movement or a change: for in this case there would be a common subject that ensures the continuity of the process; even in substantial change, there must be some common substratum, namely prime matter.[65] If the creation of the universe were a change, there would be a common subject of the evolution. According to some Gnostics, the first sentence of the Bible refers to some pre-existing matter used by the Creator when he shaped the world: in this opinion the expression '*in principio*' means that the world was formed out of a pre-existing material principle.[66] In Aquinas' view creation is a total causation; it does not presuppose anything—it produces things from nothing. Hence creation could not be a change since there is no common subject that persists and secures the continuity of the process.[67] Not even time may be regarded as a common subject, since it begins with the making of the universe. In an Aristotelian perspective time is linked to movement and change: it implies an awareness of the successive instants in the evolution of the world or of the internal development of a conscious being. Consequently time starts when the world begins to exist, it is linked to the existence of the material universe: this reality constantly changes, but its coming to be through creation was not a change.[68]

According to Plotinus the world is a necessary emanation from the highest principle, the One; it must be basically good since it flows from the supreme perfection. A similar issue is treated by Aquinas, who states that the world does not spring from the creator through necessity of nature, but through a voluntary act.[69] The author is referring to divine nature: he declares that the universe does not necessarily proceed from it. If the creative act were necessary, God could not exist without producing the cosmos; in a sense the world would belong to the essence of God, since the latter would

---

65   *De Potentia* 3, 2: Dicendum, quod in mutatione qualibet requiritur quod sit aliquid idem commune utrique mutationis termino.

66   Cf. Tertullianus *Adversus Hermogenem*, 2, 1-5.

67   *De Potentia* 3, 2: In creatione autem non est aliquid commune aliquo praedictorum modorum. Neque enim est aliquod commune subiectum actu existens, neque potentia. Divine causation is related to being; God is the ultimate cause of the being of all beings. As being involves everything, it is the perfection of whatever exists: so the divine Creator does not use any pre-existing material.

68   *De Potentia* 3, 2: Tempus etiam non est idem, si loquamur de creatione universi; nam ante mundum tempus non erat.

69   *De Potentia* 3, 5: Dicendum quod, absque omni dubio, tenendum est quod Deus ex libero arbitrio suae voluntatis creaturas in esse produxit nulla naturali necessitate.

imply the making of the world.[70] No real distinction could exist anymore between God and the world: the cosmos would coincide with the divine substance. This doctrine inevitably leads to pantheism.

Aquinas presents a number of arguments to support his view. The cosmos is an orderly whole that is oriented toward an end: it is not some totality of things brought together by chance or accident. Is this orderly disposition the result of nature? In a sense, yes; yet nature could not be regarded as the first cause of this arrangement; prior to nature is the activity of the will: an agent that originates a voluntary act sets for himself his own goal and moves himself to this end.[71] Nature also tends toward an end and moves to it: voluntary activity, however, is prior to nature, since the agent determines the end and drives himself to it. So the activity of the divine will is prior to that of nature.[72] Moreover, the activity of nature is directed to one single effect that is similar to its cause: nature always produces something akin to it. In the case of divine creation there is a tremendous distance between the perfection of the creator and the sensible world, which in addition displays a great variety of beings.[73] Furthermore, the activity of an agent is characterized in agreement with the proper features of that cause, for in a sense the effect pre-exists in its cause. As to the divine creator, he is an intelligent substance: creatures pre-exist in him in an intelligible way. There is a close connection between thinking and willing: the will performs what the intellect plans. In this sense divine creation must be a voluntary act.[74] Finally the divine creator does not depend upon anything outside himself: his creative activity coincides with his substance. Of course, what is created is distinct from the divine perfection, but the act of creating remains within the divine substance: that is only possible because God creates by his intellect and will. So the creative activity remains identical with the divine substance, whereas the world is distinct from it.[75]

Does the creation of the world involve any deliberative process? Aquinas does not mention any deliberation in this context; he explicitly discards it.[76]

---

70 In Aquinas' view God must be fully master of his activity (*sui actus dominus*); that will not be the case if what he does flows from his nature; in this hypothesis he will be *quasi ab alio actus* (*Contra Gentiles* 2, 23, 995). Aquinas is very cautious: only free decision fully belongs to the divine principle.

71 *De Potentia* 3, 15: Unde agens per voluntatem sic agit propter finem, quod praestituit sibi finem et seipsum quodammodo in finem movet, suas actiones in ipsum ordinando.

72 *De Potentia* 3, 15: Unde oportet quod primum ordinans in finem, hoc faciat per voluntatem; et ita Deus per voluntatem creaturas in esse produxit, non per naturam.

73 *De Potentia* 3, 15. The argument is important with respect to human activity: this latter could not be free if it depended upon a Creator producing the world by necessity of nature.

74 *De Potentia* 3, 15: Quod autem est in intellectu, non proceditur nisi mediante voluntate; voluntas enim est executrix intellectus et intelligibile voluntatem movet; et ita oportet quod res creatae a Deo processerint per voluntatem.

75 *De Potentia* 3, 15: Per hoc igitur Deus agit quidquid extra se agit, quod intelligit et vult.

76 *De aeternitate mundi*, c. 4 (p. 56): Etiam voluntas non est necessarium quod praecedat duratione effectum suum, nec agens per voluntatem, nisi per hoc quod agit ex deliberatione, quod absit ut in Deo ponamus.

As a matter of fact, deliberation would imply some uncertainty and hesitation on behalf of the creator. True, the creative act must be fully autonomous, but it could not be the outcome of a search or a reflection. That creation is a voluntary act and not a necessary process of divine nature, means that the supreme intellect conceives the making of the universe and performs it through an activity of the will. Needless to say, in God will and intellect coincide with the divine substance.

In the light of our previous considerations it is possible to make a brief comparison between Plotinus and Aquinas regarding the topic of this study:

1. Both authors agree in repudiating any kind of metaphysical dualism. According to Plotinus there is ultimately only one single principle, the One, uncompounded and immutable; it is beyond being and is the source of all lower levels of perfection. The One coincides with the supreme goodness. As for Aquinas, he also maintains that all beings proceed from one creative principle; in his view it is a proper characteristic of creation to be all-embracing: creation does not presuppose any pre-existing matter, it is at the origin of being in all beings. In this sense the most perfect Being produces all beings in whatever they are.

2. Plotinus and Aquinas do not fully agree concerning the way in which lower beings are produced. According to Plotinus the three higher hypostases participate in the creative activity: from the One proceeds the Intellect in which all immutable Ideas are included; from the Intellect springs Universal Soul which contains all seminal reasons shaping the sensible universe. In this view the highest principle is the immediate cause of only one lower perfection. This doctrine is not accepted by Aquinas: in his opinion there is one creator, who is the immediate cause of the 'beingness' of all beings. Creation is an activity that could belong only to an infinite being: the divine creator could not communicate this activity to any lower reality. So the divine creator is the constant and immediate cause of all beings in the universe.[77]

3. In Plotinus' view, as in Aristotle's teaching, the world never came to be; it always exists, without beginning. Yet the universe is not properly eternal; it is not beyond time, since it is constantly moving and changing.[78] It could not have a beginning since the creation of the cosmos is not the result of a deliberative process on the part of the highest Principle: such a process would involve some uncertainty or hesitation, which are incompatible with the supreme perfection. As for Aquinas, his teaching is shaded: from a philosophical viewpoint it is impossible to demonstrate

---

77 *Contra Gentiles* 2, 21, 974: Relinquitur igitur quod nihil aliud praeter Deum potest creare, neque sicut principale agens neque sicut instrumentum.
78 In his treatise on eternity and time Plotinus defines eternity as a life that always remains identical in itself, and always present to itself in its totality (III 7, 3, 16-17).

that the world ever commenced. Some authors have attempted to prove that the cosmos came to be, but their arguments are not fully convincing. On the other hand, Aristotle's argumentation, aimed at showing that the world never began, is also defective. On the basis of philosophical reasoning it is impossible to demonstrate either that the world always exists or that it had a beginning: appealing to divine revelation, Christians believe that the universe is not everlasting.

4. The notion of creation is central with respect to our topic. In Plotinus' view creation is not a free decision, a result of a deliberative process: it is essentially contemplation, although it includes a dynamic and volitional aspect. Contemplating its own perfection the creative principle necessarily produces some imitation of it. In other words, contemplation is not a passive viewing, it is rather a dynamic intuition of the perfection that is contemplated: loving its own perfection, the contemplating principle produces an image of it. In Aquinas' view creation is a voluntary act, it is not a necessary process stemming from divine nature. Yet Aquinas discards any deliberation: creation is a free decision on the part of the creator in the sense that it is fully autonomous and independent; there is no necessity of nature. In this respect there is certainly a difference between Plotinus and Aquinas, although it may be difficult to clarify.

5. Since in Plotinus' doctrine creation is contemplation necessarily producing an imitation of what is contemplated, the link between lower beings and the creative cause is necessary: the creative cause necessarily produces the lower beings, which in a sense belong to the perfection of their origin. Since the world necessarily proceeds from the higher hypostases, it is not really distinct from them. Aquinas clearly intends to avoid that kind of pantheism; the world is not evil, it is fundamentally valuable, not because it necessarily flows from the highest perfection, but because the divine creator, as the supreme being, is the source of all beings: since being is the perfection of all perfections, the divine creator is not a principle of evil, but of goodness. Of course not all imperfection is excluded from the universe: humans are free, they are responsible for their conduct. This freedom is possible because the creation of the world is not a necessary emanation: human freedom is a participation in the freedom of the divine creator.

Two apologies of the world: the one of Plotinus implies a pantheistic view, entailing some degradation of man's personal destiny and responsibility. The apology of Aquinas is essentially based on the notion of creation as an autonomous act that is the origin of a transcendental causation, an act that produces the being of all beings. In Aquinas' teaching being coincides with perfection and goodness.

Reason and Experience in Plotinus

ANDREW SMITH

One of the criticisms which any metaphysical system must face, and particularly so since Kant, involves the careful examination of the principles and base on which its edifice has been constructed. I am not here concerned with such vexed questions as to whether there are such things as *a priori* statements, a premiss on which all classical metaphysics must stand, but rather with the looser question as to the motivating force in metaphysical enquiry. It has seemed to some modern observers[1] that a metaphysical system usually takes its start from a series of leading questions, accepted views or feelings about the universe, in short, prejudices which are normally unconsciously held by the philosopher. That is, in the end, metaphysical systems, however rationally set out, rest on some unconscious notion which leads the argument in a particular direction. In this sense the Greek preoccupation with order and unity, seen for example in the Presocratics, largely determined one at least of the parameters of Greek philosophizing. This view is not, however, one which I feel particularly needs to be disputed in order to reinstate classical metaphysics. It may be argued that it is in the nature of any kind of research or thinking that a way must first be suggested which is then followed up. Some of the greatest of modern scientists themselves speak in similar terms of inspiration or of the sudden idea which is then pursued relentlessly. Or are we again involved in Plato's problem that we must know what we are looking for before we can identify and find it?[2] In any case it remains a deep and interesting puzzle whether there is an experiential ground in metaphysical enquiry and, if there is, what it might be.

These questions certainly occur when one reads the *Enneads* of Plotinus, for he took for granted and worked within most of the accepted and traditional concepts of Greek philosophy. For example the basic concern for order and intelligibility which led the Presocratics to search for an originating cause, a unifying explanation of the world, is accepted by Plotinus as an important challenge which led to his notion of the One, the utterly transcendent cause of all coherence. Plotinus, of course, argues for the necessity of unity at all levels, but it never occurs to him to doubt the importance of the question, an example of the subconscious acceptance

---

1 Cf. Morris Lazerowitz, *The Structure of Metaphysics* (London, 1955), pp. 67-9.
2 *Meno* 80e.

of a particular philosophical insight as a leading idea. Nor is it at all clear whether Plotinus' metaphysical world view was servant to an inner experience or vice versa.

Speaking of his three hypostases, the One, Intellect and Soul, he observes:

> And just as in nature there are these three of which we have spoken, so we ought to think that they are present also in ourselves.[3]

However, what is particularly interesting about Plotinus is that he often does bring out into the open, in a way not seen in any other Greek philosopher, an awareness of the role which actual experience, as opposed to rational or discursive argument, plays in his metaphysics. This openness concerns the higher levels of reality, the end rather than the starting point of enquiry; for Plotinus constructed a metaphysical system which more than most makes claims to see beyond the realm of normal experience in order to find an explanation for phenomena here. But he does not try to conceal the difficulties which this involves. In particular he is often at pains to express his conviction that in many cases only experience of the other reality can bring us to an understanding of it. At the same time he insists on pursuing rational, demonstrative discourse as far as it can possibly take us. Of course we must not forget that Plotinus would not have considered such experience to be subjective, but rather a contact with objective reality and thus a sort of empirical datum.

In this article I wish to explore the way in which Plotinus balances and interweaves argument and experience. I will take my material largely from two treatises (VI 7 [38] and VI 9 [9]) which deal with the difficult levels of Intellect and the One.[4] The subject of *Ennead* VI 9 is the Good or the One. In the first two chapters the role of unity is explored in a discursive way, beginning with the need that any entity has for unity if it is to be an entity at all. Examples are given from the world of sense experience: an army, chorus, flock; Plotinus then moves to a higher level of reality: health, beauty; then to Soul; and finally to Intellect. Each of these is unified but none is unity or oneness itself. He establishes that there must be something beyond these, the One itself. But so far he has described it only indirectly by showing how Soul and Intellect cannot in themselves be such unity.

Now in the third chapter he is ready to turn to the One itself. But he begins with a change of key[5] by expressing the difficulty we have in

3 V 1, 10, 5-6. All Plotinus translations are taken from A. H. Armstrong's Loeb edition.
4 On VI 7 see Pierre Hadot, 'Structure et thèmes du Traité 38 (VI 7) de Plotin' in *Aufstieg und Niedergang der römischen Welt* II 36, 1 (Berlin, 1987), pp. 624-76.
5 For a similar transition, see V 5, 4, 7-9: 'Now we long to see, if it is in any way possible, what is the pure, real One, unrelated to anything else. At this point then you must rush to the One, and not any longer add anything to it, but stand absolutely still in fear of departing from it.'

knowing the One. For with the One we move beyond form; we enter the formless and have a fear of entering nothingness. The very expression suggests a personal experience at this point:

> It (the soul) slides away and is afraid that it may have nothing at all. Therefore it gets tired of this sort of thing, and often gladly comes down and falls away from all this, till it comes to the perceptible and rests there as if on solid ground; just as sight when it gets tired of small objects is glad to come upon big ones.[6]

Yet to balance this there follows an epistemological rather than psychological explanation for the difficulty. When we first know the One, he explains, we become identical with it; the very identity of subject and seen object prevents our awareness in any normal sense of the fact that we have grasped it.[7] In the first two chapters Plotinus had argued discursively to absolute unity from the lowest manifestations of unity in the physical world and upwards through Soul and Intellect. He once again suggests the same upward path, but now *internally* within the individual. There is also a suggestion of moral as well as intellectual progress in the words: 'and become freed from all evil' (κακίας τε πάσης ἀπηλλαγμένον εἶναι).[8] This tone of virtual exhortation is kept up for some lines. At one point we are told to entrust ourselves to Intellect (τὴν ψυχὴν τὴν αὐτοῦ νῷ πιστεύσαντα).[9] The final section of the chapter then returns to establishing the nature of the One.

Chapter four again brings up the difficulty (ἀπορία) of dealing with the One, which lies beyond normal knowledge; we must go beyond reason (λόγος) and knowledge (ἐπιστήμη). We note the phrase 'from reasonings to vision' (ἐκ τῶν λόγων ἐπὶ τὴν θέαν)[10] and the almost emotional appeal in the long following sentence. And yet the solution to these difficulties lies in the use of reasoning, for we need the λόγος or reasoned argument which brings assurance (πίστις). Reasoned argument, then, is essential. Plotinus next clearly states that the following paragraphs will help to bring up arguments to aid conviction: 'but as for what [the enquirer] disbelieves because he is deficient in his reasonings, let him *consider* the following' (ἃ δὲ ἐν τοῖς λόγοις ἀπιστεῖ ἐλλείπων, ὧδε διανοείσθω).[11] We are

---

6 VI 9, 3, 6-10: ἐξολισθάνει καὶ φοβεῖται, μὴ οὐδὲν ἔχῃ. διὸ κάμνει ἐν τοῖς τοιούτοις καὶ ἀσμένη καταβαίνει πολλάκις ἀποπίπτουσα ἀπὸ πάντων, μέχρις ἂν εἰς αἰσθητὸν ἥκῃ ἐν στερεῷ ὥσπερ ἀναπαυομένη. οἷον καὶ ἡ ὄψις κάμνουσα ἐν τοῖς μικροῖς τοῖς μεγάλοις ἀσμένως περιπίπτει.
7 Cf. V 8, 11.
8 VI 9, 3, 19-20.
9 VI 9, 3, 23.
10 VI 9, 4, 13-14.
11 VI 9, 4, 34-5.

here asked to use reasoning (διάνοια). There is then a resumption of argument in chapter five. We naturally ask whether any new arguments are given here beyond what has already been presented in the earlier sections. In a sense what is now presented to us is basically the same as that offered in chapters one and two, i.e. the hierarchy of reality from the physical world to the One. But whereas this hierarchy was earlier explored in terms of increasing unity, in chapter five we are required by Plotinus to conduct a more fundamental enquiry. I say 'required' because Plotinus does not offer here the arguments which establish the positions he wishes us to accept, for he has done this elsewhere[12] and sees no reason to repeat them here. The first requirement is that we establish for ourselves the existence of a type of reality other than the material (ἄλλη φύσις), secondly that Soul is derived from Intellect, and thirdly a more exact delineation of the nature of Intellect.

I think it is particularly important to point out in passing that although Plotinus seeks to explore those higher reaches of metaphysics which were left deliberately vague by Plato, he nevertheless frequently returns to basics such as here to the establishing of incorporeal reality. The great treatise VI 4 and 5 on the omnipresence of being concentrates on the notion of being in this way, without involving the added complication of the distinctions within and above being. And Porphyry considered it appropriate to dwell on the same topic in a similar way in *Sententiae* 40.

What Plotinus has to say about Intellect in chapter five is largely a repetition of what has already been said, but with further explication. For example the analogy of science helps further to explain the nature of Intellect.

> For Intellect is not divided as are the rational principles which are already thought one by one, nor are its contents confused; for each one proceeds separately; it is as it is in our bodies of knowledge, where all the items are in a partless whole and yet each of them is separate.[13]

It is important to note how Plotinus stresses that this treatment of Intellect is provided by reason: 'argument says that it must necessarily exist' (φησὶν αὐτὸ ὁ λόγος ἐξ ἀνάγκης εἶναι).[14] The amount of space devoted here to Intellect, the third of the subjects he required to be examined, in comparison with the other two points which are summarily dealt with, seems to be intended to help us to grasp the One, since it is precisely by

12 For the nature of incorporeal reality see especially VI 4 and 5, and for the derivation of Soul from Intellect V 1 and 2. Although these treatises were written after VI 9 they certainly reflect basic ideas which would have been covered many times in the course of Plotinus' long teaching career.

13 VI 9, 5, 16-20.

14 VI 9, 5, 21-2.

analogy with Intellect that we are shortly to learn more about the One. The implication is that it will be helpful to have as clear a picture of Intellect as possible. This approach to the One through Intellect may be seen in the fresh presentation of the One to which he now turns. Plotinus chooses to express himself in one long, complex sentence, which I reproduce below divided into its three sense units (24-38: τὸ δὴ πρὸ τοῦ ... ὑπ' αὐτῆς οὖσαν). This sentence reflects, in its very structure, the main thought of this whole section—knowledge of the One depends on Intellect. The two have to be played off, as it were, against each other.

> Now that which is prior to what is most honourable among real beings, given that there must be something before Intellect which wants to be one but is not one, but in unitary form, because Intellect is not dispersed in itself but is in reality all together with itself and its nearness after the One has kept it from dividing itself, though it did somehow dare to stand away from the One
>
> —that which is before this Intellect, this marvel of the One, which is not existent, so that 'one' may not here also have to be predicated of something else, which in truth has no fitting name, but if we must give it a name, 'one' would be an appropriate ordinary way of speaking of it, not in the sense of something else and then one;
>
> this is difficult to know for this reason, but can be better known from its product, substance—and it is intellect which leads to substance—and its nature is of such a kind that it is the source of the best and the power which generates the real beings, abiding in itself and not being diminished and not being one of the things which it brought into being.

Here we begin with the One ('That which is prior') but are brought immediately to Intellect in a series of subordinate clauses which establish its identity. The return to the One ('This marvel of the One') is in negative terms. The difficulty of pinning it down is expressed: 'it is difficult to know' (χαλεπὸν μὲν γνωσθῆναι), a difficulty which we overcome only be knowing it through its offspring, Intellect: 'from its product' (γιγνωσκόμενον δὲ μᾶλλον τῷ ἀπ' αὐτοῦ γεννήματι). This then leads to a more positive delineation of the One as source of all that is best, a power which generates reality whilst remaining undiminished in itself, i.e. a return to Intellect as our viewpoint. Experience and argument, then, are both expressed by the very structure of this sentence; for the difficulty of knowing the One is seen in the broken progression of thought and the need for personal ascent, reflected later in the phrase 'wanting to unify our souls' (VI 9, 5, 40-41: τὴν ψυχὴν ἑνοῦν θέλοντες). Moreover knowledge of the One comes through analogy—a concept which is restated at the end of the chapter: 'these correspond to those higher things' (VI 9, 5, 45:

ὁμοίως ἀεὶ ἐκείνοις ἐν ἀναλογίαις), and which is applied in chapter six
where we are told not to restrict its unity to that of a point or number.
This chapter again returns to controlled argument, firstly on the nature
of the One as infinite power, and secondly on its simplicity which depends
on its self-sufficiency—in this case taking his premiss of self-sufficiency
from Plato.[15]

Chapter seven turns away again from strict argument to exhortation
and to yet greater use of metaphor as, for example, in the use of 'touch'
(VI 9, 7, 4: θίγειν), and of vivid image, e.g. that of Minos and Zeus or
the One compared to a father. The treatise ends in much the same spirit
of mystical exhortation and exploration, often in images, of our
relationship to the One, e.g., the image of the centre of the circle used to
illustrate our relationship to the One. On several occasions in this final
chapter ideas, arguments and images are repeated or picked up again,
giving one less the impression of a systematically built up argument as of
a constant circling around the same point, the One, in an attempt to cast
light on it from different sides. So, for example, the Eleusinian mysteries
are alluded to in 9, 46: 'whoever has seen, knows what I am saying'
(ὅστις εἶδεν, οἶδεν ὃ λέγω)[16] and again in chapter eleven we return to the
mysteries for the image of the inner and outer sanctuary used to illustrate
that the One can be known only by someone who has actually experienced
it. Why this is so has been explained discursively in chapter ten. The
circle image is found both in chapter eight and also picked up again in
10, 16–17. Analogy, an important linking idea, also reappears in 8, 12 in
the circle image and in 8, 24; in both passages we are asked to dematerialize
the analogy. The theme reappears in chapter eleven where we are told
that we have an image of the One in ourselves—παρ' ἑαυτῷ ἐκείνου
εἰκόνα—which is described as a likeness—ὁμοίωμα. If we are conscious of
ourselves as one with the One we know we have an image of the One.
We must then go further, to the archetype, to an experience of the One
itself.

We are presented, especially in the final chapter of this treatise, with a
collection of interwoven themes which in their presentation reflect that
circling around the One which Plotinus earlier in the treatise says is the
appropriate approach,[17] and which in their constant change from
exhortation to discursive exploration reflect that transition from reasoning

15 *Philebus* 20d 3; 60c 4.
16 An Eleusinian expression; cf. Plot. I 6, 7, 2 and Pausanias I 37, 3 ('Those who know
   the mystery of Eleusis and those who have read Orpheus will know what I am talking
   about').
17 VI 9, 3, 52-4: 'We run round it outside, in a way, and want to explain our own
   experience of it, sometimes near it and sometimes falling away in our perplexities
   about it.' Cf. II 2, 2, 13 on the soul circling around god.

(λόγοι) to vision (θέα) in which both have a vital and mutually supportive role. It does not after all seem to be the case, as I perhaps implied at the beginning, that one uses reason to a certain point and then abandons it to achieve the highest level. The ladder is not taken away as irrelevant. It is true that one must transcend reason, but discursive thought is a constant attendant.

I would like now to return to chapter four of VI 9, which is of especial interest because of the way in which it balances discursive thought and experience in its most explicit and objective form, the personal experience Plotinus thinks we can have of the One (or even of Intellect). The difficulty of conceiving unity leads Plotinus to say that we must transcend reason—ὑπὲρ ἐπιστήμην τοίνυν δεῖ δραμεῖν—where ἐπιστήμη is λόγος or reasoning. We advance from reasoning to vision—ἐκ τῶν λόγων ἐπὶ τὴν θέαν—and the philosopher can only point the way: 'as if showing the way to someone who wants to have a view of something' (ὥσπερ ὁδὸν δεικνύντες τῷ τι θεάσασθαι βουλομένῳ). We note here the personal nature of the effort to vision expressed by the word 'wants' (βουλομένῳ). Yet as we saw before he concludes by saying that our failure to reach the One may be due to a failure in *reasoning*: 'through lack of reasoning to guide him and give him assurance about the One' (δι' ἔνδειαν τοῦ παιδαγωγοῦντος λόγου καὶ πίστιν περὶ αὐτοῦ παρεχομένου). And he later refers to lack of trust in reason: 'he disbelieves because he is deficient in his reasonings' (ἐν τοῖς λόγοις ἀπιστεῖ ἐλλείπων).

Before coming to any conclusion on the relationship of experience to reasoning in this passage it may be useful to say a few words about πίστις and similar expressions in the *Enneads*. Πίστις in Plotinus bears neither the pejorative connotation of Platonic πίστις which is very low in the epistemological scale, nor does it signify a trust in some higher order—a means of overcoming an epistemological barrier—but is rather connected with the soul's reasoning power and the conviction which reasoned demonstration brings. It may sometimes be extended to embrace rational discourse about the Intelligible world. The experience of the One, however, is a vision which goes beyond πίστις. The usage of Plotinus may be likened to Aristotelian πίστις in the sense of conviction which comes after demonstration, *firmitas persuasionis* in the index of Bonitz.[18] Proclus has no fewer than three different levels of πίστις in a passage of his *Platonic Theology* in which he distinguishes a πίστις at the level of Intellect—κατὰ νοῦν ἐνέργειαν—from a higher πίστις which brings unity, as well as the normal Platonic πίστις at the lowest level.[19] For Plotinus, of course, the higher stage of union with the One transcends πίστις.

---

18 John M. Rist, *Plotinus: The Road to Reality* (Cambridge, 1967), p. 232.
19 I 25 and especially p. 111, 2 (Vol. I Saffrey-Westerink).

And so πίστις is associated with demonstration and reasoning (ἀπόδειξις, διαλογισμός), both of which are seen as a form of knowledge (ἐπιστήμη).[20] Philosophical argument (λόγους τοὺς φιλοσοφίας) can be said to bring us to πίστις.[21] Philosophical thought (κατανόησις) and 'firm confidence in the existence of the immaterial' (πίστις ἀσωμάτου) form the second stage of ascent for the philosopher.[22] This analysis of the usage might allow us to give a more precise meaning to phrases such as τὴν ψυχὴν τὴν αὑτοῦ νῷ πιστεύσαντα, 'entrusting his own soul to Intellect', cited above. It surely means not an unqualified self-surrender but an acceptance of what intellect indicates based on rational confidence.[23] Persuasion, πειθώ, is the active aspect of the state of mind of πίστις. And as such it is found in the same relationship to λόγος, argument. Thus in VI 5, 11, 4-7 we have the association of ἀπόδειξις, πειθώ and παραμυθία:

> Well it has already been demonstrated in many ways that it is so; but a bit of encouragement is required, though not the least but the greatest reason for confidence is that nature expounded as it is.[24]

Παραμυθία, a favourite expression of Plotinus, is rightly interpreted by McKenna, in his translation 'intellectual satisfaction', as rational argument.[25] That such argument may be taken as far as the explanation of Intellect may be discerned from I 2, 1, 52 where persuasion is the accompaniment of an argument touching the nature of the archetypes at the Intelligible level: 'but we must make our argument persuasive . . .' (δεῖ δὲ πειθὼ ἐπάγειν τῷ λόγῳ).

There is, however, one passage which on the surface at least seems to demote πίστις by placing persuasion and πίστις at the level of soul and necessity (ἀνάγκη) at the level of Intellect:

> Has then our argument demonstrated something of a kind which has the power to inspire confidence? No, it has necessity not persuasive force; for necessity is in Intellect but persuasion in the soul.[26]

20 VI 9, 10, 5-6.
21 I 3, 1, 34.
22 I 3, 3, 6.
23 Cf. V 1, 3, 2, where πιστεύσας is similar in meaning.
24 VI 5, 11, 4-7: ἀποδέδεικται μὲν οὖν ἤδη πολλαχῇ, ὅτι οὕτως. δεῖ δέ τινων καὶ παραμυθίων, καίτοι οὐχ ἐλάχιστον, ἀλλὰ μέγιστον εἰς πειθὼ ἦν ἐκείνη ἡ φύσις οἷα ἐστὶ διδαχθεῖσα.
25 Cf. Plut. 395F (παραμυθίας πρὸς τὴν ἀπορίαν); 929F; Simplic. *in Phys.* 361, 19; Plut. *an. proc.* 1014A πιστούμενοι τῷ εἰκότι καὶ παραμυθούμενος in the context of his arguments for a creation of the world in time. Note the reference to ἀπόδειξις a few lines later. Cf. also Plut. 1012B.
26 V 3. 6, 8-12: ἆρ᾽ οὖν τοιοῦτον ὁ λόγος ἔδειξεν, οἷον καὶ ἐνέργειαν πιστικὴν ἔχειν; ἢ ἀνάγκην μὲν οὕτως, πειθὼ δὲ οὐκ ἔχει. καὶ γὰρ ἡ μὲν ἀνάγκη ἐν νῷ, ἡ δὲ πειθὼ ἐν ψυχῇ

There is, however, nothing surprising in this, for Plotinus often changes the emphasis of his evaluation of the different levels of reality depending on the point from which he is viewing them. Here intellect is being more sharply distinguished from soul level than in some of our other texts. Strictly speaking even Intellect is 'experienced' by us in so far as it lies above the level of discursive reasoning. But placing necessity (i.e. certainty) at the level of Intellect does not preclude its being also found at the discursive level. It is simply that the sort of necessity meant in this passage transcends that found in demonstrative reasoning. For elsewhere[27] necessity also characterizes discursive reasoning, so that convincing argument ($\pi i\sigma\tau\iota\varsigma$) can be said to lead to what is reasonable and necessary ($\varepsilon\ddot{\upsilon}\lambda o\gamma o\nu$ $\kappa\alpha i$ $\dot{\alpha}\nu\alpha\gamma\kappa\alpha\tilde{\iota}o\nu$). And so there is another kind of necessity at the discursive level.

I would like to conclude by considering a passage in VI 7, which brings us back clearly to the contrast with which we began between experience and reasoning. In the middle of this treatise we are presented with a transition from the level of reasoning to what lies above. In chapter eighteen Plotinus says that we cannot be satisfied in our search for Goodness with an argument for the goodness of the Intelligibles based on their derivation from the One. The argument must be pressed further: 'but the discussion is anxious to grasp the reason for their goodness' ($\dot{\alpha}\lambda\lambda\dot{\alpha}$ $\pi o\theta\varepsilon\tilde{\iota}$ $\dot{o}$ $\lambda\acute{o}\gamma o\varsigma$ $\lambda\alpha\beta\varepsilon\tilde{\iota}\nu,$ $\kappa\alpha\tau\dot{\alpha}$ $\tau\acute{\iota}$ $\tau\dot{o}$ $\dot{\alpha}\gamma\alpha\theta\dot{o}\nu$ $\alpha\dot{\upsilon}\tau\tilde{\omega}\nu$).[28] The discursive enquiry ($\lambda\acute{o}\gamma o\varsigma$) must be pursued. This is reflected in chapter nineteen; in our search we must not rely on the desire ($\ddot{\varepsilon}\varphi\varepsilon\sigma\iota\varsigma$) of soul, something which is described as an affection ($\pi\acute{\alpha}\theta o\varsigma$), but should rather use demonstrations ($\dot{\alpha}\pi o\delta\varepsilon\acute{\iota}\xi\varepsilon\iota\varsigma$). The enquiry is pressed home: 'our rational discourse seeks the reason why' ($\langle\dot{o}\rangle\lambda\acute{o}\gamma o\varsigma$ $\tau\dot{o}$ $\delta\iota\acute{o}\tau\iota$ $\zeta\eta\tau\varepsilon\tilde{\iota}$);[29] and only at the end of the passage do we have a hint that reason will not take us as far as the One: 'while discourse has not arrived there' ($\lambda\acute{o}\gamma o\upsilon$ $\mu\dot{\eta}$ $\varphi\theta\acute{\alpha}\nu o\nu\tau o\varsigma$). Another discursive argument is tried in chapter twenty. But the Goodness which lies above Intellect cannot be discerned by reason: 'the things that have intellect . . . seek Intellect from their reasoning, but the Good even before reason' ($\nu o\tilde{\upsilon}\nu$ $\mu\grave{\varepsilon}\nu$ $\dot{\varepsilon}\kappa$ $\lambda o\gamma\iota\sigma\mu o\tilde{\upsilon},$ $\tau\dot{o}$ δ' $\dot{\alpha}\gamma\alpha\theta\dot{o}\nu$ $\kappa\alpha i$ $\pi\rho\dot{o}$ $\tau o\tilde{\upsilon}$ $\lambda\acute{o}\gamma o\upsilon$).[30] The distinction of levels is clearly drawn. And yet the following chapters continue to pursue the matter discursively, a course of action that Plotinus is clearly aware of when he admonishes us at the beginning of Chapter 21: 'we must be bold' ($\ddot{\omega}\delta\varepsilon$ $\tau o\acute{\iota}\nu\upsilon\nu$ $\tau\varepsilon\tau o\lambda\mu\acute{\eta}\sigma\theta\omega$).

The same phenomenon is found within a few lines at the beginning of chapter forty. The context is the absence of intellection in the One. There

27 VI 5, 8, 1-5.
28 VI 7, 18, 50-1.
29 VI 7, 19, 17.
30 VI 7, 20, 21.

is firstly a reference to actual experience of the One—from such experience
we can know that there is no intellection there: 'those who have had a
contact of this kind would know . . .' (εἰδεῖεν ἂν οἱ προαψάμενοι τοῦ
τοιούτου). What follows is significant. For instead of ascent from reasoning
or intellection to what lies beyond, from knowledge to vision, we now
have the reverse order; reason is brought into play after the appeal to
experience: 'but we do need to add some words of encouragement to
what has been said' (δεῖ γε μὴν παραμύθια ἄττα πρὸς τοῖς εἰρημένοις κομίζειν).
And these παραμύθια are to be a mixture of persuasion (πειθώ) and necessity
(ἀνάγκη). The persuasion here is not the conviction of experience but the
confidence inspired by demonstrative proof ('necessity'). If we look back
to VI 9, 4, we can see a similar movement; for there starting with the
difficulties of approaching unity he concludes by pointing out the need
for λόγος.

The impression which these considerations lead to is that Plotinus'
thought can move in two ways. Firstly there is discursive argument based
on traditional Hellenic ideas, e.g. the discussion of unity and the need for
unity. There lies behind this particular line of enquiry a conviction that
unity is an important philosophical topic; this is an experience or inner
conviction which Plotinus shared with a wide spectrum of the philosophical
tradition. But there is, secondly, a mode of philosophical enquiry,
operating with respect to Intellect and the One, in which there is a
constant oscillation between experience of the One (or of Intellect) and
discursive reasoning about it. The 'experience' here may arguably have
similar psychological roots to that experience we have just referred to of
a deep conviction about the orderliness and eventual unity of reality; it is,
however, of a more intense kind, is clearly and openly recognized by
Plotinus, and is, moreover, accepted by him as an actual datum, as part
of the given reality of our situation. Yet whilst this actual experience of
unity may act as a stimulus to the discursive examination of the One, it
does not, I think, provide the premiss for establishing the One. That is
the task of reason.

In the end, of course, our souls can experience a kind of unity with
the One in which we are cut off from all else including our rational self.
The ultimate goal is the 'flight of the alone to the alone' (φυγὴ μόνου πρὸς
μόνον) as stated at the end of VI 9. But it is an experience which can
neither be reached nor communicated without reasoning or philosophical
enquiry. And however difficult it may be to discern the exact relationship
of reason and experience, it is abundantly clear from the rhythm of a
treatise like VI 9, from its constant pendulum-like swinging between
reason and experience, that reasoning is not a menial servant to a higher
activity but lies at the core of Plotinus' thought. Philosophizing remains
central, an interpretation which is also manifested in Plotinus' hesitation
elsewhere in deciding who *we* truly are, a tendency to locate the self both
at the transcendent level *and* at the level of discursive reasoning.[31]

---

31 Cf. A. Smith, *Porphyry's Place in the Neoplatonic Tradition* (The Hague, 1974), pp. 41-
   7; id. 'Unconsciousness and Quasiconsciousness in Plotinus', *Phronesis* 23 (1978), p. 293.

The Rationality of the Real
Proclus and Hegel

JOHN J. CLEARY

INTRODUCTION

Although system-building in philosophy has fallen into disrepute in this century, it is not because the perennial temptation to systematize has been finally overcome by something definitive like Gödel's incompleteness proof in mathematics. On the contrary, it is usually when some attempt to construct a system has failed that philosophers become temporarily disenchanted with the whole systematic approach, only later to resume their efforts from a new direction.[1] In view of this historical pattern, I think it is legitimate to wonder about the philosophical attraction of systems. Thus, taking Proclus and Hegel as ancient and modern systematizers respectively, I want to consider some questions about their motivation for constructing systems. For instance, why does Proclus systematize the metaphysical tradition stemming from Plato, Aristotle and Plotinus, given that these were aporetic rather than systematic thinkers.[2] Arguably, his concept of system is drawn from mathematics, as evidenced by his commentary on Euclid and by his Elements of Theology, so perhaps he wished to construct a definitive science based on this Greek model. But I want to suggest that religion was also a motivating factor, since we know from the Life written by his follower Marinus that Proclus zealously practised cult worship and theurgy. Thus, he may be completing the Iamblichean project of justifying pagan theology against the Christian faith, or he may be constructing a systematic science of theology as his own unique project.

1 For instance, one could take the Vienna Circle to be reacting against Hegelian systematizing, though one of the goals of their 'unity of science' project was to assemble a unified encyclopedia of the sciences.
2 Despite persistent attempts to reconstruct Plato's 'unwritten doctrine', it is clear that his extant dialogues are unsystematic in the sense that each constitutes its own dialogical space which is not systematically related to other dialogues. Although Aristotle does develop a body of doctrine in his own name, he cannot be said to have constructed a philosophical system in any modern sense, because he sharply differentiates the sciences from each other and adopts an aporetic approach in all of his inquiries. While one could reconstruct some kind of Neoplatonic system from the writings of Plotinus, his so-called *Enneads* are unsystematic in that they were written in response to specific questions rather than as a means of setting out any systematic doctrine.

From the philosophical point of view, however, he seems to be searching for some ultimate ungrounded hypothesis from which to deduce all of reality in a consistent fashion. Although Proclus represents his work as the completion of a Platonic project, it seems that he is pushing too far Plato's search for some adequate hypothesis grounded in language. Not even in the *Parmenides,* which was taken by Neoplatonists to exemplify dialectical theology, does Plato construct the sort of demonstrative science that Proclus presents in his *Elements of Theology.* So we must raise a question about what philosophical problems are being resolved through the construction of such a systematic science. But perhaps we should also entertain the possibility that Proclus had lost sight of the traditional problems of metaphysics, since his system seems to contain petrified answers to the old problems about the one and the many, cause and effect, prior and posterior. Thus, if one wishes to rehabilitate Proclus as an original thinker, one must show how he contributed to the Neoplatonic tradition by systematizing it.[3]

There are some clear parallels with Hegel, who resurrected systematic philosophy in the 19th century after the scepticism of Hume and the critical philosophy of Kant seemed to have buried it forever. In the Introduction to his *Encyclopedia*, for instance, he suggests that system satisfies the desire of reason for completeness through the progression from and return to first principles as a genuine ground. According to him, philosophy cannot be a scientific production without being systematic in such a way as to include all particular principles of the empirical sciences.[4] Like Plato before him, Hegel criticizes these special sciences for their lack of self-reflection and, on the basis of this critique, he makes rather sweeping claims for the superiority of reason. But Hegel's critique of Newton in his *Dissertation* on the planets also tells us something about his own conception of Nature as an objective embodiment of Absolute Spirit.[5] His major criticism is that such notions as gravity and inertia had not been properly deduced in a systematic way, so that they appear to be accidental rather than essential characteristics of natural bodies. Perhaps this critique is also motivated by Hegel's desire to justify metaphysics as a science, in view of the success of Newton's general theory of gravitation, which Kant viewed as a leading paradigm of scientific knowledge.

3   The typical view about Proclus' lack of originality is to be found in A. C. Lloyd's contribution to the *Cambridge History of Later Greek and Early Medieval Philosophy* (ed. A. H. Armstrong, Cambridge, 1967) where he claims (p. 311) that generally the concepts and hypostases of Proclus are not original but are derived from predecessors like Plotinus, Iamblichus and Syrianus. For spirited defences of Proclus as an original thinker one should consult W. Beierwaltes, *Proklos, Grundzüge seiner Metaphysik* (Frankfurt, 1965) and J. M. P. Lowry, *The Logical Principles of Proclus'* ΣΤΟΙΧΕΙΩΣΙΣ ΘΕΟΛΟΓΙΚΗ *as Systematic Ground of the Cosmos* (Amsterdam, 1980); cited below as *LPP.*

4   G. W. F. Hegel, *The Logic of Hegel* from *The Encyclopedia of the Philosophical Sciences*, trans. W. Wallace (Oxford, 1892), p. 24.

5   G. W. F. Hegel, *Dissertatio Philosophica de Orbitis Planetarum* (1801) translated by W. Neuser into German as *Philosophische Erörterung über die Planetenbahnen* (Weinheim, 1986); cited below as *Dissertation.*

Since the time of Hume and Kant, however, metaphysics has been steadily losing its legitimacy as a scientific enterprise. By contrast with mathematics and experimental physics, it seems to lack any definite procedure for deciding whether its claims are true or false. Although metaphysical arguments usually conform to the rules of logic, one can only reach true conclusions if one's initial assumptions are true. While the same holds for mathematics, it can be defended as a purely formal discipline concerned only with internal consistency, since there appears to be no independent 'reality' against which one might test its conclusions. But then perhaps a similarly consistent philosophical system could have just as good a claim to being true. If this argument seems plausible then it may help us to appreciate the perennial attraction of Platonism with its emphasis upon the internal consistency of a logical system of Ideas. In this article, I discuss Proclus and Hegel as two eminent exponents of such systematic rationalism in the history of philosophy.

It will be immediately obvious that my choice of thinkers is partly dictated by the fact that Proclus acknowledged the influence of Plato, and that Hegel, in turn, confessed himself to have been deeply influenced by both Plato and Proclus. But while these evident connections guide my initial approach to Proclus and Hegel, I sometimes take issue with their interpretations of Platonism. For instance, Proclus presents his *Elements of Theology* as an unhypothetical science according to the model of Euclid's *Elements*, though there is little solid evidence (despite reports about an 'unwritten doctrine') that Plato developed such a higher science. In order to show that Proclus adopted a mathematical model for his theology, I use his commentary on the first book of Euclid together with his *Elements of Theology*. In the case of Hegel, I correlate his remarks on Plato and Proclus in the *Lectures on the History of Philosophy*[6] with his conceptions of dialectical and speculative thinking as these are revealed in his *Logic*. Perhaps it is an unintentional example of 'the cunning of Reason' that, just like Proclus, Hegel's own philosophical programme seems to involve some creative misunderstandings of the Platonic tradition.[7]

I: MATHEMATICS AS A PROCLINE MODEL FOR SYSTEMATIZATION

We can see the attractions of a comprehensive system for Proclus (*in Crat.* 1.10–2.4) in his arguments for the superiority of what he calls Parmenidean dialectic over Aristotelian syllogism.[8] This hypothetical method is held to be superior to syllogism because it directs our attention more to the

---

6   G. W. F. Hegel, *Vorlesungen über die Geschichte der Philosophie. Werke* 19 (Frankfurt, 1971); cited below as *Vorlesungen*.

7   For instance, as Beierwaltes has shown, Hegel's own concept of dynamic negation as an integral element of the One is clearly a misunderstanding of Proclus' concept of the One; cf. W. Beierwaltes, *Platonismus und Idealismus* (Frankfurt, 1972), pp. 177–8.

8   My conventional references to Proclus' works are as follows: *in Crat.* = *In Platonis Cratylum commentaria*, ed. G. Pasquali (Leipzig, 1908); *in Eucl.* = *In primum Euclidis elementorum*

interrelationship of the Forms, through its affirmative and negative conditionals. Reflecting the same methodological preoccupation with system, Proclus insists (*in Parm.* 982.11–15; *Pl. Th.* I.9. 40, 10–12) on the correct order in the use of dialectic; i.e. division, definition, demonstration. Proclus promotes division as a method of teaching definitions, even though this method was rejected by Aristotle precisely because of its ontological presupposition that there is a single basic division of all classes and subclasses of reality. In contrast to Speusippus and later Platonists, Aristotle thought that this presupposition is not true of reality, and so he gave only a preliminary and secondary role to dialectical or 'logical' inquiry by comparison with scientific or 'physical' inquiry. In this scheme of things, the Aristotelian theory of the syllogism is not a part of philosophy but rather its instrument or *organon*.

From this perspective, we can appreciate Proclus' comparison of Platonic and Aristotelian logics in his commentary on Plato's *Cratylus*.[9] His criticism of Aristotle's logic as being merely about empty names shows that he regards Plato's dialectic as having a firmer grasp on reality. He also insists that a chain of hypotheses gives a better access to the truth, presumably on the assumption that reality is mapped out by such a logical structure. Finally, Proclus claims that this kind of dialectic is superior to syllogistic because its premises are reached by division which cuts reality at its natural joints, as the butcher metaphor of Plato's *Phaedrus* suggests. All of these claims underline the importance of Platonic dialectic as a guide to reality for Proclus, so we should study his related methodological conceptions. According to remarks in his *Platonic Theology* (I.10.45. 19–46.22), the series of hypotheses in Plato's *Parmenides* gives a chain of reasoning in which the first are derived from the fewest, simplest, and most self-evident ideas, which are sometimes called 'common notions'. The subsequent hypotheses are less simple and greater in number, and they follow from previous hypotheses just as if it were a geometrical system. The most important point, however, is that for Proclus the order of procession among divine realities can be traced by means of a mathematical model which seems to be adopted from Euclid.

At the beginning of the first prologue to his Euclid commentary, Proclus distinguishes mathematical being from the simplest partless realities, and from divisible things which are the most complex. After arguing for this ontological division, Proclus attributes it to Plato on the grounds that it corresponds to his distinction between different types of knowing. Thus intellect is held to correspond to indivisible realities because of their purity and freedom from matter. By contrast, opinion corresponds to divisible things in the lowest level of sensible natural objects; whereas understanding goes with intermediate things such as the forms studied by mathematics. While

---

librum commentarii, ed. G. Friedlein (Leipzig, 1873); *in Parm.* = *In Platonis Parmenidem commentaria*, from *Opera inedita*, ed. V. Cousin (Paris, 1864), 617–1258; *Pl. Th.* = *In Platonis Theologiam libri sex*, ed. E. Portus (Hamburg, 1618).

9 For an excellent recent study of this and related logical issues in Neoplatonism one should consult A. C. Lloyd, *The Anatomy of Neoplatonism* (Oxford, 1990); cited below as *AP*.

marking it as inferior to intellect, Proclus argues that understanding is more perfect, more exact, and purer than opinion:

> For it traverses and unfolds the measureless content of Nous by making articulate its concentrated intellectual insight, and then gathers together again the things it has distinguished and refers them back to Nous.[10]

In spite of appeals to Plato's authority and the use of familiar language from the *Philebus* (58–9), I think that here we have something unique to Proclus; namely, epistemological and ontological grounds for composing his *Elements of Theology* along Euclidean lines. The crucial point for this project is that (mathematical) understanding is a means by which the unitary content of intellect is reflected in a multiple form that makes it accessible to our discursive thinking. Although he insists that mathematical objects are multiform images which only imitate the uniform patterns of being, one suspects that Proclus finds them indispensable for obtaining access to the completely unitary objects of intellect. At least, this is a natural way to interpret the metaphor about mathematicals standing in the vestibule (ἐν προθύροις) of the primary forms, announcing their unitary and undivided and generative reality (*in Eucl.* 5.2–3).

My interpretation seems to be supported by Proclus' treatment of Limit and Unlimited both as mathematical principles and as principles of being as a whole. According to his *Elements of Theology* (*ET*, 89–90), these are the two highest principles after the indescribable and utterly incomprehensible One. By contrast with the One, which remains (μονή) always in itself without procession, these transcendent principles do give rise to an ordered procession (πρόοδος) of things that appear in their appropriate divisions. Noetic objects, for instance, by virtue of their inherent simplicity, are the primary participants because their unity, identity, and stable existence are derived from the Limit, while their variety, fecundity, and otherness are drawn from the Unlimited (*ET*, 90–2). While mathematical objects are also the offspring of the Limit and the Unlimited, Proclus emphasizes (*in Eucl.* 6.7 ff.) that some secondary principles are involved in the generation of this intermediate order of things. Although he does not identify these principles, his examples suggest that they are principles in arithmetic and geometry which are seen as reflections of the primary principles of Limit and Unlimited. In the mathematical order of being, he says, there are ratios proceeding to infinity (reflecting the Unlimited) but controlled by the principle of the Limit. For instance, number is capable of being increased indefinitely, yet any number you choose is finite. Likewise, magnitudes are indefinitely divisible, yet the magnitudes distinguished from one another are all bounded, and the actual parts of the whole are limited. From these examples, I think it is clear that the Unlimited is reflected in the multiplicity of number and in the divisibility

---

10 *In Eucl.* 4.12–14: translation by G. Morrow, *Proclus. A Commentary on the First Book of Euclid's Elements* (Princeton, 1970), p. 3.

of the continuum, both of which are controlled by some principle which reflects the Limit. Since mathematics presents such an accessible model for the characteristic activity of these principles, it is little wonder that Proclus finds it so indispensable for understanding how they function throughout the intelligible realm, which is the subject-matter of his theology.

But the most important evidence, of course, is Proclus' own explicit discussion (*in Eucl.* 21.25 ff.) of the contribution of mathematics to all branches of philosophy, and especially to theology. According to him, mathematics prepares the mind for theology by showing through images that apparently difficult and obscure truths about the gods are evident and irrefutable. For instance, it shows that numbers reflect the properties of transcendent beings (ὑπερουσίων), and it reveals the powers of the intellectual figures within the objects of the understanding. It is not at all clear what Proclus has in mind, even though he refers to Plato's many and wonderful teachings (δόγματα) about the gods by means of mathematical forms. This reference to some unwritten doctrines is not clarified in any way by the subsequent references to the secret theological teaching of the Pythagoreans, the so-called 'sacred discourse'[11] of Philolaus, and the treatise of Pythagoras on the gods. Apparently, all of these displayed the same tendency to clothe theology in mathematical garments, but we are not given any more information as to what precise form this took. In any case, given the Neopythagoreanism of Proclus himself, it is at least significant that he should cite these as precedents for his own approach to theology. It seems to indicate the general direction that he will take, though none of its details.

II: THEOLOGY AS PROCLUS' SYSTEMATIC SCIENCE

I propose to treat the *Elements of Theology* as a self-contained rational system about which one can ask internal and external systematic questions.[12] For instance, why does Proclus give primacy to the proposition (*ET*, 1) that 'Every manifold in some way participates unity'? To begin an unhypothetical science, he needs something that is presupposed by every other proposition but it is difficult to see how *ET*, 1 fits the bill. Perhaps one clue is to be found in the sort of proof given; i.e. *reductio per impossibile*. Thus he supposes the opposite of the proposition to be the case; i.e. that there is a

11   Morrow (ibid., p. 19, n. 42) notes that this ἱερὸς λόγος is cited frequently by Iamblichus in his so-called *Life of Pythagoras*, and by Syrianus in his commentary on Aristotle's *Metaphysics* (10.5, 123.2, 140.16, 175.6, Kroll), and by a contemporary of Proclus, Hierocles of Alexandria, in his commentary on the *Carmen Aureum* (I.464 Mullach). Morrow speculates that these so-called 'sacred writings' may have been an invention of late Neopythagoreanism, though he does not doubt that Proclus takes them seriously.

12   Lowry (*LPP*) has adopted a similar approach to this work as a systematic treatise but he has completely ignored its mathematical dimensions, while also paying scant attention to the religious motivation for Proclus' system.

manifold which in no way participates unity. Then he shows that, however one interprets this supposition, it leads to impossibilities. As a result, by indirect proof, he has established that every multitude in some way participates unity. The second proposition ('All that participates unity is both one and not-one') is proved in a straightforward way from the meaning of participation in unity; i.e. that something has unity as an effect and is not pure unity. So this something is one, in the sense of being affected by unity, but is also not-one because the unity is by addition and not by itself.

The next logical step in the argument is represented by *ET*, 3: 'All that becomes one does so by participation of unity.' The key point in this proof is that becoming one implies participation of unity, and so rules out the possibility that it is one absolutely. So this leads straight on to *ET*, 4 ('All that is unified is other than the One itself') which is proved indirectly with the help of the previous two propositions (*ET*, 2 & 3). Dominic O'Meara claims that Proclus regarded *ET*, 4 as the first principle of his system, while treating the previous propositions as part of the way to such a principle.[13] Whatever the case may be, *ET*, 5 ('Every manifold is posterior to the One') shows some signs of an emerging system of priority and posteriority, with its important conclusion that there is a transcendent One which is also participated by every plurality. Subsequently (*ET*, 6) he establishes the basic point that no plurality is indefinitely divisible but is composed either of unified groups or of units.

According to Dodds, the first six propositions deal with the One and the Many, which was a basic topic of Greek dialectic.[14] From the systematic point of view, however, we can still ask why these propositions are chosen as primary for the subsequent development of the system. Perhaps the best way to answer this question is to explore the internal connections and dependencies of propositions within the whole system. For instance, there seems to be no good reason why the system should not begin with *ET*, 7: 'Every productive cause is superior ($\kappa\rho\varepsilon\tilde{\iota}\tau\tau o\nu$) to that which it produces.' As Dodds has pointed out, this is arguably the basic principle on which the whole structure of Neoplatonism is founded. The proof is similar to that given for *ET*, 1 in that it works by the elimination of alternative possibilities and does not depend on any previous propositions. So why does Proclus not place it at the head of his system? The answer depends partly on the Greek tradition of dialectical inquiry and partly on Proclus' own system in which the existence of the One is first established before its causative role is elaborated. I think that the One and the Many also reflect the principles of Limit and Unlimited, which come directly after the transcendent One.

13 D. J. O' Meara, *Pythagoras Revived: Mathematics and Philosophy in Late Antiquity* (Oxford, 1989), p. 204. He finds some vital evidence in the *Platonic Theology* (II.66, 1–9) where Proclus identifies a thesis from Plato's *Parmenides* ('The One, if it is one, may not be many' —137C) as the very first concept of a science proceeding from the intellect.
14 E. R. Dodds (tr. & comm.), *Proclus. The Elements of Theology* (Oxford, 1933), pp. 3–7 (Cited below as *PET* to distinguish it from the propositions themselves, cited as *ET*).

But these connections are not established immediately, since the next proposition (*ET*, 8) argues for the unity and transcendence of the Good or final cause. The argument depends on the self-evident (to the Greek mind) assumption that all things which exist desire the good. From this assumption it is argued that the primal good is beyond all such things because, if they desire the good, it is evident that none of them can be identical with it. In Procline jargon, if they 'participate' the Good then they cannot be the Good absolutely (ἁπλῶς), just as things which 'participate' the One cannot be identical with it. Here the guiding maxim accepted by Proclus (*Th. Pl.* II.7, 101) is the Plotinian one (III 8, 11; 9, 3; V 5, 13) that the addition of characteristics diminishes what is absolute. The basic notion is that what is simple, like absolute goodness, is made less perfect by any addition because that emphasizes some aspect at the expense of others. Since Proclus realizes that all definition involves some denial, he asserts that absolute goodness is indefinable and hence completely transcendent, thereby making a typical Neoplatonic transition from the logical to the metaphysical order of things.

Given the complete primacy of absolute goodness, the next two propositions (*ET*, 9 & 10) establish the intermediate position of what is self-sufficient (τὸ αὔταρκες) between simple goodness and what is not self-sufficient. *ET*, 9 states that everything which is self-sufficient either in its existence or in its activity is superior to what is not self-sufficient but rather dependent upon another existing thing as the cause of its completeness. It also notes that the self-sufficient has more likeness to the Good itself, though it is not itself the primal good because it participates good. This partly anticipates *ET*, 10, which claims that everything which is self-sufficient is inferior to the unqualified Good. According to Proclus, the self-sufficient is that which has its good from and in itself, but that also implies that it participates good and so is not identical with the Good itself which transcends participation and fulfilment. These two propositions establish the self-sufficient as an Iamblichean 'mean term' between the unqualified Good and things which are good merely by participation. The self-sufficient resembles the Good itself in that its goodness is self-derived, and it resembles good things in so far as its goodness inheres in the not-good or the less-than-good. The assumption of Iamblichus (adopted by Proclus as a general rule) is that it would be impossible to bridge the gap between the Good itself and good things without something intermediate which shares some characteristics of each. It is such an assumption (based on the use of mean terms in mathematical proportion) which leads to the typical Neoplatonic multiplication of entities by filling up the intermediate spaces in a triadic fashion. This seems to be the logical ground for Proclus' introduction of henads between the One and the whole noetic realm, although he also has religious reasons for bringing them into his system. It would be quite consistent with the religious aspects of his Pythagoreanism to suggest that Proclus saw these henads as combining both the principles of Limit and Unlimited as actual and potential elements (*ET*, 159). This is reflected at lower levels in his system because he regards all Being as a mixture or synthesis of Limit and Unlimited, just as Plato's *Philebus* had suggested.

In *ET*, 13 systematic unity begins to emerge through the identification of the Good with the One. The argument (such as it is) is that, if unification is in itself good, and if all good tends to create unity, then the unqualified Good and the unqualified One merge as a single principle which makes things both one and good. Apart from some intriguing terminology, the argument seems to provide no more than bald assertions of previous principles and conclusions. However, it does give a clear connection between two previous groups of propositions, which dealt with the One and the Many (*ET*, 1–6) and with causes (*ET*, 7–12), respectively. Although the One and the Good are not identified explicitly anywhere in Plato's dialogues, Dodds (*PET*, p. 199) thinks that Proclus is justified in representing this as Platonic doctrine, but I see it more as an illustration of the sort of creative misunderstanding involved in systematizing an unsystematic tradition.

According to the plausible divisions supplied by Dodds, the next 11 propositions (*ET*, 14–24) set out the Neoplatonic schema for a vertical stratification of reality. For instance, *ET*, 14 classifies all things as either unmoved, or intrinsically moved or extrinsically moved. As Dodds rightly emphasizes, this is not just a logical schema but also an ontological division of reality, which combines the Aristotelian unmoved mover with the Platonic self-moving mover, even though Aristotle's views seem to have developed in opposition to those of Plato. From the historical viewpoint, therefore, Proclus' *reductio* argument for the existence of an unmoved mover is worth examining. If we suppose all extrinsic movement to be derived from an agent, which is itself in motion, then we have either a circle of communicated motion or an infinite regress. But neither is possible, according to Proclus, because the sum of existence is limited by a first principle (*ET*, 11), and the mover is superior to the moved (*ET*, 7). So there must be something unmoved, which is the first mover.

One noteworthy point about the argument is Proclus' conception of the unmoved mover both as a productive and as a final cause, which gives the previous propositions about such causes an important role in the proof. An unaristotelian implication of this conception is that the unmoved mover is treated as the primary member in a chain of downward causation. Another example of creative synthesis by Proclus appears in his argument for the necessity of something self-moved as a link between the unmoved mover and the externally moved thing. Suppose that all things are at rest, what will be the first thing set in motion? By definition it cannot be the unmoved mover, nor can it be the externally moved thing, since its motion is communicated from outside. By elimination, therefore, the self-moved must be the first thing set in motion, as a kind of mean term (μέσον) between the unmoved mover and that which is extrinsically moved. Here we see the Iamblichean rule of mean terms used to fill up a perceived gap left by Aristotle's uncertainty over the place of self-moving souls in his cosmology.

    In connection with the development of the Procline system, the movement
out from and back to the One is outlined in *ET*, 25 to 39, which deal with
the spiritual motions of procession and reversion. For example, *ET*, 25 states
that whatever is complete proceeds to generate those things which it is
capable of producing, thereby imitating the one originative principle of the
universe. The argument depends upon the assumption that this first principle,
on account of its own goodness, is by a unitary act constitutive of all that is,
since the Good is identical with the One (*ET*, 13) and action under the form
of goodness is identical with unitary action. In a similar way, principles inferior
to the One are impelled by their own completeness to generate further
principles inferior to their own being (*ET*, 7). The reason for such impulsion
is that the Good is constitutive of all things (*ET*, 12), and so whatever is
complete is by nature productive within the limits of its power. Here there
is a direct connection between degrees of reality and of productiveness in
the following way. The more complete is the cause of more, in proportion
to the degree of its completeness, since the more complete participates the
Good more fully; i.e. it is nearer to the Good or is more akin to the cause of
all. The basic rule of this hierarchy is that whatever constitutes a larger class
of things comes nearest to the universal performance of these functions,
while a like service to a smaller class stands at a further remove. The explicit
corollary of this rule is that the principle most remote from the beginning of
all things is sterile and a cause of nothing. Proclus seems to be referring here
to unitary and primary matter, which stands sterile at the lowest point in the
system whose highest point is the fruitful One.[15] Dodds (*PET*, p. 212) reads
this proposition as a formal statement of the Plotinian law of emanation,
whose implicit panzoism is extended to the hierarchy of cosmic principles.
But it is also possible to read the proposition as an expression of a Neoplatonic
principle of plenitude which is connected exclusively with form and not
with any potency of aristotelian matter.[16]

    In fact, Proclus insists upon the inseparability of the similarity and difference
between the cause and its immediate product in every procession. Such
insistence conforms to the 'mean term' rule and also lays the foundations for
the opposite movement of reversion in which whatever has proceeded also
reverts in respect of its being upon that from which it proceeds (*ET*, 31). Just
as the One is the ultimate principle of procession, the Good is the principle of
reversion because all things seek to attain the Good through their own
proximate causes. Such a cause is the source of well-being for each thing and
is also the primary object of its desire. Thus, according to Proclus (*ET*, 32),
all reversion is achieved through some likeness between the reverting terms
and the goal of reversion. This gives rise to a cycle of procession and reversion

15   This gives the misleading impression that Proclus' hierarchy is linear, whereas, in fact, it
        is circular in character; so that (paradoxically) unitary matter is in a certain way nearest to
        the One.
16   This is similar to A. C. Lloyd's (*AP*, pp. 106 ff) interpretation of what he calls 'the
        Proclan rule' as an aversion from dualism.

between the principle and that which it produces (*ET*, 33), by virtue of the natural sympathy between the two. Whatever reverts by nature is said to have desire in respect of its being for that upon which it reverts. We see here the basis for natural magic in the Procline system, since likeness is the principle on which theurgy depends for its theoretical possibility. A corollary of *ET*, 34 is that all things proceed from Intelligence (νοῦς), since it is an object of desire to all things. Thus, according to Proclus, it is from Intelligence that the whole world-order is derived, even though it is eternal. This represents his attempt to reconcile Plato's talk of the 'generation' of a cosmos in the *Timaeus* with the Academic tradition that the world-order is eternal. Since the procession is logical rather than temporal, Intelligence can proceed eternally and be eternally reverted, while still remaining steadfast in its own place in the cosmos.

However, the tidiness of the Procline system appears to be upset somewhat by the introduction (*ET*, 40) of things called 'self-constituted' (αὐθυπόστατον) which get their substance from themselves, as distinct from things that proceed from another cause. At first sight it seems that such entities can find no place in the continuous system of procession and reversion to a first principle that functions as both formal-efficient and as final cause. Furthermore, one wonders why Proclus felt it necessary to introduce such entities into his neat monistic system. By way of answer, Dodds (*PET*, p. 224) suggests that he is trying to make some provision for the freedom of the human will, which was a necessary ethical postulate in Hellenistic philosophy. He argues that the concept of 'self-constituted' here does not mean 'self-caused' in the sense of being an independent principle, but rather it 'hypostatizes itself' or determines the particular potentiality that will be actualized in it. But Whittaker[17] has cast doubt upon Dodds' historical account, which also fails to explain the role of self-constituted things in the whole deductive system. Thus, I think one must seek an alternative answer by way of comparison with the place of henads as the highest self-constituted entities.

In *ET*, 40 the argument for self-constituted entities depends heavily on an earlier proposition (*ET*, 9) that whatever is self-sufficient, either with respect to being or to activity, is superior to anything that is dependent on another as the cause of its completeness. It is not a big step to the conclusion that things which are produced by themselves or are self-constituted are senior (πρεσβύτερα) to those things which derive their being solely from another. Yet the *reductio* argument by exhaustion repays scrutiny. Proclus outlines three possibilities: either there is nothing self-constituted, or the Good is such a thing, or else the principles which arise first from the Good are such things. It is through his rejection of the first possibility that we get the clearest view of the necessity of self-constituted things in his system. If there are no such things, he argues, then there will be no true self-sufficiency in

17   J. Whittaker, 'The Historical Background of Proclus' Doctrine of the *ΑΥΘΥΠΟΣΤΑΤΑ*,' *Entretiens* 21 (1974), 193–230.

anything; neither in the Good nor in things posterior to the Good. Since such a lacuna is unacceptable, it remains to decide whether the Good itself is self-constituted or only things posterior to the Good. But he argues that the Good cannot be self-constituted because it would thereby lose its unity in producing itself, since that which proceeds from the One is not-One. So he concludes that self-constituted things must exist as posterior to the first principle but as prior to things that depend completely on another cause.

This whole argument establishes the intermediate place of self-constituted things in the Neoplatonic hierarchy between the transcendent first principle and lower entities that have only external causes. In *ET*, 41 these latter are distinguished from self-constituted entities in terms of what has its existence 'in another', as distinct from what exists 'in itself'. Here the self-constituted is identified with that which can exist in its own right without inhering in a substrate, just as soul can exist without body, and intelligence without soul. These parallels are reinforced by *ET*, 42 and 43 which state that whatever is self-constituted is capable of reversion upon itself and vice versa. I think we can take Proclus to be referring to the capacity for self-reflection which is a characteristic function of the higher faculties of the soul.

But Proclus also argues (*ET*, 44) from their self-reflective activity to the independent existence of self-constituted things. As Dodds (*PET*, p. 225) points out, this is an essential step for the proof of the immortality of self-constituted entities, which he gives in the subsequent propositions (*ET*, 45–51). In *ET*, 45, for instance, he argues that they are without temporal origin because everything having such an origin is in itself incomplete and needs the perfective activity of something external. By contrast, whatever produces itself is perpetually complete, since it is always immanent in its cause as the principle that perfects its being. The corollary of this (*ET*, 46) is that everything self-constituted is also imperishable because a condition of perishability is that something can be separated from its cause. If we assume that having parts or being complex is another such condition, then the imperishability of self-constituted things is also supported by the proposition (*ET*, 47) which establishes that they are simple; i.e. without parts. Such a conclusion is confirmed by *ET*, 48 which claims that whatever is not perpetual is either composite or has its subsistence in another, while *ET*, 49 holds that whatever is self-constituted is perpetual. Finally, *ET*, 50 and 51 together establish that whatever is self-constituted transcends the things that are measured by time with respect to their existence. Dodds (*PET*, p. 227) claims that Proclus here introduces the distinction between temporal existence and temporal activity in order to allow the human soul to engage in such activity, even though it has immortal existence as a self-constituted entity (*ET*, 191).

With reference to Proclus' own philosophical and spiritual motivation for system-building, however, perhaps the most illuminating problems arise from his introduction of henads as independent entities between the transcendent One and the whole noetic realm. The difficulties associated with these entities have already been well discussed by Dodds (*PET*, pp. 257–60) and Beutler,[18] so that I can focus my questions on their function in his system. It is clear that their introduction is motivated by Proclus' desire to give the traditional gods a leading role in his system of theology, even though Homer's lusty anthropomorphic figures become metaphysical abstractions in the process. Yet I think that this transformation, which Dodds (*PET*, p. 260) regards as 'one of time's strangest ironies', is precisely what Proclus needs to justify theurgy as a religious practice. If the henad which stands at the head of each hierarchical series has 'processed' in continuous steps to the lowest intelligible things, then it is possible to return to the deity by retracing these steps. Such a return corresponds to what Plotinus had already spoken about in terms of mystical union with the One, without providing any theoretical or practical guidance on how it might be achieved. Even though Proclus takes the One to be completely unknowable and inaccessible, the positing of henads seems intended to supply intermediaries by means of which divine power can be exercised and recognized. This move also has important implications for divine providence, about which Proclus wrote at least two treatises; i.e. *de providentia et fato*, and *de decem dubitationibus circa providentiam*.[19]

In contrast to the earlier Greek religious tradition (which belongs mainly to the poets), it is noteworthy that Proclus feels obliged to give a formal deductive proof (*ET*, 113) of polytheism. Along with being an argument against Christian monotheism, this represents a solution to the Plotinian problem of bridging the gap between the transcendent One and the rest of reality by appealing to the Iamblichan rule of mean terms. But perhaps the most problematic proposition (*ET*, 114) is that every god is a self-complete henad and, conversely, that every self-complete thing is a god. The long-standing difficulty here is how the gods can be self-complete ($\alpha\dot{v}\tau\sigma\tau\epsilon\lambda\dot{\eta}\varsigma$) if they owe their divine character to participation in the One. Similar difficulties have already been raised about the 'self-sufficient' and 'self-constituted' things, which do not fit comfortably into a hierarchical causal series that begins with the One. The problem is merely compounded by the subsequent proposition (*ET*, 115) which claims that, as a self-complete henad, every god is above Being, Life, and Intelligence. Although Proclus sometimes uses the term 'gods' more generally and loosely, he posits henads (i.e. gods in the strict sense) as transcending the three Plotinian hypostases. This indicates, I think, that he is using the henads to bridge the gap which Plotinus left between One and the rest of reality. But, as Dodds (*PET*, p. 261) points out, such a metaphysical doctrine can only be squared with traditional theology by a rather artificial use of the principle that everything is in everything but appropiately ($o\dot{i}\kappa\epsilon\dot{i}\omega\varsigma$) in each. However, the very fact that Proclus makes such efforts to insert the traditional cult gods into his system shows that reli-

18. R. Beutler, 'Proklos' in Pauly-Wissowa, *Realenkyklopaedie der klassischen Altertums-wissenschaft*, Band XXXIII, 1 (1957), cols. 186–247.
19 *Tria Opuscula*, ed. H. Boese (Berlin, 1960), pp. 3–108, 109–71.

gious theory and practice were important motives for composing the *Elements of Theology*.

This intermediary role of the henads becomes clearer with the proposition (*ET*, 116) that every god is participable, except the One which transcends all participation. Since the henads are self-complete unities that are most like the One, they are most closely linked to it but not by participation. However, they themselves are linked to lower unities by participation, and so a henad will stand at the head of each order (συστοιχία) which proceeds downward by participation. This is another way of understanding the proposition (*ET*, 117) that every god is a measure of things existent. The claim is that, since each henad has the character of unity, it defines and measures all the manifolds of existents (οὐσίαι). Proclus' proof also appeals to his very first proposition (*ET*, 1) that manifolds are essentially indeterminate and so require unity for their determination. But, consistent with the Procline division of reality, it is the manifolds of existents (ὄντα) that are measured by the henads, while the Forms serve as measures for the manifolds of generated things (γιγνόμενα). Here the systematic principles of Limit and Unlimited in Proclus' thinking about the divine are reflected throughout the system, thereby providing further theoretical foundations for the theory and practice of theurgy.

Finally, let me consider briefly those propositions (*ET*, 119–24) that bear directly or indirectly on the question of divine providence. The foundation is laid with the claim (*ET*, 119) that every god is (as distinct from having) supra-existential (ὑπερουσίως) excellence. It follows (*ET*, 120) that every god has the essential function of exercising providence towards the universe; i.e. the bestowal of good things upon the secondary existences which thereby convey the good to all things. By way of evidence for providence as an appropriate activity of the divine, Proclus points out that the term 'providence' (πρόνοια) itself refers to an activity prior to Intelligence (πρὸ νοῦ). While we may regard this as mere word-play, it is typical of the Platonic tradition to search for evidence in the wisdom of language. For Proclus the term 'providence' itself indicates that it belongs appropriately to the henads which he places beyond Intelligence in his own system, by way of opposition to Plotinus. In order to safeguard the transcendence of the gods Proclus emphasizes that they maintain their substantial unity, even while exercising providence towards secondary existences. Thus the gods are in no danger of becoming busybodies, since their goodness shines on everything like the light of the sun and each thing partakes in their providence according to its own limited capacity. In contrast to the one-sidedness of Aristotle and the Stoics, Proclus triumphantly reconciles providence with the transcendence of the gods through his system of procession and reversion.

III: PHILOSOPHY AS HEGEL'S SYSTEMATIC SCIENCE

I find it significant that Hegel resisted the defamation of Proclus as a religious zealot (*Schwärmerei*) by contemporary historians of philosophy like Brucker

(1742), Tiedemann (1793) and Tenneman (1807). Clearly, this revaluation of Neoplatonism played an important role in his own view of history as the development of Absolute Spirit found in art, religion, and philosophy. Thus it is understandable that Hegel should read the history of philosophy as more ordered and rational than perhaps it was in fact. Though he acknowledges that there may have been contradictions (i.e. reverses) at the particular levels, he insists that they are 'taken up' (*aufgehoben*) within the truth of the whole. This has the rather paradoxical result that the history of philosophy is no longer history in our usual sense, but rather an idealized retrospective on the development of Absolute Spirit from the point of view of principles and ideas which reflect the manifestation of Spirit in Hegel's own time. If we view such self-centeredness (which Aristotle also displays) in philosophers as typical of their hermeneutical situation, we may find some truth in Hegel's schematic reconstruction of history. In such an idealized history, Plato is treated as the discoverer of speculative Dialectic because he recognized the identity in difference of being and non-being, one and many. Aristotle is also very important as the first thinker to grasp the concept of pure actuality through his notion of the divine as 'thought thinking itself'. This is taken to be an anticipation of Hegel's own notion of self-conscious Reason.[20]

But Hegel's greatest praise is reserved for Proclus, because he introduced triadic thinking into his theology. He is praised especially for not dealing with the triad as three abstract parts but rather as one concrete totality which retains and fulfils all three determinations. For Hegel the crucial conceptual advance is that the internal differentiations of the Idea are retained in the whole. Thus he regards Proclus as the leading thinker among the Neoplatonists, and as more advanced than Plotinus (*Vorlesungen* § 473). This passage helps to clarify Hegel's admiration for Proclus, though even more remarkable is his interpretation of the mystical tendencies in Neoplatonic philosophy as speculative thinking (§ 484). Such an interpretation of Proclus is undoubtedly influenced by Hegel's own conception of religion as an aspect of Absolute Spirit which is brought to its conceptual fulfilment through philosophy. Hegel's *Logic* outlines the way in which Spirit moves from an abstract and empty universal toward a concrete universal that is in-itself and for-itself. The traditional distinction between form and content is supposedly overcome in this logic, whose function is to follow the inner movement toward the truth of the whole (cf. *Logik* I, § 31; II, § 356).

In his Introduction to the *Logic*, which is the first part of Hegel's *Encyclopedia of the Philosophical Sciences*, we find ample evidence for the religious motivation behind his own philosophical system, when he identifies Truth or God as the common object of philosophy and religion. Hegel also cites the

---

20   Gadamer has shown that this is a misunderstanding on Hegel's part, just as is his interpretation of Plato's *Sophist*, though these are good examples of 'creative' misunderstanding; cf. H.-G. Gadamer, *Hegels Dialektik* (Tübingen, 1971) trans. P. C. Smith, *Hegel's Dialectic* (New Haven, 1976), chap. 1.

anthropological evidence for a distinction between mankind and the lower animals in terms of a capacity for religion and philosophy. Furthermore he claims (§ 6) that the content of philosophy is Actuality understood as the core of truth for the world of consciousness, both inward and outward. Since philosophy is different only in form from other modes of becoming acquainted with the same reality, it must be in harmony with experience, which may even serve as an extrinsic means of testing the truth of a philosophy. But, according to Hegel, the highest and final aim of philosophic science is to bring about a reconciliation of self-conscious reason with the Reason which is in the world; i.e. Actuality. On this basis he defends the controversial propositions contained in the preface to his *Philosophy of Law*; namely, that what is reasonable is actual, and that what is actual is reasonable. Behind this stands his religious belief in divine government for the world, whose philosophical meaning is that God is the supreme and only true Actuality. In the *Logic* Hegel distinguishes Actuality not only from the fortuitous but also from the categories of existence and other modifications of being. Indeed, his thesis about the actuality of the rational involves a rejection of the traditional distinctions between idea and reality, and between 'is' and 'ought'. For him philosophy is about an Idea or Actuality whose phenomenal aspects are represented by external objects and social conditions.

However, Hegel also acknowledges the right of the empirical sciences to be called philosophical, and he even accepts as a principle that one must be in touch with their subject-matters, either through the external senses or through our intimate self-consciousness. Although these sciences begin with experience, he argues that their aim is to provide general propositions about what exists and that it is this feature which makes them philosophical. Yet, according to him, such empirical knowledge cannot deal with objects like freedom, spirit, and God, whose scope and content is infinite. This shortcoming requires one to move to the higher viewpoint of speculative philosophy which assumes that Mind or Spirit is the cause of the world, and this means that morality and religion can arise from and rest upon thought alone. Furthermore, the demand of subjective reason for necessity is not satisfied by the empirical sciences because of two defects of method; namely, that the universal propositions are not connected with particulars, and that their principles are postulates which are neither accounted for nor deduced. When reflection tries to remedy these defects it becomes the sort of speculative thinking that belongs to philosophy.

Yet Hegel emphasizes that such a speculative science does not neglect the positive sciences, but rather appropriates for its own structure their universal laws and classifications. In addition, however, it introduces other categories that are commensurate with the concepts typical of philosophical thought. Thus, for instance, speculative logic contains all previous logic and metaphysics by preserving the same forms of thought, while expanding into wider categories. Hegel recognizes (§ 10) the need to defend his rather extravagant claims that speculative philosophy is able to apprehend absolute objects like God, spirit, and freedom; though he thinks that such a defence is best given through his own practice of this science. Against Kant's prohibition on metaphysics, Hegel objects that the proposed critical examination of knowledge itself involves the sort of speculative dialectic that he himself uses in the philosophical science. Hence, in spite of what Kant says, philosophy must be continued so as to satisfy a craving in the most inward life of the mind, which expresses itself in thinking. Due to the narrowness of understanding, mind entangles itself in contradictions and stimulates the craving of reason to work out the solutions in itself. But, in order to overcome these contradictions, mind must rise above the dialectical to the speculative mode of thinking (§ 80–2).

Thus Hegel attributes the perennial character of philosophy to this craving for thought in the human mind. While it begins with experience, its antagonism to sense phenomena leads it to the Idea of the universal essence of these phenomena. Even the empirical sciences stimulate the mind to overcome the form in which their varied contents are presented and to elevate these contents into necessary truths. While incorporating the contents of the empirical sciences, philosophy makes such contents imitate the action of the original creative Thought and the evolution of the Absolute. Therefore, contrary to what his many critics say, Hegel does hold experience to be the real author of growth and advance in philosophy. According to him, philosophy owes its development to the empirical sciences, though it adds the *a priori* character that constitutes the freedom of thought in itself. The empirical contents are now warranted as necessary and no longer dependent on the evidence of facts, which themselves become illustrations and copies of the original and self-sufficient activity of thought. Incidentally, this view about the higher role of philosophy throws a different light on Hegel's *Dissertation,* where he tries to establish the necessity of Newton's laws of planetary motion.

Hegel also claims (§ 13) to have some insight into the inner necessity of the origin and development of philosophy, which is reflected externally in the history of philosophy. From the historical point of view, the stages in the evolution of the Idea seem to follow each other by accident but Hegel thinks that this cannot be the case because the Architect directing the work is the one living Mind whose nature is to think and to bring its own essence to self-consciousness. For him the latest development in philosophy is the result of all the preceding systems, and so must include their principles. Thus philosophy will be the fullest, most comprehensive, and most adequate system of all. Here we can see the philosophical and religious motivations that lie behind Hegel's interest in system as an expression of the Absolute.[21]

21 In Hegel's doctrine of Essence (§ 112 & 159) we find more evidence for the religious motivation behind his philosophy, when he insists that the absolutely infinite God is identical with the inner essence of things, and so should not be treated as some supreme other-worldly being. See also his discussion of the compatibility of necessity and providence within the divine as Actuality (§ 147–9).

He is particularly insistent that the system of philosophy, whose principle is universal, cannot be put on the same level with any other system whose principle is particular. The same evolution of thought that is presented externally in the history of philosophy is also presented in the system of philosophy itself within its own internal medium of thought. Thinking which is genuine and self-supporting must be intrinsically concrete, and when it is viewed in its universality, it is the Idea or the Absolute. For Hegel the science of this Idea must form a system because truth is only possible as a universe or totality of thought. Thus philosophy cannot be a scientific production unless it forms a system whose universal principle is to include every particular principle. Due to its encyclopedic character, philosophy does not give a detailed exposition of particulars but rather outlines the principles of the special sciences and the notions of chief importance in each. But, unlike ordinary encyclopedias which present bits of knowledge in a wholly extrinsic arrangement, the encyclopedia of philosophy must form a system because it presents the necessary internal relationships between its constituent parts (i.e. Logic, Philosophy of Nature, Philosophy of Mind). By contrast with the positive sciences, which lack necessity and fail to ground their assumptions properly, philosophy can examine its own presuppositions dialectically and establish their necessity. In this way philosophy reaches the closure required of a complete system, like a circular line that returns to its origin.

The first part of this philosophical system is logic, which is the science of the pure Idea in the abstract medium of thought, taken as a self-developing totality of its laws. For Hegel (§ 19) God as absolute truth is the object of logic, which is the only mode of grasping the eternal and the absolute. Thus the general topic of logic is the supersensible world, by contrast with mathematics which deals with the abstractions of space and time. Hegel takes Aristotle to be the founder of logic as a purely formal treatment of the laws of thought, but he himself wishes to go beyond this view of logic as purely instrumental. For him (§ 24) logic coincides with metaphysics, as the science of things set and held in thoughts that express the essential reality of things. This identification is based on Hegel's explicit assumption (§ 23) that the true nature of reality is brought to light in reflection, which is the activity of a thinking subject. Contrary to Kant's thesis about an unknowable thing-in-itself, Hegel claims that the objective world in its own self is the same as it is in thought. For him objective thought is the heart and soul of the world or, as the ancients would say, that νοῦς governs the world. Reason is in the world as its principle, since its inward nature is universal. Thus Thought (as universal) is the constitutive substance of external things, and it is also the universal substance of what is spiritual. Hegel's absolute idealism is grounded in the assumption that Thought is the basis of everything because it is the true universal in all that nature and mind contains. Since Logic is the system of pure types of thought, Philosophy of Nature and of Mind are types of applied logic, since they represent particular modes of expressing the forms of pure thought. This is why the rationality of the real can be expressed in a philosophical system.

CONCLUSION

Taking Proclus and Hegel as leading examples of systematic thinking, I have argued that religion provides one of the deep motivations for the construction of systems in philosophy. Since these two illustrate pagan and Christian thinking, respectively, it is obvious here that 'religion' must be taken in a very general sense; i.e. a belief in the divine governance of the world. This divine power is typically identified as an intelligent and ordering force, so that it is usually assumed that Intelligence rules the world and creates a rational world-order. Therefore, if one wishes to understand this intelligible cosmos, it follows that one must construct a rational system that reflects the ordering principles of intelligence. However, as we have seen in Proclus and Hegel, there may be different conceptions of what constitutes a rational system; i.e. mathematics or speculative dialectic.

22   This paper was written during a period of sabbatical leave from Boston College which I spent as a von Humboldt fellow at Heidelberg University in 1990. I would like to thank my host professors, Hans-Georg Gadamer and Wolfgang Wieland, for the academic and personal contact which made my sojourn in Heidelberg so rewarding and enjoyable. I also wish to acknowledge the financial support for my research, which was provided by Boston College and the von Humboldt Foundation.

Friendship and Beauty in Augustine

EOIN CASSIDY

INTRODUCTION

One of the first recorded references to friendship in Augustine's writings is to be found in Book I of the *Soliloquia*. The following is an extract from this book:

> On account of wisdom I want to have, or fear to be without other things, such as life, tranquillity and friends. What limit can there be to my love of that beauty, in which I not only do not begrudge it to others, but I even look for many who will long for it with me, sigh for it with me, possess it with me, enjoy it with me. They will be all the dearer to me the more we share that love in common.[1]

It is a fine passage which situates the mutual attraction of friends for each other in the context of the desire for the eternal beauty of wisdom. Approximately ten years later (*c*.397) Augustine wrote the celebrated *Regula ad servos Dei*. Centred on the apostolic ideal of fraternal love expressed through the related motifs of unity and unanimity, the *Rule* concludes with the following passage: 'Observe these precepts with love as lovers of spiritual beauty, exuding the fragrance of Christ'.[2]

Recent detailed research into the *Rule* of Augustine has highlighted both the significance of this phrase as providing the context for the *Rule* and the fact that the *Rule* expresses Augustine's ideal of true friendship (a friendship 'in Christ').[3] If this analysis is correct it suggests that Augustine not only wished to highlight the importance of friendship for the monastic life but that he also wished to situate this ideal in the context of the love of spiritual beauty.

In the Augustinian *corpus* these are the only two texts which suggest that there is a link between the attractiveness of, or desire for friendship and the

---

1 *Soliloquia* I, xxii; *The Soliloquies*, trans. T. Gilligan (Washington, 1948).

2 *Regula ad servos Dei* VIII, 2; Augustine of Hippo and his Monastic Rule, trans. G. Lawless (Oxford, 1987).

3 The most authoritative commentary on the significance of the reference to spiritual beauty in the *Rule* of St Augustine is that of Luc Verheijen, O.S.A. 'Éléments d'un commentaire de la Règle de saint Augustin, XV: Comme des amants de la beauté spirituelle', *Augustiniana* 32 (1982), 88–135. The significance of the ideal of friendship to Augustine's vision of the monastic life has been highlighted by Tarsicius Van Bavel. Interestingly, Van Bavel also situates Augustine's references to friendship in *Epistle* 73 to Jerome (404) in the context of Augustine's love for the monastic ideal. 'The evangelical inspiration of the Rule of Saint Augustine', *Downside Review* 93 (1975), 83–99.

quest for beauty. Notwithstanding the undoubted importance of the *Rule* in expressing the mature philosophy of Augustine the question must be asked, whether the connection between friendship and beauty is coincidental, or whether it reflects something which lies at the heart of Augustine's theory of friendship. At first sight it might seem unusual to suppose that there is, in Augustine's writings, a link between the interpersonal and aesthetic dimensions of human nature, particularly given the scarcity of textual evidence with which to support this claim. However, as this article will illustrate, the motifs of friendship and beauty are indeed linked by Augustine in a manner which suggests that it is impossible to understand the nature of the human quest for either one without reference to the other. Essentially what this implies is that, for Augustine, the universal desire for friendship can only be adequately explained in the contest of a relationship which both transcends and yet fulfils human friendship, namely, the love of spiritual beauty. It also implies that the love for, or possession of, spiritual beauty is never something which is achieved by one outside the context of the love of community expressed through the ideal of friendship in Christ.

One value of this study of the relationship between friendship and beauty is that it allows us to situate Augustine's theory of friendship in the wider perspective of classical thought, particularly that of Plato who both in the *Symposium* and the *Phaedrus* likewise explained the attraction of friendship in the context of the desire for that which is beautiful. It also provides one with an insight into the extent and limits of the influence of Plotinus on the philosophy of Augustine. Undoubtedly Augustine's theory of beauty and the significance which he attached to the quest for beauty was influenced by the perspective outlined by Plotinus in the *Enneads*. In keeping with the Platonic perspective enunciated in both the *Symposium* and the *Phaedrus*, Plotinus was concerned to affirm the ontological status of the beautiful and, in consequence, the metaphysical roots of the human quest for fulfilment. In addition, Plotinus was conscious of the specifically religious nature of the desire to contemplate beauty. It was this unity of the metaphysical and religious character of the quest for beauty, discerned by Plotinus, which was to provide for Augustine the perspective around which his writings on beauty were ordered. Nevertheless, as shall be shown, it is precisely the recognition, on Augustine's part, that there is an essential relationship between friendship and beauty which allows one to recognize that his aesthetic philosophy cannot be understood simply by analogy with that of Plotinus. Unlike the perspective proposed by Plotinus, the possession of beauty in the context of Augustine's philosophy is a goal which is necessarily a *bonum commune*, not merely in the sense that it is universally desired, but rather that its possession is something which is only desired and achieved to the extent that it is desired and achieved in community.

Finally, and most importantly, the recognition that there is in Augustine's writings an essential relationship between friendship and beauty provides one with a framework within which to understand Augustine's explanation of the universal desire for friendship, specifically the desire that friendships be eternal. As was correctly recognized in classical Greek philosophy, it is not possible to adequately explain the attraction of friendship either by having recourse to the superficial attraction of likeness or complementarity of opposites or by proposing reasons of pleasure or utility. In particular, the Greeks saw that the attempt to base friendship on purely pragmatic or utilitarian grounds could never hope to resolve the conflict of interests reflected in the desire for independence (αὐτάρκεια) and the desire for the love of a friend. The theories of friendship of both Plato and Aristotle are a testimony to their shared viewpoint that it is only if friendship is situated in the context of a developed metaphysical theory that the relational character of human nature can be accepted and thus the universal desire for friendship can be understood. Although Augustine's philosophy does not share the same preoccupation with the ideal of αὐτάρκεια as was to be found in Greek culture, he does, nevertheless, share the Greek view that utilitarian concerns could never adequately explain the universal desire for friendship. For Augustine, it was the distinction between a love for that which is transitory and that which is eternal that provided the critical insight which demanded that he reflect at length on the true basis for the love of friendship. The unsatisfactory nature of relying on a love which is transitory is nowhere more clearly expressed than in the *Confessions*, where he reflects on his own state of mind after the death of his unnamed friend of his youth: 'I lived in misery, like every man whose soul is tethered by the love of things that cannot last and then is agonized to lose them.'[4]

Illustrating, as it did for Augustine, the folly of misplaced friendships, the death of this unnamed friend forced Augustine to look to a horizon that transcended the limited perspectives of either pleasure or utility. It will be shown that Augustine's recourse to the motif of beauty, one which explains the attractiveness of friendship in the context of a teleological vision of human nature, reflects this recognition on his part of the need to situate friendship within the larger perspective of metaphysics. Furthermore, situating friendship in the context of the love of beauty allowed Augustine to give due prominence to the spiritual basis of the attraction of friendship.

The question must now be addressed as to what evidence there is in Augustine's writings to support the view that the attractiveness of friendship can be explained in terms of the desire for beauty. Where does one find evidence of a recognition that the relationship of friendship possesses beauty and facilitates the ascent to the beautiful? As we have already noted there is very little direct textual evidence of an essential connection between friendship and beauty. However, Augustine's vision of the beauty of friendship is strikingly illustrated in the choice of motifs which he uses to describe the nature of friendship. Without exception, they are the same motifs which he

4 *Confessiones* IV, vi, 11; trans. R.S. Pine-coffin (Harmondsworth, 1961).

associates with beauty or by which he describes the attraction of beauty. These include those of unity, truth, harmony, virtue, order and benevolent love. Some of these reflect the influence of Neoplatonist aesthetic philosophy; nevertheless, what is uniquely Augustinian is the recognition that they also express the essential characteristics of true friendship.

THE BEAUTY OF FRIENDSHIP

What is the beauty of friendship? If one were to count simply by the amount of attention accorded to a particular motif there is no doubt but that it is the quality of unity in the relationship of friendship which Augustine saw as expressing its beauty. From his very earliest memories of friendship until the end of his life, Augustine always recognized the power of attraction of this unity in love and it was the motif which dominated his reflections on friendship in the *Confessions*. One notes, for example, the following passage in which he reflects on the death of the unnamed friend:

> Because I was his second self I wondered that he should die and I remain alive. How well the poet put it when he called his friend the other half of his soul. I felt that our two souls had been as one, living in two bodies, life to me was fearful because I did not want to live with only half a soul. (IV, vi,11)

If the attraction of unity is recognized in almost all of the classical treatments of friendship, it is also, in classical literature, the motif which is most closely associated with that of beauty. In particular it is that around which Plotinus' treatment of beauty is structured. Karl Svoboda summarizes the aesthetic theory of Plotinus: 'Il enseignait que tout est ce qu'il est parce qu'il est un (V 3, 15), que tout tend à l'unité (VI 2, 11) que tout les choses existent par l'Un (VI 9, 1).'[5]

Undoubtedly the writings of Plotinus on this theme exercised an influence on Augustine, nevertheless their perspectives are not identical; firstly, there would not seem to be any absolute identity between beauty and the 'One' in the philosophical system of Plotinus, because, for him, the form of beauty includes the concept of limit: the 'One' can be properly designated as beauty, but only in so far as it is the cause of the beautiful.[6] For Augustine there is no such difficulty in identifying beauty with unity. The 'One' is simultaneously both beauty and the cause of beauty. Secondly, while accepting alongside Plotinus the identification of limitlessness with the 'One', Augustine will nevertheless always insist on an equally important motif, namely, that

5   Karl Svoboda, *L'esthétique de saint Augustin et ses sources* (Brno, 1933), pp. 42–3.
6   Cf. J. M. Rist, *Plotinus : The Road to Reality* (Cambridge, 1967), p. 65. Nevertheless it must be added that, with Plotinus, the extent to which the One as creator of beauty is independent from that which it has created is not clear.

the 'One' is a unity in love. This is an association which one does not find in the writings of Plotinus. In the perspective from which Augustine writes, viz., the belief in the trinitarian concept of God, beauty, as the expression of the 'One', could never adequately be described purely by the motif of simplicity. It is unity in love and that alone which is beautiful. It is this difference between unity and unity in love which goes some way to explain the very significant divergence which exists between Plotinus and Augustine, in their respective evaluations of the importance which ought to be attached to friendship in the quest for, or enjoyment of, human fulfilment.[7] For Augustine the beauty of friendship can have no other meaning than the attraction of sharing in the divine life, which is unity in love. This opinion is reinforced by the recognition that Augustine emphasized the triadic structure of true friendship—a friendship which is 'in Christ'.[8] In his later writings he articulated the view that this relationship bears the traces of the divine trinitarian life.[9]

If the early writings of Augustine focused upon the beauty of unity, one can also point to the fact that the Cassiciacum dialogues in particular highlighted the beauty of wisdom or truth. The beauty of truth is the beauty of that which is intelligible. This theme, which is central to the whole Platonic and Neoplatonic tradition, situates, for Augustine, the attractiveness of friendship in the context of the attractiveness to each other of those who desire the beauty of intelligibility. For him the goal of *contemplatio Dei* is always associated with truth. One has only to note the number of times he will compare this present life with eternal life by using the biblical passage: 'Now we see as in a glass darkly, then we will see face to face.'[10] The delight by which we are attracted to this goal of truth is particularly well expressed in the following passage from one of his commentaries on John's Gospel, where he identifies God with the truth to which we are attracted:

7   J. O'Meara, *The Young Augustine* (London, 1980), p. 155, states that Plotinus' essay 'On Beauty' informed Augustine of a spiritual Trinity. This, nevertheless, should not obscure the immense difference which exists between the respective understandings of Trinity in the Plotinian and Christian schemata. The trinitarian unity in love, including as it does the characteristics of equality and reciprocity, is not compatible with Neoplatonism.

8   This is particularly highlighted in the following passage: 'What does the soul love in a friend except the soul? And, therefore, even here there are three: the lover, the beloved, and the love' (*De Trinitate* VIII, x, 14); trans. S. McKenna, *The Fathers of the Church*, 45 (Washington, 1963).

9   Plotinus (V 8, 13; VI 7, 15; VI 7, 17; VI 7, 33) speaks of that which proceeds from the Good as possessing the traces of the Good. However, nowhere does he speak of fraternal love being a trace of the One. On the contrary, Augustine, in *In Evangelium Iohannis*, tr. 14, 9; 18, 4; and 39, 5 and *De Trinitate*, 8, 10, 14, proposes fraternal love as a model of the Trinity.

10 1 Cor., 13; 12. Augustine cites this text on numerous occasions. Some of the more detailed treatments of it are to be seen in *De Civitate Dei* XXII, xxix; *Enarrationes in Psalmos* CIV, 3; CV, 27; CXVIII, vi, 1; *De Trinitate*, I, 17–19; I, 20–27; IV, 4–7; IV, 11; IV, 24; VIII, 4.

If, therefore, this which is revealed concerning the delights and earthly pleasures, to those who love them because it is true that everyone is attracted by his particular delight, how does the Christ revealed by the Father not attract us? What is it that the soul desires with more force than the truth?[11]

Regarding human friendship, the attraction or beauty of friendship is always situated in the context of the desire for truth. Using the language of Plato, it is truth which is the 'first friend'. Both Plato and Augustine realized that the recognition of the beauty of truth situates the attractiveness of friendship firmly in the context of a teleological perspective. The goal of this quest for Augustine is *contemplatio Dei*.

Mention was made of the close relationship between Plato and Plotinus in respect of their understanding of beauty. In this context it is interesting to observe the following passage from the *Enneads* which reflects the clear divergence which Plotinus discerned between his own theory and that of classical Greek philosophy:

> Nearly everyone says that it (beauty) is good proportion of the parts. . . .
> On this theory, nothing single and simple but only a composite thing will
> have any beauty. . . . But if the whole is beautiful the parts must be
> beautiful too.[12]

For Plotinus, it is the single, the simple, which is beautiful, rather than proportion and measure. These latter, being essentially quantitative, could not be appropriate to express the absolute unity and simplicity of spiritual realities. In contrast with this view, Augustine will never cease to insist in his writings on the beauty of proportion, measure or harmony. In fact, some of the most expressive passages on beauty are to be found in the *De Ordine* which is devoted to describing the harmony that reflects the right ordering of the parts to the whole.[13] From the earliest Cassiciacum dialogues he identified beauty with harmony, the harmony of rhythmic measure which occupies an important role in the *De Musica*, a theme repeated in both the *Confessions* and the *Enarrationes in Psalmos*.[14] In fact, Augustine observed that the proportion, harmony and equality evoked by music testify in a unique way to the objective existence of beauty. Interestingly, this emphasis on harmony reflects

11. *In Evangelium Iohannis*, tr. XXVI, 5. *Tractatus on the Gospel of John and his first Epistle*, trans. J. W. Rettig, (Washington, 1968). Among the many references to love which is directed to wisdom or truth, cf. *Confessiones* VI, x, 17; X, xxiii, 33–4; *Contra Academicos* I, i, 4; *Epistula*, CLV: 1–2; *Sermo Denis* XVI, 2. In *In Evangelium* tr. XXXIV, 9; XL, 8, the emphasis is on the eschatological nature of the goal of truth which is desired.

12. *Enneads* I 6, 1, 21–30, trans. A. H. Armstrong (London, 1966).

13. *De Ordine* II, 51; II, 14. Cf. also *Confessiones*, VII, xiii 19; VII, xvi, 22.

14. Interestingly, when speaking of the beauty and harmony of rhythmic measure in music, Augustine will frequently use the image of friendship. It reflects the importance which he attaches to the association between friendship and harmony. Cf. *De Musica* I, 23; II, 25; II, 26; III, 1; V, 16; VI, 27. Beauty is identified with harmony of rhythmic measure

more the classical Stoic understanding of beauty,[15] and Augustine's ready embracing of this perspective undoubtedly owes much to the Stoic influence on his writings of this early period.

For Augustine, the beauty of harmony is pre-eminently expressed in the attraction of peace, the beauty of which he never ceased to extol. In fact, alongside that of unity, it is this longing for peace which most characterizes his later writings. The following passage from his commentary on the *Psalms* is only one of many which speak of the delight evoked by the beauty of peace:

> Love peace my brethren. Greatly we are delighted when the love of peace cries from your hearts. How greatly does it delight you! . . . With how great beauty has the perception of peace smitten your heart![16]

Book XIX of *De Civitate Dei*, which contains the most detailed analysis of this theme in the Augustinian corpus, repeats this emphasis on the delight, the sweetness of peace. It also includes a lengthy description of peace as that perfectly ordered and perfectly harmonious fellowship in the enjoyment of God and a mutual fellowship in God (XIX, xiii, 1). It is a definition which, interestingly, accurately reflects that celebrated definition of true friendship which is found in the *Confessions*: 'Blessed are those who love you, O God, and love their friends in you' (IV, ix, 14). In consequence, it is not surprising that Augustine sees the beauty of friendship in terms of the attractiveness of peace and harmony. Particularly in his later writings, the desire for friendship and peace are almost synonymous, or at least the desire for friendship is nearly always situated in the context of both the longing for peace and the difficulty of attaining to it. Furthermore, it is this recognition of the difficulty of attaining peace which highlights one of the more significant developments in Augustine's theory of friendship during the course of his life, namely, the increasing recognition that true friendship is attained only in eternal life.[17]

or number in *De Ordine*, I, 2; II, 3; II, 40–3; *Confessiones* X, xxxiii, 49; *Enarrationes in Psalmos* XXXII, ii, S. 1; LXIV, 3; LXXXVI, 1; CXLVII, 2; CXLVIII; CXLIX, 2. In *Confessiones*, IV, xvi, 30 and in *De Musica*, Book VI, Augustine expresses reservations about placing too much emphasis on the role of music in revealing beauty. However, in *Enarrationes in Psalmos*, XXXII, ii, S. 1, 5; XCI, 5, and CXLIII, 10, he reflects on the similarity of the harmony of a virtuous life and that of music. In *De Quantitate Animae*, X–XXIII, the virtuous life is shown to possess the type of harmony or beauty associated with geometric proportion.

15 The rational character of harmony which is clearly expressed in the identification of beauty with number is the most graphic sign of the Stoic influence on Augustine's aesthetic theory in these early writings. Cf. in particular *De Musica*, VI, 2–5; 17–24. Note the role assigned to reason, ibid., VI, 24. Cf. also *De Ordine* II, 43–8, where Augustine seems to imply that it is the very existence of number which guarantees the rational structure of reality.

16 *Enarrationes in Psalmos* CXLVII, 15. Expositions on the book of psalms; trans. J. H. Parker. (London, 1847–1853).

17 Cf. *In Evangelium Iohannis*, tr. XXXIV; LXXVII, 1–5; XXX, 7; *De Civitate Dei*, XIX, v–xii; *Epistula*, LXXII, written to Jerome.

The unanimity which alone secures the harmony or peace of friendship is difficult to attain because of the misunderstandings and/or lack of knowledge[18] which are inevitable components of this life. In keeping with the classical tradition, Augustine always maintained both that unanimity is only possible between the virtuous, i.e., on the basis of justice, and that it is only the mutual attraction of the virtuous to each other which creates the unanimity that is friendship.[19]

Augustine frequently adverts to the beauty of virtue or, more precisely, the beauty of righteousness. In a particularly fine passage from one of his commentaries on the *Psalms* there is the following:

> You do not yet love righteousness! you are still a servant: be a son. But of a good servant is made a good son. Now you act through fear: you will learn to act also through love. For there is a beauty in righteousness. Punishment may deter you, but righteousness has its own comeliness; it seeks men's eyes; it inflames its lovers. For this the martyrs . . . shed their blood. What did they love when they renounced all things? For were they not lovers? . . . Whoever does not love is cold and harsh. There should be love, but only of that beauty which seeks the eyes of the heart. Let there be love, but of that beauty which with praise of righteousness inflames the mind. Men exclaim, they cry out aloud, they say everywhere, How good! How excellent! What do they see? Righteousness they see in which an old man bowed down is beautiful.[20]

The beauty of righteousness is pre-eminently an interior beauty, one which Augustine will always insist is only seen with the eyes of the heart, or by a person with a pure heart.[21] It is the beauty that is only recognized by the virtuous person, and consequently it is only the virtuous who are attracted by this beauty. It is in this context that Augustine affirmed that friendship is only possible between the virtuous. As Augustine states in a celebrated letter to Caecilianus, dated 412: 'You will be his friend in proportion as you are an enemy to his evil deeds.' (*Epistula* CLI, 12)

18 Cf. *De Civitate Dei*, XIX, v–xii.
19 Cf. *Contra Academicos* III, 13; *Epistula* XXVII; XXVIII; XXXI; CCLVII. In particular note *Epistula* CLXXXVII, 41, where he treats of the basis of friendship in terms of the ties of religion (*religio*) and kindness (*benevolentia*); *Enarrationes in Psalmos*, XXXIX, 4 situates the basis of friendship in goodness; *Epistula* CXXX. 4; *Epistula* CLV, 15; and *Epistula* CXCII, 1, emphasise the link between unanimity with oneself, God, and the other. *De Civitate Dei*, XIX, xvi, recognises the link between friendship in society and the existence of justice. *De Trinitate*, IX, vi, 11, situates the basis of friendship in the beauty of faith.
20 *Enarrationes in Psalmos* XXXII, ii, S. 1, 6, translation amended. See also *Epistula* CXX, 20; *In Evangelium Iohannis* tr. III, 21; *De Trinitate* VIII, vi, 9; *Enarrationes in Psalmos* XXXII, ii, S. 2, 6; XLIV, iii, 14 and 29; LXIV, 8.
21 Foreshadowed in this by Plotinus, Augustine stresses the importance of an ordered soul or purity of heart. Among the numerous references to this theme in Augustine's writings, cf. the following: *De Trinitate*, VI, xii, 15; XIV, xx, 24 and 44; *Enarrationes in Psalmos* CXL, 2; *De Civitate Dei* XXII, xxix.

For Augustine the attraction of friendship lies in the mutual attraction to that interior beauty constituted by virtue. Interestingly, in an earlier work, *De Quantitate Animae* (388), Augustine will also use the aesthetic motif to describe virtue: he compares the equality, the harmony of a circle to that of a virtuous life.[22] Beauty in Augustine's mind is always associated with order. The virtuous is pre-eminently the ordered person, the one who possesses an ordered love. In consequence it is not surprising that Augustine will insist that the beauty of righteousness is the highest beauty. It is also the only beauty which will ultimately lead us to the goal of *contemplatio Dei* (the contemplation of spiritual beauty). As he says, unless one possesses this beauty, one possesses no beauty, and whoever possesses this interior beauty is beautiful all over.[23] It is in this context that Augustine insists that the attraction of friendship cannot lie outside the mutual attraction to that interior beauty constituted by virtue.

Closely related to the theme of harmony is that of order. In what way is the beauty of friendship associated with the attractiveness of order? And how does Augustine understand the beauty of order?

In the course of his treatment of peace in Book XIX of *De Civitate Dei*, Augustine combines the concepts of order and harmony in a way that would suggest their virtual identity. However, order always reflects a particular way of being, or right order of being in the world, namely that the inferior should always submit to the superior. In addition it expresses the ontological character of the aesthetic motif.[24] The attraction of being is always understood in terms of the beauty of order and vice versa. One of the earliest of Augustine's writings, entitled *De Ordine*, is devoted to an analysis of this theme, namely the beauty of creation. In many ways Augustine's identification of the beauty of the world with its order reflects the classical treatment of the issue of Divine Providence.[25]

In order to affirm the order of the world, Augustine goes to some lengths in *De Ordine* to establish that there is an inner harmony to the conflict between contrasts.[26] In this he is faithful to the approach of Plotinus. However, the specifically Augustinian perspective is not focused upon the beauty of the world, but rather on the beauty of God. In this work, and particularly in the *Enarrationes in Psalmos*, the motif of order is seen as a way of showing that the beauty of creation reflects the beauty of the creator or the divine artisan.[27] Both express the ontological character of beauty and allow,

22 *De Quantitate Animae* XVI, 27.
23 *Enarrationes in Psalmos* XLIV, 3, (AD 403). Beauty is always associated with order and is used by Augustine as a way of extolling the beauty of creation. Cf. ibid., CXLIII, 6; CXLVIII, 15; CXLIV, 1–15.
24 *De Ordine* I, ix; I, xi; II, ii. It is a theme which has its roots in classical Platonism. Cf. *Timaeus* 29a, 30a.
25 Karl Svoboda points to the Stoic and Neoplatonic explanation of the issue of divine providence in terms of the motif of order. Cf. ibid., pp. 42–3.
26 *De Ordine* I, vii, 18.
27 Cf. *Enarrationes in Psalmos* XXXIX, 8; LXXXIX, 4; CXLVIII, 15.

or indeed demand, that one ascend from the contemplation of the beauty of creation to the goal of *contemplatio Dei*.

One of the clearest examples of the evolution in Augustine's thought from an intellectualist to a voluntarist understanding of human nature can be seen in the way he moves from placing emphasis on the order of reason to the order of love. In *De Ordine* reason is seen as the principle of order, in his later writings the stress will uniformly be placed on the importance of the *ordo amoris*. Although love is never envisaged as excluding reason, Augustine will increasingly emphasize that one ascends by the path of love, rather than by that of reason.

The question remains as to how far the attraction of friendship can be attributed to this love of order. The first thing to note is that, for Augustine, order is always synonymous with peace, whether it be peace within the individual or in society. Now, the natural instinct for peace at the level both of the individual and of society was something whose importance he never minimized. It is the theme around which both the *Confessions* and the *De Civitate Dei* are structured, and in both the human being is defined in terms of this longing for peace or rest. In consequence, Augustine was always acutely aware of the importance of the beauty of peace or order in explaining the attractiveness, and thus the basis, of friendship.

The identification of order with being provides us with another perspective by which we can address this issue. The beauty of friendship is always linked by Augustine to the love of that which is eternal. This is vividly illustrated in his lengthy treatment, in Book IV of the *Confessions*, of the folly of placing one's love in that which is transitory. It is in this context that he situates the attractiveness of the ordered love which he defined as a friendship 'in Christ'. It alone is eternal.[28] Thus the beauty of friendship, or the beauty of ordered love is ultimately, in Augustine's mind, identified with the beauty of being itself.

Finally, one must examine the attractiveness of love itself. If the beauty of friendship is related to that of ordered love, Augustine will stress the attractiveness not of order alone, but also of love. This becomes increasingly evident in his writings from the year 407 onwards, and reflects a significant development in Augustine's understanding of the significance of love.[29] If, in his early writings, love is seen as the path by which the goal of beauty is

---

28   Cf. *Confessiones* IV, ix, 14.
29   Cf. Athanase Sage, *La vie religieuse selon saint Augustin* (Paris, 1972). Sage places particular emphasis on the date (407), primarily because of the significance of Augustine's commentary on the first Epistle of St. John in highlighting the identity which exists between fraternal love and the love of God. This development in Augustine's view of the significance of fraternal love is also particularly evident in Book VIII of *De Trinitate*. T. Van Bavel, *Introduction to the Spirituality of St. Augustine* (New York, 1980), p. 77, suggests that the development began a little earlier. In this context, note *Epistle*, 73, 10 (403–4), to Jerome, which situates friendship in the context of the love of love.

attained, then, in his later writings, love is not only identified with the path to that goal, but becomes synonymous with the goal itself.

The most sustained treatment of this theme is to be found in the *Tractatus in Epistulam Iohannis* (407). The whole work is devoted to the analysis of the view that God is love. Specifically verse ix. 9 focuses upon the identity which exists between God and beauty; included in it is the following passage:

> How will we become beautiful? In loving the one who is eternally beautiful. The more love grows in you, the more beauty grows; because love is the beauty of the soul.[30]

Just as was observed earlier, when treating of the beauty of virtue, love expresses that interior beauty is only discernible by those who are pure in heart. However, what is particularly interesting about this passage is that not only is love seen as the way to the attainment of beauty, but growth in love is envisaged simultaneously as growth in beauty. Love and beauty are, in fact, synonymous. Furthermore, love is identified as beautiful because it is identical with God who is beautiful. Augustine can equate love and beauty precisely because in God they are both one. Earlier, in the same verse, there is the following passage:

> In loving him, we have become his friends; but it was as enemies that he has loved us in order that we would become his friends. He loved us first, and he has granted us that we might love him. As yet we loved him not; in loving him we become beautiful.[31]

What is clarified here is that it is not my love which is primarily beautiful, but rather God's love for me. What is further revealed here is the character of God's love which is beautiful. It is essentially a benevolent love, one which desires to create friendship out of enmity. A theme which Augustine will frequently repeat is that God loved us when we were ugly in order that we might be beautiful, deformed so that we might be formed.[32]

---

30   *In Epistulam Iohannis*, tr. IX, 9, trans., J. W. Rettig for an understanding of the significance of the motif of spiritual beauty in Augustine's mature writings cf. Luc Verheijen, 'Éléments d'un commentaire de la Règle de saint Augustin, XV: Comme des amants de la beauté spirituelle', *Augustiniana* 32 (1982), 88–135.
　　For other texts which treat of the relationship between the love of God and becoming beautiful or like God, cf. *Epistula* CXVIII, 2, (410/11)—love is directed at the beauty of the Lord; ibid., CXX, (*c*.410)—in becoming like God one becomes beautiful; *Enarrationes in Psalmos* XCIX, 5 (412)—the measure of growth in love is the measure of growth in likeness.

31   Ibid. Augustine always emphasized that friendship was a graced relationship. In *Epistula CLV* (414) he explicitly distinguishes on this basis Christian from non-Christian piety. The clearest examples of Augustine's recognition that fraternal love depends upon God's prior love for us is to be seen in the group of commentaries *In Evangelium Iohannis*, tr. LXXXV, LXXXVI and LXXXVII; also ibid., XXXII, 2; LXV, 2. Note also *Epistula* CCXVII; *Enarrationes in Psalmos* XXXV, 7; *De Catechizandis Rudibus* I, iv, 11; *Sermo Denis* XVI, 2–3.

32   Cf. in particular *In Epistulam Iohannis* tr. IX, 9 and *Enarrationes in Psalmos* XLIV, 3. Note also CIII, I, 4–6 and CXXXII, 10.

The love which, for Augustine, is beautiful—which is attractive—is always that which is benevolent and it is precisely this beauty or attractiveness of benevolent love which creates friendship out of enmity. It is this understanding of love which allows us to understand the phrase which Augustine uses on more than one occasion, viz., 'Whoever loves men ought to love them either because they are just, or in order that they might be just.'[33]

Benevolent love not only expresses the relationship of friendship, but it is equally that which creates the relationship. It is precisely benevolent love which is the source of the attraction of friendship. If Augustine recognizes that friendship is frequently based on need, nevertheless he continuously insists that in the last analysis, the only adequate foundation for this ideal of true friendship is the mutual attraction of benevolent love. The only love which is beautiful is that which images the benevolent love of God.

Finally, the recognition in the above passage that we can become beautiful only because God loved us first, situates friendship in the context of a 'graced' relationship. It is God's gift of his love for us which is the basis of human friendship as well as friendship with God. This allows us to see the significance, for Augustine, of the often repeated theme that God not only loved us while we were deformed, but that he became like us, i.e., without form or comeliness, in order that we might be formed in him.[34] If Augustine shares with the Neoplatonists the view that the possibility of the attraction of friendship depends upon the recognition of one's likeness to the other, an attraction which is constituted by the mutual sharing in beauty, he will be alone in placing this idea in the context of the doctrine of grace. The theme of grace was one which not only marked all his writings, but one which, as he always recognized, was the crucial point which differentiated his writings from those of Neoplatonism.

FRIENDSHIP AND BEAUTY:
THE RECOVERY OF THE CLASSICAL PERSPECTIVE

As was mentioned at the outset of this article, one of the values of this study of the relation between beauty and friendship is that it situates Augustine's

---

33 *De Trinitate* VIII, vi, 9. Cf. also *Epistula*, LXXIII, 10; *De Trinitate*, VIII, VI, 9; *Sermo* CCCXXXVI, ii, 2, (date and authorship uncertain). There are many references which illustrate the importance which Augustine attaches to *benevolentia* in this context. Cf. *In Epistulam Iohannis*, tr. VI, 1—the beginning of love is generosity. Cf. also *Epistula* XLVII and *Epistula* CLV. *In Evangelium Iohannis*, tr. LXXXV, 3, speaks of service being the way to friendship. *De Diversis Quaestionibus* LXXXIII, q. 71, situates the desire for friendship in the context of the desire to imitate Christ's benevolent love. *Epistula* CXXX, written to Proba, and *Epistula* CLXXXVI, written to Paulinus, see friendship as the desire to lead others to Christ: cf. also ibid., CXLVII, 5, written to Paulina, and CLV, 4, written to Macedonius. Love is identified with benevolence, *Enarrationes in Psalmos* CXXI, 1; XXXI, ii, 5.

34 Cf. *Enarrationes in Psalmos*, XXVI, ii, 10; XLIV, 3; CIII, i, 4–5.

theory of friendship in the context of classical Greek philosophy, particularly that which is to be seen in the dialogues of Plato.

In company with the other Greek philosophers Plato was concerned with reconciling the two seemingly contradictory desires for friendship and independence (αὐτάρκεια). In the classical Greek culture the possession of wisdom was always identified with the independence of the sage. It was to the attainment of this goal of αὐτάρκεια that they envisaged human life being ordered. In this perspective, how does one explain the attractiveness of friendship other than in purely pragmatic terms as an aid to the achievement of an independence which does not include the relationship of friendship? This problem was nowhere more clearly expressed than in one of Plato's earliest dialogues, the *Lysis*, which was devoted to the topic of friendship, where he states that if one does not possess virtue there is no basis for the attraction of friendship and if one does possess virtue one has no need of a friend. The dialogue ends inconclusively, a testimony to the difficulty of resolving this problem. Nevertheless, there is contained in the *Lysis* the seeds of what was to provide Plato with what was, for him, a satisfactory solution to the question at issue. In *Lysis* 219d he introduces the idea of the 'first friend' (πρῶτος φίλος), 'for whose sake all other things can be friends'. It is the Good or the Beautiful which is understood to be the first friend and, in consequence, it is in virtue of one's desire for the Good or the Beautiful that one is attracted to a friend. Rather than a view of human nature in which friendship is explained in terms of an already achieved likeness in respect of the mutual possession of virtue, the idea of the πρῶτος φίλος shifts the focus for understanding the basis of the love of friendship to a dynamic, teleologically orientated vision of the person. Friendship is explained in terms of a goal which both transcends and yet fulfils the relationship, namely the desire for the Good or the Beautiful. It is this perspective which governed Plato's subsequent references to friendship and is particularly evident in the *Gorgias*, the *Symposium* and the *Phaedrus*, the latter two dialogues situating friendship exclusively in the context of the desire for the beautiful. The kinship (οἰκειότης) or natural affinity between friends is twofold. Firstly, there is the recognition of a mutual sharing in or possession of beauty and, secondly, there is the recognition of the mutual desire for beauty. It is not simply a question that one needs friends in order to ascend to contemplation of beauty. Certainly friendship is explained in terms of the desire for beauty but desire is not to be understood simply as poverty seeking fulfilment, because that neglects the emphasis which Plato places upon the recognition of one's kinship to each other as a result of our mutual sharing in beauty.[35] Those who love beauty are in and through that very love united in community. Both the *Symposium* and the *Phaedrus*[36] testify to Plato's conviction of the

35 In particular cf. *Symposium* 205c–206a and 221e–222a.
36 For a detailed treatment of the communitarian nature of the quest for spiritual beauty cf. *Phaedrus* 244a–257b.

essentially communitarian nature of the contemplation of beauty. The goal to which friendship aspires, while it transcends the relationship of friendship, is nevertheless never conceived as being exterior to that relationship. Paradoxically, what Plato seems to be suggesting is that the independence or the freedom which accompanies wisdom is not achieved in opposition to friendship, but rather is only to be found in and through the very relationship of friendship.

For Plato, the significance of the relationship between friendship and beauty is twofold. Firstly, it marks a recognition on his part that the only adequate explanation for the attractiveness of friendship is one which situates it in the context of a developed metaphysical theory, one which explains friendship in terms of the nature and destiny of the human person. This is the sense in which Plato affirms that friendship can only be explained in terms of the desire for beauty. Secondly, what the relationship between friendship and beauty also illustrates is that the desire for and the contemplation of beauty cannot be achieved outside of the context of friendship. It is not only the goal of the contemplation of spiritual beauty but also the means by which one ascends which is essentially communitarian. It is precisely in the experience of the beauty of friendship that one recognizes or remembers the beauty which one ought to desire and through this remembrance of one's natural affinity to beauty one is enabled to desire it. In recognizing that one cannot desire that of which one is ignorant, Plato sees, in the experience of friendship, the educational environment which is essential if beauty is to be desired and contemplated.

The philosophy of Plotinus in many respects reflects the philosophical legacy of Platonism. However, with regard to the ideal of friendship the contrast between Platonism and Neoplatonism could not be more striking. It is not that there are no references to friendship to be found in the *Enneads*, the contrary is in fact the case.[37] Where they occur, for the most part they either are used to emphasize that quality of unity in love so cherished by Plotinus,[38] or they situate friendship in the context of the spiritual ascent of the soul.[39] However, despite this superficial similarity with the Platonic perspective, particularly the educational focus which he gives to friendship in the process of this conversion of the soul, friendship for Plotinus, unlike Plato, does not constitute an integral part of human nature. Even in the process of this ascent the friend is not really needed: one is able to find in oneself all that a friend can offer; one may find the inspiration to ascend in the beauty present in one's own soul. If friendship is thus relatively insignificant in the ascent to one's τέλος, then the attainment of the goal which one desires and to which one is ordered actually excludes friendship. The theory of emanation excludes

37   The following references to φιλία as cited in the *Lexikon Plotinianum* (Leiden/Leuven, 1980), occur in the *Enneads*: III 2, 2, 4; IV 4, 40, 6; V 1, 9, 6; VI 7, 14, 20; VI 7, 24, 27.
38   III 2, 2, 4; VI 7, 14, 20.
39   For references to the friend as spiritual guide, cf. I 4, 15 and 24.

any possibility that the union with the One could be described as in any way comparable to a reciprocal relationship, and there is no evidence that Plotinus regarded the unity of love which constitutes one's union with the One as a unity that is only achieved in community. In effect, with the philosophy of Plotinus one has the clearest example of a philosophy which values αὐτάρκεια as the ideal of the solitary life.[40] Even if Plotinus himself supported and aided the quest for wisdom among his disciples, his was a quest whose ultimate goal was conceived in independence of others. It is not without some reason that many commentators see in Plotinus the one who was primarily responsible for the relative demise of friendship as an ethical category in the writings of late antiquity.

If the importance which Plato attached to friendship in the desire for the beautiful reflects a significant difference between the perspective of Platonism and Neoplatonism, then, Augustine's theory of friendship marks a recovery of the early Platonist perspective and is an illustration in this respect of Augustine's independence of Neoplatonism. The link between friendship and beauty in Augustine's writings highlights, in a manner similar to that in Plato's philosophy, both the need to situate the attractiveness of friendship in the context of a developed metaphysical theory and the recognition of the interpersonal nature of the human τέλος as symbolized by the contemplation of spiritual beauty. Particularly in this latter respect, the perspectives of both Plato and Augustine are in marked contrast to that of Neoplatonism.

However, the specific emphasis which Augustine placed upon the relationship between friendship and beauty highlights not only his independence of Neoplatonism, but also of classical philosophy in general. What is most noticeable about Augustine's treatment of the relationship between friendship and beauty is the way in which it allows him to highlight the religious and specifically Christian outlook within which he wrote. In particular it offered a way of illustrating the fact that the human being is created in the image of God. For Augustine, friendship which is in Christ was a particularly apt vehicle for reflecting or imaging beauty which was always identified by him with the presence of God. Friendship 'in Christ' not only expressed the ideal of unity in love, but also reflected the trinitarian character of the divine life. For Augustine, friendship also proved a particularly apt model for illustrating the central role which is accorded to the doctrine of grace in the Christian schema. It offers a prime example of the fact that salvation can only be achieved to the extent that it is offered and received as a gift. To emphasize, as Augustine did, that one ascends to the contemplation of spiritual beauty only by way of the gift of love recalls the truth to which Augustine himself was dedicated: 'The good I do is done by you in me and by your grace' (*Confessions* X, iv, 5). Finally, what the linking of friendship to beauty also clearly highlights is the communitarian nature of the goal of the Christian life and the communitarian nature of the path by which that goal is achieved.

40 Cf. I 6, 6 and 9–10.

Augustine's commitment to the ideal of the monastic life, one which is reflected in his love of friendship, is ample testimony to his recognition of the centrality of community within the Christian context.

CONCLUSION

To conclude, the motif of beauty in Augustine's writings has allowed us to see that the basis of friendship is situated firmly in the context of the desire for, or delight in, the love of God. The desire for unity, truth, order, peace, virtue and benevolent love all find their focus in the desire for beauty, and Augustine always recognized that God alone is truly beautiful. In addition, while agreeing with the classical tradition that the experience of likeness provided the only acceptable basis for the attraction of, or delight in friendship, he nevertheless insisted that this likeness always referred primarily to one's likeness to God. For him, it was inconceivable that one could attain a likeness either to oneself or to another without first becoming like God, because ultimately the very existence of being is itself dependent upon, or is an expression of, this likeness to God. In this fashion, Augustine's insistence on situating friendship in the context of the love of spiritual beauty points inescapably to a metaphysical and religious foundation for friendship, namely our ontological dependence on God.

Time, Space and Matter in the *Periphyseon*

An Examination of Eriugena's Understanding of the Physical World

DERMOT MORAN

Eriugena has unusual theories of space, time and matter, theories which have led him to be called an immaterialist in the manner of Berkeley, or a critical idealist in the manner of Kant.[1] He may properly be termed an immaterialist with regard to his theory that sensible corporeal bodies are only apparently corporeal—for him physical bodies are a collection or assembly of incorporeal, insensible properties. He is labelled an idealist for his theory of place and time as categories in the mind, prior to all objects, and within which all empirical objects are contained. On this basis, the claim has been made that Eriugena is an original thinker and that his views should be accorded a respectful place in the history of philosophy. This article will examine Eriugena's originality with regard to his theory of the nature of the material world.[2] It will emerge that Eriugena indeed holds an immaterialist account of matter and of physical things, but that there are nuances in his theory which need to be addressed.

Eriugena's views are complicated, indeed somewhat confused. The confusion stems partly from the multiplicity of his sources—drawing as he did on both the Greek and Latin Christian traditions; partly from the general misinformation concerning the world which was current in the encyclopaedic knowledge of the day; partly from his own attitude as a philosopher of synthesis and mediation. Eriugena is very loose in his use of philosophical terminology; for example, in the distinction between essence (οὐσία, *essentia*) and substance (ὑπόστασις, *substantia*). His aim is to deliver the secret, hidden knowledge (Eriugena's phrase is: *gnostica scientia*) to achieve salvation and

---

1 The nineteenth century commentators on Eriugena noticed the comparison with Kant. See T. Christlieb, *Leben und Lehre des Johannes Scotus Erigena in ihrem Zusammenhang mit der vorhergehenden und unter Angabe ihrer Berührungspunkte mit der neueren Philosophie und Theologie* (Gotha, 1860); see also W. Beierwaltes, 'The Revaluation of John Scottus Eriugena in German Idealism', in J. J. O'Meara and L. Bieler, eds., *The Mind of Eriugena* (Dublin, 1973), pp. 190-9.

2 A version of this paper was first read at the Conference on 'Johannes Scottus Eriugena and the Neoplatonic Tradition', held by the National Committee for Philosophy of the Royal Irish Academy, Dublin, 22-23 May 1989. I would like to thank Fran O'Rourke for his instructive comments.

although a knowledge of physical theory (φύσικη θεωρία) is important for this end, Eriugena does not believe we should argue endlessly about competing theories. As with Augustine and the early Christian Fathers, there is little interest in absolute accuracy regarding the physical world; indeed there is a general belief (stemming ultimately from Plato's *Timaeus*) that the visible world is not completely knowable as it is not true being, but rather belongs to the sphere of becoming.[3] Despite these qualifications, Eriugena has a very clear vision of the goal towards which his thought is moving. Φύσις, nature, understood as a dynamic process of self-manifestation, at once manifesting itself as Creator and created, and in the same dialectical process withdrawing into its nameless origin, stands as the absolute frame of his thinking. Matters of consistency are subordinated to the task of explicating this dynamic concept of φύσις. Eriugena speaks of God as the 'divine cosmographer' (*divinus cosmografus*, III.710c) whose work is recounted in the physical (φυσική, III.705b) level of understanding Scripture. To understand this work belongs to the fourfold division of wisdom (*quadriformis sophiae divisio*, III.705b).

Given this complexity of doctrine, our aim is first of all to give an exposition of Eriugena's complex views on the nature and genesis of the physical world and, secondly, to interpret them as to their originality. We shall see that Eriugena argues that corporeal nature is in fact not fully real but is totally dependent on incorporeal nature—the realm of the 'intellectuals' and 'intelligibles', and that this incorporeal nature is in the last analysis beyond comprehension. Nevertheless, its mysterious, marvellous and ineffable ways may in part be catalogued, and we shall follow Eriugena's attempt to do this.

I: THE CATEGORIES CONTAIN THE CREATED UNIVERSE

Eriugena's philosophy of the spatio-temporal created world is based, like that of all the major NeoPlatonists, on his interpretation of Aristotle's *Categories*. The visible world is enclosed by the categories. Eriugena did not know Aristotle at first hand. Porphyry and Boethius as well as Martianus Capella were important sources for Eriugena on the nature of the Aristotelian categories, but the key source was the widely circulated Pseudo-Augustinian *Categoriae decem*.[4] The *Categoriae decem* lists the categories in the order in which Aristotle himself lists them, and Eriugena follows this order.[5] Eriugena

---

3   Eriugena probably knew the *Timaeus* in the Latin translation of Calcidius, whose commentary he cites in the *Annotationes in Marcianum*, ed. C. Lutz (Cambridge, Mass., 1939), p. 10 [7,10] and p. 22 [13,23]. Eriugena refers to Plato 15 times in the *Periphyseon*.

4   Porphyry's *Isagoge* and his two Commentaries on the *Categories* (one now lost) were most important for shaping the medieval reaction. Porphyry did not think the categories were about things (τὰ ὄντα, τὰ πράγματα) or genera of being, nor were they simply grammatical categories about words; they were about 'vocal significant sounds (φωναί) which signify things'. Porphyry disagrees with Plotinus' rejection of the categories and accepts that they apply to the sensible world.

5   Aristotle himself gives different lists of categories in different places. In the *Categories* there are ten, and the *Topics* follows this list; but *Metaphysics* XIV.2.1089b20 lists only

treats of categorial problems in his Commentary on the *De nuptiis Philologiae et Mercurii* of Martianus Capella, and in the *Periphyseon*, especially in Book I.463a–489b and Book II.588b–89a. In Book II.588b the categories are listed in Greek and are treated as answers to questions (what? how great? and so on) as in Aristotle's *Topics*. Eriugena, while taking his list of categories from Aristotle, appears not to accept Aristotle's table of ten categories as definitive.

Eriugena holds that the categories do not apply to the divine 'uncreated' world. Following Augustine, he argues that the categories do not apply to God, since he is infinite, and the categories as the widest genera define or delimit things in certain ways. The categories describe everything other than God:

> Aristotle, the shrewdest among the Greeks, as they say, in discovering the way of distinguishing natural things (*naturalium rerum discretionis*), included the innumerable variety of all things which come after God and are created by him in ten universal genera which he called the ten categories, that is, predicables. For, as he holds, nothing can be found in the multitude of created things and in the various motions of minds (*variisque animorum motibus*) which cannot be included in one of these genera. (I.463a17-23)[6]

Eriugena sees only the christianized Aristotle—the categories mark the distinction between a timeless God and a temporal, created reality.[7] God is outside the categories and so categorial terms such as substance and accident do not apply to him. Augustine and Boethius both agreed that God can have no accidents and Eriugena repeats this view. Eriugena also develops Augustine's view that God is not properly called substance into a general thesis that God is beyond substance, *supersubstantialis*.

It is true that the categories tell us the nature of the highest grades of reality—for Eriugena there really exists such an entity as the most general substance, the most general quality and so on, down to the most specific

three—substances (*οὐσίαι*), passions (*παθή*) and relation (*τὸ πρός τι*). Brentano in his book, *On the Several Senses of Being in Aristotle*, trans. R. George (Berkeley, 1975), p. 50, assumes that Aristotle did want to have a determinate number and that ten was that number (on Neopythagorean grounds). Possibly Aristotle was already reducing a number of the categories (action, passion, position, having) to movement (*κίνησις*), a category suggested by Plotinus.

6   Sheldon-Williams' translation, Vol. 1, p.85. In this essay we shall refer to the Periphyseon in the following way: for Books One, Two, Three, we shall make use of I.P. Sheldon-Williams' edition, *Iohannis Scotti Eriugenae Periphyseon (De Divisione Naturae)*, Volume 1 (Dublin, 1968); Volume II (Dublin, 1970); Volume III (Dublin, 1981). For Books Four and Five we shall refer to the text as printed in Migne, *Patrologia Latina*, Vol. CXXII. A translation of all five books by I. P. Sheldon-Williams, corrected by J. J. O'Meara is available in J. J. O'Meara, ed., *Eriugena. Periphyseon (Division of Nature)* (Montréal, 1987).

7   Eriugena adopts from Maximus Confessor the notion that the category which stands between God and creation is the category of time (or the conjoined categories of place and time).

species and individuals. At times Eriugena speaks as if the world itself is made up of these widest genera, intermediate species and individuals. The categories are for him the names of the ultimate constituents of the universe. Regarding universals, Eriugena appears in these passages to be a realist of the Platonic kind.[8] He sometimes speaks as though God were the highest being, the highest substance, the most universal category. Yet, at the same time, this highest essence, *οὐσία*, 'contains' all things and is present in all things. Therefore God 'runs' through all the genera and species as well as being above them and containing them. Everything else depends on him in some way. Substance therefore is a name for the highest being. Of course Eriugena will always modify this with a Dionysian *via negativa* where God is ultimately beyond being, beyond substance and beyond life, beyond even non-being itself. To speak of the highest *οὐσία* is permitted, and God may be called that *οὐσία* so long as we reserve the right to apply apophatic negations at a more advanced stage of the discussion.

Despite their inapplicability to the divine realm, the categories are most important in Eriugena's thought—to such an extent that I. P. Sheldon-Williams thought the *Periphyseon* was really a work on the categories.[9] It is through the categories that Eriugena is able to think the nature of created reality. Eriugena is an innovator in his application of the categories and is not slavishly following Aristotle. In fact, his outlook on the categories differs from that of Aristotle in a number of interesting ways which I briefly list here:

1. The categories do not apply to God or to the primary causes (II.588b).[10] The categories apply only to created reality. Aristotle holds that the category of substance also applies to the eternal intelligences in the upper world.

2. Eriugena states that the ten Aristotelian categories are not complete— others could be added if the author had more time for the analysis.

3. The categories can be structured in different ways, e.g. subsumed under the wider categories of rest and motion (II.597a). Eriugena implies that the categories can actually be subsumed under higher and more general

8   The philosophical discussion on the nature of universals which dominated twelfth century philosophy actually began in the ninth century (with Ratramnus of Corbie for example), but never clarified the terms sufficiently. Eriugena sees the logical classes as ontological categories, but sometimes says that these divisions are purely our mind's ways of viewing things, and have existence *in mente* rather than *in re*. For him, the unfolding of the world through the categories is both the unfolding of the divine will, and also a product of human knowing or human *θεωρία*.

9   See Sheldon-Williams, Vol. I, p. 5. See also Sheldon-Williams' essay in A.H. Armstrong, ed., *The Cambridge History of Later Greek and Early Medieval Philosophy* (Cambridge, 1967). The standard work on Eriugena remains M. Cappuyns, *Jean Scot Erigène: sa vie, son œuvre, sa pensée* (Louvain, 1933). On the categories, see also J. Marenbon, *Early Medieval Philosophy* (London, 1983). See also, J. Marenbon, 'John Scottus and the *Categoriae decem*', in W. Beierwaltes, ed., *Eriugena: Studien zu seinen Quellen* (Heidelberg, 1980).

10 He cites Augustine's *De Trinitate* at *Periphyseon* I.463b but he could just as easily have cited Boethius' *De Trinitate*, Ch. 4.

(*superior et generalior*, I.469b) categories of motion and rest, which themselves can be subsumed under the greatest category of the All (*universitas*, Greek: τὸ πᾶν, I.469b19). This is in line with Plotinus' discussion of the categories.[11] Eriugena divides the categories under the higher categories of rest and motion: four of the categories are at rest (οὐσία, quantity, situation and place), the other six are in motion (I.469a).

4. The categories intermingle and interpenetrate so that it is difficult to distinguish what belongs precisely to any one category: 'almost all the categories are so interrelated (*concatenata*) that they can scarcely be distinguished from one another in a definite way' (I.472b-c).

5. Quantity is the first accident; this is a variation from the tradition of Martianus Capella, Calcidius and Boethius, for which authors quality is primary (I.497a). Indeed as we shall see in our discussion of material bodies, quantity operates in the physical world as the underlying substance.[12]

6. The categories can be divided into those which are circumstances (περιοχαί, *circumstantiae*, I.471c) standing around substance, and those which can be genuinely seen as accidents (Eriugena uses the Greek term συμβάματα, rather than Aristotle's term συμβεβηκός; Latin: *accidens*, I.471c). This is a crucial point to which we shall return.[13]

7. Οὐσία in itself is incorporeal; so also are the other categories because they depend on οὐσία: 'therefore all the categories are incorporeal when considered in themselves' (I.479a).

8. However some of the categories combine through a '*coitus*' to give the appearance of corporeality (I.479a).

9. The categories of place and time are metaphysically prior to the things enclosed in those categories (I.482b).[14]

The context of the discussion of the categories in Book One of the *Periphyseon* is their applicability to God. Augustine and Boethius had already raised this question in their writings on the Trinity, arguing that God cannot have accidents, and indeed that God is not truly substance but is supersubstantial (see, for example, Augustine, *De Trinitate* IV.11). Boethius denies

11   John P. Anton, 'Plotinus' Approach to Categorial Theory', in R. Baine-Harris, ed., *The Significance of Neoplatonism* (Norfolk, Va., 1976), pp. 83-100.
12   Sheldon-Williams, *Periphyseon*, Vol. I, p. 232, n. 98.
13   In treating accidents as circumstances, literally 'standing around' the substance, Eriugena is reflecting accurately the meaning of the Greek term περιοχαί, which referred to the villages lying outside the polis of Athens.
14   Eriugena cites Augustine's *De musica* VI as the source of this view. Augustine says that the number of places and times precedes the things that are measured by them. This 'transcendental' turn allows Eriugena to argue that things conform to the measure of the mind rather than the other way around. This transcendental shift is theologically inspired: God's knowledge produces things, it is not things which produce the knowledge of them.

that God is in any place, and explains that he is not in time but is eternal—
meaning here present to all times, just as omnipresent means present to all
places. Eriugena will say that God is really more-than-substance (*supersubstantialis*) and that it is only by metaphor that the category of substance
applies to him.

II: THE PRIMARY CATEGORY: SUBSTANCE

Let us examine the category of substance in more detail. Eriugena, following
the tradition of Aristotle and Augustine, understands substance as that which
stands by itself, which has *per se* subsistence (I.470b), and is that upon which
everything else depends (*fulciri* I.470b26; Aristotle's word is ὑπάρχειν).
Aristotle in the *Categories* sees everything as either a substance or 'either
predicable of a substance or present in a primary substance' (iv.2a33-35).
Eriugena simplifies this scheme. For him there are essentially only two kinds
of being: everything is either a subject and has being in and through itself
(*per se*), or is in a subject, and has its being in something else (*in aliquo*).[15]
Οὐσία has being in and through itself. Accident for Eriugena exists in another
(*in aliquo*), and has a natural desire for the subject to which it adheres, an
appetite (*appetendum*) for being.

The Aristotelian tradition is wedded to a Neoplatonic outlook, which
dissolves Aristotle's plurality of substances into a single essence. As a Neoplatonist, Eriugena accepts that ultimate reality is one. In so far as the One is
nameable at all it may be called essence or οὐσία, but this οὐσία cannot be
known and in fact all we ever know are emanations out from the essence
which are termed ὑποστάσεις or substances (*substantiae*). Οὐσία in itself is
accessible neither to sense nor to intellect (I.471b). These substances or
hypostases are emanations from the hidden One, and do not in themselves
have ultimate reality. Eriugena's original term for them is the primary causes
(*primordiales causae*, II.529b). They occupy the second level of his four-fold
division of nature.

Eriugena's understanding of οὐσία derives directly from Dionysius and
Maximus and indirectly from Proclus. For the Greek Christian tradition
οὐσία is the hidden infinite source from which particular ὑποστάσεις
(substances) 'radiate' or emanate, the precise nature of this emanation never
being clarified in Greek Christian thought. Maximus in particular provided
the triadic conception of being as a trinity of essence, power and operation

15 Eriugena does not display a grasp of the problem to which Porphyry and others were
    referring—a problem which continues to haunt discussion of the categories; rather
    Eriugena speaks of them both as logical and as ontological descriptions of things. This is
    partly due to the fact that, for Eriugena, logic (*logica, dialectica*) is both the structure of
    argument and also the structure of being. See D. Moran, *The Philosophy of John Scottus
    Eriugena. A Study of Idealism in the Middle Ages* (Cambridge, 1989), pp. 123-53.

(οὐσία, δύναμις, ἐνέργεια, essentia, virtus, operatio, I.507c27-8). This trinity means that an entity is understood as not revealing itself as it is in itself, but only through its powers and operations, and its 'circumstances'. This οὐσία in its trinity is timeless and outside of space (I.507d); all other things exist in time and space. There is an unknown underlying source of all things (which must be one because there exists nothing which could differentiate it) and there exist also the spatio-temporal manifestations of all things—a view which might call to mind Hindu thought or that of Schopenhauer.[16] Above all else Eriugena wants to emphasize the infinity and incomprehensibility of this underlying substratum.

Following Maximus, Eriugena first argues that the primary ontological distinction is that between uncreated (unmanifest) and created (manifest) being. This distinction corresponds to the distinction between the realm of the timeless and placeless and spatio-temporal reality. At *Periphyseon* I.481b-c Eriugena quotes Maximus' assertion that everything apart from God 'is understood to be in place, with which time is always and in every way simultaneously understood'. Secondly, Eriugena—here adapting Aristotle's distinction between subject and what is in a subject or said of a subject— argues that there are only two kinds of thing: namely substance and accident, or, as he also puts it, 'subject' and 'what is in a subject'. Regarding the reduction of all things to substance and accident, it is the opinion of 'dialecticians', according to Eriugena at I.470d, that everything which is exists precisely in so far as it belongs in one of the following four classes: subject, in a subject, of a subject, in and of a subject.[17] Eriugena knows very little about Aristotle's own conception of substance, but he does attempt on the basis of his knowledge of the categories to reclassify the determinations of 'subject', 'in a subject', 'of a subject' and 'in and of a subject' into a simpler scheme. Eriugena reduces these four to two at I.470d. 'Subject' and 'of a subject' are identified: to say 'Cicero' is to say 'man'. We are saying the same thing; all that differs is the degree of generality: one is an individual and the other is a species (I.471a). The species is complete in the individual and the individual fully represents the species, therefore 'subject' and 'of a subject' can be identified. Then 'in a subject' and 'in and of a subject' are merged into one by Eriugena. We are left with a simple twofold classification—'subject' and 'what is in a subject', i.e. substance and accident. This clears the way for the further reduction of everything to one incorporeal essence, God or *natura*.

Regarding the division of the world into timeless and temporal: strictly speaking God is not properly called οὐσία. God is indefinable, and hence is neither a defined substance (*diffinita substantia*, II.591a1) nor a defined subject (*diffinitum subiectum*, II.591a2). God is infinite and unbounded and hence not

16 Schopenhauer was impressed by this aspect of Eriugena.
17 Eriugena could have found this classification in Aristotle. Sheldon-Williams in his edition, Vol. I, p. 102, refers to Boethius' *Commentary on the Peri Hermeneias of Aristotle*, ed. Meiser, i. 3, p. 57, 28 -58; ii, 3, p. 68, 9-10.

a 'what'. None of the categories applies to God and for that reason he has no place: 'because it [the divine essence] is infinite and uncircumscribed and does not allow itself to be located by any intellect nor by itself.'[18] Nevertheless God may be described as the place of all things (*locus omnium*, II.592c24), or the 'place of places' (*locus locorum*). Indeed metaphorically God may be called Place or Time because he is the cause of all places and times (I. 468c). On the other hand, all bodies are contained within their essences or substances and cannot, while they remain bodies, overstep the limits of their natures (II.590c). It is a very important principle for Eriugena that things are contained by their essential definitions, and God is not so contained being infinite, hence he is also indefinable. Now essential to defining and delimiting are the categories of place and time, since substances in the ordinary created world are what they are by virtue of their location in space and time. When things return to God at that point they overstep (Eriugena uses the Latin verb, *transcendere*) their given natures (I.483a). In a crucial addition to the text, transcendence of nature is explained—to transcend one's nature means that one's nature is no longer apparent or manifest. For Eriugena creation is manifestation, but in the *reditus* the individual manifest essence is absorbed and hidden in the unmanifest whole, as air is no longer seen when light shines.[19]

III: ACCIDENT AND MATTER AS A COLLECTION OF ACCIDENTS

Next let us examine the meaning of accident and specify more precisely the relation of substance to accident in Eriugena. Although all accidents by definition are those which are 'in a subject', some accidents are outside the substance and so determine it in special ways. Grouping the accidents according to whether they are outside or inside the substance: those which 'stand outside' appear to be quantity, place, time and situation (*locus, tempus, quantitas, situs*). Since we do not know οὐσία, we end up knowing only that which surrounds substance. Eriugena cites Maximus as his authority for this notion (I.471c).[20]

Eriugena has modified the theory of the categories by importing Eastern Greek thinking found in Maximus and also in Basil. This tradition argues that place, time and quantity are not strictly speaking accidents, but are circumstances, literally bystanders (περιοχαί, I. 471c7), surrounding the invisible ungraspable essence.[21] Οὐσία can only be known by its circumstances (*circumstantiae*, I.471b34; *circumstantes*, I.471c7). These are not strictly speaking accidents because they are outside (*extrinsecus*) substance, yet they cannot

18 *Periphyseon* II.592c25-592d26: quia infinita est et incircunscripta et a nullo intellectu neque se ipsa locari, id est diffiniri et circunscribi permittit.
19 This passage at *Periphyseon* I.483a-b is added to the Rheims version of the manuscript in Eriugena's supposed hand. It is surely an authorial addition.
20 See Maximus, *I Ambigua* xiii, PG XCI. 1225.

exist apart from it. Eriugena uses the image of a centre around which the circumstances revolve; οὐσία is at the centre of the revolutions of time and the dispositions of place, quantity and situation. All the other categories, however, are genuinely in the subject; these he terms accidents or συμβάματα (I.471c8). This theory is a development of Gregory of Nazianzus and other Eastern writers, but it also bears some similarities to Sorabji's portrayal of the Aristotelian interpretations of Simplicius and the Christian, John Philoponus.[22] It is definitely not the classical Aristotle. This is an instance of Eriugena's unresolved adoption of two conflicting sources—on the one hand he wants a simple ontology of substance and accident, on the other a threefold classification of substance, circumstance and accident. Nevertheless, as we shall see, the theory of circumstance is crucial to his explanation of the nature of matter.

At I.478c Eriugena says that none of the categories is in fact accessible to sense. Οὐσία itself transcends the senses and the other categories are either in or around οὐσία so that they also in themselves are not known to the senses. The argument is simple: if οὐσία is incorporeal, then its accidents must also be incorporeal since they inhere in it (or stand around it):

> You are aware, I think, of the fact that none of the aforesaid ten categories which Aristotle defined, when thought of by itself, that is, in its own nature, in the light of reason, is accessible to the bodily senses. For οὐσία is incorporeal and the object of no sense, while the other nine categories are about it or within it. But if the former is incorporeal, surely it must be apparent to you that everything which is either attached to it or subsists in it (*omnia quae aut ei adhaerent aut in ea subsistunt*) and cannot exist apart from it is incorporeal? Therefore all the categories are incorporeal when considered in themselves (I.478c).[23]

Eriugena goes on to explain that some of these categories 'commingle' (*coitus*) with one another to produce the effect of corporeality:

> [Some] of them, however, by a certain marvellous commingling with one another (*earum tamen [quaedam] inter se mirabili quodam coitu*), as Gregory says, produce visible matter, while some appear in nothing (*in nullo apparent*) and remain for ever incorporeal. For οὐσία and relation, place, time, action, passion are not reached by any bodily sense, while quantity and quality, situation and condition, when they come together

21 All these terms are derived from Greek words which contain the prefix 'περί' meaning 'about' or 'around'. See M. Cristiani, 'Lo spazio e il tempo nell'opera dell'Eriugena', *Studi Medievali* 14 (1973), 39–136. At I.471b Eriugena refers to a Gregory and his commentator Maximus. Cristiani treats this as a very important passage and understands the Gregory here to be Gregory of Nazianzus. See also M. Cristiani, 'Le problème du lieu et du temps dans le livre Ier de *Periphyseon*', in J. J. O'Meara and L. Bieler, eds., *The Mind of Eriugena* (Dublin, 1973), pp. 41–8.
22 Richard Sorabji, *Matter, Space and Motion* (Cornell, 1988).
23 Sheldon-Williams' translation, Vol. I, pp. 119–21.

and constitute matter, as we said just now, are normally perceived by bodily sense (I.479a).[24]

Eriugena sees material bodies as made up of a congruence of accidents. The terms he gives to this congruence are varied; it is termed *concursus* (I.498b23, I.503a4), *contemeratus coitus* (I.498b26-7), *armonia* (I.501b9), *confluxus* (III.713 c19), *conventus* (III.714a31), *synodus* (III.714a33). The most frequent terms are *concursus* and *coitus* (e.g. III.712b7).[25]

The Gregory referred to in this passage is Gregory of Nyssa. The work is *De hominis opificio*, Chapter XXIV (PL XLIV.212d),[26] or in its original Greek title, Περὶ κατασκευῆς ἀνθρώπου. It was written in 379 to supplement his brother Basil's *Hexaemeron*. It gives an account of the creation of man on the Sixth Day. An important work, it was translated into Latin four times between the sixth and the sixteenth century; the earliest translation being that of Dionysius Exiguus who entitled it *De conditione hominis*. Eriugena called it *De imagine*.[27]

In Chapter XXIV, Gregory is wondering how an immaterial God could have produced a material world. Gregory refers to the categories of quantity and quality. When we think of a body, according to Gregory, we can formulate different ideas about it—that it is two cubits long, heavy and so on; these ideas can be separated from each other, and from the idea of the body in itself. When they have all been removed, no idea of the body remains. There is no underlying subject of predication, no ὑποκείμενον.[28] Gregory argues that matter is not co-eternal with God, but is composed of qualities mingled together. Each of the qualities on its own is grasped as an intellectual idea which is incorporeal (we can for example distinguish the idea of colour from the idea of weight). For Gregory these qualities are ideas independent of one another and independent of any substratum; it is only when thought together that we get the idea of materiality. When all the ideas are withdrawn, the idea of body itself dissolves.

Eriugena accepts this view, but is more specific about which accidents are active in the production of our idea of body. They are: quantity, quality,

24 Sheldon-Williams' translation, Vol. I, p. 121.
25 Eriugena is committed to the view that all nature acts harmoniously, so this coming together of qualities to form bodies is not chaotic or disordered. Many of Eriugena's terms suggest an analogy with the sexual act. Through an act of congress, things are produced. This notion would reappear in later writings of the medieval alchemists.
26 There is a similar idealistic passage in Gregory's work *De anima et eius resurrectione* which, however, appears to have been unknown to Eriugena.
27 See M. Cappuyns, 'Le *De imagine* de Grégoire de Nysse traduit par Jean Scot Erigène', *Recherches de théologie ancienne et médiévale* 32 (1965), pp. 205-62. See also, Philip Levine, 'Two Early Latin Versions of St. Gregory of Nyssa's Περὶ κατασκευῆς ἀνθρώπου', *Harvard Studies in Classical Philology* 63 (1958), 473-92. It is translated by W. Moore and H.A. Wilson in *Gregory of Nyssa. Selected Works and Letters*, The Nicene and Post-Nicene Fathers, Vol. 5 (Grand Rapids, Michigan, 1972), pp. 387-427. A new Greek edition of Gregory of Nyssa's text is in preparation by Carlos Steel of the University of Leuven.
28 Richard Sorabji, *Matter, Space and Motion*, p. 53.

situation and condition. As far as I have been able to determine, this selection of a group of categories as productive of corporeality is original to Eriugena.

Another possible source for Eriugena's theory is Gregory's brother, Basil, who had already commented on the nature of sensible substance in his *Hexaemeron* 1.8.21a-b, where he says:

> Let us recommend to ourselves concerning the earth, not to be too curious what its substance is; nor to wear ourselves out by reasoning, seeking its very foundation; nor to search for some nature destitute of qualities, existing without quality of itself; but to realize well that all that is seen around it is related to the reason of its existence, forming an essential part of its substance. You will end with nothing if you attempt to eliminate by reason each of the qualities that exists in it. In fact, if you remove the black, the cold, the weight, the density, the qualities pertaining to taste, or any others which are perceptible, there will be no basic substance.[29]

Gregory and Basil presumably inherited this idea from Plotinus who argued that sensible substances are a mere conglomeration (συμφόρησις) of matter and qualities.[30] What is at issue in Basil's case is the nature of the material substance of the earth. He is arguing that earth is coldness, solidity, hardness and nothing more. There is nothing underlying these qualities of earth, holding them up, as it were. Basil is trying to rule out the question: what gives a foundation to the earth? Actually at the beginning of the same chapter Basil indicates that there are two kinds of substance—that accessible to the mind, and that accessible to the senses, so he may only be ruling out a self-subsisting underlying material substance.

With regard to the theory that physical things are really incorporeal, it is clear then that Eriugena drew on the Greek Christian tradition, which in turn drew its account of matter from Plotinus. Eriugena accepts the Greek view that creation is manifestation, appearance (φαινόμενον), that it is a spatio-temporal interval (διάστημα) underlying which is the mysterious infinite reality of hidden οὐσία.[31] Eriugena defines creation as manifestation (*creatio, hoc est in aliquo manifestatio*, I.455b) and indeed as self-manifestation. In Book III he speaks of the One, Nature, as creating itself by self-manifestation: it 'creates itself, that is, allows itself to appear in its theophanies' (III.689a-b).

29 Trans. by Sr. Agnes Clare Way, in *Saint Basil. Exegetical Homilies*, Fathers of the Church series, Vol. 46 (Washington, 1963), p. 14. Sorabji calls attention to this passage in his study on *Matter, Space and Motion*. Sorabji maintains that both Basil and Gregory are committed to what he terms 'the bundle theory of substance'; a substance is nothing other than the collection of its properties.

30 Sorabji, *Matter, Space and Motion*, p. 51. See Plotinus *Ennead* VI 3, 8, 19-37. The term συμφόρησις itself comes from Epicurus.

31 Eriugena uses the word *creatio* for creation, but also the terms *processio, descensio, emanatio*. Indeed he also translated Dionysius' Greek term πρόοδος as *exitus*. There is one instance of Dionysius using the term θέσις instead of the more usual πρόοδος in a quotation from Scripture.

Given Eriugena's account of substance and accident as immaterial and incorporeal, we now turn to a more detailed treatment of Eriugena's understanding of matter in order to understand his account of the constitution of physical things.

IV: MATTER AND THE FOUR ELEMENTS

Greek physics saw the physical corporeal world as made from the four elements. What role do the elements play in Eriugena's theory? Eriugena sees the four elements as stumbling blocks in his attempt to reduce everything to the immaterial causes. Here he did not look to Dionysius who has no real discussion of material bodies, but turned instead to Gregory of Nyssa's *De imagine* and Augustine's *De Genesi ad litteram*.

Eriugena explores various theories concerning the nature of the four elements in a series of exchanges between the participants in the dialogue. The junior interlocutor, Alumnus, has a theory that the four elements are each produced by two causes—namely the two qualities which are specific to each element. Thus fire is produced by warmth and dryness (II.604a-b). Alumnus claims this is a theory supported by the *sapientes mundi*, the wise natural philosophers. Nutritor, Eriugena's mouthpiece, rejects this theory on the grounds that qualities cannot be the causes of substances and in any case do not exist on their own (II.605a8-605b13). Nutritor has his own theory, namely that fire is an incorporeal substance. This incorporeal fire in turn descends from the most general substance (*generalissima essentia*, II.605b15) whereas the quality warmth descends from the most general quality (*generalissima qualitas*).[32] The four elements then are contained in the causes—general or universal essence and accident.

In themselves the four elements are simple, incorporeal and not known by the senses (II.606c), and are called 'pure' by Eriugena. They are four effects of the most general substance (II.606c). The four qualities although they are opposites are also the result of the one cause, namely the most general quality (*generalissima qualitas omnium qualitatum*, II.606d). In the peaceful concord of universal nature (*ineffabilis universalis naturae pacifica concordia*, II.606d5-607a6) they all co-exist. Eriugena relocates the elements in the hierarchy of being. Rather than being at the lowest level, above unformed matter and below individual corporeal things (especially below living things), the elements are actually very high on the scale—they are incorporated into the primary causes, and are either themselves those causes, or principles (*rationes seminales*) contained in the causes. In Book V Eriugena says that the elements are drawn back so that they will all be contained by fire: water changes into vapour and vapour into flame and flame returns to

---

32   It is part of his theory to reify the universals and see them as the highest principles of being. The highest genus of substance contains all the other particular and general substances, the highest genus of 'accident' contains all general and particular accidents. In Eriugena's terms the lower is always 'contained in' the higher.

the element of fire (V.953a). Fire then returns to its causes in substance and quality. Eriugena regards 'the natural stability of substances and the mutability of natural qualities' to be the two components which make up the natural creature (V.958b-c). All things return into substance and quality.

To take the example of the element fire: there are, according to Eriugena, really two fires—the invisible insensible fire (*ignis per se invisibilis*, II.608b27) which is incomprehensible in itself and dwells in the causes (II.604c23-25), and the visible fire which is sensible and corporeal and proceeds from it like a ray (*radius visibilis*, II.608b).[33] A forerunner of this theory is to be found in Plato's *Timaeus* 53a-54b, where the four elements are forms which exist in themselves, but also which have traces or likenesses in this world.[34] Alumnus believes that even this lower fire would itself be invisible where it does not mingle with grosser natures. Thus he maintains that the actual sun's rays are invisible in themselves (and incomprehensible to the senses of animals, II. 608b) but as the rays from the sun move downwards they mingle with grosser natures until they can be seen. First it mingles with ether, then with air, until it is reflected by bodies so as to reveal itself in colours. This explanation is typically Neoplatonic and depends on a theory of emanation. Eriugena speaks of a gradual descent (*gradatim descendit*, II.608b32-33) of the ray from the hidden causes to the material sensible realm.

The teacher goes further and stresses that the fire which departs from its source still carries with it the immaterial fire which is its cause (II.609a)—the cause remains in the effect. Eriugena's account is suitably triadic: there is first the immaterial 'father' fire; second, the ray or 'son' fire (which also is

---

33   At *Periphyseon* II.608b Eriugena speaks of the invisible fire begetting from itself the visible ray (*de se gignit*). This is analogous to the Father giving birth to the Word, or to the act of creation whereby the created world proceeds from the invisible primary causes.

34   The idea of two fires derives from the *Timaeus* 48e-53c. See Sorabji, *Matter, Space and Motion*, pp. 32-5. For Plato the elements can change into one another e.g. fire into air, or air into water. Fire then is not a 'this' but a 'such'. In *Timaeus* 51b-c Plato asks if there is a self-subsisting fire, a fire-in-itself; or does only sensible fire exist, which on Plato's account could not be fully real? Originally the elements existed only as shadows or traces (ἴχνη) of themselves, so the creator began to mark them out and give them form in shapes and numbers. Fire is a solid body for Plato and has been constructed. Fire is constructed from the pyramid shape. It also appears as if fire gains the sensible qualites it has—namely warmth and dryness when considered in conection with the human domain. Possibly in itself it does not have these qualities. But Eriugena picks up on this to describe an immaterial insensible fire and then a sensible fire that flows forth from it. Cornford in his book, *Plato's Cosmology* (London, 1937), pp. 180-1, interprets Plato to mean that fire is a bundle of properties, and certainly Albinus and other Middle Platonists follow him here. (See Sorabji, ibid., p. 33). But Eriugena seems to be opting for a different explanation, whereby sensible fire is an emanation of intellectual fire, which itself is somehow contained in the genus of substance. I agree with Sorabji (p. 35) that Plato appears to be talking of fire not just as a bundle of properties but as things endowed with properties. There is a form of fire. But there is indeed an ambiguity and it is interesting to see what Eriugena does with that ambiguity.

immaterial but can become visible when mingled with the other elements), and third, the brightness (*splendor*) which is a result of the fire. These three are taken to be an image of the Trinity (II. 609a-b). Eriugena explicitly says the brightness proceeds (*procedit*) from the Father fire through the ray (*per radium*)— a typical Latin Trinitarian formulation. Eriugena then drops the discussion of the elements and proceeds to a discussion of the vestiges of the Trinity.[35] Clearly his investigation into natures (*naturarum inquisitio*, II.608a5) has the intention of showing that the invisible Trinity is present in all natural processes.

In Book I.479a-b Eriugena maintained that the four elements are bodies in themselves (*corpora per se*), but they are of such a fine nature that in themselves they are invisible, and elude every mortal sense (*sensus mortalis*). In Book III.701a Eriugena repeats the view that all bodies are made of the four elements which themselves are incorporeal and invisible; but he goes on to list the five greatest bodies (*maxima corpora*), earth, water, air, ether and heaven (*terra, aqua, aera, aethera, caelum*). This lists the four elements in a different way: they are now ranked as cosmic zones: the lowest is earth, and ether stands for the realm of fire which is highest, below the firmament which Eriugena calls '*caelum*'.[36]

Despite the apparent solidity and corporeality of the elements from which physical things are formed, the visible world is nonetheless really incorporeal but appears solid due to a concourse of accidents.[37] Eriugena cites Gregory of Nyssa as his authority on the nature of matter and material things: 'matter is nothing else but a certain composition of accidents which proceed from invisible causes to visible matter.'[38] Then he gives the explanation: material things are corruptible. If material things had a simple and immutable essence then they would not be corruptible—'for genera and species and ἄτομα (Eriugena uses the Greek ἄτομα to mean 'individuals') are eternal and endure for the very reason that there is in them something which is one and indivisible which can neither be dissolved nor destroyed.' For each element

---

35   Eriugena's digression into the vestiges of the Trinity may be prompted by thinking of the manner in which fire is a vestige for Plato. But it is noteworthy that both Eriugena and Plato take fire as their main example of an element. Eriugena says little of the other elements except to give etymological definitions of their natures and to argue that all things are made up of a commingling of all the elements. In Periphyseon III.714b Eriugena explains that fire is called 'πῦρ' in Greek because it penetrates all things through their pores (*per poros*, 714b).

36   See Sheldon-Williams, Vol III, p. 318 note. Eriugena's use of the notion of ether is not developed further.

37   Here Sorabji has not noticed that two aspects of the tradition are maintained together: material things are mere 'bundles of properties', yet on the other hand they have (or are really) essences which are invisible and are real bearers of properties.

38   *Periphyseon* I.479b-c: Nil aliud dicens materiam esse nisi accidentium quandam composi-tionem ex invisibilibus causis ad visibilem materiam procedentem, trans; Sheldon-Williams, Vol. I, p. 120. This definition appears faulty as it includes the *definiendum* in the definition; however, the main idea is clear—matter is a visible effect produced from invisible causes.

there is an invisible incorporeal substance and also an emanation which in the last instance will be shifting and transitory.

In Book III.712a–715a Eriugena returns to the account of the four elements, deriving their nature from traditional etymologies of their Greek names. Again he stresses that material bodies are not composed of the substances of the elements which are indestructible and immutable, but of the qualities of those substances (III.712b). All bodies are made up of coldness, dryness, moistness, warmth, but this time Eriugena adds that bodies are made up of the elements together with superadded forms (*formae*, III. 712b4). What is the nature of these superadded forms? Corporeal entities consist of matter and form. Eriugena argues that every body has actually two kinds of form—a stable substantial form and a fluctuating 'qualitative' form, which is receptive of accidents and accounts for change in a body. Things change when different qualitative forms mingle with the unstable flux which is unformed matter. The unstable forms themselves are created from the coming together of quantity and quality. Eriugena calls this form the qualitative form (*forma qualitativa*, III.701d25) which is fleeting and insubstantial. Thus he says that the scriptural statement 'Heaven and Earth shall pass away' means that unformed matter and qualitative form will pass away but not the stable four elements out of which things are made, nor their 'substantial form' (*substantialis forma*, III.702a). Here he sees the elements as belonging to the sphere of the unchanging incorporeal substantial forms, whereas physical things as we know them come together into unstable forms due to the commingling of the categories of quantity and quality supported by unformed matter.

Eriugena has a peculiar view of these stable substantial forms which remain in their genera and are eternal. He says that they are free of the *concursus* (III.702d31) of accidents, whereas the bodies (*corpora*) which are subject to change are the commingling of accidents. Pure substances have no accidents. Eriugena goes on to explain that each substantial form is one and is neither multiplied nor diminished:

> For that form, for example, which is called 'man' is no greater in the infinite multiplication of human nature into its indivisible species than in that unique and first man who became the first to partake of it, nor was it less in him than in all whose bodies are multiplied out of him, but in all it is one and the same and in all it is equally [whole] and in none does it admit any variation or dissimilarity. . . . But that form which is joined to matter so as to constitute body (is) always variable and changeable and dispersed among diverse differences by accident. For it is not from natural causes that the manifold differences of visible forms proceed in one and the same substantial form, but they come from without. For the dissimilarity of men one from the other in feature, size and quality of their several bodies, and the variety of custom and conduct result not from human nature, which is one and the same in

all in whom it exists . . . but from things which are understood about it (*circa eam*), namely from places and times, from generation, from quantity and quality of their diets, their habitats, the conditions under which each is born, and to speak generally, from all things that are understood about (*circa*) the substance, and are not the substance itself. (III.703b–c)[39]

In Book One Eriugena gives a slightly different account of the constitution of physical bodies. Here he acknowledges that some may think there is a contradiction between the account of matter as a commingling of the four elements, and the account of matter as the coming together of quantity and quality with οὐσία (I.495d–496a). But there is no contradiction to those who know that the world is really a concourse of the categories of accident. Quantity (*quantitas*) and quality (*qualitas*) combine together to produce a *quantum* and a *quale* which is the physical body as spatially extended (*spatiose*, I.497a13).[40] The other accidents are superadded to these two. Here quantity serves as a 'second subject' (*secundum subiectum*, I.496a9) after οὐσία. Quality, Alumnus says, has been established to be the cause not only of matter but also of form (I.496c). The Master quickly points out that οὐσία is the source of substantial form (I.497c)—and indeed God is the absolute form of all things (*forma omnium*, I.502a).[41]

V: THE NATURE OF LIGHT

Although he says little about individual elements, he does focus on the nature of light, presumably because of its importance in the biblical cosmology of *Genesis*. Light is the first born of creation, and is quasi-divine.

Though light is not itself one of the four elements, it seems to belong to them, because its nature is fire (*natura lucis est ignis*, I.521a). It appears to have two aspects. Sensible light (*lux sensibilis*) fills the whole universe and is

---

39 Sheldon-Williams' translation, Vol. III, p. 219.

40 The distinction between a quality and what has quality is made in the *Categories* of Aristotle in VIII 10a27. A body is a real thing—but it is like a shadow which is a commingling of body and light (501c). At I.501c–d Eriugena digresses to give an account of the nature of shadows and argues that they are cones on the other side of a body from the light, whether they be finite or infinite. Here Eriugena appears to be allowing for the possibility of an infinite shadow (if we accept the interpolation in Eriugena's supposed hand to the text of Rheims). This is a textual interpolation of an expansive scientific kind which has not been given due notice by commentators. An infinite shadow would be very confusing in his system as it would postulate an infinite body, or a body the same size as the sun, so that the shadow thrown is not a cone but an infinitely long cylinder. This may represent a mistake on the part of the author.

41 Eriugena's invocation of the Augustinian phrase *forma omnium* for God was noticed and praised by Nicholas of Cusa in his annotations to *Periphyseon* Book One. The phrase recurred in the 12th century where Amaury of Bene held that God was the form of all things, a view which was condemned as heretical in 1210 and 1225.

actually immutable in itself and immobile (I.520d).[42] Eriugena then says that this light has a vehicle (*vehiculum*)—the solar body (*solare corpus*, I.520d15) which is in eternal motion and from which light radiates out in such a way that it fills everywhere at once. The light itself is immobile but its vehicle is ever moving. In Book I.521b Eriugena cites Dionysius (*Celestial Hierarchy* IX. 3. 206c-d) and Basil (*Hexaemeron* II. 7. 45a, 48b) in support of the view that light is everywhere in the universe and is essentially timeless, changeless and immutable.[43] In fact, Eriugena modifies this slightly to say that light is everywhere except for a small space near the earth which it leaves empty so that night (the earth's shadow) can come.

In Book III Eriugena notes that Basil and Augustine differ in their account of the nature of the light which was created on the First Day: was it fire as Basil had thought (III.693c)? Or was it the creation of the heavenly powers as Augustine had thought? Eriugena, true to his spirit of synthesis, is not prepared to choose between these authorities but adds a third possibility—it is the succession of the causes into the effects, i.e. the manifestation of effects. Through the processsion of light, the effects become manifest, because Christ is the light of the world. We are given to understand that the true light is incorporeal and not available to the senses, but the sensible light is an emanation from the divine light. Eriugena is aware of a darkness above the light.[44] In part his interest is governed by his theological understanding of the '*lux inaccessibilis*', the inaccessible light in which God dwells. This highest light, *lux per excellentiam*, is in fact to our eyes a darkness. Therefore above the light, a realm of darkness is postulated, though this darkness is really superessential light which dazzles the mind.

VI: THE SUN, MOON, STARS, PLANETS

So far we have seen that corporeal bodies, the elements and even light appear to be corporeal—but in reality their essences are invisible and incorporeal. Is this also true of the great solar bodies? If light is incorporeal, are the 'light-filled' bodies (the sun, moon and stars) also incorporeal?

The Neoplatonists believed that the sun is the cause of both colour and sight. The sun both produces the ray of light and enables the eye to receive the ray. Eriugena inherited this Neoplatonic view of the sun, but he also inherited conflicting accounts of the nature of the solar body. Eriugena is

---

42 Eriugena uses the words *media spatia* here to refer to the whole cosmic region between the ether and the earth which is filled by light.

43 Eriugena could also have cited Gregory of Nyssa's *De hominis opificio* XXI.3 on this account.

44 This notion was already articulated by Origen in the Περὶ ἀρχῶν (*De principiis*) and in his *Commentary on John*. Plotinus (following Alexander of Aphrodisias) holds light to be incorporeal (see for example VII, 5, 5). The Neoplatonic tradition in general regarded light as incorporeal, and Eriugena is following in this tradition.

unsure of the size of the sun and, in fact, cites Basil in Book III, showing that the sun is of an immense and unmeasurable size, that is, 'infinite' (*infinitas*, III.721d31-2).[45]

In regard to the location of the sun in the heavens, at least three times Eriugena puts it in a central position. At III.722b11 he puts the solar orbit (*ambitus solis*) in the centre of the cosmic circles (*in medio totius spatii*), i.e. between the earth and the outer sphere which circumscribes the sensible world. Similarly at III.697d he says the sun is in the middle region of the world (*medium mundi [spatium]*) and equidistant from the earth and the fixed stars. Of what nature is the body of the sun (*corpus solare*)? It is a body between the physical and the celestial or spiritual.

It draws some of its characteristics from the upper world of the fixed stars (which are light and cold, pale and 'spiritual', III.697c36), and some from the lower region (which is hot and ruddy coloured, III.698a18). The sun draws these opposite characteristics into balance and hence achieves its own medium hot colour. The sun draws its kind of corporeality (*corpolentia*, III.697d10) from lower natures, but it receives its spirituality from the natures above it. Since it has light then it must possess the element fire. In fact it is made up of the four elements like all the celestial bodies, Eriugena says at III.695d. Nevertheless, he denies that the sun is a wholly physical entity; rather it is a quasi-spiritual being. Already, at III.695a, Eriugena had theorized (cutting across his fourfold division of nature) that there is a threefold division of created being: that which is wholly body (*omnino corpus*), wholly spirit (*omnino spiritus*), and something which is an intermediate (*medium quod nec omnino corpus est nec omnino spiritus*) between the two. This is reminiscent of Proclus' positing of an intermediate realm between the intelligible and the sensible regions. Eriugena has an intelligible world (wherein the four elements live in their immaterial purity in the reasons and primordial causes) and a sensible world; the sun acts as a dividing line between the two. The sun therefore shares in both the corporeal and the incorporeal realms and gives a concordant harmony (*concors armonia*, III.695c26) to the whole universe.

Given Eriugena's view that time is what separates the Creator from the created world, it is not surprising that the sun, which measures time in the world, should be at the perimeter of the created universe, between the sensible and spiritual regions, and measures both. This Eriugena could have found in Maximus. Furthermore, the sun is the cause of what is below it. The causes of all things are gathered together as one in the sun, '*simul et uniformiter*'. The primary causes proceed into the reasons (*rationes*), which themselves proceed into the incorporeal simple elements, and these in turn as fire and light and produce their vehicle, the sun, and from it all other things flow forth (III.696a). Eriugena does not use the sun as the explanation

45 Eriugena argues that the size of heavenly bodies is computed from the size of their shadows. But the sun casts no shadow, therefore it is immeasurable. 'Infinite' here means immeasurable.

of the nature of time. Following both Augustine and Basil, who themselves are following Plotinus, Eriugena held that time was not dependent on the movement of the heavenly bodies as Aristotle had thought. For Eriugena, Scripture confirms that the sun could stand still in the heaven and yet time would continue to pass.[46] We shall return to the nature of time.

Given Eriugena's spiritualization of the cosmos, is it fair to draw a cosmological theory about the actual movements of the planets from Eriugena's text? Scholars are divided over which cosmological system is presented in the text, but perhaps we are reading it too literally in attempting to find a coherent theory, since Eriugena's aim is to show only the manner in which this world derives from invisible causes. Eriugena himself is partly responsible for giving the misleading impression that he is a cosmologist in the traditional sense, since he parades his knowledge of nature, drawing on Pliny and other classical sources, and is forced into a cosmological description which may not fit well with his hierarchical metaphysical description of the cosmos.[47]

The question of whether, in Eriugena's account, the planets revolve around the sun or the earth is complex. Evidence leans towards the view that Eriugena believed some of the planets revolve around the sun (III.698a). At III.697d, Eriugena sees Saturn, since it is cold and pale, to be closer to the stars, and the sun, since it is intermediate, to hold a middle position in the universe. This could be interpreted as saying that the sun is in a fixed position and does not move; Eriugena says it has a 'natural situation' (*naturalis situs*, III.698a), like the balance point on a scales. On the supposed authority of Plato's *Timaeus*, Eriugena suggests that Mars, Jupiter, Venus and Mercury revolve around the sun (*circa solem*, 698a22). Eriugena is here confusing Plato with his faulty recollection of Calcidius. In Book One of the *Annotationes in Marcianum*, Eriugena cites Calcidius as claiming that all planets revolve around the sun, whereas in Plato's *Timaeus* (38c) the planets revolve around the earth.[48] Prudentius of Troyes was obviously correct when he reported

46 I am grateful to Professor James J. McEvoy of the Institut Supérieur de Philosophie, Louvain, for pointing out to me the importance of the sun as a symbol of life, energy, time, truth and justice. Indeed Eriugena at one point speaks of the '*sol iustitiae*'. In the *Homilia*, the forms of all bodies are said to proceed from the sun.

47 P. Duhem, *Le système du monde: histoire des doctrines cosmologiques de Platon à Copernic*, Vol. III (Paris, 1915, reprint 1958) is responsible for first attributing to Eriugena a system of planetary movement close to that of Tyco Brahe, based on the Heraclidean system he found in the *De nuptiis Philologiae et Mercurii* of Martianus Capella. Two studies by R. von Erhardt and E. von Erhardt-Siebold: *The Astronomy of Johannes Scotus Erigena* (Baltimore, 1940), and *Cosmology in the Annotationes in Marcianum: More Light on Eriugena's Astronomy* (Baltimore, 1940), have given a more balanced picture, pointing out that Eriugena does not depart from the information available in Pliny and is describing not a heliocentric physical theory but a metaphysical system where the sun is a quasi-divine principle which separates and mediates between the invisible timeless world of the primary causes and the visible temporal world of the effects.

48 *Annotationes in Marcianum*, ed. C. Lutz (Cambridge, Mass., 1939), p. 22, lines 20-8 [13,23]. In fact Calcidius nowhere says that the planets revolve around the sun.

that Eriugena was drawn to new and daring cosmological speculations by his reading of Martianus. However it is more correct to say that Eriugena misread Martianus to provide support for his own heliocentric theory. There is no doubt that Eriugena believes that some or most of the planets go around the sun. The problem is: what does 'around' (*circa*) mean here? The planets change colour as they traverse different regions in space. This is explained as their becoming pale when they are above the sun and getting ruddier when they traverse the regions below the sun. Duhem points out that Eriugena is departing from tradition in his explanation of this phenomenon. Bede had explained it differently, saying that colour depended on the depth into the waters about the world into which the planet wandered.[49] Eriugena may not be saying that the centre of the orbits of these planets is the sun, but only that, in their orbits, the planets go above and below the sun. In fact at III.715d Eriugena concedes that the 'opinions of the natural philosophers' (*opinio sapientum mundi*) on these matters are many and varied and have never been reconciled. It is possible therefore to hold any opinion which is 'likely and conformable to reason' (*verisimile aut rationi conveniens*).

Concerning the moon, Eriugena is similarly perplexed. The centre of its orbit is the earth (III.717c), but opinions vary as to its size. Some say it is equal in size to the earth (III.720a), but Eriugena following Martianus holds that its amplitude is one sixth that of the earth. Eriugena also produces some calculations to measure the distance from the moon to the earth and from the sun to the moon.

Eriugena rejects the view that there are waters above the sun— incidentally on this point disagreeing both with Basil (III.694c) and with Augustine (III.694d)—and argues that the waters above the firmament referred to in *Genesis* are in fact the 'spiritual reasons' (695d33-696a34) from which all things derive, including the four elements.

We must mention here that Eriugena appears to believe in the existence of the world soul. All living bodies participate in the most general or universal life (*generalissima vita*, III.728d-729a) which is the form of life. This form is called by the philosophers 'the universal soul' (*universalissima anima*, III.729a14-15). Eriugena speaks of this soul as if it were an emanation of the divine life, and in fact identifies it with the Holy Spirit.[50] Eriugena goes further and claims that no creature, whether sensible or intelligible, can survive without direct participation in this Life. It is not just the support of living things, but of all things. It operates like the sun, but is greater than the sun in that it penetrates to the core of each thing (III.729a-b).

Eriugena has a new hierarchical picture: God emanates as the Verbum, who in turn emanates as the Spirit. Both Son and Spirit are in a sense the life of this world and contain the primary causes of all things. The primary

49   P. Duhem, *Système du monde*, Vol. 3.
50   Augustine was disturbed over the problem of the existence of the world soul (*Retractiones* i, 5, 3; i, 11, 4). If it existed then it must be a creature. Eriugena on the other hand identifies it with God.

causes produce the seminal reasons, which in turn produce the elements, which produce visible bodies. The reasons are as superior to the elements as the elements are to the physical bodies (III.696a). The four elements themselves do not partake of time or place but are above those regions, yet the elements are associated with time and place since these are contained within them. The reasons and causes on the other hand are completely above time and place. If man had not sinned then he would know precisely the boundaries of this world, but his present sinful state means that many things are now hidden from him (III.723c).

VII: UNFORMED MATTER

All things proceed from οὐσία through the causes (which themselves are contained in the Verbum, who is the light of the world) and then through their reasons, a process which at some point involves the sun and sensible light. Gradually there is a spreading outwards of the 'divine ray' until the whole cosmos is generated into its particular species and forms. First in rank among all things to be produced is unformed matter (*materia informis*). All things are created timelessly and there is really no before and after in the order of production, nevertheless there is an order of value which places some things higher than others.[51] At I.499c Alumnus says that after God, unformed matter is the most important thing to inquire into, since many important questions depend on it. Eriugena wonders where it comes from, what it is, whether it is definable, and whether it is accessible to sense or to intellect. The authority of the Fathers establishes that prime matter, like God, is indefinable (I.500a). It is incorporeal. Eriugena quotes Augustine as having given what comes closest to a definition: 'matter is the mutability of mutable things which is receptive of all forms.'[52] He supports this with definitions drawn from Plato's *Timaeus* and Dionysius' *Divine Names*.[53] At III.701c Eriugena repeats his definition of unformed matter but introduces new elements into the discussion. Here he sees matter as pure flux (*instabilis inundatio*, 701c22) and explains change as coming about through the mingling of this flux with the unstable qualitative forms which we have already discussed. In fact, unformed matter is identified with the waters beneath the heaven of the simple elements in the cosmological hierarchy (III.702a). For Eriugena matter is both the bottom rung of the cosmic hierarchy and also expresses the formless nature of the spiritual world. This is similar to Proclus' view that matter is the last emanation from the One and yet because it is single and undifferentiated is also next to the One.

51 Eriugena struggles with this in his *Hexaemeron*. On the one hand, he wants to argue that human nature is highest and so was created last, on the other hand he argues that those things which come first in order were created first. He solves this dilemma by saying that there are two ways of regarding the same thing—as it is in the causes and it is produced in the effects (III.704b).

52 I.500c: Mutabilitas rerum mutabilium omnium capax omnium formarum informis materia est. See also III.701c-d.

53 *Timaeus* 48e-51b. Dionysius, *Divine Names*, IV. 729a.

Given that all things proceed from *οὐσία* which contains the most general essence and the most general quality and the most general life, from which derive all other things, including the four elements, and given that all physical reality is nothing more than a combination of immaterial qualities and equally immaterial forms, what need is there in Eriugena's system for prime matter (*materia informis*)? As a Christian he believes the world is formed out of nothing (*ex nihilo*), and is concerned to reject as false the claim that the things of this world are made out of a pre-existent matter. Especially in Book III Eriugena denies that there can be such a thing as pre-existing matter, and argues that the nothing from which all things are made is God. For Eriugena creation *ex nihilo* really means creation *ex Deo*. To generate from nothing means to generate from God. Eriugena understands non-being to be of two distinct kinds: there is non-being through transcendence (*nihil per excellentiam*), which God enjoys and from which nothingness he generates both his own nature and also all existing things; and there is pure nothingness of privation (*nihil per privationem*). In the first sense, unformed matter means God; in the second sense unformed matter can only stand for nothing at all—by which Eriugena means the opposite of *οὐσία* (III.634c-d).

Despite the equation of non-being with God, Eriugena retains the concept of unformed matter in his system, and gives it the lowest place in created reality. At III.636c it is stated that God, who made the world from unformed matter, made unformed matter from nothing at all (*de omnino nihilo*). Unformed matter is almost nothing (*prope nihil*). It does not exist on its own, and is merely a capacity to receive qualities. Prime matter is certainly not place and Eriugena rejects the view that God prepared a place into which he would put creation (643c)—or into which he would diffuse himself. God needs no place. Prime matter then is not place or extension. Neither is it the ultimate subject as in the Aristotelian system. The ultimate subject for Eriugena is always divine *οὐσία*. If prime matter has any function at all in Eriugena's system—and indeed it seems something of an embarrassment to him, something that must be explained away—it simply serves as another name for the mysterious hidden recesses of the primary causes from which all creation emerges. Since corporeality is created by the categories and by the invisible primary causes (sometimes identified with the categories), what need is there for a pure potentiality?—except that Eriugena believes it is what is receptive of qualitative form, and qualitative form turns out to be a conglomeration of accidents that accrue around the substantial form which remains in the primary causes. Receptivity or potentiality is not something for which Eriugena has a more detailed account. Receptivity, possibility and potentiality are all somehow emanations of the Word which is power (*δύναμις*), and which contains all things in itself in their potencies.

According to the five modes in which things may be said to be or not to be, prime matter is on the side of the things that are not. It escapes being because of the excellence of its nature (I.443a23) and hence is classified beside God, as it were. Prime matter is essentially incorporeal and despite appearing as corporeal matter when mingled with qualitative form, in itself it remains eternal and incorporeal and is really a name for the hidden darkness of God or his primary causes, which exist in the Word, which is one with God the Father. Matter then is incorporeal.

VIII: THE CATEGORIES OF PLACE AND TIME

Finally let us look briefly at two of the ten categories, those which—after substance—are most important and which are said to differentiate individuals: the categories of place and time. Eriugena's theories on place and time are unique and radical. Let us note here that Eriugena uses the word 'space' (*spatium*) when speaking of the cosmos, but he uses the word 'place' (*locus*) when speaking of the category. It is not clear how he understood the two to be related.

In Book One (468c-d) Eriugena calls place and time created things, and says they are that within which the rest of the world is contained (i.e. all things excluding οὐσία which is timeless and non-spatial). They are 'that without which nothing can exist' (ὧν ἄνευ τὸ πάν, I.468c). Here Eriugena says that everything within time and place moves; but time itself also moves and place itself is in a place (468d). For place to be in a place means that place is defined by God, who is the place of all places (*locus locorum*, I.468d3, III.643).[54] Eriugena goes on to argue, as we shall see, that place is definition and definition is in the mind; therefore place is in the mind. Before discussing this thesis, let us look at the traditional account of the category of place.

Aristotle says almost nothing about place (τόπος) in the *Categories*, but devotes considerable attention to it in *Physics,* Book 4, where he discusses the nature of the infinite, place and the void. It is here that Aristotle criticizes Plato's confusing account of space (Χώρα) in the *Timaeus* and gives his own definiton of place as 'the primary motionless boundary of that which contains' (Book 4, ch. 4, 212a20). For Aristotle place is the inner containing surface by which one body enfolds another body. A body is in a place if it is contained by another body, if it is not contained by another body then it is not in a place. The void (τὸ κενόν) is place deprived of a body (208b26-27), it is an interval (διάστημα, 213a29) in which there is no sensible body. Aristotle believes a void is impossible. But he also believes that the universe as a whole (everything contained within the outer sphere) is not in any place, since it is not contained by any other body. The outer sphere itself, relative to the others, may be referred to as 'up', while the centre (towards which heavy bodies tend) is down. Eriugena also denies that there

---

54 In Book III, in his discussion of the creation of dry land on the third day, Eriugena argues that this means all things are made in their eternal reasons and also marked out for their particular time and places because God is the time of times and the place of all things (III.699c12-13: *locus omnium et tempus temporum*).

is an absolute up or down in the universe. Strictly speaking, when one considers the universe as a whole there is no 'up' or 'down' (*sursum et deorsum*, I.467a), but up and down emerge only from a consideration of the parts. This is standard Aristotelian thinking. Furthermore, Aristotle denies that place is equivalent to the form of the body, because things in motion are going towards their proper place and are not in their place, whereas they do have their form. Similarly, for Aristotle, place is not the matter of a thing.

Later Neoplatonists developed very complex theories of place and time.[55] Plotinus disagreed with Aristotle that place and time were necessary as separate categories. Indeed he argued that place and time were measurements, then as such they would be contained in the category of quantity.[56] Afterwards, Porphyry, in his *Commentary on the Categories of Aristotle*, agrees that place and time can only be present if quantity is present but he does not deny that they are proper categories in their own right. Eriugena several times refers to time and place as quantitative measures, and follows Augustine in holding that what measures is prior to the measured, hence place and time are prior to the things in space and time, a view which would not necessarily have found sympathy with Aristotle.[57]

Eriugena also denies that place is to be identified with the matter of a thing (I.488a), since earth is more properly the matter of a thing but it is not its place. He thus rejects the view that earth is the place of things. Similarly, air is not the place of certain bodies (I.488d), and the same is true of the other elements. If the elements were the places of bodies, when things decay they would return to those elements; there they would simply be air or light and hence they would have no definite place. We must either conclude that things have no definite place, or else that the elements are not the correct places of things. For Eriugena no right thinking person could agree with the suggestion that things might have no place (I.489a). He rejects the view that everything which surrounds a body can be taken to be its place. He gives the example of colour—if colour surrounds a coloured body, is colour the place of that body? That is an absurdity: a quality cannot be a place—presumably because they belong to different categories (I.489a-b).[58] What then is place?

Eriugena gives a definition: 'place is nothing else but the boundary by which each thing is enclosed within fixed terms.'[59] Eriugena states that there are many kinds of places and even that there are incorporeal places which

55   See Richard Sorabji, *Time, Creation and Continuum* (London, 1983).
56   Plotinus, III 7, 7 disputes the view that time is a measure of motion. For him time comes from the unquiet soul's rebellion which produces the sensible cosmos.
57   The full metaphysical analysis of place which Eriugena gives is an amalgam of commentaries on the *Categories*, including the pseudo-Augustinian *Categoriae decem*, and *De nuptiis Philologiae et Mercurii* of Martianus Capella, as well as the *Hexaemeron* of Basil and *De opificio mundi* of St. Gregory of Nyssa. Eriugena also refers to St. Augustine's account of the measurement of place and time in *De musica*.
58   At this point Eriugena is led into a digression to argue that οὐσία is not a body.
59   I.474b: Nil aliud est locus nisi ambitus quo unumquodque certis terminis concluditur. Sheldon-Williams, Vol. I, p. 110.

bound incorporeal things. The boundary, limit or form of all rational and intellectual spirits is the Word of God, the boundary of irrational spirit is sensible things, the boundary of bodies is the four elements. Place is boundary. Nutritor goes further: 'place is constituted in the definitions of things that can be defined' (I.474b). The definitions of all things are contained in the knowledge (*scientia*) of the liberal arts, therefore the liberal arts are the places of things which can be defined. All things find their place in the arts. Eriugena concludes that place is in the mind, since the arts are in the mind. His argument is as follows:

> What contains is other than what is contained.[60]
> Bodies are contained in their places, therefore place is not a body.[61]
> Place is definition.[62]
> Definiton exists in art and every art is in the mind.[63]
> Place exists only in the mind.[64]

Eriugena is running together the logical notion of place as definition, which involves placing a thing in the sense of locating it in the fixed scheme of science (from which he draws the conclusion that definition is place), and the more problematic statement that, since place is definition, therefore place in a real sense resides in the mind, since all knowledge and science has no other being but in the mind. The ambiguity of the term 'place' (*locus*, τόπος), which can have a grammatical-logical meaning as well as a physical meaning, is responsible for this confusion.

Eriugena's purpose is clear: he is arguing in respect of place what Augustine and Plotinus hold in respect of time, namely, that it exists in the mind, and through it the mind measures things. Thus he now rejects as foolish those who say that earth is the place of animals, water is the place of fish, air is the place of birds and ether is the place of the planets. The true place of everything is its essential definition, which is changeless, and which as λόγος or rationale is preserved in the mind. Whose mind? Clearly Eriugena means the human mind, since he has just been talking about the liberal arts as containing the definitions of all things. The human mind has the power to define, hence all things which it defines are set in their proper places. Of course, the human mind, since it transcends definition and place, cannot define itself, and hence it is located in no place. We are half-way towards the Kantian theory that space and times are the forms of outer and inner intuition which organize all appearances. Of course, since the Word is the true knowledge (*cognitio*) of all things, then the true definitions are

60   I.478b26-7: Aliud est enim quod continet et aliud quod continetur.
61   I.478 c27-29: Corpora continentur locis suis; aliud igitur est corpus et aliud locus. Body is in the category of quantity, definition in that of place.
62   I.475b17: Locus omnis quia diffinitio est.
63   I. 475b15-17: Si enim diffinitio omnis in disciplina est et omnis disciplina in animo, necessario locus omnis, quia diffinitio est, non alibi nisi in animo erit.
64   I.475b17: Non erit nisi in animo.

contained in the Word, but there is no suggestion that the restored human self is any less omniscient than the Word; indeed Eriugena explicitly says that unfallen man is omniscient. The unfallen human mind (Christ, pre-fall humans and humans after the return of all things) is the place of all things. But is Eriugena ruling out that the fallen mind also constitutes the places of things? There is no evidence to suggest that Eriugena denied that the fallen mind functions in the same way, in fact his discussion of the liberal arts makes it all the more likely that he is referring explicitly to the fallen mind. We may conclude that the fallen mind gives us the individual places for all things. Whether these are the same places as those given by the unfallen mind is another question. While Eriugena does not discuss this point, his linking of place with time should be sufficient to suggest a possible answer.

> For I am here following the Greeks, who do not hesitate to assert that everything which moves through space must also move in time, while everything that lacks motion through space must also be without motion in time. For these two, space and time, must either both be present together, or both equally absent, for it is impossible to separate the one from the other.[65]

The fallen mind generates the places and times of this material corporeal world. The unfallen mind generates the eternal timeless ordering of things in their true invisible places.

One final point we should note—God, the angels and human minds all escape being defined and hence none of these is in a place. Human nature itself is without place, and indeed has a kind of omnipresence, similar to that of God.

IX: TIME

Now let us look at Eriugena's concept of time. In some ways the derivation of time is one of the most difficult features of Neoplatonism. As we have seen, Eriugena, following Augustine (and indeed Basil and Plotinus), sharply distinguishes the supra-temporal and temporal worlds. In Book III Eriugena distinguishes between the timeless region beyond the firmament and the region of time and place within it. In this he is following the Greek Christian writers in particular. Of course the *Timaeus* distinguishes between true being and becoming and sees time as a moving image of eternity. Eriugena's thought is within that general framework. As a Christian, he has even more reason to separate created from uncreated by the recognition that created things have a beginning in time, and indeed says that all created things are subject to time. Yet Eriugena will in fact argue finally that creature-

---

65 V.1001a; Sheldon-Williams' translation, in O'Meara, ed., pp. 688-9. Eriugena is distancing himself from Augustine who thought that spiritual substances did not move (V.1000d).

hood can be understood in two ways—as eternal in God, or as temporal in place and time (III.677a-b), and that creatures are eternally made (*aeternaliter facta*). Although time is a feature of the creation of the cosmos, it is not the defining feature: created for Eriugena simply means manifested or caused, and even eternal things (i.e. the causes themselves) may be created.[66] Time and place are actually modes in which the mind categorizes and orders things. There are two general modes of viewing (*duplex speculatio*, III.704b)—one way sees things temporally and spatially in the effects, the other sees things time-lessly in the causes.

That is not to say that time is unreal, rather there are two kinds of time. Eriugena holds that God proceeds into time in the creation of all things (III.678c-d), so that creation is a self-manifestation of the eternal in time. This means that God really did intend to generate the temporal domain. Yet Eriugena speaks as if there is a 'true' or special time in which creatures are truly themselves. Another corrupting, 'deviant', time is introduced by the fall of human nature. Strictly speaking, there are not two times, but the one time seen in two different ways. In one view, things unfold naturally from their seminal reasons into their individual natures. In the other way, time introduces corruption and death. These two times will be restored into one by the return of all things. This return Eriugena always says is not itself a temporal movement but an eternal dialectical moment which is interwoven with, and indistinguishable from, the divine emanation outwards (πρόοδος). Time is a created thing, but it must have an 'eternal' counterpart—the 'form of time' which is fully itself. As emerges in Book V, this eternal counterpart to time is the endless spiritual movement of souls in the return. Through the fall new characteristics were added to this form of time so that time appears to be both limiting and corrupt. What distinguishes Eriugena from other Neoplatonic accounts of time is that he gives to human nature the possibility of seeing both temporally in the fallen mode, and also seeing things *sub specie aeternitatis*. Humans have a *duplex intentio* or *duplex consideratio* that allows them to see the created world in both its apparent (temporal) and real (eternally temporal) ways.

What are Eriugena's sources for this understanding of time? His view comes very close to Plotinus' account, which Eriugena could not have known directly. Although one would expect a strong influence from Augustine, especially *Confessions* Book XI, Eriugena does not discuss Augustine's thesis that time is the *distentio animi*.[67] Yet it is clear from what we have said that

---

66 Book III.677a states that creaturehood may be understood in two ways: 'the one relating it to its eternity in the divine knowledge . . . the other to its temporal establishment which was, as it were, subsequent in itself'.

67 Augustine, *Confessions*, Book XI. 26. For Plotinus time is a distention of life (III 7, 11). Callaghan in his article, 'A New Source for St. Augustine's Theory of Time', *Harvard Studies in Classical Philology* 63 (1958), 437-54, says Augustine could have found this view either in Basil's *Adversus Eunomium* or in Gregory of Nyssa's *Contra Eunomium* (although this is problematic). Is Eriugena really influenced by Basil? Sorabji and others have argued

Eriugena, in agreement with Augustine, sees time, like place, to be part of the defining power of the mind.

Did Boethius influence Eriugena on this point? This is difficult to judge. Eriugena uses the notions of eternity (*aeternitas*) and sempiternity (*sempiternitas*) without particularly distinguishing them, and even quotes St. Paul (Rom. 1:20) as saying that eternity is everlasting (III.690a).[68] It is more likely that Eriugena took his view of time from Dionysius and Maximus. In Book III Eriugena quotes from Dionysius to say that God is the eternity of things and the time of things, and uses the word *saeculum* to translate Dionysius' word αἰών (III.682a-b). Dionysius discusses time (χρόνος) and eternity (αἰών) in *De divinis nominibus* X. For him God may be called 'time' or 'eternity' but he also precedes time and eternity (937b). Dionysius says that not everything called eternal in the Scriptures is truly eternal—it may just mean very old; time refers to things which are in the process of change. Scripture speaks of a 'temporal eternity' and an 'eternal time' (940a). Eriugena also adopts this paradoxical manner of speaking. Time, for Dionysius, is related to becoming (γένεσις); eternity, with being (τὰ ὄντα). Dionysius clearly states that eternal things are not to be thought of as co-eternal with God who is beyond eternity. These things are more rightly thought of as between time and eternity. Dionysius is not more specific—but he does not appear to be articulating the doctrine of the inseparability of time and space. It is clear that Eriugena's thinking on time here owes a great deal to Dionysius.

The Greek Christian view of time (in Dionysius and Maximus) derives from Proclus and Plotinus who saw time as an aspect of the general soul (Ψυχή). As J. F. Callaghan puts it:

> Plotinus is thinking of the universal principle of soul that creates the world and everything in it, and time is simply the productive life of this creature's soul, in which life, the universe and all its motions have their existence; in this sense the universe is said to be in time. Time, for Plotinus, therefore, is the power that produces motion, not the measure of it. Time may be said to exist in the individual souls of men, but here too it is conceived not in a psychological but in a meta-physical sense; it is that which produces the motions of men, not that which measures them.[69]

Time is a διάστασις ζωῆς, a distention of living soul (III 7,11). Added to this Neoplatonic view, in Maximus, there is a quasi-Aristotelian view of place as

that Basil produces a radical view of time in antiquity but there is no evidence that Eriugena was especially influenced by it. Eriugena appears to be following Maximus.

68   The concept of sempiternity only appears in the *Periphyseon* when he is quoting that passage of Scripture, except for one passage at III.654a where Eriugena speaks of numbers being eternal (*aeterna*) and the reasons being sempiternal, though he seems to equate these two terms.

69   J. F. Callaghan, ibid., pp. 436-7.

the limit of a body. When the two traditions merge in Eriugena, we have the view of place and time as containers of the physical world, which since they are not first principles, must themselves be contained in something else, namely, the mind.

What is Eriugena's conclusion regarding the nature of time? Is it real or unreal? Clearly time has some reality, because Eriugena (following Dionysius) sees God as descending into time and he is at pains to defend the reality of the Incarnation. Following Dionysius, he says that God can be called 'time', but he also believes God is extended in time in a certain way. Here Eriugena is not just referring to the *inhumanatio* of God in the incarnation. He is referring to the πρόοδος or *exitus* of God from himself—the manner in which God extends himself, timelessly into time. God manifests himself in all things as those very things themselves, as Eriugena states forcefully in Book III.678c-d:

> It follows that we ought not to understand God and the creature as two things distinct from one another, but as one and the same. For both the creature, by subsisting, is in God; and God, by manifesting Himself, in a marvellous and ineffable manner creates Himself in the creature, the invisible making itself visible . . . the infinite finite and the uncircumscribed circumscribed and the supratemporal temporal.[70]

God is both in time and beyond time. In this sense time is a mode of the divine being, a distention of the divine mind. The divine mind as it were 'spreads' itself out in time. There is, however, a second emanation of time, due to the fall. Here we need to see that time is also a distention of the human mind—especially the fallen mind. Time now emerges as a force of death and corruption rather than being simply a new modality of the infinite nature of God. Here time is the species under which humans view the world—they see it as temporal and thus as finite and enclosed. Is time in this sense then a 'form of intuition' in the Kantian manner? Allowing for the different philosophical context, I would argue that Eriugena's concept of time can be considered as Kantian, in that time is really a matter of the perceiver rather than the perceived. Eriugena also stresses, however, that we can either see the world under its aspect of time or under its aspect of eternity. Furthermore, human beings although they see the world through the framework of time are themselves in their essence beyond time, and in that sense they cannot define themselves and are unlimited. It is the business of philosophy to lead them from their limited, temporal, to their unlimited, timeless selves. Humans have a twofold power to see things temporally or eternally. It is this twofold power that accounts for human transcendence, and gives humans the Janus-faced ability to look towards their cause and creator and also look to the cosmos and its created being. Through the human mind (including the perfect human and divine mind of the Word) all things come to be and all things are contained and defined.

70   Sheldon-Williams' translation in O'Meara, ed., p. 305.

X: CONCLUSION

What I have tried to do in this article is show the complexity of Eriugena's cosmological model and to provide some detail on his views about categorial reality—substance, quality, time and space, in so far as these categories are relevant to his theory of the generation of the physical world. It will be noticed that I have not dealt with the fourfold division of nature; this is Eriugena's portmanteau scheme for all of being and non-being, and it was introduced by him to keep his complex cosmology coherent. Eriugena was struggling with the great handicap of a faulty manuscript tradition (with regard to Aristotle and Plato), and was trapped into a world-view from which he endeavoured to escape but which he had to accommodate. It is a mark of the sheer genius of his intellect that he was able to keep together all of the divergent aspects of the Platonic, Aristotelian and Christian strands of the tradition. But no one can step completely outside of his time, and the attempted revolution in thought which Eriugena proposed was unintelligible to his day, as is evident from the misinterpretation of his cosmological theories by his followers.

Immateriality and Intentionality

GERARD CASEY

L'excellence de la Raison ne dépend pas d'un grand mot vuide de sens (l'immaté-rialité); mais de sa force, de son étendue, ou de sa Clair-voyance.

Julien de la Mettrie[1]

La théorie de l'intentionnel joue un rôle essentiel dans une métaphysique réaliste. Seule, elle permet une explication cohérente de l'extériorite du monde et de sa con-naissance par l'esprit de l'homme.

André Hayen[2]

One cannot go far in the reading of St Thomas Aquinas and other medieval writers without coming across a multiplicity of usages of the Latin term for 'being' or 'to be', *esse*, such as *esse intentionale, esse intelligibile, esse naturale, esse sensibile* and so on.[3] It is not always easy to appreciate the distinctions which these terms are intended to mark and if one is inclined to scepticism one might indeed suspect that these are distinctions without a difference. However, such a judgment would be both precipitate and incorrect. Even if the distinctions marked by such terms are not immediately perspicuous it is essential, if one wishes to understand and appreciate the thought of the medievals, that one come to understand them. Within the compass of a short paper it will not, of course, be possible to be compre-hensive, so I shall investigate the notions of immateriality and intentionality with a view to clarifying their relationship.[4] In so doing, I hope some light

1 *L'Homme machine* in *Œuvres Philosophiques* Volume I (Paris 1987), p. 65.
2 *L'Intentionnel selon saint Thomas* (Paris, 1954), p. 13.
3 In the passage cited from the *Summa Theologiae* in footnote 17 below, the terms *esse intentionale, esse intelligibile, esse naturale, esse materiale* and *esse immateriale* all occur together in just seven lines of Latin.
4 This paper concerns itself with just a very small part of a large and interesting area of philosophy. In addition to the works cited in the body of the paper, readers interested in this topic may wish to consult some or all of the followings works: Robert W. Schmidt SJ, *The Domain of Logic according to Saint Thomas Aquinas* (The Hague, 1966); J. Peghaire CSSp, *Intellectus et Ratio selon S. Thomas D'Aquin* (Paris, 1936); Victor Kal, *On Intuition and Discursive Reasoning in Aristotle* (Leiden, 1988); Henry Veatch, *Intentional Logic* (New Haven, 1952); Irving Thalberg, 'Immateriality', *Mind* 92 (1983), 105–13; John N. Deely, 'The Ontological Status of Intentionality', *The New Scholasticism* 46 (1972), 220–33; Richard E. Aquila, 'The Status of Intentional Objects', *The New Scholasticism* 45 (1971), 427–56; Mark McCarthy, 'Meaning and Intentional Objects', *Semiotica* 23 (1978), 165–90; Christian Koch, 'The Being of Idea: The Relationship of the Physical and the Nonphysical in the Concept of the Formal Sign', *Semiotica* 66 (1987), 345–57; John Deely, *Introducing Semiotic: Its History and Doctrine* (Bloomington, 1982); Walker Percy, *The Message in the Bottle* (New York, 1954).

will be thrown on what Bernard Lonergan refers to as 'matters intermediate between metaphysics and psychology'.[5]

Why should we, or St Thomas for that matter, be concerned with these notions? The answer to this question for St Thomas (and for those of us who take him as a guide in these matters) seems to be that without such concepts we will find it difficult to make sense of the fact of knowledge. Human knowing is so patently evident that we seldom if ever stop to think how strange it really is. Not only strange but, in cosmic terms, rare. And yet knowledge is an amazing phenomenon. So far as we know, in the entire material universe, only animate creatures on one small planet in an obscure solar system in a remote galaxy give any evidence of being able to know. And among these animate creatures only one kind gives evidence of having the capacity to be able to know that it knows. Trees do not know the world in which they live (at least so far as we know); still less do rocks and mud evince any interest in what is going on around them.[6]

The peculiarity of knowledge lies in its double aspect. It seems clear that when I know something, I am changed in some way—knowledge, then, involves a certain modification of the knowing subject. This modification, however, is of a special kind. When sunlight falls on the sunbather and the beach pebble, both alike are warmed but only the sunbather is aware of being warmed. Unlike all other accidental modifications of a subject, then, the modification of the subject which results in knowledge permits the subject to stretch out (*intendere*) towards something else other than itself.[7] This directedness of knowledge towards something other than itself is often termed 'intentionality'.[8]

5 Bernard J. Lonergan SJ, *Verbum: Word and Idea in Aquinas* (Notre Dame, 1967), p. xiv.
6 Referring to the three notions mentioned in the title of his essay 'Intentionality, Immateriality and Understanding in Aquinas', *Heythrop Journal* 30 (1989), 150–9, Stephen Theron says that 'we tend to expect intentionality to prove the most difficult of these notions, immateriality to belong merely to the history of ideas, understanding to be no trouble at all. In fact understanding, the fundamental notion, is the most mysterious of the three' (p. 150).
7 Jacques Maritain gives the following summary definition of knowledge: 'Knowing appears to us to be an immanent and vital operation that essentially consists, not in making, but in being; to be or become a thing—either itself or other things—in a way other than by an existence that actuates a subject. This implies a union quite superior to the union of matter and form which together comprise a *tertium quid*, and it supposes that the known object is intentionally made present to the faculty thanks to a *species*, a presentative form. Finally, intellectual knowledge is accomplished thanks to a mental word or concept, a presentative form uttered by the intellect within itself, and in that form the intellect intentionally becomes, in terminal act, the thing taken in this or that one of its intelligible determinations.' Jacques Maritain, *The Degrees of Knowledge*, trans. Gerald B. Phelan, (London, 1959), pp. 117–18.
8 William McDougall writes: 'Intelligent activity implies not merely representations of objects or events . . . but also a mental reference to the object represented; it involves awareness of the object, thinking of the object, or, as we may conveniently say, thinking the object.' *Modern Materialism and Emergent Evolution* (London, 1929), p. 45. While he

How is it possible for a being or mode of being to be of or about something other than itself? As Anthony Kenny puts it: 'What makes a picture of X to be a picture of X, what makes an image of X to be an image of X, what makes a thought about X be about X?'[9] Kenny believes that 'one of the most elaborate and also one of the most puzzling accounts of the harmony between the world and thought is Aquinas' doctrine of the immaterial intentional existence of forms in the mind.'[10]

How does St Thomas' theory work? According to Kenny, the connection between thought and reality is established by form. The form bicycle exists in an individual and material way (*esse naturale*) in the real bicycle; and in a universal and immaterial way (*esse intentionale*) in the mind. Because it is the same form (in some sense of 'the same') it makes the knowledge to be of bicycles rather than of automobiles; because the form exists in two distinct ways it allows the knowledge to be knowledge of bicycles rather than the production of an ethereal velocipede. Maritain puts it succinctly:

> Another kind of existence must, then, be admitted; an existence according to which the known will be in the knower and the knower will be the known, an entirely tendential and immaterial existence, whose office is not to posit a thing outside nothingness for itself and as a subject, but, on the contrary, for another thing and as a relation. . . . In virtue of that existence, the thing exists in the soul with an existence other than its own existence, and the soul is or becomes the thing with an existence other than its own existence. (*Degrees*, p. 114)

In the course of his article, Kenny discusses Peter Geach's[11] and Bernard Lonergan's[12] accounts of Aquinas on intentionality and he argues that neither author is entirely correct in his interpretation of Aquinas.[13] According to Kenny, Geach takes Aquinas' doctrine of intentionality to amount to the claim that a form individualized by matter is a constitutive principle of the thing in its physical existence outside the mind, while the identical form individualized in the intellect is a constitutive principle of the thing as it exists in the intellect. The problem with this interpretation, as Kenny correctly points

---

admits that 'we do not know, and probably never shall know or be able to explain, how a physical stimulus to a sense-organ or nerve evokes or results in a sensation, an idea or a representation', he is emphatic in his insistence that 'the essence of our mental life, in its aspect as intelligence, is not a mere succession of sensations, ideas, or representations of things, but a thinking of things' (p. 56).

9 Anthony Kenny, 'Intentionality: Aquinas and Wittgenstein', in *The Legacy of Wittgenstein* (Oxford, 1984), p. 61. Cf. Kenny's earlier essay 'Intellect and Imagination in Aquinas' in Anthony Kenny (ed.), *Aquinas: A Collection of Critical Essays* (Notre Dame, 1976).

10 Ibid. Note the immediate connection which Kenny makes here between immateriality and intentionality although he goes on to say that 'intentional existence and immaterial existence are not the same thing' (p. 65).

11 Peter T. Geach, 'Form and Existence' in *God and the Soul* (London, 1969).

12 Lonergan, *Verbum*, pp. 147–51.

13 Kenny, ibid., p. 66.

out, is that in the intellect there are no individualized forms as such, but only universals.[14]

On the other hand, according to Kenny, Lonergan's interpretation distorts Aquinas' account by replacing identity of form with mere similarity. Lonergan does indeed speak of 'assimilation' in reference to species rather than of formal identity, seeming thereby to suggest that similarity somehow replaces identity. Furthermore, Kenny takes Lonergan's claim[15] that Aquinas' understanding of the Aristotelian maxims (the sense in act is the sensible in act; the intellect in act is the intelligible in act) has shifted in meaning from identity in second act to assimilation on the level of species to be a distortion of Aquinas' own position. Now while I have some sympathy with Kenny in his efforts to understand Lonergan on this point, and while it may not be perfectly clear what Lonergan means positively by this claim, it does not seem to constitute a denial of the formal identity of the knower and the known in the act of knowledge. Lonergan says:

> The form of the knowing must be similar to the form of the known, but also it must be different; it must be similar essentially for the known to be known; but it must differ modally for the knower to know and not merely be the known. Modal difference of forms results from difference in recipients: the form of color exists naturally in the wall but intentionally in the eye because wall and eye are different kinds of recipient; similarly, angels have a natural existence on their own but an intentional existence in the intellects of other angels. Thus, the negative concept, immateriality, acquires a positive content of intentional existence; and intentional existence is a modal difference resulting from difference in the recipient. (*Verbum*, p. 151)

Lonergan does not, *pace* Kenny, appear to be denying the identity of form and substituting mere similarity in its place. He is instead affirming the necessity for identity in difference and difference in identity. The identity is identity of form; the difference is one of modality of existence; on the one hand, *esse naturale*—on the other, *esse intentionale*. On this point, Lonergan's account seems to me to be close, if not identical, to the one which Kenny himself offers.

We may perhaps find an additional clue to Lonergan's meaning if we pay attention to an earlier passage in which he claims that Aristotle's account of knowledge by identity is, although correct, incomplete:

> Inasmuch as faculty and object are in act identically, there is knowledge indeed as perfection but not yet knowledge of the other. Reflection is required, first, to combine sensible data with intellectual insight in the

14 Geach's account has the merit of enabling the intellect to have direct knowledge of singulars without any need for converting to phantasms. This might in itself constitute part of a solution to the problem of knowledge but it could not be a solution according to the mind of St Thomas.

15 Lonergan, ibid., p. 148.

expression of a *quod quid est*, of an essence that prescinds from its being known, and then, on a deeper level, to affirm the existence of that essence. Only by reflection on the identity of act can one arrive at the difference of potency. And since reflection is not an identity the Aristotelian theory of knowledge by identity is incomplete. (*Verbum*, p. 72)

It seems clear then that Lonergan is not denying the necessity of formal identity; he is simply questioning its sufficiency. In a footnote to the passage just cited, Lonergan adds the clarifying comment that 'to the Aristotelian theorem of knowledge by immateriality Aquinas has to add a further theorem of knowledge by intentionality. The difference between the two appears clearly in the case of one immaterial angel knowing another immaterial angel without the former's knowledge being the latter's reality.'[16]

It is significant that Lonergan's example is given in terms of angelic knowledge, for here the issues are conceptually clearer than they are in the case of human knowledge. Attempts to understand human knowledge are complicated by the form/matter composition of the human subject with the resultant two-tier epistemogenetic structures. The point of the illustration is that immateriality (which is the root of all knowledge) is not sufficient of itself to ground knowledge. If Raphael knows Gabriel, the mode of immateriality by which this knowledge takes place in Raphael is not the same mode of immateriality by which Gabriel exists in himself. The cognitive mode of immateriality is *esse intentionale*, the ontological mode of immateriality is *esse naturale*. St Thomas puts it thus:

> One angel knows another by means of that angel's species existing in his intellect. This species differs from the angel of which it is the similitude not as material being (*esse materiale*) differs from immaterial being (*esse immateriale*) but as natural being (*esse naturale*) differs from intentional being (*esse intentionale*). For an angel himself is a form which subsists in natural being, but not so his species, which is in the intellect of the other angel. There it has only intelligible being (*esse intelligibile*). Likewise, the form of colour has natural being (*esse naturale*) on the wall while it has only intentional being (*esse intentionale*) in the medium by which it is conveyed to the eye.[17]

In a paper written some years ago on Thomistic angelology, I assumed that *esse intentionale* was a purely psychic mode of existence.[18] Effectively, I took

16 Ibid., p. 72, n. 115. Cf. Mortimer J. Adler who, in 'Sense Cognition: Aristotle vs Aquinas', *The New Scholasticism* 42 (1968), 578–91, rejects the whole notion of intentional beings.

17 *ST*, I, 56, 2, ad. 3: Unus angelus cognoscit alium per speciem ejus in intellectu suo existentem; quae differt ab angelo, cujus similitudo est, non secundum esse materiale, et immateriale, sed secundum esse naturale et intentionale. Nam ipse angelus est forma subsistens in esse naturali, non autem species ejus quae est in intellectu alterius angeli; sed habet ibi esse intelligibile tantum; sicut etiam et forma coloris in pariete habet esse naturale, in medio autem deferente habet esse intentionale tantum.

18 An extensively revised version of this paper has since been published as 'Angelic Interiority', *Irish Philosophical Journal* 6 (1989), 82–118.

esse intentionale to be a lexical equivalent of *esse intelligibile*. However, while the passage just cited may seem to suggest the equivalence of *esse intelligibile* and *esse intentionale*, the illustrative example given at the end of the passage concerning the form of colour on the wall and in the transmitting medium would seem to indicate that intentional existence (*esse intentionale*) is not solely an intrapsychic mode of existence (and hence, whatever else it might be it could not be equivalent to *esse intelligibile*) but is something capable of being supported in non-psychic beings as well.[19]

John Peifer cites this passage and goes on immediately to claim that intentional existence 'must be an *im-material* existence, for it is the existence a form enjoys in a cognitive faculty whose root condition is immateriality.'[20] But as the passage cited makes clear, intentional existence is also a mode of existence which a form can enjoy in the sensitive medium, and the sensitive medium is certainly not a cognitive faculty. St Thomas, in this passage, denies that intentional existence is natural existence. Only if the further assumption is made, that natural existence equals material existence, can Peifer's conclusion obtain. I am not denying that Peifer may ultimately be right in his judgment that intentional existence must be immaterial existence (indeed I shall myself be concerned to argue that it cannot be simply material)—however, his attribution of that immateriality to cognitive faculties alone on the basis of this text ignores the crucial example.

It might be thought that this passage is an aberration, a rare instance of a careless use of examples by St Thomas. But this is not so. St Thomas expresses the very same idea in a passage from his Commentary on the *de Anima*:

> But a spiritual change is that according to which a species is received in the sense organ *or in the medium* through a mode of intention, and not through a mode of natural form. For the sensible species is not received in the sense according to that being which it has in the sensible thing (Emphasis added).[21]

Again, the contrast drawn is that between a natural mode of existence and an intentional mode of existence, not between a material mode of existence and an immaterial mode of existence.

From these passages it seems clear that not only is intentional being an intrapsychic mode of existence but that entities can somehow exist in an intentional form in the medium between object and organ. This, of course means that intentional existence is not, then, simply intrapsychic existence in a cognitive power but rather existence which is in some way (perhaps

19 On the point at issue St Thomas speaks of *esse intelligibile tantum* while in the illustrative example he speaks of *esse intentionale tantum*.
20 John Peifer, *The Mystery of Knowledge* (New York, 1964), p. 60.
21 *In II de An.*, 14, 418: Immutatio vero spiritualis est secundum quod species recipitur in organo sensus aut in medio per modum intentionis, et non per modum naturalis formae. Non enim sic recipitur species sensibilis in sensu secundum illud esse quod habet in re sensibili.

essentially) relatable to a cognitive power, either actually in that power or else in a medium between sensory object and sense organ.[22]

With these passages in mind, let us try to determine in a preliminary way the interrelationship of these concepts. We are dealing with two sets of distinctions: on the one hand, the distinction between *esse naturale* and *esse intentionale*; and, on the other hand, the distinction between *esse intelligibile* and *esse sensibile*. *Esse naturale* is the objective, extramental existence which a thing possesses in itself and not as the result of being known (by any finite knower). *Esse intentionale*, on the other hand, is either intrapsychic existence in a cognitive power (sensory or intellectual) or else a mode of existence in a medium in some way relatable to a sensory cognitive power.

There is a crucial ambiguity in the use of the term *esse intelligibile*. In one sense of the term, *esse intelligibile* is simply whatever is the object of the intellect, that which is either immaterial itself or potentially so. In contrast to *esse intelligibile* in this sense we have *esse sensibile*: *esse sensible*, the object of the senses, is material and corporeal and is therefore, as such, unintelligible. This distinction between *esse intelligibile* and *esse sensibile* drawn thus with respect to their objects is all on the *esse naturale* side of the *esse naturale/esse intentionale* distinction. There is, however, a second sense of *esse intelligibile* in which it connotes not the mode of existence of the object which is understood but the mode of existence of such objects in the understanding. Used in this sense, *esse intelligibile* falls on the *esse intentionale* side of the *esse naturale/esse intentionale* distinction.

Kenny claims that the coincidence of immateriality and intentionality take place only in respect of intellectual cognition and not in respect of cognition as such.

> Intentional existence and immaterial existence are not the same thing. A pattern exists, naturally and materially, in a coloured object; it exists, intentionally and materially, in the eye or, according to Aquinas, the lucid medium. Gabriel is a form which exists immaterially and naturally in its own right; it exists immaterially and intentionally in Raphael's thought of Gabriel. The characteristic of intellectual thought, both of men and angels, is that it is the existence of a form in a mode which is both intentional and immaterial. (p. 65)

The distinctions embodied in this paragraph might be set out in the following way:

---

22 Maritain suggests that it may be necessary to admit an intentional manner of existing in orders other than that of knowledge so as to explain how the power of the artist passes, as it were, into the artist's brush through his hands. I shall make use of this passage when I come to develop the notion of supervenience below.

	ESSE NATURALE	ESSE INTENTIONALE
ESSE MATERIALE	Mode of being of material things	Mode of being of things in sense organ or medium
ESSE IMMATERIALE	Mode of being of immaterial things	Mode of being of things in intellect *(esse intelligible)*

This is a very neat formulation, relating natural being, intentional being, material being, immaterial being and intelligible being. The only problem is that it appears to neglect some pertinent texts of St Thomas. St Thomas refers to the reception of form in the sense organ or in the medium as a spiritual immutation: on Kenny's schema it is simultaneously intentional and material. But given that St Thomas considers the spiritual and the material to be contraries, it is difficult to see how the reception of form in the sense organ or the medium could be at once spiritual and material.

There is, then, something of a puzzle with the category created by combining intentional existence with material existence. It cannot possibly be material existence in the same way as we have material existence in the combination of natural existence with material existence. It would seem then that an entity need not be material or immaterial simply as such, but relatively material or immaterial *vis-à-vis* other things. Kenny seems to admit as much:

> But intentional existence is not, as such, completely immaterial existence. The form in the eye lacks the matter of gold, but not the matter of the eye; it is an individualized form, not a universal. And according to Aquinas the redness exists intentionally not only in the eye but in the lucid medium through which I see it. (p. 73)

The problem here is that if, by virtue of these considerations, the form in the eye is not completely immaterial, neither is it, by virtue of the same considerations, completely material. This means then that in the schematization, the relationship between *esse materiale* as *esse naturale* and *esse materiale* as *esse intentionale* is analogous rather than univocal, for the form of the gold as it exists in the eye does not inform the matter of the eye in precisely the same way as it informs the matter of the gold. This is, presumably what St Thomas means by calling it spiritual immutation as distinct from natural form.

> There are two kinds of immutation, one natural, and the other spiritual. It is a natural immutation when the changing form is received

in that which is immuted according to *esse naturale*, as heat in the thing heated; it is a spiritual change when the changing form is received in the thing immuted according to *esse spirituale*, as colour in the pupil, which does not thereby become coloured. So, the operation of the senses requires a spiritual immutation by which the intention of the sensible form comes to be in the sense organ. Otherwise, if a natural immutation sufficed for sensing, all natural bodies would sense when altered.[23]

The editor of the Blackfriars edition of the *Summa Theologiae* notes that 'sense knowledge implies a non-materiality while yet being the act of an organ. It is intentional and psychic, even in its humblest forms, and not a physical reaction merely. The retinal image in the eye is not an "impressed species".'[24]

Now the question we have already skirted becomes acute. Is the intentional as such immaterial, or is it, as Kenny suggests, immaterial only in regard to intellectual cognition but not in regard to sensory cognition? To focus the discussion, I shall trace the course of a dispute on the nature and extent of immateriality in sensory cognition which took place in the late 1960's between Mortimer Adler and John Deely.[25] The dispute focuses on whether or not sense-perception is immaterial.

In *The Difference of Man and the Difference it Makes*,[26] Adler had held that Aristotle and Aquinas do not try to establish the immateriality of the intentional as such but only the immateriality of conceptual acts, such as judgment,

---

23 *ST*, I, 78, 3: Est autem duplex immutatio, una naturalis, et alia spiritualis. Naturalis quidem, secundum quod forma immutantis recipitur in immutato secundum esse naturale, sicut calor in calefacto. Spiritualis autem, secundum quod forma immutantis recipitur in immutato secundum esse spirituale: ut forma coloris in pupilla, quae non fit per hoc colorata. Ad operationem autem sensus requiritur immutatio spiritualis, per quam intentio formae sensibilis fiat in organo sensus: alioquin, si sola immutatio naturalis sufficeret ad sentiendum, omnia corpora naturalia sentirent, dum alterantur.
    Cf. *ST*, I, 78, 1: 'The lowest of the operations of the soul is that which is performed by a corporeal organ and by virtue of a corporeal quality. Yet this transcends the operation of the corporeal nature; because the movements of bodies are caused by an extrinsic principle, while these operations are from an intrinsic principle.' (Infima autem operationum animae est, quae fit per organum corporeum, et virtute corporeae qualitatis. Supergreditur tamen operationem naturae corporeae: quia motiones corporum sunt ab exteriori principio; huiusmodi autem operationes sunt a principio intrinseco.)
24 St Thomas Aquinas, *Summa Theologiae* (London, 1970), Notes by Timothy Suttor, p. 130, note b. Stephen Theron, in his otherwise excellent article, seems to be in error on this point. He asks 'what in the sense faculty corresponds to the intelligible species in the mind?' He answers, correctly, 'the internal sense-image' but then goes on, incorrectly, to identify this internal sense-image with the 'retinal image, auditory vibration, etc.' (p. 152). As we have just seen, St Thomas emphatically denies that natural change is sufficient to account for sensation.
25 See Mortimer Adler, 'Intentionality and Immateriality', *The New Scholasticism* 41 (1967), 312–44; Mortimer Adler, 'The Immateriality of Conceptual Thought', *The New Scholasticism* 41 (1967), 489–97; John Deely, 'The Immateriality of the Intentional as Such', *The New Scholasticism* 42 (1968), 293–306; and Mortimer Adler, 'Sense Cognition: Aristotle vs. Aquinas', *The New Scholasticism* 42 (1968), 578–91.
26 Mortimer Adler, *The Difference of Man and the Difference It Makes* (Holt, 1967).

conception, and inference (pp. 216–17). But as John Deely points out, whatever Aristotle may or may not have believed, St Thomas articulates and defends the nature and extent of the intentional as such precisely on the basis of immateriality. Thus, Aquinas claims that

> Things which have souls have a twofold being. One, material, in which they are like other material things; the other, immaterial, in which they have something in common with superior substances.
>
> The difference between the two kinds of being is this: in accordance with material being, which is contracted by matter, any given thing just is what it is and no more, as this stone is nothing other than this stone: but in accordance with immaterial being, which is broad, and, in a way, infinite inasmuch as it is not terminated by matter, a thing is not just that which it is but is also other things, in a certain way. That is why all things are contained in superior immaterial substances, as in universal causes.
>
> But in lower things there can be found two grades of immateriality. One grade is completely immaterial, and this is intelligible being. In the intellect things have being and are without matter and without the individuating conditions of matter and also without material organs. Sensible being is midway between the two (i.e. between purely immaterial being and purely material being). For in the senses, a thing has being without matter but not without the individuating conditions of matter nor without the corporeal organs. For sense is of the particular, intellect of the universal.[27]

St Thomas explicitly states that there are two grades of immateriality in inferior things. One kind is entirely immaterial and this is intelligible being. It is in the intellect not only without matter but without the individuating conditions of matter, and without the assistance of corporeal organs. Sensible

27 *In II de An.*, 282–4: Huiusmodi autem viventia inferiora, quorum actus est anima, de qua nunc agitur, habent duplex esse. Unum quidem materiale, in quo conveniunt cum aliis rebus materialibus. Aliud autem immateriale, in quo communicant cum substantiis superioribus aliqualiter.

Est autem differentia inter utrumque esse: quia secundum esse materiale, quod est per materiam contractum, unaquaeque res est hoc solum quod est, sicut hic lapis, non est aliud quam hic lapis: secundum vero esse immateriale, quod est amplum, et quodammodo infinitum, inquantum non est per materiam terminatum, res non solum est id quod est, sed etiam est quodammodo alia. Unde in substantiis superioribus immaterialibus sunt quodammodo omnia, sicut in universalibus causis.

Huiusmodi autem immateriale esse, habet duos gradus in istis inferioribus. Nam quoddam est penitus immateriale, scilicet esse intelligibile. In intellectu enim res habent esse, et sine materia, et sine conditionibus materialibus individuantibus, et etiam absque organo corporali. Esse autem sensibile est medium inter utrumque. Nam in sensu res habet esse sine materia, non tamen absque conditionibus materialibus individuantibus, neque absque organo corporali. Est enim sensus particularium, intellectus vero universalium.

being is midway between the two, for, in the senses it has its being without matter, but nevertheless, not without the individuating conditions of matter, nor without the assistance of corporeal organs.[28] Deely adds that 'not only are the intentionality of perceptual actuations and the intentionality of conceptual actuations analogical, and not univocal, in the doctrines of Aristotle and Aquinas . . . but there is an immateriality which is proper to both these levels precisely as intentional, which immateriality is likewise . . . analogical and not univocal.' In *The Difference of Man* Adler had accepted that intentionality is analogical (though he was later to retract this view in 'Sense Cognition: Aristotle vs Aquinas') and Deely presses him to accept that the immateriality associated with these analogical intentionalities is similarly analogical.

Adler in his response to Deely admits his interpretative error and accepts that St Thomas was concerned to establish the immateriality of the intentional as such. He still, however, denies the immateriality of the *quo* of sense cognition. He tries to show the Thomistic position to be either untenable or self-contradictory. He distinguishes two positions which he calls, for convenience, the Aristotelian and the Thomistic. According to Adler these two positions agree in many points. For both the Aristotelian and the Thomist, the form of the thing known must be received in the knower without the matter of the thing known. The knower is a knower precisely because he can receive forms in this way. The form received is the *quo* of cognition, that is, it is that by which cognition is effected and not, as such, the object of cognition. The phantasm as the *quo* of sense cognition is indispensable to knowledge of singulars and the concept as the *quo* of intellectual cognition is indispensable to knowledge of universals. Finally, both positions agree that the sensible form is received in a power that is corporeal while the intelligible form is received in a power which is incorporeal.[29]

Thus far, according to Adler, the two positions are essentially identical. Now we come to the difference(s). According to the Thomistic position the phantasm as the *quo* of sense cognition must be immaterial in a sense analogous to the immateriality of the concept as the *quo* of intellectual cognition. Two grades of immateriality are involved; one in which the *quo* is subject to the individuating conditions of matter, and another in which the *quo* is not subject to the individuating conditions of matter. In Adler's opinion, there appears

28 Cf. *ST*, I, 84, 2, where Thomas says that 'the nature (*ratio*) of knowledge is opposed (*ex oppositio se habet*) to the nature (*ratio*) of materiality'. He goes on to say that 'the more immaterially a thing receives the form of the thing known, the more perfect is its knowledge. Therefore the intellect which abstracts the species not only from matter, but also from the individuating conditions of matter, has more perfect knowledge than the senses, which receive the form of the thing known, without matter indeed, but subject to material conditions'. Cf. *In II de An.*, 24, 551–4.

29 One might have some reservations about the propriety of attributing corporeality to powers. Powers are capacities and capacities, while they may be located in and exercised through corporeal entities, are not themselves corporeal.

to be a contradiction here. It seems that the phantasm must be at once material and immaterial; immaterial if it is to be the *means* of cognition; and material if it is to be the means of cognition of the *singular*. This apparent contradiction can be resolved by distinguishing between the entitative being of the phantasm and the intentional being of the phantasm. Entitatively, the phantasm is an act of a corporeal power (it would perhaps be better to say 'a power exercised through a corporeal organ') and as such is corporeal; intentionally, it is the relation between the knower and the known.

Adler admits that drawing this distinction may remove the appearance of contradiction, but he believes that it does so at an unacceptably high cost. How, for example, if this distinction is drawn, is one to account for the conditions of materiality still attaching to the sensitive *quo* in its intentional being? If to be intentional is to be as such immaterial, why should the conditions of materiality attach to phantasm in its intentional being?

Adler raises this point only to drop it as not being immediately relevant to his concerns. In my opinion, however, it is precisely the point that needs to be discussed, for the distinction between the entitative and intentional being of the phantasm, or between its physical ground and its function, is the key to the solution of the problem. Instead Adler proceeds to refute Deely's conception of what intentional being is, namely, some kind of intersubjective entity. Adler flatly denies that there can be such a thing as intentional being in this sense. 'There is . . . no inter-subjective mode of being; for everything that exists either is a subject (i.e. a substance) or in a subject (i.e. as an accident). This amounts to saying that if intentional being must be identified with inter-subjective being in order to distinguish intentional from entitative being, then there are no intentional beings—no existent nonentities.'[30] I find myself in complete agreement with Adler on this point.

Adler rejects the charge that without the notion of intentional being we would be unable to explain the phenomenon of knowledge, pointing out the agreement between the Aristotelian and Thomistic positions in the areas listed above. He claims that the distinction between entitative and intentional being need not be postulated in order to account for knowledge. Again, I can agree with Adler here if what he is rejecting is Deely's intersubjective account of intentional being.

Adler now proceeds to give his own positive account. While the phantasm is entitatively corporeal and the concept is entitatively incorporeal, they are both intentional for the same reason, namely, that they are the acts of cognitive powers. The form received in sense cognition is immaterial only in the sense that it is received in the sensory power without the matter which it informed *in re*. It is only in this sense that it is immaterial. The phantasm exists as a *quo* in another kind of matter, 'a kind of matter that is invested with cognitive power and so can be called "cognoscitive matter".'

30   Mortimer Adler, 'Sense Cognition: Aristotle vs. Aquinas', 582.

So, if it is immaterial in that it is separated from its matter *in re*, it is material in that it exists in another kind of matter. The concept, by contrast, is doubly immaterial; immaterial by abstraction from the material conditions *in re*; and immaterial in that it exists in a power which is not material. In regard to its mode of being, the phantasm is wholly material, while in regard to its mode of being the concept is wholly immaterial. In regard to their being received without the matter of the entity known, both phantasm and concept are immaterial. This distinction suffices to explain the data. No postulation of different kinds of being is required.[31]

In all of this, Adler sees himself siding with what he takes to be the economical Aristotelian position as against the more expensive Thomistic position. However, as is well known, Aristotelian exegesis is not simple. In interpreting Aristotle one can go two ways. If one takes a physicalist interpretation of aisthesis as the norm and interprets the discussion of the reception of form without matter in *De Anima* II, 12 in that light, then one will have insuperable problems understanding Aristotle's account of the intellect. One might even go so far as to call the Aristotelian doctrine of the intellect 'a museum piece' as does a recent translator.[32] If however, one takes Aristotle's account of the intellect as normative, then one can interpret this account of αἴσθησις in *De Anima* II, 12 more benignly, which is indeed what St Thomas does in his commentary.

Aside from the fact that the notion of cognoscitive matter is intrinsically obscure, Adler's concerns can be met without denying the need for *esse intentionale*. Adler's concerns seem to be prompted by what he sees as an unnecessary multiplication of entities in the same order of being, a concern which is fueled by Deely's doctrine of intersubjective being. But the distinction of *esse intentionale* and *esse naturale* is not (or need not be) characterized as a distinction between two entities in the same order of being. While the relationship of intentionality supervenes upon physical being (material or

---

31 Adler has a point. Much of the difficulty in comprehending discussions on these topics results from taking the term 'immaterial' and its synonyms and antonyms as being simply univocal. It is quite clear, however, that the contrary terms, 'material' and 'immaterial', can be used simply in a contrastive fashion rather than as having an absolute significance. 'Something is said to be immaterial if it is less particular, more generic, or on a logically higher plane than whatever is said to be material with respect to it. In other words, it here functions as an essentially relational and contrastive term.' (Eike-Henner W. Kluge, 'Immateriality and Perceptual Awareness', *Proceedings of the American Catholic Philosophical Association* 52 (1978), 135.) Kluge makes this remark in the course of distinguishing two basic uses of the term 'immaterial'. The one I have just cited she calls its logical use; another use, which she calls qualitative, is 'superficially more prosaic in that it seems to center in the simple claim of qualitative difference between the corporeal and the mental realm.' 135. Cf. Ernan McMullin, *The Concept of Matter in Ancient and Mediaeval Philosophy*, (Notre Dame, 1963); and *The Concept of Matter in Modern Philosophy*, (Notre Dame, 1963). See also Bernard Lonergan, *Verbum*, p. 143, on the analogy of matter.

32 Aristotle, *De Anima* (translated with an introduction and notes by Hugh Lawson-Tancred), Penguin Books, 1986, p. 92.

immaterial) and cannot subsist apart from such physical support it is not itself a physical entity. It is something over and above whatever, as it were, carries it. Intentionality can supervene upon a physical and material medium (*in medio deferente*) or organ, or it can supervene upon a physical and immaterial concept. It would seem then not to be an really distinct mode of being but rather a formally distinct mode of being of cognitive objects and operations which is physically dependent on a carrier.[33] This view of things is borne out by Maritain:

> The concept in its entitative role and as modification of the subject, and the concept in its intentional role and as formal sign, are not two distinct things (indeed, intentionality is not exactly a thing-in-itself but, rather, a mode). These are two formal aspects or two distinct formal values *of the same thing,* [emphasis added] the intentional role being of importance only to knowing, the entitative function, to the being of nature (in this case, of the soul itself). . . . As thing or entity, the concept is an accident, a quality or modification of the soul; but arising, as it does, within the soul as a fruit and an expression of an intellect already formed by the *species impressa* . . . this quality, this modification of the soul which is the concept, has . . . the privilege of transcending the entitative, informing activity it exercises and of being present in the faculty after the manner of a spirit. . . . Thus, the concept exists in the intellect not only in an entitative manner and as an informing form, but also as a spiritual form, not absorbed in actuating a subject so as to form a *tertium quid* with it, and therefore actuating, on the contrary, or rather, terminating, the intellect intentionally and in the line of knowing, in that it expresses the object and renders it transparent. (pp. 125–6)

Thus understood there is nothing essentially mysterious about intentionality or at least, nothing more mysterious than, say, colour which is supported by a physical medium yet is actualized only in the presence of an entity with a suitable receptor.[34] In *The Degrees of Knowledge* Maritain has a fascinating section which is meant to be illustrative of the necessity of the intentional not only in the cognitive order but in other orders as well. He gives the example of the painter. Everything on the canvas is caused, in one sense, by the brush yet it is obvious that the brush is only a carrier, as it were, by means of which a causality superior to that of the brush is borne. If you look for art in the brush you will not find it; you will find just wood, hair, and paint.

33 Lonergan agrees that there is a sensitive apprehension of the universal in the particular without which it would be impossible for the intellect to reach the abstract universal (p. 30). If it were true that the sense apprehended the particular and only the particular and in no way touched on the universal, it would simply not be possible for such sensitive apprehension to be the material cause of our knowledge of the abstract universal. On this point Lonergan is in essential agreement with Adler who makes a very similar distinction in the context of the differentiation of animal and human cognition.

34 Compare the account of perception which Plato gives in the *Theaetetus* (155D–157E) and which he never repudiates.

Examine everything entitative about the medium that transmits sensible quality and you will only find the properties and movements—the wave movements and others—that the physicist sees in them. You will no more find quality there than you will find the soul under a scalpel. Yet quality passes through it, *secundum esse intentionale*, since the sense will perceive it when the wave or vibration reaches the organ. It is like a dream of a materialistic imagination to want, with Democritus, to have quality pass through the medium entitatively, or, since it is not there entitatively, to deny, with the votaries of modern 'scientism' that it could pass through it at all. (*Degrees*, 114–15)

Let us take another example. Suppose you go into a record shop and ask for Scarlatti's Harpsichord Sonatas. You are given a circular piece of metal-coated plastic enclosed in a plastic case. In what sense have you been given Scarlatti's Harpsichord Sonatas? Sonatas are not, as such, purely physical objects—whereas what you have just bought is, or appears to be. In its purely physical capacity the disc you have just purchased can be used as a makeshift frisbee, or as a thing to put your cup of coffee on, or as something to be mounted over the fireplace and admired. However, if it is placed in the appropriate equipment which is then operated, the disc will generate electronic signals which, if converted into air waves by the appropriate movement of corrugated circular pieces of cardboard will, if a sentient being is within a certain delimited range, result in the hearing of music.

What should strike one about this account is the number of 'ifs' which appear in it, the number of conditions which have to be satisfied. The hearing of the Sonatas only comes about if all these conditions are satisfied. Does this mean that the Sonatas are not actually in the piece of metal-coated plastic? Yes—they are not actually there. But there is a difference between this piece of metal-coated plastic and another in that one will, if all the conditions are satisfied, produce Scarlatti's Harpsichord Sonatas while the other will not. The music is, therefore, virtually present in the plastic, that is to say, the plastic has the power to produce them in the appropriate circumstances.[35]

What is also striking about the example given is the number of levels of supervenience which occur. The electronic supervenes upon the physical; the mechanical supervenes upon the electronic; and the auditory supervenes upon the mechanical. Scarlatti's Harpsichord Sonatas can be said to be there on all the various levels, yet it is only on the final level that they attain a fully actualized status. Since their existence at the various other levels tend towards this fully actualized status, the virtual mode of existence at these levels may be said to be intentional. The music is carried by a variety of physical, electronic, mechanical conditions.

Similarly, meaning in language is supervenient upon a complex system of materially perceptible signs. It takes an effort of the imagination to realize

35 This explanation of supervenience is not unlike Locke's account of secondary qualities. See *An Essay on Human Understanding*, Book II, Chapter VIII, section 23.

this although it is immediately evident to us when we hear a completely foreign language being spoken for the first time.

If we call to mind the old Scholastic tag 'the sense in act is the sensible in act' we can see that it is validly convertible, that is 'the sensible in act is the sense in act'. We can generalize this principle in the following way; the (passive) powers embodied in physical energy interchanges can be realized only in their assimilation by the (active) powers of the appropriate receivers.

Another Scholastic tag runs 'whatever is received is received according to the mode of the receiver.' An appreciation of this point will, I believe, solve Adler's puzzle as to why the conditions of materiality should attach to the sensitive *quo* of knowledge which is immaterial. Cognitive capacities are not physical things. Even our sensory cognitive capacity is not such a thing. However, it is exercised through a corporeal organ and in its operation is conditioned by such exercise.

> The primary sense organ is that in which such a potentiality δύναμις resides. These are then the same, although what it is for them to be such is not the same. For that which perceives must be a particular extended magnitude, while what it is to be able to perceive and the sense αἴσθησις are surely not magnitudes, but rather a certain principle λόγος and potentiality of that thing.[36]

It is important to be clear as to the significance of the 'im' in 'immaterial'. According to Yves Simon, when we speak of immaterial existence in connection with knowledge what is signified by the term 'immaterial' is the form's emancipation from matter with respect to the conditions which matter imposes on form when that form is a constitutive principle of a real being. The immaterial existence of form involved in sensitive knowledge can be misunderstood in two ways: first, if it is not realized that despite its emancipation from matter in some respects, the form still retains the individuating factors consequent upon materiality; and second, if the distinction is not grasped in such a way as to allow for the existence of a thing in itself and its existence in knowledge. 'To obviate these misunderstandings it is advisable to employ the term intentional existence, a term fashioned by scholasticism to capture an insight of Aristotle and which signifies the existential modality which a thing takes on in awareness.'[37]

Is intentionality then, as such, immaterial? Yes—in that it is a mode of being which supervenes upon a material base and which can be actualized only in the presence of a being with an immaterial receptive capacity.

---

36   Aristotle, *De Anima* 424 a 24–8, trans. D. W. Hamlyn, (Oxford 1968).
37   Yves Simon, *Introduction à l'ontologie du connaître*, p. 17.

Der Übergang von der Physik zur Metaphysik im thomistischen Gottesbeweis

WOLFGANG KLUXEN

Der thomistische Gottesbeweis gehört sicher zur den am häufigsten untersuchten, kritisierten und diskutierten Lehrstücken der Scholastik. Ich will dem keine weitere Analyse hinzufügen. Es geht mir nur um einige interpretatorishe Hinweise, die weniger auf den Beweisgang selbst eingehen als auf die Stellung des Gottesbeweises in der thomistischen Gesamtkonzeption der theoretischen Philosophie. Dies geschieht nicht nur in historischer Absicht, vielmehr geht es zugleich und vor allem um ein Strukturmoment des 'Thomismus' als einer permanenten Möglichkeit metaphysischen Denkens. Das meint nicht notwendig die thomistische Schultradition, die nicht selten den Gottesbeweis isoliert und dann ihm eine Vollkommenheit und gar Originalität zuspricht, die er gar nicht hat und nicht zu haben braucht. Seine eigentliche Bedeutung wird eher zu klären sein, wenn man ihn in den Systemzusammenhang einordnet, in dem er bei Thomas steht.

Der durch die Tradition klassisch gewordene Text, den ich für die folgenden Überlegungen zum Ausgangspunkt nehme, ist jener aus der *Summa theologiae* (I, 2, 3), der die berühmten *quinque viae* enthält. Der Artikel steht unter der Frage *utrum deus sit*. Welche Bedeutung diese einfache Formel hat, sieht man am Vergleich mit anderen Formeln. So fragt Duns Scotus: *utrum in entibus sit aliquod ens infinitum*, oder elementarer: *utrum sit aliqua natura prima*. Er bringt schon damit zum Ausdruck, daß die Frage in einem bestimmten philosophischen Zusammenhang, nämlich dem von *ens* und *natura*, gestellt und beantwortet wird. Thomas spricht im Kontext seines *theologischen* Hauptwerkes ohne weiteres von 'Gott', und der Schluß des Beweises nimmt ausdrücklich das Wort auf: *quod omnes nominant deum*. Dies *nominare* muß man unterstreichen: vorausgesetzt ist ein *quid nominis*—wir würden sagen, eine 'Bedeutung'—, ganz im Sinne der Beweislehre des Aristoteles, und mit der Bezugnahme auf diese Bedeutung endet der Beweis. Man hat Thomas wegen der Identifizierung des von ihm bewiesenen 'ersten Bewegers' mit dem Offenbarungsgott kritisiert, da dieser letztere eben nicht bewiesen sei; Thomas überschreite in unerlaubter Weise die Grenze, die dem philosophischen Gedanken gesetzt ist. In Wahrheit steht es in der theologischen Summe anders: Von Anfang an ist vom Offenbarungsgott die Rede, dem die im Beweis selbst nachgewiesenen Bestimmungen als erster Beweger, erste Wirkursache usw. ohne Zweifel—nämlich nach dem Offenbarungsverständnis—zukommen.

Hier wird nicht ein philosophisches Ergebnis nachträglich mit dem theologisch Vorausgesetzten identisch gesetzt; vielmehr wird umgekehrt von der Theologie ein philosophischer Beweisgang in ihren Kontext einbezogen, und dans ist etwas grundsätzlich anderes.

Im Sinne der aristotelischen Wissenschaftslehre kommt es für die Theologie, die sich als Wissenschaft ausformen will, zuerst darauf an, sich ihres *subiectum* zu versichern, genauer seines *quia est.* Was nun dieses *est* besagt, erklärt Thomas im Rahmen der folgenden *Quaestio* (I, 3, 4 ad 3): es besagt lediglich das *esse copulae*, das will sagen: Sätze mit dem Subjekt 'Gott' sind sinnvolle Sätze. Es genügt für den Gottesbeweis unter theologischem Aspekt der Nachweis, daß es einen Gegenstand gibt, der sinnvoll mit dem Namen 'Gott' bezeichnet werden kann. Es braucht nicht verlangt zu werden, daß der Nachweis selbst alle Aspekte berücksichtigt, die möglich oder sinnvoll sind. Der Nachweis braucht nicht gleichsam die ganze Gotteslehre zu erbringen. Er muß vor allem wirksam, also wissenschaftlich überzeugend sein und eindeutig—in welcher Begrenztheit des Aspektes auch immer—einen Gegenstand nachweisen, der von allen anderen durch eine Eigenschaft unterschieden ist, die nur dem geglaubten Gott zuzuschreiben ist.

Diese auszeichnende Eigenschaft haben wir darin zu erblicken, daß der Nachweis auf allen fünf Wegen zu einem 'Ersten' führt, das aus sich selbst jene Bestimmtheit besitzt, auf welche der jeweilige Beweisweg ausgerichtet ist. Ganz streng genommen ist es dabei nicht einmal notwendig, daß die Einzigkeit dieses Ersten im Beweis selbst aufgewiesen wird (tatsächlich fehlt der Aufweis für die Einzigkeit des ersten Bewegers bei Thomas), denn das Nachweisziel, das *quia est* des Subjekts der Rede von Gott, ist auch ohne den Einzigkeitsbeweis erreicht. Die Wirksamkeit, die wissenschaftliche Überzeugungskraft des Beweises liegt darin begründet, daß er auf eine Basis in der Erfahrung bezogen ist—mit Recht steht die *manifestior via* am Anfang, welche die unmittelbare und jedermann zugängliche Erfahrung der Bewegung zum Ausgang nimmt. Das kann man allgemeiner formulieren: Basis des Beweises ist jene Ebene, zu welcher der Mensch kraft seiner erkenntnismäßigen Ausstattung unmittelbaren Zugang hat, und das ist bei Thomas die Ebene der *quidditas rei sensibilis.* Die wissenschaftliche Behandlung dieser Ebene geschieht aber, aristotelisch gesprochen, in der Physik. Der Gottebeweis setzt in diesem Sinne physikalisch an.

Die physikalische Basis ist beim ersten Weg ganz klar: 'Bewegung' ist der Grundbegriff der Physik im aristotelischen Sinne. Auch die Wirkursächlichkeit des zweiten Weges ist deutlich eine physikalische Kategorie. Der dritte Weg, der vom Möglichen und Notwendigen ausgeht, spricht klar vom ersteren im aristotelischen Sinne als von dem, was 'gelegentlich ist und dann auch wieder nicht' (*possibile esse et non esse*); das ist der Begriff des *corruptibile*, der auf die Welt unter dem Monde zutrifft. Ebenso ist auch das 'Notwendige' konkret gemeint: Es meint zunächst die 'Himmel', die im Gegensatz zur Welt unter dem Monde zwar 'notwendig', aber nicht 'aus sich' notwendig sind.

Auch der vierte Weg muß trotz der allgemein klingenden Rede von den *gradus entis* auf einen möglichen physikalischen Sinn hin geprüft werden. Der zentrale Gedanke ist, daß das 'Seiende' der ersten und obersten Stufe—wobei durchaus ein kategorial beschränktes Seiendes gemeint sein kann—Ursache aller ihm nachgeordneten Stufen ist. Das Beispiel vom Feuer, das in der Gattung des 'Warmen' das 'Erste' ist und daher alles andere Warme verursacht, dürfte deutlich machen, daß der Satz 'quod est primum in aliquo genere, est causa cuiuscumque existentis in illo genere' Geltung in Bereich der Physik beansprucht, ja sich darin ausweist. Auch der fünfte Weg, welcher die Zielbestimmtheit einsichtsloser Naturen auf die Zielbestimmung durch eine vorgeordnete intelligente Ursache zurückführt, bleibt im Rahmen eines Sachverhaltes, der in der physikalischen Erfahrung ausgewiesen ist.

Wenn das nun zutrifft, dann erscheint auf allen diesen Wegen 'Gott' als das jeweils einem physikalisch begründeten, kategorial beschränkten Ansatz korrespondierende 'Erste', dem von diesem Ansatz her keine weitergehende Bestimmung als die eben darin nachgewiesene beigegeben werden kann. Man darf aber noch hinzufügen, daß alle fünf Wege innerhalb des Horizontes der *einen* Welt liegen, welche diejenige unserer Erfahrung ist und welche in der Physik wissenschaftlich ausgelegt wird. Das fünffach aufgewiesene Erste ist das Korrelat jener Welt, welche durch die aristotelische Physik erfaßt ist: das, so scheint es, ist das Ergebnis.

Nun wird eine solche rein physikalische Deutung des thomistischen Gottesbeweisses gewiß auf Bedenken und Einwände der Thomisten und der Thomaskenner stoßen. Zunächst kommt es aber auf die Feststellung an, daß diese Deutung insofern möglich ist, als der Text eine Grundlage zu ihrer Ausführung bietet. Es gilt weiter zu sehen, daß der so verstandene Beweis immer noch den Anforderungen der Theologie entspricht, welcher es allein auf das *quia est* ihres *subiectum* ankommt. Dies gilt unter der Voraussetzung, daß der 'physikalische' Gott nicht notwendig wiederum selbst als ausschließlich physikalische Größe aufgefaßt werden muß.

Diese Voraussetzung ist nun im aristotelischen Kontext bereits dadurch erfüllt, daß der Gottesbeweis lediglich als *demonstratio quia* geführt wird. Eine solche Beweisführung ist dann notwendig und auch einzig möglich, wenn wir von dem zu Beweisenden keine unmittelbare Erkenntnis besitzen, die uns einen Zugang zu seinem Wesen oder Wesensbegriff eröffnen würde. Die wissenschaftliche Behandlung ist dann nicht auf Grund der Definition möglich, die wir nicht haben, aber anstelle der Definition kann die 'Wirkung' eingesetzt werden; genauer dürfte man vielleicht sagen: der Begriff, der anläßlich einer Wirkung oder einer gewirkten Präsenz als ein solcher des diese Wirkung oder Präsenz veranlassenden Seienden gewonnen wird. Dies Prinzip gilt allgemein, nicht nur für die Gotteserkenntnis. Es gilt andererseits nicht nur für die philosophische Gotteserkenntnis, sondern auch für die theologische, sofern es sich bei der Offenbarung prinzipiell auch wieder um eine bloße Wirkung Gottes, eine gewirkte und nicht eine unmittelbare

Präsenz handelt. Wesentlich ist dabei, daß aus der Begrenztheit der Wirkung, die in einer solchen *demonstratio quia* zur Basis genommen wird, nicht geschlossen werden darf, daß das Nachgewiesene ausschließlich in der begrenzten Dimension zu halten sei, die der Beweis eröffnet. Der physikalische Gott kann also sehr wohl noch die Dimension des 'göttlichen Gottes' besitzen. Es wäre sogar eine Position möglich, bei der sich der Theologe mit dem physikalischen Gott begnügt, da dessen Nachweis das erforderte *quia est* in zureichendem Maße beibringt, und die Erkenntnis des 'göttlichen Gottes' rein aus der Offenbarung zu gewinnen sucht, ohne weitergehenden rationalen Anspruch. Solche Position liefe allerdings auf einen philosophischen Agnostizismus hinaus, sie überspränge die Metaphysik. Eben das ist nicht die Einstellung des Thomas, sondern eher die des Maimonides, und sie wird von Thomas kritisiert.

Bei Thomas folgt auf den physikalisch angesetzten Gottesbeweis nicht der Sprung in die Offenbarungsaussage, sondern die inhaltliche Entfaltung eines metaphysischen Gottesverständnisses. Dies geschieht natürlich im theologischen Kontext, aber diese Abfolge ist nicht nur durch diesen, sondern ebenso durch den philosophischen Sachzusammenhang bedingt. Auf die Frage *an sit* folgt konsequent die Frage *quid sit*, und es ist klar, daß diese weitere Frage nicht mehr in irgendeinem Sinne 'physikalisch' zu behandeln ist—auch wenn Thomas sie dann als Frage danach verstanden wissen will, *quid non sit*. Es findet so ein Übergang statt, von der Physik des Gottesbeweises zur Metaphysik der Gotteslehre: so muß man es wenigstens sehen, wenn man die physikalische Deutung der fünf Wege akzeptiert.

Es scheint nun schwer zu denken, daß gleichsam nachträglich zu einem physikalischen Gedankengang eine metaphysische Bedeutung seines Resultats konstruiert wird. Daher wohl haben viele Thomisten den Gottesbeweis von vornherein als metaphysischen verstehen wollen. Das hat aber wieder entgegengesetzte Schwierigkeiten. Am ehesten gelingt es beim vierten Weg, der freilich als Beweis am wenigsten überzeugend ist. Am schwierigsten ist es gerade beim ersten Weg, den Thomas als den 'offenkundigsten' und damit wohl auch als den wirksamsten bezeichnet. Man kann kaum den Ausweg wählen, innerhalb der fünf Wege den einen als physikalisch, den anderen als metaphysisch zu kennzeichnen. Sie sind ganz parallel gebaut, und es ist nötig, sie darum als 'Wege' des einen Beweises zu verstehen, nicht als gänzlich unterschiedene, gar verschiedenen Wissenschaftsdisziplinen zugehörige Gedankengänge.

Wer also den von Anfang an metaphysischen Charakter des Gottesbeweises behaupten will, hat die Frage zu beantworten, ob denn schon der Ansatz *aller* Wege den Charakter hat, den Thomas für den entscheidenden der Metaphysik hält. Dies ist nach dem Text von *In Boeth. de trin.* 5, 2 und 3 die *separatio*, die 'Trennung' von der Materie und von der Bewegung. Dies meint ausdrücklich nicht, daß nur immaterielles Seiendes als Gegenstand der Metaphysik in Frage kommt; aber am materiellen Seienden zielt die metaphysische Betrachtung auf solche Strukturen ab, die ihrem Wesen nach nicht auf Verwirklichung in Materie angewiesen sind, die insofern 'getrennt' zu betrachten sind. Man muß hinzufügen, daß sich hier sofort die Frage des Ausweises stellt. Der im Sinne der 'Abrennung' metaphysische Charakter einer Struktur des Seienden muß aufgezeigt werden, wenn er sich zuerst in einem materiellen Seienden zeigt. Der definitive Nachweis, daß Metaphysik in diesem Sinne ein sinnvolles Vorhaben ist, wird erst dadurch geliefert, daß die Existenz eines wesentlich immateriellen Seienden bewiesen wird. Das ist bei Thomas konstante Lehre, auch wenn der Ausdruck *separatio* sich nur im zitierten Text findet.

Es scheint mir nun deutlich, daß im *Ansatz* des Gottesbeweises die *separatio* eben nicht vorausgesetzt ist. Der Ansatz steht klar auf der Ebene des materiellen Seienden unserer Erfahrung. Ebenso deutlich scheint mir aber, daß das Resultat des Beweisganges nicht mehr innerhalb der physikalischen Welt liegt. Das in jedem der fünf Wege nachgewiesene Erste ist gerade dadurch Erstes, daß es nicht mehr in eine Reihe gehört, innerhalb deren ein *regressus* stattfinden kann. Es ist in keiner dieser Reihen die Nummer Eins, von der ab fortlaufend gezählt wird, sondern ist stets das nicht mehr hinzuaddierbare Eine, dem gegenüber alles andere 'Zweites' ist. Der physikalisch nachgewiesene Gott ist Korrelat der physikalischen Welt in der Weise, daß diese im ganzen, als physikalische, ihm gegenübersteht, er selbst aber gerade nicht mehr physikalische Größe ist. Es gibt also keinen physikalischen Gott. Der Nachweis erbringt vielmehr das *quia est* des im strengen Sinne metaphysischen Gottes.

So viel, scheint mir, kann man schon auf Grund der Formulierung des Gottesbeweises sagen, und es folgt dann, daß im Gottesbeweis selbst der Übergang von der Physik zur Metaphysik geschieht. Das bedeutet jedoch nicht, daß die Metaphysik erst nach dem Gottesbeweis anfangen kann und ihn sich gleichsam von der Physik als deren Grenzresultat vorgeben lassen, schließlich gar die bei der Wesensanalyse Gottes einzusetzenden Begriffe aus ihm entnehmen muß—was dann ja konsequent zu fordern wäre. Thomas entspricht solcher Forderung in keiner Weise: die auf den Gottesbeweis folgende Gotteslehre ist nicht Entfaltung von dessen Resultat, sondern bringt die Ergebnisse von Analysen zum tragen, die ihn gar nicht einmal voraussetzen, sondern viel früher angesetzt sind, nämlich beim ersten Begriff: beim 'Seienden, das als erstes vom Verstand aufgefaßt wird'. Klassisches Beispiel solcher Analysen gibt schon das Frühwerk *De ente et essentia*, und die Gotteslehre selbst gibt deren eine Fülle.

Dies 'ersterkannte' Seiende erscheint nun nicht gleich als jenes *separatum*, als welches es formell Gegenstand der Metaphysik ist, sondern in kategorialer Vielfalt und in der konkreten Bestimmtheit der *quidditas rei sensibilis*. Die Analyse setzt deshalb bei jenem bestimmten Seienden an, das als primäre Bedeutung dieses Begriffs unmittelbar erkennbar ist, nämlich bei der zusammengesetzten Substanz (*substantia composita*). Die in der Analyse entwickelten

Begriffe sind zunächst an dieser ausgewiesen und für sie gültig. Aber es sind Begriffe von *Prinzipien* des Seienden, die entwickelt werden: Materie und Form, Potenz und Akt, Wesen und Sein, und dies sind nicht wieder Begriffe einer Substanz oder überhaupt eines materiellen Etwas, eines *quod est*, sondern eines 'Wodurch', eines *quo est*. Solches gehört zum Seienden, ist innerhalb seiner antreffbar, und so zeigt sich in den Prinzipien der materiellen Substanz eine Bedeutung von 'Sein', die Materialität nicht einschließt. Das besagt aber, daß der Begriff des Seienden selbst nicht auf den Bereich des materiellen Etwas muß eingeschränkt werden. Das Seiende 'als Seiendes' kann demnach 'getrennt' gedacht werden. Das gilt dann auch für die mit ihm konvertiblen Bestimmungen, die Transzendentalien.

Es bleibt jedoch bestehen, daß diese Begriffe zunächst nur am materiellen Seienden ausgewiesen sind, dessen Existenz uns unmittelbar zugänglich ist. Man kann demnach, im Sinne der modernen Unterscheidung von Ontologie und Metaphysik, von einer Ontologie reden, deren eigentlich metaphysischer Sinn noch offen bleibt. Obwohl Thomas diese Unterscheidung nicht kennt, dürfte sie dennoch etwas bei ihm treffen; denn er ist, mit Aristoteles, der Meinung, daß alle diese Analysen zur 'Physik' gerechnet werden müssen, wenn es kein anderes Seiendes als eben von dieser erfaßbares gäbe: sie wäre dann die Erste Philosophie (so z. B. *Met.*V, 1 und Thomas, *In Met.*V, l.1). Anders ist es, wenn ein immaterielles Seiendes existiert, in welchem die immaterielle Bedeutung auch erfüllt wird, nämlich als Bedeutung für ein Etwas, ein *quod est* immaterieller Art. Ein solches ist uns nicht unmittelbar gegeben, da wir auf die Ebene der *quidditas rei sensibilis* angewiesen sind. Aber wenigstens kann sich seine Existenz, sein 'Daß' oder '*quia est*' auf dieser Ebene durch seine 'Wirkung' zeigen, als Existenz eines 'Etwas', das eben 'nicht' materiell ist, dessen Washeit also nur durch die Negation der materiellen Bestimmungen gekennzeichnet werden kann, die am erfahrungsweltlich antreffbaren Seienden vorliegen.

Das ist genau die Struktur des Gottesbeweises, sofern er einen physikalischen Ansatz nimmt und zur Negation der physikalischen Bestimmtheit des nachgewiesenen 'Ersten' fortschreitet. Nach Erreichen dieses Resultats kann dann die zuvor schon entwickelte 'Ontologie' sogleich in ihre eigentlich 'metaphysische' Bedeutung eintreten: sie kann die immaterielle Bedeutungsdimension ihrer transzendentalen und ihrer Prinzipienbegriffe zu einer Wesensanalyse entfalten. Angesichts der Tatsache freilich, daß diese Begriffe ihren Ausweis am materiellen Seienden haben, wird diese Analyse wesentlich in einer negativen Operation bestehen, nämlich in der 'Abtrennung' der immateriellen Dimension von dem Kontext, in dem sie erstmalig erschienen ist. Ferner wird die Bestimmung des immateriellen Wesens der Weise entsprechen, wie die ontologische Analyse die immaterielle Dimension erreicht hat: einmal in der Weise des Prinzipseins, zum anderen in der Weise der Anwesenheit durch 'Wirkung'. Beides zusammen ist daran schuld, daß die Metaphysik das immaterielle Seiende nicht zu ihrem *subiectum* hat—als unmittelbaren Gegenstand, dessen Prädikate sie aufsucht—, sondern nur als *principium subiecti.* Wenn ihr unmittelbare Gegenstand das *ens commune* ist, so gewinnt sie diesen *als metaphysischen,* als welcher er zugleich *separatum* sein muß, erst auf einem Umwege.

An diesem Umweg—wenn man ihn so nennen darf—hat der Gottesbeweis seinen systematischen Ort, ja er hat für die Metaphysik eine zentrale Stelle. Freilich hat er diese nicht schon insofern, als er an eine Grenzposition der 'Physik' führt, sondern sofern er in den Gesamtprozeß des metaphysischen Diskurses eingefügt ist, also ihm schon eine 'Ontologie' vorausliegt, die dann nach ihm 'metaphysisch' zum tragen kommt. Das verleitet natürlich manche Interpreten zu dem Versuch, den Beweis selbst als ein Stück metaphysischen Diskurses verstehen zu wollen. Gerade bei den *quinque viae* bedarf es jedoch erheblicher Anstrengung, um diese Deutung dem höchst knappen Text abzuringen: er ist eher geeignet, solche Anstrengung zu vereiteln.

Wie ein eigentlich metaphysischer Gottesbeweis aussehen würde, ließe sich wieder am Vergleich verdeutlichen. Das eindrucksvolle Muster gibt Duns Scotus im *Tractatus de primo principio* (wobei gleichgültig ist, ob die Schrift ganz aus seiner Feder stammt): Da wird der Gottesbeweis aus der Entfaltung der Transzendentalienmetaphysik, welche die Ordnung des Seienden im ganzen auslegt, entwickelt, faßt sie zusammen und erbringt in einheitlichem Zuge sogleich die gesamte metaphysische Gotteslehre; und das geschieht in höchst sorgfältig abgesicherten, logisch zwingenden Schritten. Auch Thomas bringt gelegentlich solche metaphysischen Gesamtsichten, so schon in *De ente et essentia,* aber es ist immer noch strittig, ob sie als 'Beweis' gemeint sind: wo ein solcher beabsichtigt ist, nämlich als Antwort auf die Frage *utrum deus sit,* da finden sich jene Argumente (und verwandte), die in den fünf Wegen klassisch formuliert sind. Von diesen gilt aber, daß sie keineswegs die gesamte vorentwickelte Ontologie zusammenfassen; sie ist in ihnen nicht einmal für ihre Wirksamkeit vorausgesetzt. Schon gar nicht wird aus dem Beweis die Gotteslehre inhaltlich entwickelt: er zielt nur auf das sozusagen punktuelle *quia est* dessen, dem der Name 'Gott' zugesprochen werden kann, und es kommt nur auf den Übergang von der Physik zur Metaphysik an.

Verglichen mit hohen metaphysischen Erwartungen, die sich etwa an Duns Scotus nähren, ist der thomistische Gottesbeweis geradezu dürftig. Genau so aber entspricht er der Funktion, die ihm in einem aristotelischen Konzept der theoretischen Philosophie zukommt. Es ist primär gerade diese systematische Funktion, die er auszufüllen hat, und wie das zu geschehen hat, dafür hat die aristotelische Schule hinreichend Beispiele gegeben. Es ist folgerichtig, wenn Thomas gerade im Gottesbeweis diesen Beispielen folgt. Er schreibt nicht gerade ab, aber die Vorlagen—von Aristoteles bis Maimonides—liegen auf der Hand. Thomas hat es nicht mit Gegnern, oder gar mit Atheisten oder Religionskritikern, zu tun, sondern mit einer Wissenschaft, welche den Gottesbeweis als integrales Stück ihrer Weltdeutung mitbringt. Dieser bedarf also weder besonderer begrifflicher Anstrengung noch gar der genialen Originalität: wer den Text im Lichte der aristotelischen Tradition liest, welche Thomas benutzt, kann es nur lächerlich finden, wenn gewisse Thomisten darin eine 'Meisterleistung' erblickt haben. Andererseits ist auch eine Kritik verfehlt, die nicht wahrnimmt, wie präzis begrenzt seine Funktion ist, und ihm eine Leistung abverlangt, die er nicht beansprucht. In beiden Fällen liegt der Fehler darin, daß der Text isoliert und nicht an seinem systembestimmten Ort gesehen wird, dem er angemessen ist.

Durch die Deutung als, sozusagen punktueller, 'Übergang' wird der thomistische Gottesbeweis metaphysisch entlastet. Auf der anderen Seite wird er natürlich mit dem Verdacht belastet, seine Geltung müsse dann auch von jener aristotelischen Physik und deren Weltbild abhängen, die man wissenschaftsgeschichtlich als überholt und erledigt anzusehen hat. Aber das ist nicht ganz so einfach, wie es scheint: die moderne Naturwissenschaft ist nicht einfach an dieselbe Stelle getreten wie die aristotelische Physik; sie hat eine andere Perspektive eingenommen, ihr erkenntnistheoretischer Anspruch liegt völlig anders, und es ist keineswegs klar, ob sie und wie sie ontologischen Sinn hat. Zwar ist das konkrete Weltbild des Aristoteles ersetzt. Aber es bleibt möglich, seine Physik als ontologischen Text zu lesen, der nicht im Modus moderner Wissenschaft Faktenzusammenhänge konstruiert, sondern eher phänomenologische Analyse treibt. In dieser Qualität kann er Gesichtspunkte und Einsichten enthalten, die nicht dem kritischen Urteil des 'Überwundenseins' unterliegen. Thomas kann in seiner geschichtlichen Lage selbstverständlich nicht umhin, sich auf das 'Weltbild' des Aristoteles zu beziehen, das für ihn wissenschaftlich maßgeblich sein muß. Doch ist im Gottesbeweis auffällig, daß er die aristotelischen Ausgangsbegriffe—Bewegung, Wirkursächlichkeit, Notwendigkeit, Teleologie und auch Stufung (ein im Aristotelismus der Tradition durchaus enthaltener Begriff)—nicht am Weltbild exemplifiziert, wie bei seinen Vorlagen oft geschieht, sondern sich an ihre allgemeine ontologische Bedeutung hält—, ein Merkmal, das scheinbar den 'metaphysischen' Interpretationsversuchen entgegenkommt. Aber es ist nicht schon eine Metaphysik, sondern vielmehr, was in der Sprache der Phänomenologie eine 'Regionalontologie' unserer Erfahrungswelt heißen könnte, auf die sich Thomas bezieht. In ihr gilt es dann jene Punkte auszumachen, die den Übergang zur Metaphysik insofern ermöglichen, als sie die Existenz eines erfahrungstranszendenten Seienden bezeugen.

Die Gültigkeit dieser 'Regionalontologie' ist natürlich die Voraussetzung für die Gültigkeit der 'fünf Wege', und so fühlen sich Thomisten gehalten, sie zu verteidigen. Sieht man aber auf die strukturelle Einordnung und die Funktion, die der Gottesbeweis systematisch hat, so erkennt man zuerst, daß diese fünf Wege nach Beweistauglichkeit—unter den gegebenen geschichtlichen Voraussetzungen—und eben punktuell, nicht wieder 'systematisch' gewählt sind. Es müssen nicht fünf, und es müssen nicht diese fünf sein, und Thomas selbst ist, wie die Parallelstellen zeigen, nicht auf sie festgelegt. Von da aus ist der Schritt nicht groß zu der weitergehenden Frage, ob der thomistische Gottesbeweis auch *prinzipiell* derart an die Vorgabe der aristotelischen 'Regionalontologie' gebunden sei, wie er es historisch ist, oder ob man ihn von dieser so lösen könne wie man ihn vom Weltbild des Aristoteles lösen muß.

Diese Frage hat nur Sinn, wenn man das thomistische Konzept der Metaphysik auch in veränderter geschichtlicher Lage für sinnvoll, also für eine permanente Möglichkeit metaphysischen Denkens hält. Sie stellt sich dann im Hinblick auf ein Weltverständnis, das durch die aristotelische Ontologie nicht mehr zureichend ausgedrückt ist, in dem aber jene Ansätze zu suchen sind, deren ontologische Erfassung jenen Übergang zur Metaphysik rechtfertigt, der für das Gesamtkonzept grundlegend ist. Freilich werden sie wohl kaum auf der Ebene einer Wissenschaft zu finden sein, die sich methodisch gegen jede Ontologie abschließt; so ist von ihr aus erst recht kein Gottesbeweis als wissenschaftlicher zu führen. Aber bedarf es in unserer geschichtlichen Lage eines wissenschaftlichen Beweises, um sich ontologisch des *quia est* dessen zu versichern, 'den alle Gott nennen?' Gewiß ist diese Versicherung notwendig, aber die thomistische Metaphysik hängt sicher nicht davon ab, daß sie auf Grund aristotelischer Physik geschieht.

God's Presence in the World

The Metaphysics of Aquinas and some Recent Thinkers (Moltmann, MacQuarrie, Rahner)

MAURICE CURTIN

There are those who hold that God is not present but absent or non-existent. They are the secularists or secular humanists. Their philosophy is gradually changing the life and thinking of many persons throughout the world. On the other hand, those thinkers who hold that God is present and supremely relevant differ widely in explaining his presence. I have selected from their number, Moltmann, MacQuarrie and Rahner.[1]

But why call upon Aquinas? Is it reasonable to expect a contribution to a contemporary problem from somebody belonging to a distant age and to a completely different cultural context, and writing in a style now completely unfamiliar and outmoded? The article which follows is intended as an answer. Aquinas indeed is not contemporary in time. But he is contemporary in thought in so far as he expresses truths that are relevant to all time because they transcend time.

I: SOME RECENT THINKERS

God in Creation; The Ecological Theology of Jürgen Moltmann

Moltmann's Gifford Lectures of 1984–5 are published as *God in Creation: An Ecological Doctrine of Creation*.[2] Moltmann is indeed very conscious of the present ecological crisis due to man's misconceived domination over nature. And so all through his lectures he emphasizes the presence of God through his Spirit; he emphasizes too a cosmic eschatology in which not only man but the whole of creation will be gloriously transformed. But one thing he makes clear: he will have nothing to do with the notion of causality.

---

1 Partly, but not entirely for lack of space I have omitted: Richard Swinburne, *The Coherence of Theism* (Oxford, 1977); Grace Jantzen, *God's World, God's Body* (London, 1984); Matthew Fox, *Original Blessing: A Primer in Creation Spirituality* (Santa Fe, 1986). Swinburne does not deal with God's real presence in the world, but with the logical coherence of the concept of an omnipotent spirit (pp. 97–125). Jantzen is really reviving an ancient error; her speculation or hypothesis would be the negation of God's transcendence (cf. p. 127). Fox would replace the word 'theism' by 'panentheism'. Is it merely a matter of terminology? (cf. pp. 88–92).

2 Jürgen Moltmann, *God in Creation: An Ecological Doctrine of Creation* (London, 1985).

> If we are to follow the concept of God's transcendence in relation to the world with an understanding of this divine world-immanence it is advisable to eliminate the concept of causality from the doctrine of creation, and indeed we have to stop thinking in terms of causation at all; for the causality approach allows us to conceive only of the transcendence of the divine *causa prima* which, since it is divine must also be *causa sui;* but creating the world is something different from causing it. (p. 14)

In place of the principle of causality Moltmann would have the principle of mutual interpenetration (cf. pp. 13–17, 86–93). This latter principle he describes as an intricate web of unilateral, reciprocal and many-sided relationships.

> In this network of relationships, 'making', 'preserving', 'maintaining', 'perfecting' are certainly the great one-sided relationships, but 'indwelling', 'sympathizing', 'participating', 'accompanying', 'enduring', 'delighting', and 'glorifying' are relationships of mutuality which describe a cosmic community of living between God the Spirit and all his created beings. (p. 14)

It is a question whether this accumulation of descriptive phrases amounts to an explanation.

A Dialectical Theology of God's Presence: John MacQuarrie

MacQuarrie's Gifford Lectures of 1983–4 are published as *In Search of Deity: An Essay in Dialectical Theism.*[3] I will concentrate on two themes: his critique of what he calls classical theism, especially in its doctrine of transcendence and immanence, and secondly, his dialectical concept of God, again with special attention to God's presence in the world.

According to MacQuarrie there is 'traditional theism' and there is 'classical theism'. Traditional theism, in addition to the teachings of theologians and philosophers, contains a vast penumbra of popular prescientific beliefs. Classical theism would leave aside these beliefs and uphold only what is upheld at an academic level:

> I shall tighten up the concept of theism and consider it in its strongest form as expounded by its best representatives, especially Thomas Aquinas. . . . (This is) the usage of writers among whom are both critics and admirers of his work. (p. 31)

MacQuarrie himself is both a critic and an admirer. It is his criticism which now concerns us. The main fault in Aquinas' theistic teaching, he repeatedly points out, is a lack of balance:

> Unfortunately, no matter how carefully classical theism is formulated, it still tends to present a distinctly 'monarchical' view of God, that is to

3 John MacQuarrie, *In Search of Deity: An Essay in Dialectical Theism* (London, 1984).

say, God is one-sidedly transcendent, separate from and over and above the world. The transcendence and majesty of God are not sufficiently qualified by recognition of his immanence and humility. (p. 31; see pp. 177–81)

To say, with Aquinas, that the existence of the world depends on God's will as on its cause is to speak 'as if God were not only a monarch but a somewhat capricious one' (p. 36).

Any doctrine which stresses the total otherness of the creator, the complete externality of the creation and the infinite difference between them, has a concealed tendency towards deism, or even eventually, atheism. (p. 35)

What is the alternative to classical theism? MacQuarrie answers:

The alternative I shall develop I am calling 'dialectical theism' (p. 14). When I speak of 'dialectical theism' I am not speaking of some weak compromise. 'Dialectic' is to be understood in the strong sense of the clash of opposites; for instance, God is not half transcendent and half immanent, but wholly immanent. This may sound like a contradiction. It is so in terms of the logic of the finite, but not of the logic of the infinite. (p. 15)

In Chapter 13, 'A Dialectical Concept of God', we find that 'clash of opposites', of God as being and as nothing, as one and as many, as knowable and as incomprehensible, as transcendent and as immanent. It is the last mentioned opposition which concerns us. How is God both transcendent and immanent? MacQuarrie has already set aside the idea of First Cause. Instead, he posits in God's fullness of being an inner differentiation into what he calls three 'modes' which he goes on to describe, (not with his usual clarity and lightness of touch). I paraphrase: The primordial mode of his being is God in his superexistence and transcendent otherness. The expressive mode is God coming out from his hiddenness and mystery to bring a cosmos into being. Finally, there is the unitive mode, God as forming a new and richer unity of himself and his creation, a unity of himself and his creation, which includes distinctness. It is in the expressive and unitive modes that God is immanent, present in the whole of his creation (pp. 174–9).

The 'Mediated Immediacy' of God: Karl Rahner

I base myself on two sections of *Foundations of the Christian Faith*: 'Some Basic Epistemological problems' (pp. 14–23) and 'Finding God in the World' (pp. 81–9).[4] His epistemology is certainly basic. There are two kinds of knowing; there is a conceptual knowing, a categorical knowing, in which

4 Karl Rahner, *Foundations of Christian Faith: An Introduction to the Idea of Christianity* (London, 1978).

reality is mediated to us through a concept. This kind of knowing is sparked off by the everyday experiences of life and is elaborated into theoretical or scientific constructions (pp. 14–21). But there is another and a more fundamental kind: there is a non-conceptual or preconceptual knowing in which reality becomes immediately present to us without any concept. This is the kind of knowing which operates not for any and every experience of life but only for those deepest experiences in which we are confronted, challenged, by the very meaning or purpose of existence. On such occasions the reality of the infinite object of our deepest aspirations can never be captured by a concept; we tend towards it as a horizon (pp. 20–1). This transcendental knowing must be followed by reflection and conceptual knowing, must be steeped again in its deep experiential origins. Preconceptual knowing is *a priori*, unthematic; conceptual knowing is categorical, thematic, scientific.

God can be known by each of these kinds of knowledge. We need not delay over the conceptual knowledge, such as in the Five Ways. Rahner fully accepts the philosophy of Aquinas concerning this knowledge (cf. pp. 68–71, 86–8). It is the transcendental knowledge which concerns us. Rahner explains it thus:

> The original knowledge of God is not the kind of knowledge in which one grasps an object which happens to present itself directly or indirectly from outside. It has rather the character of a transcendental experience. Insofar as this subjective, non-objective luminosity of the subject in its transcendence is always orientated towards the holy mystery, the knowledge of God is always present unthematically and without name, and not just when we begin to speak of it. (p. 21)

Rahner later expands his treatment of this transcendental knowledge of God as 'holy mystery' (cf. pp. 57–68).

We pass to 'Finding God in the World' (pp. 81–9). Rahner is concerned not so much with God's existence in the world as with our finding him. The problem is that God is everywhere and he is nowhere, everywhere as the ground of everything that is, nowhere as an existent within the world (cf. pp. 81–3).

> The presence of God as the transcendental ground and horizon of everything which exists and everything which knows (and this is a presence of God, an immediacy to him) takes place precisely in and through the presence of the finite existent. (p. 83)

> As God he does not have to find a place by having something else which is not him make room. (p. 93)

The 'mediated immediacy to God' is not a contradiction: the categorical appearance of the finite existent in its concreteness and finiteness does not in itself reveal God himself 'but only in its character of pointing to the modality of this transcendental relationship to God which gives immediacy' (p. 85). In other words in the transcendental knowledge of God, the intellect is not a neutral faculty but is oriented towards him as the source of salvation.

II: AQUINAS

God is in all things and in all places

Contemporary thinking is dominated by the opposition of the transcendence and the immanence of God. Aquinas does not use the terms of a later age, 'transcendence' and 'immanence': the idea that they vary in inverse ratio would be foreign to him. He uses the word *praesentia*, but not in our sense of 'presence'. *Praesentia* means 'awareness', in particular, the 'awareness that one in charge has of all that is under his authority. Thus, for Aquinas the presence of God means that awareness of God as lord of creation, to whose gaze all things are naked and open. For Aquinas then the word is neither 'immanence' or 'presence', but that most fundamental of all terms: 'being', or more precisely, 'being in'. With that one word we are introduced immediately into the very heart of metaphysics. His thinking, however, was not timeless, unconditioned by history. He was well aware of those contemporaries who denied the omnipresence of God: the Manichaeans who excluded God from the material world, some Platonists who held that his providence extended only to the highest things, and the Averroists who excluded him from individual corruptible things. It is no wonder then that he treats of God's presence in a great variety of contexts: in connection with God's knowledge in Book One of the Commentary on the *Sentences*, treating of divine providence in the Third Book of the *Summa Contra Gentiles*, with respect to creation and conservation in Questions Three and Five of *The Power of God (De Potentia)*, and in dealing with God's infinity in the *Summa Theologiae*, which is the principle source for this theme. It is scarcely necessary to recall that his thinking is analogical, not univocal or unidimensional; thus, to interpret presence, nearness or distance spatially would be to miss everything.

God is in all things as the cause of being

I base myself on the *Summa Theologiae* I, 8. It will clarify the problem if we hear some of the objections and the replies to them:

a. What is in a thing cannot be above that thing. But God is infinitely above every created thing. Therefore, he cannot be in any created thing. Aquinas replies: God is infinitely above every created thing because of the perfection of his nature; but he is in everything because he is the cause of the existence of everything (*ST*, I, 8, 1 ad 1; cf. *In I Sent.*, 37, 1, 1 ad 1).

b. What is in a thing is contained by that thing. But God cannot be contained in a thing. Rather he 'contains', that is, 'sustains' everything in being. Aquinas answers: although bodily things are said to be in a thing as contained by the thing, spiritual things are said to be in something as 'containing', 'upholding' the thing, just as the soul upholds the body or sustains it (cf. *ST*, I, 8, 1, ad 2; *In I Sent.*, 37, 1, 1).

c. To be everywhere means to be in all places. But God cannot be in a place at all, and still less in all places, because he is incorporeal. Aquinas answers: God is not in a place as a body is in a place; a body is in a place because its dimensions or surface touch the surface of the encompassing body. But God is incorporeal and he is in a place because of the power or influence he exerts upon it (*ST*, I, 8, 2 ad 1).

What is the fundamental reason of God's presence in all things? It is that he and he alone is the cause of the very being, the very existence, of each and every thing. And he causes not only the beginning of existence but the continuation of existence as well, just as the sun causes light in the atmosphere as long as the air is lighted up:

> God is in all things not as part of their essence or as an accident but as an agent cause is present in that upon which it acts. It is necessary that every agent cause be joined to that upon which it acts immediately and to make contact with it by its active power. This is the reason why the mover and the moved must be together. But since God is being itself by his very essence it is necessary that created existence should be his proper effect; just as to cause something to burn is the proper effect of fire; and God causes this effect (existence) in things not only when they first begin to exist but as long as they are preserved in being just as light is caused in the atmosphere as long as the atmosphere is lighted up. (*ST*, I, 8, 1)[5]

The general principle, derived from Aristotle's *Physics,* need not detain us. Since an effect is that which comes from a cause, an immediate effect that would be disjoined, isolated, from its cause would be unintelligible. What does it mean to say that God is the cause of being, and that being, existence, is the proper effect of God? Misconceptions must be forestalled: firstly, there is no one definition of cause which will be applicable univocally both to God and to created causes. The concept of cause is neither univocal, nor yet equivocal, but analogical. Secondly, created causes are real causes producing real effects. They really act; they are not mere occasions for God to act, letting his activity pass through them like the window pane that gives no light itself but lets the light pass through. But God alone is the cause of existence; existence is his proper effect because his very essence is to be; he is subsistent being. A thing acts in accordance with what it is; just as a singer sings, or a builder builds, a fish swims, or a bird flies, so God and God alone causes things to be.

Things have not a kind of shadowy existence in a 'world of possibles', where God would intervene and confer real existence on them. This is a trick of the imagination; the 'world of possibles' is an unreal world, a non-existent

5   Cf. *In I Sent.*, 37, 1, 1; *Contra Gentiles* 3, 68; *De Potentia* 3, 1, and 4, *De Potentia* 5, 1, and 2.

world; there is no such thing as a real essence already complete and waiting for existence to come upon it; it is not real: it is just nothing. Hence God's presence in the whole world or in an individual thing is not the filling up of a pre-existing vacancy; his presence is not something following on his absence.

> The first effect is existence itself which is presupposed by all other effects and itself does not presuppose any other effects; therefore, it follows that to cause existence as such is the effect of the first cause alone in accordance with its own power. (*De Pot.*, 3, 4)

This is but one of many statements, and possibly the clearest, setting forth the altogether unique power of God over the very existence of things. As for the presence of God it is not something either before or after his giving of existence. His presence is his giving of existence and his giving of existence is himself; God's presence is God. Created causes of themselves cannot give existence. Altogether they are real causes, their causal power is limited; Aquinas uses various phrases to convey a single truth: God alone is his existence; no creature is its existence, all creatures *have* existence.

This is the fundamental reason why God alone can give the beginning of existence. It is also the reason why God alone can preserve things in existence:

> Just as it would imply a contradiction that God should make something which was not created by him; so too would it be if anybody were to say that God should make something which would not need to be kept in existence by him. (*De Pot.*, 5, 2)[6]

As for created causes, their causal power, though real and effective, is qualified, limited: hence Aquinas speaks of them as being causes 'only of the becoming of things' (*secundum fieri tantum*), only of being causes of such and such, not of being simply so called (*esse tale*, not *esse*), of operating not solely by their own power, but by the power of the first cause (*ex influentia causae primae*).

God is present in the inmost being of things

There are grades of 'being in': at the very centre of the thing, on the periphery, or in between the two. Aquinas is not content with saying that God is in things, he goes further; God is in the very inmost centre of each thing, at the very core of its being:

> As long therefore as a thing has existence, so long is it necessary that God should be present to it according to the degreee that it has existence. But existence is that which is inmost in each thing and which is deepest in everything; since it is the formal reality in respect to everything which is in a thing, as is clear from what has been said above. (*ST*, I, 7, 1) From which it follows that God must be in all things and that too in their inmost being. [*ST*, I, 8, 1)

6 Cf. *CG,* 3, 65; *ST,* I, 104, 1.

Intimus does not mean 'intimate'; it means 'inmost' or 'innermost'. Another point; let us note that emphatic position of *et intime* at the end. Aquinas does not say 'God is inmost in things', but 'God is in things and that too in their inmost being'. The same emphasis can be seen in his Commentary on the *Sentences:* 'it is necessary that God should be in each thing in its inmost being, just as the existence of the thing which is of all things innermost' (*In I Sent.*, 37, 1, 1).

And so we come to the kernel of the argument; it turns on the comparison of essence and existence. Is existence the inmost reality in things? At first sight it does not seem to be. An essence can be consideed as fully constituted in everything that is necessary to it, before existence supervenes upon it. Therefore it would seem that essence is something interior in things, inmost in them, and that existence is something adventitious, something exterior. But Aquinas, in effect, points out that this would be to look at things from a material point of view, to approach things from a genetic or evoluntionary viewpoint, not from a formal or metaphysical viewpoint. Metaphysically existence is most formal in things.

Existence is the greatest perfection of all realities, because it is related to everything else as perfection is related to what can be perfected. Nothing has any perfection except in so far as it is. Hence existence is the ultimate perfection of everything and even of forms themselves. Hence it is related to everything else not as a receiver is related to something which is received, but rather as something which is received to a receiver (*ST,* I, 4, 1 ad 3). In other words, there are two ways of looking at things: the ascending order, the order of emergence, and the descending order, the order of participation. The latter is the metaphysical viewpoint; it is the viewpoint of Aquinas. He sees created things as sharing in their infinitely varied but limited ways in the being of the creator whose very essence is *to be.*

Aquinas and Spinoza agree on one thing: every determination is a negation. Side by side with their positive aspect, for example, being a rose or being a lion, essences have their negative aspect: a rose is not a daffodil, and a lion is not a gazelle. And neither the lion, nor the rose has of itself the perfection of existence. Essence, therefore, connotes determination to one species or grade of being; implying limitation, negation. And what is a negation cannot be at the centre, cannot be inmost; it can only be exterior to something positive, and that positive thing is existence; existence is at the centre. Likewise existence in things is their deepest reality. And the reason is the same: being is not founded on non-being—that would be the very definition of nihilism—it is the very opposite, non-being is founded on being. And so the conclusion follows: God, because he is the cause of existence, is at the very inmost reality of everything that exists. Chronologically, God's giving of existence and of his presence are at the same instant; ontologically, his giving of existence is first as it is the foundation of the relation of presence, a relation which is real on the side of the creature and notional on the side of God.

And so it can be said that God's presence to me precedes my presence to myself. No hyperbole, simply ontology.

God is present in all things as absolutely distinct, totally independent

Twentieth century theology and religious thinking are dominated by the opposition of transcendence and immanence, with a strong emphasis on immanence. Aquinas was not unaware of the polarity (see, for example, *ST*, I, 8, 1 ad 1). But for him, God's transcendence, far from being opposed to his immanence, is the very reason for his immanence. If God were not transcendent, that is, totally independent of the created universe, he would no longer be the universal and proper cause of existence (*ST*, I, 3, 8, and *ST*, I, 13, 11). And if he were not the proper cause of existence, he would not be the present in things, inmost in each one.

God is present in things as a simple being in composite beings

God is simple; he has no parts of any kind whatsoever. A being that has parts is dependent on the parts and subsequent to them, and thus dependent on an agent cause to bring those parts together (*ST*, I, 3, 7). All other things are composite; they have parts; at least their essence ('what they are') is really distinct from their existence ('that they are'). The simplicity of God is the simplicity of perfection, the simplicity of the fullness of being, not like the simplicity of a mathematical point which is the simplicity of imperfection, having the minimum reality. And so arises the question: how are we to conceive the presence of God in all things? Aquinas answers:

> It must not be thought that God is everywhere in such a way that he is divided up according to different places, a part of him here, a part of him there. (*CG*, 3, 68)

He is altogether outside the domain of continuous quantity because by his simple power he touches everything. God is not only beyond continuous quantity but also, by reason of his fullness of being, he is beyond the possibility of measurement; he is immeasurable, immense. What measure or independent standard could really be applied to him? His immensity, an absolute attribute, must be distinguished from his omnipresence which is a relative attribute; if God had not created the world, he would still be immense; but he would not be omnipresent because there would be no world for him to be present in.

God is present in all things as the ultimate end of their existence

Until now the focus has been on God as agent cause; he gives being or existence to things and he preserves them in existence. But a more fundamental question arises: Why does he give them being? Why does he preserve them in existence? These are necessary and inevitable questions. Merely to see things issuing from their efficient causes, to see products coming forth from their generative processes, is not to understand them in a fundamental way; it is not to know them in the full sense of knowing. It would be like the ancient Pre-socratics who viewed the world merely as a machine. We know how decisively Aristotle rejected this error, and before him, Anaxagoras. First among causes is the end, the final cause, 'the cause of causes'.

Aquinas has a passage, about as succinct and comprehensive as one could wish for, on the philosophy of final cause, on teleology:

> First among all causes is the final cause. The reason for this is that matter does not acquire a form except in so far as it is acted upon by an agent cause: for nothing can move itself from being potentially something, to being actually something. But an agent cause does not act except to attain some end (*ex intentione finis*). (*ST*, I–II, 1, 2)7

In this passage we have the broad and full concept, not the narrow concept of cause as a merely physical force impelling something forward extrinsically. Cause is an analogical concept not because causes are four in number but because they cause in four different ways. Let us concentrate on the final cause. Every agent acts for an end. This principle is absolutely universal; it holds for man in all his actions, even indeliberate. It holds without any metaphor or anthropomorphism for the things beneath man; it holds even for God himself, only that he does not act for a final cause because nothing in God is caused; but God acts for an end, and that end is himself.

The agent need not know the end, but some superior agent must know the end, some supreme intelligence (The Fifth Way). The end need not exist in reality; it moves, attracts the agent as it exists in his active powers in the form of an élan, an aim, an intention. Note the phrase *ex intentione finis* in the above passage. The *intentio* is the dynamic tendency inscribed in the agent, in every agent, without which it would never determine itself to act. It should be kept in mind that when we speak of the end 'moving' the agent, we are using 'move' in a metaphorical sense, in the sense of 'attracting', not in the sense of impelling.

Let us now ask the fundamental question: why is God present in all things? The answer is that he is present because he is the end or purpose of all things. Nowhere in the writings of Aquinas does this emerge more clearly than in Book 3 of the *Summa Contra Gentiles*. Chapters 64 to 68 are a veritable treatise on God's presence and God's providence. 'As a consequence it is clear that God must be everywhere and in all things.' These are the opening words of Chapter 68. As a consequence of what? He is present because he is 'the cause of operation of all things that operate' (Chapter 67). And he is the cause of operation because nothing acts except by divine power (Chapter 66). But nothing would exist so as to operate if God did not preserve things in being (Chapter 65). But why does God preserve things in being? Because he rules

---

7 Cf. *CG*, 3, 2; *In I Met.*, 4, 70–1 and *ST*, I, 5, 2 ad 1).

them by his providence, because he is the end or purpose of all things (Chapter 64).

So runs the argument, called by logicians a chain argument or enthymeme. Instead of going backward from Chapter 68, it would be possible to go forward from Chapter 64. The conclusion would be the same; God is present in things not only because he keeps them in existence, but more fundamentally because he wants to draw them towards himself. In order that things may attain their end he has placed in them an immanent urge or striving or law. Let us listen to one of his modern commentators, Walter Farrell:

> Everything in the universe hustles eagerly to this goal of goodness each in its own way; man with alert steps along the dangerous road of knowledge and love, brutes with the unerring aim of instinct, the inanimate world with the blind plodding step of physical necessity devoid of all knowledge.[8]

As we reflect on God's presence in the universe, we must try to see not only his creating and sustaining hand but also his inviting, providing and guiding hand as well.

God is present not as a blind force but as all seeing and supremely intelligent

This is the first consequence or aspect of God's providence. He is translucently aware of all things, foreseeing, or rather seeing everything, knowing the minutest detail of each individual thing and of the whole cosmos. This is the special meaning of 'presence' when Aquinas says that God is in all things by his essence, by his presence, by his power (cf. *ST*, I, 8, 3). No human ruler could achieve this all seeing vision.

God is present in things not as gaining but as giving

This is the second aspect of God's providential presence. When we say that God created things for himself and conserves or preserves them for himself, how are we to understand 'for himself'? We do not mean that God can gain anything from his creatures; he is infinitely rich. We mean that he gives existence to things so that his infinite goodness and riches can be shared, diffused; *bonum est diffusivum sui*.

> It must be said that to act in order to fulfil a need belongs only to an agent that is imperfect, that is able to act and to be acted upon. But this cannot be said of God. Therefore he alone is supremely liberal because he acts not for anything he can gain only on account of his goodness. (*ST*, I, 44, 4 ad 1)

God is the supreme, the only true altruist. Human agents even in their most admirable and most disinterested actions will always stand to gain something for themselves.

8 Walter Farrell, *A Companion to the Summa*, I (London, 1941), p. 63.

God is present in things not as visible but as unseen

This third consequence is in the nature of a caution. The existence of God is not a kind of immediate inference from man's infinite aspirations; that would be a modern form of the ontological argument. God indeed is the end that attracts man, and attracts everything else too. But the end need not exist in reality, and most often does not exist: now, for example, all we see is a green field; soon there will be a house in the field; but the house already exists in the mind and intention of the prospective owner, architect and builder. Sometimes indeed the end will never exist; a mirage in the desert will entice the weary traveller not less powerfully because it is a mere illusion; the El Dorado gave no less courage to the conquerors because it was a vain hope. We are brought back to the principle that the end excercises its causality as an intention. And this holds even when the end is God himself. If we do not prove his existence in some other way and if we are relying on our desires alone, then for all we know, we may be yearning for a non-existent God.

III: AQUINAS AND RECENT WRITERS COMPARED

How is one to compare thinkers who seem to belong to different worlds: Aquinas to the world of highly developed technical scholastic philosophy, and the modern writers to the world of more free flowing, more diffuse, more descriptive, and accessible religious writing? There is another difference: Moltmann, MacQuarrie, Rahner seem to be reacting against what they consider to be an overemphasis on God's transcendence. Aquinas approaches the consideration of God's presence from a more impartial standpoint. Let us now compare each in turn with Aquinas, remembering that their idea of God's presence will depend on their idea of God's nature. For Aquinas God's presence in things is the presence of a being whose very essence is to exist and who is present as creator, sustainer, provider, and who is at once inmost and absolutely transcendent.

The God described by Moltmann in his ecological theology is a God who is immersed in things by his Spirit, a God who is always with his people, lending the whole cosmos to a glorious transformation. This is an enriching biblical theology. The theology of Aquinas is also biblical but less obviously so. But when we come to the explanation of God's presence we see the immense difference. Moltmann has no place for the notion of cause; what he gives us is a description of God's presence, not an explanation: God is present as 'indwelling', 'sympathizing', 'glorifying' (*God in Creation*, p. 14). 'The creator is not an unmoved mover of the universe' (p. 87). Creation is explained as a kind of contraction and expansion of the divine substance itself, a kind of self-limitation followed by a diffusion of self (pp. 86–93). This is far removed from the causal metaphysics of Aquinas. In rejecting the use of causal analysis is Moltmann trying to posit or to presuppose a kind of extension within God himself? And if this is so, what of that perfect simplicity of God who is present in the world as the unextended in the extended?

Moltmann's thinking is really determined by a conscious choice described at the beginning of his work:

> If a doctrine of creation is to be ecological, it must try to get away from analytical thinking, with the distinction between subject and object, and must try to learn a new communicative and integrating way of thought. Modern thinking has developed by way of an objectifying, analytical, particularising and reductionalistic approach. (*God in Creation*, p. 2)

A distinction has to be made: there is an analysis, a material analysis, which is downward and reductionist; but there is another analysis, which is meta-physical, which is upwards and which seeks the highest explanation of things, the first cause. We must first distinguish before we can unite, and a causal analysis can never be dispensed with.

MacQuarrie rejects the view of God presented by Aquinas, who, he says, is among the best representatives of classical theism (cf. p. 31). This view of God he regards as too monarchical, too transcendent, too remote, not sufficiently qualified by God's immanence and humility. This rejection cannot be based on the texts of Aquinas himself who explains as clearly as one could wish why God is not only in things but is inmost in them; far from being opposed, his immanence which is altogether unique, is based on his transcendence. MacQuarrie's own view of God's nature is achieved by what he calls a dialectic, a selection of what is best in all the religious thinkers from antiquity to our own time. But the danger is that the dialectic can degenerate into the eclectic unless based on metaphysics, that is, unless it is based on being.

We have already seen the three modes of God's being, the primordial mode, the expressive mode, the unitive mode (*Search for Deity*, pp. 174–5). Later on he would favour a modification of the classical doctrine of creation by some form of Plotinus' doctrine of emanation (pp. 178–9); God should be regarded as imparting something of himself, especially to higher orders of creation. In these pages MacQuarrie bears a resemblance to Moltmann. But how can God, a simple being—in the strict philosophical sense of simple—go out of himself and return to himself? There is indeed a dipolarity, but it is not in the deity; it is the dipolarity between God, who is subsistent and simple, and creatures who have their existence from God and who are of necessity composite.

Unlike Moltmann and MacQuarrie whose approach is from ontology, Rahner approaches the consideration of God's presence from epistemology. In an article on the metaphysics of God's presence it would be a lacuna not to say something about epistemology because epistemology, as a critical and fundamental reflection on our knowledge, is an intrinsic part of metaphysics. Aquinas too has an extensive epistemology of God and of his presence; it is the famous question twelve of *Summa Theologiae I*. But the difference is significant: the epistemological parenthesis of Aquinas is a reflection upon God whose existence and whose presence are already securely established; for Rahner epistemology is a presupposition, something to be investigated and decided beforehand, as a basis for philosophy and for the knowledge of God's existence. Again, Rahner sets great value on what he calls non-conceptual knowledge, a knowledge which is unthematic, fundamental, transcendental. Is there a non-conceptual knowledge of God? Aquinas would agree that there is; it is the knowledge of the beatific vision (cf. *ST*, I, 12, 9 and 11). But as long as we are in the conditions of this life, a non-conceptual knowledge of God is not possible. Things act in accordance with their nature, and man comes to know things, also spiritual things, even God, by means of his psychophysical nature, that is by means of concepts derived from material things (cf. *ST*, I, 12, articles 2, 3, and 11). Indeed whether in this life or the next God's presence will always remain to the created intellect incomprehensible, a mystery.

Rahner has much to say about immediacy, even 'mediated immediacy', but what he is referring to is the immediacy of God to our knowing. When Aquinas speaks of immediacy he means the immediacy of things to the first cause of their existence. Rahner is right to emphasize the orientation or dynamism of man. But that dynamism must be considered more closely, located more correctly. Is it right to speak of a dynamism of intellect as such? Is it not the role of the intellect to present to the appetitive powers a choice of goods, of objectives, in a way that is neutral, impartial? There is indeed a dynamism in the appetitive powers, as their very name applies. It is the intention (*intentio*) of which we have spoken. But unless we have an independent proof, the object of even our deepest yearnings may be a good which is merely imaginary.

I have left to the end those for whom God is an absentee, namely, the secular humanists. What they need, at least at the beginning, is a Socrates rather than an Aquinas. They must somehow be brought to ask: 'Has man any other needs and yearnings than those that we affirm and promote: the complete realization of human personality, a heightened sense of personal being, a more humane social framework?' Their unspoken presupposition is that God and man are rivals in the achievement of these aims. On the contrary, God is neither a rival nor an absentee but the ever present source of our existence and the ultimate destiny of our striving. To bring them around to this realization is the first step. At a further stage is philosophy; academic philosophy may be only for the few. Historically it was a philosophy, eighteenth century deism, which was the fount and origin of secular humanism. There is another philosophy, that of Aquinas, which is the basis of a more satisyfing humanism, a humanism which encompasses not just some but all of man's aspirations.

Divine Immutability and Impassibility Revisited

GERALD HANRATTY

Shortly before his death the philosopher Jacques Maritain addressed an urgent appeal to theologians. At a time when loss of faith, rebellion against God and spiritual despair were widespread, there was 'an immense problem' which was insulated against critical reflection by almost impregnable linguistic barriers. The problem, which presented itself in such an acute form, was the perennial one of the use of our concepts and language to refer to God and his attributes. More specifically, the venerable tradition which ascribed the attributes of immutability and impassibility to God had contributed to the decline of belief in a century which had witnessed unprecedented levels of oppression and suffering. 'If people realised', Maritain wrote, 'that God "suffers" with us and is even more vulnerable than we are to all the evils which ravage the earth, the situation would undoubtedly change and many souls would be delivered from unbelief.'[1]

Predictably, there was no facile repudiation of Thomistic philosophical and theological principles in Maritain's tentative proposals for an amelioration of the enigma of human suffering and divine impassibility. In so far as suffering was a privation and a mark of imperfection, it could not be ascribed to God. Nevertheless, St Thomas' magisterial account of analogical predication could be extended to comprehend experiences and insights which were frequently expressed in poetry and mystical literature but could not be accommodated in the unwieldy rational categories of classical theology. In his account of analogical predication, St Thomas insisted that our capacity to ascribe specific perfections to God was narrowly circumscribed and that the divine perfections differed essentially (*secundum rationem*) from those which were accessible to us. Our faltering attempts to analogically extend our concepts and language were trivial in comparison with the unlimited sea of unnamed and unnameable perfections in the divine nature. But it was precisely this radical agnostic strand in St Thomas' theology which opened the door to an adjustment of the tradition which insisted on divine immutability and impassibility. Human suffering—and the sublime values so often associated with it—simply had to be replicated in the inscrutable depths of the Godhead. 'It is only in a metaphorical sense', Maritain asserted, 'that we can deploy the concept and word "suffering" in our reflection and talk about God. Nevertheless, we must admit that among the divine perfections there is a *nameless* and eternal

---

1 Jacques Maritain, 'Quelques réflexions sur le savoir théologique', *Revue Thomiste* 77 (1969), 25.

exemplar of suffering and of the personal nobility so often associated with it.'[2] This concession, Maritain argued, would at least erase the false and unchristian image of a remote and insensitive deity who remained eternally indifferent to the struggles and sufferings of his creatures.

Maritain's plea is only one in a chorus of voices from various points on the theological and philosophical spectrum which calls for the modification or abandonment of the traditional emphasis on divine immutability and impassibility. At the most general level it is argued that classical theology, with its stress on God's changeless perfection, is incompatible with the modern sensibility which sets a higher value on change and development. This criticism is frequently linked with the further charge that classical theology, because of its indiscriminate borrowing from the Greek metaphysics of being, could neither assimilate nor transmit the most profound truth of Christian revelation—that God is love. Furthermore, many critics share Maritain's view that classical theology engendered an image of a perfectly self-contained and serenely unconcerned monarchical Creator. And this image contributed in turn to the emergence and wide diffusion of the many varieties of atheistic humanism.

In response to these apparently conclusive objections many theologians have drawn on the resources of Process Philosophy in their attempts to construct a more appropriate Christian theology and a more credible account of the mysteries of Creation, Incarnation and Redemption. In the original Process perspective of A. N. Whitehead it is simply assumed that an immutable and impassible God is not 'religiously available'. Whitehead's complex metaphysical system is based on categories such as creativity, change, relation and temporality. Moreover, these categories extend into the theological sphere, since God is not exempt from the general metaphysical principles which are discernible in the intra-cosmic domain. In the Whiteheadian scheme, then, God is envisaged as the highest instantiation of the 'creativity' or dynamism which pervades all levels of reality. Whitehead also distinguishes two poles or natures in God. There is a 'primordial' and self-contained, if unconscious and un-actualized, nature. The 'consequent' nature, on the other hand, represents the actualized or conscious dimension of the divinity. Most importantly, there is an open-ended relationship of mutual dependence between God and the world. 'Neither God, nor the World', Whitehead argues, 'reaches static completion. Both are in the grip of the ultimate metaphysical ground, the creative advance into novelty. Either of them, God and the World, is the instrument of novelty for the other.'[3] In this framework there is, of course, no place for a self-subsistent God who creates the world without recourse to any pre-existing material and sustains it by his omnipotent power. Instead, Whitehead's God is a function of the universal

2   Ibid., p. 23.
3   Alfred North Whitehead, *Process and Reality: An Essay in Cosmology* (New York, 1960), p. 529.

dynamism or 'creativity' and depends on the world in his ongoing project of self-creation and self-actualization. Moreover, this metaphysical scheme, which places God and the world in relationships of mutual dependence, effectively rebuts the standard objections to the immutable and impassible God of classical theology. As a participant in the cosmic process and a sympathetic collaborator in human existence, God is susceptible to the vicissitudes and afflictions of the human condition. In a frequently quoted phrase, God is taken to be 'the great companion—the fellow-sufferer who understands'.[4]

Whitehead's critique of classical theology—and his dipolar understanding of the divine nature—have been revised and expanded by numerous successors. For one of the most influential contemporary representatives of Process thought, Charles Hartshorne, God is 'the Worshipful One', who, although surpassing in perfection all others, must nevertheless 'in some respects be self-surpassable'. It follows that there is a capacity for change or the acquisition of further perfection in God. Drawing on the Whiteheadian legacy, Hartshorne elaborated a dipolar theology in which the 'abstract' or absolute dimensions of God are complemented by 'concrete' or relative and dependent dimensions. But while Hartshorne's worshipful and unsurpassable One is closer to traditional theology than Whitehead's demiurgic fellow-sufferer, his God is nevertheless affected by the cosmic process. Even more importantly, Process theology makes possible a coherent and persuasive articulation of the crucial truth of Christianity—that God is love:

> A deity who cannot in any sense change or have contingent properties is a being for whom whatever happens in the contingent world is literally a matter of indifference. Such a being is 'impassive' toward all things, utterly insensitive and unresponsive. This is the exact denial that 'God is love.' It means that nothing we can possibly do, enjoy, or suffer can in any way whatever contribute a satisfaction or value to the divine life greater or different from what that life would have possessed had we never existed or had our fortunes been radically other than they are. Strange that for so many centuries it was held legitimate to call such a deity a God of love, or purpose, or knowledge.[5]

Because Process thought seems to resolve what are perceived as the antinomies of classical theology, and because of its theoretical cohesion and attunement to modern sensibilities, theologians in both the Catholic and Protestant traditions believe that it provides a framework for a credible modern formulation of the Christian faith. Thus David Tracy argues, with only minor reservations, that Process thought supplies the most appropriate conceptual and linguistic instruments for a viable contemporary apologetics. For Tracy, 'the dipolar concept of God is at once internally coherent as a concept, true to our common experience, and true to the Scriptural meaning

---

4 Ibid., p. 532.
5 Charles Hartshorne and William Reese, *Philosophers Speak of God* (Chicago, 1953), p. 20.

of God.'[6] From a 'creative neo-Thomist' standpoint, and with greater reservations than Tracy concerning the compatibility of Process metaphysics with Christian faith, W. Norris Clarke nevertheless admits that discussion with Process thinkers has convinced him that the traditional strict insistence on divine immutability and impassibility must be modified. While there can be no compromise on God's status as the absolute and supremely perfect creative cause of the universe, the Thomist thesis—that God is not really related to or affected by his creatures—is ill-adapted to the modern mentality. Distinguishing between 'the infinite Plenitude of God's intrinsic inner being and perfection' and his 'relational consciousness', Norris Clarke has no hesitation in affirming that God is really related to and affected by his creatures at the level of his relational or personal consciousness. Moreover, in the context of this new and more appropriate personalist understanding of divine perfection and of the mutual relations between God and creatures, we can conclude that our suffering is sympathetically replicated in the divine consciousness. Like Maritain, Norris Clarke argues that we should 'admit in the divine consciousness something corresponding to what we would call compassion (suffering-with-us, wounded love etc.) but purified of all that would be genuine imperfection'.[7]

Taking up the appeal of David Tracy and others for a viable modern apologetics and theology, Joseph A. Bracken advocates an even more extensive utilization of Process metaphysics in the construction of 'a neo-Whiteheadian synthesis of Christian belief'. Since Process is the basic metaphysical principle, there can be no question of ascribing immutable perfection to God. Following Hartshorne's line, Bracken argues that God, although unsurpassable by others, can nevertheless acquire further perfection. And when the doctrine of the Trinity is understood in the light of Hartshorne's metaphysics, God is found to be 'a community of three divine persons who are constantly growing in knowledge and love of one another and who are thus themselves in process even as they constitute the divine community as a specifically social process.'[8]

Since Process theologians believe that the confluence of Christianity and the Greek metaphysics of being and substance was responsible for a distorted understanding of God as an immutable and impassible being, it is not surprising that they have elaborated a revised Christology in the light of their purified concept of revelation. From a standpoint in which it is assumed that God is capable of further self-actualization and is really related to and

6 David Tracy, *Blessed Rage for Order: The New Pluralism in Theology* (New York, 1975), p. 179.

7 W. Norris Clarke, *The Philosophical Approach to God: A Neo-Thomist Perspective* (Winston-Salem, 1979), pp. 99–100.

8 Joseph A. Bracken, *The Triune Symbol: Persons, Process and Community* (Lanham, 1985), p. 7. For a further attempt to construct a theology of the Trinity on Process foundations, see John J. O'Donnell, *Trinity and Temporality: The Christian Doctrine of God in the Light of Process Theology and the Theology of Hope* (Oxford, 1983).

dependent on the world, Christ is seen as a particularly significant illustration of general metaphysical principles. In the words of one of the most prominent exponents of Process Christology, Norman Pittenger, Christ is the 'chief exemplification . . . of those "principles" which are required to explain, make sense of, and give the proper setting for whatever goes on in the entire process of God in relationship to man and man in relation to God.'[9] Or, in another key, Christology is presented according to the exigencies of Hartshorne's dipolar theology. On the one hand, faith in Jesus Christ points to God's 'abstract', independent, or absolute nature; but it also reflects his 'concrete' or dependent nature which 'is conditioned by the relativities and contingencies of world process, even to the point of appropriating that process at each of its successive stages into its own destiny.'[10]

With notable exceptions such as Norris Clarke, theologians who draw on Process thought admit that, since change is the ultimate principle of reality, the time-honoured ascription of immutability and impassibility to God must be abandoned. In response to the standard modern criticisms of classical theology, and in order to elaborate a specifically Christian understanding of God, others have found appropriate categories for a modification of the intransigent traditional emphasis on divine immutability and impassibility in Hegel's philosophy. Towards the end of an exhaustive account of Hegel's speculative penetration of Christian revelation, Hans Küng concludes that, since the Hegelian system proposes a dynamic and dialectical conception of God or Absolute Spirit, it is a congenial framework for a distinctively Christian theology. Because the system portrays God as a dialectical being or a coincidence of opposites, it is an apt instrument for the comprehension of the Christian mysteries of the incarnation, passion, and death of the Son. And in Küng's view, the Hegelian understanding of the divine nature avoids the pitfalls of the traditional theology which envisaged God as an inert and insensitive monarch:

> The living God is for Hegel the one who moves, changes and undergoes a history, who does not rigidly *remain* what he is, but *becomes* what he is. And he is the God who does not stubbornly remain within himself in a lofty posture of splendid isolation above the world, but who comes out of himself and externalizes himself in the becoming of the world, a movement which comes to a climax when God himself becomes man. According to Hegel this God is the true, the Christian God; and so according to him the true God is the one who as infinite fullness comprehends all antitheses in unity in himself. He does not pallidly hover, severed from everything else as a grey Absolute, but lives in many forms as the one, all-encompassing Spirit. It is the God

9   Norman Pittenger, *Christology Reconsidered* (London, 1970), p. 68.
10 Thomas W. Ogletree, 'A Christological Assessment of Dipolar Theism' in *Process Philosophy and Christian Thought*, ed. Delwin Brown, Ralph E. James, Jr., and Gene Reeves (Indianapolis, 1971), p. 346.

who does not suffer antitheses to congeal statically in themselves, but thrusts them out into the world, suffering along with them and reconciling them into unity; it is the God who, precisely in this externalization into the world, which reaches its revealed pinnacle in the incarnation and death on the cross, manifests the inmost depths of his heart. In brief, according to Hegel, the true God is the one who is both finite and infinite, both God and man in unity.[11]

Although Küng has some reservations about the pantheistic and deterministic features of Hegel's system, he is convinced that it is a more apt vehicle for a truly Christian theology than the Greek metaphysics which resolutely excluded life and becoming from the divine nature. Küng does not question God's unlimited perfection; but, he argues, the venerable insistence on divine impassibility cannot be verified in Scripture. Instead, 'it occurred more in the form of a self-evident axiom, taken over in practice from Plato's theory of God.'[12] Nor can the biblical references to divine immutability be translated without remainder into the categories of Greek metaphysics. Whereas the Parmenidean, Platonic, Aristotelian, and Stoic theologies portrayed God as a self-subsistent and static being, biblical references to God's immutability should not be construed in a metaphysical sense but rather 'in the historical sense of his essential fidelity to himself and to his promises, guaranteeing permanence and continuity in his action'.[13]

In a somewhat different key, reflection on the significance of the crucifixion is taken as a point of departure for a revision of classical theology and an exclusion of the extraneous metaphysical influences which obfuscate the true face of God. From the standpoint of a theology of the cross, Jürgen Moltmann argues that the crucifixion is the absolutely unique—and scandalous—event which demolishes all philosophical idols and demands a 'revolution in the concept of God'. For such a revolutionary theology the attributes of immutability and impassibility are marks of deficiency rather than perfection. In Moltmann's words, 'a God who cannot suffer is poorer than any man. For a God who is incapable of suffering is a being who cannot be involved. . . . And because he is so completely insensitive, he cannot be affected or shaken by anything. . . . But the one who cannot suffer cannot love either'.[14] However, Jesus' experience of abandonment and his death on the cross reveal that suffering, and therefore love, are constitutive of God's nature. Moreover, it is the cross which brings into view the dialectical, and therefore trinitarian, nature of God. The cross, on which the Father and Son are alienated from each other, represents a contradiction and even a

11   Hans Küng, *The Incarnation of God: An Introduction to Hegel's Theological Thought as Prolegomena to a Future Christology*, trans. J. R. Stephenson (Edinburgh, 1987), pp. 433–4.
12   Ibid., p. 525.
13   Ibid., p. 533.
14   Jürgen Moltmann, *The Crucified God: The Cross of Christ as the Foundation and Criticism of Christian Theology*, trans. R. A. Wilson and John Bowden (London, 1974), p. 222.

'bifurcation' in the divine nature. But it also reveals that suffering in all its forms is incorporated into the life or history of God. Even more importantly, the cross is the supreme manifestation of God's reconciling love. For it is from the mutual separation and suffering of the Father and Son on the cross that the Spirit of reconciliation and salvation proceeds. 'Because this death took place in the history between Father and Son on the cross on Golgotha,' Moltmann writes, 'there proceeds from it the spirit of life, love and election to salvation. . . . There is no suffering which in this history of God is not God's suffering; no death which has not been God's death in the history of Golgotha. Therefore there is no life, no future and no joy which have not been integrated by his history into eternal life, the eternal joy of God.'[15] In Moltmann's view, this revolutionary conception of a suffering and therefore loving God is the only effective antidote to the widespread phenomenon of protest atheism which has emerged in response to the traditional portrayal of God as an all-powerful and invulnerable creator and ruler.

With less enthusiasm for revolutionary novelty, Eberhard Jüngel and Heribert Mühlen also argue that the traditional conception of a changeless and impassible God must be revised in the light of a theology of the cross and the trinity. Like Moltmann, Jüngel believes that Christian revelation leads us to dialectical thinking in our attempts to elucidate the divine reality. The cross can only be understood therefore in terms of a radical self-differentiation in God; the crucifixion and death of the Son is a revelation of the supreme paradox that God is 'a living unity of life and death'. But even in the separation of God from God on the cross, unity is maintained through the loving and reconciling bond of the Spirit. And according to Jüngel, we simply cannot explicate this Christian revelation of God's nature by means of the classical category of inert and invulnerable being. There must be a significant adjustment, therefore, in the classical doctrine of God. 'For this distinction between God and God based on the cross of Jesus Christ', Jüngel writes, 'has destroyed the axiom of absoluteness, the axiom of apathy, and the axiom of immutability, all of which are unsuitable axioms for the Christian concept of God.'[16] Like Küng, Jüngel acknowledges that theology is indebted to Hegel for this decisive reformulation of the Christian doctrine of God. For his part, Mühlen is convinced that, since classical consciousness has been superseded by a modern mentality which envisages reality as a dynamic and evolving whole, theology must be dehellenized. In a cultural context where the questions and experiences which lead to belief in God are frequently suppressed, new ways must be found to present the true face of the Christian God. But this urgent apologetic task 'is almost impossible within the traditional horizon of the all-cosmic understanding of being from

---

15   Ibid., p. 246.
16   Eberhard Jüngel, *God as the Mystery of the World: On the Foundation of the Theology of the Crucified One in the Dispute between Theism and Atheism*, trans. Darrell L. Guder (Edinburgh, 1983), p. 373.

which only the omnipotent and apathetic face of the Platonic God addresses us'.[17] Once more, then, a theology of the cross is seen as an effective antidote to classical or 'deistic' theology and as a viable horizon for a contemporary 'personalistic' understanding of the revealed God. From this horizon, the metaphysical or 'theo-ontological' attributes of immutability and impassibility are interpreted in terms of God's unfailing presence to his people. Seen from the perspective of salvation history, biblical and dogmatic references to God's immutability do not designate his inert, invulnerable, and self-contained being; rather, they encapsulate his abiding fidelity to his covenant and his promises to his people.[18]

In response to the insistent modern demands for the dehellenization of Christianity and the elaboration of a theology which would show the true face of God, even more traditionally-minded theologians take the line of Maritain and Norris Clarke in arguing for some amelioration of the long-standing emphasis on God's metaphysical immutability and immunity from suffering. Thus, while Jean Galot accepts that God's being is indeed eternally and immutably perfect and that this metaphysical attribute cannot be reduced to his abiding fidelity to his promises, he nevertheless concludes that classical theology was unduly influenced by Greek philosophy. This unwarranted influence is particularly evident in the Thomistic thesis that God is not really related to his creatures. This framework exaggerates God's metaphysical isolation and precludes a full appreciation of the doctrine of the Incarnation and of the revealed truth of God's love for his creatures. In Galot's words, God 'takes the initiative in establishing real relations with human persons. Hence it cannot be said that on his part these relations are not real, whereas they are real on the part of the human beings who turn to him. It is God who confers reality on his covenant with men and who by his actions, his involvement, cements very profound relationships of love with mankind.'[19] In our stumbling attempts to understand God's being and his real involvement with his creatures, we are compelled, Galot argues, to acknowledge a distinction in the divine nature. From an abstract standpoint, God is, as the tradition maintained, the immutably perfect and transcendent pure act of

---

17 Heribert Mühlen, *Die Veränderlichkeit Gottes als Horizont einer zukünftigen Kreuztheologie: Auf dem Wege zu einer Kreuztheologie in Auseinandersetzung mit der altkirchlichen Christologie* (Münster, 1969), p. 9.

18 Mühlen's understanding of biblical and dogmatic references to divine immutability is shared of course by Hans Küng and other contemporary theologians. See: Wilhelm Maas, *Unveränderlichkeit Gottes: Zum Verhältnis von griechisch-philosophischer und christlicher Gotteslehre* (München/Paderborn/Wien, 1974); Wolfhart Pannenberg, 'The Appropiation of the Philosophical Concept of God as a Dogmatic Problem of Early Christian Theology' in *Basic Questions in Theology*, Vol. 2 (London, 1971), pp. 119–83. According to Pannenberg, 'the fact that God does not change in his acts is an expression not of an immutability constitutive of his essence but rather of his free momentary, humanly unanticipatible decision, just as much as his creative activity. It is identical with the faithfulness of God' (pp. 161–2).

19 Jean Galot, *Who is Christ?* (Chicago, 1980), p. 277.

existing. But God's involvement with creatures in Creation and Incarnation indicates that there is a mutable and free expression which is distinct from the necessary order of his being. 'The love at work in salvation conforms to the love proper to the eternal divine being', Galot writes, 'but remains distinct from it. Its fundamental characteristic is precisely that it is freely given and cannot be reduced to the necessary being of God.'[20] On the basis of this distinction between the necessary and free orders of the divine nature, Galot also argues that God freely chooses to subject himself to suffering. Drawing on Moltmann and others, Galot concludes that love and suffering are inseparable and that revelation testifies that the passion of the Son is replicated in the Father. However, suffering does not involve any diminution in God's unlimited perfection. When we attribute suffering to God, we are not referring to the immutable intra-divine relationships of love between the Persons of the Trinity but to the supremely free and gratuitous love which God offers to his creatures. Once more, we must distinguish between the necessary and free orders in the divine nature. 'In God', Galot argues, 'we must not confuse the free and gratuitous love which he offers to humanity with the intra-divine love which remains completely invulnerable. However profound the divine suffering, it can never impinge on the necessary sphere of God's being.'[21]

Responding to the modern objections to classical theology, Hans Urs von Balthasar also accepts that, if God is absolutely immutable and impassible, there cannot be an adequate appreciation of divine self-emptying in the mystery of salvation. Von Balthasar traces a tentative line of development through what can only be a 'narrow pass'. On the one hand, the force of the dogmatic affirmations of divine immutability and impassibility must be preserved; but in the light of the doctrine of the Trinity and the *kenosis* of the Son in the Incarnation and Passion, we must ascribe an extra dimension to God—an inexhaustible 'supra-fullness' or 'ever-more'—which is not expressed in the clearcut dogmatic affirmations of immutability and impassibility. A theology of the cross thus leads to the paradoxical conclusion that immutability and 'supra-mutability', and impassibility and supreme vulnerability, are mysteriously united in God. Von Balthasar agrees therefore with the assertions of a contemporary exegete that revelation 'compels us to modify the traditional conception of divine immutability' and to accept that 'God himself is really affected by the suffering of the Son, although this suffering brings no diminution to his divinity.'[22] In a more radical key Walter Kasper highlights the baneful influence of Greek philosophy on classical theology.

20 Ibid., p. 276.
21 Jean Galot, *Il Mistero della Sofferenza di Dio* (Assisi, 1975), p. 149.
22 Hans Urs von Balthasar, *Pâques le Mystère*, trans. R. Givord (Paris, 1981), p. 37. There is a valuable account of von Balthasar's thought on divine immutability and impassibility in Gerry O' Hanlon SJ, 'Does God Change?—H. U. von Balthasar on the Immutability of God', *Irish Theological Quarterly* 53 (1987), 161–83. Von Balthasar's position is reflected in François Varillon, *La Souffrance de Dieu* (Paris, 1975).

In a philosophical context the existence of God was affirmed in response to questions about the ultimate ground of the existence, unity, and meaning of all things. But the philosophers' God was a metaphysically isolated unmoved mover. 'Because he never changes he can never do anything', Kasper comments, 'no life goes out from him, he is dead. Nietzsche's "God is dead" is therefore only the final implication of this form of Western metaphysics.'[23] It is essential, therefore, to subject the traditional conception of an immutable God to a Christological critique which will focus on the historical involvement of the biblical God of life and love. And in Kasper's view the Idealist philosophies of Fichte, Schelling and Hegel are more appropriate instruments for Christian theology than the categories of Greek metaphysics.[24]

The fact that Christianity encountered Greek culture at such an early stage undoubtedly exercised a profound influence, not only on its missionary strategy, but on the apologetics and theology of the church of the early centuries. In the apostolic and post-apostolic ages the conceptual and linguistic resources of Greek philosophy were deployed in order to implant the Christian seed in the dominant culture of the Mediterranean world. Since Christians claimed from the beginning that they possessed superior answers to the search for truth and salvation, they simply had to translate the content of revelation into the philosophical idiom which had already attained a universal perspective. Yet, although Christian apologists and theologians drew freely on the Greek philosophical tradition in their defence and explication of revelation, and although many of them believed that philosophy represented a providential anticipation of the conclusive revelation in the coming of the Logos, they tenaciously safeguarded the original revelation and repelled all attempts to assimilate Christianity to any of the varieties of Greek philosophy. On a range of crucial issues, including God's transcendence, the origin of the universe, the distinction and relations between the Creator and his creatures, divine and human freedom, the question of evil, and the nature and destiny of the human soul, the early Church gradually extracted the distinctive implications of revelation. The greatest challenge was to construct a metaphysical framework which would accommodate the essential truths that God is love and that the relations between the Creator and his creatures are in the order of charity and gift rather than necessity and fate.[25] Furthermore, it was on this distinctive metaphysical base that the early

---

23 Walter Kasper, *Jesus the Christ*, trans. V. Green (London/New York, 1977), p. 82.
24 See *Jesus the Christ*, p. 183. It is worth noting that Kasper changed his position on the role of metaphysics in the development of classical theology. Referring to the confluence of the biblical and philosophical traditions in classical theology, Kasper writes: 'Even, and in fact precisely, the God who is conceived with the help of the categories of classical metaphysics is not a dead God but in the highest possible measure a living God.' Cf. *The God of Jesus Christ*, trans. Matthew J. O' Connell (London, 1983), p. 150.
25 On the emergence of a distinctive metaphysics in early Christianity, see Claude Tresmontant, *La métaphysique du christianisme et la naissance de la philosophie chrétienne* (Paris, 1961). For a sympathetic discussion of the encounter between Christianity and Greek culture, see Werner Jaeger, *Early Christianity and Greek Paideia* (Oxford, 1969).

Church gradually built an elaborate doctrinal and dogmatic structure. It is significant, therefore, that it was against a background of Greek, most notably Platonic, philosophy that the protracted trinitarian and christological controversies occurred. From the beginning Christianity had to give an account of its totally novel claim that Jesus Christ was true God and true man. The attainment of conceptual and linguistic clarity about the Incarnation, and the condemnation of Arius' denial of the divinity of the Logos at the Council of Nicea in 325, represented a radical break with a theology which was based on the Platonic legacy. According to Thomas G. Weinandy, 'the *homoousion* doctrine has utterly purged Christianity of the Platonic One and all its implications.'[26] Moreover, reflection on, and fidelity to, the sources of revelation led to an equally radical break with Platonic and Stoic notions of emanation. From the perspective of the Greek metaphysics of the One, and the concomitant assumption that all emanations from the One are imperfect or secondary realities, there could be no coherent expression of the revealed truths that the one God is a trinity of persons, each of whom is really and truly divine and one of whom, the Son or Logos, became man.

For the most part, the trinitarian and christological controversies of the early Christian centuries were concerned with the adaptation of Greek philosophical categories to the exigencies of a theology of charity, liberty, life and grace. There is no basis therefore for the frequently repeated charge that the early Church borrowed indiscriminately from Greek philosophy and thus compromised the original force of revelation. The goal of apologetic and patristic reflection was the precise articulation of the truths contained in the sources of revelation. In order to explain, safeguard, and propagate these truths, the early Church had to translate the concrete, descriptive and kerygmatic language of the Bible into explanatory or philosophical categories. And the transposition of the religious experience of the biblical authors into the modes of theological and philosophical understanding gave rise in turn to the doctrinal formulations of the decisive ecumenical Councils of the early Church.[27]

In the light of the protracted and often contentious course of doctrinal development in the early Christian centuries, there is no justification for the claim that the God of patristic and classical theology was a remote, inert and impassive monarch. Yet, as the Church appropriated and articulated its faith

---

26 Thomas G. Weinandy OFM. Cap., *Does God change? The Word's Becoming in the Incarnation* (Massachusetts, 1985), p. 16.

27 Cf. Aloys Grillmeier SJ, *Christ in Christian Tradition: From the Apostolic Age to Chalcedon (451)*, trans. John Bowden (London/Oxford, 1975), pp. 555–556: 'On closer inspection, the christological "heresies" turn out to be a compromise between the original message of the Bible and the understanding of it in Hellenism and Paganism. It is here that we have the real Hellenization of Christianity. The formulas of the Church, whether they are the *homoousios* of Nicea or the Chalcedonian Definition, represent the *lectio difficilior* of the gospel, and maintain the demand for faith and the stumbling-block which Christ puts before man. This is a sign that they hand on the original message of Jesus.'

during these centuries, it unhesitatingly ascribed the attributes of immutability and impassibility to the supremely perfect Creator and Lord. The contentious issues arose from the need to reconcile the truths concerning Creation, the Trinity, and God's entry into history through the incarnation of the Son with divine unity, immutability and impassibility. At the dawn of the Age of Scholasticism the consensus reached by patristic theology was re-affirmed by St Anselm of Canterbury (1033–1100), for whom it was at once a truth of faith and reason that 'the Divine nature is beyond doubt impassible, and that God cannot at all be brought down from his exaltation nor toil in anything which he wishes to effect'.[28] But it was of course St Thomas Aquinas, who, during the high tide of Scholasticism, elaborated the most comprehensive defence of the venerable tradition. Since the advocates of a revision or abandonment of the traditional emphasis on divine immutability and impassibility generally accept that St Thomas' system represents the apex of classical theology, the remaining pages of this essay will attempt, against the background of modern objections, to summarise and explain the Thomistic arguments for the ascription of immutability and impassibility to God.

ST THOMAS ON DIVINE IMMUTABILITY

Throughout his career St Thomas never doubted that the biblical evidence, the traditional teaching of the Church, and theological and philosophical reflection warranted the attribution of immutability to God. But for St Thomas, as for his patristic forbears, the immutable God who revealed himself in the Old Law—and definitively in the incarnation of the Logos—was a loving and provident Creator and Lord rather than a remote, inert and insensitive despot. Since critics of St Thomas' version of classical theology believe that the ascription of immutability to God is incompatible with the revelation of his love, providence and freedom, it is essential to establish the precise meaning of the Thomistic affirmation of divine immutability and the contours within which that affirmation is made. Because St Thomas was acutely sensitive to linguistic usage, he knew that the word 'immutable'— and various cognate expressions—can have either positive or negative connotations when they are used with reference to finite or created realities. Since these expressions are used to refer to the states of beings as disparate as angels and rocks, they are deployed in analogical rather than univocal or equivocal senses. However, the thread which links the various uses of these expressions is their reference to a lack or absence of motion. But since there are different kinds of motion, and since motion can be either a desirable or undesirable attribute depending on the kind of being to which it is ascribed, the absence or lack of it can have either positive or negative connotations.

Following Aristotle, St Thomas defines the motion which occurs in material things as the actualization of something which is in potency in so far

28   Saint Anselm: *Basic Writings*, trans. S. N. Deane (La Salle, 1962), p. 190.

as it is in potency. This kind of motion comprehends both substantial and accidental changes, and since it necessarily involves the constituent principles of act and potency, it embraces both perfection and imperfection. In another key this kind of motion is described as an 'imperfect act' or the 'act of the imperfect', since it is predicated of something which has a capacity for further actualization or perfection. According to St Thomas, then, the lack or absence of this kind of motion can have positive or negative connotations depending on the status of the particular material natures to which immovability is ascribed. Thus, in so far as a being which is capable of motion remains in a state of rest, it has failed to attain a perfection which is appropriate to its nature. In this context rest or immovability has the negative connotation of inertia or stagnation. But since rest or immovability can also refer to the completion of motion and the attainment of a perfection or goal, it can also have positive connotations. However, the attribution of rest or immovability to corruptible material natures is always ambivalent, since the prime matter or fundamental principle of potency in such natures cannot be simultaneously actualized by all the forms they are capable of receiving.

St Thomas observes that there is a similar ambiguity in the ascription of immovability to things which can scarcely move. When, for example, immovability is predicated of an invalid or an animal which lacks self-motion, it obviously has negative connotations. But its connotations are clearly positive when it designates the enduring, or relatively indestructible, qualities of a rock or mountain. Furthermore, there is a sense in which immovability can be predicated of the constitutive principles of material things. When prime matter and substantial and accidental forms are considered in abstraction from their constitutive roles in material natures, immovability can be ascribed to them. In this context, however, immovability always refers to the intrinsic incompleteness, and therefore imperfection, of these principles. In Thomistic cosmology, however, the heavenly bodies have no potentiality for the reception of further substantial forms, and, on the plane of accidental change, are subject only to local motion. The heavenly bodies thus possess higher grades of being and goodness than their corruptible earthly counterparts. And since they are not subject to substantial change, the immovability ascribed to them has the positive connotation of the highest actualization or perfection on the plane of created material realities. Finally, in the Thomistic hierarchy of created beings, angels or separated substances occupy a unique position. Since angels are subsistent immaterial forms, which are not subject to the kind of motion which is an imperfect act and have no potentiality for non-existence, they enjoy a singularly stable kind of existence. And when they are described as 'immutable and invariable in being', these attributes encompass the highest peaks of created perfection.

Besides the motion which is an 'imperfect act' or an 'act of the imperfect', St Thomas also identifies a 'broad' or 'improper' type of motion which he designates as an 'operation', an 'act of a being in act', or an 'act of the perfect'. Whereas, in an imperfect act, the action is transmitted to an external mobile object, the action does not emerge from the agent in an operation. In a contemporary idiom, the first kind of motion always involves 'transient' action, while an operation is an 'immanent' action which perfects the agent itself. The higher-order spiritual operations of knowing and willing in angels and humans are prime instances of immanent actions. But the sensitive operations of animals, and the relatively self-sufficient operations of plants, also testify to the presence of lower-order immanent actions. St Thomas again identifies different ways in which immovability is associated with imma-nent action. In an obviously pejorative sense, things which are incapable of immanent action can be characterized as immovable. But there is another sense in which immovability can be ascribed to things which are capable of immanent action. And since this kind of immovability signifies immunity from the potentiality, and therefore imperfection, which is inherent in things capable of only transient action, it has positive connotations. Here again there is a scale of perfection which extends from the higher-order operations of knowing and willing in spiritual beings to the relatively imperfect operations of things at the lower end of the hierarchy of creatures which possess immanent action. Considered from an abstract standpoint, immanent action, as the 'act of a being in act', involves no potentiality and is therefore free from imperfection. However, since creatures are inherently contingent and incomplete, even those which possess the higher forms of immanent action have potentiality for further development or perfection which can only be attained through appropriate forms of motion. In so far as creatures lack some perfection or motion for which they have a potentiality, their immovability has negative connotations. But in so far as they have attained some degree of perfection, their immovability is positive.

For St Thomas, then, there is an inescapable ambivalence in the ascription of immovability to creatures. References to a lack or absence of either transient or immanent motion can designate an unactualized and therefore defective state of a creature. Or, they can mean that a creature has been actualized in some respect and has thus attained a stable and desirable condition. Again, it can be said that when a creature is considered from the standpoint of its perfectibility or openness to change and development, immovability represents a disordered or deficient status. But if a creature is considered from the perspective of the perfection which is instantiated in it, the ascription of immovability means that it has been actualized or perfected in some respect which is appropriate to its nature. It follows that the most perfect creatures enjoy the highest grades of immovability and that those which occupy 'the lowest rank in goodness and the lowest grade in being' are most susceptible to motion or change. Since angels enjoy the simplest and most invariable kinds of immanent motion and are not subject to substantial and accidental changes, they occupy the highest rank on the scale of created perfection. Yet even angels are mutable inasmuch as they exercise their power selectively and can orient their wills towards good or evil. Inanimate bodies, on the other hand, since they lack immanent motion and are most amenable to the vicissitudes of transient motion, are furthest removed from the perfection of angels. In the light of his examination of the various ways in which immovability can be ascribed to creatures, St Thomas concludes that only an absolutely perfect being which has no capacity for further actualization or change can be called immovable or immutable in an unqualified sense. The ascription of immutability to such a being has no negative connotations. Differing radically from creatures, this unconditionally perfect being is the One whom St Thomas recognizes as God.[29]

In ascribing immutability to God, St Thomas wishes to highlight the radical disjunction between the divine and created orders. On the speculative plane, however, his most original insights were his identification of a composition of essence and existence in all contingent or created beings and his inference that, while essence is really distinct from and in a relation of potency to the act of existing (*esse, actus essendi*) in created beings, there is no such distinction in God. From this original speculative standpoint *esse*, which actualizes or confers existence on essences, is the crowning perfection of all created or composite beings; in St Thomas' emphatic phrase, *esse* is 'the act of all acts and the perfection of all perfections.'[30] Across the spectrum of created beings, however, *esse* is specified or limited by the essences which it actualizes or renders existent. But for St Thomas, composite, contingent, and therefore imperfect, realities testify to the presence of a source or cause which is pure actuality and unlimited by any kind of potentiality or imperfection. This unique and transcendent being, whose 'to-be (*esse*) is his very essence',[31] is of course God. As the 'first-being' (*primum ens*) or 'being in the highest degree' (*maxime ens*), as 'the cause of to-be in every other being' (*aliquid quod omnibus entibus est causa esse*), and as the One who possesses 'the entire plenitude of the perfection of all to-be' (*omnem plenitudinem perfectionis totius esse*) God is the unreceived, unlimited, and absolutely perfect actuality of pure existence. In St Thomas' most concise formulae, God is 'the self-possessed act of existing' (*ipsum esse subsistens*) or 'the very infinite act of existing' (*ipsum esse infinitum*).

The God encountered in the conclusions of St Thomas' five ways is the only appropriate response to the fundamental questions of why there is something rather than nothing and why things, which are contingent, nevertheless remain in existence. The ways are designed to elicit a recognition of God as the ultimate and supremely perfect efficient, exemplar, and final cause of all

29 For this account of St Thomas' treatment of the ascription of immutability to creatures I have drawn on the invaluable work of Michael J. Dodds OP, *The Unchanging God of Love: A Study of the Teaching of St Thomas Aquinas on Divine Immutability in View of Certain Contemporary Criticism of this Doctrine* (Fribourg, 1986), pp. 39–66.

30 *De Potentia*, 7, 2 ad 9: Esse est actualitas omnium actuum . . . et perfectio omnium perfectionum.

31 *ST*, I, 13, 11.

contingent realities. In the light of St Thomas' identification of God as the unreceived and unlimited act of existing, it is simply a caricature to say that he borrowed indiscriminately from Greek metaphysics or that the God of Thomistic theology is a remote, inert and apathetic being. From the numerous affirmations of divine immutability in St Thomas' works it is clear that he is concerned with God's absolute perfection as the pure or unlimited act of existing and that he wishes to contrast this uniquely dynamic perfection with the imperfection which is always found in creatures. Thus, a succinct outline of the arguments for divine immutability in the *Summa Theologiae* begins with God's unique status as the first and completely perfect being in whom there is no trace of potency (*absque permixtione alicujus potentiae*). And since there can be no change without potency, it follows that God is not subject to any of the varieties of motion or change which are familiar to us. The second argument turns on divine simplicity. Change, in its various manifestations, is inexplicable without the presence of composition in the beings which are subject to change. But since all forms of composition, including that of essence and existence, are excluded from God, he must be absolutely simple (*omnino simplex*) and thus immune from change. Finally, St Thomas points out that mutable beings necessarily acquire something which they did not previously possess when they change. However, God is the infinite act of existing and possesses eternally the fullness of perfection of all to-be. It is impossible for God to need or acquire anything and he must therefore be completely immutable (I, 9, 1).

As the creative first cause of all things and the One to whom creatures owe their continuance in existence, St Thomas' God is far from being a remote and uninvolved deity. 'As long as anything remains in existence', St Thomas writes, 'God must be present to it . . . The act of existing is the most profound dimension of any being . . . It follows that God is present in all things in the deepest possible way.'[32] St Thomas' original theological synthesis, which portrays God as the transcendent pure act of existing and yet emphasises his radical immanence in creatures, is complemented by a striking agnosticism concerning the divine nature. Immediately after the elaboration of the Five Ways to God's existence in the *Summa Theologiae*, St Thomas admits that 'concerning God we cannot know what he is but rather what he is not' (*de Deo scire non possumus quid sit, sed quid non sit*).[33] Even revelation and grace, since they are transmitted in ways which are adapted to our finite condition, do not enable us to comprehend the infinite divine act of existing. St Thomas ratifies a venerable mystical tradition when he insists that through 'the revelation of grace which we receive in this life . . . we are united with God as with an almost unknown being' (*ei quasi ignoto conjungamur*).[34] Against

32 *ST*, I, 8, 1: Quandiu igitur res habet esse, tandiu oportet quod Deus adsit ei . . . esse autem est illud quod est magis intimum cuilibet, et quod profundius omnibus inest . . . Unde oportet quod Deus sit in omnibus rebus, et intime.
33 *ST*, I, 3, Prol.
34 *ST*, I, 12, 13 ad 1.

the background of the numerous modern criticisms of classical theology, it is crucially important that the Thomistic ascription of immutability to God does not imply any positive insight into the divine nature. The significance of the ascription lies rather in its evocation of unlimited actuality or perfection and in its exclusion of creaturely imperfection from the essentially unknowable God.

St Thomas' careful delineation of the horizons within which our theological knowledge and language are confined casts further light on the significance of divine immutability. For St Thomas, our affirmation of God's existence and our faltering attempts to speak about him are extrapolations from our knowledge of finite and contingent realities which evince a relationship of dependence on a first and universal cause. The way of causality (*via causalitatis*) is therefore the basis of our theological knowledge and language. In our discovery of God as the first cause of both the motion or change and the imperfect immutability which we find in creatures, and, even more fundamentally, as the ultimate cause of the existence of creatures, we are led to acknowledge his surpassing perfection as the unreceived act of existing. While our affirmation of God's existence through the way of causality does not enable us to comprehend or designate his nature, we can nevertheless assert that he is exempt from the mutability and contingency which characterize creatures. 'All changeable and defectible things', St Thomas writes, 'must depend on a first principle which is immovable and exists necessarily' (*oportet autem omnia mobilia et deficere possibilia reduci in aliquod primum principium immobile et per se necessarium*).[35] The disjunction between the divine and created orders receives further emphasis through the deployment of the way of negation (*via negationis/remotionis*) which safeguards God's transcendence, incomprehensibility and ineffability. The guiding principle of the way of negation is that creatures must in some way resemble their Creator, while the limitations and imperfections associated with the creaturely mode of existence must be denied of God whose boundless perfection we cannot comprehend. St Thomas insists that 'concerning names which are predicated of God according to the way of negation . . . they in no way designate his substance but rather the removal of something from him.'[36] Through the way of negation, therefore, we systematically exclude from God all forms of creaturely motion in so far as these entail limitation and imperfection. But in our ascription of immutability to God we obviously do not mean that he is lifeless and inert like lower-order creatures. Instead, we concentrate on the kinds of perfection, and therefore immutability, which we find in higher-order creatures. And in so far as even these kinds of immutability are limited and imperfect, we exclude them in order to point, however tentatively, to God's timeless, incomprehensible and unnameable perfection.

35 *ST*, I, 2, 3 ad 2.
36 *ST*, I, 13, 2. De nominibus quae de Deo dicuntur negative . . . manifestum est quod substantiam eius nullo modo significant, sed remotionem alicuius ab ipso.

These tentative gestures of the way of negation are supplemented in turn by the way of eminence (*via eminentiae*) through which we can attain a limited but nonetheless genuine knowledge of some divine attributes and predicate corresponding names in an 'absolute and affirmative sense' (*absolute et affirmative*). Our capacity to identify certain divine attributes and predicate the corresponding names is based on our knowledge that, as 'the excelling cause' (*excellens principium*), God must possess in an eminent way the perfections found in creatures' (*Deus in se praehabet omnes perfectiones creaturarum, quasi simpliciter et universaliter perfectus*).[37] While the ways of causality and negation safeguard divine transcendence and incomprehensibility, the way of eminence ensures that theology is not confined to limp and ineffectual gestures and that our theological language is not limited to the ambivalent and imaginative plane of metaphorical discourse. St Thomas is of course aware that biblical language is frequently metaphorical and that such vivid and evocative language is an appropriate instrument for the communication of religious experience and for use in prayer and devotion. But he is also convinced that theology requires a rigorous conceptual and linguistic framework in order to extract and communicate the truth which is conveyed in metaphorical language. Through a judicious use of the way of eminence we conclude that God must possess certain perfections and that the corresponding names can be 'properly predicated of him' (*proprie dicuntur de Deo*).[38] These names designate perfections such as goodness, life, and knowledge which must be in God in a way which surpasses (*secundum eminentiorem modum*) the created forms which are familiar to us.

To clarify the nature of predication according to the way of eminence St Thomas also distinguishes between the mode of signification (*modus significandi*) and the reality signified (*res significata*) by divine names. The mode of signification of these names is conditioned by our limited human perspective which is directed primarily to our material environment. But in predicating these names of God we prescind as much as possible from their ordinary usages and recognize that what they really signify is instantiated only in God.[39] According to St Thomas, this distinction between the mode of signification and the actual signification applies to all names predicated of God. Moreover, it is essential to remember that the ascription of various attributes and the predication of corresponding names does not imply that there is either division or plurality in God. Instead, while the ascription and predication proceed according to the limitations of our understanding and language, they nevertheless refer in their actual signification to God in his pre-eminent unity, simplicity and perfection. As our theological concepts and language are extrapolations from our knowledge of and talk about creatures, so the starting point for the predication of immutability according to the way

37 Ibid.
38 *ST*, I, 13, 3 ad 1.
39 Cf. *ST*, I, 13, 6.

of eminence is our knowledge of immutability as it occurs in creatures. Whereas the way of causality leads to the conclusion that God is the 'immovable and perfect cause' of changeable and contingent creatures, and the way of negation excludes creaturely mutability and immutability (in so far as they lack some perfection), we can affirm through the way of eminence that, since God is boundlessly actual and perfect, he must possess in a pre-eminent way the kinds of creaturely immutability which have the most desirable connotations. The affirmation of divine immutability in the three ways is at once a bulwark against the presumption that our concepts and language actually encompass the divine nature and an acknowledgement of the incomprehensibility and surpassing perfection of God. In the *De Veritate* St Thomas vividly contrasts the timebound and perishable creatures of our environment with the unfailing and eternal perfection of God, who, 'in so far as—and because—he is immutable, admits neither *has been* nor *will be*' (*in quantum ratione suae immutabilitatis non novit fuisse vel futurum esse*).[40]

Having excluded all traces of creaturely potentiality, mutability and imperfection from God, St Thomas has to bring the light of reflection to bear on the mysteries of the Trinity, Creation and Incarnation. In order to attain some limited insight into the inner divine life, St Thomas has recourse to his account of the immanent operations of knowing and willing. Since these operations are acts of a being in act and in themselves entail no potency or imperfection, they can be ascribed to God according to the way of eminence and afford a glimpse into the infinitely perfect triune divine life. For St Thomas, the 'procession' or 'generation' of the Son from the Father can be compared with the procession of the concept or mental word in our immanent operation of knowing. And our immanent operation of willing or loving furnishes an appropriate analogy for the procession of the Holy Spirit from the perfectly reciprocal love between the Father and Son. Most importantly, the tri-personal God of Thomistic theology is a perfectly actualized and therefore unchanging communion of knowledge and love rather than a static and apathetic deity. And because God is an unchanging exchange of knowledge and love between the three divine persons, there can be neither increment nor loss in the divine nature.

Contemporary critics of classical theology argue, however, that this unchanging divine perfection and self-sufficiency cannot be reconciled with the doctrines of Creation and Incarnation. From the critical perspective it is clear that if God is a self-contained absolute who has no real relation with creatures, he must be a remote and impassive deity. However, St Thomas' denial that God is really related to creatures emerges from his reflection on the unique causality represented by the divine creative act. In all instances of finite transient causality, St Thomas argues, the causal action mediates between—and is common to—the agent and the effect. But since God is the infinite act of existing and transcends the entire created order, there can be

40   *De Veritate* 21, 4 ad 7.

no intermediate action or motion between the Creator and his creatures. Moreover, since the divine creative act is identical with the divine act of existing, and since the creative act does not involve either motion or change (*non fit per motum vel per mutationem*) or depend on pre-existing material, it follows that 'creatures are really related to God, whereas God has no real relation to creatures but only a relation according to our way of thinking in so far as creatures depend on him.'[41] In excluding any real relation to creatures on God's part, St Thomas wishes to underline the fundamental difference between the divine creative act and the transient causality which we observe in creatures. All that is not God depends totally and unconditionally on the infinite divine act of existing which is the first and universal cause. 'Creation', St Thomas insists, 'does not entail any change, but is rather the intrinsic dependence of the creature on the source which confers existence on it' (*non enim est creatio mutatio, sed ipsa dependentia esse creati ad principium a quo instituitur*).[42] Since creation is the ultimate and universal causal act, it follows that, although God is not really related to creatures, his presence to them is more intimate and fundamental than that which obtains in the reciprocal real relations between creatures. 'The simple conferral of existence', St Thomas writes, 'is the distinctive effect of the divine creative act and this effect takes precedence over all others' (*illud autem quod est proprius effectus Dei creantis est illud quod presupponitur omnibus aliis, scilicet esse absolute*).[43] St Thomas' characterization of God's presence to creatures as a relation 'according to reason' or 'according to our way of thinking' can suggest that his presence is insignificant or remote. In the light of contemporary misunderstandings and objections, the expression 'actual relation' can more effectively designate, as Thomas G. Weinandy suggests, the supremely dynamic and intimate relation between the Creator and his creatures.[44]

When St Thomas turns his attention to the mystery of Incarnation, he has recourse again to the principles of his theology of Creation. In view of the outcome of the early christological and trinitarian controversies and the continuous teaching of the Church, St Thomas is convinced that the real significance of the Incarnation can be upheld only in a context which safeguards divine immutability. If the incarnation of the Logos means that God undergoes change, it follows that either it is not really God who is man or that God is not truly man. For St Thomas, the incarnational act requires that God be immutable. 'The mystery of the Incarnation', he writes, 'is not accomplished through God being changed in any way from the state which

41   *ST*, I, 13, 7. Cum igitur Deus sit extra totum ordinem creaturae, et omnes creaturae ordinentur ad ipsum, et non e converso, manifestum est quod creaturae realiter referuntur ad ipsum Deum; sed in Deo non est aliqua realis relatio ad creaturas, sed secundum rationem tantum, inquantum creaturae referuntur ad ipsum.
42   *Contra Gentiles* 2, 18.
43   *ST*, I, 45, 5.
44   Cf. *Does God Change?* pp. 94–5.

he enjoyed from all eternity, but rather through his having united himself to the creature in a new way or having it [i.e. the creature] united to himself.'[45] Through the incarnational act, therefore, a union or relation is effected between the person of the Word and the human nature. In the Thomistic framework this union or relation, like that between the Creator and his creation, 'is not really in God, but only in our manner of thinking, since God is thought to be united to a creature inasmuch as the creature is united to God who remains immutable'.[46] Here, as in the Creator-creature relation, there is no intermediate action or motion between the divine Word and the human nature to which the Word is united. Only in this way can the full significance of the Incarnation—that it is truly the divine Word who is man and that the Word is really man—be upheld. For St Thomas, however, the preservation of the Word's immutability and the inference that the Word is not really related to the human nature do not mean that the Incarnation is an illusory or ephemeral event. Rather, the union of the divine and human natures in the person of the Word is such that the actions and passions of the human nature can be ascribed to the Word. Like the presence of the Creator to his creation, the union or relation of the Word and the human nature is a most intimate or 'actual' bond. The real significance of St Thomas' theology of the Incarnation, according to Thomas G. Weinandy, is that 'the Logos is understood to be related, and actually is related, not by some effect of change in him, but because the manhood is really related to him. It is because the manhood is really related to the Logos as he is that he becomes and is man, and man understands him in a new way as man.'[47]

ST THOMAS ON DIVINE IMPASSIBILITY

In Thomistic theology, impassibility is an inescapable implication of God's unlimited actuality and perfection. As the range and intensity of the objections show, however, the exclusion of suffering from God presents particular difficulties to modern sensibilities. Thus the voice of protest atheism insists that a God who cannot experience suffering is an unworthy distraction from the urgent task of alleviating pain and injustice. From within the horizon of belief, on the other hand, it is often asserted that, since Calvary is the supreme testimony to God's love, mercy and compassion, the affirmation of divine impassibility cannot be reconciled with God's self-revelation in the crucifixion and death of the Son. For his part, St Thomas recognized that

45 *ST*, III, 1, 1 ad 1: Incarnationis mysterium non est impletum per hoc quod Deus sit aliquo modo a suo statu immutatus in quo ab aeterno non fuit: sed per hoc quod novo modo creaturae se univit, vel potius eam sibi.
46 *ST*, III, 2, 7 ad 1: Haec unio non est in Deo realiter, sed solum secundum rationem tantum: dicitur enim Deus unitus creaturae ex hoc quod creatura unita est ei, absque Dei mutatione.
47 *Does God Change?* p. 98.

suffering is frequently associated with the sublime human virtues of love, mercy and compassion. Nevertheless, although suffering—either in the form of personal 'crosses' or compassionate solidarity with others—is often the occasion of heroic virtue, it is neither desirable nor praiseworthy in itself. Instead, suffering always represents a lack of some desirable good and is therefore evil. In St Thomas' words, 'a being suffers in so far as it is deficient and imperfect' (*patitur autem unumquodque, secundum quod est deficiens et imperfectum*).[48] And since the fundamental principles of Thomistic theology preclude the ascription of any deficiency or imperfection to God, it follows that he is in no way subject to suffering.

For St Thomas, biblical and devotional allusions to divine suffering must be understood in metaphorical senses. It is significant, therefore, that many critics of the classical theological thesis admit that our language is metaphorical when we ascribe suffering to God or that divine suffering differs radically from the varieties of suffering known to us. In his call for a revision of the Thomistic emphasis on divine impassibility Jacques Maritain argues that God's suffering does not entail any imperfection, that the concepts and language which we use to refer to it are metaphorical, and, in the final analysis, can only point to inconceivable and unnameable dimensions of the divine nature. 'We have to admit', Maritain writes, 'that this mysterious perfection which in God is the unnamed exemplar of suffering in us, is an integral part of the divine beatitude—a perfect and exultant peace which infinitely transcends our conceptual powers and burns in its flames what from our perspective is apparently irreconcilable.'[49] Following a similar line, Hans Urs von Balthasar also believes that God is at once impassible and vulnerable to suffering in ways which exceed our finite intellectual capacities. Responding to the criticisms of Process theologians and the demands of modern sensibilities, W. Norris Clarke concedes that there is 'something corresponding to what we would call compassion (suffering-with-us, wounded love, etc.)' in the divine consciousness. In order to safeguard divine perfection, however, both Norris Clarke and Jean Galot distinguish God's intrinsic inner being which is unaffected by suffering from his relational or intentional consciousness and the free and gratuitous love which he offers to creatures. While God is immune from suffering in his intrinsically perfect inner being, he is mutable and vulnerable in his free and contingent relations with creatures. Even more radical critics of the classical theological thesis, who believe that suffering and death are constitutive features of the divine nature, admit that God's passion and death differ radically from their human counterparts. According to Jürgen Moltmann, God, unlike creatures, is not subject to 'unwilling suffering as a result of an alien cause'. Nor does he suffer 'because of a deficiency in his being', but he rather chooses to submit himself to 'active suffering, the suffering of love, in which one voluntarily

48   *ST*, I, 25, 1.
49   'Quelques réflexions sur le savoir théologique', 21–2.

opens himself to the possibility of being affected by another.'[50] In the light of these revisionary approaches, however, the Thomist response must be that only those attributes which in themselves entail no limitation or imperfection can be ascribed to God according to the way of eminence. And since suffering is always due to some deficiency, it is incompatible with God's unlimited actuality and perfection.

Opposition to the classical theological thesis of divine impassibility is generally based on the perception that a God who cannot suffer must be an impassive and indifferent being. To exclude suffering from God, Maritain, Galot and others argue, is to deny his loving and compassionate nature. From Moltmann's perspective, God's loving solidarity with suffering humanity is verified in the affliction, abandonment and death which reach to his inner trinitarian being. 'To recognize God in the Cross of Christ', Moltmann writes, 'means to recognize the cross, inextricable suffering, death and hopeless rejection in God.'[51] On another point of the spectrum, Process theology is inspired by Whitehead's dismissal of the religiously unavailable God of classical theology in favour of a sympathetic 'fellow-sufferer who understands'. The objections of both protest atheists and revisionary theologians are encapsulated in François Varillon's assertions that 'a Father who cannot suffer would be a Father without tender love' and that, whereas suffering is an imperfection in the order of being, 'it is the summit of perfection in the order of love.'[52]

According to St Thomas, however, it does not follow that loving solidarity with others must necessarily find expression in compassionate suffering. Rather, compassionate suffering, like all forms of suffering, is evil in so far as it is due to limitation and imperfection. But when compassionate suffering is accepted in response to, and in solidarity with, the suffering of others, it is praiseworthy and good. In response to the question whether the pain of sadness is always evil, St Thomas argues that, as shame is an appropriate reaction when someone is guilty of evil conduct, so compassionate sadness is good 'when something else [i.e. the suffering of others] is presupposed (*ex suppositione alterius*).'[53] Yet, although human compassionate suffering is often the occasion of heroic virtue, the ascription of such suffering to God would detract from the perfection of the divine nature. For St Thomas, the ascription of compassionate suffering to God is an unwarranted extrapolation from our observation of the association between loving solidarity with others and compassionate suffering. Even in this sensitive area, however, we cannot suspend the carefully formulated rules which enable us to obtain a limited appreciation of God's unlimited perfection. 'We must remember', St Thomas writes in his *Commentary on Job*, 'that one and the same attribute can

---

50   *The Crucified God*, p. 230.
51   Ibid., p. 277.
52   *La Souffrance de Dieu*, p. 21, p. 71.
53   *ST*, I–II, 39, 1.

be either good or evil according as it is ascribed to different natures. . . . But there cannot be anything evil in the most perfect good. Nevertheless, it can happen that something which pertains to divine goodness is evil when it is found in human nature. Thus it is blameworthy in a human person not to have compassion in so far as compassion signifies suffering, whereas divine goodness demands this precisely because of its perfection.'[54]

Even in human compassionate suffering we can distinguish the love which inspires the compassionate person from the actual suffering which is undergone in solidarity with others. Moreover, it is this generous love, rather than the concomitant suffering, which we admire and value in instances of compassionate solidarity with others. Thus it is the love which is expressed in Mother Teresa's compassionate solidarity with the poor of Calcutta which inspires universal admiration. And it is clear that if Mother Teresa were to sympathetically assume the suffering of even one of the afflicted whom she encounters, her capacity to heal, comfort and console would be curtailed or even extinguished. Such considerations help us to appreciate that, while human compassionate suffering testifies to the presence and power of love, it is nevertheless a limited perfection which cannot be extended to God who is perfect, unlimited and unchanging love. According to St Thomas, God is merciful and loving, not because he sympathetically identifies himself with the sufferings of creatures, but rather because he can overcome the afflictions of creatures through his infinite love and mercy. 'God's unlimited mercy is manifested in the bestowal of the fruits of mercy', St Thomas writes, 'but divine mercy is not itself subject to suffering.' Furthermore, 'God cannot be compassionately afflicted by the suffering of another. But he is supremely capable of dispelling the affliction of another; and such affliction is always traceable to some deficiency.'[55] Due to our finite perspective, and our frequent observation of the conjunction of sacrificial suffering and love in our world, we cannot comprehend God's infinite and unfailing love which is not subject to suffering. Yet the logic of divine perfection and transcendence demands that the imperfection and evil of suffering must not be attributed to God. When we think or speak about God's love and mercy, we must acknowledge the infinite gulf which separates the divine modes from their human counterparts. And for St Thomas, it is in the gratuitous and unrestricted qualities of divine mercy that God's transcendence and omnipotence are most clearly revealed: 'Mercy, which is indeed generous to others and brings relief

54   *Expositio super Iob ad litteram* X, vs. 3: Sed considerandum est quod aliquando diversis naturis unum et idem potest esse bonum et malum . . . non enim potest in summo bono aliquid mali esse; sed potest contingere quod aliquid malum est in homine quod ad divinam pertinet bonitatem, sicut non misereri secundum quod misericordia in passionem sonat in homine quidem vituperatur, quod tamen divina bonitas ex sui perfectione requirit.

55   *ST*, I, 21, 3: Misericordia est Deo maxime attribuenda: tamen secundum effectum, non secundum passionis affectum . . . Tristari ergo de miseria alterius, non competit Deo; sed repellere miseriam alterius, hoc maxime ei competit, ut per miseriam quemcumque defectum intelligamus.

to them in their needs, belongs principally to one who stands above. It follows therefore that mercy is proper to God and that it is the most spectacular manifestation of his omnipotence.'[56]

It is in the incarnation of the Son or Word, and more particularly in his suffering and death on Calvary, that we receive the definitive revelation of God's unlimited mercy and love. Because contemporary exponents of a theology of the cross present apparently persuasive arguments for the admission of suffering into the divine nature, it is essential to outline St Thomas' reasons for his fidelity to the tradition of divine impassibility in the light of the sacrificial suffering and death of Christ. Predictably, St Thomas' theology of the cross is based on his account of the union of the divine and human natures in the *hypostasis* or person of the Word. Far from being an ephemeral or accidental conjunction, this union is such that the attributes which belong to either nature can be ascribed to the *hypostasis* or person: 'Since there is one *hypostasis* of both natures, the same hypostasis is indicated by the name of either nature. . . . Thus what belongs to the divine nature can be predicated of the man and what belongs to the human nature can be predicated of God.'[57] But although both divine and human attributes are predicated of the unitary *hypostasis* or person, the incarnational act and hypostatic union require that we distinguish between the subject of the predication and 'the reasons for the predication of each class of attribute' (*distinguuntur tamen quantum ad id secundum quod utrumque praedicantur*). It is because the Incarnation means that the Word truly is man that we can ascribe the suffering and death on Calvary to the divine person. But as God's immutability must be preserved if God is to be truly man in the Incarnation, so God—or the divine nature of the Word—must remain impassible if it is to be God who really suffers as a man. The logic of the Incarnation demands that Christ really suffered on Calvary; but this suffering occurred in the human nature which was united to the person of the Word. 'In the mystery of the Incarnation', St Thomas concludes, 'we affirm that the Son of God suffered, yet we deny that the divine nature suffered.'[58] In Thomistic theology, therefore, the Cross is seen as a particularly apt revelation of divine mercy and love. In his suffering for us and with us in his humanity, Christ revealed God's nature in a manner which is accessible to us. Because we can only understand and appreciate suffering as it occurs in our world, the ascription of such suffering to the divine nature would detract from God's unlimited perfection and actuality. Rather than being a revelation of a suffering God, the Cross

---

56　*ST*, II–II, 30, 4: Pertinet enim ad misericordiam quod alii effundat; et, quod plus est, quod defectus aliorum sublevet; et hoc est maxime superioris. Unde et misereri ponitur proprium Deo: et in hoc maxime dicitur eius omnipotentia manifestari.

57　*ST*, III, 16, 4: Cum sit eadem hypostasis utriusque naturae, eadem hypostasis supponitur nomine utriusque naturae . . . Et ideo de homine dici possunt ea quae sunt divinae naturae: et de Deo possunt dici ea quae sunt humanae naturae.

58　*ST*, III, 16, 5 ad 1: In mysterio incarnationis dicimus quod filius Dei est passus, non autem dicimus quod natura divina sit passa.

shows an infinitely loving and merciful God who can overcome suffering and redeem us from sin and death. When we reflect on the revelation of God's mercy and love in the crucified Saviour, we must acknowledge that 'Christ, in his Godhead, was incorporeal and impassible' (*quod Christus secundum deitatem est incorporeus et impassibilis*).[59]

For many contemporary theologians and philosophers the thesis of divine impassibility is an archaic obstacle to Christian apologetics and the life of faith. Christ's mission on Calvary, it is argued, obviously consisted in the revelation of a God who suffers and therefore sympathizes with us in our tribulations. For the classical theological tradition, and specifically for the Thomistic elaboration of this tradition, there are insuperable objections to the abandonment or revision of the thesis of divine impassibility. At the most basic level, the admission that God is either subject to suffering or voluntarily submits himself to suffering detracts from his unlimited and unfailing perfection and love. Nor is this objection overcome by the concession that divine suffering differs radically from human suffering. Since all the varieties of suffering known to us reflect the imperfections and limitations of our condition, their significance cannot be altered or extended so that they can be ascribed to God. Our faltering attempts to think and speak about the transcendent and infinitely perfect divine reality must safeguard the truth expressed by St Bernard on the occasion of the death of his brother: 'Though God is incapable of suffering, He is not incapable of compassion, He whose especial prerogative it is ever to have mercy and to spare.'[60] In order to evoke a response to God's surpassing love and mercy, mystics, poets, theologians and prayerful believers can avail themselves of the treasury of metaphorical language. But although metaphorical language nourishes our theological reflection and facilitates our devotion, it points, in the words of a notable twentieth-century upholder of divine impassibility, to 'Christ our Lord above us, and, encompassing all and penetrating all, God—not a Sufferer, but indeed the Sympathizer, God Joy, the Ocean of Joy, our Home.'[61]

---

59   *ST*, III, 16, 8 ad 2.
60   Cited in Baron Friedrich von Hügel, *Essays and Addresses on the Philosophy of Religion*, second series (London, 1926), p. 194.
61   Ibid., p. 213.

Aquinas and the Act of Love

MICHAEL NOLAN

Newman's Anglican days made him acutely aware of how the language of Catholicism sounds strange in unaccustomed and indeed suspicious ears and how readily misunderstanding ensues. Infallibility is taken to be a claim to be right on everything, the Immaculate Conception is confused with the Virgin Birth, and the remission of sins becomes a permission to continue in evil ways. It is, he saw, a general problem in dealing with the unfamiliar, and he wondered what a hostile foreigner would make of the maxims of the laws of England. Might he not, reading in Blackstone's incomparable Commentaries that 'the power and jurisdiction of parliament is so transcendent that it cannot be confined either for causes or persons within any bounds' see a blasphemous claim to divine omnipotence? Might not the assertion that 'the king can do no wrong' seem an arrogant claim to divine sinlessness? In truth, of course, all that is meant is that in English law there is no higher authority than Parliament and that the King cannot be sued in his own Courts: nothing more. Newman could but ask the hostile foreigner to abide a while and abate his hostility.

Aquinas, writing in a highly technical Latin and within a philosophy and theology alien to modern ears, is no less prone to be misunderstood, and the modes of misrepresenting him, often unwitting, are many. What he has to say about marriage and related issues has been the object of recent attacks: often he is read as if he were a Lutheran or Calvinist. It may be well to note some of these types of error before dealing with his own understanding in these matters.

There is, for instance, straight mistranslation. Thus in a recent television discussion[1] it was claimed Aquinas held that 'masturbation is a more serious sin than rape.' It is true that Aquinas says that what he calls unnatural acts (bestiality, sodomy and masturbation) are a more serious type of sexual sin than what he calls *raptus*. But *raptus* does not mean rape in the sense beloved of the panting readers of the national dailies, and the learned professor who made the equivalence is a manifest uncle of the schoolboy who thought that the Pope bestowed on Henry VIII the title of Fido the Offensive. *Raptus* is a technical word in Roman civil law, and in medieval as well as current canon law means rape in the sense of 'the act of carrying away a person, especially a woman, by force' (*Oxford English Dictionary*)—what we commonly call abduction. That this is Aquinas' meaning of the term is shown by his explicit reference to canon law (*ST*, II-II, 154, 1), and equally by his assertion that

1 Channel 4 Television, 7 September 1990.

the crime of *raptus* is committed even if intercourse does not actually follow (*ST*, II–II, 154, 7). He is dealing with a law meant to protect women against a forced consent to marriage: it is a crime to abduct them with a view to sexual intercourse, even if this does not occur. It presumes that any apparent consent to intercourse in these circumstances is not true consent and it makes any attempted marriage invalid.

It may of course be said that *raptus*, even in the sense of abduction, is a more serious crime than masturbation. The suggestion shows the need to read Aquinas carefully. The passage in question refers, not to the seriousness of an individual deed but the seriousness of *types* of sexual sin. Aquinas does *not* say that every sin of masturbation is more serious than any sin of *raptus*. He distinguishes between the seriousness of types of sin in the same way as civil law distinguishes between the seriousness of types of crime, but accepts, as does civil law, that the seriousness of an individual and specific act depends on the circumstances (*ST*, I–II, 72, 3 & 7). In English law burglary, for which the maximum sentence is fourteen years, is a more serious crime than theft, for which the maximum sentence is ten. But it would be ludicrous to suggest that in English justice a person who breaks a neighbour's window at nine o'clock on a summer's evening and takes a flowerpot— which is burglary—has committed a more serious crime than someone who slips through the open door of an old man's house and takes his life-savings from under his bed—which is theft. Similarly, murder is a more serious crime than causing grievous bodily harm, but would one say that Irish justice takes killing a brutal spouse in a quarrel to be a worse offence than torturing a child for pleasure—yet one is murder and the other the causing of bodily harm? A case of *raptus* could be a willing elopement, or it might involve the repeated violation of a woman for the vilest of motives. Masturbation might be the hesitant act of a person in distress, or the act of someone watching lecherously while others abuse a child. The relative seriousness of *individual* acts is not a matter that can be decided in writings on moral theology or in a statute. As sins, they are matter for a confessor, as crimes, for a judge and jury.

Aquinas' understanding of the seriousness of types of sexual sin turns on the extent by which a type of act differs from the matrimonial act, which he takes as normative. He sees rape (in the modern sense) as being a serious sin precisely because it lacks the consent which is necessary for marriage (*In IV Sent.*, 41, 1, 4).

There is a further consideration. We tend to see sins as offences against a commandment or law: Aquinas sees them as offences against a virtue, and he categorizes them as such. The more important a virtue, the more grievous a sin—more precisely, type of sin—against that virtue. He classifies sexual sins in his discussion of chastity, and injuries to the bodily integrity of another person in his discussion of justice (*ST*, II–II, 65). But an individual act may be a sin against more than one virtue. Aquinas considers the moral principles applying to such acts (*ST*, I-II, 73, 6 & 7): their variety is obviously infinite and he confines himself to some illustrations which do not include rape in the modern sense. But in his system rape is manifestly a double sin: a sin against chastity and a sin against justice. And since justice is a more important virtue than chastity (*ST*, II-II, 161, 8), then rape is principally a sin against justice. It was not, one may note, a crime that medievals took lightly. William the Conqueror decreed that a rapist should have his eyes gouged out and his testicles cut off; the Statute of Westminster in 1364 made it a hanging offence, and continental jurists were scarcely less imaginative.

Aquinas is open also to the dangers of the infelicitous translation of his highly technical medieval Latin. Thus Noonan in his scholarly work *Contraception*[2] translates *Utrum luxuria quae est circa actus venereos possit esse peccatum* as 'Can the lechery which pertains to the venereal act ever be a sin?' (p. 245). There are strange things here. The plural *actus venereos* is translated as the singular 'venereal act' and the singular is then turned into the typical by the addition of the definite article: 'the venereal act'. *Circa* is rendered as 'pertaining to' when 'in' or 'accompanying' would have sufficed. Moreover *luxuria* is translated as 'lechery' and again the definite article is added. Webster (a fair test, since Noonan is American) gives lechery to mean 'inordinate indulgence in sexual activity', while the Oxford Dictionary gives 'habitual indulgence of lust, lewdness of living'. But Aquinas is dealing with *luxuria* as one of the seven deadly sins where the normal translation is 'lust'. Moreover in using the word 'lechery' Noonan departs from the usage of the two standard translations of Aquinas, both of which translate *luxuria* as 'lust'. At best, from his point of view, Noonan might have translated: 'Can lust in venereal acts be a sin?'—which rings very differently from 'Can the lechery which pertains to the venereal act ever be a sin?' But what is most curious is that Noonan ignores the definition of *luxuria* which Aquinas gives in his answer to this very question: *hoc autem pertinet ad rationem luxuriae, ut ordinem et modum rationis excedat circa venerea* which I translate: '*luxuria* means "to exceed the order and measure of reason in venereal acts"'. Aquinas writes:

> Venereal acts (*usus venereorum*) are very necessary for the common we-lfare, and precisely because of this they must take place in accordance with the rules of reason. . . . *Luxuria* is a transgression (*excedat*) of these rules and as such is certainly sinful. (*ST*, II-II, 153, 3)

It is as though Aquinas had asked 'Whether gluttony in eating is a sin' and this were translated 'Whether the gluttony that pertains to the act of eating can ever be a sin'—a phrase that suggests, if it does not explicitly assert, that all eating is somehow gluttonous.

One moves on from mistranslation to the failure to distinguish between the different meanings of words. Ranke-Heinemann[3] makes the bizarre

2 John T. Noonan Jr., *Contraception* (Cambridge, Mass., 1965), p. 245.
3 Ute Ranke-Heinemann, *Eunuchs for Heaven*, (London, 1990), p. 281.

accusation that 'Masturbation in the view of St Thomas was a vice more damnable than intercourse between mother and son.' This presumably turns on Aquinas' assertion that incest is a lesser sin that sodomy and other 'unnatural' sins. The word 'incest' conjures up gothic images of dark deeds in hidden places, but in the present context (in which he makes explicit reference to canon law) Aquinas is using it simply to mean sexual relations between people within the forbidden degrees of consanguinity—for example, a relationship between second cousins. But he distinguishes sharply between two forms of consanguinity and hence between two types of incest: that between parents and their children, and that between people descended from the same parents or grandparents. Prohibitions on relations between the latter, which would scarcely be called incestuous in the usage of modern English, vary from culture to culture, he says. It is quite other with relations between mother and son, or between father and daughter. These are forbidden by natural law, most of all relations between mother and son, for here the son would not show his mother the respect that is her due. He is aware that a union of father and daughter can be fertile, but insists that it is wrong because it disturbs the appropriate relationship between them (*In IV Sent.*, 40, 1, 3). He even expresses his horror of such relationships by re-telling Aristotle's folktale of the stallion that covered its mother and then in shame threw itself over a cliff. Thus parent–child relations and masturbation are both unnatural, though in different ways, and Ranke-Heinemann's allegation is simply untrue.

One moves on to selective quotation. The precise reason why a male or female child is conceived on a particular occasion was not known in the middle ages, as it is not today. (It depends on which type of sperm the ovum receives and this is said to happen at random—that is, what determines it on a particular occasion is not known). We do know today that in some species it depends on the time of day or on the environmental temperature. Aquinas accepts that it may be due to some such circumstance. He does indeed write that a female child may be conceived because the wind is from the south and this is much trumpeted as evidence that he regarded a woman as 'a freak product of environmental pollution' (Ranke-Heinemann, p. 165). But if he says that a female child is conceived because of a southern wind (which, after all, is warm and pleasant), he equally writes that a male child may be conceived because the wind is from the north—and this is cold and harsh. Yet he does not commit himself to this. The sex of the child, he thinks, may be determined by the wishes of the parents. Indeed in the 'state of innocence'—in Utopia—this would certainly be the case and parents would as often choose to have a girl as a boy, for the completion of the human species requires that there be both men and women and that each person should have a partner (*ST*, I, 99, 2).

These instances show some of the difficulties of understanding Aquinas. Yet, beyond such technical difficulties, there are deep conceptual problems.

Aquinas—and the remark is not facetious—is a Catholic and the English-speaking world is—as Newman stressed—Protestant. Aquinas lived in a culture which was soon to produce Dante and Boccaccio, and the figures of Beatrice and *La figlia del suo figlio* and the mirthful women of the Decameron. Modern English developed in the world of Milton and Satan and sinful Eve, a world in which the word concupiscence—which simply means desire—came to mean 'sinful desire', and even sin itself. The *Oxford English Dictionary* indicates the change: concupiscence is 'eager or vehement desire; in Theological usage, the coveting of "carnal things", desire for "things of the world"'; it adds a second meaning: 'especially, libidinous desire, sexual appetite, lust'. The 'theological usage' is that of Lutheran, not scholastic, theology. In Aquinas concupiscence carries no moral value in itself but is morally good or bad according as it is directed by reason and will to a morally good or bad object (*ST*, I-II, 24, 1). To read Aquinas as though every time he uses the word *concupiscentia* he means concupiscence in the English sense is rather like taking a German who says '*Ich habe Lust*' to be in a state of sexual arousal.

But the difference in the meaning of concupiscence is rooted in a deeper difference in the meaning of original sin. For Luther the sin of Adam positively damaged human nature, for the scholastics it did not. Luther himself was quite aware of the difference. He writes:

> The scholastics argue that original righteousness was not a part of human nature but, like some adornment, was added to man as a gift, as when someone places a wreath on a pretty girl. The wreath is certainly not a part of the virgin's nature; it is something apart from her nature. It came from outside and can be removed again without any injury to her nature. Therefore they maintain about man and about demons that although they have lost their original righteousness, their natural endowments have remained pure, just as they were created in the beginning. But this idea must be shunned like poison, for it minimizes original sin. Let us rather maintain that righteousness was not a gift which came from without, separate from man's nature, but that it was truly part of his nature . . . so, after man has fallen from righteousness into sin, it is correct and truthful to say that our natural endowments are not perfect but are corrupted by sin. (*Lectures on Genesis* 3, 7)

He stresses his difference from the scholastics:

> Nothing was more common and received more general acceptance in the schools than this thesis [that our natural endowments are still perfect]. (Ibid.)

His own account of the effects of original sin is simply stated:

> Original sin really means that human nature has completely fallen; that the intellect has become darkened, so that we no longer know God and his will and no longer perceive the works of God; furthermore

that the will is extraordinarily depraved, so that we do not trust the mercy of God and do not fear God. (Ibid. 2, 17)

Of procreation he writes:

It is a great favour that God has preserved woman for us—against our will and wish, as it were—both for procreation and also as a medicine against the sin of fornication. In Paradise woman would have been a help for duty only. But now she is also, and for the greater part at that, an antidote and a medicine; we can hardly speak of her without a feeling of shame, and surely we cannot make use of her without shame. The reason is sin. In Paradise that union would have taken place without any bashfulnss . . . Now, alas, it is so hideous and fright-ful a pleasure that physicians compare it with epilepsy or falling sickness. Thus an actual disease is linked with the very activity of procreation. We are in the state of sin and death; therefore we undergo this punishment, that we cannot make use of woman without this horrible passion of lust, and, so to speak, without epilepsy. (Ibid., 2, 18)

It is only right to add that Luther insists that marriage is honourable:

Marriage should be treated with honour; from it we all originate, because it is a nursery not only for the state but also for the church and the kingdom of Christ until the end of the world. (Ibid., 4, 1)

The scholastic account of original sin, which will be discussed later, may be gathered from Luther's criticisms and contrasts. He writes:

It is a cause for great errors when some men minimize this evil [original sin] and speak of our depraved nature in the manner of the philosophers, as if it were not depraved. Thus they state that the natural endowments have remained unimpaired not only in the nature of man but in the devil. But this is obviously false. (Ibid. 3, 1)

He again contrasts his position with that of the medievals:

See what follows if you maintain that original righteousness was not a part of nature but a sort of superfluous or superadded gift. When you declare that righteousness was not a part of the essence of man, does it not follow that sin, which took its place, is not part of the essence either. Then there was no purpose in sending Christ, the Redeemer, if the original righteousness, like something foreign to our nature, has been taken away, and the natural endowments remain perfect. What can be said that is more unworthy of a theologian? Therefore let us shun those ravings like real pests and a perversion of the Holy Scriptures. (Ibid., 3, 7)

For Luther, all of these defects of human nature constitute concupiscence (Ibid. 2, 17). He criticizes the scholastics for limiting the meaning of the word to what he calls 'wretched and hideous lust'. As we shall see, this is most certainly not the meaning of the word in Aquinas at least, and, I suspect, in many other scholastics.

The penetration of Luther's ideas into the English-speaking world is obvious in the Book of Common Prayer. Article 9 reads:

> Original sin standeth not in the following of Adam (as the Pelagians do vainly talk), but it is the fault and corruption of the Nature of every man that naturally is engendered of the offspring of Adam; whereby man is very far gone from original righteousness, and is of his own nature inclined to evil, so that the flesh lusteth always contrary to the spirit; and therefore in every person born into this world, it deserveth God's wrath and damnation. And this infection of nature doth remain, yea in them that are regenerated; whereby the lust of the flesh, called in the Greek (φρόνημα σαρκός), which some do expound the wisdom, some sensuality, some the affection, some the desire, of the flesh, is not subject to the Law of God. And although there is no condemnation for them that believe and are baptized, yet the Apostle doth confess, that concupiscence and lust hath of itself the nature of sin.

It is quite difficult for anyone who has grown up in a culture in which the words concupiscence and original sin have these meanings, to read the scholastics without carrying forward the notion that these words imply depravity of some degree. To this must be added a further difficulty, again deriving from—or perhaps one should say best illustrated by—a Protestant thinker: the Kantian feeling that a truly moral act cannot be pleasurable and if pleasurable is not truly moral.

Aquinas of course accepts the notion of original sin, but accepts it precisely in the sense which we have seen criticized by Luther: 'an adornment, added to man as a gift . . . it came from outside and can be removed without any injury to nature.' He distinguishes between deficiencies, evils and faults. A deficiency is simply the absence of something, such as the absence of life in a stone. An evil is the absence of something that should be there, such as blindness. A fault is an evil arising from a voluntary act, such as sin. Now human nature has obvious deficiencies: man finds it hard to fix his mind on God, who is his true goal; emotions run riot and overwhelm reason; illness and distress end in death. These things, as such, are deficiencies arising from the mere fact of being human and seen in this way they are most certainly (*proculdubio*) natural deficiencies. But since man in Adam was constituted in 'original justice', a state in which deficiencies were overcome by the gift of God, and since that state was lost through sin, then, looked at from that viewpoint, the deficiencies are penalties for sin and are due to it (cf. *In II Sent.*, 30, 1, 2). He puts the same point in another way:

> It would have been possible for God at the time he made Adam to have created another man and to have left this man in his natural

condition. That man would have been mortal and subject to suffering, and he would have experienced the battle of concupiscence against reason . . . but the state of that man would not be a state of sin or penalty. (*In II Sent.*, 31, 1, 2, ad 3)

It follows that there is no way by which, looking at man as he is today, we could come to know of the existence of original sin—unless revelation taught us that is the case. We know of it only through faith (*In II Sent.*, 30, 1, 1, ad 1). Aquinas disagrees with the modern theologians who believe we can observe the 'fallen-ness' of man.

This enables us to understand what he means when he says something is 'due to original sin'. One may think of two men doing heavy work on a farm on which both were born. One won a lottery, gave up his work, drank his way through the money and is back on the farm again. The other has spent all his life on the farm. Both are suffering the strain of labour, but only of the first can one say that he is suffering the price of his foolishness, or that his suffering is due to his foolishness. In one sense it is due to his foolishness but in another sense his backache is due to precisely the same causes that give his fellow-worker backache—arduous labour. His foolishness has not altered his physiology: it is not the cause of his backache in the sense in which heavy labour is the cause.

What Aquinas takes original sin to be we can see in his discussion of the fate of unbaptized infants who die 'in the state of original sin'. (One recalls that in his thinking Adam and Eve had the destiny of seeing God *in sua essentia*—face to face, as it were; that they lost this destiny through sin, as did their descendants, and that it is restored by baptism.) He argues that they will experience neither physical or mental suffering. He writes:

> Any penalty should be proportionate to the fault. The defect which is passed on from generation to generation and which does indeed meet the definition of fault, is not a taking away or corruption of any good which belongs to human nature as such, but is a taking away or corruption of something which had been added to human nature. And this fault is the fault of this individual person only in so far as the human nature with which he was born could, and was meant to, have this additional good and does not have it. Hence no other penalty is due to that individual person except that of not being able to reach the goal which the added good would have enabled him to reach and which cannot be reached by human nature as such. But this goal is the vision of God. Hence the lack of this vision is the one and only penalty of original sin after death. (*In II Sent.*, 33, 2, 1)

He explains that a physical punishment can be applied only if a person has done wrong, but the person who dies unbaptized has in fact done no wrong and should not therefore be punished. He goes on to argue that they are equally free from mental unhappiness. They will be completely happy, he says; they will know God as fully as human nature permits, they will know they do not see God face to face, and this will not cause them any unhappiness either. (*In II Sent.*, 33, 2, 1)

Aquinas is of course aware of a long tradition which asserts that original sin is concupiscence. (The precise meaning of that assertion merits examination, which I would hope to undertake elsewhere.) As so often, he accepts the words but gives them his own meaning. Concupiscence is either habitual or actual. Now actual concupiscence, concupiscence experienced here and now, cannot be bad in itself (otherwise, he says, it would be a sin to be thirsty), but it would be bad if directed to a bad object—a yearning for heroin, say. Habitual concupiscence is the capacity or disposition to experience actual concupiscence. Now, as a fact, we can erupt into evil desires and that capacity or disposition so to erupt is a deficiency, and since that deficiency is due to original sin—'due' in the sense described above—it is, *materialiter sed non formaliter*, original sin. This distinction between actual and habitual concupiscence is subtle, but is essential for understanding what Aquinas has to say on marriage.

If Aquinas' theology is different from that which floats in the minds of English-speakers, his philosophy is equally strange to ears tutored by Descartes and Locke. If one asks a person today to show you 'a thing' he will point to a stone or a car or another inanimate object. If one asked a medieval thinker to show you a thing he would have pointed to a flower, perhaps, or a baby. For moderns, the world is basically a physical object or set of physical objects from which all else is derived either by the processes of evolution—and these are seen as basically random processes—or by the work of man. Such derived objects are not fundamentally real and have no meaning or significance within themselves. Such meaning and significance as the man-made enjoys comes from the man who made it or the person who uses it. It follows that its structure tells us nothing of God. At best he is the creator of the physical world. All else is accidental.

For Aquinas the world in all its aspects is full of meaning. It is sacred, and as such is not just to be used by us as we wish. Aquinas in fact has an attitude to reality which we would today call an ecological sensitivity. Many now feel that forests are not simply 'things' which we can destroy at will to provide our daily papers, nor animals simply 'objects' which we can exterminate to provide aphrodisiacs (the rhinoceros) or domestic ornaments (the elephant). Something of what Aquinas means by 'natural' is to be found when we say that it is unnatural to rear hens in batteries or calves in darkened pens, or when we prefer foods 'with no artificial preservatives'. The concept of 'natural' comes under much attack when it is used by theologians. Curiously, its meaning is quite clear to weight-lifters, a group rarely noted for their intellectual subtlety, but fully capable of grasping—if that is the word—the difference between natural food, of which they can eat any variety, and 'artificial substances', which they must eschew. *Ex ore gigantium* . . . In Aquinas, though he naturally never uses the term, our own body is an ecological object, indeed for us the primary such object.

This belief in the goodness of nature leads him to say that a person is born with certain incipient virtues. Reason already possesses the basic rules for understanding the world and the will has a natural desire for good, though these need to be developed by virtuous acts (*ST*, I-II, 63, 1).

The belief equally leads him to write of procreation:

> Granted that the material (*corporalis*) world has been made by God, and is good, it is impossible to argue that what needs to be done to conserve that world—something which in any case we are naturally inclined to do—is wrong. So since nature inclines us to produce children, it is impossible to say that the acts by which a child is conceived are always wrong and that it is impossible to perform them virtuously. (*In IV Sent.*, 26, 1, 3)

Anyone who denies this, he says, is 'insane' and must believe that the material world was created by an evil god, and that, he says, is the very worst of heresies (Ibid.). The marriage act is not only not sinful; is meritorious (*In IV Sent.*, 26, 1, 4). He considers counter-arguments. Some authorities have said that the marriage act is 'excused' by virtue of the good values associated with marriage. But what is excused is sinful. Hence the marriage act is sinful. He replies that we excuse something that looks bad, but is not bad, or at least is not as bad as it looks. Now if the marriage act looks bad it is because it seems to show a loss of selfcontrol. Hence the word 'excuse' is sometimes used of it without implying it is really bad (*In IV Sent.*, 26, 1, 3, ad 4).

We can understand his point if we reflect on some of the occasions when we do say 'Excuse me'. We say it when we sneeze in company, or need to blow our nose repeatedly. We have done nothing morally wrong: why then ask to be excused? Aquinas thinks that we ask to be excused when in some way we have behaved with limited self-control. We say it too when we come by accident upon a couple in a delicate situation. Then, in the best tradition of investigative journalism, we make our excuses and leave—but we are not asserting that they are necessarily doing anything wrong.

He considers the argument that the marriage act is so abundantly delightful that the pleasure is excessive and must therefore be evil. He replies that whether pleasure is excessive or not should not be judged from its abundance but from whether it arises from doing what it is reasonable to do. But the marriage act is reasonable and the objection fails.

He even considers—and one must remember that the arguments Aquinas deals with were often put to him by ingenious and mischievous students— the difficulty that a couple in congress cannot raise their mind to God, to which he replies, more or less, that there is a time for everything (*ST*, II, 153, 2, 2).

He considers the objection that the marriage act is '*turpe*', shameful or perhaps indecent. His reply to this merits special attention for it is often misunderstood. He says that the 'shamefulness' of the marriage act '*non est turpitudo culpae sed poenae*': it is not the shamefulness of fault but of penalty (*In IV Sent.*, 26, 1, 3, ad 3). The language is highly technical, but the distinction is one we readily use. If you are invited to dinner and are found stealing the spoons, that is shameful: the shamefulness of wrongdoing. If while at table you are beset by a bout of hiccups that too is shameful but not in the same way. It is but one of many things in human life which are shameful—better perhaps, shame-making—but in no way wrong, things which we seek to do in private: the relief of natural needs, etc. Aquinas calls this the 'shame of penalty' because he thinks that in the 'state of innocence' such things would be fully under our control, not semi-controlled as they are now. The fact that a couple would be embarrassed if caught in the marriage act does not, for him, imply in the least that they are doing anything wrong.

One may disagree with Aquinas as to what makes sexual activity 'indecent'. It remains that the civil law regards sexual activity in a way in which it does not regard eating or drinking, and forbids it in public. The features of sexual activity that cause the law to regard it in this way are precisely those that Aquinas is indicating. Accusing him of hypocrisy in this matter is like accusing society of hypocrisy because on the one hand it publicly celebrates marriage and on the other accuses any couple performing the marriage act in public of behaving indecently.

None of this is meant to suggest that Aquinas approves in the slightest of sexual activity outside marriage. He does not. But neither does he regard the marriage act as sinful. As we have seen, he explicitly says it may be meritorious.

The connection he makes between the marriage act and original sin is easy to misunderstand. Original sin is inherited through the marriage act, not because the act is pleasant, but because it is the only way in which *anything* can be inherited. Consider a deposed king and queen. Any children born to them could be said to have lost their inheritance, but the same could not be said of any child they might adopt. Aquinas illustrates his point with a fanciful example. Suppose, by some miracle, a child was produced using material from its father's finger. That child would not incur original sin because he is not in a true sense his father's child and cannot inherit from him. (*ST*, II-I, 81, 4).

What then of the relation between original sin and the pleasures of the marriage act? Aquinas argues that actual delights of intercourse cannot possibly transmit sin because they can be experienced without sin, as in the marriage act. And even if the delights are themselves sinful (as in an adulterous relationships) they still do not transmit sin. What children inherit from their parents is the capacity for concupiscence, and concupiscence, as we have seen, is, *materialiter*, original sin. Formally, of course, original sin is the fact that 'original justice' was not transmitted. Aquinas writes:

> The libido which transmits original sin to children is not actual libido. For even if, by some miracle, there were no actual libido, original sin would still be transmitted. (*ST*, II-I, 82, 4, ad 3)

Aquinas' meaning may be shown by an analogy. Suppose that a father could transmit to his children a disposition to anger. That disposition would be transmitted to his children no matter what his mood at the actual time his children were conceived. It would not really matter whether on the occasion of any particular act of intercourse the father was in vile temper or unaccustomedly mild: the child's inherited dispositions would be those of the father.

It is worthwhile to notice some further things Aquinas has to say about the pleasures of marriage. (He calls them '*delectationes*' which is better translated 'delights'.) Inquiring whether the marriage act is meritorious, he considers the claim that 'merit lies in difficulty, as does virtue, but the marriage act is delightful [and hence cannot be meritorious]' and replies that marriage itself is difficult: merit does not require that the marriage act be also difficult (*In IV Sent.*, 26, 1, 4, ad 4). He is aware that some have stressed St Paul's reference (1 Cor. 7, 6) to 'concession'—which, it should be noted, may well not have referred to the marriage act but to abstention from the marriage act—and observes 'there is no reason why a person availing of a concession should not merit, because the good use of the gifts of God is itself meritorious' (*In IV Sent.*, 26, 1, 4, ad 3). Then when inquiring whether marriage is a sacrament he considers the problem that sacraments derive their efficacy from the passion of Christ, but marriage [i.e. the marriage act] is delightful and answers: 'even if marriage is not like the passion of Christ in its suffering, it resembles it in the love he showed' (*In IV Sent.*, 42, 1, ad 3).

The reference to love leads us to inquire how far Aquinas talks of love between husband and wife. Rather than the word 'love' (*amor*) itself he uses its derivative 'friendship' (*amicitia*). He writes:

> The greatest love would appear to exist between husband and wife, because they are united not only in the act of carnal copulation, which even in animals produces a sweet relationship (*suavis societas*), but also in the total sharing of family life (*totius domesticae conversationis consortium*). (*CG*, 3, 123)

He believes that the friendship of husband and wife is 'honourable, useful, and delightful'. He also believes that it is pre-figured in the Creation story. Man and woman were directly created by God (*ST*, I, 92, 4), one from the earth, the other from Adam's side. Aquinas sees this as signifying that between husband and wife there should be an alliance (*socialis conjunctio*). Eve was not taken from Adam's head, because a wife should not rule over her husband, and she was not taken from his feet because a wife is not subject to her husband as a slave is (*ST*, I, 92, 3).

Why he does not primarily use the word 'love' is clear from what he has to say about friendship:

> Not all love is friendship, but only the love in which we wish the
> other person well. If we love something for our own sake, as when we
> love wine . . . that is not the love of friendship. . . . But in friendship
> there must be mutual love and there must be sharing. (*ST*, II-II, 23, 1)

'A friend wishes to be in the company of his friend and share his life with him
(*familiaris conversatio*)' (*ST*, I-II, 65, 5). Love brings about union: a real union
with the person when physically present, and a union in the mind when
absent (*ST*, I-II, 28, 1). Each wishes to have access to the inner world of the
other. The lover is not satisfied with a superficial knowledge of the beloved:
he wants to know every single detail. What is good for the beloved is good
for him, what is bad for the beloved is bad for him (*ST*, I-II, 28, 2). Love
produces ecstasy: the lover is out of his mind (*ST*, I-II, 28, 3) and of course
jealous (*ST*, I-II, 28, 4). It never does to forget that Aquinas came from Italy.

What he has to say about marriage is more complex than has been assumed,
and the present article does not presume to offer a definitive treatment of
this topic. He certainly takes chastity to be a Christian virtue, and virginity
to be a virtue as a mode of chastity and to be 'more excellent' than marriage.
But he makes it clear that he is talking about states rather than about
individuals, and quotes Augustine: 'How does the virgin, solicitous for the
things of the Lord as she may be, know that some hidden weakness of mind
does not make her not ready for martyrdom, while the [married] woman
(*mulier*) she sees as inferior to her may even now be ready to drink the
chalice of the Lord's passion' (*ST*, II-II, 152, 4). He says that virginity is not
the greatest virtue, and faced with the scriptural phrase that virgins follow
the Lamb wherever he goes he replies that they may indeed follow the Lamb
but are not necessarily those who follow Him most closely (Ibid.). He notes
Augustine's assertion that feminine blandishments throw a man down from
the peak of (spirituality, presumably) but argues that they do not interfere
with the practice of everyday virtue (*ST*, II-II, 153, 2, ad 1).

He accepts the tradition deriving from Augustine that marriage has three
goods: the good of offspring, the good of faithfulness and the good of being
a sacrament, but he interprets these quite widely. The good of offspring is
not merely procreation of children but also 'their upbringing and the sharing
of life-work that this brings about between husband and wife': this sharing
too is a good of marriage (*In IV Sent.*, 31, 1, 2, ad 1). The good of
faithfulness is not principally the exclusion of other partners: it lies rather in
giving to each other what is due—i.e. intercourse (Ibid., ad 3). The *bonum
sacramenti* is not merely the lifelong quality of marriage but everything else
that this signifies (Ibid., ad 7). He regards the procreation of offspring as the
most essential element in marriage but the sacramental unity as the most
worthy (*In IV Sent.*, 31, 1, 3). He says that the intention of realizing either
the good of offspring *or* the good of faithfulness legitimates the act of
marriage (*In IV Sent.*, 31, 2, 2)—which is not to say that the good of

faithfulness could legitimate an unnatural act, for this, by definition, is not an act of marriage. And of course an intention need not be something that is actually present in consciousness here and now: a man on a journey does not have to keep his point of arrival in mind while he takes every single step (*ST*, I-II, 1, 6, ad 3).

He does say that it is sinful to perform the marriage act purely for pleasure (*In IV Sent.*, 31, 2, 2) and some may think this rigorous. But what of the husband who comes home half-drunk, incapable of showing his wife true affection, yet demanding what he is pleased to call his rights? There are those who would be angry that Aquinas should call this only a venial sin. The distinction he draws between the spouse so set on pleasure that he would have intercourse with anyone and the spouse who at least remains faithful to his partner has been criticized as unlikely to be of practical use[4] but Aquinas— who taught in a university and was certainly no innocent—may have been thinking of the workings of phantasy. Indeed sometimes when reading his critics on this point one wonders whether to sympathize with their lack of imagination or admire their manifest avoidance of erotic literature.

Aquinas accepts that what he calls 'the carnal conjunction' makes for sweetness between the partners, but he says this only once (see above) and does not put this effect at the center of his account of marriage. He is not a great romantic. Equally he will be misunderstood if his language is taken in a Lutheran sense: if original sin is seen as a deformity or depravity in human nature; if concupiscence is taken formally to mean original sin and to be as such sinful in its very nature; if statements that something is caused by sin are taken as referring to an actual effect of sin within human nature and not as referring to a lost inheritance, and if '*bonum prolis*' is taken as referring to the conscious intention of procreating a child here and now. It would be equally wrong to imply that Aquinas anticipates, or would have sympathy with, current attitudes. But as Max Beerbohm noted, it is difficult to keep up with the leaders of modern thought as they disappear into oblivion.

4 John T. Noonan Jr., *Contraception*, p. 251.

Does Natural Theology Rest upon a Presumption?

PATRICK MASTERSON

I

In this article I wish to examine and evaluate some features of the contention that an objective proof for the existence of God is an illusory project. It is deemed illusory, not because such proofs have in the past been shown to be defective, but rather because such a project can be shown to be in principle unrealizable. For it can be shown that the intended goal of such a demonstration, namely an effective affirmation of God, cannot be achieved simply by logical reasoning from objectively known true premises but only through recourse to certain presumptions which arise from freely adopted or culturally conditioned attitudes and commitments. The arguments of natural theology, it is claimed, do not work apart from these presumptions.

This is a view which is held not just by atheists but also and increasingly by theists themselves, and it is with versions of the view proposed by this latter group that I will be chiefly concerned in this paper. I argue that whereas commitment does play a role in attaining an affirmation of God it is less crucial than is commonly maintained.

The objections against a demonstrative argument for God which I propose to consider arise from the distinctive character of the intended conclusion of such an argument on the one hand, and of the premises of such an argument on the other, rather than from any general critique of the formal deduction relating conclusion to premises. However, as will be seen, the consideration of these objections does have some bearing upon an appreciation of the sort of argument which is involved in the enterprise of natural theology.

II

The first type of objection to be considered then is one which arises from the sort of reality which is envisaged in the conclusion of the argument, namely a divine reality or God. It is objected that because of the unique nature of the deity any affirmation of him is necessarily a self-involving affirmation and therefore quite different in kind from the impersonally affirmed conclusion which is characteristic of a demonstrative argument. The affirmation of God is called self-involving because it implies a certain attitude on the part of the person who makes the affirmation and commits him to certain behaviour—all of which presupposes that more is involved in attaining the affirmation than mere intellectual ability to draw a conclusion from premises in accordance with generally accepted rules of logic.

One could illustrate this objection in various existentialist sources, e.g. in Kierkegaard's account of truth as subjectivity or Marcel's distinction between problem and mystery. However, it can also be illustrated in a more analytic and linguistic idiom. The example I have in mind is the work of Donald Evans who has adapted Austin's account of the illocutionary force of utterances to elucidate the self-involving character of theistic discourse.

Evans distinguishes sharply between scientific assertions and theistic or religious assertions. Amongst the criteria whereby these two kinds of assertion can be distinguished he mentions a) one that has to do with the logic of such assertions and b) one which has to do with the conditions for understanding them. Thus scientific assertions are a) logically neutral and b) comprehensible impersonally. By contrast theistic assertions are a) fundamentally not logically neutral but rather self-involving, and b) not comprehensible impersonally.

A scientific assertion is said to be logically neutral in the sense that 'I give assent to it without committing myself to future conduct (other than verbal consistency), and without implying or expressing any personal attitude for or against what is asserted. If the scientific assertion were not neutral, agreement between scientists would depend partly on each one's personal commitments and attitudes, especially his moral commitments and attitudes.'[1] This logical neutrality is not to be confused with *psychological* neutrality about the issue in question nor with absence of belief about the issue. It refers rather to the requirement that scientific language be neutral in its public meaning.

Scientific assertions are not only logically neutral, they are also comprehensible impersonally. In saying that scientific assertions are comprehensible impersonally, Evans does not dispute the uninteresting fact that all comprehension or understanding is 'personal' in the sense that it is persons who understand. The point he wishes to make is that the conditions for understanding such assertions are intellectual and scientific, not intimately personal. Given sufficient intelligence and adequate scientific training anyone can understand a particular scientific assertion regardless of one's personal attitudes concerning what the assertion is about, and regardless of one's moral, aesthetic, or spiritual appreciation of what the assertion is about. The comprehensibility of a particular scientific assertion is not directly dependent upon such profoundly personal conditions.

By contrast with scientific assertions, Evans speaks of theistic or religious assertions as not logically neutral and not comprehensible impersonally. They are not logically neutral because in their primary use, upon which all other uses are parasitic, they are self-involving. They express or imply attitudes

---

1 Donald Evans, 'Differences between Scientific and Religious Assertions', *Science and Religion,* ed. I. G. Barbour (London, 1968), p. 113.

and involve commitments to certain lines of behaviour. They do not simply express a factual content which is either true or false. Thus the assertion 'God made the world', though formally similar to the assertion 'Smith made the table', has a radically different illocutionary force. It is radically self-involving because it implies as part of its meaning an attitude to the world including oneself which regards it as a totally dependent gift of existence from a being worthy of worship. The affirmation of God as maker of the world can never have merely constative illocutionary force because in virtue of the public linguistic conventions governing its meaning there is no conceivable context in which it would not logically involve consequences for attitude and action.

Likewise, the affirmation of God is not, according to Evans, comprehensible impersonally. A real experiential understanding of the logically self-involving assertions of theistic discourse can arise only in the context of certain depth experiences such as experiences of the numinous, experiences of profound interpersonal encounter, or striking aesthetic or moral experiences. Such depth experiences are mysterious and elusive, and their occurrence presupposes that their subject has fulfilled various personal conditions, e.g. has cultivated certain aesthetic, moral or speculative dispositions. Consequently, since an affirmation of God is achieved only in the context of such depth-experiences involving personal pre-conditions it cannot, like a straightforward scientific assertion, be said to be comprehensible impersonally.

These considerations concerning the self-involving character of theistic discourse and the special conditions involved in its effective comprehension elucidate Evans' contention that any proposed *demonstration* of God's existence must be judged inadequate. In advancing this contention he writes: 'The conclusion to a quasi-scientific teleological argument, however, is a flat Constative (non-Commissive and non-Behabitive) which is impersonal (non-expressive); no act of worship is performed in the utteran·e, no religious feeling-Response is expressed, and no religious way of life is adopted. . . . In so far as the teleological argument is quasi-scientific and does not depend on any particular attitude or onlook, we surely cannot go beyond the conclusion in Hume's *Dialogues*, that "the cause or causes of order in the universe probably bear some remote analogy to human intelligence". Such a conclusion lacks both positive religious relevance and psychological certainty.'[2] Having indicated that the cosmological argument is similarly defective he observes: 'On the other hand, the cosmological argument, like the teleological argument, can lose these defects if it pays the price of becoming attitude-dependent; that is if the argument is reinterpreted so that one does not expect an inquirer either to *understand* it fully or to give his *assent* to it unless he adopts an attitude which resembles the biblical Creation-onlook, then the conclusion *will* be religiously relevant and psychologically certain—once he adopts the required attitude.'[3]

2 Donald Evans, *The Logic of Self-Involvement* (London, 1969), pp. 263–4.
3 Ibid., p. 266.

Evans' main point is that God is such that an effective affirmation of him must be logically self-involving in a way which is beyond the scope of the impersonally affirmed and logically neutral factual conclusion of a scientific or demonstrative argument. Hence it is futile to look for an objective demonstration of the existence of God such as the traditional 'proofs' envisage.

To this it might be objected that even if a metaphysical proof does not as such guarantee the self-involving commitment which is integral to an effective affirmation of God it is nevertheless a logical precondition of such commitment—a necessary if not sufficient condition. In other words, philosophically, the commitment in question would be justified only because of prior knowledge of the truth that in fact finite beings really depend upon an infinite cause—and this is what a metaphysical argument claims to establish. It may well be that an effective affirmation of God is not achieved until the transcendent cause, in which such an argument terminates, is personally acknowledged as involving consequences for attitude and action. But that the argument itself proceeds impersonally from logically neutral premises about the world to a logically neutral conclusion about its cause does not render it irrelevant to a committed acknowledgement of God. On the contrary it is precisely because it is intrinsically independent of personal attitude and behaviour that it can satisfy the truth conditions of such commitment.

III

It is at this point, however, that the second kind of objection against an objective demonstration of God's existence which I propose to consider makes its presence felt. It is an objection not so much about the relevance of the conclusion of such a demonstration to an effective affirmation of God, as about the reliability of the premises from which the conclusion is derived. In effect, the objection would dispute the claim that the conclusion is drawn strictly from impersonally comprehensible and logically neutral assertions about the world. On the contrary, it would claim that the premises from which the conclusion is derived, and therefore the conclusion itself, can be shown to involve presuppositions which are a function of attitude or sheer commitment rather than objective reliable evidence.

This kind of objection has given rise to two rather different appraisals of the significance of the arguments of natural theology—one radically critical, the other somewhat more benign. The more benign appraisal is that the arguments of natural theology cannot be said to prove the existence of God but do at least show that his existence is possible. The more critical appraisal sees the objection as indicating that the arguments of natural theology represent a wholly misconceived and misleading approach to the reality of God. Let us briefly consider each of these two viewpoints.

The writings of John Hick provide a clear example of what I have called the somewhat more benign critique of the traditional arguments of natural theology. He claims that these arguments do not prove the existence of God but merely show the possibility of his existence. They do not *prove* the existence of God because the account of the world which they propose does not warrant the conclusion to a transcendent cause of the world unless one resorts to a presumption about the ultimate intelligibility of being—a presumption which is a matter of commitment or faith and not a matter of evidence or proof. Thus the traditional proofs argue in one form or another that the world is ultimately unintelligible unless God exists. According to Hick: 'the force of these arguments depends upon the decisive ruling out of one alternative, namely that the world is ultimately inexplicable, so that we shall be driven by force of logic to the other conclusion that God exists. But the difficulty of finding an agreed premise arises again at this point. For it is precisely this excluding of the non-theistic alternative that apparently is not and cannot be accomplished by logical considerations alone. It rests upon a fundamental act of faith, faith in the ultimate "rationality" of existence; and this is part of the larger faith which the atheist refuses. He believes on the contrary that the universe is devoid of ultimate meaning or purpose and the question why there is anything at all has no meaning and therefore no answer.'[4]

The same point is also made by Ronald Hepburn in an article in *Philosophy*.[5] He discusses the fact that common to the pattern of all arguments for the existence of God is a claim that reality is completely intelligible. He points out that this claim can neither be substantiated by argument nor accepted as self-evident since there is no obvious contradiction in saying that not all there is may be knowable—in other words that some data may elude or resist intelligible explanation, no matter to what level or viewpoint the matter is pursued. If one presumes that being is completely intelligible one commits oneself to seeking to overcome the *prima-facie* counter-evidence to the claim provided by situations of incomplete intelligibility. But if one has not presumed the complete intelligibility of being, the counter-evidence might make one doubt the reasonableness of any such presumption. In fact the argument for God is constructed from a combination of such counter-evidence and the presumption of the complete intelligibility of being. For example, the contingency of objects of experience and the regress of causal dependence are taken to show that the world of experience is in itself incompletely intelligible. This, in combination with a presumption about the complete intelligibility of being, provides the basis for an inference to God as a transcendent principle of ultimate intelligibility. But one might equally well take the indications of incomplete intelligibility as counting against a presumption of the complete intelligibility of being and thereby deprive the argument of an essential premiss.

4 John Hick, *Arguments for the Existence of God* (London, 1970), xiii.
5 Cf. Ronald Hepburn, 'Method and Insight', *Philosophy* 48 (1973), 153–60.

Thus the plausibility of a theistic argument rests upon commitment to a presumption rather than upon assent to indubitable evidence. But one might as readily adopt an alternative presumption as Flew does in formulating what he calls the Stratonician presumption, according to which the presumption must be that the qualities observed in things belong to them by natural right so that the characteristics we claim to discern in the universe as a whole must be accepted as the underivative characteristics of the universe itself. Hence, any quest for intelligible explanation must ultimately terminate in the acceptance, however unintelligible, of how things happen to be as a matter of brute fact.[6] As Russell puts it in his famous debate with Copleston: 'I should say that the universe is just there, and that is all.'[7]

According to Hick the fact that the arguments of theism rest upon a presumption about the intelligibility of being undermines their probative force. Since, however, one cannot rationally decide between the presumption underlying theism and the presumption underlying naturalism, the proofs—by articulating the implications of one option—do at least establish the possibility of the existence of God. However, the actual existence of God is another matter and in conclusion he insists that: 'It is logically inappropriate to seek to settle the question by means of proofs. If there is a God, this is a fact which must be known by some other way than by means of philosophical argumentation.'[8]

This claim that an *a posteriori* proof of God's existence is impossible because it must involve a presumption which begs the question is a serious objection. It raises the basic issue of how we can use the principle of intelligibility of being to establish the existence of God if this principle can be held to be universally valid only if God exists. The objection might also be formulated in terms of other alleged properties of being, such as goodness and unity. Thus, for example, a moral argument for the existence of God would seem to depend upon some claim about the intrinsic goodness or perfection of being such as an assertion that *ens et bonum convertuntur*. But the universal validity of this too would seem to depend upon the reality of a good God.

I will return presently to discuss some aspects of this crucial objection. However, before doing so I wish to refer to the more radical version of the objection to a demonstrative argument from objective premises about the world to the existence of God as its transcendent cause.

IV

This version of the objection is not content to point out that because the arguments of natural theology involve commitment to a presumption they

6 Cf. Anthony Flew, *God and Philosophy* (London, 1966), chap. 3.
7 Cf. B. Russell & F. Copleston, 'A Debate on the Existence of God', reprinted in *The Existence of God*, ed. John Hick (London, 1964), pp. 167–91.
8 Ibid., p. 19.

merely establish the possibility of the existence of God. It sees them rather as obscuring the true significance of the commitment upon which they are parasitic and as suggesting a wholly inappropriate approach to the reality of God. This view is given clear and radical expression by D. Z. Phillips in an essay entitled 'Faith, Scepticism and Religious Understanding'.[9]

Phillips argues that whether there is a God is not something anyone could find out by way of arriving at a matter of fact answer. God's existence is not a matter of fact which might conceivably not have been. It therefore cannot be established as though it were a matter of fact. It makes no sense to envisage God's existence as either a fact or not a fact to which some process of rational argument might be relevant in deciding which alternative is true. The question of the reality of God is a question of the possibility of sense and nonsense, truth and falsity *in religion*. The criteria of what can sensibly be said of God can be found only within religion. It is a mistake to look for external reasons for believing in God as though one could settle the question of his existence without referring to the religious form of life of which belief in God is a fundamental part.

Philosophy can explore the meaningfulness of talk about God only from within the presupposed context or religion. In coming through religion to see that there is a God one does not come to see that an additional being exists. One comes rather to see a new meaning in one's life and to attain a new kind of understanding. Discovering that there is a God is not like establishing that something exists within a familiar universe of discourse. It is rather a discovery of a new universe of discourse. We must not impose an alien conception of rationality on religious discourse nor assume that the distinction between the real and the unreal comes to the same in every context. We must not suppose that God's reality is to be construed as an existent amongst existents. As Kierkegaard puts it: 'God does not exist. He is eternal.' Seeing that there is a God is synonymous with seeing the possibility of eternal love. It one rises above the dimensions of contingent temporal love such as self-love, erotic love and friendship to an acknowledgement that there is an eternal love which will not let one go whatever happens one thereby attains the affirmation of God. In the context of religion, which is the only one appropriate to a discussion of God, belief, understanding and love can be equated. What it means to affirm the reality of God can only be apprehended in and through the context of a lived religious commitment to eternal love. Such commitment precludes any distinction between the commitment and the grounds for the commitment. The arguments of natural theology are both irrelevant and potentially misleading. They are neither a necessary theoretical basis for a subsequent commitment, nor a means of establishing the possibility of God. The commitment has an absolute priority and it is through it alone that the reality of God is attained. The truths of

9 Cf. D. Z. Phillips, 'Faith, Scepticism and Religious Understanding', *Faith and Philo-sophical Enquiry* (London, 1970), pp. 13-34.

theistic discourse arise within a religious form of life and it is a mistake to
look for a philosophical argument which would establish their truth or even
their possible truth. It is a basic mistake to suppose that 'the relation between
religious beliefs and the non-religious facts is that between what is justified
and its justification, or that between a conclusion and its grounds.'[10] There
are no trans-field criteria of rationality through which the truths of theistic
discourse, which arise only within religion, could be evaluated. They can be
understood and assessed only through an insider's grasp of the religious form
of life of which they are a part. There can be no philosophical justification of
commitment to God outside the religious form of life of which it is a part.

V

This brief overview has highlighted some of the chief current objections to
the idea of an objective demonstration of the existence of God as envisaged
in traditional natural theology. They operate, as we have seen, at various
levels of criticism. There is the relatively innocuous objection that the proofs,
because they are impersonal must be transformed, through incorporation
into a self-involving context and idiom, if they are to achieve their intended
goal of an effective affirmation of God. There is the more basic objection
that the proofs themselves involve an undecidable assumption about the
intelligibility of being and therefore can at best be said to have established
not the existence of God but merely the possibility of his existence. Finally,
there is a radical claim that natural theology has no independent relevance to
the question of the reality of God. This is an issue which is resolved
exclusively through an autonomous, self-sufficient religious commitment.
From this perspective the endeavours of natural theology are at best an
eludication of an already achieved religious knowledge of the reality of
God—at worst a misleading approach to the question of the reality of God.

   This last mentioned view is certainly the most radical in terms of its
consequences for natural theology as traditionally envisaged. It renders the
traditional proofs either unnecessary or ineffectual and misleading—unnecessary for believers and ineffectual and misleading for non-believers. They are
unnecessary for believers since, far from being a logical pre-condition of
their belief in God, it is their belief in God which is the precondition of the
proofs being in any way useful. For non-believers they are ineffectual
because they cannot generate the religious form of life through which alone
the reality of God is attained, and they are misleading because they give a
false impression about what is involved in attaining the reality of God.
Although thus undermining natural theology, the view claims to safeguard
the affirmation of God from any attack by making it primarily a matter of

10   D. Z. Phillips, 'Religious Beliefs and Language Games', ibid., p. 101.

lived commitment which those who find themselves involved in, or freely commit themselves to, a religious form of life will *ipso facto* find acceptable, and those who are not so involved cannot even hope to understand and therefore can in no relevant sense criticize.

This view has been styled 'Wittgensteinian Fideism' because it embodies the Wittgensteinian theme that religion is one of the ultimate given forms of life, each with a unique discourse of its own which is quite in order as it is, since it sets its own criteria of coherence, intelligibility and rationality.[11] If such a view were to be accepted, it would undermine natural theology not simply in the sense that it would show it to involve an uncompelling presumption but in the more radical sense that it would show it to be a wholly misconceived project of trying to subordinate an autonomous form of life to inappropriate criteria of rationality and reality.

However, such a view need not be accepted and there are, I believe, good reasons why it should not be accepted as an adequate guide to an appraisal of theistic discourse. It seems to me that what this view ultimately involves is the claim that a demonstrative *a posteriori* argument from the world to God is impossible not just because the ultimate nature of the world is unknowable but rather because there is no such reality as *the* world of which God could be the explanation. There is, e.g. the world of the Greek, and the world of the Christian, the world of magic and the world of science, the world of sensuality, and the world of morality, the world of belief and the world of unbelief. Each of these worlds embodies a form of life with its own criteria of rationality and reality. It is the task of the philosopher to systematically describe such forms of life through which men deploy a world around them. But it is not his task to establish that one world is more real or more true than another since there are no context-independent criteria of truth and reality transcending the individual forms of life themselves.

It can be objected that this view involves a philosophically unacceptable isolation and absolutization of supposedly autonomous forms of life. Undoubtedly the philosopher's first task is to render a faithful account of lived experience in its various dimensions and varied expression. But surely what characterizes the philosophical, and more specifically the metaphysical, undertaking is that it does not remain at the level of factual description but rather seeks to test the legitimacy of the proposed facts, aims at a critical appraisal of the totality of experience and seeks to determine the *right* beyond the *fact*. It aims to discriminate between what might seem to be so and what really is so, and pursues the investigation of this reality to its adequate and ultimate foundation. To abandon this quest for what is ultimately, universally and necessarily true for every intelligent being (even though not all may recognize this truth) would seem to deprive philosophy of its very *raison d'être*. But to confine the discussion of reality and truth to *within* a number of

11   Cf. K. Nielsen, 'Wittgensteinian Fideism', *Philosophy* 42 (1967), 191-209.

wholly independent contexts or forms of life would be in effect to do just this. It would be to accept a form of conceptual relativism which undermines the significance of rational debate on the main topics of traditional philosophical interest.

Moreover, quite apart from these general philosophical consequences of such a view, there is a particular consideration which shows it to be a singularly unfruitful line for a theist to pursue. Theism, as generally understood, involves the affirmation of God as the personal Creator of a real finite world which stands in a non-mutual real relationship of absolute dependence upon him. This account of God and the world is intended as an affirmation of how things really are, whether or not somebody recognizes it, believes it, or is committed to it being so. The affirmation of God thus involves the acknowledgement of a trans-human absolute principle of meaning and value which determines how all things really and truly are. It means that reality, truth and rationality are not, in the final analysis, contextually dependent upon compartmentalized human forms of life which allow of no trans-field appraisal of their objective validity. It means admitting at least that some forms of life are more adequate and true to how things really are than others—however difficult it may be in practice to get at the real truth. It means accepting that there is an independent meaningful reality against which forms of life can, in principle, be measured and denying that it is meaningless to raise the question of the truth or falsity, rightness or wrongness, of a form of life taken as a whole.

The view which we have been discussing must consider such appraisal and objective discrimination of whole forms of life meaningless. Hence, far from being the necessary philosophical prolegomenon to an authentic and invulnerable affirmation of God, it is in fact incompatible with the necessary consequences of such an affirmation. In it the difficulties of natural theology are bypassed at too great a price. However, although this attempt to save the intellectual respectability of an affirmation of God by making it a function of commitment to an autonomous form of life is not, I believe, a viable position, it nevertheless highlights the issue involved in the second objection, mentioned above, against any alleged demonstration of the existence of God. This is the objection which claims that at best the arguments of natural theology, merely establish the *possibility* of the existence of God. For they must presuppose the principle of the total intelligibility of being, which, as an undecidable presupposition, is adopted in virtue of an ultimate free commitment.

This is a view with which until recently I have been in sympathy. However, I am increasingly persuaded that it is one which must be very carefully weighed and refined, if it is not to be vulnerable to the kind of objection which I raised to the view described as 'Wittgensteinian Fideism'. For it is not clear how the two views can be said to be significantly different if both ultimately rest upon an autonomous commitment—either to a particular form of life or a freely adopted picture of reality—whose truth, as distinct from that of some other and even contradictory view of reality, cannot be decided on a basis of any objective rational consideration. Surely if the affirmation of God deriving from an argument of natural theology is not to appear fundamentally arbitrary it must claim to satisfy the necessary truth conditions of such an affirmation. It may be difficult to determine just what would count as the necessary truth conditions of such an affirmation. However, if the ontological significance of such an affirmation is not to be undermined, these conditions must relate to how things actually are and not merely to some human option such as a *gratuitous* commitment to the radical intelligibility of being. A commitment to intelligibility may indeed be a relevant factor in an argument for God, but it is at least as important that this commitment itself be seen to be really intelligible and in some way objectively justified. To this end I would like in the remainder of this paper to reflect in a general way on some important aspects of a metaphysical argument for the existence of God.

VI

The existence of God is said to require metaphysical demonstration because God as such is not experienced directly or immediately within the world of experience. Moreover, since we have no *a priori* means of proving his existence, it must be established *a posteriori* through an explication of the metaphysical implications of the world of experience. If we can eludicate this relationship between such metaphysical reflection and its experiential foundation we will be in a better position to decide whether or not natural theology rests upon an unjustified presumption or arbitrary commitment.

I mentioned above that what specifically characterizes the metaphysical enterprise is that it does not remain at the level of factual description but seeks rather to test the legitimacy of the proposed facts, to reach a critical justification of the totality of experience and determine the right beyond the fact which renders experiences coherent and vindicates its intelligibility.[12] In the *Phaedo* Plato witnesses to this driving force of metaphysical enquiry to know why things should be as they are, when he describes how he was never satisfied to know simply that things were as they were but sought rather to see all things in the light of the form of the Good and thus come to an understanding of their ultimate meaning and value.[13]

But how does such an enterprise avoid the charge that it is merely a manipulation of the hard facts of experience—either by subjecting them to an arbitrarily adopted *a priori* principle asserting the radical intelligibility of

12   These observations on metaphysical thinking are indebted to J. Ladrière's valuable Preface to C. Winckelmans de Cléty's *The World of Persons* (London, 1967), xii–xxi.
13   Cf. *Phaedo*, 96a–99d.

the real, or imposing upon them the conception of reality and rationality of some particular form of life. If we confine our attention to recording the supposedly hard facts of experience we will not discover any *rationale* which founds and makes the totality of the facts of experience possible. On the other hand if we appeal to some universal principle or principles through which the facts may be comprehended, such principles must appear to be arbitrarily assumed unless we can show that they have a foundation in the given reality of experience. But if what is given is only a collection of isolated empirical facts, we have no real basis for the affirmation of these principles through which the facts might be really comprehended.

The first step in overcoming this dilemma is one which denies that the reality of our experience which grounds metaphysical reflection, including the arguments of natural theology, is adequately described as a collection of empirical facts. What is really given, prior to philosophical reflection, is not an opaque collection of unconnected sense data, which in classical empiricism is what is meant by the world of experience; but rather a richer texture of experience which includes not only sense experience but also the intelligent human experience of reaching real understanding and affirming real value. Thus prior to explicit metaphysical reflection, both temporally and foundationally there is the experienced—more than sensory—reality of a familiar and coherent world of communicating intelligent subjects united, with some measure of success, in a common project of reaching intelligent and responsible solutions to practical, scientific and moral problems. In other words, metaphysical reflection which aims to elucidate the *ultimate rationale and value* of reality is rooted in a world of experience which manifests evidence of real intelligibility and value. Hence, the move from the facts of experience to seeking their ultimate rational justification arises not as an arbitrary construction imposed on brute atomic data but as an appropriate response to the solicitations of phenomena which present themselves as manifestations of an intelligibly articulated reality.

The quest for an adequate *rationale* for reality is a quest which develops as a wholly reasonable attempt to elucidate the intelligible source which manifests limited evidence of its reality in our pre-philosophical lived experience of real intelligibility and value. As one writer observes: 'It is remarkable, for example, that men communicate with each other, form lasting and profound friendships, sometimes sacrifice themselves for one another, respect other persons quite differently from things, value creativity, build universities, and are incurably attracted by the ideal of fidelity to understanding. These facts are odd if the world of which these intelligible subjects are a part is a radically absurd.'[14] In effect, the quest for an intelligible foundation of reality is *responsible*, in the literal sense of being a justified response to the manifest indications of experienced reality.

14   Michael Novak, *Belief and Unbelief* (London, 1966), p. 145.

The metaphysical affirmation of God proposes itself as this ultimate rational foundation of reality as humanly experienced. Now, as I have emphasized, this humanly experienced reality includes the experience of some real satisfaction of a specifically human need for meaning and value. We enjoy the fulfilling experience of, to some extent at least, actually understanding features of the world and actually apprehending and promoting objective moral values. Involved thus in the reality of human experience is both an acknowledgement of and an exigency for intelligibility and value. How can the affirmation of God be rationally adduced as the only vindication of this real acknowledgement and real exigency? In outline, any such argument would involve in the first place a thematization of the experiential insight and requirement that being must be ultimately such that the world of human experience should be rationally justified, and secondly a disclosure through metaphysical analysis that this intelligible foundation is not to be adequately found within the intrinsic resources of the world of experience.

Although easy to propose, this project of analysing the intrinsic resources of the world of experience and judging it to lack a required intelligible foundation is an exceedingly tall order and it is not perhaps surprising that most people have abandoned it as a naïve and futile ambition. Inasmuch as there is today any rational enquiry into the underlying conditions of the possibility of experience it tends to terminate either in a positivistic or existentialist descriptive account of how as a matter of ultimate brute fact the world of experience happens to be intrinsically constituted. Thus, in the positivist idiom, Flew writes: 'the universe itself is ultimate; and hence . . . whatever science may from time to time hold to be the most fundamental laws of nature must, equally provisionally, be taken as the last word in any series of answers to questions as to why things are as they are. The principles of the world lie themselves "inside" the world.'[15] On the other hand, the existentialist, working within a phenomenological perspective, will accept as an ultimate matter of fact that man happens to exist as a precarious source of meaning and value grafted through his body to a world of hazard, absurdity, ambiguity and contingency. From such viewpoints an affirmation of God will appear as an unjustifiable presumption or option—an appraisal with which many contemporary theists are, as we have seen, and in my view with self-defeating consequences, quite happy to agree.

However, one need not agree with such an appraisal and implicit in what I have been saying is a basis for the contention that the affirmation of God as the adequate *rationale* of the world of human experience can be objectively justified. This basis is our pre-philosophical but distinctively human apprehension that experienced reality is not just a concatenation of empirical data but a manifestation of intelligible structure and value. The argument for God is the working out of the implications of this apprehension that intelligibility

15   Anthony Flew, ibid., p. 194.

and value are characteristic of being, which therefore cannot be ultimately a negation of them. The argument would be a reflective itinerary of metaphysical analysis, back along the intelligible contours of reality from its self-manifestation in human experience to the ultimate ontological source which adequately grounds and vindicates the intelligibility and value revealed in this experience.

In such an argument the move beyond the finite world to God is made not as an arbitrary *option* for intelligibility rather than unintelligibility but as the rationally appropriate response to a really required legitimization of experience—a legitimization which is shown to be unavailable within the intrinsic resources of the finite world. How such insufficiency of the finite world is effectively shown is of course an exceedingly complicated issue and can be approached in various ways including, e.g. the five ways of St Thomas. In one manner or another these ways would involve showing that any account of reality exclusively in terms of the internal structure of this world can on reflection be seen to exhibit a gratuitousness and facticity, which if accepted as ontologically ultimate, would contradict our initial apprehension of real intelligibility and value. The point is partially made by Wittgenstein in the *Tractatus* where he writes: 'The sense of the world must lie outside the world. In the world everything is as it is and happens as it does happen. *In* it there is no value—and if there were it would be of no value. If there is a value which is of value, it must lie outside all happening and being-so. For all happening and being-so is accidental. What makes it non-accidental cannot lie *in* the world, for otherwise this would again be accidental. It must lie outside the world.'[16]

The indirect causal affirmation of God as the transcendent justifying principle of the reality of our experience does not wholly dissipate for us the mystery of being. In a sense it even deepens it. Yet it has a genuinely explanatory value in that it shows *why* the world which we apprehend is not contradictory, which it surely cannot be since it actually exists and what is contradictory is precisely what cannot exist.

VII

If the view which I have outlined is correct what conclusions can be drawn from it? In the first place it would follow that it is misleading to say that natural theology rests upon a presumption in the sense of intrinsically presupposing an arbitrarily adopted principle or an unjustifiable commitment to a religious form of life. On the contrary, the arguments of natural theology must be seen as the *rational* justification of the affirmation of God. They would be seen to establish this affirmation through a reflective eludication of the *rationale* or sufficient reason of reality which is *implicitly* acknowledged in

16   Ludwig Wittgenstein, *Tractatus Logico-Philosophicus* (London, 1922), 6.41.

our apprehension of intelligibility and value as characteristic of reality. One can therefore say that an affirmation of God is primarily a function of reason rather than commitment, because, as Aquinas observes in the *De Veritate*, an affirmation of God is implicit in all our typically human apprehension of intelligibility and value.[17] And making explicit what is implicit is properly a work of rational reflection rather than arbitrary commitment.

However, if the metaphysical argument for God is thus an explicitation of what is implicit in our pre-philosophical experience, it is so only in respect of a particular view of such experience. This is a view of human experience as apprehending being not just as empirical datum but as exhibiting intelligibility and value which invite rational investigation of their justifying source.

Undoubtedly this is a controversial view of experience and is not, particularly in the present age, one which is reached effortlessly as something which goes without saying. There is, I think it is fair to say, a cultural prejudice against such a view which finds expression, for example, in a pervasive and unquestioned positivistic outlook, or in the outlook of those who because they discuss morality and even the human subject exclusively in terms of the will and its capacities such as sincerity and courage, cannot, on moral grounds, entertain the possibility of a normative realism demanding intellectual moral insight into real objective goodness and value. For these and other reasons the thematization of experience indicated above may be dismissed as mere wishful thinking or an arbitrary stacking of the cards of experience from which to produce a desired conclusion, namely, the existence of God. Kierkegaard voices this objection in the *Philosophical Fragments* where he argues against the objective validity of any proof for God on the grounds that it is derived from a highly idealized interpretation of experience in which the conclusion is already presupposed. Thus he writes: 'I merely develop the ideality I have presupposed, and because of my confidence in *this* I make so bold as to defy all objections, even those that have not yet been made. In beginning my proof I presuppose the ideal interpretation, and also that I will be successful in carrying it through: but what else is this but to presuppose that the God exists, so that I really begin by virtue of confidence in him?'[18]

Does this objection then not draw us back inevitably to the view that the arguments of natural theology rest upon a commitment or a presumption? Certainly in the case of Kierkegaard it did, but it need not do so. For the theist can claim, and I think must claim if he wishes to defend the full ontological import of an affirmation of God, that his thematization of experience is not an arbitrary idealization of this experience but rather an adequate and objectively accurate account of it. This claim that experienced reality is

17   St Thomas, *De Veritate*, 22, 2 ad 1: Omnia cognoscentia cognoscunt implicite Deum in quolibet cognito. Sicut enim nihil habet rationem appetibilis nisi per similitudinem primae bonitatis ita nihil est cognoscibile nisi per similitudinem primae veritatis.
18   Søren Kierkegaard, *Philosophical Fragments* (Princeton, 1962), p. 53.

objectively apprehended as exhibiting an intelligibility and value which invite rational investigation of their justifying source is of course a claim which must be validated. It does not go without saying and, as I have indicated, very different views of experience commend themselves to the contemporary consciousness.

The theist, however, need not be unduly disconcerted by the observation that there are conflicting descriptions of experienced reality. He can readily agree that what experienced reality may itself be like and what people suppose or say it is like are not necessarily identical and he can argue the case for his account as more adequate and objectively justified than the alternative accounts.

However, although he can thus come to grips with the objection that people have different views of experienced reality he must resist the, at first sight more convenient, suggestion that the reality experienced is wholly relative to the discourse through which it is described. There is a basic difference between, on the one hand, claiming that people conceive and speak of reality differently, and on the other hand claiming that people conceive different realities.[19] In the first case there is the possibility of rational discrimination between alternative conceptions with a view to determining which conception represents the true or at least the more adequate account of reality. If, on the other hand, one accepts that people conceive different realities there is no independent criterion whereby the truth of one rather than another conception might be decided, since the meaning of 'truth', 'rationality' and 'reality' will be variously determined by the respective conceptual systems. One would be back into the domain of ultimate commitments or unquestionable forms of life. This, as we have seen, is where many believers such as Phillips stand. He writes: 'Religious language is not an interpretation of how things are but determines how things are for the believer. The saint and the atheist do not interpret the same world in different ways. They see different worlds.'[20] This, as I have indicated, would appear to be a counterproductive view for a theist to espouse since it is difficult to see how it avoids making the reality of God contextually dependent upon one of a range of possible human viewpoints.

The theist, therefore, cannot without undesirable consequences retreat within an impregnable universe of discourse which places his account of experienced reality beyond discussion. Rather he must defend, in the face of competing views, the objective truth of his account of experience. I have indicated that concretely this will involve *defending* a claim that reality is experienced as manifesting an intelligibility and value which invite reflective analysis of their ultimate *rationale*.

19 This point is very effectively made by Roger Trigg in *Reason and Commitment*, (Cambridge, 1973).
20 D. Z. Phillips, ibid., p. 132.

How such a claim might be most effectively supported is a large and complicated issue. Here I can merely reiterate my suggestion that it can be most fruitfully pursued through attentive consideration of our specifically human *activity* of understanding and evaluating. We attain our most decisive apprehension of reality, not when we are half asleep, or in a state of idle reverie, or when we unthinkingly accept a prevailing ideology, but rather when we are alertly and inquisitively engaged in attaining intelligent insight into the objects of consciousness and the requirements of truly moral behaviour. In effect, the experiential grasp of objective intelligibility and value is not attained through the senses but through the persevering activity of intelligence. Reflecting upon such activity of intelligence, through which we are enabled to acknowledge intelligibility and value as characteristic of reality, we apprehend a dynamic exigency which impels us to rationally pursue the justifying source of this intelligibility and value. This rational pursuit of how reality must ultimately be if its experienced manifestation is to be possible articulates itself in the argument for God.

The validity of this approach to the nature, resources and implications of experience is, I would suggest, verifiable in principle by any intelligent subject. However, in the final analysis one must, I believe, also admit that it involves presuppositions and a certain commitment. For example, it presupposes that one consciously and concernfully pursues the path of intelligent enquiry into meaning and value. It also presupposes a readiness to attend to the metaphysical significance of what such enquiry yields and to undertake the quest for an ultimate justifying principle which it inspires. In a word, it involves an openness to the metaphysical in man and a commitment to its metaphysical explication.

That such openness and commitment are quite in order can, I think, be rationally defended. But equally clearly there are many factors in contemporary culture which tend to obscure and stultify them. Hence, *in practice*, it might transpire that only a person already either culturally or existentially committed to a religious form of life will be disposed to accept the proposed appraisal of experience.

We seem thus, in conclusion, to be drawn closer than perhaps anticipated, to Evans' view of effective theistic argument as self-involving in the sense that, in practice, it involves certain personal preconditions, and the adoption of a religious or quasi-religious attitude. However, and this is the important point, such acknowledgement of the *de facto* relevance of preconditions and commitment to acceptance of a theistic argument does not undermine the *de jure* status of the argument as intrinsically a valid demonstration of God's existence from objectively true premises. Any preconditions or commitment involved are of psychological rather than logical significance. In particular, the meaning and truth of the components of the argument are not intrinsically relative to any commitment it involves. Hence, notwithstanding the weight of current opinion to the contrary, I submit, in conclusion, that natural theology is open to rational debate concerning the objective truth or falsity of its arguments. It does not and indeed, in view of its intended object, cannot rest upon a non-rational presumption.

L'Existence de Dieu Aujourd'hui

FERNAND VAN STEENBERGHEN

Après avoir sapé les bases de la métaphysique dans la *Critique de la raison pure*, Kant a eu la sagesse de mettre en valeur l'"impératif catégorique' (c'est-à-dire l'obligation morale) et les trois postulats de la raison pratique qui le fondent: la liberté (et donc la responsabilité) de la personne humaine, l'immortalité de l'âme et l'existence de Dieu, garant de l'ordre moral. Ces trois thèmes sont toujours actuels, car ils le resteront tant qu'il y aura des hommes. Le troisième—l'existence de Dieu—est le plus fondamental, car il conditionne les deux autres: la responsabilité morale relève, en dernière analyse, du Législateur souverain et l'immortalité de l'âme n'acquiert son sens profond que si elle est éclairée par la doctrine du Rémunérateur divin du bien et du mal.

Mais l'existence de Dieu est contestée par l'athéisme contemporain. Il y a toujours eu des athées dans l'histoire des hommes, mais l'athéisme n'a jamais atteint les proportions, les prétentions scientifiques et l'agressivité que nous lui connaissons aujourd'hui. Les origines historiques, les causes et les différentes formes de l'athéisme ont été abondamment étudiées; ces problèmes ne seront pas abordés ici.

Du côté des théistes, l'unanimité est loin d'être acquise lorsqu'il s'agit de fonder l'affirmation de Dieu et ce fait pose des problèmes. Les diverses voies d'accès à la connaissance de Dieu sont-elles toutes valables? Si oui, comment s'explique leur diversité? Si non, quelles sont les tentatives inopérantes et, dès lors, inacceptables? Comment opérer la sélection des voies satisfaisantes?

Il est évident que la valeur d'une preuve de l'existence de Dieu dépend de la valeur de la philosophie au sein de laquelle cette preuve est élaborée. Nous retrouvons donc, à propos de ce problème capital, le 'scandale' de l'histoire de la philosophie, c'est-à-dire la déroutante multiplicité des opinions, non seulement divergentes, mais souvent contradictoires. Sans doute, ce scandale peut être surmonté dans une large mesure par le travail de l'historien, puis par celui du philosophe.[1] Il reste cependant que des désaccords importants opposent entre eux de nombreux penseurs et que, finalement, chacun doit choisir sa voie en s'efforçant de faire le choix qui offre les meilleures garanties de vérité, c'est-à-dire de fidélité au réel.

Les choses étant telles, je voudrais tenter de voir où nous en sommes, aujourd'hui, dans la solution du problème de l'existence de Dieu. En

---

1 Voir, à ce sujet, F. Van Steenberghen, *Études philosophiques*, 2e éd. (Québec, 1988), pp. 61-8. On peut montrer, en effet, que les oppositions entre philosophes sont souvent plus apparentes que réelles. Lorsqu'elles sont réelles, elles s'expliquent souvent par les contingences historiques et n'ont alors qu'une portée très relative. Enfin, malgré tous les obstacles, l'humanité progresse dans la conquête de la vérité.

explorant la situation actuelle de la recherche dans le camp des théistes, il apparaîtra que, dans ce domaine comme en beaucoup d'autres, les hommes n'ont pas travaillé en vain, car des positions sont définitivement dépassées et des vérités importantes sont acquises. Il va de soi qu'il ne saurait être question d'examiner ici l'immense littérature contemporaine qui traite du problème de l'existence de Dieu: il y faudrait un gros volume. Sur la base d'une connaissance suffisante des orientations de cette littérature, il s'agira de dégager un certain *status quaestionis* et d'en donner un bref commentaire.

Une première thèse semble solidement établie: elle concerne la 'définition nominale' qu'il faut formuler au point de départ de la recherche de Dieu. Thomas d'Aquin enseigne, à la suite d'Aristote, que, lorsqu'on se propose de démontrer l'*existence* de quelque chose, il faut commencer par dire de quoi on parle. Autrement dit, il faut fixer le sens qu'on donne au mot par lequel on désigne l'objet dont on veut démontrer l'existence. Ainsi, lorsqu'on entreprend de démontrer l'existence de 'Dieu', il faut préciser d'abord quel sens on donne au terme 'Dieu'. Il s'agit donc d'une 'définition nominale', c'est-à-dire de la définition du *nomen*, du substantif 'Dieu'. Le bien-fondé de cette requête est assez évident, car il serait dépourvu de sens de vouloir établir l'existence d'un X indéterminé. Il est très important de satisfaire à cette requête si l'on veut faire du bon travail, clair, précis, efficace.

Encore faut-il bien choisir cette définition nominale. Comment procéder? Le choix de la définition nominale qui s'impose dépend du contexte social et culturel dans lequel on entreprend l'enquête sur l'existence de Dieu. Ce contexte est, pour nous, celui des grandes religions monothéistes, qui professent l'existence de Dieu et qui entendent par le terme 'Dieu' *l'Être suprême personnel qui a créé l'univers et le gouverne par sa providence*. C'est l'existence de ce Créateur personnel et provident que l'athéisme rejette et que nous voulons démontrer. Dès lors la définition nominale qui s'impose aujourd'hui peut se formuler ainsi: nous entendons par le terme 'Dieu' *le Créateur provident de l'univers* (*provident* implique évidemment *personnel*).

En formulant cette première thèse, nous dépassons de nombreuses positions historiques dont l'insuffisance nous apparaît clairement aujourd'hui. En voici quelques exemples.

Prenons d'abord le cas d'Aristote. Il connaît les croyances de ses compatriotes, il sait ce qu'ils entendent par 'les dieux'; mais, comme philosophe, il n'admet pas leurs conceptions anthropomorphiques de la divinité. Pour lui, l'Être suprême est le *Premier Moteur*, c'est-à-dire l'Être immatériel qui meut éternellement la première sphère, celle qui englobe tout l'univers matériel. Démontrer l'existence de Dieu, c'est donc, pour Aristote, établir l'existence nécessaire du 'Premier Moteur'. Définition nominale tout à fait insuffisante à nos yeux, car le Premier Moteur du Stagirite n'est ni Créateur, ni Providence. Ce n'est pas le 'vrai' Dieu.

Autre exemple. Dans son *Proslogion*, S. Anselme propose, comme définition nominale de Dieu, *Id quo maius cogitari nequit* (Un Être tel qu'on ne peut en concevoir de plus grand). On a contesté la valeur de la démonstration par laquelle Anselme établit l'existence de Dieu ainsi 'défini'. Mais le premier et le principal défaut de sa démonstration est l'insuffisance de la définition nominale dont elle part, car cette définition ne permet aucune connaissance *précise* et *distinctive* de Dieu: pour un matérialiste, par exemple, l'Être tel qu'on ne peut en concevoir de plus grand est un être matériel puisque, pour le matérialiste, on ne peut concevoir que des êtres matériels; pour Aristote, on vient de le voir, l'Être le plus grand que l'on puisse concevoir est le Premier Moteur.

Lorsqu'on prend connaissance des 'cinq voies' célèbres par lesquelles S. Thomas prouve l'existence de Dieu dans sa *Summa theologiae*, on constate d'abord qu'il n'observe pas lui-même la règle qu'il a établie, car il ne commence pas par donner une définition nominale de Dieu. Mais chacune des cinq voies *s'achève* par une définition nominale distincte. Après avoir démontré l'existence d'un Premier Moteur, il ajoute: *et hoc omnes intelligunt Deum*. Au terme de la *secunda via*, qui établit l'existence d'une Cause efficiente première, il déclare: *quam omnes Deum nominant*. La *tertia via* prouve qu'il existe un Être nécessaire par soi et conclut: *quod omnes dicunt Deum*. La *quarta via* prétend établir l'existence d'un Être suprême, cause de tous les autres; S. Thomas ajoute: *et hoc dicimus Deum*. Même conclusion à la *quinta via*, qui établit l'existence d'un Être intelligent qui ordonne tous les êtres de la nature vers leur fin.

Voilà donc cinq définitions nominales différentes. Sont-elles satisfaisantes? Seule la *quarta via* définit Dieu comme *Créateur* de l'univers. La *quinta via* le définit comme l'*Ordinateur intelligent* des êtres de la nature, ce qui n'est qu'un aspect de la providence. Aucune des cinq voies ne présuppose la définition *minimale* que nous avons formulée parce qu'elle est indispensable pour caractériser le vrai Dieu que reconnaissent les grandes religions monothéistes; le Créateur provident de l'univers.

Notons qu'une définition nominale ne préjuge pas la solution qui sera donnée au problème qu'elle permet de poser d'une manière claire et précise: il se pourrait, par exemple, que quelqu'un arrive à démontrer l'existence du Créateur, mais pas de sa providence.[2]

Voici un deuxième acquis: le progrès de la pensée philosophique et les exigences de rigueur que ce progrès comporte nous permettent d'éliminer comme inopérantes certaines preuves de l'existence de Dieu proposées au cours de l'histoire. Dans la synthèse philosophique de leurs auteurs, ces démonstrations leur paraissaient satisfaisantes, mais elles ne le sont plus à nos yeux. Citons, à titre d'exemples célèbres, la preuve de S. Augustin par les vérités éternelles, l'argument dit ontologique de S. Anselme (dont il a été

---

2   Pour un examen plus complet de la question de la définition nominale de Dieu, voir F. Van Steenberghen, *Dieu caché* (Louvain, 1966), pp. 27-44. Traduction anglaise: *Hidden God*, Louvain, 1966, pp. 24-38.

question plus haut) et la *quarta via* de S. Thomas. Les exposés de ces trois grands docteurs ne sont pas dépourvus d'intérêt, car ils contiennent des vues suggestives, qui méritent notre attention; mais l'articulation logique de ces preuves ne nous satisfait plus et ne résiste pas à la critique.[3]

Avant d'aborder l'examen des preuves de l'existence de Dieu que nous considérons aujourd'hui comme valables, il est important de noter que beaucoup de considérations proposées au cours de l'histoire en faveur de l'existence de Dieu ne sont pas des preuves proprement dites, mais ce qu'on peut appeler des 'préparations psychologiques', c'est-à-dire des observations ou des réflexions qui disposent l'esprit à chercher Dieu, en écartant des préjugés, en éveillant la curiosité ou l'inquiétude, en secouant l'indifférence religieuse de tant d'hommes superficiels. On peut compter parmi ces préparations psychologiques les *arguments d'autorité*, basés sur le consentement universel de l'humanité, la convergence de nombreux penseurs éminents, le témoignage des saints; ensuite les *présomptions* en faveur de l'existence de Dieu: on montre que, sans Dieu, l'ordre moral n'a pas de base solide, l'ordre social est menacé; les *acheminements* vers les preuves: on décrit, par exemple, la fragilité des êtres matériels, la beauté de l'univers, l'ordre que révèlent les lois de la nature, la finalité des êtres vivants. Tous ces faits peuvent être les amorces de la preuve cosmologique, dont nous allons parler maintenant.[4]

Déjà dans la Bible, la contemplation de l'univers corporel est proposée comme la voie qui doit conduire l'esprit humain à la découverte du Créateur. Tel est le sens des deux textes qui sont régulièrement cités pour appuyer la doctrine définie au premier Concile du Vatican touchant la connaissance naturelle de Dieu: *Sagesse*, 13, 1-9 et *Rom*, 1, 20-23. Pour l'auteur de la *Sagesse*, les païens sont inexcusables d'avoir ignoré le vrai Dieu, Créateur de l'univers: tout en admirant ses œuvres, ils n'ont pas reconnu leur Auteur et ils ont adoré des créatures, captivés par leur beauté. S. Paul reprend cette doctrine et il ajoute que, tout en connaissant le Dieu suprême, les païens ont préféré le culte des idoles. Ces textes scripturaires ne précisent pas comment la considération du monde créé révèle l'existence du Créateur.

Au cours des siècles la réflexion des penseurs chrétiens sur ces textes de l'Écriture a donné naissance à plusieurs formes de la preuve qu'on peut appeler l'*argument cosmologique*, car il s'agit d'une preuve de l'existence de Dieu qui s'appuie sur la considération du *cosmos*, c'est-à-dire de l'univers matériel.

---

3 Ibid., pp. 65-94; *Hidden God*, pp. 56-81. On trouvera, dans ces pages, la critique de plusieurs preuves de l'existence de Dieu que je ne mentionne pas ici. D'autres tentatives inefficaces pourraient être citées. Par ailleurs je ne veux pas me prononcer sur la valeur de certaines démonstrations qui, tout au moins dans leur présentation, ne me paraissent pas rigoureuses. Un seul exemple: le livre, si riche et si nuancé, du P. J. Delanglade, *Le problème de Dieu* (Paris, 1960).

4 Ibid., pp.52-64; *Hidden God*, pp. 45-55.

Une première forme de cette preuve exploite les indices de *dépendance* que manifeste le monde corporel: les êtres corporels sont sujets à des *changements* multiformes; dans leur formation et dans leur évolution, ils sont les *effets* de causes multiples; ceux qui commencent et cessent d'exister (c'est le cas des êtres vivants) trahissent par là leur *contingence*. En partant de ces faits, on démontre qu'il existe, à l'origine du monde corporel, au moins une Source immuable de tous les changements, au moins une Cause incausée, au moins un Être nécessaire par soi ou absolu. On aura reconnu, dans cet exposé, les trois premières des cinq 'voies' proposées par S. Thomas dans la page célèbre de la *Summa theologiae* déjà évoquée plus haut. Elles s'inspirent toutes trois d'Aristote et de son école. Elles invitent à chercher l'Absolu au-delà des êtres corporels, car ceux-ci sont changeants, causés et contingents.[5]

Une deuxième forme de la preuve cosmologique s'appuie sur l'*ordre* admirable que révèlent les lois de la nature. C'est la démonstration qui s'inspire le plus directement de la Bible: non seulement des deux textes classiques rappelés plus haut, mais de nombreux psaumes, qui décrivent les beautés de l'univers créé, du livre des *Proverbes*, qui célèbre la divine Sagesse dans la création, du livre de *Daniel*, qui appelle toutes les créatures à bénir le Seigneur. Cette preuve par l'ordre est esquissée dans la *Summa contra Gentiles* de S. Thomas, mais la science actuelle lui fournit une base incomparablement plus riche et plus solide. Einstein (avec bien d'autres savants) était saisi d'admiration au spectacle des lois physiques et du fait qu'elles peuvent s'exprimer en formules mathématiques rigoureuses: ces lois font de l'univers un système de relations intelligibles et elles révèlent, à l'origine de l'univers matériel, une Intelligence prodigieusement puissante et vraiment géniale.[6]

La troisième forme de la preuve cosmologique est apparentée à la précédente, mais s'en distingue cependant: c'est celle qui fait état de la merveilleuse *finalité* qui se manifeste dans le monde de la vie. C'est la cinquième voie de la *Summa theologiae*; S. Thomas l'a exposée plusieurs fois au cours de sa carrière et, à la fin de sa vie, dans le prologue de son commentaire sur le IVe évangile, il l'a appelée *via efficacissima*. C'est en tout cas celle qui est la plus accessible aux gens simples.

Certaines personnes croient encore que les théories évolutionistes de Lamarck et surtout de Darwin expliquent adéquatement l'origine de la vie et sa prodigieuse évolution, ce qui rendrait caduque la preuve de l'existence de Dieu par la finalité. Il n'en est rien. Au contraire, les données actuelles de la biologie moléculaire permettent d'étoffer surabondamment la preuve traditionnelle. Les facteurs de l'évolution invoqués par Lamarck, Darwin ou d'autres (influence du milieu, sélection naturelle, mutations accidentelles du code génétique etc.) rendent compte de certains aspects de l'évolution; mais

5 Sur les trois premières voies de la *Summa theologiae*, leur efficacité et leurs limites, voir F. Van Steenberghen, *Le problème de l'existence de Dieu dans les écrits de S. Thomas d'Aquin* (Louvain-la-Neuve, 1980), pp. 165-205.
6 Sur la preuve de l'existence de Dieu par l'ordre de l'univers, voir ibid., pp. 123-6.

ils n'expliquent ni l'origine des mécanismes merveilleux qui sont à l'œuvre dans la formation et la croissance des êtres vivants, ni la finalité qui apparaît partout dans les organismes vivants. De nouveau, ces faits requièrent l'existence d'une Cause souverainement intelligente et puissante.[7]

Je suis très attiré par une quatrième forme de la preuve cosmologique: celle qui met en lumière la nécessaire *origine temporelle* du monde corporel. Les philosophes qui ont ignoré ou qui rejettent la doctrine de la création sont acculés à penser que le monde, étant incausé, a toujours existé. Or, la matière étant en évolution continuelle, un monde éternel dans le passé impliquerait une évolution sans commencement et, dès lors, une série *infinie* d'événements passés: en effet, si la série était finie, on pourrait remonter, par la pensée, jusqu'au premier événement, lequel marquerait le commencement de l'évolution et le commencement du monde. Or c'est là le point faible qui condamne l'hypothèse d'un monde éternel dans le passé: l'infini quantitatif est impensable et impossible.[8] Celui qui a compris cela saisit avec évidence que le monde matériel a commencé d'être et d'évoluer; dès lors ce monde ne saurait être absolu ou incausé, car il serait évidemment absurde de soutenir que, n'existant pas, l'univers s'est donné lui-même l'existence. Il dépend donc d'une Cause créatrice, totalement affranchie du temps, c'est-à-dire éternelle au sens strict du terme (sans commencement, sans fin et sans succession); et pour être éternelle en ce sens, cette Cause doit être immatérielle.

Chose remarquable, la science actuelle est pleinement gagnée à l'idée d'un univers qui a *commencé* son évolution il y a 15 à 20 milliards d'années. Sans doute, la science positive, limitée par ses méthodes, ne peut aller plus loin: elle établit que l'histoire de notre univers a commencé par ce qu'on appelle le 'Big bang' (l'explosion de l'atome primitif); elle ne peut remonter plus haut, s'interroger sur l'origine de cet atome: elle laisse ce problème à la philosophie.[9]

Malgré la rigueur logique et l'intérêt humain des différentes formes de la preuve cosmologique que nous avons discernées, cette preuve souffre d'une certaine faiblesse, conséquence inévitable du point de départ qui lui donne son nom: le cosmos, le monde matériel. En raison de ce point de départ, aucune des voies que nous avons tracées ne permet de conclure immédiatement à l'existence d'une *Cause créatrice unique*. La première voie

7 Sur la preuve de l'existence de Dieu par la finalité, voir ibid., pp. 52-71 et 229-35; F. Van Steenberghen, 'La cinquième voie, *ex gubernatione rerum*', dans *Quinque sunt viae*, Studi Tomistici 9 (Città del Vaticano, 1980), pp. 84-108. Sur l'évolution voir F. Van Steenberghen, *Études philosophiques*, pp. 199-230.
8 Cf. F. Van Steenberghen, *Études philosophiques*, pp. 189-98.
9 Rappelons, en terminant cette enquête sur la preuve cosmologique, que divers aspects de cette preuve ont été exposés d'une manière à la fois très vivante et très savante par M. Claude Tresmontant dans son livre récent: *L'histoire de l'univers et le sens de la création* (Paris, 1985).

conclut à l'existence, au-delà du cosmos, d'*au moins un* Être immuable, incausé et nécessaire de soi. La deuxième et la troisième établissent l'existence d'*au moins une* Intelligence ordonnatrice de l'univers corporel. La quatrième voie prouve l'existence d'*au moins une* Cause immatérielle et éternelle de l'univers corporel. Mais comment prouver qu'il n'existe qu'*un seul* Être immuable, incausé, nécessaire de soi, qu'*une seule* Intelligence ordonnatrice et qu'elle est créatrice? N'existe-il pas, indépendamment de l'univers matériel, des êtres finis immatériels? S'il en existe, sont-ils causés ou incausés? S'ils sont causés, dépendent-ils de la même cause, ou des mêmes causes, que l'univers matériel?

Ne pensons pas trop vite que ces questions sont superflues. Nous sommes tellement habitués à penser le 'Dieu unique et créateur', que nous ne voyons plus la pertinence des questions que je viens de poser. Pour parvenir au *Créateur unique* que professe le monothéisme, il faut prolonger les voies cosmologiques et, à cette fin, il est indispensable d'entrer dans le domaine de la réflexion métaphysique. Voici pourquoi.

Il s'agit de démontrer qu'il existe un *Être suprême unique*. Pour le faire, la raison humaine ne dispose que d'un seul moyen: établir l'existence d'un *Être infini*, c'est-à-dire d'un Être qui ne s'oppose à rien, qui n'est limité par rien parce qu'il est la plénitude de l'être. Car, ne s'opposant à rien, l'Être infini est nécessairement *unique*: la formule 'plusieurs êtres infinis' implique évidemment contradiction puisque, si ces êtres sont plusieurs, ils s'opposent et sont donc finis. Or, pour démontrer l'existence de l'Être infini, il faut démontrer que *tout être fini* est causé dans son être même ou créé. C'est ce que la métaphysique établit en étudiant l'être fini, soit dans son être, soit dans son agir. Au terme de cette démonstration, il apparaît que l'ordre tout entier des êtres finis dépend, dans son être même, d'un Créateur infini et donc unique. La preuve métaphysique de l'existence de l'Être infini est vraiment la 'voie royale', la démarche rationnelle indispensable à la démonstration rigoureuse et complète de l'existence de Dieu, 'le Créateur provident de l'univers'. Car, que le Créateur soit aussi 'provident', se déduit aisément du fait que, comme Créateur, il précontient éminemment toutes les perfections de ses créatures.

On peut rejoindre la preuve métaphysique à partir de la conclusion de la quatrième voie cosmologique. Celle-ci établit que l'univers matériel, ayant commencé d'exister, a été créé par une Cause immatérielle et éternelle. Mais une cause créatrice doit précontenir adéquatement son effet, puisqu'elle le cause dans la totalité de son être. Elle ne saurait donc être finie, car l'être fini s'oppose tout entier aux autres êtres finis et ne saurait donc les précontenir adéquatement. La cause créatrice de l'univers matériel est donc l'Être infini et unique.

Si le Créateur ne s'était pas révélé aux hommes, s'il n'avait pas établi avec eux des relations d'ordre 'surnaturel', nous ne pourrions le connaître que par les démonstrations rationnelles que nous venons de rappeler. Car, dans cette hypothèse, toute *expérience* de Dieu serait exclue et nous ne pourrions l'atteindre que par la raison discursive. Mais le judaïsme et, après lui, le christianisme se présentent à l'humanité comme des religions qui doivent leur existence à des initiatives de Dieu lui-même. Le judaïsme se réclame des révélations de Jahvé aux patriarches, à Moïse et aux prophètes. Le christian-isme est fondé sur la foi en l'incarnation du Fils de Dieu, qui a apporté au monde la 'Bonne Nouvelle' du Royaume de Dieu. Ces faits entraînent comme heureuses conséquences des *expériences religieuses* authentiques, portant sur la présence et sur l'action du Créateur. Ces expériences se sont présentées sous différentes formes au cours de l'histoire: les plus sublimes ont été les contacts multiples du Christ avec ses contemporains; Bergson a mis en valeur le témoignage des grands mystiques chrétiens, qui, dans les formes supérieures de la contemplation, ont joui d'une intimité extraordinaire avec les Personnes divines; l'action du Tout-Puissant peut aussi être perçue dans les miracles dûment critiqués: ceux de Lourdes, par exemple, ou ceux qu'on rencontre dans la vie des saints, Jean Bosco, le curé d'Ars et tant d'autres.

Ces voies de l'expérience religieuse authentique sont particulièrement importantes aujourd'hui, vu l'état d'esprit de la plupart de nos contempo-rains: fermés à toute réflexion métaphysique, ils ont le culte de l'expérience sous toutes ses formes. Même en philosophie, les courants empiristes dominent et toute connaissance métempirique est souvent frappée de suspicion.

Nous n'exploitons pas assez ces voies de l'expérience religieuse. Tout procès de canonisation comporte l'examen rigoureux de plusieurs miracles récents. Quel usage faisons-nous de ces dossiers précieux? On ne parle plus guère que sporadiquement des miracles de Lourdes. La vie de Marthe Robin, décédée en 1981, a été, pendant un demi-siècle, une accumulation de miracles extraordinaires, parmi lesquels le fait qu'elle a vécu de longues années sans boire et sans manger; mais son premier biographe, l'abbé Peyret, parle avec beaucoup de discrétion de ces faits absolument inouïs; pourtant, si Dieu réalise ces merveilles, n'est-ce pas pour réveiller la foi dans nos pays rongés par le matérialisme jouisseur?

Au terme de cet aperçu qui résume l'état actuel du 'dossier' relatif aux preuves de l'existence de Dieu, il est réconfortant de constater que ce dossier est plus riche et plus solide que jamais. On notera aussi la remarquable *convergence* des différentes voies que nous avons explorées. Cet ensemble est vraiment impressionnant. Il m'est difficile de comprendre qu'un homme intelligent, ouvert aux problèmes philosophiques les plus fondamentaux et averti des positions actuelles des sciences de la nature, puisse se déclarer athée. Je puis comprendre qu'il y ait des *agnostiques*: des gens qui, accaparés par toutes sortes d'occupations terrestres, ne se donnent pas le temps d'étudier le problème religieux. Je puis aussi comprendre qu'au spectacle du mal, certaines personnes mettent en doute la *providence* du Créateur. Mais soutenir que l'univers est incausé, et donc éternel, que les lois de la nature sont l'effet du hasard, de même que les performances des vivants, ce sont des thèses indéfendables, aujourd'hui plus que jamais.

A la lumière de l'exposé qu'on vient de lire, je voudrais examiner, dans une dernière section de cette étude, certaines formules qu'on rencontre souvent dans la littérature religieuse actuelle, mais qui sont très contestables. On parle de 'ceux qui croient en Dieu'; on déclare 'Je crois que Dieu existe' ou 'Je crois en l'existence de Dieu'; un théologien se propose d'expliquer 'Pourquoi je crois en Dieu'. Que signifient exactement ces formules? Sont-elles défendables?

Croire, c'est *admettre une affirmation comme vraie sur le témoignage d'autrui.* 'Croire que Dieu existe', c'est donc admettre comme vraie l'affirmation 'Dieu existe' sur le témoignage de quelqu'un. De qui? Il est certain que beaucoup de gens admettent que Dieu existe sur le témoignage de personnes jugées honnêtes et compétentes: leur curé, un théologien, voire un philosophe. Mais tel ne devrait pas être le cas d'un chrétien cultivé et certainement pas le cas d'un théologien. Ceux-ci doivent *savoir* que le Créateur existe; éclairés par la définition du premier concile du Vatican, ils savent que Dieu peut être connu par la raison et ils doivent s'efforcer de comprendre les preuves valables de l'existence de Dieu.

L'acte de foi 'surnaturelle' ou de foi 'divine' ne se définit pas autrement que l'acte de foi humaine: croire les vérités révélées, c'est *les admettre comme vraies sur le témoignage de Dieu* qui les a fait connaître aux hommes. Selon la formule traditionnelle, 'credere est assentire veritati revelatae propter auctoritatem Dei revelantis'. La valeur morale de cet acte tient au fait qu'il est un hommage à la véracité divine. Cette définition reçue, on ajoute communément, comme corollaire évident, que l'acte de foi surnaturelle présuppose une double connaissance préalable: il faut savoir que *Dieu existe* et qu'*il a parlé*. C'est ce qu'on appelle, à la suite de S. Thomas, les *praeambula fidei*. Cette doctrine traditionnelle est pur bon sens. Comment pourrais-je croire quelque chose *sur l'autorité de Dieu* sans savoir d'abord que Dieu existe et qu'il a parlé?

S'il en est ainsi, un nouveau corollaire de la doctrine de l'acte de foi s'impose: l'existence de Dieu ne saurait faire l'objet d'un acte de foi surnaturel, *c'est-à-dire motivé par l'autorité de Dieu révélant*. En effet, si je sais que Dieu a révélé, je sais déjà qu'il existe et, dès lors, je ne saurais plus le 'croire'.

C'est la thèse qu'on peut lire dans le *Traité élémentaire de philosophie* publié autrefois par des professeurs de l'Institut supérieur de philosophie de Louvain. Critiquant le traditionalisme de Louis de Bonald, l'auteur de la *Théodicée* écrit: 'en tout cas, l'existence de Dieu ne peut faire l'objet d'un acte de foi divine'.[10]

Or cette affirmation de bon sens a heurté un théologien calviniste, le pasteur A. Lecerf, et elle a fait bondir Étienne Gilson. Et comme la *Théodicée*

10   Cf. *Traité élémentaire de philosophie à l'usage des classes,* 7e éd. (Louvain, 1926), p. 22.

est, dans le *Traité élémentaire*, l'œuvre de Mgr Mercier, c'est au Cardinal Mercier que Lecerf et Gilson on adressé leurs protestations.[11] En fait, pour les dernières éditions du traité, le Cardinal Mercier avait confié le soin de revoir et, éventuellement, de compléter son texte, au chanoine N. Balthasar, son successeur dans la chaire de théodicée à Louvain. Et c'était Balthasar qui avait introduit le bout de phrase litigieux. Mercier était mort en 1926. Balthasar estima qu'il devait prendre la responsabilité du passage incriminé et répondre aux objections formulées à l'adresse de son maître illustre; il le fit dans une note publiée en 1937.[12]

Dans cette note, Balthasar cite un texte de S. Thomas qui donne la clef de l'interprétation judicieuse du passage critiqué par Gilson: *quamvis Deum esse simpliciter possit demonstrari, tamen Deum esse trinum et unum et alia huiusmodi quae fides in Deo credit, demonstrari non possunt; secundum quae est actus fidei credere Deum.*[13] Autre chose est de *savoir* que Dieu existe, autre chose est de *croire* qu'il est un en sa nature et trois en ses personnes (et tous les autres mystères révélés). Savoir que Dieu existe est un préambule indispensable de la foi surnaturelle. Le *Traité élémentaire* avait donc pleinement raison lorsqu'il écrivait: 'Le croyant admet l'objet de sa foi en s'appuyant sur l'autorité de Dieu. Cet acte *suppose* donc en lui la connaissance rationnelle de l'existence de Dieu et du fait historique de la révélation.'[14]

Malgré la note justificative du chanoine Balthasar, Gilson a récidivé un quart de siècle plus tard, dans *Le philosophe et la théologie*.[15] Il y attaque de nouveau le passage du *Traité élémentaire* déjà visé en 1936, mais ne l'attribue plus au Cardinal Mercier. Il connaît donc la note de Balthasar, mais ne la mentionne pas. Avec comme conséquence que son biographe ignorera, lui aussi, la réplique du professeur de Louvain.[16] Gilson maintient sa thèse voisine du fidéisme, qui fait de l'existence de Dieu le premier objet de la foi surnaturelle, fondée sur l'autorité de Dieu révélant. Pour la défendre, il invoque cette fois un texte de l'*Épître aux Hébreux*. A propos de la foi du patriarche Hénoch, l'auteur inspiré déclare: 'Sans la foi, il est impossible d'être agréable à Dieu: car celui qui s'avance vers Dieu doit croire qu'il existe et qu'il se fait le rémunérateur de ceux qui le cherchent'.[17] Gilson

---

11   Cf. A. Lecerf, *De la nature de la connaissance religieuse* (Paris, 1931); É Gilson, *Christianisme et philosophie* (Paris, 1936), pp. 87-8.

12   N. Balthasar, *Le chrétien peut-il croire de foi divine en l'existence de Dieu?* dans la *Revue néoscolastique de philosophie*, 1937 (40), pp. 67-74.

13   Thomas d'Aquin, *In III Sent.*, 23, 2, 2.

14   *Traité élémentaire* ..., t. II, p. 23.

15   Cf. É. Gilson, *Le philosophe et la théologie* (Paris, 1960), pp. 86-88.

16   L. K. Shook, *Étienne Gilson* (Toronto, 1984), pp. 204-5. Le P. Shook constate que le traducteur de *Philosophie et christianisme*, R. MacDonald (New York–London, 1939) n'attribue plus le texte litigieux à Mercier, mais à un de ses disciples. Il ajoute: 'It is not known whether Gilson or Phelan authorized this change' (p. 205). Le P. Shook ignore manifestement la note de Balthasar.

17   *Lettre aux Hébreux*, 11, 6.

conclut de ce passage que la foi en l'existence de Dieu n'est pas seulement *possible* pour le chrétien, elle est nécessaire, indispensable au salut.[18]

Nouvelle confusion entre le Dieu connu par la raison et le Dieu connu par la révélation. Dans son commentaire au texte de l'*Épître aux Hébreux*, Dom Paul Delatte écrit très justement: 'Il est une large différence entre le Dieu qui est pour l'intelligence la conclusion d'une inférence rationnelle, et le Dieu sur qui l'âme s'appuie par la foi. Autre est la croyance à un Être suprême, préambule aux vérités de la foi, autre la relation intime, confiante, où nous entrons avec Dieu par la foi.'[19]

C'est bien cela. L'acte de foi que requiert l'*Épître aux Hébreux* est évidemment un acte de foi surnaturelle, qui présuppose la connaissance de l'existence de Dieu et du fait qu'il a parlé. Cela étant acquis, le premier objet proposé par Dieu à notre adhésion de foi est son propre mystère: l'existence du Dieu-Trinité; ensuite ses desseins miséricordieux envers l'humanité et la félicité divine qu'il promet à ses fidèles serviteurs. On retrouve cette révélation primordiale dans les formes antiques du *Credo*: 'Je crois en *Dieu le Père* tout-puissant . . . Et en *Jésus-Christ son Fils* unique . . . Je crois au *Saint-Esprit*'; 'Je crois en un seul *Dieu, Père* tout-puissant . . .'

Quant au fond du problème, Gilson en 1960 ne voit toujours pas qu'il est *dépourvu de sens* de 'croire' que Dieu existe sur le témoignage de Dieu lui-même. C'est une contradiction dans les termes, car, si l'on *croit* que Dieu existe, c'est qu'on ne le *sait* pas; mais si l'on connaît le témoignage de Dieu, c'est qu'on *sait* qu'il existe.

Supposons un agnostique qui découvre l'existence de Dieu en lisant l'évangile de S. Matthieu. Sur quoi repose son adhésion? D'abord sur le témoignage de l'évangéliste, dont il admet la compétence et la sincérité. Ensuite sur le témoignage de Jésus de Nazareth, qui parle souvent de son Père céleste et qui confirme sa mission religieuse par de nombreux miracles. Il croit donc que Dieu existe sur ce double témoignage, et non pas sur celui de Dieu lui-même.[20]

Nous vivons dans un monde empoisonné par le scepticisme, l'incertitude généralisée, le désarroi intellectuel. Contaminés par ce poison, beaucoup de chrétiens souffrent du même scepticisme et se réfugient dans un fidéisme plus ou mois avoué: on croit sans avoir de raisons claires de croire. Je me souviens de ma stupeur et de ma colère lorsque j'ai lu, il y a quelques années, dans un hebdomadaire catholique, cette phrase ahurissante: 'Il est évident (sic!) qu'on ne peut pas démontrer l'existence de Dieu.' J'ai demandé (en

---

18 É. Gilson, *Le philosophe et la théologie*, pp. 76 et 89-90.
19 Dom Paul Delatte, *Les épîtres de saint Paul replacées dans le milieu historique des Actes des apôtres* (Louvain–Paris, 1929), t. II, p. 428.
20 Au début du livre II de son dialogue *De libero arbitrio*, S. Augustin demande à son ami Evodius comment il s'y prendrait pour faire connaître Dieu à un athée de bonne foi. Evodius répond qu'il ferait appel au témoignage des apôtres qui ont vécu avec le Christ. Sur cette preuve, voir F. Van Steenberghen, *Dieu caché*, pp. 271-7; *Hidden God*, pp. 231-6.

vain) à la rédaction de rectifier, en rappelant la définition dogmatique du premier Concile du Vatican sur la possibilité de connaître avec certitude l'existence de Dieu. L'homme cultivé (à fortiori le théologien) *sait* que le Créateur existe et qu'il a parlé aux hommes; sachant cela, il *croit* de foi divine tout ce que Dieu a révélé, à commencer par le mystère de sa vie trinitaire. Telle est l'authentique doctrine catholique, en parfaite harmonie avec les exigences légitimes de la raison.

Mind and Heart in Natural Theology

JOSEPH McCARROLL

INTRODUCTION

In the *Republic*, Plato describes the different ways of speaking about the divine as 'types of theology' (379a: τύποι περί θεολογίας). For him, thus, false propositions, as well as true ones, have to be recognized as theologies. In a striking interpretation of this passage, Eric Voegelin suggests that true views about the divine emerge originally as articulations of openness to God, while false ones have to be understood ultimately as rationalizations of spiritual closure.[1]

The present article examines some aspects of this question. The first section notes the contemporary cultural amnesia regarding religion, especially the tendency to reduce religious beliefs to symptoms of emotional and psychic immaturity or disorder, rather than recognizing them as appropriate and realistic responses to the objectively existent divine reality. The second section distinguishes the spontaneous open response in which we come to know and love God through the world from the more theoretical approach in which we subject this spontaneous response to analysis. The third section returns to the development of theoretical analysis by the classical philosophers and underlines their insistence that philosophical contemplation has an inherent theophanic quality, a view retained and expanded in the Christian intellectual tradition, for example, by Clement. The fourth and final section presents Voegelin's analysis of Plato's account of the 'types of theology' as articulations of open and closed states of soul.

I: RECOVERING FROM THE MODERN CLOSURE TO RELIGION

One of the effects of the 'closing of the mind' through higher education which Allan Bloom has analysed, is that a reductionist misinterpretation of religious beliefs has become part of the enlightened viewpoint among the educated.[2] The conventional wisdom now is that religious beliefs lack

---

1 Eric Voegelin, *Order and History*, Vol. III, *Plato and Aristotle* (Baton Rouge, 1957), p. 67.

2 Allan Bloom, *The Closing of the American Mind* (New York, 1987). Like Camus in *The Myth of Sisyphus*, Bloom in this book seems to diagnose the various symptoms of existential alienation from within. The overlong and rambling quality of the study seems to be due to the author's failure to break through to the religious closure that lies at the heart of the wide range of phenomena examined.

objective cognitive validity. They are not true knowledge that puts us in contact with God. Rather, they are to be explained away as projections of psychic immaturity, insecurity or disorder, and can be thrown aside as one acquires the scientific knowledge which is rendering them redundant. The authority often relied upon is Freud. In *The Future of an Illusion* (1927), he holds that religious beliefs are illusions generated as wish fulfilments.

Children, Freud argues, are helpless and dependent. They are aware of their plight and terrified by it. This arouses in them a need for protection from a loving figure. The protection is provided by the father. The situation of the adult in the universe is somewhat similar, he suggests. He too is dependent, aware of it, and terrified by his vulnerability. The religious belief in the benevolent providence of God who rules the universe like a loving father arises, Freud claims, as an illusion, a wish fulfilment, to provide security against the dependence that is part of the human condition, and the dread and anxiety it engenders.

As an argument it is far from rationally compelling. In the first place, the sequence of feelings attributed to the child is not convincing. Most children are cared for immediately and continuously by their parents so there is no reason for them ever to experience the great feeling of being at risk and the horror arising from it to which Freud refers. When they grow hungry they are fed. When they cry, they are picked up and surrounded with affection. The notion that they are aware of their dependence and feel terror because of it seems more like an adult projection; and even if it did occur, it would be an abnormal situation. In the second place, even if a child did feel such a terror and it aroused a need for protection, the dependence, fear or need do not bring the father into existence. Either he is really there or else he is not. Belief in a non-existent protector and provider would not be of any value to an abandoned infant. In the third place, even in Freud's own account of what is supposed to happen in the origin of belief in God, what takes place in the adult is not what takes place in the child. The child needs and has a real father; the adult, in Freud's theory, needs but lacks a divine protector so he invents an imaginary one. The analogy is defective. In the fourth place, as Paul Vitz has recently noted, Freud explicitly says that the opinions presented in *The Future of an Illusion* 'form no part of analytic theory' but are only 'personal views'.[3]

As Vitz shows, Freud found the psychology of projection in Feuerbach's *The Essence of Christianity* (1841), which he had studied enthusiastically as a young man.[4] Vitz proceeds to play Freud at his own game by proposing a neurotic explanation of atheism as arising in part from defective fathering. The child who receives adequate loving fathering is thereby given a solid foundation of personal emotional development which later places no

3   Paul Vitz, 'The Psychology of Atheism and Christian Spirituality', *Anthropotes* 4 (1990), 95.
4   Ibid.

obstacles in the way of his discovering the existence of God who loves us like a father. The child who does not, however, is deprived thereby of part of his emotional and personal development and this obstructs at a later stage the recognition of God. Vitz uses Voltaire, Feuerbach, Marx, d'Holbach, Nietzsche, Camus, Sartre, Russell and Freud himself as test case histories.[5]

The difficulty with any age is to gain sufficient theoretical distance from it to see its characteristic blindspots. It is perhaps an indication that we are at last beginning to shift into a post-modern age that we now possess the theoretical apparatus needed to recover from the modern closure to religion.[6] The closure to religion has itself become the focus of theoretical analysis, for example, by Martin Buber in *The Eclipse of God* (1952), and more extensively by Eric Voegelin in 'The Eclipse of Reality' and throughout his work.[7] When the reductionist view of religion becomes widely accepted among the educated elite, and through them becomes part of the public opinion, its true nature as a misinterpretative closure fades from public awareness and a substantial deformation of man's response to the divine follows.

> In this 'climate of opinion', to be characterized as a state of public unconsciousness, it becomes incumbent on the true philosophers, who are always rare, to regain consciousness through regaining its historical stratification.[8]

The present article seeks to make a contribution to this recovery of consciousness by recalling some aspects of the question of openness and closure that have been analysed by philosophers in the past.

II: RESPONDING TO GOD THROUGH THE WORLD AND ANALYSING THIS RESPONSE

St Thomas identifies a variety of acts and habits that have God as their direct or indirect object, such as charity and prayer.[9] A man can respond to God in different ways. There is religious experience: the divine presence discerned in the heart. There is a response to revelation and grace; there is a more recondite recognition of a divine pull in the philosophical life of reason, and

---

5   Ibid. 97-101.
6   Cf. George William Rutler, *Beyond Modernity: Reflection of a Post-Modern Catholic* (San Francisco, 1987). Voegelin has examined the notion that we all live in an 'age' in The Drama of Humanity, the Walter Turner Candler Lectures delivered in 1967 at Emory College, Georgia (from a transcript of a sound recording), and in 'Equivalences of Experience and Symbolization in History', *Philosophical Studies* 28 (1981), 91-2.
7   Eric Voegelin, 'The Eclipse of Reality', in *Phenomenology and Social Reality*, ed. Maurice Natanson, (The Hague, 1970), pp. 185-94.
8   Eric Voegelin, *Order and History*, Vol. IV, *The Ecumenic Age*, (Baton Rouge, 1974), p. 176.
9   *ST*, II-II, 81-91.

there is a response to God through the world. It is with the latter two that we are here concerned.

The same individual may participate in several or even all of these modes of religious response, and in so far as he is brought up within a living religious tradition, the different modes are likely to be intertwined and to encourage one another. Consequently, they may not be readily distinguished.

For present purposes, it is helpful to distinguish between a more spontaneous response to God through the world, and a rationally mediated reflection on that initial response in the philosophical mode. Those who experience the former very often do so as part of a spiritual life within a tradition in which it is bound up with other modes of response. They are little inclined, or equipped sometimes, to distinguish it or to subject it to any kind of critical clarification. Their focus is on God and on their relationship with him, and not on an analysis of the steps through which they 'reach' God through the world. With the author of *The Imitation of Christ*, they agree that it is better to feel these things than to be able to define them.

For those more inclined to philosophical reflection, the focus can fall on a critical scrutiny of the steps through which this 'reaching' takes place. The danger for them is that they may come to neglect the cultivation of the spontaneous response in which they discover, rediscover or otherwise respond to God through the world, and end up concentrating on an abstract analysis of formal arguments then seen as 'proofs for the existence of God', even to the extent of considering that they do not know that God exists until they have found an analysis of such arguments that is perfect. In this way, 'reaching' God through the world could be displaced by 'proofs for the existence of God'.

They run the risk of concluding that because their articulated account of this or that 'proof for the existence of God' shows it to be flawed, it follows that God does not exist. This is to mislocate the inadequacy. The formal elaboration is difficult: the spontaneous 'reaching' of God through the world is not. Bernard Lonergan remarks: 'I do not think it difficult to establish God's existence.'[10] And again, he says: 'our knowledge of God is both earlier and easier than any attempt to give it formal expression.'[11] With these words of encouragement, let us consider briefly some examples of the more spontaneous response to God through the world.

> Praise the Lord from the earth, sea creatures and all oceans,
> fire and hail, snow and mist, stormy winds that obey his word;
> all mountains and hills, all fruit trees and cedars,
> beasts, wild and tame, reptiles and birds on the wing (Ps. 148, 7-9).

> Let the sea and all within it, thunder;
> the world, and all its peoples.

10   Bernard Lonergan, *Philosophy of God, and Theology* (London, 1973), p. 55.
11   Bernard Lonergan, *Insight* (New York, 1957), p. 683.

Let the rivers clap their hands
and the hills ring out their joy
at the presence of the Lord (Ps. 97, 7-9).

What experience is being expressed by these lines and by all those like them throughout the Bible? They give their own reply:

The heavens proclaim the glory of God
and the firmament shows forth the work of his hands.
Day unto day takes up the story
and night unto night makes known the message (Ps. 18, 1-4).

There are perhaps three moments or stages in this experience. First we are moved by something we meet, for example, the snow, frost, hailstones and ice in Psalm 147, 16-17. Something about it strikes a chord deep within us— its beauty, its power, its order, its superabundance, its sheer existence or its mysteriousness. As soon as we come to know it somewhat, we are moved thereby to love it a little with that emotionally charged acceptance which Crowe, following St Thomas, calls *complacentia*.[12] Next, without any notice-able intellectual difficulty or agonizing, it moves us further to a small under-standing of the God who lies behind it. The 'moving' or 'drawing' referred to here is not any occult matter but a prompting of further understanding: this marvellous thing which has awakened wonder in us prompts us to understand that it was made by God, that even now he holds it in being, that whatever perfections it has, he has in infinite abundance. But this understanding is achieved spontaneously rather than analytically. It is a swift meditative ascent from creature to Creator. The emphasis in this simple kind of meditative ascent is not on these earlier steps, but on the higher, lighter *complacentia* which follows on the hint of God which we have been given. This love of God shifts naturally into any of a variety of other responses: praise, rejoicing, giving thanks, giving glory, and most characteristically, adoration.[13] This response to God through the world articulates itself in a form of prayer. As the beauty of the original aspect of the world which caught our attention leads us to consider and celebrate the beauty of God from whom it derives, so the beauty of the creature and its Creator inspire a beauty in the prayer, as we can see for example in Psalm 103 or in Hopkins' 'Pied Beauty'.

In an introduction to a 1916 reprint of the Book of Job, G. K. Chesterton gives a good description of the typical atmosphere and style of this kind of prayer:

(God) unrolls before Job a long panorama of created things, the horse, the eagle, the raven, the wild ass, the peacock, the ostrich, the

12 Frederick Crowe, 'Complacency and Concern in the Thought of St Thomas', *Theo-logical Studies*, 20 (1959), 1-39; 198-230; 343-95.
13 *ST*, II-II, 81–91.

crocodile. He so describes each of them that it sounds like a monster walking in the sun. The whole is a sort of psalm or rhapsody of the sense of wonder. The maker of all things is astonished at the things he has himself made. . . . Job puts forward a note of interrogation; God answers with a note of exclamation.[14]

The amazing everyday things in the world arouse in man a wonder that prompts him to go beyond them to the greater wonder, God, who lies behind them, and to celebrate him and them, often in an exclamatory style. Chesterton's work is relevant to our theme for two other reasons. It provides a compact interplay between an unusual responsiveness to the beauty, order and gratuitous givenness of things, an obviously authentic personal ascent from them to God beyond them, and a somewhat undisciplined intellectual elaboration of these events of the soul. In his work, therefore, we can observe natural theology at its moment of emergence from personal spirituality, as the wonder-laden exclamatory response to God through the world shifts from prayer to reflective meditation.[15]

The other aspect of his work that is relevant to the present theme is his acute realization that our sensitivity to the marvel of created things can become dulled and often needs to be re-aroused. This is important, if as is suggested here, natural theology needs constantly to take care not to lose touch with its proper engendering experience, the response to God through the wonder-weighted aspects of the world. This is a theme explored also by Patrick Kavanagh in his poem 'Advent'.

Kavanagh hopes through 'the dry black bread and the sugarless tea of penance' to regain 'the spirit-shocking wonder in a black slanting Ulster hill' and the 'heart-breaking strangeness in dreeping hedges'. A receptivity has been lost, through too much pleasure, but also through what he calls 'testing' too much, a closed reasoning that blunts and numbs sensitivity by trying to 'analyse' things in a wrong way. The Advent of the title, therefore, refers first to the period of purgation needed to re-vitalize him to the wonder of ordinary things that is found so effortlessly in 'a child's soul'. It has a further meaning, however. What he seeks is not just the recovery of a merely poetic or naturalistic sensitivity. It has a religious dimension. The rebirth he strives for, symbolized by the starting of a new year, will enable him to recognize in everyday things, not just their own beauty, but also 'God's breath' within them. Thus, the Advent of preparation and ascesis will be followed, as the year is reborn, by an actual Advent, the rebirth in the soul of the responsiveness to the presence of God through the things in the world: 'And Christ comes with a January flower.'

14   G. K. Chesterton, Introduction, *The Book of Job* (London, 1916), p. xxiii.
15   See for instance, the chapter on his early Notebook in Maisie Ward's *Gilbert Keith Chesterton* (London, 1945), pp. 56-64, or the experiences described by him in *Orthodoxy* (London, 1939), culminating on pp. 127-28.

As Kavanagh's poem shows, this prayer in response to God as manifested through the world found a ready home within the Christian tradition. St Paul is aware not only of man's response to God through the world, but also of the specifically intellectual derailment that can follow if it is wilfully prevented from flowering in prayer:

> For what can be known about God is plain to them, because God has shown it to them. Ever since the creation of the world, his invisible nature, namely, his eternal power and deity, has been clearly perceived in the things that have been made. So they are without excuse; for although they knew God they did not honour him as God or give thanks to him, but they became futile in their thinking, and their senseless minds were darkened (Rom. 1, 19-21).

And this wilful truncation originates in and generates a volitional closure:

> You must no longer live as the Gentiles do, in the futility of their minds; they are darkened in their understanding, alienated from the life of God because of the ignorance that is in them, due to their hardness of heart; they have become callous (Eph. 4, 17-19).

The same interplay between the cognitional darkening of understanding and the volitional *sclerocardia* is to be found when we move from a consideration of the spontaneous response to God through the world to a consideration of the more theoretical or philosophical analysis of this response in natural theology.

III: NATURAL THEOLOGY AND THE THEOPHANIC QUALITY OF PHILOSOPHICAL REASON

The spontaneous response to God through the world is universal, although it is articulated differently according to the degree of compactness or differentiation of the one who makes the response. Voegelin has drawn attention to the range of ways in which reason goes in search of the ground of existence even within the compact mode of consciousness. In *The Ecumenic Age*, he surveys a variety of kinds of 'mytho-speculation', and notes their equivalence to the noetic exploration which our tradition calls natural theology.[16] And in the second of his *Drama of Humanity* lectures, 'The Epiphany of Man', he examines two such symbolisms, one, a dialogue between Gargi and the wise man Yajnavalkya from the Upanishads, and the other from the Essene Apocalypse of Abraham.[17] The experience which concerns the present theme is the properly philosophical or theoretical one. This is not universally present or available. It was differentiated at a particular historical site and moment and spread from there. Its emergence has been

16　*The Ecumenic Age*, pp. 60-4.
17　*The Drama of Humanity*, Lecture 2, 'The Epiphany of Man', 31-4.

studied by, among others, Snell, Jaeger and Voegelin.[18] The original rootedness of the philosophical life of reason in a specific type of religious
experience is symbolized by Voegelin's description of those who made this
breakthrough as 'the mystic philosophers'.[19]

As Plato articulated in a dramatic and symbolic manner, for the first
philosophers theory was not just technique. It was theophanic. Philosophical
reasoning was experienced, understood and practised as spirituality. In the
Republic Plato describes the ascent (ἐπάνοδος), from the cave of illusion to the
vision of the Good. The symbolism is patently religious: imprisonment,
conversion and ascent, culminating in a vision of the transcendent source of
being and life, goodness and knowledge.[20] Beneath the rich symbolism we
discern a spirituality of liberation in which the soul is released from the
limiting demands and deceits of practicality, from the distorting pulls of the
passions and of self-interest, and from the disorientation of wrongly-formed
character. Gradually it discovers its proper, purely intellectual finality and
begins to respond to it. The theoretical, or as Voegelin calls it 'noetic', mode
of reason comes into its own. As it does so, it begins to orient itself towards
the truth of things as they are in themselves, and not just as self-interest
misrepresents them to us. Spontaneously, once set free to follow its inherent
orientation, reason goes in loving search of the ultimate ground of reality.
Slowly it becomes clear that the goal of that search is the divine, and that the
divine is transcendent. The intellect discovers that the philosophical quest is
itself a theophanic response to the presence of the divine in the soul and in
the universe. The philosopher realizes that the divine ground is drawing him
towards itself in and through the truth-search of theoretical reasoning and
contemplation.[21]

In his more subdued style, Aristotle continued the differentiation of what
he termed the 'theoretical life' (βίος θεωρητικός), through a deeper analysis
of human understanding. He found that intellect, νοῦς, is the highest power
in the human soul, and also the most divine (τὸ θειότατον). It is the ruling
part (τὸ κύριον), of the soul, and the right order of personal existence is
established by allowing νοῦς to exercise its natural governing function in the
formation of character. The man who achieves this learns to distinguish true
goods from merely apparent ones, and to desire, to love and act, according
to the truth. Such a man is a mature or wise man (σπουδαῖος), one who has

18   Bruno Snell, *The Discovery of the Mind: The Greek Origins of European Thought*, trans. T.
     G. Rosenmeyer (New York, 1960); Werner Jaeger, *Paideia: The Ideals of Greek Culture*, 3
     volumes, trans. Gilbert Highet, (Oxford, 1965); Werner Jaeger, *The Theology of the Early
     Greek Philosophers*, trans. Edward S. Robinson (London, 1967); Werner Jaeger, *Aristotle:
     The Fundamentals of His Development*, trans. Richard Robinson (London, 1967); Eric
     Voegelin, *Order and History*. Vols. II and III, *The World of the Polis* and *Plato and Aristotle*
     (Baton Rouge, 1957).
19   Eric Voegelin, *The World of the Polis*, chaps. 8 and 9, p. 239.
20   Eric Voegelin, *Plato and Aristotle*, pp. 59, 96, 112-17.
21   Eric Voegelin, 'Reason: The Classical Experience', in *Anamnesis*, trans., ed., Gerhart
     Niemeyer (Notre Dame, 1978), pp. 89-115.

attained full human stature. He differs from other men in that he sees the truth in each class of things, and indeed is himself the very norm and measure (*κανὼν καὶ μέτρον*), of right order and moral truth in human affairs.

Aristotle identified the specific activity proper to human intellect: theoretical activity (*θεωρητικὴ ἐνέργεια*), and distinguished the theoretical habits needed to develop it. As moral action and practical work are perfected by the practical virtues of prudence (*φρόνησις*) and art (*τέχνη*), so the life of reason is perfected by the noetic virtues that fit it to reach its proper object, the truth. Thus, understanding (*νοῦς*) is the virtue that perfects the ability to grasp first principles; scientific knowledge (*ἐπιστήμη*) governs right reasoning from these to true conclusions; and wisdom (*σοφία*) is the master-virtue, integrating *νοῦς, ἐπιστήμη* and *φρόνησις*. Its proper object is the truth about the highest realms of being, especially the divine and all things in relation to the divine. The philosopher is the man who has acquired the virtue of wisdom, and his proper occupation is the theoretical contemplation of the divine and of all things in relation to it.

Theory in this original sense is for Aristotle the highest form of activity possible for man and in it he finds his highest possible kind of happiness. It is when he is engaged in contemplation that man most resembles and approaches the divine. Aristotle goes so far as to coin a word to describe the religious significance for man of this activity: to engage in noetic contemplation is for man, he says, to achieve immortality, *ἀθανατίζειν*.[22]

St Thomas resumed Aristotle's analysis of intellect and found in it a suitable analogue for his understanding of the divine nature and also an adequate basis for analysing the natural desire to see God which stands as the foundation of his study of the meaning of human existence and moral action. God is the infinite substantial act of understanding. Human intellect is a bare incarnate capacity to understand: as such it is naturally a desire to see God in his essence, and is open to an obediential elevation through grace by which it would be made able to participate somehow in the divine life.[23]

The discovery of the theoretical mode of reason by the classical philosophers, especially Plato and Aristotle, opened the way for the development of what our tradition calls natural theology. Thomas is careful to distinguish, but not to oppose, the ways of reason and revelation. The philosophical differentiation of reason opens the possibility not only of a response to God through the world, but also of a more reflective analysis of this spontaneous response. But a man does not have to be outside faith to follow this path.

22   *Nicomachean Ethics*, X, vii, 1177a14-b35; see Eric Voegelin, *Plato and Aristotle*, 293-341; Bernard Lonergan, *Verbum: Word and Idea in Aquinas*, ed. David B. Burrell (Notre Dame, 1967), pp. 120, 185; Eric Voegelin, *Anamnesis*, p. 103; James V. Schall, *Reason, Revelation, and the Foundations of Politics* (Baton Rouge, 1987), pp. 38-62.

23   James E. O'Mahony, *The Desire of God in the Philosophy of St Thomas Aquinas* (Cork, 1929); Patrick K. Bastable, *Desire for God: Does Man Aspire Naturally to the Beatific Vision? An Analysis of This Question and Its History* (Dublin, 1947); Henri de Lubac, *The Mystery of the Supernatural*, trans. Rosemary Sheed (London, 1967); Bernard Lonergan, 'The Natural Desire to See God', in *Collection* (New York, 1967), pp. 84-95.

Rather, reason has a partial autonomy within faith, and its exploration of the world leads to the discovery and rediscovery of the existence of God and to some analogous understanding of what God is like, which complements, rather than seeks to replace or compete with what is known by faith.[24]

The religious closure that has spread throughout much of Western culture since the Enlightenment has affected natural theology, challenging its validity and leading to a loss of awareness of the significant role it played in Christianity. Voegelin notes, however, that 'The technical superiority of Christian over Greek metaphysics was itself a factor in the victory of Christianity over paganism in the Roman Empire.'[25] In particular, Christianity forces a sharp recognition of the utter transcendence of God and poses ineluctably the question of the relationship between him and his creatures. Although 'the classic movement, as well as its continuation by the Hellenistic thinkers, had provided the noetic instrument for the re-symbolization' of the relationship between God and creation, circumstances in the late imperial period were not ripe for the swift or wholesome completion of this intellectual task.[26] As Lonergan notes, 'the shadow of infelicity hung too heavily over the Empire for thinkers to be balanced.'[27] As a result, all the factors combined so that 'it took another twelve hundred years for the problems of contingent and necessary being to be articulated by the Scholastic thinkers.'[28]

This articulation was the achievement of Thomas. The basis of Christian theology, Voegelin says, and the 'centrepiece of Thomistic theology', is the *analogia entis*. Here, the technical language and method required to speak correctly about God and the world's relationships with him are developed.[29]

Voegelin's evaluation of the significance of natural theology is a much needed corrective to the underestimation brought about so often by contemporary neglect and attack:

> History shows us . . . a progressive differentiation between the domain of transcendent Being and the domain of being that is immanent, but that participates in the *Lex aeterna*. In the writings of a Saint Thomas, this differentiation arrives at its maximum, and it is this that I consider the highest degree of reason.[30]

24 See for example, *Contra Gentiles* 1, chaps 3-12.
25 Eric Voegelin, *The New Science of Politics* (Chicago, 1952), p. 80, n. 7.
26 Eric Voegelin, 'The Gospel and Culture', in *Jesus and Man's Hope*, Vol. 2, ed. Donald G. Miller and Dikran Y. Hadidian (Pittsburg, 1971), p. 83.
27 Bernard Lonergan, 'The *Gratia Operans* Dissertation: Preface and Introduction', *Method* 3 (1985), 27.
28 Eric Voegelin, ibid.
29 Eric Voegelin, *From Enlightenment to Revolution*, ed. John H. Hallowell (Durham NC, 1975), p. 26; Eric Voegelin, 'On Christianity', a letter to Alfred Schütz in January 1953, published in *The Philosophy of Order*, ed. Peter J. Opitz and Gregor Sebba (Stuttgart, 1981), p. 455.
30 Eric Voegelin, 'Les perspectives d'avenir de la civilisation occidentale', in *L'Histoire et ses interprétations: Entretiens autour de Arnold Toynbee*, ed. Raymond Aron (The Hague, 1961), p. 161; cited in Eugene Webb, *Eric Voegelin: Philosopher of History* (Seattle, 1981), p. 73, n. 1.

He continues with the observation that since Thomas' achievement, progress in that area has been overtaken by decline: 'We are today on the descending slope, that of regression, in which we see re-established the confusion between the two domains of being.'

In every age, the practice of theory is complicated and sometimes threatened by attempts, varying in success, to remove it from its spiritual and theophanic context. These efforts to disengage the critical techniques from their normative context in the ascent towards the divine ground are backed up by sceptical assaults, often using these very techniques, on the existence and reality of the divine and of the moral truth made manifest through the ascent. In such situations, the response has to be an attempt to recover and protect the theophanic quality and origin of philosophical reason.

Thus, Clement of Alexandria seeks to recover the theophanic dimension of philosophy on a Christian foundation by an appeal to the Gospel. With a gentle irony, he contrasts the quarrelsome and sceptical argument of his more sophisticated opponents with 'our barbarian philosophy':

> Our barbarian philosophy, on the other hand, has no place for any sort of strife. What it says is: 'Seek and you shall find; knock and it shall be opened to you; ask and you shall receive' (Mt. 7, 7; Lk. 11, 9). Investigation by question and answer is, I think, knocking on the door of truth, asking that it may be opened. When the door, which has been barring the way, is opened by investigation, scientific contemplation (ἐπιστημονικὴ θεωρία) of the truth begins.[31]

IV: NATURAL THEOLOGY
VOEGELIN'S RECOVERY OF PLATO

In the essay on which he was working before his death, Eric Voegelin examines the intimate relationship between theoretical analyses of natural theology and the existential stances of the thinkers who elaborate them. He starts with the observation that

> (The) language of supposedly analytic discourses on the questions of divinity has stabilized, by cultural consensus, on a level of compactness which does not sufficiently distinguish between the paradoxic structure of the divine-human encounter in the search, and the symbols arising in reflection on the culturally concrete expressions of the search.[32]

31 Clement of Alexandria, *Strom.*, VIII, I; cited in Bernard Lonergan, *The Way to Nicea* (London, 1976), pp. 117-18.
32 Eric Voegelin, '*Quod Deus Dicitur*', *Journal of American Academy of Religion*, 53 (1985), 569-84. An earlier analysis of some of the same questions appears in Eric Voegelin, *Conversations with Eric Voegelin*, ed. Eric O'Connor (Montreal, 1980), pp. 125-29. Page references within the following paragraphs are to '*Quod Deus Dicitur*'.

Misinterpretation arises, he suggests, when original symbols are not treated as expressions of somebody's personal experience and search for the meaning of his existence; in other words, when they are detached and interpreted apart from their engendering spiritual experience. Instead, they are studied on their own, apart from their motivating existential context, as propositions or opinions to be evaluated in terms of their logical compatibility with the modes and rules of discourse or discovery proper to everyday practicality or the scientific study of sensible phenomena.

To get behind this distorting procedure and to recover analytically the awareness that such symbols are to be interpreted in the light of the religious tension that gave rise to them, Voegelin returns to the *Proslogion* of Anselm. Here, the theoretical search is set within the context of prayer. Like Clement, Anselm understands his theoretical search is set within the context of an interpersonal exchange between the thinker and God. He prays that he may receive understanding of the original symbols of his faith. Like this faith, his theoretical search for the meaning of the faith as a theologian is rooted in and dynamized by the living desire of his soul for God. Like Clement, too, he quotes the words of Christ: 'Ask and you shall receive, that your joy may be full.' Clearly, like Clement also, he recognizes that the initiative in the search, as in the faith, lies with God. And he responds 'with the joyful counter-movement of his quest (XXVI)' (p. 575).

Voegelin asks what it was that led Anselm to move from this kind of language, in which the theophanic and personal dimensions of the search are evident, to the language of 'proofs for the existence of God' and the other abstract terminology. The shift is prompted, he suggests, by the encounter with a practical or theoretical non-believer. The practical non-believer is someone whose existential state is like that articulated in Psalm 13: 'The fool says in his heart, "There is no God"'. Voegelin notes that the modern connotation of 'silliness' misses the meaning that the word *nabal* had in Hebrew. 'The fool of the Psalm is certainly not a man wanting in intellectual acumen or worldly judgment'; nor does it refer to 'as differentiated a phenomenon as dogmatic atheism'. It refers, rather, to 'a state of spiritual dullness that will permit the indulgence of greed, sex and power without fear of divine judgment' (p. 577).

The fact that a type has to be singled out for comment means that it has become a significant social trend. Voegelin draws attention to the importance of the social situation constituted by 'the mass phenomenon of men who do evil rather than good because they do not "seek after God and his justice", who "eat my people like bread" because they do not believe in the divine sanction for acts of unrighteousness. The personal contempt for God will manifest itself in ruthless conduct towards the weaker man and create general disorder in society' (p. 577). The situation formed by a preponderance of such people puts pressure on the life of reason but probably does not suffice to bring about the shift from prayer to proofs, to which he refers.

Voegelin suggests that what accentuates the closure to the point at which it is felt necessary to respond by constructing proofs for the existence of God, is the entry into Christianity of the Hellenistic and later continuations and derailments of the philosophical tradition.

To understand this phenomenon Voegelin returns to Plato's analysis of the challenge posed to the philosopher by existential closure. The differentiation of philosophical reasoning makes possible its deformation, and when that deformation acquires sufficient social support it threatens the philosopher's response to the divine. Plato responds to this threat by analysis.

In the *Laws*, Plato presents a set of negative propositions concerning the divine and its relationship with man and the world:

> It seems that no gods exist.
> Even if they do exist, they do not care about man.
> Even if they care, they can be propitiated by gifts.[33]

These opinions seem to have been common currency in the Sophistic schools. The fact that they were in such general use implies, for Voegelin, that 'the contempt for the gods had grown into a general loss of experiential contact with cosmic-divine reality. The triadic patterns of negative expressions appear to have developed as an expression for the resultant contraction of man's existence' (p. 578).

Man is always free to reply to the divine invitation either by acceptance or by refusal. When refusal gains social dominance it generates a cultural demand for new 'theologies', which rationalize it by denying the reality of that which moves us from beyond. This is the function which Plato imputes to the three propositions cited in the *Laws*. Voegelin comments:

> The folly of responding to the divine appeal by denial or evasion is just as much a human possibility as the positive response. As a potentiality it is present in every man, including the believer; and in certain historical situations its actualization can become a massive social force. (p. 576)

When this happens, it undermines the plausibility or credibility of the philosopher's tension towards the divine.

It is in response to this threat that Plato elaborates in the *Laws* what has since come to be known as a proof for the existence of God. We see here the moment of birth of the part of philosophy that has since grown into natural theology.

What prompts the shift from prayerful response to God to defensive proofs of his existence is the intrusion of a powerful public opinion dominated by an existential alienation such as finds articulation in the three opinions presented. Natural theology, therefore,

---

33 Eric Voegelin, ibid., p. 577; cf. *Laws*, Bk X, 885b.

is neither modern nor ancient; it is rather the argument that will recur whenever the quest for divine reality has to be resumed in a situation in which the 'rationalization' of contracted existence, the existence of the fool, has become a mass phenomenon. (p. 578)

Plato's central insight into this process, however, regards the origin, status and function of the negative propositions.

That the negative propositions are not a philosopher's statement concerning a structure in reality, but express a deformation of the 'heart', is the insight gained by Plato. (p. 579)

The existential closure articulated in the Sophistic propositions, the *ἄνοια*, is not basically a theoretical error. It is a *νόσος*, a disease of the soul, a spiritual disorder.

In the second book of the *Republic*, Plato elaborates a technical vocabulary for diagnosing this disease. He distinguishes two levels of meaning in the three propositions that express the inverted philosophy of existence.[34] A more superficial degree of falsehood attaches to the three negative propositions in the sense that God does exist, he does rule the universe with complete justice and benevolence, and he cannot be fooled or bought off by mechanical religious observance or material bribes unsupported by moral reform of conduct and soul.

The deeper and more substantial falsehood is the existential attitude that moves a man to identify with these three propositions as expressive of his experience of life. The negative opinions are symptomatic of an underlying existential alienation.

The 'ignorance within the soul' (*ἐν τῇ ψυχῇ ἄγνοια*) is 'truly the falsehood' (*ἀληθῶς ψεῦδος*), while the falsehood in words is only 'the after-rising image' (*ὕστερον γεγονὸς εἴδωλον*). The false words, therefore, are not an 'unmixed falsehood' as is the 'essential falsehood' (*τὸ μὲν δὴ τῷ ὄντι ψεῦδος*) in the soul. The verbal falsehood, the 'rationalization' we may say, is the form of truth in which the diseased soul expresses itself (*Republic* 382). (p. 579)

The negative propositions, while false in the sense that the understanding of reality which they express is incorrect, have at least a truth as accurately articulating how that objective reality 'looks' from within alienated consciousness. Through them, in other words, we may learn something of the distortion within the soul of the person who finds them an adequate view of reality. They tell us how a person 'sees' reality. They are 'true', therefore, in the sense that they are 'the syndrome of a disease that affects man's humanity and destroys the order of society' (p. 579).

34 Eric Voegelin, *Plato and Aristotle*; see pp. 31-6 on the analysis of inverted existence in the *Gorgias*, and chap. 3 on the *Republic*.

It is in the context of this dialectical analysis of the existential stances underlying and engendering various positions in natural theology that Plato coins the technical term 'theology'. The negative propositions are, Plato says, τύποι περὶ θεολογίας, types of theology (379a). They have to be classified as false theologies, whereas the analysis advanced by the philosopher to counter them is true theology. Both types, however, the negative as much as the positive, have to be recognized as theologies because both spring from and articulate types of response to the divine. The true and false propositions are 'the verbal mimesis respectively of man's existence in truth or falsehood' (p. 580). The propositions have no autonomous truth of their own, but have to be referred back to their engendering experiences, man's answering or failing to answer the divine invitation. Voegelin concludes:

> The two types of theology together represent the verbal mimesis of the human tension between the potentialities of response or non-response to the divine presence in personal, social and historical existence. (p. 580)

There are, therefore, conditions of interiority that ground the untruth of the negative propositions in the false theologies. By the same token, however, there are conditions of spirituality to be fulfilled in order that the positive propositions of natural theology be authentically 'held' by a particular individual. These centre around a deliberate effort to achieve and maintain a tension of sanctity, of openness and response to the divine, reached through the world, and, if one seeks to be a philosopher, through the active culture of meditation. The personal response to God through the world should be maintained and the theophanic quality of philosophical reason should be discerned and acknowledged. Without some such foundation of personal response to God through the world and through reason, the 'holding' of even a correct natural theology degenerates into a mechanical remembering and repetition of phrases not really understood. The truth of the propositions that constitute natural theology, Voegelin insists,

> is neither self-evident, nor a matter of logical proof; they would be just as empty as the negative ones, if they were not backed by the reality of the divine-human movement and counter-movement, of the Prayer answering the appeal in the soul of the proponent. (p. 580)

CONCLUSION

The focus in the present article has been the interplay between the cognitional and volitional components of natural theology. There is a perennial need to recall this interplay because, as experience has shown, natural theology seems ever in danger of being caught up in the derailment of the noetic tension into what Voegelin has called the 'new intellectual game with imaginary realities in the imaginary realm of thought, the game of propositional metaphysics'.[35]

To lessen the likelihood of such derailment it is necessary to repeatedly re-insert natural theology within its engendering experiences of order, the primary response to God through the world, and the secondary reflection on this in the noetic mode of reason. In both of these, there is an interplay between intellect and will.

The spontaneous response takes the form of a prayer in which the emphasis falls on the wonder evoked by some features of the world, and even more, by the God who lies beyond them and whose glory they manifest. The style is often exclamatory. This kind of response is more universal although it varies, both in experience and symbolism, according to the degree of compactness and differentiation. People vary in their responsiveness to this elementary experience of order due to natural endowment, but there is also a volitional aspect. The sensitivity to the wonder of the world and to the glory of the God reflected in it can be dulled to a large extent and may need to be re-awakened. In both of these cases, a volitional factor comes into play. Again, as the passages from Paul intimate, if the meditative ascent from the world to God is blocked deliberately, because of a volitional disorder, further intellectual and volitional disorder is produced.

Natural theology arises from theoretical reflection on this earlier spontaneous response. Theory as such, however, is not universal but emerged at specific historical sites and developed along definite historical lines of transmission, one of which was the Christian tradition. Here also an element of volitional commitment is needed. As Plato suggests in the tale of the cave, effort is required to tear oneself away from the illusions, to turn oneself around, to face the greater brightness of the sun and to ascend from the cave. To live the life of reason requires discipline, and as it calls for a sharp break with widely held social opinions, it also calls for an autonomy that can deal with some solitude and perhaps even social isolation and antagonism.

More essentially, however, the philosophers discerned at the core of the noetic tension a theophanic quality. In following the path of theory, they were responding to a pull from the divine. As in all such responses, man is free and can respond to the divine invitation either by acceptance or by refusal. Theory is not for human beings effortlessly detached intellection. To give free rein to human understanding so that it may follow the scent of truth in a truly unrestricted manner demands the development of a character in which the passions are ruled by the moral virtues. Here too, then, a volitional component is indispensable.

As the response to the world can become opaque to the divine presence beyond it, so too the philosophical life of reason can become closed. Voegelin follows Plato in seeing such an existential closure as the ultimate originating

35   Eric Voegelin, *The Ecumenic Age*, p. 43.

source of false propositions about the divine. Here too, a volitional component intervenes. Existential closure motivates the construction of opinions that function as its rationalization. When these gain significant social support, they begin to undermine the plausibility of the philosophical quest for the divine through the life of open theoretical reason. This, in turn, prompts the philosopher to respond with a counter-critique of the false opinions and their existential foundation. From such a defensive response, Voegelin suggests, arises the elaboration of what comes to be known as natural theology. From the perspective of this recognition of the interplay of the intellectual and volitional elements in natural theology, therefore, theological propositions may be termed 'true' or 'false' according as they represent theoretical articulations of existential openness or closure.

What Voegelin means by existential openness and closure, and by 'true humanity' and the 'untrue man' is not something obscure. Elsewhere he calls it existence in truth or untruth, and he gives the following succinct description of both states:

> In an age that has good reasons to doubt the validity of large parts of classic and scholastic metaphysics, it is therefore of the first importance to disengage from the metaphysical efforts of the past the truth of existence that has motivated and informed them.
>
> I have again used the expression 'truth of existence'. We can now define it as the awareness of the fundamental structure of existence together with the willingness to accept it as the *conditio humana*. Correspondingly we shall define untruth of existence as a revolt against the *conditio humana* and the attempt to overlay its reality by the construction of a Second Reality.[36]

Finally, Voegelin is open to the possibility that even on this secondary and reflective level, natural theology is a sort of prayer:

> In search of the meaning of such demonstration (setting aside the previously mentioned usefulness of symbols for protective and defensive functions) there seems to suggest itself the possibility that demonstrations of this type are a Myth of the Logos offered by the Intellect as a gift of veneration to the constitution of being.[37]

36   Eric Voegelin, 'On Debate and Existence', *Intercollegiate Review* 3 (1967), 150-1.
37   Ibid., p. 150.

Nature, Surnature, Culture, en Philosophie de la Religion

GEORGES VAN RIET

Lorsque la réflexion philosophique se porte sur la religion en vue de la situer et de la comprendre, tout en respectant son originalité, elle est tentée de la rapprocher pour le moins des notions de nature, de surnature et de culture. Nous nous proposons d'examiner ces rapprochements en nous inspirant de la tradition philosophique inaugurée par Aristote, car c'est d'elle que les deux premiers de ces termes ont reçu leur signification originaire.

I: NATURE

Dans la tradition aristotélicienne, on considère que le terme de nature est le plus fondamental. Par nature, on entend ce qu'est une chose du fait de sa 'naissance', ce qu'elle est 'en elle-même', initialement, avant tout développement et donc aussi avant toute éventuelle déformation. La nature n'est pas seulement un état initial, elle est une structure qui implique une sorte de canon, ou de règle, pour apprécier les états ultérieurs; rien, en effet, ne se développe 'comme il convient', sinon selon sa nature. Doit être considéré comme une déformation ce qui se produit contre sa nature; est accidentel, sans importance et sans raison d'être, ce qui 'advient' à une nature sans en résulter ni s'y opposer. La nature, c'est l'essentiel, le fondamental.

Pour préciser ce qu'il entend par nature, Aristote distingue, d'une part, ce qui résulte de la nature et, d'autre part, ce qui a lieu par hasard ou ce qui résulte de l'intelligence humaine dans l'art ou la technique.

Le hasard peut produire les mêmes effets que la nature, mais 'par accident'. Ses effets n'ont rien de propre ni de spécifique; ils ne peuvent rien nous apprendre; le hasard ne rend compte ni de la constance ni de l'ordre des phénomènes observés. Ainsi, si je vais au marché pour acheter des légumes et que je rencontre un débiteur qui doit me restituer une dette, je ne peux conclure que, pour recouvrer une dette, il faut aller acheter des légumes.

Sont des êtres de la nature ceux qui ont en eux-mêmes, à titre essentiel, un principe de mouvement et de repos, tels, par exemple, les corps élémentaires, les plantes, les animaux, les hommes. Les mouvements locaux, la croissance et la décroissance, les altérations qualitatives, sont considérés comme leur fait à eux; ils se produisent en raison d'une inclination qui leur est intrinsèque. Mais nul ne reconnaît pareille inclination aux objets de l'art, considérés comme tels: si l'on enfouit dans la terre un lit en bois et qu'il germe, il n'en résulte pas un autre lit; s'il pourrit, c'est en tant qu'il est du bois, et non en tant qu'il est un lit. L'art ou la technique sont des causes extrinsèques de changement; ils peuvent se trouver dans le même sujet, mais par accident: quand un médecin se guérit lui-même, il guérit, non comme médecin, mais comme malade.

Il faut remarquer que, pour Aristote, sont appelés 'naturels' les changements 'conformes à la nature' (κατὰ φύσιν). Ainsi, manifestement, ceux qui sont le résultat de propriétés des êtres naturels (une pierre se meut vers le bas, qui est son lieu naturel); la nature est dans ces cas leur cause adéquate. Mais sont également 'conformes à la nature' et donc 'naturels' les phénomènes qui résultent d'une cause extérieure, si celle-ci agit dans le même sens que la nature et ne fait qu'accroître l'intensité du mouvement (ainsi une pierre projetée vers le sol; ainsi aussi l'art, l'éducation, la médecine); cette cause extérieure est alors appelée une puissance (δύναμις) active.

Sont au contraire appelés hors nature (παρὰ φύσιν) les phénomènes dus à une force extérieure (βία) qui contrarie la nature et lui imprime un mouvement 'forcé' (une pierre jetée en l'air); de manière générale, est dû à la violence ce dont le principe est extérieur à celui qui est l'objet de l'action sans que celui-ci y ait aucune part.

Pour l'être qui en est le principe, le terme d'un mouvement naturel est une fin, un bien, une perfection, un acte, une plénitude d'être. L'être naturel l'obtient par son activité. La finalité établit dès lors une corrélation entre l'essence d'un être de la nature, ses opérations et sa fin.

La Nature (prise comme un tout) agit en vue d'une fin (comme l'art, mais sans délibération ni réflexion) et cette fin, c'est encore la Nature, mais cette fois comme forme. On peut y distinguer:

1) les mouvements tels que les altérations, les générations et corruptions, dans le monde sublunaire des quatre éléments: ils dépendent des mouvements du ciel, moteurs spirituels;

2) de manière éternelle et parfaite, le mouvement local circulaire du ciel (constitué par le cinquième élément, la quintessence, l'éther);

3) les divers types d'activités de l'homme: la theoria et la praxis, qui sont des opérations immanentes, et la poièsis, qui produit une oeuvre extérieure. La fin dernière de ces activités est le 'bonheur', à savoir un bien 'achevé' mais fini, auquel on ne peut rien ajouter; c'est le meilleur possible, 'étant donné les circonstances'. Il consiste, soit dans un équilibre entre les diverses fonctions dont l'homme est capable, soit dans son activité la plus haute, la contemplation (mais, à vrai dire, en cette vie c'est plutôt une idée limite).

La Nature, ainsi entendue, renvoie à un Premier Moteur Immobile, Acte pur, premier appétible, fin dernière de tout ou cause finale suprême (mais non pas cause efficiente) de tout mouvement; il est pure intelligence; son acte est de se penser soi-même; c'est en fonction de lui que sont constitués l'ordre et le mouvement du monde.

Saint Thomas d'Aquin a repris Aristote. On dit qu'il l'a complété par Platon ou par le néoplatonisme. Mais il l'a surtout complété par deux thèses originales qui suffisent à le classer, non plus parmi les disciples des grands philosophes, mais parmi les maîtres.

D'après la première de ces thèses, la perfection fondamentale n'est pas la Forme, ni l'Idée, mais l'*esse*, l'exister. L'exister est ce qu'il y a de plus intime et de plus formel dans les réalités offertes à notre expérience; c'est l'acte, au sens le plus fondamental, l'acte premier. Dans les réalités multiples que nous observons, cette perfection se trouve 'déterminée', 'limitée', par l'essence; par rapport à l'exister (qui est acte), l'essence est 'puissance'. Comme pour Platon les êtres sensibles pouvaient être multiples dans leur espèce par participation à l'Idée-Forme, ainsi pour saint Thomas les êtres finis s'expliquent tous par une commune participation à un exister qui est identique à son essence ou dont l'essence est d'exister, qui est donc un Exister subsistant et,—en un sens inconnu des Anciens,—un être 'infini' (non plus indéfini, indéterminé, mais positivement illimité).

L'Exister est la définition de Dieu ou, si l'on veut, sa 'propriété': Dieu seul existe vraiment, au sens plein du mot. Le fini 'participe' à ce qui est le propre de Dieu; il est 'créé'. On ne peut se représenter l'acte créateur; si l'on veut le comparer avec l'art, on doit préciser que Dieu crée sans matière, *ex nihilo*; qu'il crée 'librement', mais sans délibération ni choix entre des 'possibles'; qu'il ne vise d'autre fin que lui-même. Du côté du créé, la création n'est qu'une relation de totale dépendance existentielle.[1]

Le créateur est souverainement libre, mais éminemment 'raisonnable'. Le propre de la raison est d'ordonner vers une fin:[2] la finalité aristotélicienne, loin d'être compromise par la création, se trouve au contraire radicalement fondée et garantie. Les diverses natures particulières, les 'lois' de leur développement, la fin à laquelle elles tendent, sont voulues par Dieu: l'ordre naturel' devient, de par la création, un ordre divin. L'optimisme de Platon et d'Aristote, qui orientait la nature vers le bien et le meilleur, reçoit une justification métaphysique: si une inclination naturelle ne peut être vaine, c'est parce qu'elle traduit la motion du Premier Moteur.[3]

La seconde thèse originale de saint Thomas concerne l'homme. Pour lui comme pour Aristote, l'homme est composé d'âme et de corps, de forme et de matière; mais, pour saint Thomas, en raison de son intellect, qui est la faculté de connaître non seulement l'essence des choses sensibles mais l'exister dans toute son ampleur, l'âme humaine a son exister propre; elle ne résulte pas de la génération, mais est créée par Dieu, de façon immédiate, comme subsistante; elle fait participer le corps à sa propre subsistance; elle est

---

1 *ST*, I, 45, 3: Creatio in creatura non est nisi relatio quaedam ad creatorem ut ad principium sui esse.
2 *ST*, I-II, 90, 1: Rationis est ordinare in finem
3 *In Eth. Nic.*, I, 2, 21. Naturale desiderium nihil est aliud quam inclinatio inhaerens rebus ex ordinatione primi moventis quae non potest frustrari.

incorruptible. Dans le créé, l'intellectualité est la perfection la plus haute qui se puisse concevoir; elle fait 'ressembler' à Dieu autant que faire se peut.[4]

A l'intellect correspond la volonté, appétit intellectuel. En tant que nature (*voluntas ut natura*), la volonté tend nécessairement au bien dans toute son ampleur; mais, en tant que raison (*voluntas ut ratio*), c'est-à-dire dans son exercice, ou dans ses actes élicites qui ne sont que des inclinations correspondant à des objets présentés par l'intellect,[5] elle est au pouvoir de l'homme, en ce sens que celui-ci peut, soit la laisser s'épancher, soit la suspendre: il dispose d'un 'libre arbitre' par lequel il se dirige lui-même vers sa fin; parmi les actes de l'homme (*actus hominis*), seuls les actes libres sont des actes humains (*actus humani*).

Ces deux thèses originales entraînent des conséquences importantes lorsqu'il s'agit de déterminer la fin de l'homme et la manière dont elle peut être atteinte.

Dieu est la fin à laquelle tout le créé est ordonné; non pas qu'il soit constitué par l'action des choses (comme la victoire par le combat des soldats), mais en tant qu'il préexiste et que les choses, en agissant, acquièrent une plus grande ressemblance avec leur Créateur. Dans l'ordre universel, toute puissance existe en vue de son actuation; la matière première existe pour la forme des éléments, celle-ci pour celle des mixtes, celle-ci pour l'âme végétative, celle-ci pour l'âme sensitive, celle-ci enfin pour l'âme intellective: la fin dernière de toute la génération est donc l'âme humaine.[6] Pour chaque chose, la fin est constituée par son activité propre: pour l'âme humaine, la fin est l'intellection. La fin de l'intellect est la fin dernière de toutes les actions humaines, et donc de l'homme tout entier.[7] Or l'intellect est fait pour tout connaître de la manière la plus parfaite possible; sa fin, qui est le bonheur de l'homme, sera donc de connaître Dieu, non seulement comme cause de tout, mais tel qu'il est en lui-même: toute créature dotée d'intelligence désire, par nature, voir la substance divine.[8] Si l'âme humaine ne peut trouver son bonheur que dans la vision immédiate de Dieu, c'est parce qu'elle est créée immédiatement par Dieu.[9]

Comment l'homme va-t-il atteindre sa fin? Que doit-il faire pour y parvenir?

A la différence des êtres sans raison, dont les actions résultent de manière nécessaire de leur nature, l'homme connaît sa fin comme telle; il connaît

---

4 *In III Sent.*, 10, 2, 2, 1: Homo in quantum per creationem producitur in participatione intellectus producitur quasi in similitudinem speciei ipsius Dei, quia ultimum eorum secundum quae natura creata participat similitudinem naturae increatae est intellectualitas.

5 *ST*, I, 87, 4: Actus voluntatis nihil aliud est quam inclinatio quaedam consequens formam intellectam

6 *CG*, 3, 22: Ultimus igitur finis generationis totius est anima humana.

7 *CG*, 3, 25: Finis igitur intellectus est ultimus finis totius hominis.

8 *CG*, 3, 57: Omnis intellectus naturaliter desiderat divinae substantiae visionem.

9 *Quodl.*, 10, 17: Quia anima immediate facta est a Deo, ideo beata esse non potest nisi immediate videat Deum.

non seulement la chose qui est sa fin, ainsi que le fait également l'animal non rationnel, mais il saisit sa fin comme fin, (*la ratio finis*), et le rapport entre moyens et fin. Aussi, quoiqu'il ait (par sa volonté *ut natura*) une inclination nécessaire au bien en général, ou au bien sans limites, il ne rencontre ici-bas que des biens finis et il peut déterminer librement (par sa volonté *ut ratio*) ceux qu'il voudra rechercher. Il n'est pas physiquement contraint, mais moralement obligé d'orienter tous ses actes vers la fin que lui a assignée la nature, d'établir une hiérarchie ou de respecter un ordre entre les multiples biens finis. La raison lui dicte à cet effet les règles qu'il doit observer dans l'usage des biens matériels, dans ses relations avec autrui, et dans ses rapports avec Dieu. Ces règles concernent dans les deux premiers cas ce qu'on peut appeler au sens strict la 'moralité' de ses actes; dans le troisième, leur caractère 'religieux': elles visent en effet à le sanctifier en le 'reliant' à Dieu.

Appuyée uniquement sur les considérations qui précèdent, qui ne relèvent que de la raison interprétant la nature, la religion telle qu'on l'entend ici peut s'appeler une *religion naturelle*. Elle prescrit à l'homme de poser librement des actes dans lesquels il rend hommage à Dieu comme à celui qui l'a créé, qui accroît la valeur de ses actes en sorte qu'ils le conduisent à sa fin, et qui lui accordera finalement la béatitude.[10] Dans une religion naturelle la créature rationnelle se réfère donc à trois interventions divines.

La première est celle de sa création, par laquelle elle est immédiatement ordonnée à Dieu.

La troisième, qui résulte de la première, est celle de l'accomplissement final de sa destinée. A la différence d'Aristote, saint Thomas estime que la béatitude parfaite (qui consiste pour lui dans la vision de Dieu) ne peut être obtenue en cette vie. Mais la séparation d'avec le corps ne suffit pas à la procurer à l'âme; l'ange, forme pure, n'en jouit pas par nature; par son acte créateur Dieu est sans doute ontologiquement présent, mais il faut qu'il intervienne pour se rendre intentionnellement présent; on sait qu'il le fera, puisqu'on a discerné dans l'homme un désir naturel de voir Dieu, et que pareil désir ne peut être vain, étant mis en nous par le créateur; mais il reste que Dieu seul peut nous mettre en possession de la fin à laquelle il nous destine.

La deuxième intervention découle des précédentes. Si c'est Dieu qui nous a créés et qui nous accordera la béatitude parfaite, c'est lui aussi qui, par sa Providence, rendra 'méritoires' les actes 'humains' que nous posons en cette vie et en fera des étapes qui nous acheminent vers notre fin. Alors que, selon l'ordre de l'univers créé, les natures irrationnelles inférieures sont sans cesse aidées par les supérieures (ainsi, l'eau de la mer, par elle-même, se porte vers le centre, mais sous l'influence de la lune est soumise au flux et au reflux), la nature rationnelle ne peut, dans ses actes libres, être aidée que par Dieu seul.[11]

10 *CG*, 3, 120: Offert se mens nostra Deo quasi suae creationis principio, quasi suae operationis auctori, quasi suae beatitudinis fini.

11 *ST*, II-II, 2, 3: Sola autem natura rationalis creata habet immediatum ordinem ad Deum.

Laissant de côté l'acte créateur (dont le sujet créé, comme tel, est le résultat et auquel, par conséquent, il ne prend aucune part), on peut se demander si les deux autres interventions divines (qui concernent des actes de l'homme) n'ôtent pas à la religion son caractère 'naturel'. Il semble que non. 'Naturel', en effet, a deux sens, tant chez saint Thomas que déjà chez Aristote:

> Il signifie, d'une part, ce qui a en soi un principe suffisant dont quelque chose résulte nécessairement, si rien n'y fait obstacle; ainsi il est naturel à la terre de se mouvoir vers le bas. . . . Mais, d'autre part, on appelle naturel ce qui a une inclination naturelle vers quelque chose, bien qu'il n'ait pas en soi le principe suffisant dont cela résulte nécessairement; ainsi on dit qu'il est naturel qu'une femme conçoive un enfant, bien qu'elle ne puisse le faire sans l'intervention d'un homme. . . . C'est en ce second sens qu'il est naturel au libre arbitre de tendre vers le bien.[12]

De manière générale, d'ailleurs, pour qu'un mouvement soit 'naturel', il suffit que le sujet ait la puissance passive qui l'ordonne à une perfection nouvelle, ou encore qu'il ait une inclination naturelle à recevoir celle-ci; il n'est pas requis qu'il possède la force active pour l'acquérir.

On peut estimer que le double sens que peut prendre le terme de 'nature' risque de créer une équivoque, précisément dans le cas de la religion, puisqu'il y s'agit de célébrer les interventions de Dieu. Pour l'éviter, certains théologiens du moyen âge ont appelé 'nature' (ou 'nature pure') ce qu'un sujet peut faire par ses seules forces, et 'surnature' ce qui en lui résulte d'une intervention divine ou de la grâce de Dieu. Arrêtons-nous à cette dernière notion.

II: SURNATURE

Pour saint Thomas, dans la créature rationnelle, relève de la nature ce qu'elle tient du fait de sa création, notamment son ordination à Dieu et son désir naturel de voir Dieu, mais relève de la grâce ou de la surnature ce qui dépasse les forces (ou le pouvoir actif) de sa nature quant à l'obtention effective de la vision béatifique: 'quoique l'homme soit incliné par nature vers sa fin dernière, il ne peut l'atteindre par les forces de sa nature, mais uniquement par grâce, et cela en raison de l'éminence de cette fin.'[13]

---

12 *De Veritate*, 24, 10, ad 1: Aliquid dicitur naturale *dupliciter*. *Uno modo* cuius principium sufficiens habetur ex quo de necessitate illud consequitur, nisi aliquid impediat; sicut terrae naturale est moveri deorsum. . . . *Alio modo* dicitur aliquid alicui naturale, quia habet naturalem inclinationem in illud, quamvis in se non habeat sufficiens illius principium ex quo necessario consequatur; sicut mulieri dicitur naturale concipere filium, quod tamen non potest nisi semine maris suscepto. . . . Hoc autem modo libero arbitrio est naturale tendere in bonum.
13 *In Boeth.*, VI, 4, 5: Quamvis homo naturaliter inclinetur in finem ultimum, non tamen potest naturaliter illum consequi, sed solum per gratiam, et hoc est propter eminentiam illius finis.

Certains ont voulu faire relever aussi de la grâce l'ordination de l'homme à la vision de Dieu; mais cette position semble intenable, car, s'il en était ainsi, la vision 'béatifique' (c'est-à-dire celle qui rend bienheureux) ne se présenterait plus comme un 'bien', comme une perfection et une fin; à fortiori, elle ne serait plus l'objet premier d'une recherche moralement obligatoire, ni la source de toute obligation; dépassant tout désir naturel, elle ne serait plus désirable, car le principe et le fondement de tout ce qui peut nous attirer est ce qui nous attire naturellement.[14]

Entendue au sens strict, la notion de 'surnaturel' vise à rendre compréhensible la manière dont Dieu, qui nous a créés et dotés d'une nature, nous sanctifie et nous conduit à notre fin. En dépit de ce que suggèrent certaines expressions courantes, elle ne caractérise pas proprement l'intervention divine elle-même (comme l'"aide surnaturelle' de Dieu), ni non plus son résultat (comme la 'béatitude surnaturelle'), mais des réalités créées surajoutées à la nature, dont on postule l'existence pour rendre intelligibles, dans une interprétation métaphysique, certaines interventions de Dieu. On le voit mieux par les deux exemples suivants, l'un relatif à l'intelligence, l'autre à la volonté.

Notre intelligence trouvera sa suprême perfection dans la vision de Dieu; elle ne peut y parvenir par ses seules forces; Dieu doit l'y aider. Comment concevoir son intervention? L'expérience montre que, pour accomplir l'acte de voir, trois conditions sont requises: un organe (les yeux), un objet (les choses), et une lumière qui éclaire l'objet et le rend ainsi effectivement visible. De même, pour l'acte de penser, il faut une faculté (l'intellect passif, qu'Aristote comparait à une tablette sur laquelle rien n'est écrit), des données sensibles déjà appréhendées par nos sens, et une lumière qui les rend intelligibles (l'intellect agent). Pour jouir de la vision béatifique, dira-t-on, nous disposons de notre intellect passif, capable de connaître la totalité de l'être; Dieu, d'autre part, est ontologiquement présent dans toute sa création; mais pour que nous voyions Dieu, il faut que nous soit accordé un don surnaturel, dont la fonction est analogue à celle qu'exerçaient la lumière pour la vision oculaire, l'intellect agent pour la pensée, et qu'on appelle la 'lumière de gloire'; celle-ci ne vient pas surélever notre intellect passif, qui est, comme on l'a dit, le degré d'être le plus élevé auquel une créature peut accéder dans sa participation à Dieu, mais elle nous rend Dieu intentionnellement présent.

En cette vie, c'est notre volonté qui est aidée par Dieu; c'est en effet par nos actes libres que nous nous dirigeons vers notre fin. Or Dieu ne peut mouvoir notre volonté, comme si celle-ci était simplement mue et n'était en aucune façon le principe de son mouvement, car le principe d'un acte volontaire doit nécessairement lui être intrinsèque. Il ne peut pas davantage la mouvoir comme on meut un instrument, car si un instrument est un

14 *De Veritate*, 22, 5: Appetibile quod naturaliter appetitur est aliorum appetibilium principium et fundamentum.

principe de l'action, il ne peut, à son gré, agir ou ne pas agir. Même mue par Dieu, il faut que notre volonté demeure elle-même la cause efficiente de son acte; or aucun acte n'est produit de manière parfaite par une puissance active, s'il ne lui est pas connaturel grâce à une forme qui soit au principe de l'action et qui rende l'action spontanée et délectable. Il faut donc que Dieu crée en nous une 'forme surajoutée à notre puisssance naturelle' qui nous incline à agir de la manière dont le fait une vertu acquise (ou une habitude). C'est ainsi que saint Thomas explique que la charité surnaturelle, est un don créé, surajouté à notre libre arbitre et indispensable pour rendre méritoires nos actes moralement bons.[15] Un don analogue est requis pour expliquer métaphysiquement l'acte de foi. L'objet de la foi est le même que celui de la vision béatifique; nous pouvons ici-bas y adhérer par un acte complexe qui relève de l'intelligence et de la volonté. La foi n'est pas une vision, elle concerne des réalités encore absentes; l'intellect y adhère, mais sans évidence, sur ordre de la volonté,[16] ce qui fait d'ailleurs que l'acte de foi est un acte libre. Pour que cet acte ait effectivement lieu, est requis un don surnaturel, le *lumen fidei*. En dépit de son nom, cette 'lumière de foi' n'est pas accordée directement, ni au sens propre, à l'intelligence, mais à la volonté libre; elle ne permet pas de découvrir dans l'objet de foi des aspects nouveaux qu'on ne découvrirait pas sans elle, ni de voir cet objet, de le saisir comme 'présent', dans une évidence surnaturelle; elle nous fait adhérer intellectuellement à l'objet des 'vérités' de foi parce qu'il représente pour nous un (vrai) 'bien'.

On notera que les divers dons surnaturels ne sont pas connus en eux-mêmes, ni mieux connus que ce qu'ils ont pour mission d'expliquer; on les pose par une induction métaphysique et on les dote des propriétés requises pour 'intérioriser' et rendre 'quasi-naturels' les effets des interventions de Dieu. Ce qui risque cependant de rendre cette interprétation métaphysique assez vaine, c'est que le surnaturel est du créé; or, là où la nature ne sufffit pas en raison de l'infinie distance qui la sépare de Dieu, comment des dons créés surajoutés à la nature réussiraient-ils à nous unir à Dieu? Saint Thomas connaît l'objection, mais la réponse qu'il y fait est étonnamment brève et n'emporte pas nécessairement l'adhésion: l'efficacité d'une forme, dit-il, est en proportion de la vertu de l'agent qui donne cette forme.[17]

Par ailleurs, l'intérêt des dons surajoutés à la nature, c'est qu'ils dépendent d'une certaine façon de notre liberté: bien que nous ne puissions pas les acquérir par nos propres forces, nous devons les accueillir librement et nous avons le pouvoir de les refuser (en péchant). En outre, aux yeux des théologiens, ils dépendent, plus que la nature, de la liberté de Dieu; d'où le

---

15 *ST*, II-II, 23, 2: Oportet quod, si voluntas moveatur a Spiritu Sancto ad diligendum, etiam ipsa sit efficiens hunc actum; nullus autem actus perfecte producitur ab aliqua potentia activa nisi sit ei connaturalis per aliquam formam quae sit principium actionis.
16 *ST*, II-II, 2, 9: Ex imperio voluntatis.
17 *ST*, II-II, 23, 2, ad 3: Efficacia formae est secundum virtutem agentis qui inducit formam.

nom de 'grâce' par lequel on les désigne. C'est d'ailleurs par crainte de porter atteinte à la liberté de Dieu que certains contestent la thèse thomiste du désir naturel de voir Dieu: ils redoutent que l'on conclue du désir naturel à l'exigence du surnaturel. Saint Thomas connaît cette difficulté:

> D'après certains, tout procède de Dieu selon son bon plaisir; d'autres prétendent que c'est selon une exigence. Les deux opinions sont fausses: la première supprime l'ordre nécessaire qui existe, l'un par rapport à l'autre, entre deux effets divins; la seconde prétend que tout procède selon la nécessité de la nature. Il faut choisir une voie moyenne, et dire que ce que Dieu veut d'abord procède de son bon plaisir, mais que ce qui est requis à cet effet procède selon une exigence, en présupposant cependant (la première volonté): en ce sens que cette exigence ne signifie pas que Dieu est débiteur à l'égard des choses, mais bien à l'égard de sa propre volonté, car c'est pour exécuter sa volonté qu'est exigé ce qui est dit procéder de Dieu selon une exigence.[18]

Il semble que, pour saint Thomas, la création des êtres et le pardon des péchés relèvent de la simple volonté ou du bon plaisir de Dieu, mais que, en présupposant la décision de créer des êtres intelligents, sont au contraire 'exigées' la conservation dans l'être, l'aide de la grâce ici-bas et, si le péché n'y fait pas obstacle, la vision béatifique.

La notion de surnature étant quelque peu précisée, et distinguée de celle de nature (pure), la religion, que nous estimions devoir être appelée 'naturelle' lorsqu'on y entendait la nature dans un sens large, devrait, lorsqu'on distingue nature et surnature, être dite *à la fois naturelle et surnaturelle*. Dans la terminologie adoptée, on ne peut plus la dire simplement naturelle; mais on ne peut pas davantage la dire simplement surnaturelle, car elle caractérise des actes humains et aucun acte humain n'est purement surnaturel. Si l'on distingue nature et surnature, on ne les oppose pas; elles ne sont pas antithétiques, mais complémentaires; prises isolément, ni l'une, ni l'autre, ne suffit pour spécifier la religion.

Telle que nous l'avons entendue, nous avons étudié la religion dans son essence. A ce titre, elle constitue la 'religion universelle', valable (et obligatoire) pour tout homme, et elle peut de surcroît être appelée la 'vraie' religion, celle où Dieu intervient effectivement. Lorsqu'on distingue religion vraie

18 *De Veritate*, 6, 2: Potest solvi quaedam controversia quae inter quosdam versabatur, quibusdam dicentibus omnia a Deo secundum simplicem voluntatem procedere, quibusdam vero asserentibus omnia procedere secundum debitum a Deo. Quarum opinionum utraque falsa est; prima enim tollit necessarium ordinem qui est inter effectus divinos ad invicem; secunda autem ponit omnia procedere secundum necessitatem naturae. Media autem via est eligenda; ut ponatur ea quae sunt a Deo primo volita procedere ab ipso secundum simplicem voluntatem, ea vero quae ad hoc requiruntur procedere secundum debitum, ex suppositione tamen: quod tamen debitum non ostendit Deum esse debitorem rebus, sed suae voluntati, ad cuius expletionem debetur id quod dicitur procedere secundum debitum ab ipso.

(au singulier) et religions fausses, on présente ces dernières comme si elles étaient le fait de l'homme seul, et comme si les diverses interventions divines qui y sont évoquées n'étaient que le produit inconsistant de l'imagination humaine.

Mais il reste qu'en fait l'essence de la religion se réalise plus ou moins bien dans les diverses religions concrètes, comme d'ailleurs aussi dans les divers individus qui se réclament d'une même religion. Cependant, ni l'ignorance (invincible), ni l'erreur (commise de bonne foi), ne privent une religion de son caractère essentiellement surnaturel (ni, bien sûr, de son caractère essentiellement naturel). Rappelons l'adage: A celui qui fait ce qu'il peut, Dieu ne refuse pas sa grâce.[19] Faire ce qu'on peut relève de la nature (pure); c'est un acte du libre arbitre.

Ce serait, nous semble-t-il, confondre le genre avec l'espèce que de prendre pour des synonymes le 'surnaturel' et le 'révélé'. C'est pourtant ce qui se fait souvent; et on les oppose tous deux au 'naturel'. Nous dirions plutôt que la révélation, —sauf si on l'entend dans un sens très large, comme une 'révélation universelle' faite à tout homme et dont l'organe est la raison humaine, —se réfère à des hommes qui en furent les bénéficiaires privilégiés et exclusifs, tels les 'prophètes' qu'on cite dans l'histoire. La religion révélée est alors une religion historique ou positive.

Du point de vue 'apologétique' (ou des raisons d'adhérer à une religion déterminée), citons pour terminer la classification kantienne des diverses espèces de religions:

> La religion (considérée subjectivement) est la connaissance de tous nos devoirs comme commandements divins. Celle où je dois savoir au préalable que quelque chose est un commandement divin pour le reconnaître comme mon devoir, est la religion révélée (ou qui exige une révélation). Au contraire, celle où je dois savoir par avance que quelque chose est mon devoir avant que je puisse le reconnaître comme commandement de Dieu, est la religion naturelle. Celui qui déclare que seule la religion naturelle est moralement nécessaire, c'est-à-dire un devoir, peut se nommer aussi rationaliste (en matière de foi). S'il nie la réalité de toute révélation divine surnaturelle, il se nomme naturaliste. S'il admet la révélation en soutenant que la connaître et l'admettre comme vraie n'est pas pour la religion une condition nécessaire, on pourrait l'appeler un rationaliste pur. Mais s'il croit que la foi en elle est nécessaire à la religion universelle, on pourrait l'appeler un pur surnaturaliste en matière de foi.[20]

19 *De Veritate*, 24, 15, ad 2: Est consuetum dici quod si homo facit quod in se est, Deus dat ei gratiam. *In IV Sent.*, 20, 1: Deus, qui dat omnibus abundanter, nulli gratiam denegat qui quod in se est facit ut se ad gratiam praeparet. *CG*, 3, 159: Deus enim, quantum in se est, paratus est omnibus gratiam dare. . . . Illi soli gratia privantur qui in seipsis gratiae impedimentum praestant.

20 E. Kant, *Die Religion*, éd. Meiner, pp. 170-1.

III: CULTURE

Si l'on peut définir avec plus ou moins de précision les termes de nature et de surnature, il est au contraire très difficile de cerner celui de culture.

Aujourd'hui le terme de culture a deux sens différents, qui résultent de deux manières de considérer le même objet, à savoir, d'une part par la réflexion commune et son prolongement philosophique, d'autre part par les méthodes des sciences positives. On pourrait symboliser cette différence d'un mot, en disant que dans le premier cas on parle généralement de 'la' culture (au singulier), et dans le second 'des' cultures (au pluriel). Voyons cela de plus près.

Dans le langage courant et en philosophie, la culture est un complément apporté à la nature. Elle s'applique à tout ce qui peut être 'cultivé', c'est-à-dire développé, éduqué: les champs (agriculture), les jardins (horticulture), les poissons (pisciculture), les enfants (puériculture) et, bien sûr, les hommes. Chez ceux-ci, la culture peut être générale, ou particulière (culture scientifique, artistique, classique; culture des sciences, des lettres, des arts, de l'esprit, du cœur, des sentiments); elle peut aussi concerner le corps (culture physique). Entendue sans qualification, elle est définie dans les dictionnaires comme le 'développement de certaines facultés de l'esprit par des exercices intellectuels appropriés ou, par extension, l'ensemble des connaissances acquises qui permettent de développer le sens critique, le goût, le jugement': ou encore comme 'l'ensemble des aspects intellectuels d'une civilisation'. On oppose alors l'homme cultivé au barbare, au sauvage, au primitif, à l'homme inculte, grossier, ignare ou ignorant. —Quant à la civilisation dont la culture désigne les aspects intellectuels, on la définit comme 'l'ensemble des caractères communs aux vastes sociétés les plus évoluées, ou l'ensemble des acquisitions des sociétés humaines, ou l'ensemble des phénomènes sociaux (religieux, moraux, esthétiques, scientifiques, techniques) communs à une grande société ou à un groupe de sociétés,'[21] ou 'l'ensemble des opinions et des mœurs qui résulte de l'action réciproque des arts industriels, de la religion, des beaux-arts et des sciences.'[22]

Ayant partie liée avec le social, ce qui relève de la culture est souvent appelé de nos jours 'socio-culturel', mais n'est pas mieux défini pour autant, et moins encore dans le langage courant que dans les dictionnaires. Ainsi, pour ne citer qu'un exemple, on pouvait lire dans un quotidien, sous le titre 'La démocratie culturelle dans l'Europe de 1992', les lignes suivantes:

> Dans des domaines aussi variés que le sport, les loisirs, l'écologie, la solidarité sociale, l'éducation des adultes, la musique, le théâtre, les groupes folkloriques, des associations ont fleuri et ont suscité un nouveau dynamisme dans la vie socio-culturelle. Diverses initiatives spécifiques

21 P. Robert, *Dictionnaire alphabétique et analogique de la langue française.*
22 E. Littré, *Dictionnaire de la langue française.*

focalisent, en outre, le dynamisme des membres de ces associations: des concours de créativité, la Fête de l'Europe, des voyages à Strasbourg, le tour de l'Europe des jeunes à vélo. L'objectif visé par ces associations? Faire une Europe qui ne soit pas uniquement fondée sur l'économie, et suivre un chemin de crête qui passerait entre l'incontournable problématique politique et économique et l'aspect socio-culturel de la Communauté.[23]

Pour clarifier quelque peu la nébuleuse qu'est, dans le langage courant, la notion de culture, et la confronter avec celles de nature et de surnature, nous reprenons quelques indications à l'ouvrage de Mgr A. Dondeyne, *Foi chrétienne et pensée contemporaine*.[24] L'auteur y entend le terme de culture dans un sens très large, où il est d'ailleurs synonyme de civilisation, et il discerne dans la culture deux structures, l'une 'horizontale', l'autre 'verticale'.

Selon sa structure horizontale, la culture est à la fois subjective et objective. L'homme a pour tâche de devenir plus homme, de s'humaniser; il le fait en 'se cultivant' ou en développant ses diverses facultés; en ce sens on parle de culture physique, de culture de l'intelligence, du cœur, du sens esthétique. Mais cette culture du sujet ne peut se réaliser que par la médiation d'une culture objective: l'homme ne s'humanise qu'en humanisant le monde, en transformant la nature brute par une série de créations telles que la technique, les œuvres d'art, le langage oral ou écrit, les lois, les institutions sociales, etc. Les deux aspects de la culture sont inséparables; l'un appelle l'autre: ils s'influencent mutuellement. Pour l'homme, qui est un esprit incarné, tout enrichissement de la vie intérieure passe par le détour d'une 'expression', d'une extériorisation ou d'une objectivation. Celle-ci fournit une détermination, un contenu, aux actes du sujet et constitue en même temps, non pas une cause, mais une invitation et un tremplin pour de nouveaux actes. Ainsi, l'artiste crée des œuvres qui, à leur tour, vont, non pas causer, mais éveiller et en tout cas affiner, notamment chez d'autres, le sens du beau. Coupée de la subjectivité qui l'a créée et dont elle peut favoriser le dynamisme, la culture objective, comme toute expression, est fatalement ambiguë: les créations, les inventions et les découvertes les plus remarquables peuvent devenir avilissantes.

Outre sa structure horizontale, la culture présente une structure verticale, en ce sens qu'on peut y discerner une hiérarchie de niveaux.

Un premier niveau culturel concerne les valeurs vitales et les biens matériels, tels que l'habitat, le vêtement, l'hygiène, le confort, et, par extension, tout ce qui relève de l'"économie'. L'intérêt de ce premier niveau, c'est qu'on y remarque aisément, sur des exemples simples, la finalité inhérente à la recherche d'une valeur quelconque et le rapport entre culture subjective et culture objective. En l'occurrence, dans le cas des valeurs vitales, la

23   *La Libre Belgique*, 1-1-1988.
24   Albert Dondeyne, *Foi chrétienne et pensée contemporaine* (Louvain, 1951), pp. 188-201.

recherche est de l'ordre de la raison fabricatrice ou de la technique instrumentale. Les instruments sont des moyens en vue d'une fin. En tant que tels, ce ne sont pas des objets 'naturels': il n'y a ni marteau, ni toit, ni vêtement, en dehors de l'activité qui insère un objet donné dans la recherche de la fin vitale que l'on poursuit. Certes, cette insertion ne se fait pas de manière arbitraire. Mais la nature du matériau n'égale jamais sa valeur instrumentale; c'est son emploi qui lui confère une nouvelle réalité, une qualité 'culturelle'. Or l'invention ne concerne pas uniquement les moyens; par delà les moyens, elle porte sur la fin elle-même, en l'occurrence sur les valeurs vitales. Cellesci, en effet, ne sont pas déterminées indépendamment des moyens qui y conduisent: on ne peut les penser concrètement, leur assigner un contenu, qu'à travers les déterminations que leur apporte la technique. Ces déterminations sont, à leur tour, des instruments en vue d'une recherche ultérieure. La valeur, ou la fin, est toujours à la fois élaborée et dépassée par les moyens mêmes qui la servent; elle n'est pas donnée, au préalable, de manière positive et précise, comme si on pouvait en déduire les moyens qui permettent de l'atteindre: elle constitue plutôt une norme négative qu'il faut respecter pour éviter un échec certain.

Un second niveau culturel est constitué par les valeurs culturelles entendues au sens courant et étroit du mot, à savoir par les valeurs spirituelles particulières, telles qu'on les atteint par les sciences désintéressées, les créations artistiques et, dans une certaine mesure, par les institutions politiques et sociales.

Un troisième niveau culturel comprend les valeurs morales, c'est-à-dire celles qui visent directement le 'respect' et la reconnaissance, en soi et en autrui, de la personne humaine comme totalité ou en ce qui constitue sa 'dignité', sa valeur de fin pour soi, de sujet de droits et de devoirs. Parmi ces valeurs, il faut citer le respect de la vie et de la mort, de la vérité, de la liberté, l'amour désintéressé, inconditionnel et fidèle, par lequel se crée une société authentiquement humaine.

Ces trois premiers niveaux peuvent être appelés 'profanes', en tant qu'ils se distinguent d'un dernier niveau, celui des valeurs 'religieuses', par lesquelles l'homme recherche une communion avec l'Absolu. —En vérité, Mgr Dondeyne hésite quelque peu à considérer la religion comme un niveau culturel; il écrit: 'En un sens, elle nous fait sortir du monde de la culture, puisqu'elle nous ouvre sur le transcendant, l'au-delà du monde. . . . Cependant elle se reflète dans la culture et, en ce sens, elle constitue une sphère culturelle à côté et au dessus des autres, enveloppant toutes les autres' (p.199).

Chacun des quatre niveaux culturels possède une relative indépendance ou autonomie; comme en témoigne l'expérience, on rencontre des hommes plus cultivés à certains niveaux qu'à d'autres. Et cependant, on le constate également, les quatre niveaux sont aussi en quelque mesure interdépendants et peuvent s'influencer mutuellement; chacun est, pour les autres, une sorte de 'situation', dont l'influence n'est jamais déterminante, mais demeure toujours ambiguë.

La double structure, horizontale et verticale, de la culture, —celle-ci étant d'ailleurs prise dans un sens très large, —et l'ambiguïté qui caractérise, les uns par rapport aux autres, les aspects qu'on y distingue, sont susceptibles d'être diversement interprétées. En outre, on peut, pour élaborer une interprétation, recourir à différentes philosophies. Désirant comparer la notion de culture à celles de nature et de surnature, nous nous inspirerons, ici comme plus haut, de la tradition issue d'Aristote.

On trouve, nous semble-t-il, dans cette tradition, bien que sous d'autres termes, ce qui est visé aujourd'hui par la 'culture'. Sans doute, il s'agit principalement de la culture subjective, mais celle-ci est sans cesse mise en relation avec la culture objective, notamment parce que, selon Aristote, on ne connaît le sujet que par le détour des objets auxquels il se rapporte. D'ailleurs, dans la Grèce du Ve siècle, les sciences, les arts, la philosophie, étaient en plein essor; l'homme était considéré comme essentiellement sociable: la cité était démocratique, la justice était rendue par des tribunaux populaires, les rhéteurs jouaient un rôle important. Par tempérament, Aristote était un fin observateur autant qu'un remarquable dialecticien. On peut dès lors penser que tout l'invitait à réfléchir à la culture, du moins à ses trois niveaux 'profanes'; s'il néglige le niveau 'religieux' proprement dit, on ne peut oublier que sa conception du Premier Moteur et du Bien suprême sera complétée, plus que réfutée ou corrigée, lorsque son œuvre sera connue et passionnément étudiée en milieu chrétien, juif et islamique. C'est d'ailleurs à saint Thomas autant qu'à Aristote lui-même que nous recourrons pour éclairer quelque peu les rapports entre nature et culture.

D'un mot, chez ces philosophes, ce qu'on entend généralement aujourd'hui par 'culture subjective' (au sens large), à savoir le développement de certaines facultés de l'homme, se retrouve dans les 'vertus', (ce terme étant, lui aussi, entendu au sens large). Qu'est-ce donc qu'une vertu?

La vertu se classe parmi les 'habitus', et ceux-ci parmi les 'dispositions'. Une disposition est une qualité qui résulte d'un certain ordre entre des éléments multiples. Une disposition peut être passagère, telle par exemple celle qui résulte d'une passion. Mais lorsqu'elle se stabilise au point de constituer une acquisition durable du sujet qu'elle qualifie, elle devient pour lui un $\pi\tilde{\omega}\varsigma$ $\check{\varepsilon}\chi\varepsilon\iota\nu$, une $\check{\varepsilon}\xi\iota\varsigma$, une manière d'être, en latin un *aliquo modo se habere* ou un *habitus* (terme dont dérivent les mots français d'habileté, d'habilité, d'habitude), à savoir une qualité caractéristique de ce qu'il est. Il y a des habitus entitatifs; ils qualifient l'état dans lequel nous sommes, le rendent plus harmonieux ou le dégradent; ainsi la santé, la beauté, ou leurs contraires. Il y a des habitus opératifs; ils qualifient nos manières d'agir, selon qu'elles sont bonnes ou mauvaises; ils viennent compléter celles de nos puissances d'agir (ou de nos facultés) qui sont à la fois actives et passives, c'est-à-dire celles qui ne sont pas la source unique de leurs opérations, mais ne sont pas non plus mues déterminément par leurs objets. On ne les rencontre donc ni dans les choses matérielles, ni dans des facultés actives (comme l'intellect agent); mais on peut les trouver dans l'intellect potentiel, dans la volonté, également dans les facultés sensibles (dans la mesure du moins où celles-ci participent à la raison en pouvant lui être soumises).

> Par nos facultés nous avons le pouvoir (ou nous sommes capables) de faire quelque chose, tandis que par les habitus nous devenons, non pas capables ou incapables de faire quelque chose, mais 'habiles' ou 'inhabiles' pour faire bien ou mal ce dont nous sommes capables. Les habitus ne nous confèrent ou ne nous ôtent donc aucun 'pouvoir' (ou aucune capacité); ce que nous acquérons par eux, c'est d'agir bien ou mal.[25]

Du point de vue psychologique, les habitus opératifs exercent trois fonctions principales; en déterminant une faculté, ils l'orientent vers un terme unique, et apportent ainsi à l'agir d'abord une certaine constance; ensuite, une promptitude, qui dispense de longuement réfléchir quand l'action est urgente; enfin, une facilité, une aisance, qui rend l'action attrayante; par ces trois fonctions, ils jouent un rôle analogue à celui de la nature. S'ils orientent nos facultés dans le sens qui convient à la nature ou selon ce que dicte la raison, ils ont sur les autres une 'supériorité' ou une 'excellence' (ἀρετή) et on les appelle des 'vertus'; celles-ci se définissent donc comme des habitus opératifs bons selon lequels on peut agir quand on le veut; elles rendent bon le sujet lui-même, ainsi que ses œuvres.

On l'aura remarqué, le terme 'vertu' a un sens très large; il désigne ce qui rend excellent non seulement, comme dans son acception courante actuelle, notre agir moral, mais également notre activité intellectuelle, artistique, poétique, technique, là où nous parlerions aujourd'hui plutôt de 'talent', d''habileté' ou de 'compétence'.

D'où viennent les vertus? Quelle est leur cause? A quoi doivent-elles leur naissance, leur croissance, leur diminution, leur disparition?

Envisageons d'abord ces questions dans le domaine profane.

D'après Aristote, les vertus sont de bonnes 'habitudes'. Ce n'est pas par un effet de la nature ni contrairement à la nature qu'elles naissent en nous; la nature nous prédispose à les acquérir, elle en offre les 'germes', les 'commencements' (*semina, inchoationes*); à nous de les développer par l'exercice répété de certains actes: des activités semblables créent en effet des dispositions correspondantes. C'est en forgeant que l'on devient forgeron, c'est en jouant de la cithare que l'on devient cithariste; c'est en posant des actes de courage, de justice, de tempérance, que l'on devient brave, juste, modéré. La qualité de l'exercice n'importe pas moins que l'exercice lui-même; nul ne devient bon cithariste en s'exerçant mal ou sous la conduite d'un mauvais maître qui lui aura laissé prendre de mauvaises habitudes.[26]

25 *CG*, 4, 77: Per potentiam sumus potentes aliquid facere, per habitum autem non reddimur potentes vel impotentes ad aliquid faciendum, sed habiles vel inhabiles ad id, quod possumus, bene vel male agendum. Per habitum igitur non datur neque tollitur aliquid posse, sed hoc per habitum acquirimus, ut bene vel male aliquid agamus.

26 *Eth. Nic.*, II, 1.

Comment la répétition des actes fait-elle naître l'habitude? Saint Thomas explique que, lorsqu'une faculté, à la fois active et passive, et par là capable d'être diversement orientée,—la volonté, par exemple,—se porte sur un objet déterminé, elle se trouve de ce fait disposée d'une certaine façon à son égard. Si cela se reproduit plusieurs fois, cette disposition se renforce, de telle sorte qu'elle devient comme une forme qui détermine l'orientation de la faculté vers un terme unique, à la manière dont le fait la nature.[27] Et c'est pour ce motif qu'on dit que l'habitude est une seconde nature.[28] La croissance, la décroissance, la disparition des vertus s'expliquent de manière analogue; elles proviennent respectivement de la multiplication, de la diminution, ou de la non-réitération des actes spécifiques qui leur ont donné naissance. Les vertus dues aux actes sont appelées des vertus 'acquises'.

Tout ceci est dit de manière abstraite, à l'aide de catégories métaphysiques. Pour être plus concret, il faudrait détailler les nombreuses vertus que l'homme peut acquérir selon les divers buts qu'il se propose. On verrait mieux comment, en tant qu'il se cultive, l'homme n'est pas un être 'naturel', mais, selon une terminologie plus récente, un être 'historique' et 'social'.

Un être historique, car la culture subjective requiert des exercices répétés, et donc du temps. Par l'exercice, nos facultés se modifient au niveau de leurs habitus; les actes qui en relèvent, et dont on dit qu'ils se répètent, ne sont pas rigoureusement semblables; ils deviennent 'meilleurs'; l'apprentissage nous fait progresser. Nous changeons, et le monde qui nous entoure change; il devient 'familier', culturel. La culture objective sert de médiation au développement de la culture subjective, tant pour nos actes 'immanents' dont l'objet nous demeure intérieur que pour ceux qui produisent une œuvre qui nous est extérieure: ainsi l'objet d'une méditation silencieuse, d'une réflexion, d'un projet, se modifie du fait de notre activité et tant qu'elle se poursuit, tout comme celui d'un travail manuel, d'un art ou d'une technique.

En outre, l'homme est, par nature, un être social. Aucune activité humaine, fût-elle la plus intime, aucune vertu, fût-elle la plus personnelle, ne peut être exercée, sans que joue, de manière réelle et efficace, sinon explicitement consciente, une relation aux autres. Aucun vivant ne survient s'il n'a été engendré; aucun homme ne se cultive sans avoir été éduqué; aucune pensée ne prend forme sans un langage, au moins intérieur, qui l'exprime. Plus l'homme accède à ce qu'il a de plus inaliénable, sa personnalité, plus il s'ouvre aux autres. Réaliser la communion des personnes, tel est le but profane le plus élevé que l'homme peut se proposer.

Mais, on l'a dit, ce but profane n'est pas le but suprême de l'homme; celui-ci est d'ordre religieux. L'homme a en lui un désir naturel de voir Dieu; il ne peut toutefois réaliser ce désir par ses seules forces, ni à l'aide de quoi que ce soit de créé. Mais, avec la grâce de Dieu, il peut poser des actes

27 *ST*, I-II, 58, 1: Consuetudo quodammodo vertitur in naturam et facit inclinationem similem naturali.
28 *Virt.*, 9: Et propter hoc dicitur quod consuetudo est altera natura.

(de foi, d'espérance, de charité) qui ont Dieu pour objet et qui se traduisent de manière expresse dans le 'culte', de manière plus implicite mais non moins réelle dans la moralité. D'après saint Thomas, pour que ces actes demeurent des actes humains, libres, dont nous sommes les maîtres, il faut que Dieu nous accorde, comme complément à nos facultés qui les produisent, des 'vertus surnaturelles'.

A la différence des vertus profanes, qui sont des vertus 'acquises', les vertus surnaturelles sont des vertus 'infuses'. Dieu seul est la cause immédiate de leur naissance en nous, et aussi de leur croissance; mais leur diminution ou leur disparition tient à nous, qui pouvons, par le péché, mettre un obstacle aux dons de Dieu.

Les vertus infuses relèvent-elles encore de la 'culture'? On peut penser que leurs expressions culturelles et morales relèvent en quelque manière de la culture objective; mais prétendre saisir ces expressions sans les rapporter à ce qu'elles expriment, c'est leur ôter leur caractère spécifique, les dénaturer, en l'occurrence les profaner; ce projet est aussi réducteur que celui d'étudier des textes en négligeant leur sens. La question majeure est donc de savoir si les vertus infuses elles-mêmes relèvent de la culture subjective.

Elles n'en relèveraient, semble-t-il, que si, d'une manière ou d'une autre, on y découvrait, comme dans les vertus acquises, le reflet du caractère historique et social de l'homme, à savoir une situation qui est influencée par nos actes et par ceux d'autrui, de sorte que, pour l'individu et pour l'humanité, les actes religieux soient comme un tremplin pour des progrès ultérieurs. En est-il ainsi?

A première vue, on pourrait penser que non, car, précisément en ce qui concerne leur 'cause' ou la manière dont nous en disposons, la différence semble grande entre la vertu acquise et la vertu infuse. Rappelons-le, par rapport aux valeurs profanes, une faculté qui est à la fois active et passive constitue, en dépit de son indétermination, le principe suffisant d'un acte bon; la répétition de ces actes lève progressivement l'indétermination de la faculté, et crée l'habitude bonne, la vertu dite 'acquise'; dans ce processus de 'répétition', on a noté la place laissée à l'apprentissage, à l'éducation, aux exemples, bref, à autrui, et, d'autre part, l'effet psychologique, la constance, la facilité et la promptitude. —Par rapport aux valeurs religieuses, la faculté ne suffit pas pour l'acte bon, même pas pour le tout premier; Dieu doit intervenir; il le fait par la vertu dite 'infuse'. Celle-ci semble donc constituer pour la faculté, non pas une perfection qui lui permet d'agir mieux qu'elle ne le faisait initialement, mais un nouveau 'pouvoir' requis pour qu'elle puisse tout simplement agir. Cette différence entre vertu acquise et vertu infuse est si grande qu'on peut se demander si ce n'est pas sans quelque équivoque ou abus de langage que la seconde est appelée un habitus et une vertu. Quant aux effets psychologiques des vertus infuses, ils sont généralement indiscernables, ce qui s'explique aisément s'il est vrai que pareils effets résultent de l'habitude et que les vertus infuses ne sont pas des habitudes.[29]

29 *Virt.*, 10, ad 14 et 15.

On peut néanmoins estimer que les vertus infuses relèvent elles-mêmes de la culture subjective, et ceci pour deux raisons principales.

D'abord, parce que Dieu, de qui nous les recevons gratuitement, ne nous les accorde que sous certaines conditions. Saint Augustin définissait la vertu comme une bonne qualité de l'esprit, que Dieu crée en nous sans nous.[30] Saint Thomas rectifie cette définition en remarquant qu'elle ne s'applique pas aux vertus acquises et qu'elle ne vaut pas non plus, en rigueur de termes, pour les vertus infuses; celles-ci, en effet, sont causées en nous par Dieu sans que nous en soyons les auteurs, mais non pas sans que nous y consentions; quant à ce qui est fait par nous, c'est également Dieu qui en est la cause, mais non sans que nous en soyons les auteurs; Dieu lui-même, en effet, agit au sein de toute volonté et de toute nature.[31] Dieu est la cause efficiente de l'infusion des vertus surnaturelles, mais notre 'consentement' en est une condition; on peut même dire qu'il en est la condition nécessaire et suffisante, car à celui qui fait ce qu'il peut Dieu ne refuse pas sa grâce. Or pareil consentement signifie que nous accueillons librement le don divin, que nous l'assumons, que nous l'incarnons dans notre conduite concrète à la manière d'une inspiration constante de notre action; il nous faudra donc sans cesse le réinventer dans les situations toujours changeantes de la vie. Sont en effet infuses non seulement les vertus théologales (de foi, d'espérance, et de charité), qui ont Dieu pour objet et pour fin, mais également les vertus morales qui orientent vers Dieu sans avoir Dieu pour objet (telle par exemple la tempérance pratiquée par esprit de pénitence, en vue de plaire à Dieu). Ces vertus morales infuses sont comme l'épanouissement des vertus théologales dans notre vie profane; aux vertus morales acquises, dont la règle est la raison, elles ajoutent une motivation religieuse, un 'supplément d'âme'.[32]

En outre, bien que nos actes ne puissent pas produire une vertu infuse, ils peuvent cependant y 'disposer',[33] et, lorsqu'ils se répètent, les actes produits par une vertu infuse n'engendrent pas une nouvelle vertu ou une vertu acquise, mais 'renforcent' la vertu infuse et lui permettent de 'croître'.[34] A l'égard des vertus infuses, notre intervention est donc loin d'être négligeable; bien qu'elle soit de l'ordre de la causalité simplement 'dispositive', ses effets

---

30 *Virt.*, 2, et 9, 1: Virtus est bona qualitas mentis quam Deus in nobis sine nobis operatur.

31 *ST*, I-II, 55, 4, ad 6: Virtus infusa causatur in nobis a Deo sine nobis agentibus, non tamen sine nobis consentientibus, et sic est intelligendum quod dicitur 'quam Deus in nobis sine nobis operatur'; quae vero per nos aguntur, Deus in nobis causat non sine nobis agentibus; ipse enim operatur in omni voluntate et natura.

32 *ST*, I-II, 63, 3, ad 2: Virtutes theologicae sufficienter nos ordinant in finem supernaturalem, secundum quamdam inchoationem, quantum scilicet ad ipsum Deum immediate; sed oportet quod per alias virtutes infusas perficiatur anima circa alias res, in ordine tamen ad Deum.

33 *Virt.*, 10, ad 17: Licet virtus infusa non causetur ex actibus, tamen actus possunt ad eam disponere.

34 *ST*, I-II, 51, 4, ad 3: Actus qui producuntur ex habitu infuso non causant aliquem habitum, sed confirmant habitum praeexistentem. *Virt.*, 10, ad 19: Actus virtutis infusae non causant aliquem habitum, sed per eos augetur habitus praeexistens.

ressemblent étrangement à ceux de la causalité efficiente que nous exerçons à l'égard des vertus acquises. De ce point de vue, les vertus infuses relèvent, à l'instar de ces dernières, de la culture subjective; pour qu'elles naissent et croissent, nul n'ignore combien importent l'effort personnel, la pratique, l'éducation, l'aide d'autrui.

Si ces considérations sont fondées, on peut conclure que la religion, qui nous avait paru à la fois *naturelle* (en tant qu'elle répond aux vœux de la nature) et *surnaturelle* (en tant qu'elle est le fruit d'une intervention divine), peut également être dite *culturelle* et constituer le niveau supérieur de la culture subjective en tant qu'elle exige, pour naître et se développer, la répétition de certains actes, l'enseignement, l'éducation, l'exemple, la tradition, et qu'elle s'exprime et s'objective dans des formes qui doivent sans cesse être reprises et réinventées.

Quant à la culture, nous l'avons, elle aussi, considérée d'un point de vue philosophique ou dans son essence, en discernant dans sa structure un aspect subjectif et un aspect objectif, ainsi qu'une hiérarchie de valeurs. A chacun des quatre niveaux qui y ont été distingués, elle demeure intrinsèquement liée à la nature; on le voit au mieux lorsqu'on conçoit la culture subjective comme une acquisition de 'vert1us'. Celles-ci ne résultent pas déterminément de la nature, mais elles ne sont pas non plus simplement des 'habitudes' dues à la répétition d'actes semblables. Ce sont de 'bonnes' habitudes, c'est-à-dire qu'elles orientent vers un terme qui constitue une 'valeur', un bien, une perfection, un parachèvement, de la nature. La nature les contient en germe, elle leur sert donc de norme au moins négative; la fin de la nature humaine, la 'destinée' de l'homme, quoiqu'elle ne prenne des contours définis que par l'activité qui y mène, se trouve cependant comme prédessinée dans la nature elle-même. Or l'homme a le pouvoir d'agir mal, ou contrairement aux vœux de la nature; la répétition d'actes mauvais engendre de 'mauvaises' habitudes ou des 'vices'. Les vices, loin de constituer des éléments de culture, s'opposent à la culture et forment donc une sorte d'"anti-culture'.

La notion de culture à laquelle aboutit la réflexion philosophique a dès lors un caractère nettement appréciatif. Elle évoque un idéal auquel tout homme, en raison de sa nature ou en tant qu'il est homme, a le droit et le devoir de tendre. En ce sens, la culture humaine est fondamentalement une, et donc essentiellement la même pour toute l'humanité car, en dépit des distinctions de race, de sexe, de langue, d'histoire, de situation économique, psychologique ou sociale, les hommes ont tous la même nature, la même destinée et la même dignité: en tant que tels, ils ont tous droit au même respect.

Certes, cette notion de culture est abstraite; mais elle est aussi univoque: elle garde le même sens dans chacune de ses applications concrètes. Celles-ci sont multiples et donc différentes les unes des autres; mais elles ne diffèrent que par des éléments étrangers au contenu propre de la notion; par rapport à ce contenu, qui représente une essence, les éléments différentiels sont contingents, accidentels, négligeables puisqu'ils étaient, de fait, négligés (ni inclus, ni exclus) dans la notion abstraite; ils viennent s'ajouter à la notion lorsqu'on veut exprimer le concret: on parlera de culture classique, de culture française, de culture contemporaine, etc. Les éléments qui particularisent la culture ne sont pas eux-mêmes d'ordre culturel (pas plus que la grandeur ou la couleur d'une fenêtre ne sont elles-mêmes des fenêtres); ils ne méritent donc pas le 'respect' qu'on porte à ce qui est humain.

La culture, dans sa pureté notionnelle, évoque un idéal; dans le concret, cet idéal se réalise plus ou moins bien; les réalisations particulières, qui sont par quelque côté déficientes au regard de l'idéal, peuvent être évaluées, jugées, classées. Etant donné que les quatre niveaux de valeurs sont assez autonomes, il arrivera même que certaines particularisations ne font plus place aux niveaux supérieurs (de la morale et de la religion); on n'a pas affaire pour autant à d''autres cultures', mais à des 'demi-cultures', à des formes tronquées de la culture. En outre, si les mots gardent un sens, on refusera d'appeler 'culture' ce qui relève de l''anti-culture', à savoir ce qui contrarie le développement de la nature.

Comme le dit le Concile de Vatican II:

> C'est le propre de la personne humaine de n'accéder vraiment et pleinement à l'humanité que par la culture, c'est-à-dire en cultivant les biens et les valeurs de la nature. Toutes les fois qu'il est question de vie humaine, nature et culture sont aussi étroitement liées que possible.[35]

A l'heure actuelle, le terme de culture se prend généralement dans un autre sens que celui qui vient d'être évoqué. Il s'emploie le plus fréquemment au pluriel; on insiste sur les différences entre les cultures; on souligne la relativité foncière de toute culture, on s'abstient d'ailleurs de toute référence à la nature ou à une norme quelconque.

D'un mot, la culture fait l'objet de sciences positives, telles que l'anthropologie, l'ethnologie, la sociologie. Ces sciences, en raison de leurs méthodes, observent des faits, et tentent d'induire des lois résultant de concomitances constantes. On y néglige par conséquent la culture subjective, ainsi que les quatre niveaux auxquels s'intéressait la réflexion philosophique; on y étudie les faits sociaux, et en particulier leur transmission. On entend dès lors par culture:

> l'ensemble des formes acquises de comportement qu'un groupe d'individus, unis par une tradition commune, transmettent à leurs enfants. Ce mot désigne donc, non seulement les traditions artistiques, scientifiques, religieuses et philosophiques d'une société, mais encore ses techniques propres, ses coutumes politiques et les mille usages qui caractérisent sa

---

35 *Gaudium et spes*, 53, 1.

vie quotidienne, modes de préparation et de consommation des aliments, manières d'endormir les petits enfants, mode de désignation du président du Conseil, etc.[36]

On décrit donc les mentalités, les us et coutumes, les mœurs, les idées et les valeurs, et on les met en relation avec la vie collective. La culture est l'ensemble des caractères propres à la vie d'une société.

Les faits sociaux sont étudiés souvent selon une méthode qui rappelle celle de la linguistique chez de Saussure, pour qui ce qui compte, dans une langue, ce ne sont pas les termes considérés isolément mais leurs 'écarts différentiels', car le système linguistique est un ensemble où tout se tient, où il n'y a ni dehors ni termes absolus mais uniquement des relations internes, des rapports de dépendance mutuelle. Les faits culturels semblent cependant constituer, au sein des faits sociaux, un groupe distinct de celui des faits économiques et politiques.

Cette nouvelle signification du terme de culture ne comporte qu'une seule difficulté, mais qui est d'importance: la 'culture' ne désigne qu'un simple fait constaté, et on lui attribue néanmoins une 'valeur', comme on le faisait dans l'ancien usage du mot. On ne classe plus les cultures; mais on les déclare toutes de même valeur; on proclame qu'il faut les 'respecter', les 'reconnaître' dans leur 'identité' ou dans leur 'différence' d'avec les autres. D'un mot, on recourt subrepticement à des attitudes philosophiques, au moment même où l'on se félicite d'y avoir échappé grâce à la science.

A nos yeux, la confusion entre les deux sens du terme de culture constitue un des plus redoutables dangers auxquels nous sommes actuellement exposés. Valoriser sans raison et indistinctement tout ce qui se présente, c'est en réalité tout dévaloriser. L'entreprise est d'autant plus grave qu'elle concerne ce qui mérite le plus d'être respecté: si la religion constitue la valeur suprême, qui dépasse même la moralité, on ne peut la réduire à un fait socio-culturel, sinon en rejetant sa prétention à assurer le salut de l'homme par son union à Dieu.

36 M. Mead, *Sociétés, traditions et techniques*, 1953, p. 13.

L'Amour du Souverain Bien

Réalité et Illusion
(Malebranche, F. Lamy, Ameline)

GENEVIÈVE RODIS-LEWIS

'Induire à illusion, témérité et erreur' est une des mises en garde des articles d'Issy contre les 'voies extraordinaires' non contrôlées par les autorités ecclésiastiques (art. 27, 28; 'illusion' est répété art. 25, 29 . . .). Fénelon le reprend à plusieurs reprises dans l'*Explication des maximes des saints*:[1] 'illusion' en est aussi le mot final de la *Réponse* à Bossuet, deux fois répété dans les lignes précédentes. Mais en 1699, la condamnation à Rome de 23 propositions renvoie également à l'illusion plusieurs des thèses dont l'exposé était présenté comme 'Vrai' à propos de chaque Maxime: avant d'observer, par soumission, le silence sur ces points litigieux, Fénelon avait multiplié de vastes exposés avec une sereine assurance.[2] Or, entre le printemps de 1697 et la fin de 1699, une polémique parallèle, plus philosophique et psychologique que théologique, se développe entre Malebranche et le bénédictin François Lamy, réagissant tous deux contre le possible soupçon de quiétisme. La dénonciation de nombreuses illusions (des sens, de l'amour-propre, de la conscience superficielle) est un thème directeur de la *Connaissance de soi-même*.[3] A la fin de son tome III, F. Lamy citait, pour l'en louer, plusieurs phrases d'un 'illustre et solide' ou 'excellent Auteur',[4] contre le

---

1 L'édition, dite Lebel (imprimeur), Versailles, 1820 sq., 35 volumes, et toutes celles qui l'ont suivie, ne donnent pas cette *Explication* . . . , à cause de sa condamnation par Rome. L'édition critique d'A. Cherel (1911) suit un texte manuscrit, plus complexe que celui publié au début de 1697: nous y renvoyons, dans l'édition de la Bibliothèque de la Pléiade (t. I, Paris, 1983: Fénelon, *Oeuvres*) par J. Le Brun (auteur d'une importante thèse sur *La spiritualité de Bossuet*, 1972): l'Avertissement répète 'illusion', pp.1003-4, et annonce que chaque article sera commenté en 'Vrai' ('doctrine saine du pur amour') et 'Faux' (précisant où 'le danger de l'illusion commence': p. 1006). La fin de la *Réponse* (de Fénelon) *à l'écrit* (de Bossuet) *intitulé Relation sur le quiétisme* (p. 1097 sq.) reprend la mise en garde contre 'l'illusion' (p. 1198, *bis*) et conclut qu'il ne pouvait se taire sur ces 'erreurs impies', ni 'excuser l'illusion' (p. 1199). Les articles d'Issy sont donnés pp. 1534-8.

2 L'édition Lebel consacre au quiétisme les volumes IV à VI, avec en tête du volume IV un 'Avertissement' historique très complet (p. I-CCXXVIII, de Gosselin). Dans la Pléiade, Le Brun présente l'essentiel dans la Notice pp. 1530-45. Tous deux se limitent aux auteurs (archevêque de Paris, etc.) concernant directement Fénelon et Bossuet, sans parler de Malebranche, Lamy, ni d'Ameline. Ce dernier est absent de la plus riche étude du Père Yves de Montcheuil, *Malebranche et le quiétisme*, 1946.

3 T. I, II, III, 1697; t. IV-V, 1698.

4 T. III, c. 9, 12, p. 491; cité par Malebranche à la fin des *Trois lettres au R. P. Lamy*, 1698; édition A. Robinet, Malebranche, *Oeuvres Complètes* (désormais *OC*, suivi du tome et de la page) XIV, 127.

retour sur soi dans l'espoir de la récompense et la jouissance de la béatitude, qui nous ferait aimer Dieu: il 'mérite d'être aimé en lui-même; et . . . la douceur que l'on goûte dans son amour, nous éloigne de lui, si nous arrêtant à cette douceur, nous ne l'aimons pas pour lui-même: car alors nous nous aimons au lieu de lui'.[5] Malebranche, avant la fin de 1697, donne à la suite d'une réédition de son *Traité de morale*, comportant quelques additions,[6] un écrit d'une cinquantaine de pages, *De l'amour de Dieu*, exposant les aspects complémentaires de cette thèse, car tout amour est mû par un 'plaisir'. Ici encore il faut distinguer le réel et l'illusoire, qui s'arrête à 'de faux biens'. Le 'plaisir éclairé, lumineux, raisonnable' nous 'porte à aimer la vraie cause qui le produit, à aimer le vrai bien, le bien de l'esprit. . . . Nous faisant aimer ce que nous devons raisonnablement aimer, il nous rend plus parfaits aussi bien que plus heureux' (*OC*, XIV, 9).

A la fin, quelques lignes affirmant son 'estime et . . . amitié pour l'Auteur de la *Connaissance de soi-même*' (l'ouvrage ayant paru sans son nom), refusaient 'ce qu'il pense sur l'amour désintéressé' (ibid., p. 29). Au début, Malebranche précisait qu'il ne discuterait pas de 'tout ce qu'il y a de vrai ou de faux', en des propositions très proches de celles qui encadraient les citations faites par Lamy:[7] il se gardait de 'traiter à fond du quiétisme, bon ou mauvais' (*OC* XIV, 12). Par ce mot, Lamy se sent à son tour suspect de ce qu'il appellera 'une infâme hérésie', en accusant Malebranche: 'vous êtes l'agresseur'.[8] Il souligne alors qu'il avait supprimé la phrase des *Conversations chrétiennes* proche de la supposition dite impossible, plusieurs fois reprise par Fénelon comme sommet du cinquième amour, le plus pur: 'les bienheureux, disait Malebranche, souffriraient donc les peines des damnés, si cela était possible, sans haïr Dieu': 'loin de l'avoir voulu appliquer aux questions dont on dispute aujourd'hui, j'ai supprimé à dessein ce qui pouvait y avoir quelque rapport', précise Lamy.[9]

---

5 Ibid., p. 492 et XIV, 127.

6 *Traité de morale*, nouvelle [3e] édition, augmentée dans le corps de l'ouvrage, et d'un *Traité de l'Amour de Dieu à la fin*, Lyon, Plaignard, 1697. Lamy avait cité (t. III, c. 9, § 9, p. 487 et *OC*, XIV, 126) une phrase de I, c. 3, § 16. En 1697, Malebranche ajoute au c. 8 un nouveau §15 sur la différence entre les motifs et la fin (*OC*, XI, 102-3).

7 Juste avant cette évocation du 'quiétisme', où il s'est trouvé 'malheureusement engagé' par un de ses amis dans son dernier ouvrage, 'malgré le dessein que j'avais pris de garder sur cela un profond silence', Malebranche objecte: 'Il est vrai, dira-t-on, que les saints n'aiment point les perfections divines, à cause de ce plaisir qui les rend formellement heureux. . . . Ils aiment Dieu en lui-même et pour lui-même' (*OC*, XIV, 12: cf. Lamy, t. III, p. 486, cité *OC*, XIV, 125, § 8).

8 Répété par Lamy, *Lettres* (1699) pp. 4 et 10; cité par Malebranche, *Réponse générale*, *OC*, XIV, 139.

9 *Connaissance* . . . , t. V, fin (à pagination nouvelle) § 6, p. 11. A la fin de ses *Trois Lettres* Malebranche ne donne de ces Eclaircissements le concernant que les pp. 127-34 (*OC*, XIV, 128-31). Citant rarement Lamy, les auteurs ayant abordé cette querelle ne mentionnent pas cette suppression initiale, visant à éviter les difficultés du quiétisme. Nous la signalons dans la Notice sur le *Traité de l'amour de Dieu*, au tome II des *Oeuvres* de Malebranche (Pléiade, sous presse).

Or les auteurs qui ont abordé, ou même approfondi cette polémique, ne rappellent pas cette volonté initialement pacifique de Lamy, et son aversion manifeste pour ce quiétisme en tant qu'il est 'mauvais': nul ne met en question 'l'interprétation quiétiste du P. Lamy'.[10] La vivacité des réactions adverses est fonction du contexte historique qui s'aggrave entre le début de 1697 et la condamnation à Rome de 23 propositions soutenues dans l'*Explication des Maximes des Saints*: Fénelon pensait y avoir bien rejeté le quiétisme de Molinos, qui vient de mourir à Rome, où il était emprisonné depuis sa condamnation en 1685. Suivent le t. III de Lamy, et l'*Instruction*, de Bossuet, *sur les états d'oraison*, grossie de 130 pages de documents officiels antiquiétistes. Fénelon multiplie alors les écrits,[11] pour défendre la pureté de sa thèse, et son 'horreur' de l'hérésie, avec les débordements moraux qu'on y associe souvent. Mais il doit quitter la Cour et demeurer en son diocèse de Cambrai. Lamy reste en amicales relations avec lui par une correspondance où peu de ses propres lettres nous sont parvenues.[12] Après avoir commencé à

10 Expression de G. Dreyfus, *La volonté selon Malebranche* (1958), p. 299: elle ne cite jamais Lamy. J. Vidgrain, *Le christianisme dans la philosophie de Malebranche* (1923) le dit 'adversaire du pur amour des quiétistes', et résume Lamy (pp. 290 et 292-305), sans analyser ses réserves à l'égard de ce quiétisme. Montcheuil le cite à peine et le trouve 'vague et incohérent' (p. 104), tout en reconnaissant que Lamy rejette les erreurs quiétistes, et ne défend pas le cinquième amour des *Maximes des Saints*. Montcheuil analyse finement les relations mouvantes entre les protagonistes, et corrige plusieurs inexactitudes; (sur la confusion des prénoms avec l'Oratorien Bernard, cf. *infra*, note 31). La plus grosse est de L. Crouslé (*Bossuet et Fénelon*, 1894-1895, p. 122 croyant que Malebranche s'éloigne de . . . Bossuet, l'Auteur de la *Connaissance de soi-même*: *OC*, XIV, 29, Lamy n'étant nommé que dans l'Avertissement de la 2e édition, ibid., pp. 3-5). Montcheuil précise que *De la connaissance de Dieu et de soi-même* a paru seulement en 1741; mais cet ouvrage de Bossuet avait été publié en 1722 sous le titre: *Introduction à la philosophie ou De la connaissance de Dieu et de soi-même*.

11 *Explication* . . . , Avertissement, Pléiade, p. 1002. Le terme est repris plusieurs fois, notamment dans la correspondance. Lamy, au début des Eclaircissments ajoutés à la fin de son tome V, refuse d'être 'suspect de cette infâme hérésie' (p. 5). Sa première *Lettre* (p. 7) condamne cette 'extravagante indifférence propre à éteindre l'amour de Dieu', ces 'étranges principes qui ébranlent furieusement la morale chrétienne' et sont 'dignes d'horreur': il s'agit toujours des excès de Molinos, et non du plus pur amour: 'si je vous ai attribué des sentiments, écrit Lamy, ce n'a été que ceux que je crois les plus parfaits et que je prends pour moi-même' (*Lettre* I, p. 8).

12 Dans l'édition de Fénelon en 10 volumes in-4° (Gaume, 1848-1852; Gosselin toujours non nommé), on trouve au t. VII (Correspondance), plus de 25 lettres de Fénelon à Lamy (souvent l'encourageant à supporter ses douleurs) pour une dizaine de réponses, souvent brèves, de Lamy (plus 2, sans réponse, au t. IX, sur le quiétisme). Il y faut ajouter (t. II, *Ecrits spirituels*) cinq grandes lettres de Fénelon (les deux dernières datées de 1708) sur la prédestination et la grâce; en l'absence de réponses, on aperçoit que Lamy souhaitait une 'grâce générale', à laquelle Fénelon oppose l'étroitesse de la prédestination (d'où son abandon au pur amour, sans se fixer sur le salut). On ne saurait (comme la notice, par G. Oury, du *Dictionnaire de spiritualité*) accuser Lamy de 'pessimisme fondamental'. Nous avions fait photographier ses *Réflexions sur le traité de la grâce générale* (manuscrit des Archives de Port-Royal, à présent à Utrecht; cf. G. Lewis, *Le problème de l'inconscient et le cartésianisme*, p. 276; et pp. 219-31 sur la confrontation (psychologique

rapprocher Bossuet et Malebranche,[13] peut-être avait-il espéré, en soulignant leur accord sur l'amour de Dieu, atténuer l'hostilité de Fénelon envers l'auteur du *Traité de la nature et de la grâce*.[14] Ce fut au contraire Bossuet qui se réjouit de la protestation de Malebranche, dès 1697. En 1698, Lamy publie ensemble ses tomes IV (suite de la critique des illusions de la volupté, de l'orgueil, etc.) et V: après divers Eclaircissements, il en ajoute trois, avec une nouvelle pagination, pour protester contre la réaction de Malebranche. Celui-ci répond par *Trois Lettres au R. P. Lamy* (datées de fin juin 1698, parues à Lyon en 1699, après une réédition des *Méditations chrétiennes et métaphysiques*). Elles avaient circulé avant la sortie de l'ouvrage; et Lamy, après s'être impatienté, réplique aussitôt par quatre *Lettres* à Malebranche: les deux premières, comme le dernier Eclaircissement du tome V, accentuent son accord sur l'amour de Dieu avec certains textes du philosophe. Mais les deux dernières soulignent les textes contraires, en lui reprochant de s'être contredit, et surtout d'avoir varié en ses derniers textes pour creuser leur opposition. Malebranche publie séparément, au début de 1700, une *Réponse générale*, qui sera jointe aux textes précédents dans une dernière édition (à Lyon et à Paris). Lamy est alors astreint au silence par ses supérieurs, ce que regrette Fénelon.[15] En fait il y avait eu de chaque côté trois textes successifs; mais Lamy, jugeant ses premières citations de Malebranche pacifiques et élogieuses, et faisant commencer l'agression avec le traité *De l'amour de Dieu*, eût pu exprimer encore son humeur combative: le ton devenait de plus en plus aigre, et qui sait si Malebranche eût gardé le silence auquel il aspirait, après 'trop d'écritures'.[16]

   et non théologique) avec Nicole. Grâce à Lisa Ginzburg, nous espérons leur publication prochaine en Italie. Ils se communiquaient leurs écrits, car Nicole dans sa 1e partie répond à certaines de ces *Réflexions,* alors que l'édition complète (1715) est postérieure à leur mort (Nicole: 1695; Lamy: 1711), une édition partielle ayant paru en 1699.

13 Lamy avait défendu sans succès auprès de Bossuet une thèse de Malebranche sur la 'satisfaction' que la passion du Christ apporte pour compléter les peines des damnés (*OC*, XVIII, 464–75). Puis il avait adouci les réserves de Bossuet en lui communiquant les *Entretiens sur la métaphysique et la religion* (ibid., p. 481).

14 Sa *Réfutation*, qui lui avait été demandée par Bossuet après la parution du *Traité*, resta inédite jusqu'en 1820. Malebranche semble l'avoir ignorée (Montcheuil, p. 88).

15 *Œuvres*, t. VII, pp. 538 et 542; Malebranche, *OC*, XIX, 710 et 713: 'laisser triompher celui qui a le tort de son côté c'est vaincre le mal par le bien.'

16 'Lettre du P. Malebranche contenant une Réponse générale aux Lettres' du 'P. Lamy religieux bénédictin' s. d. (début 1700). Réponse jointe en 1707 à la 3e édition du *Traité*, suivi des *Trois Lettres*. 'Et une quatrième ou Réponse générale'. Malebranche dit à la fin: 'Ne voilà que trop d'écritures'. Il voudrait arrêter 'les brouilleries perpétuelles' qui appelle-raient 'un ouvrage immense par la multiplicité des passages qu'il faudrait transcrire . . . Enfin j'aime si peu le combat que je n'ose presque me défendre' (*OC*, XIV, 232 et 233). Lamy, ancien militaire, converti après un duel, avouait son humeur combative, mais savait parfois la dominer, largement dans ses deux premières Lettres, et pleinement en son dernier ouvrage.

Cependant Lamy n'avait pas dit son dernier mot: dès 1700, il annonce à Fénelon[17] qu'il commence un nouvel écrit sur l'amour de Dieu, sans traiter la question du 'motif': béatitude espérée ou total abandon. Le bénédictin obtient l'Approbation de ses supérieurs le 8 octobre 1710, et il aura même le Privilège royal, que Malebranche, malgré l'appui de Bossuet, n'avait pas eu pour le traité *De l'amour de Dieu*:[18] il est daté du 16 mars 1712, mais Lamy était mort en avril 1711 (probablement le 11). Depuis plusieurs années, il était réconcilié avec Malebranche.[19] *De la connaissance et de l'amour de Dieu, avec l'art de faire bon usage des afflictions de cette vie* n'est pas mentionné dans les correspondances de Malebranche, ni de Fénelon, ni dans les études sur le quiétisme. Il est également absent des quelques pages consacrées à ce 'malebranchiste' par F. Bouillier, au tome II de l'*Histoire de la philosophie cartésienne* (éd. 1868, pp. 362-73). Or au chapitre précédent sur plusieurs 'cartésiens malebranchistes', Bouillier, consacrant quelques lignes à Claude Ameline,[20] omet son *Traité de l'amour du Souverain Bien, qui donne le caractère de l'amour de Dieu, opposé aux fausses idées de ceux qui ne s'éloignent pas assez des erreurs de Molinos et de ses disciples*: l'ouvrage, dédié à l'Archevêque de Paris, a paru en 1699, avec Privilège (Paris, Fr. Léonard). Non moins ignoré des études sur le quiétisme, il s'y oppose avec vigueur, en attaquant dans la Préface (sans pagination) 'Dom. Franc. L'A' (*sic*, pour Lamy), et dans ses derniers chapitres

17 Fénelon, *Oeuvres*, t. VII, p. 567 (note se référant probablement au *Traité* posthume). Montcheuil cite cette lettre (p. 95), sans préciser quel sera cet ouvrage également absent de la bibliographie, assez abondante, de Vidgrain.

18 A Berrand, 16 décembre 1697, *OC*, XIX, 639-640: le libraire lyonnais (cf. *supra*, note 4) avait le privilège pour le *Traité de morale*, et Bossuet, qui était venu de lui-même 'offrir son estime et son amitié', ne put le faire étendre au nouveau *Traité*, dont il était 'si content' (Chauvin, ibid., p.640).

19 Lamy à Puget, 5 juillet 1708, *OC*, XIX, 789: Malebranche 'avec qui je suis raccommodé'. Du dernier *Traité* de Lamy, la *Nouvelle biographie générale* (Hoefer) dit: 'cet ouvrage posthume est estimé et rare.'

20 *Histoire de la philosophie cartésienne*, t. II, c. 17 (3e édition, 1868) p. 334: parmi les cartésiens malebranchistes de l'Oratoire, Ameline est nommé comme auteur du *Traité de la volonté* (1684) et de *L'Art de vivre heureux . . .* daté de 1694. La 1e édition est de 1667: il s'agit d'une morale optimiste, considérant, avec Descartes, la nature humaine sans les effets du péché, sur lequel Ameline insiste constamment. Cf. dans le *Dictionnaire des Philosophes* (P.U.F. 1984, dir. D. Huisman, t. I) nos notices sur Ameline et Pseudo-Ameline, et dans l'*Encyclopédie Philosophique Universelle*, t. III, *Œuvres* (à paraître P.U.F., dir. J. F. Mattéi) nos analyses de ces œuvres, avec pour C. Ameline référence au présent article. Sur F. Lamy, Bouillier évoque 'la défense du pur amour contre Bossuet' et Malebranche (sans nommer aucun de ses écrits). Au c. 7 sur Malebranche t. II, p.122, notes 1-2, il parle d'une 'citation tronquée' des *Conversations chrétiennes*, VIII, 'dans le 4e volume de la *Connaissance de soi-même*' (corriger: '3e vol.') et dit: 'Le P. Lamy répondit au traité de Malebranche par trois lettres (corriger: 'Eclaircissements') ajoutées au t. V de la *Connaissance . . .* Puis il mentionne, sans précision, les 'trois lettres' de Malebranche, et 'de nouvelles lettres' de Lamy; mais il n'y renvoie pas dans le c. 19 sur Lamy, évoquant cette polémique sur le pur amour, et il ajoute: 'Lamy aurait encore eu avec Malebranche une autre polémique au sujet du *Traité de la nature et de la grâce* que ses supérieurs lui défendirent de continuer' (p. 367).

l'*Explication des Maximes des Saints* de Fénelon. L'auteur dit avoir commencé cette étude sur l'amour de Dieu plusieurs années avant le début de la querelle autour du quiétisme.

Sans reprendre les points bien approfondis dans plusieurs études dont Fénelon et Bossuet ou Malebranche sont le centre, il nous a paru qu'en faisant connaître ces deux ouvrages, apparemment adverses, et en confrontant le dernier texte de Lamy avec ses réponses antérieures à Malebranche (rarement citées), on pouvait mieux préciser divers degrés dans ce qu'on réunit trop vite sous le nom de quiétisme. Fénelon rejette avec horreur les excès de ceux qui se 'reposent' (*quies*) totalement en Dieu, en laissant la partie supérieure de l'âme indifférente à ce que peut opérer sa partie inférieure.[21] Mais il s'efforce inlassablement de défendre l'idéal supérieur des saints qui aiment Dieu pour lui seul, sans souci de leur béatitutde, au point d'accepter l'éventualité d'une damnation éternelle.[22] Malebranche dit avoir discuté de ce 'cinquième amour' avec Lamy, qui savait ainsi qu'il lui faisait 'beaucoup de peine'.[23]

Or, sur ce point central dans la condamnation de Fénelon, Malebranche avait été le plus loin dans la phrase des *Conversations chrétiennes*, supprimée par prudence dans la première série de citations qu'en avait fait Lamy (*OC*, IV, 180; et c. 9 *De la connaissance de soi-même*, § 12, cité *OC*, XIV, 127): peut-on souffrir 'les peines des damnés' en restant 'bienheureux' et 'sans haïr Dieu'? Souvent on ne souligne guère l'incompatibilité entre cette absence de haine et l'enfer. Fénelon en citant à plusieurs reprises l'épreuve subie par saint François de Sales, qui doutant de son salut s'était libéré par un acte d'abandon,[24] admire cette parfaite indifférence à la béatitude, et condamne seulement l'"extravagance monstrueuse' qui admettrait 'de haïr Dieu éternelle-

21 Par exemple *Explication* . . . , article 11, 'Faux'; L'âme 'n'a qu'à se laisser aller sans examen à toutes les pentes qu'elle trouve en soi . . . Elle n'a qu'à demeurer sans volonté et neutre entre le bien et le mal, même dans les plus extrêmes tentations . . . C'est enseigner aux âmes à se tendre elles-mêmes des pièges, c'est leur inspirer une indolence dans le mal qui est le comble de l'hypocrisie . . . ' (Pléiade, t. I, p. 1040).
22 Fénelon avait fait ajouter aux Articles d'Issy le n° 33, pour inspirer aux 'âmes vraiment parfaites' 'une soumission . . . à la volonté de Dieu, quand même, par une très fausse supposition, au lieu des biens éternels qu'il a promis aux âmes justes, il les tiendrait par son bon plaisir dans des tourments éternels, *sans néanmoins qu'elles soient privées de sa grâce et de son amour*' (Pléiade, p. 1538. Nous soulignons ce qui rend la supposition 'impossible'). Fénelon le justifie dans l'*Explication* . . . , sur l'art. 2 ('Vrai', Pléiade, p. 1016, etc.) en nommant des Pères de l'Eglise. On cite souvent, de part et d'autre, l'acceptation par Moïse (*Exode* XXXII, 31-32) et S. Paul (*Rom.* III, 8) de sacrifier leur bonheur pour le salut de leur peuple (Ameline, c. 16, p. 113, précise qu'alors ils ont confiance en la justice de Dieu).
23 *Traité*, *OC*, XIV, 37-8; et à Berrand, 16 septembre 1697, *OC*, XIX, 639: 'il sait bien que ce n'est pas mon sentiment pour avoir discuté contre lui.'
24 *Explication*, sur l'art. 5 ('Vrai', Pléiade, pp. 1024-25) citant les *Entretiens spirituels* et la fin du c. 4 au livre 9 du *Traité de l'amour de Dieu* (S. François de Sales, *Oeuvres*, Pléiade éd. A. Ravier, p. 1025; 'les saints qui sont au ciel ont une telle union à la volonté de Dieu, que s'il y avait un peu plus de son bon plaisir en enfer, ils quitteraient le paradis pour y

ment, ou de cesser de l'aimer' (*Explication des Maximes*, art. 2, 'Faux'; Pléiade p. 1017). Lamy avait pu lire dans la 1e édition du *Traité de morale*: 'Il faut aimer l'Être infiniment parfait, et non pas un fantôme épouvantable, un Dieu injuste', comme ceux 'qui, faute d'avoir une idée juste de la divinité supposent . . . que Dieu a eu dessein de les rendre éternellement malheureux' (I, c. 8, ancien § 16, devenu 17: *OC*, XI, 104). Et Lamy est d'accord: c'est une 'extravagante disposition' que d'être 'prêt à renoncer . . . à la présence de Dieu, à sa possession, à son union, par laquelle on consentirait à le perdre à jamais, à être éternellement séparé de lui, à le haïr, à le maudire dans la suite infinie des siècles' (*Connaissance de soi*, t. V, Ecl. final 2, p. 48). Il proclame la même 'horreur' qu'a Malebranche pour le quiétisme et ses erreurs (p. 46), et rejette comme 'fureur insensée' 'cette impie et brutale indifférence par laquelle on ne voudrait rien déterminer, ni salut, ni récompense, ni bonheur, ni Dieu même' (p. 49). Laissant de côté comme Malebranche les 'voies extraordinaires' (*Amour de Dieu, OC*, XIV, 12) Lamy précise: 'Je ne suis point quiétiste. Ma contemplation n'est point absolument passive. J'éprouve que j'agis en contemplant' (*Lettres*, p. 290).

Mais, tout en évitant de citer la phrase sur les bienheureux acceptant les peines de l'enfer, Lamy avait cru trouver en Malebranche un défenseur de l'amour pour Dieu totalement détaché de l'amour-propre, dans la première citation (dès le § 9 de son c. 9) du *Traité de morale*: 'Il ne suffit pas d'aimer Dieu ou l'Ordre lorsqu'il s'accommode avec notre amour-propre. Il faut lui sacrifier toutes choses, notre bonheur actuel, et s'il le demandait ainsi, notre être propre' (*OC*, I, c. 3, § 16; *OC*, XI, 47; & cité *OC*, XVI, 126). Quel plus grand rempart contre l'amour-propre que d'accepter d'être anéanti? Ceux qui se suicident, répond Malebranche, regardent la mort comme l'anéantissement de leur être et . . . préfèrent le non-être à l'être privé du bien-être' (*Amour de Dieu, OC*, XIV, 14). Au scandale de 'la damnation du juste' par un Dieu injuste, donc 'imaginaire' (ibid. p. 25), il oppose l'hypothèse de l'anéantissement: la créature étant contingente, Dieu pouvait ne pas lui donner l'immortalité:[25] 'sans le bien et le mal-être, actuel ou futur . . . sans quelque espérance ou quelque crainte d'une autre vie, et sans la douleur

---

aller'; et *Traité* . . . p. 770: 'un cœur . . . sans aucun autre objet que la volonté de son Dieu . . . aimerait mieux l'enfer avec la volonté de Dieu que le paradis sans la volonté de Dieu . . . en sorte que si, par imagination de chose impossible, il savait que sa damnation fût un peu plus agréable à Dieu que sa salvation, il . . . courrait à sa damnation.' Mort fin 1622, il était canonisé dès 1665. Bossuet (sans citer ces phrases) discute l'autorité reconnue par Fénelon aux paroles d'un canonisé: 'on ne fait pas une règle de quelque expression extraordinaire' (p. 141: Préface sur l'*Instruction pastorale, Œuvres Complètes*, Bar-le-Duc, t. X, 1863, c. 11, pp. 135–41.

25   Pour Descartes, le dualisme rend l'âme indépendante de la mort du corps (*Méditations*, Abrégé, Adam-Tannery, IX, 10). Mais Dieu 'par son absolue puissance' eût pu déterminer que l'âme cesse d'être avec le corps. La foi complète ici la philosophie: 'puisqu'il nous a maintenant révélé que cela n'arrivera point, il ne nous doit plus rester touchant cela aucun doute' (Réponses aux 2 objections, ibid., p. 120).

qu'on souffre à se donner la mort', on préférerait être libéré de toute misère (ibid. 25-6; et 53-4). Dans son dernier ouvrage, Malebranche niera, contre Boursier, que j'aie 'le pouvoir . . . de me brûler tout vif'. Le désir invincible d'être heureux, constamment opposé à Lamy, est encore insurmontable. Cependant 'saint Laurent et d'autres martyrs' ont pu accepter de 'se laisser brûler tout vif', 'le désir naturel du bonheur' se conciliant ici avec 'la crainte d'offenser Dieu . . . , l'espérance de jouir d'un bonheur éternel et la crainte de brûler éternellement'.[26] Or Malebranche rapproche cette hypothèse 'de cette liberté imaginaire qu'on attribue aux quiétistes' et il la prolonge par celle de damnés devenus indépendants de la justice divine, 'en vivant contents au milieu des flammes' (*OC*, XVI, 66). On aperçoit ainsi comment a pu être imaginée, à partir du saint uni à Dieu sur le gril, l'impossible supposition, exaltée comme le plus haut degré d'amour.

Dès son titre, Ameline dissipe ces artifices, en désignant Dieu comme le 'Souverain Bien': en se donnant à lui, on joint béatitude et perfection. Contre 'la pleine et entière indifférence du juste pour le souverain bonheur ou pour la peine même éternelle' (p. 30), il précisera que l'enfer n'est pas simple douleur physique, mais d'abord privation de Dieu, ce qui 'enferme nécessairement une révolte éternelle', et il répète son 'horreur'.[27] Par ses définitions initiales il exclut les aberrations des 'nouveaux mystiques': 1) 'L'amour . . . est . . . l'action de la volonté qui désire de jouir d'un bien, ou qui en jouit déjà.' 2) La charité est le mouvement qui porte à jouir de Dieu. Après avoir défini convoitise et cupidité comme la révolte de la chair contre l'esprit, il donne un bon sens à 'ces mêmes termes' quand Dieu fait céder une mauvaise concupiscence à une bonne concupiscence qu'il inspire. Puis un nouveau postulat pose que l'homme ne commence à convoiter le bien que quand il commence à lui paraître doux et à lui plaire. Le suivant identifie le Souverain Bien sans lequel l'homme ne peut être heureux et la fin à laquelle rapporter toutes nos actions. C'est la jouissance propre de Dieu que saint Augustin appelle 'joie de la vérité'. Par ces prémisses, Ameline refuse donc d'emblée un amour de Dieu privé d'une béatitude spirituelle qui combat victorieusement la mauvaise concupiscence.

Son premier ouvrage, *Traité de la volonté, de ses principales actions, de ses passions et de ses égarements* (1684) développait la corruption de l'homme depuis le péché originel, en s'opposant, dès le début, à la fois à Aristote et à

---

26 *Réflexions sur la prémotion physique*, *OC*, XVI, 16; et 66 nommant 'les quiétistes'.
27 Pp. 91 et 92: ce serait un scandale de condamner aux flammes éternelles celui qui a aimé Dieu. Nous l'aimons 'comme notre fin dernière et notre souverain bien' (p. 78). Cela n'est nullement 'mercenaire' (p. 73, etc.; expression que Fénelon oppose constamment au pur amour). Ameline suggère que pour Fénelon une âme préférant sa béatitude formelle à la gloire de Dieu ferait un 'péché mortel' (pp. 153-4); mais (p. 161) il rappelle que dans son *Instruction pastorale*, Fénelon traite d'une simple imperfection, 'sans péché même véniel'. C'est très net dans l'*Explication* . . . (alors non publiée), sur l'art. 41 ('Vrai'): 'la concupiscence qui demeure toujours en cette vie n'est point un péché' (Pléiade, p. 1089).

Descartes:[28] 'nous n'examinons pas les passions en orateur, ni en physicien, mais en philosophe moral et en philosophe chrétien' (p. 4). Tout en suivant apparemment l'ordre de Malebranche dans le livre V de *La recherche de la vérité*, il remet en question la nature passionnelle de l'admiration: c'est plutôt une suspension de jugement. La 3e partie est consacrée à l'amour, auquel se subordonnent les autres passions, ce qui vient d'abord de saint Augustin. Avant d'en développer les dérèglements, il avait écrit: seul Dieu peut être aimé 'd'un amour de repos' (p. 100): l'expression n'est pas reprise en 1699, quand Ameline développe sa critique du quiétisme. Il pose comme évidentes ses affirmations 'à la façon des géomètres': après ses 'demandes ou définitions', il énonce comme vingt-six 'principes ou maximes' des citations alternées (sans références) de saint Augustin et de saint Thomas, répétant complémentairement que tous les hommes veulent être heureux. Le développement suivant, sur les vertus, unit la charité à l'Esprit Saint (p. 18), qui est 'amour subsistant' (p. 109); la méditation sur la Trinité est rare en ces textes de spiritualité morale.[29] Ameline développe ensuite l'opposition entre 'le mauvais amour de soi-même qui porte jusqu'au mépris de Dieu' (selon la formule augustinienne) et le 'bon et saint amour de soi', donné dans le second commandement 'comme le juste modèle de l'amour du prochain' (pp. 26 et 28). Il vise toujours la perfection; et de nombreux textes bibliques appuient cette attente du règne de Dieu, qu'on peut bien dire 'aimé pour lui-même', sans justifier pour autant l'indifférence au salut, qui réalise l'indissoluble union avec Celui vers lequel la vie terrestre est une longue progression, soutenue par le détachement difficile des biens sensibles. L'affirmation métaphysique chez Descartes de l'existence de Dieu comme Infini parfait, à partir de l'aspiration d'un être qui se découvre imparfait en sa finitude, devient ici subordination éthique à la source inépuisable de perfection, qui seule peut combler notre manque. 'Si c'est Dieu qui est le plus parfait des êtres, celui qui l'aime ne lui fait point d'injustice, ni à soi-même, par l'aveu de son extrême pauvreté et des richesses infinies de l'objet qu'il aime' (p. 101). Dieu n'est donc jamais instrument ou moyen de notre bonheur; le Souverain Bien est la seule véritable fin dernière (p. 102). Mieux vaut 'tirer le rideau' (p. 147) sur les désordres issus d'un acquiescement injuste au désespoir, nourri par l'orgueil secret de n'être pas comme tous, qui s'apparente au pharisaïsme. De très nombreux textes scripturaires accompagnent ces réflexions. On n'y trouve ni le nom de Malebranche, ni ses thèses propres, comme la distinction entre motif et fin qu'Ameline identifie (p. 142, dans une discussion contre Fénelon). On

---

28 Descartes, Lettre-préface aux *Passions de l'âme* (Adam-Tannery XI, 326): 'Mon dessein n'a pas été d'expliquer les passions en orateur [Aristote en traitait dans la *Rhétorique*], ni même en philosophe moral, mais seulement en physicien.'

29 A l'encontre des quiétistes, Malebranche médite constamment sur le Verbe et son Incarnation. Mais il évoque rarement l'Esprit saint, principe d'amour: *Recherche de la Vérité*, I. V, c. 4: 'la douceur inexplicable de la charité que le Saint Esprit répand dans leur cœur' (*OC*, II, 165; Pl. I, p. 522; cf. I. III-2, c. 6, *OC*, I, 446; Pl, I, p. 345).

n'a d'ailleurs aucune trace de relations personnelles entre Malebranche et Ameline, après que celui-ci ait quitté l'Oratoire dès 1661, pour exercer d'autres charges ecclésiastiques.

Au contraire, malgré les périodes de tension, Lamy retrouve par deux fois[30] l'amitié de Malebranche. Et même au plus fort de la discussion sur le pur amour, il maintient que l'Oratorien a bien avancé, en de nombreux textes, l'interprétation qu'il défend, avec des citations exactes (mais incomplètes). Il la justifie par des expressions malebranchistes; jusque dans son ouvrage posthume, où il fait la plus large part à la béatitude, (car 'l'amour seul suffit pour nous rendre heureux': p. 55), il répète: 'il ne faut pas humaniser la divinité' (préface non paginée, § 18). 'C'est humaniser la divinité, disait Malebranche, que de chercher hors d'elle le motif et la fin de son action' (*Entretiens sur la métaphysique* . . . , *OC*, XII, 201). 'Grand copiste du P. Malebranche, écrivait le P. André, il fait partout le méditatif, . . . il prend jusqu'à ses tours, ses idées, ses expressions.'[31] Doit-on en outre l'accuser de citer des 'passages tronqués et mal entendus', comme le fait Malebranche, quand il veut mettre fin à ces 'discussions inutiles' (*Lettre* 2, *OC* XIV, 97)? Certes Malebranche part du théocentrisme; dès le début de son premier ouvrage, il affirme: 'Il est évident que Dieu ne peut agir que pour lui-même; qu'il ne peut créer les esprits que pour le connaître et pour l'aimer; qu'il ne peut . . . leur imprimer aucun amour qui ne soit pour lui et qui ne tende vers lui' (*Recherche de la vérité*, *OC*, I, 10; Pl. I, p.4). 'Dieu est essentiellement heureux et parfait'; lui seul est 'la cause de sa perfection et de son bonheur, il n'aime invinciblement que sa propre substance' (*Tr. nature et grâce*, 2ᵉ p. § 54). Et il interprète souvent un verset biblique (*Prov.* XVI, 4): Dieu n'aime tout que *propter se*, pour et par rapport à lui-même. Si l'on s'attache à ces seuls textes, aimer Dieu c'est vouloir ce qu'il veut, aspirer à la perfection, sans retour sur nous-mêmes.

Mais, dès cette préface à *La Recherche* . . . , Malebranche affirmait aussi que les hommes 'aiment tous la félicité, et la perfection de leur être, et . . . ils ne travaillent que pour se rendre plus heureux et plus parfaits' (*OC*, I, 12;

---

30   La 1ᵉ brouille se termine en mai 1683, sans que la cause en soit connue: 'rien ne pouvait me consoler de la perte ou du refroidissement d'une amitié aussi précieuse que m'est la vôtre' (Lamy à Malebranche, *OC*, XVIII, 244-8. Sur la fin de la 2ᵉ, *supra*, note 19).

31   Les *OC*, XIV, pp. XIII-XXXIII donnent tout le passage de la *Vie du P. Malebranche* par André concernant la querelle avec Lamy, dont il fait un portrait sévère (pp. XXII-XXIII). André est responsable de la confusion des prénoms du bénédictin (François) et de l'Oratorien (Bernard), autre 'ami' de Malebranche: ibid., p. XVII. La rectification apparaît seulement en variante b. (texte de Lelong: 'dom François Lamy, auteur assez connu' . . . Cette erreur (signalée par Montcheuil, p. 11, n. 1) a été souvent répétée, jusque chez Delbos (*Étude de la philosophie de Malebranche*, posthume, 1924) et l'édition par D. Roustan du *Traité de l'amour de Dieu* (1923), et à l'article 'Malebranche' (par Wehrlé; *Dictionnaire de Théologie catholique*, t. IX, col. 1777 et 1779; au t. VIII, les deux Lamy sont bien distingués. Chauvin fait une autre erreur (non signalée)—Lamy aurait cité en faveur du pur amour, des passages de *La Recherche de la Vérité* (*OC*, XIX, 1972).

Pl. I, p. 5). Lamy ne peut donc accuser Malebranche d'avoir varié, quand il a toujours associé la poursuite par l'homme du bien-être et sa visée du bonheur qu'il trouvera pleinement en Dieu seul. Surtout, dans son attaque contre un livre au titre proche du sien, *L'Art de se connaître soi-même (ou la recherche des sources de la morale*, Rotterdam, 1692) du protestant J. Abbadie, Lamy a eu tort de condamner *tout* amour-propre, quand l'auteur en distinguait bien le bon amour de nous-mêmes ou désir d'être heureux.[32] En s'appuyant sur les textes de 'cet hérétique', comme dit Lamy, Malebranche réagit contre l'accusation déformante, et développe, selon son propre système, la conciliation entre l'amour de Dieu, tel qu'il nous est demandé et la poursuite de notre félicité. Ici encore les bases étaient posées dès le premier ouvrage: Dieu cause tous les mouvements qui sont dans la matière, et toutes les inclinations naturelles des esprits. Pour illustrer le principe d'inertie (qui devrait prolonger indéfiniment le mouvement en ligne droite) et le fait que les particules qui divisent la matière se pressent et tourbillonnent, Descartes évoquait ce qu'il avait appris des théologiens: 'Dieu est aussi l'Auteur de toutes nos actions, en tant qu'elles sont, et en tant qu'elles ont quelque bonté' (ou qu'elles sont droites): 'ce sont les diverses dispositions de nos volontés qui les peuvent rendre vicieuses' (*Monde*, ch. 7, Adam-Tannery, XI, pp. 46-47). Cette distinction fonde chez Malebranche le mouvement par lequel Dieu porte notre volonté vers le bien en général,[33] en nous faisant ressentir ce qu'il en a établi comme signe: plaisir sensible pour la conversation du corps, et, pour contrebalancer sa domination excessive depuis le péché originel, délectation prévenante qui nous pousse vers le bien, ce qui laisse à chacun la *liberté* de son choix. Lamy ne semble pas s'être opposé à cet aspect original de la conciliation entre grâce et liberté.[34] Avec tous ses

32 La *Lettre* I de Malebranche à Lamy défend le sentiment d'Abbadie, 'très catholique' si 'l'amour de bienveillance que nous nous portons' est 'le principe, ou le motif naturel de la charité, ou de l'amour de l'ordre' (*OC*, XIV, 56). Il cite l'accusation de Lamy 'contre les égarements d'un hérétique qui voulait introduire l'amour-propre dans le ciel': ou bien il est de mauvaise foi, ou il n'a pas compris 'assez nettement les sentiments d'Abbadie' (ibid., pp. 58 et 59)

33 'Toutes les inclinations que nous avons de Dieu sont droites.' Mais, à la différence de la matière, 'notre âme peut déterminer diversement l'inclination ou impression que Dieu lui donne ' (*Recherche de la Vérité*, I, c. 1, § 2, *OC*, I, Pl. I, pp. 26-7). La finalité vitale du plaisir et de la douleur est posée par Descartes, dans la Méditation 6 (Adam-Tannery, IX, 64-5). Malebranche développe souvent la liberté qu'avait Adam, avant la chute, d'arrêter ce message, pénible ou trop absorbant, dont le péché l'a rendu esclave. C'est pourquoi une nouvelle grâce salvatrice, par 'délectation prévenante' rétablit l'équilibre, en laissant le choix à notre liberté (*Traité de la Nature et de la Grâce*, II, §33-35, etc.).

34 F. Bouillier (*Histoire de la philosophie cartésienne,* 1e édition: 1854; 3e: 1868, t. II p. 367) déclare: 'D'après la plupart des biographes, et d'après une lettre de Fénelon, Lamy aurait encore eu avec Malebranche' (il vient de dire, p. 366, sans aucune précision, qu'il prit 'parti contre lui dans la question du pur amour') 'une autre polémique au sujet du *Traité de la nature et de la grâce*, que ses supérieurs lui défendirent de continuer', Fénelon s'indignant que Malebranche continue à écrire. (Il s'agit de l'échange de lettres sur le quiétisme: *supra*, note 15). La *Biographie universelle* de Michaud (Article Lami François, t.

contemporains, il considère comme une curieuse originalité et une fantaisie de langage la distinction de Malebranche entre le 'motif' (ou moteur: l'élan reçu de Dieu qui nous entraîne vers une jouissance) et la 'fin' (but que choisit la liberté); ils sont le plus souvent identifiés.[35] Une fois ces précisions bien établies, les thèses se rapprochent. Malebranche n'a jamais voulu louer notre amour pour Dieu en fonction du plaisir que nous y trouvons; tous considèrent les épreuves en cette vie comme une nécessaire purification. Lamy, qui a terriblement souffert en ses dernières années des douleurs de la gravelle, développe ce thème en 1703 dans *Les leçons de la sagesse sur l'engagement au service de Dieu*; et il prolonge le titre *De la connaissance et de l'amour de Dieu* 'avec l'art de faire un bon usage des afflictions de cette vie'; toute la fin du volume (p. 232-337) développe ce dernier titre, en une méditation sur l'appel du Christ à tous ceux qui souffrent: 'Venez à moi . . .' La conclusion *De la connaissance et de l'amour de Dieu* (p. 231) cite (sans nommer saint Augustin): *inquietum est cor nostrum donec requiescat in te;* et ce 'repos' final est bien distingué de l'indifférence proprement quiétiste: 'ce ne peut être que par l'ardent amour de cet objet [Dieu] qu'on peut devenir heureux'. Ainsi le dernier mot répond au sous-titre inscrit en tête de la Préface (non paginée): 'Voies sûres du bonheur et de la perfection'. Car cet amour 'nous rend non seulement parfaits, mais même heureux, et peut nous conduire à la perfection du christianisme et au Souverain Bonheur' (p. 83). L'étude des vertus qui s'associent aux divers mouvements de l'amour confirment la purification de tout ce qui est 'servile'. La charité ne cherche pas ses propres intérêts; elle 'veut devenir heureuse . . . mais elle ne le veut que parce que Dieu le veut' et reste 'pour sa gloire prête à lui sacrifier tous ses intérêts' (p. 151).

XXIII, sans date: le t. XX est de 1656) affirme qu'il a publié des 'écrits contre le *Traité de la nature et de la grâce*', et que Malebranche continua seul le combat. Dans le *Dictionnaire de théologie catholique* (t. VIII, notice de G. Bourdot), il avait attaqué Malebranche 'au sujet de son traité De la nature et de la grâce et de son Système sur l'amour désintéressé'. Or la lettre de réconciliation semble apprécier l'explication de la grâce, et Malebranche lui précise le maintien de notre liberté (*OC*, XVIII, 335-7, 2 novembre 1684), sans désaccord fondamental. Lamy en défend plusieurs thèses contre Arnauld et contre Bossuet (*supra*, note 13). Et la mise à l'écart du 'plaisir' dans l'amour de Dieu ne se réfère jamais à la grâce de délectation. Cependant son aspiration à une 'grâce générale' le sépare de Malebranche.

35 Outre le §15 ajouté au *Traité de morale* (I, c. 8) quand il précède celui de l'amour de Dieu, Malebranche reprend souvent sa distinction très précise: 'La *fin*, c'est ce à quoi l'âme tend, ce vers quoi l'âme se meut; le *motif* c'est ce qui la meut. Le motif est naturel et nécessaire, la fin est libre' (Lettre II, *OC*, XIV, 79). Fénelon et Lamy les rapprochent: le plaisir est un secours, principe ou cause efficiente de l'action, le motif est la cause finale qui attire la volonté (*Connaissance de soi*, t. V, Eclaircissement II de la fin, p. 52). Curieusement le *Dictionnaire* de Furetière donne, avec une citation de Fénelon, une définition plutôt malebranchiste—MOTIF: 'cause, raison, ce qui pousse, ce qui excite à faire quelque chose. "Les motifs d'intérêt propre, étant subordonnés à l'amour de Dieu, animent et soutiennent les hommes dans la recherche du salut" (Fénelon)'. (t. III, édition augmentée de 1727).

Ainsi Lamy, en unissant béatitude et perfection, refuse toujours ce qui l'avait choqué chez Abbadie, dont il n'avait retenu que la maladroite insistance sur notre 'intérêt': le texte de son tome III, qui a suscité la querelle, lui reprochait de soutenir 'qu'on ne peut aimer Dieu que *par intérêt*, que *par amour-propre*'. 'Quand l'amour de nous-mêmes se tourne vers Dieu, par l'intérêt du bonheur qu'il en attend, il se confond avec l'amour divin' (ch. 9, § 3; cité *OC*, XIV, 124). Par ses références à Abbadie (*Lettres* I et II *à Lamy*, et *Réponse générale*, surtout *OC*, XIV, 59, 66, 213), Malebranche montrait que le légitime amour de soi-même en son aspiration à la perfection y était bien distingué de l'amour-propre vicieux. Si le cœur de l'homme se limite aux créatures, 'ce n'est point Dieu qu'on aime, mais un fantôme qu'on se forme à la place de Dieu. Aussi est-ce un grand égarement d'opposer l'amour de nous-mêmes à l'amour divin, quand celui-là est bien réglé. . . . L'amour de Dieu est le bon sens de l'amour de nous-mêmes, c'en est l'esprit et la perfection' (Abbadie, p. 271; cité *OC*, XIV, 42). Et en insistant sur l'impossibilité de dissocier la volonté humaine et son élan vers le bonheur, Malebranche visait d'abord à préciser pour l'amour de Dieu 'en quel sens il *doit* être désintéressé';[36] (cette phrase complète dans la seconde édition (1699) le titre du *Traité de l'amour de Dieu*).

Ainsi, une fois dépassée la menace d'une confusion avec les excès du quiétisme, dont Lamy réprouve également les excès et l'illusion d'être totalement absorbé en Dieu (alors que le moi se complaît secrètement en sa supériorité), les positions de tous ces auteurs sur l'amour 'désintéressé' de Dieu rejoignent la tradition des citations multipliées par Ameline. Tous retrouvent constamment saint Augustin (sans reprendre les mêmes textes: les références à un même ouvrage sont souvent proches, mais différentes). Dans le mot de saint Paul: 'Ce n'est plus moi qui vis, c'est le Christ qui vit en moi' (Gal. II, 20), on doit souligner que le moi subsiste. De tout son être, il adhère à l'inspiration et à l'action même du Christ. L'amour demeure une union de deux volontés, quand la nôtre s'ouvre pleinement à celle de Dieu, sans renoncer à toute activité. '*Fiat voluntas tua*', dit-elle, en accueillant ce qui ne dépend pas de nous, mais en appelant aussi à *faire* ce qui nous est demandé. Le risque de ceux qui croient atteindre la plus haute perfection (dans les points dit 'vrais' par Fénelon, et cependant condamnés) est de croire qu'ils sont dès cette vie transformés jusqu'à se confondre en Dieu. Or leur connaissance demeure dans l'ombre du mystère; mais 'par l'amour, l'âme possède Dieu dès la terre, tel qu'il est en lui-même, et non pas tel qu'il

---

36 *OC*, XIV, 7. Cf. à Berrand, 2 mars 1699: 'L'amour pur et désintéressé est équivoque. Je ne rejette que celui que je crois indépendant du désir d'être heureux' (*OC*, XIV, 665). Cf. *Recherche de la Vérité*, 1. IV, c.4 (dès la 1e édition): ' . . . portés par une inclination naturelle à aimer tous les biens, nous ne pouvons devenir heureux qu'en possédant celui qui les renferme tous' (*OC*, II, 452; Pl. I, p. 412). Mais pour le 'posséder', il faut se laisser posséder par lui.

est en elle', dit Bérulle.[37] Cette sortie de soi ('extase') est sans doute une réalité vécue par quelques êtres exceptionnels. Malebranche, comme Lamy et Ameline, se garde de spéculer sur ces 'voies extraordinaires'. La réalité de cette vie unit encore charité et espérance: seule la parfaite béatitude abolira la séparation, liée ici-bas à notre limitation.

37   *Grandeurs de Jésus*, cité par J. Beaude, *La mystique*, Cerf, 1989, p. 74. Il ne faut pas,
     comme J. Vidgrain, intituler 'Le mysticisme de Malebranche' l'étude de la connaissance
     rationnelle, même si pour tout homme elle suppose l'union des esprits à Dieu (p. 341
     sq., c. 4, postérieur au chapitre sur l'amour, alors qu'il devrait le précéder). Vidgrain, en
     ce c. 3, souligne ce qui rend justement les saints exceptionnels: 'Ils aiment Dieu en lui-
     même et pour lui-même, et nullement Dieu pour eux-mêmes. Ils s'oublient et se
     perdent, pour ainsi dire, dans la Divinité, ils se rapportent uniquement à Dieu, et par la
     parfaite conformité de leur volonté avec la sienne, ils se transforment de manière que
     Dieu est tout en eux, et qu'ils ne sont rien' (*OC*, XIV, 12), cité par Vidgrain p. 304;
     Malebranche expose ici les plus hautes aspirations; cf. Fénelon, *Explication*, sur les art. 35-
     6 sur 'l'état de transformation' dont parlent tant de Pères. (Mais à la fin du 'Vrai' sur l'art.
     35, il dit l'âme pure 'transformée et déifiée', et bien que le 'Faux' rejette comme
     blasphème une 'déification . . . réelle', Bossuet dénonce ce 'langage exagératif (*Instruction
     sur les états d'oraison*, *Œuvres complètes*, t. IX, 1863, p. 476 b). Reste que la béatitude en
     est inséparable pour Malebranche, comme pour Ameline, Dieu est notre 'souverain
     Bien' et produit en nous 'le motif de son amour' (*OC*, XIV, 12).

Michael Moore (1640–1726)

COLM CONNELLAN

This essay is a first attempt at elucidating the biographical and historical details concerning a little known Irish philosopher who in his day was clearly a most important figure both in Ireland and on the Continent. Michael Moore was a Dublin diocesan priest, a philosophy professor, later rector of the University of Paris and, for a short time, Provost of Trinity College, Dublin. His name appears more usually in Latin as Morus, in English it may appear as Moore or Moor and in Irish it appeared as O'Morigh. Practically nothing is now known to us about his family or his education in Dublin. He was born in Bridge St, Dublin in 1640 and he told us himself that his father's name was Andrew. He was educated at Nantes by the Fathers of the Oratory and at the University of Paris.

The overall structure and general organisation of the University of Paris at this time is reasonably well known. The exact technical detail of administration as between faculties, nations and tribes, and colleges is not always easy to follow. The precise role of professor, master of students, junior master and senior master, procurator of a nation, rector of a college and rector of the University is not always clear to us now. Michael Moore was involved at all levels of learning, teaching and administration in the second half of the seventeenth century and the early years of the eighteenth and he was highly respected. The University consisted of four great faculties, Theology, Law, Medicine and Arts. The Arts faculty was the most famous faculty and Paris, founded in 1200, was the mother of universities. There were so many Irish masters and professors in this faculty about 1650 that they had formed their own articles of agreement. The faculty of Theology had two great schools, the college of the Sorbonne and that of Navarre. Similarly, the faculty of Arts had a number of colleges. The faculty of Arts was divided into four nations, France, Picardy, Normandy and Germany. That of Germany was divided into the tribe of the continentals and the tribe of the islanders. The Irish masters belonged to the tribe of the islanders. The register of the German nation from 1613 to 1730 still survives in Paris.[1] This is the main source for our knowledge of Michael Moore, admitted as a member of the German nation on 11 November 1662 with his degree of Master of Arts. Details of his degree of Doctor of Divinity are not available but very early in his life he was reputed for his knowledge of languages, philosophy, theology and medicine. He became professor of philosophy and eloquence at the college of Grasssins and at the college of Navarre and continued in that work for ten years.

1 Patrick Boyle CM, 'Irishmen in the University of Paris in the 17th and 18th Centuries', *Irish Ecclesiastical Record* 14 (1903), 24–45.

Paris in these years was at the centre of a major development of philosophy. Descartes had died young in 1650 and his work was quite incomplete; his teaching was condemned by the Church in 1663. Malebranche, however, much impressed by Descartes' teaching, began his serious work in philosophy in Paris in 1664.[2] Leibniz was working in Paris from 1672 to 1676 and Locke was in France from 1675 to 1680 where he was already working on his *Essay Concerning Human Understanding*. In 1672, Moore was relieved of his philosophy teaching and became professor of Latin and Greek and master of students at Navarre. In the years 1671, 1673 and 1675, he was elected procurator of the German nation.

The first documentary evidence of Michael Moore's interest in Irish affairs dates from November 1673.[3] The occasion was the introduction of the Archbishop of Dublin, Peter Talbot, to Louis XIV at the court of Versailles. Dr. Talbot brought with him 'one Mr. Moore, a priest and philosophy-professor at Paris'. This description indicates clearly that Moore was a priest in 1673—there is a suggestion that he was not ordained until 1684. Dr. Moore was present in order that he might clearly present to the King the extremity and severity of the persecution of the Irish and to ask the King to undertake their protection. The eulogy of Moore at the time of his death stated the two great loves of his life, a love of his own country and a love of the university of Paris.[4]

The story of his care of the education of the three Fleming children in Paris gives some valuable and precise dates and may indicate a link with the Moore family of Drogheda. Randall Fleming, 16th Baron of Slane, whose first wife died married Penelope Moore, daughter of Henry Moore, first earl of Drogheda, by whom he had three children, Christopher, Henry and Alice. Christopher, who would become the 17th Baron of Slane, was only seven years old when both parents died in the same year 1676. On 31 August 1677 these children were in the custody of 'Michael Moore, Gentleman, and some Popish priests' in Paris. On the 12 April 1683, they are still in the 'hands of one, Morus, an Irishman in the college of Grassins in Paris'. In June 1683, a letter from Charles II to his envoy in Paris asks him 'to restrain the said Michael Moore from arranging a marriage for the young Baron . . . and to deliver the said children to the care of their grandmother in Ireland'. There is also documentary evidence that Michael Moore had been left £1,000 for the education of the Flemings in a will dated 24 April 1683.[5]

In 1677, Moore was elected to the office of rector of the University, an honour which, at this time, he declined. One wonders whether he had some

2   Desmond Connell, *The Vision in God. Malebranche's Scholastic Sources* (Louvain, 1967), p. 7.
3   John Brady, *Reportorium Novum* (Dublin, 1955–60), Vol. II, no. 1, p. 207 (*RN*).
4   Patrick Boyle CM, 'Dr Michael Moore', *Archivium Hibernicum* Vol. V (1916), 7–16 (*AH*).
5   John Brady, *RN*, II, 2 (1959/60), pp. 377–8.

indication that he might not be continuing his work in Paris. In 1678, the Archbishop of Dublin was already in prison.[6] In 1684, Moore was recalled to Dublin by the new Archbishop, Patrick Russell and was appointed parish priest of St Catherine's and vicar general of the diocese. There is documentary evidence that he was still in Paris in March, April and July of 1685.[7] In the meantime, important political changes had begun in England and Ireland. On 6 February 1685, James II became King; on 5 June 1686, James appointed Tyrconnell (Richard Talbot) commander-in-chief of the army in Ireland; on 12 February 1687, Tyrconnell was appointed Lord Deputy. On 23 January 1688, Moore was certainly in Dublin where he attended the Dublin synod of that date as parish priest of St Catherine's and vicar general of the diocese. He was present against a the synod of 23 July 1689 as canon of Dublin diocese.[8] James had arrived in Dublin on 24 March 1689 and Michael Moore was appointed court chaplain on that day.

Richard Talbot, normally called earl or duke of Tyrconnell, was the person at the centre of everything that happened to Michael Moore between 1688 and 1690. The Talbot family had vast estates in England and Ireland— the best known estates in Ireland were Carton, Belgard and Malahide. Richard was born at Belgard and his brother Peter was born at Carton. They were Old English, they were clearly royalist and they professed their Catholicity openly. Peter was educated in Portugal and became a Jesuit. For a time, he was a professor of theology but the came to be engaged in many diplomatic missions on behalf of the rights of Catholics in England, Holland, Germany, France and Spain. He was reputed to have received Charles II into the church in 1656. He was asked to leave the Jesuits in 1659 because of his involvement in politics. There were certain reservations about his appointment as Archbishop of Dublin in 1669 though he was personally most exemplary. Peter Talbot died in 1680 after two years in prison in Dublin Castle when he lost the support of the politicians who surrounded the king. Another member of the family was Thomas Talbot, a friar, who was not so exemplary.

Richard Talbot was an outstanding royalist military man and a politician. He wanted to build up an Irish army substantially Catholic and faithful to King James, he wanted Catholics in civil administration and municipal corporations and, probably most of all, he wanted to have the Old English Catholic families restored to their lands in Ireland. He certainly succeeded in the admission of Catholics to military and civilian offices. Placing an outstanding Catholic scholar and administrator, namely Michael Moore, in charge of Trinity College was part of that general plan.[9]

6 Peter Talbot was Archbishop from 1669 to 1680; Patrick Russell from 1683 to 1693.
7 W. M. O'Riordan, *RN*, I, 2 (1956), p. 371; Patrick Boyle CM, ibid. p. 8.
8 W. M. O'Riordan, *RN*, I, 2, p. 376.
9 John Kingston, 'Catholic Families of the Pale', *RN*, I, 1 (1955) p. 80, and II, 1 (1957/8), pp. 96–103. See P. W. Sergeant, *Little Jennings and Fighting Dick Talbot*, 2 Vols. (London, 1913).

Events in Trinity College in these years are reasonably well documented in the Register of the college and in a number of histories compiled in later years. Still, the precise role of Michael Moore needs clarification. Two key dates, that of his appointment and that of his departure are not actually given in the register. The following dates and happenings, taken from the Register, are relevant to the story of Michael Moore.

19 February 1689   . . . two hundred pounds of the College money should be sent into England for the support of those Fellows that should be forc't to fly thither.

25 February 1689   Two Companies of Foot, commanded by Talbot . . . took away those few fusils, swords and pistols that they found . . . Dragoons broke open the College stables and took away all the horses . . .

1 March 1689   Most of the Fellows embark't for England. This left a Vice-Provost and four others, three of whom died within 15 months.

24 March 1689   Speech of welcome received kindly by King James.

17 June 1689   Vice-Provost and Fellows meet the King.

24 July 1689   Vice-Provost and Fellows sold a peece of plate . . .

16 Sept 1689   The College was seized on for a Garrison by the King's order . . . the Scholars were all turned out by souldiers . . .

21 October 1689   Several persons by order of the Government, seized upon the Chapel and broke open the Library. The Chapel was sprinkled and new consecrated and Mass was said in it; but afterwards being turned into a storehouse for powder, it escaped all further damage. The Library and Gardens and the Provost's lodgings were committed to the care of one Macarty, a priest and Chaplain to ye King, who preserved 'em from the violence of the Souldiers . . .

This last may be the date on which Michael Moore took over the duties of Provost. That his name should not be given in the Register at this point is surprising, when the name of his assistant, Teigue Macarty, his librarian is mentioned.[10] Though the histories of Trinity mention Moore and speak of him in a complimentary manner they do not normally refer to him as Provost. ('In France his considerable learning was better appreciated, and he ended his life as rector of the University of Paris.')[11] Moore's nomination to the duties of Provost was not by way of election, the normal procedure, but by

10 Register of Trinity College Dublin, as quoted in J. W. Stubbs, *The History of the University of Dublin* (London, 1889), pp. 130–40.

11 R. B. McDowell and D. A. Webb, *Trinity College, Dublin 1592–1952,* (Cambridge, 1982), p. 29.

appointment. There are precedents for this kind of appointment in Oxford and in Trinity about this time. It was not very acceptable to academic staff and was often referred to as a *mandamus*—a royal order. The authorities involved in the appointment of Moore appear now to us to have been James II, his Lord Deputy Tyrconnell, the Archbishop of Dublin, Patrick Russell, and the Bishops of Meath, Clogher and others. Tyrconnell is regarded as the most important person in deciding this matter. There are several clear references to Moore and Macarty being responsible for stopping the Jacobite soldiers from setting fire to the Library of Trinity. It appears from the Register that the Vice-Provost and Fellows continued to act as if they are still in charge of the College and that they did not take any notice of the caretakers Moore and Macarty. They actually kept the keys and handed them over only at a much later stage and as a result of a court order. Elections for Provost were held each November as if things were normal. The following dates from the Register are of interest at this stage of the story of Michael Moore.

20 November 1689	The Vice-Provost and Fellows met together and elected the same officers that were chosen the year before.
11 April 1690	Court at Dublin Castle . . . Mr. George Thewles and Mr. John Hall have several keys belonging to ye said College in their custody . . . forthwith to deliver the said keys to the Ltd High Chancellor, as they shall answer the same at their peril.
15 April 1690	. . . ten keys received by Fytton C (Lord Chancellor).
14 June 1690	William in Ireland
1 July 1690	Battle of the Boyne
4 July 1690	James to Paris.
15 July 1690	Fellows and Scholars return from England.
20 November 1690	The elections for the year ensuing were made as follows, Dr. Browne, Vice-Provost and Bursar . . . [12]

The story of Michael Moore's departure from Trinity is told by a number of people but it is not easy to put a precise date on it. Spring 1690 has been suggested while some prefer to say it coincided with the collapse of James II. Michael Moore, in his capacity as court chaplain, was the preacher at a Mass in Christ Church, which was used temporarily as a Chapel Royal for the King. James took offence at something which was said in the sermon. The story is simply told by Donnelly.[13] There was a report that James really wanted to have the Jesuits in charge of Trinity. Moore used the text 'If the blind lead the blind, they both fall into the pit.' The King supposed that the text referred to himself and to his friend, a Fr. Petre, who suffered from

---

12   Register of Trinity College, quoted by Stubbs, ibid.
13   N. Donnelly, *Short History of Dublin Parishes* (Dublin, 1911), Vol. 9, pp. 212–14; P. Boyle, *AH*, ibid., p. 8.

defective vision. The king gave positive orders that Moore should quit the kingdom. Moore instantly complied with the King's orders but his reply is famous 'Go, I will, without doubt, but remember, the King himself will soon be after me.' The two stories are linked—James taking offence and the possibility of the Jesuits having care and charge of Trinity College—the facts behind the stories are not entirely clear.

James was certainly under the influence of the Jesuit, Fr. Petre. In 1687, James had given a royal order to a Jesuit, Fr. Hughes, granting to the Fathers of the Society all the schools founded throughout Ireland. Still, James obviously went back on this general principle in February 1689 when he granted a charter to Donat O'Lery, priest of the diocese of Ossory, to set up a Royal College of St Canice in Kilkenny.[14] Tyrconnell's situation on this matter is not easy to discover. His brother Peter Talbot, originally a Jesuit, was asked to leave the society and later became Archbishop of Dublin. He and Michael Moore were together at Versailles, appealing to Louis XIV in 1673. However, in Tyrconnell's letter to the Queen on 2 April 1690, we find the following statement on the matter:

> As to the affairs of the King's putting the Jesuits into the Colledge here, I do not believe he ever had any such thoughts, for that would not only give great offence to all the world, I mean to England and Scotland, but very much discompose the whole clergy of this Kingdome, and, madam. you know this age will not bear being too fond of Jesuits.[15]

The account of the matter which is most frequently quoted is from the *Narrative* written by Thomas Sheridan in 1702. He had been secretary to Tyrconnell but he had serious disagreement with him—it was said that Tyrconnell once kicked him!—and he had also lost favour with James and had difficulties with two Jesuits, Petre and Johnson. The first problem for us about the *Narrative* is that it was written 12 years after the events, when James and Tyrconnell were both dead, and the work is intended as a defence of Sheridan himself. The relevant passage is as follows:

> Tyrconnell was crossed in his design of making Dublin College presently popish in order to which, as soon as he was sure of the Government . . . he sent for Mr. Moor from Paris to be Provost, a person suspected for Jansenism, and twice forced to abjure that heresy . . . Soon after he got the Catholic Bishops of Dublin, Meath, Clogher and others to recommend Mr. Moor to the King and pray that the management and conduct of that house might be put into the hands of seculars; which the King refused, either as unreasonable or else persuaded the Jesuits were fitter for that function.[16]

14 P. Boyle, *Irish Ecclesiastical Record* 14 (1903), 32.
15 John Brady, *RN*, II, 2, p. 378.
16 H. M. C. Stuart MSS vi, 1–75; See John Brady, ibid.

Caution is needed in approaching what Sheridan said.[17] Tyrconnell had not to send to Paris for Moore—he had been parish priest of St Catherine's and vicar general of Dublin since 1684 and had been certainly in Dublin since 1685. Further in the very year that this was written by Sheridan, there is documentary evidence in Paris that Michael Moore was called on to replace a philosophy professor who was teaching Jansenism. The other suggestion of this reference to Moore needs also to be critically examined. Did James refuse to sanction Moore's appointment to Trinity because the Jesuits would be more suitable? Tyrconnell's own statement is probably more accurate.

There is little information on the whereabouts of Michael Moore from the spring of 1690 until June 1691. It is a reasonable presumption that he was living quietly in Paris preparing work for publication. The pages of the register of the German nation are blank from 17 July 1685 to 12 June 1691. Michael Moore is mentioned as being present on 12 June and 23 June 1691.[18] In the Dublin diocesan lists of this period, he is still mentioned as a canon of the diocese but not as vicar general.[19] He moved from Paris to Rome and there is a suggestion that the resentment of James II had followed him to Paris. In Rome, Innocent XII valued his prudence and learning so much that he made him censor of books. He was also highly respected by Clement XI. He was appointed rector of a new seminary at Montefiascone, probably in 1691. He was also professor of philosophy and Greek, and published his *Hortatio ad Studium Graecae et Hebraicae*, in 1691.[20]

On 11 October 1692, while he was still at Montefiascone, his major work was published in Paris, *De Existentia Dei et humanae mentis immortalitate secundum Cartesii et Aristotelis doctrinam disputatio*.[21] The name of the author does not appear, probably because of the Elizabethan ban (1559) on the printing of books containing Catholic teaching. We have the precise date of the completion of the printing. the exact name and address of the printer and permission from the King to print but only six dots for the name of the author. The book contains about four hundred pages on the philosophical difficulties of the teaching of Descartes on the existence of God and on the immortality of the human mind. When Descartes first published his *Meditations* on 24 August 1641, he dedicated the work to the 'very wise and illustrious dean and doctors of the sacred faculty of Theology of Paris. . . . It was impossible to find elsewhere greater perspicacity and solidity or greater wisdom and integrity in giving judgment.'[22] Descartes thought that he was

17 J. G. Simms, *Jacobite Ireland, 1685–91* (London, 1969). John Miller, 'Thomas Sheridan and his Narrative', *Irish Historical Studies* XX, no. 78 (1976), pp. 105–28. 'The Earl of Tyrconnel and James II's Irish Policy', *Historical Journal* XX, no. 4 (1977), 803–23.

18 P. Boyle, *AH*, ibid.

19 W. M. O'Riordan, *RN*, I, 2, p. 373.

20 James Ware, *The Writers of Ireland*, ed. Harris (Dublin, 1764), Bk I, p. 290.

21 Harris' Ware mentions that this book was translated into English by a Mr Blackmore; I have been unable to find any other reference to this translation.

22 Adam-Tannery V, p. 119.

providing the best possible philosophical foundation for Catholic theological teaching, though as noted above his work was condemned by the Church in 1663. When Michael Moore published his *De Existentia Dei*, he also dedicated his work to the 'very wise and illustrious dean and doctors of the sacred faculty of Theology of Paris', appealing to their 'learning, wisdom, reliability, balance and integrity' in judging his rejection of the teaching of Descartes about God and the human mind. The teaching of Descartes was rejected by Michael Moore on purely philosophical grounds, based on the teaching of Aristotle. Moore never quotes the condemnation of the Church but mentions with surprise the popularity of Descartes' teaching.

This major work of Michael Moore deserves to be edited and studied in detail. His rejection of Descartes is still valid philosophically and it is fascinating, three hundred years later, to see what this Irish scholar said as he lived and worked at the very heart of the philosophical development of the time. The work illustrates how the writings of Aristotle were studied and used. It shows the manner in which philosophy was taught to a great many Irish students. The eloquence and style of presentation in Latin is quite remarkable. The work reveals an extensive knowledge of Renaissance philosophy, especially the work of Pomponazzi and contains a rejection of the purely mechanistic interpretation of the human body expounded by the latter.

In January 1696, Michael Moore left Italy and returned to Paris. From the eulogy delivered to the Faculty of Arts on his death thirty years later, one gets the impression that he had returned in order to live a more leisurely life, having become 'weary of the sea and the roads' after a life already full of honours and distinctions.[23] This was not to be. On 10 October 1701 he was elected rector of the University of Paris for the second time. Again, he wished to decline the honour. Patrick Boyle has a striking account of the happiness his acceptance brought to the whole university.[24] On 16 May 1702, he delivered the annual panegyric on Louis XIV. Patrick Boyle has the detail from the *Gazette de France* and from the register of the German nation on the excellence of this speech. The audience included a large attendance from all the faculties, the most distinguished of the nobility of Paris and 'there were present also the ministers and officers of the most August King of Great Britain', James III—the Pretender.[25] All the Paris sources indicate that Michael Moore was an ardent opponent of Jansenism and that he was an expert on university administration problems. From 1702 to 1726, he was principal of the college of Navarre. Between the years 1703 and 1717, he was elected on a number of occasions as procurator of the German nation. In 1712, he published a work on Logic, *Vera Sciendi Methodus*, which had a second edition in 1716, both published in Paris. Harris' Ware says it is 'written in dialogue against the Cartesian philosophy,

23 John Brady, *RN*, II, 1, p. 208.
24 *AH*, V, p. 9.
25 *AH*, V, p. 11.

DE
EXISTENTIA DEI
ET
HUMANÆ MENTIS
IMMORTALITATE
secundùm
CARTESII ET ARISTOTELIS
DOCTRINAM
DISPUTATIO
IN DUOS LIBROS DIVISA

PARISIIS,
Apud Carolum Robustel, viâ
Jacobæâ, sub Palma.

M. DC. XCII.
CUM PRIVILEGIO REGIS.

which he much depreciates.'[26] The usual reference to this work is to say that it defends Aristotle's way of knowing things as against the new method proposed by Descartes. In January 1715, he approved Cornelius Nary's Catechism for Ireland. On 29 March 1721, there is a presentation of money by Michael Moore, principal of the college of Navarre and former rector of the university, to the college of the Lombards.[27] During his time of semi-retirement, he set up a room in his own house where people could come to meet him. In spite of his great age and his broken health, he was ready each morning at dawn to help with counsel and finance the poorer deserving students of his own fatherland and to consider diligently the regulations of the university and the chronicles of his predecessors. Later on, he was practically blind and a person was employed to read for him—this person stole many of his books. He died on 16 August 1726, and was buried in the vault under the chapel of the Irish College in Paris. The eulogy, delivered in Latin, is a moving tribute to the life and work of this remarkable scholar, priest and philosopher.[28] His epitaph, written by his countryman, Mr St John, Canon of the Cathedral of Notre Dame in Paris is as follows:

Sideribus genuit faustis Hibernia *Morum*
Et *Morum* geniut Terra Britanna suum.
Quis fuit e Geminis major, si forte requiris;
Palma nimis dubia est; magnus uterque fuit.[29]

With lucky star did Ireland Moore beget,
Yet Britain too her own did once create.
Which of the twain was greater if you quest
The prize is much in doubt; for both were great.[30]

26 Ibid. This source also mentions a fourth work: 'He translated into Latin *L'Morale de Grenoble*, entitled, A Pastoral Letter. Written in French by the Lord Cardinal le Camus, Bishop and Prince of Grenoble, to the curates of his diocese. London. 1687.' At this time Moore was in Dublin.
27 *AH*, XXXV (1980), p. 52.
28 *AH*, V, p. 13.
29 James Ware, ibid., p. 289.
30 This translation of the epitaph is by Gerard Deighan, MA. I also wish to thank Dr Alan Harrison for his interest and encouragement in my research into Michael Moore.

Between Kant and Heidegger

The Modern Question of Being

RICHARD KEARNEY

Kant's Copernican Revolution transformed our view of being. It declared that being does not determine consciousness but is determined by it. Or to put it in the more technical terms of modern epistemology: the subjectivity of the subject becomes the condition for the objectivity of the object. In advocating such a radical 'critical' position, Kant brought the Cartesian primacy of the *cogito* to its logical conclusion. The ontological implications of this position were most concisely stated in Kant's celebrated—and thought-provoking—maxim that 'being is not a real predicate.' In what follows, I propose an exegetical reading of this Kantian thesis on being in the light of subsequent phenomenological interpretations by Brentano, Husserl and Heidegger.

Kant's thesis is most cogently developed in a section of *The Critique of Pure Reason* (*CPR*) entitled 'Transcendental Logic'. It arises in the context of a discussion of the ontological proof for the existence of God. For Kant—and for most post-Kantian philosophy, including Hegel—the problem of being in general is intimately bound to the problem of defining God's essence and existence. One might even argue that this legacy extends to Sartre's 'atheistic' consideration of the matter in the concluding chapter of *Being and Nothingness*. But where does the legacy begin? The discussion of the ontological proof dates back to Anselm in the eleventh century, gaining common currency in the scholastic debates of the middle ages. The proof is characterized by the attempt to infer God's existence from the *concept* of his existence. Though it underwent several significant formulations from Anselm's original presentation in *Proslogium seu Alloquium de Dei Existentia* through Bonaventure and Aquinas (who rejected it) to Duns Scotus and eventually Descartes, the proof can be broadly stated as follows: 1) major premiss—God, by his concept, is the most perfect being; 2) minor premiss—existence belongs to the concept of the most perfect being; 3) conclusion—therefore God exists.

What does this mean exactly? First, it means that the determination of God as the most perfect of all beings derives from the *idea* of his existence. As *ens perfectissimum*, God possesses every positive attribute in a perfect manner. It is inconceivable, therefore, in so far as we conceive God as perfect, that he should lack the attribute of existence. What is more, God's essence (*what* he is) can have no meaning whatsoever unless he *is*, i.e. exists in the first place. God's existence follows necessarily from our concept of his essence. We cannot think of God according to his essence, without thinking of him as existing.

Kant does not dispute the primary claim that God is the most perfect being; nor, indeed, the subsequent claim that God exists. What he does contest is the connection between the two claims—the argument that existence *belongs* to the concept of the most perfect being. Here we encounter Kant's central thesis that 'being is not a real predicate.' Being is understood by Kant to mean existence. And what he states is not simply that existence does not belong to the *concept* of the most perfect being (as Aquinas maintained in his famous objection); but that existence does not belong, in any sense, to a conceptual determination.

In a difficult and dense passage, *CPR* B 626f., Kant offers a detailed exposition of this thesis. Being, he asserts, is not a predicate of anything. It is rather 'the position of a thing or of certain determinations in themselves'. Being is not a predicate but position. By predicate Kant means something that is asserted in a judgment. Assertion is the relating of something to something and/or the combining of the two. Existence (or being) is added to the concept rather than precontained within it. Existence supervenes upon our concept; it is not a predicate extrapolated from our concept. So when Kant says that being is not a real predicate he means that it is not already part and parcel of the real content of a thing. Being comes to things from without. It is a radical exteriority. *Where* exactly it comes from is a question to which we will return below.

But first we must ascertain, or clarify, what precisely Kant means by the term 'reality'. What he does *not* mean is the external world, as in epistemological realism. Nor does reality mean actuality (being or existence). Reality, for Kant, means quite literally *thingness (Sachheit)*. Reality is the determination of a thing—what Heidegger will call the thingness of the thing. It is what belongs to the *res*. When Kant speaks accordingly about the *omnitudo realitatis*, he is referring not to the totality of things as they actually are but to the totality of all possible things. He is thinking of the whole of all real-thing-contents as possibilities—or what the scholastics called essences. *Realitas* is for Kant what *possibilitas* is for Leibniz. Or more simply put, realities are the what-contents of possible entities regardless of whether they actually exist or not. The reality of something is quite distinct from its being or existence. To summarize the comparative history of this idea, one could say that the Kantian concept of reality finds equivalents not only in the medieval concept of the *res* or the Leibnizian concept of *possibilitas*, but in the Platonic concept of εἶδος.

We here find ourselves before a fundamental Kantian distinction between *reality* and *actuality*. If reality refers to the what-content (*res*) of something, actuality refers to its existence—*that* the something exists. This distinction is reflected in Kant's claim that the two terms belong to quite different categories of understanding. Reality refers to *quality*; actuality (or existence) to *modality*. By quality Kant designates whether a predicate is ascribed to a subject or not—whether a predicate is affirmed or denied of a subject. Reality is the property of affirmative judgment. And one can say, accordingly, that every predicate is a real predicate to the degree that reality is the affirmative predicate possessing real thing-content. Hence the logic of Kant's statement that being is not a real predicate is that being is not a predicate of anything whatsoever. *That* something exists (its being-actuality-existence) is not part of *what* that something is (its reality-essence-content). Only God, in Aquinas' terms, is an entity whose existence is at one with his essence, whose reality and actuality are identical. But for a modern philosopher of finite beings such ontological correspondences seem unavailable.

So much for reality as a category of quality. What of actuality as a category of modality? For Kant, modality refers to an attitude of the knowing subject toward what is being judged. The complementary of actuality is not negation (which is the complementary of affirmation in the category of quality), but the alternative modalities of 'possibility' or 'necessity'. Actuality does not refer to the real content of something; it defines a certain modality in contrast to others (possibility or necessity). That is why to speak of imaginary entities as 'possible' is in no way to deny their reality—that is, their real contents as *Sachheit*, whatness, *quidditas*. It is simply to deny their 'actuality'. It is a way of saying, to take Husserl's famous example in *Ideas*, that even if a centaur does not actually exist, its possible existence as a fictional entity has as much 'real content' as an actually existing entity.[1] Reality is concerned with the thing's essence (the what) rather than with the thing's existence (that it exists). This is why existence is *not* a real predicate.

Kant grants, accordingly, that philosophers may legitimately refer to God as *ens realissimum*—or as Kant puts it *allerrealstes Wesen*—because he is considered the being with the greatest possible real contents. God is the being who lacks no real determination. But this judgment about God's qualitative determination makes no assertion, in Kant's view, about his actual, possible or necessary modality. The quality of being, of God as of every being, is a different matter from the modality of being.

Is this not a key point of modern philosophy? Does Kant's quality/modality distinction not anticipate, and in some respects vindicate, Husserl's claim that he phenomenologically 'reduced' world—resulting from the bracketing of existential judgment concerning the actuality of things and the resultant free variation in imagination of its essential structures—yields intuitive access to the real truth of things? The phenomenological attitude, as outlined by Husserl, could thus be said to deal with the quality of things rather than with their modality; it suspends the existential question regarding the actual being of things in order to describe their essential (real) contents.

---

1   Edmund Husserl, *Ideas*, trans. W. R. Gibson (London, 1931), § 23.

Kant's own most explicit formulation of this distinction is to be found in his famous maxim 'a hundred actual thalers contain not the least bit more than a hundred possible thalers' (*CPR*, B 627). This ostensibly untenable assertion is simply another manner of illustrating Kant's basic argument that existence is not the same thing as reality; that being is not a real predicate in the sense that it is not a determination of the concept of a thing relating to its real content. In other words, while a hundred possible and a hundred actual thalers are radically distinct in virtue of their existence, they are completely the same in virtue of their reality. They share the same what-content. The thalers in my dream have exactly the same reality as the thalers in my hand. As Kant explains: 'When therefore I think of a thing, by whatever and by however many predicates I please (even in an exhaustive determination of it), nevertheless my proceeding further to think that this thing *is* (exists) makes not the least addition to the thing (to its whatness as *res*). For otherwise, what would exist would be not exactly the same but more than I had thought in the concept, and I could not say that the exact object of my concept exists' (*CPR*, B 628). What applies here to thalers, applies equally to God. In neither case is existence to be considered as a real predicate. Or to put it in another way, the real content of the thaler or of God remains the same, regardless of whether it actually exists or not. Being is always *more* than reality. Existence is always *other* than essence. The *that* is irreducible to the *what*. Kant's thesis that being is not a real predicate thus prefigures Heidegger's notion of the 'ontological difference'.

Kant's claim that *being is not a real predicate* leads on to a second, and related, claim that *being is position*. 'The concept of position', says Kant, 'is one and the same as that of being in general.'[2] But there are problems here. If being is not a real predicate then how can it be *positively* determined? And yet to say of something that it exists, is, or has being, amounts to *positing* that thing. Thus we find the logic of Kant's thinking issuing in the following equation: *Being = existence = actuality = position*.

But what kind of position or positing is Kant talking about here? It seems that he is referring to an *existential synthesis* (A is A) rather than a *predicative synthesis* (A is B). In other words, existential positing is not the same as predication; it is not concerned with the real characteristics of something. To posit the existence of something one is obliged to go *outside* of the conceptual representation of the real-contents of that thing. Whereas predicative synthesis is preoccupied with these real-contents, it is only the existential synthesis which relates this whatness to an actual object. In other words, existential synthesis adds the actual being of the object to the real-contents of the concept. And this is why existence is 'absolute position' for Kant. It adds

2 'Der einzig mögliche Beweisgrund zu einer Demonstration des Daseins Gottes', *Kants gesammelte Schriften* II, Berlin, 1969, p. 77.

something new to the predicative content of a thing. And what is this something new? Nothing other than the actuality of being. Kant explains it thus: 'Nothing more is posited in an existent than in something merely possible (for in this case we are speaking of its predicates); but more is posited by an existent than by something merely possible, for this (existent) also goes to the absolute position of the thing itself' (*Beweisgrund*, p. 80).

To return to Kant's distinction between quality and modality, we could say that the difference between the reality and the existence of something is that between *what* is posited and *how* it is posited. The 'what' question yields the answer that actual and possible things (e.g. thalers) possess exactly the same what-content. The 'how' question, however, demonstrates that to say that something is posited as actual is to say that something *more* is posited than if it were posited as only possible. But once again we must ask what this 'more' means. Kant's arguments seem to indicate that it is the *relation* of the existent object to its concept, the rapport between the how and the what of something.

The relevance of all this to the question of the ontological argument is clear. Since existence in general is not a real predicate it does not belong to the concept of that thing. So that if I think the concept I cannot thereby attribute existence to what is thought in the concept. Unless that is, I presuppose the actuality of the thing as part of the concept. But then we are talking not of a proof, but of a tautology.

By thus exposing the weakness of the minor premiss in the ontological argument—that existence belongs to the concept of God—Kant believes he has exposed the ontological argument *per se*. While Aquinas also contested the ontological argument that God's actual existence could be derived from our concept of His existence, he did so not because he doubted that God's existence was a real predicate of his essence, but because he doubted the capacity of the finite human mind to know or understand this.[3] Kant's refutation is far more radical and raises fundamental questions about the entire modern understanding of the terms reality and existence. The single most dramatic consequence of the Kantian thesis was undoubtedly that being was now seen as position, that is, as an attitude of the human subject toward the mode of being of the object. Being is reduced to the meaning of being; and the meaning of being is equated with our understanding of being. Brentano and Husserl would call this *intentionality*; Heidegger would call it *Dasein*. In the concluding part of this essay, I will take a brief look at some of the implications of the Kantian thesis for modern developments in phenomenology and hermeneutics.

Kant's thesis that being is position was followed by two distinct interpretations. On the other hand, we find the empiricist version of position as sensible apprehension. On the other, we encounter the idealist and phenomeno-

3 Aquinas, *Summa Theologiae*, I, 2, 1 ad 2.

logical versions of being as meaningful appearance to consciousness. What both these versions share is the modern notion of *being as perception* (in the broadest sense). What separates them, however, is their radically different understanding of what is meant by perception.

Empricists understood perception as a psychological rapport between representation and sensation. And they found some support for this view in Kant's claim in the first part of the *Critique of Pure Reason*, entitled 'Transcendental Aesthetic', that sensible intuition through space and time is a precondition of objective knowledge. They thus interpreted Kant's statement that 'perception is the sole characteristic of actuality' (*CPR*, B 273) to mean that to be is to be perceived. The Kantian equation of being with absolute position was taken as stating that what exists as actual is what is perceivable by our senses. According to this view, the 'being' that is added to our knowledge of the real predicates of an object (e.g. to its colour, size, shape and other what-contents) is not some transcendent ontological substance but a psychological attitude of perception.

The phenomenological reading of Kant's equation of being and position extended the understanding of perception beyond the empirical. Like empiricism, phenomenology holds that the being of something is inseparable from our *attitude* to the relation between that thing's representational content and the object referred to by this representation. Unlike empiricism, however, phenomenology sees this relation as one of intentionality rather than of empirical correspondence between particulars.

Brentano represents a significant transition between empiricism and phenomenology. In the opening sentences of *Psychologie vom empirischen Standpunkt* (1874), he writes: 'My standpoint in psychology is empirical: experience alone is my teacher. But I share with others the conviction that a certain ideal intuition (*ideale Anschauung*) can be combined with such a standpoint.' Moreover, this ideal intuition meant, for Brentano, that certain fundamental insights into the being of things could be achieved at one stroke and without any induction (*Vom Ursprung sittlicher Erkenntnis*, 1889). Brentano's explicit departure from Mill's rejection of *a priori* knowledge clearly indicates his redefinition of our perception of being to include dimensions of experience ruled out by traditional empiricism. This was to prove the launching pad for Husserl's reformulation of perception in *Logical Investigations* (1900-1) in terms of a 'categorial intuition' of a thing's being, a perception surpassing the empirical limits of sensible intuition.[4]

Brentano's role should not be underestimated. In his Vienna lectures and later writings, Brentano replaced the term 'empirical psychology' with that of 'descriptive psychology'. He even coined the resonant term *'Psychognosie'* to convey his conviction that the human perception of being—which it is the aim of philosophy to explain—cannot be based on the methods of the

---

4 Edmund Husserl, *Logical Investigations*, Vol. 2, tr. J. N. Findlay (London, 1970), Investigation 6, Chap. 6, pp. 773-9.

natural sciences but requires a new descriptive/intuitive/phenomenological science. Brentano thus remains faithful to Kant's definition of being as position or perception; but he reformulates this to entail a dynamic relation between the perceiving subject and the object perceived. In *Psychology from an Empirical Standpoint* he refers to this relation as intentionality—no hearing without something heard, no believing without something believed, no hoping without something hoped, no striving without something striven for, no joy without something we feel joyous about etc. In other words, the *what* of something (what Kant called 'reality') is now considered ontologically inseparable from the *how* of its perception (what Kant called 'position')—perception now being understood as the intentional relation between perceiving consciousness and the thing perceived.

In this manner, the phenomenon of perception is defined as an intentional act of consciousness. The real and actual, separated by Kant under the distinct notions of quality and modality, are conjoined by Brentano under the category of intentionality. The aim of Brentano's new psychology—which set the agenda for Husserl's phenomenology—was to provide a rigorous scientific understanding of truth as self-evident. Such a category of evidence would, he hoped, counteract the relativism of his age as advanced by utilitarianism, historicism and positivism. While granting the empiricist rejection of innate ideas, Brentano clung to the notion of an 'ideal intuition' which would amplify the model of perception beyond the sensible apprehension of particulars to the intentional intuition of being. For Brentano, being is reality as intentionally perceived by a real consciousness. And, as such, it provides a solid basis for scientific truth.

Husserl shared Brentano's conviction that the categories of intentionality and ideal intuition furnish criteria for scientific rigour. He goes further than Brentano however in admitting fictional entities into the arsenal of ideal intuition. Indeed, Husserl breaks more radically with empiricism than his mentor in declaring fiction to be 'the life of phenomenology as of all eidetical science . . . the source whence the knowledge of "eternal truths" draws its sustenance' (*Ideas* § 70, p. 201). He is referring here, of course, to the practice of 'imaginative variation' whereby consciousness prescinds from the particular *fact* of something to its universal *essence*—the latter being defined as the invariant structure which is disclosed through the free variation of all its possible modes of being (i.e. as projected by fantasy or fiction).

Husserl agrees with the Kantian thesis that 'being is not a real predicate' to the extent that the categorial intuition—outlined in Investigation VI of *Logical Investigations*—is described as an intentional positing of being, irrespective of whether its properties exist actually or possibly. The being of the thing is not reducible to the nature or sum of its predicates. Its existence is irreducible to its reality. Or to put it in another way, being is the act of positing a thing's essence (its reality as *quality*) in whatever *modality* it determines (actual or possible). From the point of view of categorial intuition, the empirical status of an object is irrelevant. Fiction is as important, if not more important than fact when it comes to something's intentional being qua *phenomenon*.

In his discussion of categorial intuition in the Sixth Investigation cited above, Husserl alludes to Kant's maxim that *being is not a real predicate* (§ 43). He points out that Kant was actually equating being with existence (or position). But Husserl remarks that Kant's thesis can only be applied to the copula (this *is* white) in so far as it designates the 'belonging' of some essential property—real or imaginary—to an object. In its existential or predicative senses, the 'is' grasped by the categorial intuition is not itself part of *what* the object actually is. It is not like the colour white or any other empirically observable property of volume or texture. The 'is' is not tangible in such a basic manner. And yet it makes no sense without the support of the senses. We should think of 'sense' here in the original connotation of *aisthesis*—a phenomenological experience of meaning that precedes the dualistic opposition between sensation and understanding. The aesthetic appreciation of painting or poetry provides a useful analogy. But being, unlike aesthetic beauty, is not bound to the *whatness* of the object. Or to be more exact, the 'is' itself tells us not *what* a thing is but *that* it is—and *that* such and such properties belong to it. The categorial intuition can operate accordingly in the absence or presence of the object in so far as it designates the *belonging* of something (the colour white) to something (the chalk). What we intuit categorially is not the whiteness but the belonging, not the colour white—as in sensuous intuition—but the *being-coloured*. Categorial intuition reaches beyond and beneath the confines of sensuous intuition.

When we say that something before us *is* white, therefore, we are intuiting not just the property white but the *presencing* of this property of sense which surpasses the simple perception of particular features and aims at the total ontological identity of the object (whether this object be actually or imaginatively present to us). Categorial intuition is what enables us to see this thing *as* such and such. *Seeing this* becomes *seeing as*.

Categorial intuition goes beyond sensory intuition in two main senses therefore. First, in so far as it surpasses empirical particulars in order to grasp *ontological identity*. And, second, in that it extends the model of perception to include a grasp of the *ontological difference* between the objective status of the thing perceived and the non-objective status of the presentation of this thing. 'The appearing of things does not itself appear to us', as Husserl acknowledges, 'we live through it.'[5] This 'living through' is what categorial intuition is all about. We can only grasp the being of something to the extent that we grasp its sensible particulars *in the light of the surplus sense of its presentation*. Indeed, one could not perceive the former without the latter. The

5 Ibid., Investigation 5, Chap. 1.

empirically present particulars and the ontological presentation itself are not related discontinuously as phenomenon to noumenon but continuously as one part of the same phenomenon (entity/*Seiende*) to another (being/*Sein*).

Art and imagination can play a key role here. They can liberate intuition from direct dependence on particular sensible instances and enable us to freely vary the modes of presentation. We are thus better able to focus on the identity of a thing's 'being', and the non-empirical manner of its appearing. The 'being' of something is disclosed as that which, in its non-presentation, allows what is presented to be presented. The categorial surplus does not itself appear as an object—only as the self-effacing condition of presentation.[6]

Husserl himself comes close to a recognition of this ontological difference between modes of appearing when he observes in *Ideas* (§42) that 'a fundamental and essential difference (*Unterschied*) arises between being as consciousness and being as reality . . . a principal difference between modes of givenness'. What Husserl failed to spell out sufficiently, however, both in this passage and in the passage on categorial intuition in the Sixth Logical Investigation is the radically *ontological* nature of this difference. While Husserl represents an advance on Kant in that he develops the difference between being-as-perception and reality into the difference between being-as-consciousness and reality, he still shares with Kant the tendency to reduce both being and reality to the tenets of transcendental idealism. Husserl's phenomenology still remains subject-centred. Though he overcomes the metaphysical dualism of phenomenon and noumenon he still remains a captive of the Copernican Revolution.

In *Being and Time* and subsequent works, Martin Heidegger set out to redress this balance by pushing the Kantian and Husserl intimations of the difference between being and reality in a more 'fundamental' ontological direction. In § 83 of *Being and Time* (significantly the final section of the work) he expands on Husserl's position in *Ideas* (§ 42), adverting—in quotation marks—to the 'difference (*Unterschied)* between "consciousness" and "thing"'; and in § 63, he spells out what he calls the 'primary ontological difference between existence and reality' in terms of the difference between *Dasein* (as temporal horizon of being) and *Vorhandenheit* (as objects present at hand). As is well known, the greater part of Heidegger's remaining philosophy, written after the famous 'turn', was devoted to a relentless exploration of the ontological difference between being and beings. What began as Kant's distinction between being and reality in the first *Critique* becomes in *Being and Time* Heidegger's difference between the manner of being of *Dasein* (existence) and the manner of being of those beings which are 'objectively' present to *Dasein* (reality). The Copernican Revolution comes full circle. Western philosophy prepares for a new beginning (*ein anderer Anfang*).

---

6   Edmund Husserl, *Ideas*, §111. On the role of art and fiction see §70.

For Heidegger, Husserl's most significant contribution to this new beginning lies in his treatment of categorial intuition.[7] It is here that Heidegger locates the crucial transition from an essentialist to an existential-hermeneutic phenomenology. The decisive claims made by Husserl are: 1) that the essence of a thing is the intentional relationship between that thing and consciousness; 2) that this intentional relationship of *noesis/noema* entails a radically extended (phenomenological) model of perception; 3) that such a model embraces a categorial position or intuition of being; 4) that since this categorial intuition is not restricted to empirical facts but reaches to more fundamental dimensions of the thing's being, it involves, in the short or long term, an ontological *interpretation*. We can thus trace the lines of development from Kant's thesis that *being is position* to Husserl's thesis that *being is intuition* to Heidegger's thesis that *being is interpretation* (i.e. the meaning of being).

The most concise and comprehensive formulation of this trajectory in modern philosophy is to be found in Heidegger's own hermeneutic reading of the Kantian thesis in *The Basic Problems of Phenomenology*.[8] This is how Heidegger formulates the ontological significance of Kant's definition:

> That is real which belongs to a *res*, to a thing in the sense of a *Sache*, to its inherent or essential content, its whatness. To the thing 'house' belong its foundation, wall, roof, door, size, extension, colour—real predicates or determinations, real determinations of the thing 'house', regardless of whether it is actually existent or not. Now Kant says, the actuality of something actual, the existence of the existent, is not a real predicate. A hundred thalers do not differ in their what-contents whether they be a hundred possible or a hundred actual thalers. Actuality does not affect the *what*, the reality, but the *how* of the being, whether possible or actual. Nevertheless, we still say that the house exists or, in our terminology, is extant. We ascribe to this thing something like existence. The question arises, What sort of determination then is existence and actuality? Negatively, Kant says that actuality is not a real determination. . . . The meaning of this negative proposition is that actuality, existence is not itself anything actual or existent; being is not itself a being. (p. 43)

7   For insightful commentaries on this complex subject of Husserl's phenomenology, see J. Taminiaux, 'Heidegger and Husserl's Logical Investigations' in *Dialectic and Difference* (New Jersey, 1985), pp. 91-114; R. Cobb-Stevens, 'Categorial Intuition' in *Husserl and Analytic Philosophy* (The Hague, 1990), pp. 148-52; E. Levinas, *The Theory of Intuition in Husserl's Philosophy* (Evanston, 1973), pp. 68-81; J-L. Marion, 'Question de l'être ou Différence Ontologique' in *Réduction et Donation: Recherches sur Husserl, Heidegger et la Phénoménologie* (Paris, 1990), pp. 163-210; Jean Beaufret, 'Husserl et Heidegger' in *Dialogues avec Heidegger* (Paris, 1974), pp. 126-30; and my *Poétique du Possible* (Paris, 1984), 104-8.

8   Martin Heidegger, *Basic Problems of Phenomenology*, trans. A. Hofstadter, (Indiana, 1988), Ch. 1, § 7-9. This analysis is further developed in Heidegger, *Kants These über das Sein* (Frankfurt, 1963).

If such be Kant's *via negativa* to a definition of being, his tentative formula of a *via affirmativa,* as we saw above, is that being is identifiable with 'position in general'. Moreover, this concept of *position* is, in turn, identifiable with *perception.* Citing Kant's formula that the 'perception (which supplies the material to the concepts) . . . is the sole character of actuality' (*CPR*, B 272-3), Heidegger comments that it is perception which intrinsically reaches the actuality or existence of things. This he interprets as follows:

> The *specific character* of absolute position, as Kant defines it, reveals itself as *perception.* Actuality, possibility, necessity—which can be called predicates only in an improper sense—are not real-synthetic; they are, as Kant says, 'merely subjective'. They 'add to the concept of a thing (of something real) . . . the faculty of knowledge' (*CPR*, B 286). The predicate of actuality adds perception to the concept of a thing. Kant thus says in short: actuality, existence, equals absolute position equals perception. (p. 46)

Accordingly, to say with Kant that existence is something added to the perception of a thing's whatness (e.g. the real predicates of the whatness of a house being its doors, roofs, colour, size etc.) is to say that what is added is *not* another real predicate. This something existential refers back to the human subject; it is nothing other than perception understood, in the large sense, as the basis of all intuitive knowledge. But surely, as Heidegger objects, it is monstrous to talk of a house with a 'perception' added to it. And worse again, to talk of real predicates furnished with the subjective/cognitive property of 'absolute position'. As Kant himself fails to provide any further clarification on this key matter, Heidegger does him the hermeneutic honour of explaining what he, Kant, really *meant* to say—or at least *should* have said. In Heidegger's view, Kant's concept of existence as perception can only make sense in terms of a phenomenological understanding of perception:

> What alone can he mean? Plainly, only one thing, to say that the perception that belongs to the subject as its manner of comportment is added to the thing means the following: The subject brings itself perceivingly to the thing in a relation that is aware of and takes up this thing 'in and for itself'. The thing is posited in the relationship of cognition. In this perception the existent, the extant thing at hand, gives itself in its own self. The real exhibits itself as an actual entity. (p. 47)

What Kant was unable to unravel, in short, was the precise *phenomenological* nature of this perception. His critical terminology of *a priori, a posteriori,* subject and object, was still inadequate to a proper understanding of the way in which the 'perceiving' and the 'perceived' correspond in the phenomenon of the thing's being as 'perceivedness'. What Kant lacked was the phenomenological category of intentionality developed by Brentano and Husserl.

Equipped with this phenomenological armature, Heidegger offers the following re-reading of Kant's thesis:

> Perceiving as intentional, falls so little into a subjective sphere that, as soon as we wish to talk about such a sphere, perceiving immediately transcends it. Perceivedness belongs perhaps to the *Dasein's* intentional comportment; that is to say, it is not subjective and also it is not objective, even though we must always continue to maintain that the perceived being, the extant entity, as perceived has the character of perceivedness. This perceivedness is a remarkable and enigmatic structure, belonging in a certain sense to the object, to the perceived, and yet not itself anything objective, and belonging to the *Dasein* and its intentional existence and yet not itself anything subjective. (p. 69)

The puzzle can only be resolved by moving beyond the Kantian categories of subject/object and embracing a radical phenomenology of *Dasein*. 'The perceivedness of something extant', explains Heidegger, 'is not itself extant in this thing but belongs to the *Dasein*, which does not mean that it belongs to the subject and the subject's immanent sphere. Perceivedness belongs to perceptual intentional comportment. And this makes it possible that the extant should be encountered in its own self. . . . Perceiving takes from the extant its coveredness and releases it so that it can show itself in its own self'. (p. 70)

CONCLUSION

Kant was still a captive of the 'natural attitude'; and the methods of positive science were clearly insufficient for a proper phenomenological understanding because they asked about specific kinds of being (i.e. psychology inquired after psychical being; physics after physical being) but not after the being of things *qua being*. What Kant lacked was a phenomenological ontology of human *Dasein*. Without this, it was impossible for him to grasp that the question of the being of beings is inextricably related to the question of existence—understood phenomenologically as *Dasein*. Only with Husserl, and more explicitly with existential phenomenologists like Heidegger himself, would the equation of being-existence-position-perception be interpreted in terms of the dynamism of *intentionality* (directing oneself towards meaning) and *transcendence* (the 'toward which' of the directedness). Or to put it in the terms of scholastic ontology, phenomenology discloses intentionality as the *ratio cognoscendi* of transcendence, and transcendence as the *ratio essendi* of intentionality. The modern temptation of subjectivism is thus countered.

Heidegger concludes that what Kant's thesis—'being is not a real predicate'—*wants* to say is that *being is not a being*. However, when it came to a positive interpretation Kant was found lacking. Statements like 'being is position in general' remain unclear and ambiguous. Devoid of the conceptual method and apparatus of phenomenology, Kant was not yet in a position to redefine 'perception' as the intentional self-directedness of *Dasein* towards things. He thus failed to fully explain why *Dasein* is not one more thing amongst things—a real predicate amongst others precontained within the thingness of things. Kant's inability to go beyond the dualism of subject/ object, inside/outside, perceiving/perceived, was ultimately a failure to comprehend the intentional structure of existence as *Dasein*.

Ultimately at issue here is the *ontological difference* between *being* (existence as *Dasein*) and *beings* (essences with real predicates). Heidegger concludes accordingly that 'the task is now to pursue the structure of *Dasein's* comportments with particular regard to perception and to ask how this structure of intentionality itself looks, but above all *how it is grounded ontologically in the basic constitution of the Dasein*' (Ibid., p. 59). *Being and Time* was Heidegger's own attempt—perhaps the most influential, for better or worse, in this century—to respond to this task. Where the major thinkers of modern philosophy from Descartes and Kant to Husserl and Heidegger are in agreement, however, is that we can only understand the being of beings by reflecting on the being of our own existence. 'For it is only on the basis of the exposition of the basic ontological constitution of the *Dasein* that we put ourselves in a position to understand adequately the phenomenon correlated with the idea of being, the understanding of being which lies at the basis of all comportment to beings and guides it. Only if we understand the basic ontological constitution of the *Dasein* can we make clear to ourselves how an understanding of being is possible in the *Dasein*' (Ibid., p. 75).

Max Scheler
Phenomenology and Beyond

PATRICK GOREVAN

This article will trace the development of Max Scheler's thought from his days as a phenomenologist under the influence of Husserl and the early phenomenological movement to the far-reaching developments of his later absolute philosophy or panentheism. From being a phenomenologist who specialized in religious and ethical themes he turned to a sort of 'partnership pantheism', in which man and the world were merely a part of God, contributing to the very becoming of the deity in its fullness. Such an astonishing shift in thought needs an explanation. In this article we begin by describing Scheler as a phenomenologist, stressing the limitations this placed on his thought. We also look at Scheler's concept of being, and suggest that it contained limitations of its own, which brought Scheler to go beyond it in the direction of an absolute substance which might underpin the reality of the world in a way which his phenomenology could not.

PHENOMENOLOGY

Scheler's discovery of phenomenology is linked to his encounter with Husserl in 1901. At that time he was in search of a method which would enable him to trace the identity and activity of spirit. The noological method of Eucken, his mentor at Jena, had seemed to offer some hope. It combined a strict avoidance of reductionist explanations with an inclusion of *material*[1] elements within an *a priori* of some breadth. It was handicapped, however, by an adherence to some central Kantian dogmas. Most important among these was the thesis that intuition is necessarily phenomenal. With the help of Husserl's categorial intuition, Scheler came to a new position on the question of evidence.[2]

Scheler was also hoping to thematize the irreducible nature of ethical and other values which the Kantian system had regarded as an impoverished 'poor relation' of the more serious activities of the transcendental spirit. He wanted to find a method allowing them full citizenship in the intellectual *polis*.[3]

---

1 That is, not merely formal.
2 Cf. Preface to the second edition (published in 1922) of Scheler's *Habilitationsschrift, Die transzendentale und die psychologische Methode* (originally published in Jena, 1900), *Gesammelte Werke* (*GW*) I, p. 201.
3 For a statement of this concern, see Scheler's doctoral thesis, *Beiträge zur Feststellung der Beziehungen zwischen den logischen und ethischen Prinzipien* (Jena, 1899) *GW*, I, p. 11.

When Scheler and Husserl met, their conversation dealt with the area of intuition and perception. Scheler had come to the conclusion that the contents of the given of our intuitions were much richer than what could be included under the headings of sense-qualities and their derivatives, or of logical forms applicable to them. This insight, he mentioned to Husserl, seemed to be a fruitful starting point for a theoretical philosophy. Husserl, according to Scheler's account, expressed agreement and added that his forthcoming work on logic would contain an analogous extension of the concept of intuition, which would include intuitions of a categorial type.[4]

Some doubt the simultaneous discovery of phenomenology suggested. It is strange that Scheler should add that 'around that time' (1901) he had withdrawn his own work on logic from the printers, as a result of this new insight (*DPG*, 308). The editor of the *Collected Works* asserts that this work was withdrawn not in 1901 but around 1906.[5] This is rather difficult to reconcile with Scheler's own account. Perhaps the awareness of the phenomenological method took longer to germinate in Scheler's mind than he himself suggested.[6]

For a thorough exposé of the phenomenological method and of what Scheler hoped for from it, we must wait until 1913. In that year, which had seen the publication of *Der Formalismus in der Ethik*, he was asked by the editor of a journal called *Geisteswissenschaften* to make some brief remarks on the recent phenomenological movement whose representatives had 'found a certain alliance in the *Jahrbuch für Philosophie und phänomenologische Forschung*'.[7] The response to that request took the form of an extended essay, 'Phenomenology and the Theory of Cognition'.[8]

Scheler does not offer a 'definition' of phenomenology. He claims that it is a method which emerges from years of fruitful work, and does not admit of a ready-to-hand definition (*PTC*, 137). It is not a 'new science' or a substitute for the word 'philosophy'. It is rather an 'attitude of spiritual seeing' in which one can see or experience something which otherwise remains hidden, namely a realm of facts of a particular kind (*PTC*, 137). This notion of a realm of facts, somehow awaiting discovery by the phenomenologist, is also developed in a related essay 'The Theory of the Three Facts'.[9] Here,

---

4 'Die deutsche Philosophie der Gegenwart', *GW*, VII, p. 308 (cited below as *DPG*). See also the editor's afterword to *GW*, I, pp. 413-14.

5 Manfred Frings, 'L'état des travaux dans l'édition des *Gesammelte Werke* de Max Scheler', *Revue de théologie et de philosophie* 117 (1985), 290.

6 In an edition of this work on logic published in 1975, Jörg Willer, the editor, claims that Scheler's date must be an error, for the development which *Logik* represented over and above the *Habilitationsschrift* could scarcely have occurred in one year. Cf. *Logik* I (Amsterdam, 1975), p. 275.

7 *Der Formalismus in der Ethik*, Scheler's central work, had appeared in Volumes I and II of that journal, in 1913 and 1916. It is also available in English translation by Manfred Frings and Roger Funk as *Formalism in Ethics and Non-formal Ethics of Values* (Evanston, 1973).

8 *Selected Philosophical Essays*, trans. David Lachtermann (Evanston, 1973), pp. 136-201. This essay is cited below as *PTC*.

9 *Selected Philosophical Essays*, pp. 202-87; cited below as *TTF*.

Scheler called on phenomenological experience to furnish phenomeno-logical or 'pure' facts which come to givenness through an immediate intuition. The contents of this experience as he explains are essences and essential con-nections (*TTF*, 202).

Phenomenology is trying to get back to the things themselves, the pure facts, and tries to enter into the most immediate and vital contact with the things of the world as they are. Epistemological matters of criteria for given-ness or of mediation are anathema to it, or at least to Scheler. He is always distancing himself from what he calls the 'criteria question', wherever it may originate (*PTC*, 139). The critical philosopher, who always wants to place some yardstick or criterion of judgment between himself and what he knows, has forgotten that the yardstick can only emerge from direct contact with living reality and truth. In other words, as Scheler puts it, 'the notions of true and false themselves are in need of phenomenological clarification' (*PTC*, 140). The self-givenness and evidence of immediate intuitions are what furnish us with the ability to choose between truth and falsehood. Truth itself, however, is the evidence of immediate intuition where no choice has to be made for there is no room for doubt. He warns us against looking for a criterion for this evidence, from psychology for example. There is just no feeling or experience which will always recur when truth is present. How could one ask for a criterion or symbol of self-givenness? The idea is absurd. How can one mediate immediacy?

Each of these pure facts is an *Etwas*, a 'something', whose identity which does not change, in spite of all the variation that goes on in our sense-knowledge. They are the 'independent variable'. They have to be completely independent of symbols, even if symbols may be used to designate them and point them out (*PTC*, 144–5). Phenomenological facts differ from *natural* facts which are always mediated through the lived body and other human requirements, and from *scientific* facts which are also mediated through theories and symbols of their own, which mask rather than make clear the real identity of a content of intuition. It is a favourite theme with Scheler that phenomenology alone is capable of 'redeeming all the drafts', all that tissue of hypotheses which seem to try to explain the identities of objects, and leave us face to face with those objects as they are given (*PTC*, 145). 'Phenomenology stands or falls with the assertion that such facts do exist and that these facts and their connections are genuinely what lies at the basis of all other facts and connections, those of the natural and scientific world view' (*TTF*, 221).

Scheler's own output during these years testifies to his success in finding and describing these facts. During his phenomenological years he wrote copiously and was at the centre of the phenomenological movement. *Der Formalismus in der Ethik*, an attempt to ground ethics on values, is the most sustained work of phenomenology, but we might also mention *Wesen und Formen der Sympathie* (1913), where he offered a profound phenomenology of the emotional life.[10] It showed that we cannot reduce the life of the emotions to a series of responses to stimuli. There are intentional feelings which grasp real contents, which we call values. Another work which had a wide influence was his work on religion, *Vom Ewigen im Menschen* (1921).[11]

THE LIMITATIONS OF PHENOMENOLOGY

Scheler's attitude to Husserl became distant. He did not wish to be known as a disciple of a master. He would not ascribe to Husserl the type of role played by Kant, Fichte or Hegel in regard to their followers. 'Phenomenology is . . . more than a particular philosophical group. It is the work of a series of co-operators, with the inspiration of Husserl indeed, but not under his guidance or direction' (*DPG*, 327).

On his side, there are numerous indications that Husserl did not hold Scheler in great esteem, and that indeed he resented his sparkling and ebullient personality, which, during his years in the phenomenological movement in Munich, threatened to eclipse Husserl's own authority in the group. Scheler seems to have lacked the capacity, if indeed he felt the need, for that kind of painstaking research, for analysing and dissecting ideas in a cold and detached way, which Husserl held to be essential in the construction of an effective phenomenology. 'One needs brilliant ideas', he is supposed to have said in regard to Scheler, 'but one must not publish them.'[12] But publish them, or publicize them, Scheler did, thereby winning himself a rapid notoriety. He was soon regarded as the 'number two' phenomenologist. Husserl, however, regarded the fruits of the phenomenology practised by Scheler and his devotees as 'fool's gold'.[13]

In a conversation with H. G. Gadamer, who had encountered Scheler and discussed what he saw as his 'demoniacal' character with Husserl, the master commented: 'It is just as well that we also have Pfänder', who, Gadamer explains, 'was the driest, the least demoniacal, philosopher that you could imagine'.[14] After Scheler's death, Husserl was to refer to Heidegger and Scheler as his 'two antipodes'.[15] Perhaps the reason for many of the differences between the two is to be found in their philosophical purposes. Husserl was interested in bringing out ever more clearly and exactly the nature of the given, and thus achieving the most exact and most apodictically evident science. Scheler's aim was to apply phenomenology in the areas of emotion, religion and ethics.

10   *The Nature of Sympathy*, trans. Peter Heath (London, 1954).
11   *On the Eternal in Man*, trans. Bernard Noble (London, 1960) cited below as *EM*.
12   Herbert Spiegelberg, *Doing Phenomenology* (The Hague, 1975), pp. 280-1.
13   Herbert Spiegelberg, *The Phenomenological Movement* (The Hague, 1960) Vol. I, p. 230.
14   Hans-Georg Gadamer, 'Max Scheler, der Verschwender', in Paul Good, *Max Scheler im Gegenwartsgeschehen der Philosophie* (Bern, 1975), p. 12.
15   Letter to Roman Ingarden, quoted in Herbert Spiegelberg, *The Phenomenological Movement*, Vol. I, p. 230.

Scheler was also dismayed by what he called Husserl's eccentric turn (*eigenartige Wendung*) in the direction of a transcendental idealism. He accused Husserl of having come close, in *Ideas*, to the idealism of Berkeley and of Kant, by conceiving phenomenology as the theory of the structure of consciousness, thus rendering impossible any metaphysics based on phenomenologically grasped essences (*DPG*, 311).

Apart from these differences, Scheler was aware of the limitations of phenomenology. He had seen how they had handicapped Husserl, leading him to a kind of solipsism. In Scheler's own thought there is also a limitation of philosophy in phenomenology to dealing with essence rather than real existence. These essences were what both he and Husserl meant by 'the things themselves'. So while phenomenology's concern is to achieve a unity in knowledge, avoiding hypostatizations of subject and object, of knower and of known, there is still a danger that in the effort to achieve and guard the total unity and self-transparency of spiritual knowledge, another cleavage may open up, this time between this wonderfully self-transparent and ideal knowledge and the world of contingent existence, which is clearly not a welcome guest in such a model household.[16] If that observation can hold some weight for phenomenology in general, it is easy to apply it to Scheler too, for his concern to avoid the world of contingent facts is even more thorough-going.[17] As one recent critic of phenomenology puts it, 'Phenomenology has its own poverty. It is constitutionally incapable of exploring questions of reality.'[18]

This is apparent in Scheler's phenomenological philosophy. Scheler bases his whole system on the separation between essence and existence, which is one of the first three self-evident axioms of philosophy. We first realize that there is not nothing; then we turn to God, in the face of the utter contingency of this being, this 'not-nothing'. God, the absolute being, guarantees the existence of the contingent. Finally, the third axiom is that in every being apart from God there is a distinction of essence and existence (*EM*, 98–103).

On this dualism Scheler bases his version of phenomenology. He consistently calls for the exercise of the phenomenological reduction as a revocation of existence and of reality in order to achieve knowledge of the essences of things. This reduction, he claims, is more thoroughgoing than Husserl's and it has a distinctly *moral* ring to it, involving a 'denial' of reality and an attitude of humility rather than mastery in the face of the things themselves.[19]

16 Cf. Antonio Lambertino, *Max Scheler* (Florence, 1977), p. 46.
17 This is well illustrated by Quentin Smith in 'Scheler's Critique of Husserl's Theory of the World of the Natural Standpoint', *The Modern Schoolman* 55 (1977-8), 395-6. He points out that Husserl had seen the experience of world and the presence of logical objects as the foundation of values, while Scheler insists that value-grasping is a more fundamental and founding moment in perception.
18 Edward Vacek, 'Scheler's Evolving Methodologies', *Analecta Husserliana* 22 (1987), 174.
19 'Idealism and Realism', *Selected Philosophical Essays*, pp. 316-17.

But how can we reach the existential factor, the moment of reality and contingency? Real existence, according to Scheler, is not 'known', but is 'given' to our will in the experience of resistance: 'the *realness of a thing* . . . is only given in the intentional experience of the possible *resistance* of an object against a mental function of the type volition *qua* willing' (*EM*, 220, Scheler's emphasis). There is no continuity between contingent reality and the world of essence, at least in regard to the process of knowledge. This led James Collins to say that essence and existence, in Scheler, are not so much co-principles of being as different levels of being.[20] During Scheler's phenomenological period, the *essential* level of being is more prominent. In the later philosophy of the world-ground the sphere of *existence* and of life comes to be the more dominant.

A further limitation in Scheler's phenomenology which led him in the direction of his absolute philosophy was its lack of a concept of *substance*. Scheler's phenomenology avoids this concept which, for him, represented an 'inert and inactive I know not what'. Man, for instance, is not a substance, for he is not a single nature, merely an amalgam of spirit and life. Whatever unity he does possess is based on his reaching forward, beyond himself, towards God.[21] The material world was also non-substantial. It was merely the appearance of deeper drives and activity. Spirit could not be regarded as substantial since it was totally active.

Scheler was thus left with nothing in this world which is capable of possessing an essence and which exercises its existence in an autonomous way. Even man, the 'microcosm', is merely a reaching forward from a sub-human plethora of drives towards the absolute. But it is one thing to declare oneself opposed to a reified *substare*; it is quite another to find that one is bereft of any truly existent reality. Scheler was acutely conscious of the danger of absolute Idealism in phenomenology; he was deeply influenced by vitalist philosophy, in particular by Schopenhauer and von Hartmann; and all of this impelled him towards a philosophy which would account for real existence through the 'absolute substance', or world-ground. To this later philosophy we now turn.

THE WORLD-GROUND

The purpose of Scheler's absolute philosophy is to conceive absolute being, source of the essential structure of the world. Scheler also expects that it will be able to account for existence, which, he insists, always escapes first philosophy, which is a knowledge of essence. It will have the task of showing that, since the world around us is composed of two fundamental

20 'Roots of Scheler's Evolutionary Pantheism', in *Crossroads in Philosophy* (Chicago, 1969), p. 118.
21 'Zur Idee des Menschen', *GW*, III, pp. 182-95.

attributes—spirit and life—in the same way 'ultimate being' must contain a powerless 'infinite *ideating* spirit (and) an irrational driving force'.[22]

Scheler's new theory accounts for *existence* as Eduard von Hartmann's had done. It emerges from the thirst for reality which is to be found in the *ens a se*, the world-ground. The emergence of real existence, according to Scheler, is the fruit of a temptation in the Godhead. This timeless moment of temptation is possible because of the dualistic way the deity is now conceived. It is both powerless spirit and blind, vital will. Without the existence of the world the powerless divine spirit would remain powerless for ever. Succumbing to the urge for real existence, the Godhead 'permits' the contingent world to exist, in the hope that this will eventually lead to its own fullness, as an integration of spirit and life, through the mediation of man. Existence, therefore is not only contingent and blind, it is also linked to evil and greed within the absolute.[23]

The world-ground is the *ens realissimum* which has an identity as substances do and which can exist. It alone exists in itself and not in another. Scheler calls the world-ground 'the substance' (*SN*, II, 202, 204, 213). He goes on to link the *ens a se* at the ground of the world with substantiality so that outside of the world- ground there can be no substance (*SN*, II, 202). It is that which is in itself and is conceived in itself, for Scheler was now fast coming under the influence of Spinoza's view of substance according to which both spirit and extension are immanent in the divine substance. Nothing can exist except as a facet of the absolute.[24]

His philosophy of the world-ground does, in fact, show traces of Spinoza's rather overwhelming notion, which had become more and more attractive to Scheler in the early 1920s.[25] The religious dimensions of Spinoza were particularly compelling for him. 'Spinoza, drunk with God' was an assessment which Scheler shared. His 'passion' for the divine is barely hidden behind his geometrical methods of proceeding; he had kept only one of Descartes' three kinds of substance—the *res infinita*, reducing extension and thought to attributes of this single substance. God's existence was more certain than any other form of existence, even man's own. If Spinoza had a fault, Scheler argues, it was his inability to grant the existence, the contingency and the autonomy of *this* world.[26]

Does not this throw light on Scheler? He too finds growing difficulty in justifying the consistency of this world. All the forms of knowledge which permit us to reach it are subject to modification and do not really hold good.

---

22 'Philosopher's Outlook', in *Philosophical Perspectives*, trans. Oscar Haac (Boston, 1954), p. 8.
23 *Schriften aus dem Nachlass* II, *GW*, XI, p. 203; cited below as *SN*, II.
24 Spinoza, *Ethics*, I, trans. A. Boyle (London, 1910), Definitions 3-6 (p. 1).
25 This growing attachment to Spinoza's philosophy is seen by comparing the dismissive approach to pantheism which Scheler had in *EM*, pp. 107-9, and his remarkably favourable attitude to Spinoza in a speech delivered in Amsterdam in 1927, the 250th anniversary of Spinoza's death. Cf. 'Spinoza' in *Philosophical Perspectives*, pp. 50-64.
26 Ibid., p. 54.

By comparison with them, which offer us the world and not God, the axiological sphere—which is founded upon the religious and absolute values—offers us God as the source of all that goes to make up the sublunary world.

While one cannot think of creation without thinking of God, for Scheler and Spinoza this means that the creature is subsumed into God, not merely as the ultimate source of its existence but also for its very substantiality. Without the divinity it means nothing at all. The being of the creature is from and in God, and a true theist, Scheler admits, will not be able to countenance this (*SN*, II, 202).

So Scheler does not escape from the habit of thought for which it is necessary to discover a prior sense of being, being in the ultimate or primary sense. He occasionally even uses the word 'substance' to describe it. The pantheistic vision was prepared precisely by his denial of finite substance in the world. Once that vacuum was identified, it is filled by absolute being. While Scheler insists that the absolute being communicates spirit and drive to the finite world, it is difficult to imagine how the world thus constituted could preserve an autonomy without the bulwark of substance—that which can exist in itself. Scheler's account of absolute being as the ground of the world leaves no space for the autonomy of the world.

Scheler, much against his intentions, continues the Aristotelian search for substance. He too recognizes the need for such a prior sense of being, but ends up reifying it, placing it within the Absolute and reducing finite reality to so many attributes of the divine.[27]

THE EXPERIENCE OF BEING

Scheler's breakthrough into reality, as it has been called, is achieved at the price of an extravagant and contradictory philosophy of God, both absolute and evil, both transcendent and dependent on man. But this is not necessary if one can reach an experience of substance and existence in our conceptual knowledge. Scheler denies that this is possible.

In the first place, in regard to substance, he develops his concept of being from the denial of non-being, not from the experience of being. This makes it impossible for him to reach substantial reality, for it comes in an experience of the differences among beings as beings. For Scheler things do not differ as beings. In his enunciation of his concept of being he stresses that it applies to all the 'secondary categories of being'—quality, existent, mental or extramental, substantial or attributive (*EM*, 99).

27 Bernd Brenk in *Metaphysik des einen und absoluten Seins* (Meisenheim am Glan, 1975), p. 186, makes the point that in Scheler, as the person is to his acts, so is the world ground to its earthly attributes and manifestations—not so much lurking behind them as living through them. If this is correct, it appears to be a re-adoption of this aspect of the traditional theory of the dynamic rapport between substance and accidents.

Since the concept 'being' applies to them all in the same way, there is no question of an *analogy* of being, which might discover real differences of being, and a 'prior' sense of being, substance in the Aristotelian sense. It has been well remarked that 'it is more true that our mind is conceived in being than that being is conceived in our mind',[28] but when Scheler grounds metaphysics on 'there is not nothing', being is conceived in the mind. It is the fruit of a mental operation—the denial of non-being. The denial in question permits no analogy: it is either executed or it is not. So there can be no analogy in being, no unity in difference and no prior sense of being. Scheler had to take a different route towards substance, and identified it with the Absolute.

In the second place, turning to the question of existence, Scheler separates existence from essence so radically that existence cannot be known at all, merely felt in resistance. But can existence really not be known? True, it does not have the conceptual sharpness which Scheler demands from his essences (*Wesen, Washeit*). We cannot behold it in the evidence and clarity that the *Wesenschau* can offer. But it is somehow present when we conceive things and without it perhaps we would never manage to conceive anything.

A recent discussion, dealing with the question of whether the statement 'this exists' is tautological can, I believe, shed light on Scheler's idea of existence.[29] The question raised is: do we add anything to 'this' when we say 'this exists' or is it simply a tautological judgment? I do not think there would be any problem here for Scheler. For him, 'this' is a matter of *Wesenschau* (the beholding of essences) and 'is' is a completely different matter, namely, the existence and reality of 'this'. *Dasein* (existence) and *Wesen* (essence) are quite separate for him. So our affirming 'this is' would represent a real discovery, something which could not by any stretch of the imagination be called tautological. But most of us would find it very difficult to concur. We would agree that there is something strangely redundant about the sentence 'this room exists'. Equally it does seem to be contradictory to say 'this room does not exist'. Surely if we can talk about it as 'this room' at all it must exist in the first place?

A solution offered is that when the mind conceives its object as existing it does so by means of a judgment in which it affirms the existence of the object of its conception. This judgment employs only one concept, but it is a concept sufficiently complex to permit it to assume under different aspects the distinct roles of subject and predicate, and hence the danger that it might be regarded as a tautology. The judgment and the concept are completely in need of one another.[30]

28 Bernard Kelly, 'The Metaphysical Background of Analogy', Paper 29, Aquinas Society of London, 1958, 21.
29 Desmond Connell, 'Existence and Judgment', *Philosophical Studies* 30 (1984), 127–43.
30 Ibid., 141–2.

But the very existence of this dilemma suggests that the concept, without ceasing to be conceptual, is always reaching forward to the thing it knows as existing, when this is appropriate and in the correct way—to some things as existing in reality, to others as ideas or beings of reason or as fables. In other words, conceptual knowledge can go further than Scheler admitted. It is capable of an incomplete but genuine experience of being as existent.

We finish as we started, remembering that Scheler had sought a type of phenomenological knowledge which would cut through the undergrowth of theory, symbol and *a priori* which had blocked our access to the real. But the project failed. His phenomenology could not grasp what it meant to be real, to be substance. This was because its concept of 'being', could not admit of a radical difference within being such as substance and accident. Scheler also had to admit failure in the attempt to know the real existence of things. This was a matter for the will. It was therefore inevitable that Scheler's later philosophy should have been so extravagant and contradictory, for it represented an attempt to go beyond metaphysical knowledge.

Whitehead, Aristotle, and Substance

TIMOTHY MOONEY

The intellectual career of Alfred North Whitehead (1861–1947) was by any standards quite exceptional. In marked contrast to his contemporaries in the world of twentieth-century Anglo-American philosophy, Whitehead had an abiding interest in metaphysical problems which became more and more pronounced as he advanced in years. He stands out as one of the few recent thinkers who sought to bridge the gap between the Analytical and Continental modes of philosophizing.

Whitehead's thought can broadly be divided into three major phases. His original interests were logic and mathematics, combined with a keen awareness of the contemporary advances in physics. During his second phase he devoted himself to the philosophy of nature. In his final metaphysical period he sought to explain all of reality in one great cosmological scheme which he termed 'The Philosophy of Organism'.

Always conscious of the interaction between the concepts of philosophy and of natural science, Whitehead believed that it was necessary to formulate a new cosmology because of the breakdown of the Newtonian scheme as a complete description of reality. According to Whitehead, the fundamental flaws in this system were themselves the results of certain errors which could be traced back to almost the beginning of Western philosophy. He further argued that the most serious of these errors are closely associated with the idea of substance as originally propounded by Aristotle.

Recent years have seen a revival of interest in Whitehead's philosophy. Along with Bergson and Heidegger, he is seen as having effected a 'new departure' in metaphysics that emphasizes holism and organicism rather than substantialism and mechanistic materialism.[1] Whatever the merits of such a world–view, I do not think that Whitehead in his later philosophy actually avoids an unconscious utilization of those concepts which he criticizes in Aristotle. The first part of this essay presents Whitehead's critique of what he understands by Aristotle's substantialism. This will be followed by an exposition of Whitehead's alternative. I will finally attempt to show the particular ways in which the apparent alternative utilizes certain Aristotelian ideas.

I

If we take into account genius of insight, general equipment of knowledge, and stimulus of metaphysical ancestry, Whitehead argues, we must consider

1 See Ilya Prigogine and Isabelle Stengers, *Order Out of Chaos* (London, 1984), and Warwick Fox, 'Deep Ecology: A New Philosophy of our Time?' *The Ecologist* 14 (1984), 194–200.

Aristotle as the greatest metaphysican. He also believes that Aristotle's general conception of the physical universe remains unsurpassed as an example of inductive generalization. Whitehead nevertheless contends that the legacy of Aristotle's thought has in general been disastrous. Aristotle's emphasis on classification retarded the advance of physical science in the medieval period, for he gravely neglected the role of mathematics and measurement. We can never ignore questions as to quantities, proportions, and patterns of arrangements with other things.[2] Aristotle's philosophy also led to a serious overemphasis on explanation by final cause in the middle ages. The modern period reacted by overstressing efficient causes, so that metaphysics is now left with the task of showing the proper relationship of efficient and final causes to each other.[3] But Whitehead sees most of the problems that have ensued from Aristotle's philosophy as due to his system of logic:

> Unfortunately, owing to the way in which for over two thousand years philosophic thought has been dominated by its background in Aristotelian logic, all attempts to combine the set of special sciences into a philosophic cosmology, giving some understanding of the universe . . . are vitiated by the unconscious relapse into those Aristotelian forms as the sole mode of expression. The disease of philosophy is its itch to express itself in the forms, 'Some S is P', or 'All S is P'.[4]

In Aristotle's logic, the fundamental type of affirmative proposition is the attribution of a predicate to a subject. Many philosophers who have explicitly criticized the Aristotelian notion of substance, says Whitehead, have still been unconsciously influenced by the idea of primary substance in that they have implicitly presupposed that the subject-predicate form of proposition, which is in fact correlative to the substance-quality approach, embodies the finally adequate mode of statement about the world.[5] The difficulty is not so

2 Alfred North Whitehead, *Adventures of Ideas* (New York, 1967), pp. 142, 153 (cited below as *AI*).
3 Alfred North Whitehead, *Process and Reality* (New York, 1978), p. 84 (cited below as *PR*).
4 Alfred North Whitehead, *Modes of Thought* (New York, 1968), p. 142.
5 *PR*, 30, 75. This close association of Aristotelian Logic and Metaphysics is elsewhere seen by Whitehead as a problem of post-Aristotelian philosophy. In *PR*, 30, he states that the effect of Aristotelian logic on metaphysical categories does not seem to have been characteristic of Aristotle's own metaphysical speculations. In *PR*, 51, Whitehead says that with reference to the subject-predicate twist of mind, probably Aristotle was not an Aristotelian. And in *PR*, 137, he states that Aristotle included in his thought certain notions inconsistent with a substance-quality metaphysics. These remarks are noted by Charles Hartshorne in 'Whitehead on Process', *Philosophy and Phenomenological Research* 8 (1948), 516. Hartshorne argues that Whitehead is not so much criticizing Aristotle's treatment of substance as the reduction of it to a single definition 'neither predicable of nor present in a subject'. Yet it is this very definition, as is argued in the third part of this article, that is misunderstood by Whitehead. Hartshorne fails to note that Whitehead, in *PR*, 209, goes on to describe Aristotle as the apostle of substance and attribute and the classificatory logic which this notion suggests, having already, in *PR*, 50, condemned what he sees as

much that the subject-predicate form is incorrect in itself, but that it is unable to account for the polyadic relationships actually found in nature. Take the example of an experiencing subject who sees green in a situation distinct from but simultaneous with this same subject. There will be an essential reference to three different events, namely, to the event which is the bodily life of the observer, to the event which is the so-called situation of green at the time of observation, and to the event which is all of nature at the time of observation. Any two term proposition will conceal the diverse meanings involved in even a situation as simple as this.[6]

A still greater problem with the subject-predicate approach is that the subject—the primary substance—has been defined by Aristotle as that which is neither asserted of another subject nor is present in a subject. For Whitehead, this is equivalent to saying that the subject is an independent, individual fact. And if we ask for a full description of such an individual fact in the physical world, we are given an answer in terms of various qualities or characteristics which, when taken together, are held to constitute the real thing in question. Whitehead sees such an answer as radically incomplete:

> The answer is beautifully simple. But it entirely leaves out the inter-connections between real things. Each substantial thing is seen as complete in itself, without any reference to any other substantial thing. Such an account of the ultimate atoms, or of the ultimate monads, or of the ultimate subjects enjoying experience, renders the inter-connected world of real individuals unintelligible. The universe is shivered into a multitude of disconnected substantial things, each thing in its own way exemplifying its private bundle of abstract characters which have found a common home in its own substantial individuality. But substantial thing cannot call unto substantial thing. A substantial thing may acquire a quality, a credit—but real landed estate, never. In this way Aristotle's doctrines of Predication and of Primary Substance have issued into a doctrine of the conjunction of attributes and of the disjunction of primary substances.[7]

The doctrines of prediction and primary substance emerge for Whitehead as variations of what he calls 'The Fallacy of Simple Location'. This is the idea that a physical fact can be adequately described without reference to other regions of space and other durations of time. This is because the notion of the mere transfer of qualities cannot explain efficient causation or give any firm conclusions about other times beyond direct observation. The proper explanation of these, argues Whitehead, demands substantial interaction

---

Aristotle's idea of primary substance. The present writer regards this latter attitude as more representative of Whitehead's overall interpretation, for his analysis does not display an adequate awareness of what is actually implied in Aristotle's definition of primary substance.

6 Alfred North Whitehead, *The Principle of Relativity* (Cambridge, 1922), pp. 26-7; *PR*, 13.
7 *AI*, 132-3.

whereby 'relatedness' will be dominant over individual 'quality'. Whitehead also holds that any explanation in terms of attributes or qualities cannot unveil the real essence of a thing itself, because they are mere abstract characteristics. For example the statement 'This water is hot' involves the attribution of high temperature to a certain mass of water. But the quality of 'being hot' is an abstraction, for we can think of many diverse things that may be hot apart from this particular example. Aristotle is seen by Whitehead as having failed to recognize that such qualities do not themselves refer to particular actualities whilst not referring to others.[8]

There is yet another unfortunate consequence of the interaction between the correlative notions of substance-quality and subject-predicate. Whitehead sees Aristotle as having emphasized the meaning of substance as the ultimate subject which no longer predicted of anything else. Aristotle's notion of substance is in this way the final philosophical concept of the substratum that underlies any attribute. According to Whitehead, this idea of a substratum involves a 'static fallacy' whereby primary substances are conceived of as the static foundations of reality and as the bearers of various qualities. In this concept, the substances remain essentially unchanged and numerically identical. Now Whitehead admits that this is a useful abstraction for everyday life, and has become embedded in language, Aristotelian logic, and metaphysics. In the first two examples it can be given a certain pragmatic justification. However Whitehead goes on to state:

> . . . in metaphysics the concept is sheer error. The error does not consist in the employment of the word 'substance'; but in the employment of the notion of an actual entity which is characterized by numerical qualities, and remains numerically one amidst the changes of accidental relations and of accidental qualities.[9]

The acceptance of this erroneous metaphysical concept, says Whitehead, has destroyed the various schemes of pluralistic realism ever since. It has also been the basis of scientific materialism. Yet he sees this view as one that has been breaking down over the last few centuries. To give an example, this concept originally led to a thing like a stone being interpreted as an enduring and undifferentiated lump of material. But with the advent of the molecular theory, this original interpretation of the stone as a continuous and passive individual had to be abandoned. The original concept was now in turn applied to the agitated molecules making up the stone. Each individual molecule was seen as a self-identical unit remaining numerically one however long or short its period of endurance. This new interpretation eventually collapsed itself.

---

8 *PR*, xiii, 137; *AI*, 132.

9 *PR*, 79. See also *AI*, 276. This criticism would be far more applicable to Locke's 'Something I Know Not What' that supports qualities. Aristotle does not see a substance as a static 'substrate' (*ὑποκείμενον*) underlying qualities whilst itself without them. Whitehead's idea of substance was quite probably mediated through the tradition of classical British Empiricism.

Molecules have since been broken down into atoms and the atoms have again been divided into protons and electrons. Whitehead argues that, in addition, the energy of subatomic entities has been shown as emitting in the form of discrete quantum units that apparently dissolve into the vibrations of light. Furthermore, these emissions cannot be dissociated from these entities, which seem to exist in discrete, rhythmic periods. Thus the concept of enduring, undifferentiated substances has been finally abandoned. But this leaves us with the question as to what are the concrete facts that exhibit this attribute of wave-vibrations. And for Whitehead, the final philosophical problem is to conceive one such fact in its completeness.[10]

II

In his own system, the 'organic' or 'process' philosophy, Whitehead describes the world as a multiplicity of 'actual entities'. These actual entities are seen as the final concrete facts of which the world is made up, and Whitehead explicitly states that his central concern is to explain 'the becoming, the being and the relatedness' of these actual entities. Whitehead characterizes actual entities as processes of becoming that cannot be described in terms of static 'stuff'. He holds that the 'being' of an actual entity is constituted by its becoming, so that the two cannot be separated, and that this involves the abandonment of any notion of actual entities as unchanging subjects of change.[11]

Every actual entity is a microscopic, atomic individual. Actual entities are microscopic in that they cannot be observed, although the macroscopic material bodies we can see with our 'gross apprehensions' are no more than collections of actual entities. Because actual entities are atomic, states Whitehead, atomism is the ultimate philosophical truth. This is not to deny substantial relatedness, but only to affirm that, as the minima of reality, actual entities are indivisible in the ontological sense. As a cell complex involving other things, every actual entity is composite. In this way Whitehead sees the philosophy of organism as both an atomic and a cell-theory of reality.[12]

Whitehead states that his central concern is to explain how one actual entity can be present in another. The major part of this explanation lies in his notion of 'prehensions' of 'concrete facts of relatedness'. Prehensions are the general activities by which every actual entity grasps other actual entities into itself as part of its own process of becoming.[13] The word 'prehension' is a deliberate neologism. Whitehead seen the term 'apprehension' as too suggestive of the notion of 'cognitive apprehension', whereas the term 'prehension' better conveys his argument that an activity of grasping something need

10 *PR*, 77-9; *AI*, 156, 158.
11 *PR*, xiii-xiv, 18, 23, 29, 41.
12 *PR*, 35-6, 102, 219, 227.
13 *PR*, 20, 22, 48-57, 219.

not be conscious. Prehensions are not in fact the preserve of living beings. The experiences of living things up to and including humans are actually seen by Whitehead as complex outgrowths from the more basic prehensive activities enjoyed by all the atomic actual entities. Whitehead's system thus veers towards a form of pan-psychism.[14] Because the becoming of an actual entity is only effected in and through prehensions, argues Whitehead, we can say that the essence of this entity is that it is a prehending thing. Yet no prehension is ever anything more than a subordinate element in the entity it helps to create. None of the elements making up an actual entity ever has the same completeness of actuality as this actual entity itself.

According to Whitehead, there is an indefinite number of prehensions. Overlapping, subdividing, and supplementing each other, prehensions can be divided into other prehensions and can be combined with each other in a countless variety of ways. Yet every prehension involves three factors: the subject prehending, the object being prehended, and the 'subjective form', which is the particular way the subject prehends the object. The subjective form is partially determined by its subject, and it is partially determined by the qualitative element in the object prehended, since each pole of a relationship always affects that relationship.[15]

Whitehead divides prehensions into two major species, the positive and the negative. He calls positive prehensions 'feelings', arguing that the positive inclusion or realization of one actual entity in another is the 'feeling' of this subject for the appropriated entity. And once an actual entity has been appropriated by another, it is said to have been 'objectified' by the latter. Objectification is not a complete transfer whereby the objectified actual entity is present in its entirety in the subject that has prehended it, for Whitehead holds that the former entity can also be felt by other actual entities. As opposed to feelings, negative prehensions eliminate data from feeling. Every negative prehension is a definite act of excluding actual entities, or parts of them, from positive exclusion into its subject. As such definite acts, all negative prehensions have subjective forms, no matter how faint, for they can only reject some possibility of objectification in a particular way. It is only this subjective form of rejection that a negative prehension contributes to its subject. This contribution is made through a feeling, for all negative prehensions occur within the process that is each feeling.[16] Whitehead states:

> The negative prehensions have their own subjective forms which they contribute to the process. A feeling bears on itself the scars of its birth; it recollects as a subjective emotion its struggle for existence; it retains the impress of what it might have been, but is not. It is for this reason

14 Alfred North Whitehead, *Science and the Modern World* (London, 1985), pp. 86-9 (Cited below as *SMW*). See also *AI*, 184-5.
15 *PR*, 19, 41, 235; *AI*, 176-7.
16 *PR*, 23-6, 40-2, 221, 340.

that what an actual entity has avoided as a datum for feeling may yet be an important part of its equipment.[17]

All feelings involve negative prehensions, for all objectification involves some exclusion through these definite acts of elimination. And contained as they are within feelings, negative prehensions can be considered subordinate species of prehensions. Whitehead contends that even negative prehensions establish forms of relatedness, no matter how faint and indirect. Through all of its prehensions, every actual entity has a definite bond with every item in the universe. The bond can be that of determinate inclusion or of determinate exclusion. This doctrine of prehensions leads to what Whitehead calls 'The principle of universal relativity'. According to Whitehead:

> The principle of universal relativity directly traverses Aristotle's dictum, 'A substance is not present in a subject'. On the contrary, according to this principle an actual entity is present in other actual entities. In fact if we allow for degrees of relevance, and for negligible relevance, we must say that every actual entity is present in every other actual entity.[18]

An actual entity's process of becoming establishes this universal relatedness as the many things are gathered into the one determinate individual. For this reason, maintains Whitehead, the process of becoming can better be described as a process of 'concrescence'. This term is suitable not only because it is derived from the Latin for 'growing together', but also because the word 'concrete' suggests the idea of complete reality. Each instance of concrescence is itself an actual entity, and in each of these processes there is a succession of phases. In each phase new prehensions arise. Simpler feelings are integrated into more general complex feelings, until at last a concrete unity of feeling is obtained. This concrete unity is the completed actual entity that stands at the end of the process.[19]

Whitehead holds that at every stage the concrescence must be guided by a certain plan aimed at a certain end, and he terms this plan the 'subjective aim' of the actual entity. The subjective aim is the actual entity's 'ideal of itself', the reason why this entity is a determinate process of 'self-creation' aimed at the attainment of this same ideal. Similar to the 'entelechy' of Leibniz, the subjective aim is the 'subjective determinant' of the subjective forms of those prehensions that make up the subject's act of becoming. These prehensions 'physically clothe' the subjective aim. Not only determining how the concrescence will proceed, but also how it will terminate, the subjective aim is the final cause of the concrescence and of its component

---

17 *PR*, 226-7.
18 *PR*, 50. The idea of universal relativity would seem to depend on the existence of purely external 'weak' relations. Yet Whitehead never allows such accidental relations into the microscopic world of actual entities, though it can be argued that the notions of degrees of relevance and negligible relevance are accidental relations by other names.
19 *AI*, 236; *PR*, 26, 211-12, 237, 283.

feelings. Present in every phase and feeling of the concrescence, the subjective aim is not itself divisible into phases. It is the reason why every prehension is not merely 'concerned' with its subject at any one intermediary stage, but with its subject as it will be in its final, complete form.[20]

How do these atomic subjects make up the macroscopic world? In answering this question Whitehead characterizes every actual entity as a spatially extensive 'region' and temporally extensive 'epochal duration'.[21] The succession of these epochal durations constitutes the continuous world of appearance. Yet this 'epochal' theory of time is qualified by Whitehead. He argues that if every actual entity's concrescence is temporally extensive, it must be divisible into temporally separate sections which are themselves acts of becoming. But how can these separate acts constitute the one unitary individual? Whitehead sees the problem in the following way:

> Consider, for example, an act of becoming during one second. The act is divisible into two acts, one during the earlier half of the second, the other during the latter half of the second. Thus that which becomes during the whole second presupposes that which becomes during the first-second. Analogously, that which becomes during the first half-second presupposes that which becomes during the first quarter-second, and so on indefinitely. Thus if we consider the process of becoming up to the beginning of the second in question and ask what then becomes, no answer can be given, For, whatever creature we indicate presupposes an earlier creature which became after the beginning of the second and antecedently to the indicated creature. Therefore there is nothing which becomes, so as to effect a transition to the second in question.[22]

Whitehead seeks to overcome this difficulty by distinguishing between a 'complete' and a 'becoming' actual entity. Now according to the above argument, we can divide a concrescence into temporally separate sections, thus splitting the subjective aim. But this aim is in reality indivisible, so either the argument that extensiveness is divisible is incorrect, or else the concrescence is not after all extensive in itself. Whitehead adopts the latter position, maintaining that the concrescence is not in physical time. But he proceeds to argue that the non-extensiveness of an act of becoming does not preclude the constitution by that act of something that is temporally extensive. Whitehead's conclusion, then, is that a completed actual entity is extensive, but that the concrescence instantiating it is not extensive.[23]

The completion of an actual entity is called the 'satisfaction' of that entity. A satisfied actual entity is a fully determinate individual that briefly attains separation from other things, having drawn that which it has prehended

20 *PR*, 67-85, 235, 227, 283.
21 *PR*, 283, *SMW*, 158.
22 *PR*, 68,
23 *PR*, 35, 69, 283.

'into itself'. In this particular moment it stands out for itself alone as an absolute individual fact incapable of change or addition. Considered precisely as such an individual fact, Whitehead states, the satisfaction can be morphologically described as a 'spatialized' unit actuated by its own substantial form. Whitehead maintains that the notion of a static individual fact is nevertheless an abstraction, for being cannot be separated from becoming. In so far as the final settled individuality of a satisfaction is the concrete outcome of a process separated from the process itself, it does not enjoy the actuality of an actual entity, which is both process and outcome together. Because every act of becoming 'presupposes' its conclusion, Whitehead argues, the formal, substantial reality of an actual entity is more correctly attributable to the concrescence rather than to the satisfaction.[24] Once it attains satisfaction, an actual entity is itself prehended by other actual entities superseding it. This breaking-up of the actual entity is its 'perishing'. But perishing is also the initiation of becoming, for what has lost subjectivity becomes an object for new actual entities which, when complete, will become objects in turn. And because the parts of the various actual entities are perpetuated through successive objectifications, states Whitehead, these entities, as objects, enjoy a certain 'immortality'. For this reason every actual entity is regarded by Whitehead as a 'superject' as well as a subject, for having itself become, it reaches beyond itself in contributing to new acts of becoming. He goes on to argue that the word 'subject' should always be construed as an abbreviation of 'subject-superject', for only the latter description can bring out the final contrast between the 'organic' and 'subject–predicate' approaches.[25]

III

It will now be evident that the validity of Whitehead's organic philosophy as an alternative to an Aristotelian 'substance' philosophy involves three major claims. The first is that the subject–predicate approach is not applicable or correlative to the 'organic' notion of real relations. The second is that the idea of a concrescence aimed at producing a subject-superject overcomes the notion that a substance cannot be present in a subject. The third claim is that the notion of non-extensive becoming as the 'most real' part of an actual entity's 'life' overcomes the idea of static enduring substances which remain numerically one amidst accidental changes of quality and relation.

Concerning the 'subject–predicate' issue, it can first be remarked that Aristotle did not regard the definition of substance as that which is not asserted of a subject as an adequate description. And he could have argued that to say that a thing is not present in a subject is not to say that this thing can exist independently, but only that it is not itself a quality, a universal, or

24 *PR*, 154, 219-220, 84; *AI*, 274-5.
25 *PR*, 29, 81-5, 222, 245, 285.

a relation.[26] Aristotle would agree with Whitehead that abstract qualities cannot unveil a thing's essence, for he states that an inquiry into the 'whatness' of a substance cannot be analysed into or answered through a subject-attribute expression. The definiteness of a substance is due to form, and the fundamental matter-form relation constituting a physical substance cannot be captured in a subject-predicate sentence or subject-attribute relation.[27] Apart from these remarks, however, our central purpose is not so much to defend Aristotle as to establish a similarity between the Aristotelian and Whiteheadian descriptions of substantial relations. This should show that the subject-predicate approach is in any case no more applicable to Aristotle's description than to Whitehead's. Concerning substantial relations Aristotle states, in the *Metaphysics*, that no substance is composed of substances. But as Leclerc has noted, this statement is carefully qualified. Aristotle writes:

> Substance cannot consist of substances actually present in it; for that which is actually two can never be actually one, whereas if it is potentially two it can be one.[28]

In his work on generation, Aristotle argues that things can combine in two ways. The first involves a combination of ingredients in a compound such that these ingredients retain their own separate existence. The second way involves a blending or mixing of ingredients where these lose their separate existence. They no longer exist in the same way as they did before they are introduced into this mixture, yet they do not cease to exist. According to Aristotle:

> Since, however, some things have a potential, and other things an actual, existence, it is possible for things which combine in a mixture to 'be' in one sense and 'not-be' in another, the resulting compound formed from them being actually something different but each ingredient being still potentially what it was before they were mixed and not destroyed. (This is the difficulty which arose in our earlier argument, and it is clear that the ingredients of a mixture first came together after having been separate and can be separated again).[29]

A substance cannot be present in another because it cannot be present in its full reality. But it can be potentially present, and this is what Aristotle means when he says that what is potentially two can be one. What was once a separate entity is changed by its presence in a compound, having been

26   Aristotle, *Metaphysics*, trans. Hugh Tredennick (in two volumes: Cambridge, Mass., 1933, 1935), 1029a 10-30 (cited below as *Met.*). See also Alison Johnson, *Whitehead's Theory of Reality* (New York, 1962), p. 245.
27   *Met.*, 1041b1-30.
28   *Met.*, 1039a3-6. See also *Met.*, 1041a4-5 and Ivor Leclerc, *The Nature of Physical Existence* (London, 1972), p. 304.
29   Aristotle, *On Coming-to-Be and Passing Away*, trans. Eric Forster (Cambridge, Mass., 1955), 327b 22-34 (cited below as *De Gen.*).

deprived (even if only temporarily) of the full reality constituting it as a substance. The compound itself is not a mere aggregate of potential substances, for as Aristotle states this compound is actually something different, being one unitary individual, or in other words, an actual substance. Aristotle extends this description to cover our immediate world. The elements, the most basic substances, are all generated from each other. Thus the fundamental constituents of our sublunary world contain each other potentially, and this potentiality is actualized when one of these elements is generated by transmutation from another.[30] By virtue of their material 'content', there will also be a certain continuity between more complex entities and organisms. Because of pre-existing 'informed' matter, the coming-to-be of one thing is always another's passing away, and vice-versa. Aristotle remarks that it is a peculiarity of substance that some other substance must precede it, and, in point of time, we must hold that one actuality presupposes another, right back to the prime mover in each case.[31] Let us now consider Whitehead's notion of substantial relatedness so as to ascertain whether this form of relatedness is that of fully actual entities being present in other fully actual entities. We have noted that, according to Whitehead, the being of an actual entity cannot be separated from its becoming. Furthermore, the satisfaction does not enjoy the full actuality of an actual entity, whose substantial reality is more properly attributable to its concrescence. In this context it is interesting to consider the notion of objectification. That which is objectified is a satisfied occasion whose concrescence is worn out and completed. But if this is the case, the datum for objectification does not have the full reality it possessed when it was itself a subject. No longer becoming, the objectified entity cannot be said to be present in its full actuality in the new subject. It could of course be argued that part of the objectified entity's original subjective aim was to be a superject contributing to new becomings. Yet this is only part of its original aim, which after all aimed at a fully actual individual subject as well as at a superject. It is now no longer a subject—having perished, it is only an object. What now emerges is a considerable similarity between the Whiteheadian and Aristotelian notions of being present in a subject. For Aristotle a substance is not present in a subject in its full actuality because it no longer has this actuality for itself, only being a potential substance. For Whitehead, also, a substance is not present fully actually in a subject, for the former's only remaining aim is to contribute to the latter. It is only a component helping to make up a prehending subject, and this subject takes precedence over its objects. One wonders whether this description constitutes any real advance on that of Aristotle, in spite of the important differences between the two. An Aristotelian potential substance present in a subject is just that, an entity with the potential to exist again in its full actuality. An

30 Aristotle, *On the Heavens*, trans. William Guthrie (Cambridge, Mass., 1939), 305a32, 305b28-30.
31 *De Gen.*, 319a20-3; *Met.*,1034b15-20, 1050b3-5.

objectified actual entity, on the other hand, is only partially present in its subject, for objectification is not a complete transfer. And the objectified entity is not a potential substance. Having perished, it can never regain its subjectivity.

We now turn to Whitehead's final claim, that his theory of becoming overcomes the idea of enduring substances remaining numerically one underneath the surface-play of accidents. Now we can provisionally accept Whitehead's argument that the divisibility of an act of becoming into temporally separate sections is irreconcilable with the idea that, in a becoming, something becomes. This involves rejecting Aristotle's distinction between potential divisibility and actual division. But once we accept Whitehead's argument, the question arises as to how we are to conceive of the White-headian becoming. If such an act is not in physical time and is not even potentially divisible, we can only conceive of it as instantaneous. Our next question is whether this fits in with the overall doctrine of concrescence. Here we meet our first difficulty, for, as Chappell has noted, Whitehead's description of the internal development of a concrescence is couched in terms that effectively presuppose temporal extendedness.[32] Whitehead speaks of every act of becoming as involving a succession of phases in each of which new prehensions arise. He also states that the simpler feelings in the first phase of a concrescence are followed by subsequent integrations uniting them into more general complex feelings, culminating in a concrete unity of feeling, the satisfaction. With regard to the above description, Whitehead might argue that the real difficulty lies in the limitations of language, explaining the suggestions of temporal extendedness as linguistic abstractions thrown up in the attempt to describe the developing concrescence. But it could be argued in the same way that the idea of instantaneous becoming is itself a linguistic or theoretical abstraction. Were we able to analyse an actual entity, says Whitehead, we could only do so through the satisfaction, for an actual entity can only be felt in passage as one epochal duration. Further-more, such analysis would not reveal the growth of an actual entity's features—including that of temporal extensiveness—but only features of an already completed growth.[33] This being the case, it cannot be shown how the instantaneous is productive of the extensive. Nor has Whitehead shown how the instantaneous can be distinguished from the extensive. If the concrescence leaves us with an entity enjoying a certain quantum of time, then there can be no temporal lapse between the beginning of the concres-cence and the beginning of the satisfaction. The beginning of the extensive quantum will be indistinguishable from the beginning of its becoming. Whilst Whitehead might retort that the beginning of the becoming is simultaneously its end, this cannot be meaningfully understood within the

32 Victor Chappell, 'Whitehead's Theory of Becoming', in George Kline (ed.), *Alfred North Whitehead: Essays on his Philosophy* (New Jersey, 1963), p. 74.
33 *PR*, 227, 283.

context of a becoming that appears intrinsically incapable of analysis either in itself or from the perspective of its extensive product. And Whitehead only admits the notion of an extensive product to save the individuality of actual entities. If every becoming were immediately to change into a perishing it could not then constitute a proper unified individual. But again it has to be asked whether this solution is one that improves on Aristotle's description. According to Aristotle neither growth nor decay nor generation nor corruption can go on perpetually, there always being an unchanging something coming between them. This something need not be numerically one, for all things formally one need not be numerically one, although all things which are numerically one are formally one.[34] In addition, this something which 'comes between' is never regarded by Aristotle as something static:

> The term 'actuality' with its implications of 'complete reality' has been extended from motions, to which it properly belongs, to other things; for it is agreed that actuality is properly motion.[35]

A fully actual substance exists as an activity which is its own end in itself. Aristotle sees this as analogous to the example of teachers who consider that they have achieved their ends when they see their pupils actually performing, actuality having the meaning of complete reality. He is careful to distinguish motion as 'actuality' from motion as 'change'. The latter is incomplete, being only a means to an end. But the important point for Aristotle is that both actuality and change are processes.[36] It can be seen that Aristotle's description of a complete substance is not after all so very different from Whitehead's description of a satisfied actual entity. Both are fully actual centres of activity, the one characterized as ἐνέργεια, the other as a fully determinate 'feeling'. Whitehead diverges from Aristotle in attributing the full reality of an actual entity to its concrescence rather than to its satisfaction. Yet this does not amount to much more than a shift of emphasis within a broadly Aristotelian framework.

Having attempted to establish the close similarity between certain Aristotelian and Whiteheadian notions, it only remains for us to indicate the specific limitations of this study. We have not so much attempted to criticize Whitehead's system as to bring out his unconscious utilization of Aristotle's explanations of substantial relatedness and endurance in our immediate world. Such repetition prevents the organic philosophy from being a real

34 Aristotle, *Physics*, trans. Philip Wicksteed and Francis Cornford (in two volumes: Cambridge, Mass., 1929, 1934), 253b10–15; *Met.* 1068b6–10, 1016b35.
35 *Met.*, 1047a30–3.
36 *Met.*, 1050a18–23, 1048b19–35. From this general perspective an Aristotelian could argue that, within Whitehead's scheme, a satisfied actual entity is in fact more real than a concrescing actual entity, for the latter has not attained its final integral reality as a determinate act of feeling.

alternative to that of Aristotle, although this need not involve denying the important differences between the two systems. An outline of these differences, however, would require a far more extended work than has been here undertaken. The obvious conclusion that can be drawn from our study is that of a certain lack of familiarity on Whitehead's part with Aristotle's general understanding of our sublunary world. Whitehead may also have been relatively unfamiliar with Aristotle's understanding of the heavenly realm. God, the intelligences moving the spheres, and the ether permeating the heavens are all ideas of substance that Whitehead could more rightly criticize. None of these relate concretely to our immediate world, and they all exist eternally and unchangeably. Yet Whitehead only criticizes one of these notions briefly and indirectly, stating that Aristotle's Prime Mover is suggestive of an erroneous physics and cosmology.[37] Thus, in the main, Whitehead's critique focuses on the physical, temporal substances of our immediate world. And it is here, we have submitted, that Aristotle is least susceptible to this critique and closest to the philosophy or organism.

37   *SMW*, 216.

The Gift of Being

Heidegger and Aquinas

FRAN O'ROURKE

Nothing was happening except his being. Being was enough, it was the worship of God.

Patrick Kavanagh, *Tarry Flynn*.

I felt, as I listened, that the world was recovering its pristine freshness. All the dulled things regained the brightness they had in the beginning, when we came out of the hands of God. Water, women, the stars, bread, returned to their mysterious, primitive origin and the divine whirlwind burst once more upon the air.

Nikos Kazantzakis, *Zorba the Greek*.

The phrase 'gift of being' suggests a twofold motif. Initially and most immediately, it expresses being as it is offered to our experience. Being is given to us in every engagement and involvement with the world. A primary question in philosophy concerns the nature of this encounter. Being is in every sense the primordial datum. What does this mean? What is that which is given—what is the role of the receiver? Such is the question of cognition as raised in epistemology. A yet more fundamental meaning of the term 'gift', however, raises the most radical of all possible questions: What is the source of that which is given? Does not the given, as gift, require a giver? And why, ultimately, is there such a gift?

It would be foolhardy in a brief article to seek a comprehensive response to these most fundamental of questions, which are so simply raised merely upon linguistic reflection. Here I wish to put forward some few comments relevant to the theme, focusing upon the contrasting and complementary perspectives of Thomas Aquinas and Martin Heidegger on the occurrence of being and its presentation to man; being as it is given in our knowledge and as a reality given in and to itself. The possibility of dealing adequately with the latter, more profound, question relies upon the approach adopted with regard to the first.[1]

---

1 Many valuable studies have been written on Heidegger and Aquinas. In addition to those mentioned in footnotes, I gratefully acknowledge my debt to the following: Bertrand Rioux, *L'être et la verité chez Heidegger et saint Thomas d'Aquin* (Paris, 1963); Raúl Echauri, *Heidegger y la metafísica tomista* (Buenos Aires, 1970); Johannes B. Lotz, *Martin Heidegger und Thomas von Aquin* (Pfullingen, 1975) and *Vom Sein zum Heiligen. Metaphysisches Denken nach Heidegger* (Frankfurt, 1990); Jozef Van de Wiele, *Zijnswaarheid en Onverborgenheid. Vergelijkende studie over de ontologische waarheid in het thomisme en bij Heidegger* (Leuven, 1964);

The status of Aquinas as one of the most original thinkers of all time is beyond dispute. In philosophy of being, he successfully exercised his skill at synthesizing and deepening the insights deriving from the many tributaries of tradition which he inherited. His vision however was novel in much and profound throughout. Time alone will determine the place merited by Martin Heidegger in the history of philosophy. From his early major work *Being and Time* to the lecture 'Time and Being' he has played the role of a giant, to use the image he has borrowed from Plato, in awakening again an interest in the question of Being at a time when it had fallen into disuse. The question of Being is the most significant to which the mind can rise in speculation and the most profound facing each one in the challenge of personal destiny. Heidegger has recalled it vividly at a time when it had been long forgotten, emphasizing that for things 'to be' does not signify the same as what they are. This is the error of essentialism which dominated metaphysics for centuries. There are those who would claim, however, that the question of being was not only posed by Aquinas centuries earlier, but brought to light in a way which, unknown to Heidegger, responds to his call for a mode of thinking which goes beyond that-which-is to an original thinking of what it means *to be*.

For Heidegger, the question of all questions is the search for the meaning of Being. Today the question has fallen into oblivion. What remained hidden in mystery to the thinkers and poets of old has assumed, it seems, a clarity which renders all questioning of its nature unnecessary. Yet the mystery remains. 'We are familiar with beings—but Being? Are we not overcome with dizziness when we try to determine it or even grasp it in itself? Is not Being in some way similar to Nothing?'[2] Aristotle remarks: 'Like the eyes of bats in the light of day, so it is with our vision towards those things which are by their nature most apparent of all.'[3] Most apparent of all is the very Being of beings, and yet faced with the question of Being we approach the borders of complete darkness.[4] Plato notes that the question of Being arises when we become perplexed with the meaning of the word 'being', which we formerly thought we had understood.[5] Although we lack a clear concept, nevertheless we have, according to Heidegger, a vague and average understanding of Being (*SZ*, 5). Our search is thus guided by what is sought. We do not *know* what 'Being' means; yet in asking 'what is Being?', we are already in an understanding of the 'is', which, although not grasped conceptually, lies within our question.

John D. Caputo, *Heidegger and Aquinas. An Essay on Overcoming Metaphysics* (New York, 1982). I am also greatly indebted to the published articles and unpublished writings of Desmond Connell.

2   *Kant und das Problem der Metaphysik*, p. 204 (*KM*).
3   *Metaph.* 993b, 9–11.
4   *Was heißt Denken?* (Tübingen, 1971) p. 47 (*WD*); *KM*, 204.
5   *Sophist* 244a; quoted by Heidegger, *Sein und Zeit* (Tübingen, 1967), p. 1 (*SZ*).

This pre-reflective awareness, indeterminate yet constant and far-reaching, is so primitive that it cannot itself be called into question. Were it not for this 'preontological understanding of Being' (*SZ*, 15) man could not be the unique being he is, however wonderful his other abilities (*KM*, 205). This primitive awareness belongs ultimately to the essential constitution of man's existence and makes the question of Being both possible and necessary. 'Man alone of all beings, summoned by the voice of Being, experiences the wonder of all wonders: that beings are.'⁶ Man alone can ask: 'Why are there beings rather than nothing?' (*WM*, 42) But in this question lies an even more original one: What is the meaning of Being which is already understood in this question? (*KM*, 201)

The oblivion of Being, Heidegger explains, is a neglect of the difference between Being and beings, i.e. of the 'ontological difference'. In order to think Being once more, it is necessary to pass beyond metaphysics and return both to the element of thinking from which it rises and to the dawn of western thought in which the true nature of Being was first glimpsed. Dwelling upon Descartes' image of philosophy as a tree, the roots of which are metaphysics, its trunk physics, and the branches all the other sciences, Heidegger asks: 'In what soil do the roots of the tree of philosophy have their hold?' (*WM*, 7) Metaphysics has strayed from the origins of true thinking and lost its hold in the authentic element of thought. There is needed, therefore, an 'overcoming' of metaphysics, a return both to the historical beginning of early thinking and to the abiding realm where man is mindful of what is truly worthy of thought: Being itself (*WM*, 9).

THE GIFT OF THOUGHT

Heidegger's best statement of what he considers the true nature of thinking is perhaps a course of lectures given in 1952 under the title *What is Called Thinking? (Was heißt Denken?)*. The word for thought is derived, he tells us, from *Gedanc*, which originally signified 'the gathered and all-gathering thinking that recalls' (*WD*, 92). It is man's primal orientation of heart and spirit, his innermost nature which reaches towards the utmost limits of everything that is. In its origin, Heidegger claims, the word expresses moreover the essence of memory and thanks which lie close to the meaning of the verb 'to think'. 'Thought signifies: memory, meditation, gratitude.'⁷

The thinking that recalls in memory is the original thanks; for in giving thanks, the heart recalls in thought where it belongs (*WD*, 158). Memory, Heidegger suggests, means much more than the power to recall. It is man's entire disposition in intimate and steadfast recollection of the things which

6   *Was ist Metapysik* (Frankfurt, 1969), pp. 46–7 (*WM*).
7   *WD* 149: 'Gedanc bedeutet: Gedächtnis, Andenken, Dank.'

speak essentially in thoughtful meditation. Memory is originally the same as devotion (*WD*, 92). It carries a special tone of piety and prayer because it signifies the essential relation of recollection to what is 'holy and graceful' (*WD*, 158: *das Heile und Huldvolle*). Memory is the constant and attentive abiding in thought of everything which is present to the heart. Heidegger understands 'thought' as the inclination of the heart in its deepest meditation upon things. Understood in its original meaning, memory signifies the same as thanks. 'In giving thanks the heart gives thought to what it has and what it is' (*WD*, 93). The heart is, as it were, enthralled—not in submission, but in a devotion in which it hearkens to the realm where it originally belongs.

It is appropriate that we give thanks for the things we receive. 'Original thanking is the thanks for oneself' (*WD*, 93). That for which we first and always owe gratitude is our essential nature, which Heidegger asserts is thinking itself: 'In it resides the real endowment of our nature for which we owe thanks.' We give thanks for thinking by devoting ourselves to what of itself is most worthy of thought. In thinking what is most worthy of thought we think, and thereby thank, authentically. Heidegger tells us such thanksgiving is not a recompense, but remains rather an offering through which we allow what gives itself for thought to remain in its essential nature (*WD*, 158).

From Parmenides he discovers that the essence of thinking is determined by what is to be thought: ἐὸν ἔμμεναι—the Presence of what is present, the Being of beings. Thinking is truly thinking only when it recalls ἐόν, the duality of beings and Being. This is what is truly given for thought. What is so given is for Heidegger the gift of what is most worthy of question, and thus most needful of the thought of man (*WD*, 149).

In his *Introduction to Metaphysics* (1935) Heidegger had declared that man was the place needed by Being in order to reveal itself.[8] In *Letter on Humanism* (1947) Heidegger understands man as 'thrown' into the 'clearing' where he guards the truth of Being so that beings may reveal themselves in the light of Being.[9] The standing in the 'clearing' or lighting-process of Being, Heidegger now calls the 'ex-sistence' (*Ek-sistenz*) of man (*BH*, 66–7). The clearing itself, however, is Being. Ex-sistence is simply 'the place of the truth of Being in the midst of beings' (77). In ex-sistence lies the nature of man as guardian of Being, so much so that Heidegger declares: 'the essence of man is essential for the truth of Being.'[10] However, this does not signify that human thought is the ground for the Presence of Being, but rather indicates the essential 'belonging together' of Being and man.

8   *Einführung in die Metaphysik* (Tübingen, 1966), p. 156: 'Das Wesen des Menschen ist innerhalb der Seinsfrage gemäß der verborgenen Anweisung des Anfangs als die Stätte zu begreifen und zu begründen, die sich das Sein zur Eröffnung ernötigt' (*EM*).

9   *Platons Lehre von der Wahrheit. Mit einem Brief über den Humanismus* (Bern, 1954), p. 75: 'Der Mensch ist vielmehr vom Sein selbst in die Wahrheit des Seins 'geworfen', daß er, dergestalt ek-sistierend, die Wahrheit des Seins hüte, damit im Lichte des Seins das Seiende als das Seiende, das es ist, erscheine' (*BH*).

10 *BH*, 94: '…das Wesen des Menschen ist für die Wahrheit des Seins wesentlich.'

As one who thinks, man is open to Being. He is related to Being and so answers to it. Indeed, for Heidegger, 'man is essentially this relationship of responding [to Being], and this alone.'[11] Thought perfects the relation between man and Being. It does not make or produce this relation but offers it to Being as what has been given over to itself by Being (*BH*, 53). Thought allows itself to be called into the service of Being in order to speak its truth. Thought is in a twofold manner the thought of Being. Evoked by Being, thought belongs to Being (*gehört*), and in belonging also attends to it in hearing (*hört*) (*BH*, 56).

In authentic thought human existence dwells in nearness to Being: 'Man is the neighbour of Being.'[12] For the most part, however, he overlooks what is closest and clings to what is next removed. Nearer, however, than the nearest of things, yet more distant to ordinary thought than the farthest thing of all, says Heidegger, is nearness itself, i.e. the truth of Being (*BH*, 77). 'Being is farther than everything that is, yet nearer to man than every being, be it a rock, an animal, work of art or machine; be it an angel or God. Being is nearest of all. Yet its nearness remains what is most distant from man. He relates always and first of all only to beings' (*BH*, 76). The concerns of man are with the things which lie at hand. He has lost his call to think in a thankful way the truth of Being. Being still awaits to become worthy of thought (*BH*, 65). Heidegger expresses man's vocation: 'Man is not the lord of beings. Man is the shepherd of Being.'[13] He can never be the master but at best the servant of Being. His first service is to give thought and heed to the Being of beings (*WD*, 142).

The task of thought is to recover its roots in the ground of Being; take it into its care, receive its message and attend to its call. Thus alone will man find true 'autochthony' or self-rootedness and dwell once more in nearness to Being. How is this achieved? 'The way to what is near', says Heidegger, 'is always the longest, and thus the hardest for us humans. This way is the way of meditative thinking.'[14] Meditative thinking is the opposite of calculative thinking, which is characteristic of modern science and technology. More significantly, it has been the way of philosophy in its search for Being since early times—when the original Greek experience of truth as attunement to the revelation of Being (ἀλήθεια) gave way to conformity and correctness of ideas (heralded by Plato, and canonized in Aristotle's words: 'Falsity and truth are found, not in things themselves . . . but in the understanding.')[15] With the division in experience between subject and object, truth was sought as certitude, and the mysterious presence of Being was lost. Calculation is

11 *Identität und Differenz* (Pfullingen, 1957), p. 18: 'Der Mensch ist eigentlich dieser Bezug der Entsprechung, und er ist nur dies' (*ID*).
12 *BH*, 90: 'Der Mensch ist der Nachbar des Seins.'
13 *BH*, 90: 'Der Mensch ist nicht der Herr des Seienden. Der Mensch ist der Hirt des Seins.'
14 *Gelassenheit* (Pfullingen, 1959), pp. 21-2 (*G*).
15 *Metaph.* E, 4, 1027b, 25ff.

concerned instead with the correctness and objectivity of representative predication—attained in judgments by which man assumes power and control over the things which are. Being in itself, however, is given only in a pre-predicative experience.

That which from the beginning is closed to calculation, and yet in its mystery is closer than every being, attunes man in his essence to a truth which logic cannot grasp. Determined by what is totally 'Other' than beings, Heidegger calls such thinking 'meditative' or 'essential' (*WM*, 48–9). 'Essential thinking looks to the slow signs of the incalculable and sees in this the unthought arrival of the ineluctable' (*WM*, 50). Obedient to the truth of Being, such thought helps Being find a place in the history of man. It is an occurrence of Being itself (*WM*, 47). Rather than reckon with beings, it is devoted to the truth of Being and answers the call in which Being claims man for itself.

Heidegger understands man's response to Being as a kind of 'sacrifice' or 'offering': 'In this offering is expressed the hidden thanking which alone does homage to the grace with which Being has endowed the nature of man with thought in order that he may take over . . . the guardianship of Being' (*WM*, 49). How is such thinking to be achieved? According to Heidegger, 'it is enough if we dwell on what lies near and meditate upon what is closest' (*G*, 14). However, this does not imply that such thought happens by itself, any more than does calculation. It requires at times an even greater effort. It needs care and vigilance. Yet, it must also be able to bide its time, to wait and hope as does the farmer, that the seed will come up and ripen (*G*, 13).

Meditative thinking requires what Heidegger calls: 'releasement toward things' and 'openness to the mystery' (*G*, 24–5). In this way we will approach the things of the world, yet remain free in our relation with them. We 'let them rest in themselves as something which is not our most inward and proper concern . . . as things which are nothing absolute, but themselves depend on something higher' (*G*. 22–3). Our relation to the world, says Heidegger, will thus become wonderfully relaxed and simple. We remain open to the hidden mystery of things which everywhere touches us deeply, yet reveals itself only in withdrawing.

Being cannot be grasped in thought. It eludes every effort to lay hold of it: 'We never come to thoughts. They come to us.'[16] Heidegger says hopefully: 'We must do nothing . . . but wait' (*ED*, 35). In releasement we remain open for what is granted as a gift. We do not wait for anything, but leave open what we are awaiting. Knowledge occurs within an open horizon into which thoughts emerge. In this way we achieve the original truth of beings as they unfold within their Being. Things truly reveal themselves, according to Heidegger, under the vigilance of mortals. 'The first step toward such vigilance is that away from thinking that merely represents—that is, he explains—to the thinking that responds and recalls.'[17]

16   *Aus der Erfahrung des Denkens* (Pfullingen, 1954), p. 11 (*ED*).
17   *Vorträge und Aufsätze* II (Pfullingen, 1967), p. 54.

POETRY AND THOUGHT

As a unique example of original thinking and utterance, Heidegger points to poetry. He writes: 'Poetry may serve as an excellent example of a non-objectifying thinking and saying.'[18] But this conceals at first the difficulty of the relationship between thought and poetry as understood by Heidegger. For he sees them as both intimately related, yet essentially distinct in nature and role. Poetry is not just another way of thinking, but a unique and creative way of knowing. The exact relation between them Heidegger leaves unclear, although he gives an indication: 'Considered from the point of view of the essence of Being, it remains undecided how poetry, thanking and thinking are related to one another and yet distinct. Presumably, thanking and poetry arise in different ways from fundamental thought, which they require, although unable in themselves to be thought.'(*WM*, 51)

A line from Hölderlin hints at the fundamental value of poetic thought: 'Full of merit, yet poetically dwells man on this earth.'[19] Although man 'merits' much while 'dwelling on the earth', such merit never reaches the foundation of human existence. This is a gift the origin of which poetry alone can reveal. In this sense human existence 'is fundamentally poetic'. 'In poetry—says Heidegger—man is reunited on the foundation of his existence. There he comes to rest, not indeed to the seeming rest of inactivity and emptiness of thought, but to that infinite state of rest in which all powers and relations are active' (*HD*, 45). To 'dwell poetically' is, according to Heidegger, 'to stand in the presence of the divine and be touched by the nearness of the essence of things' (*HD*, 42).

Poetry and thought are primarily alike in their meditative nature. Opposed to calculative thinking, which dominates beings as objects, poetry and thought are open to what is essential. Heidegger writes: 'Obedient to the Voice of Being, thought seeks the Word which will utter the truth of Being . . . Out of long-guarded speechlessness and the careful clearing of the domain thus illumined, comes the utterance of the thinker. Of like origin is the naming of the poet.' But while poetry and thinking are most alike in their care of the word, they are 'at the same time remotely distant in their essence. The thinker utters Being. The poet names what is holy' (*WM*, 50–1).

The exact relation between Being and the Holy is not explained by Heidegger. Many commentators suggest they are in fact the same, but viewed from different aspects.[20] Richardson asks if we may infer 'that the

18 *Phänomenologie und Theologie* (Frankfurt, 1970), p. 47.
19 'Voll Verdienst, doch dichterisch wohnet / Der Mensch auf dieser Erde.' See *Erläuterungen zu Hölderlins Dichtung* (Frankfurt, 1971), p. 33 (*HD*).
20 J. B. Lotz writes: 'The "Holy" signifies poetically the same domain as that presented to thought as "Being". In each it is the final, total realm, and the supporting ground of all beings which is not itself a being, but also not nothing'. *Sein und Existenz* (Freiburg, 1965), p. 184. Richardson remarks: 'The most striking designation of Being, and one that

Holy designates Being in its positivity, while Being as such comports both
positivity and negativity, revealment and concealment in the coming-to-pass
of a-letheia'.[21] Heidegger nowhere gives so explicit a formulation, merely
hinting at its characteristics in his commentaries on Hölderlin. Heidegger
feels a profound kinship with this great Romantic. In an age when the gods
have 'withdrawn' because of a lack of piety, the poet stands between men
and gods, waiting to utter for his fellow mortals what he discovers as holy.
And the philosopher, recognizing the oblivion of Being, and the blindness of
men to its mystery in the face of beings, urges them to meditate upon the
wonder of wonders: that Being is. Each shares a piety or humility in the
hope of a return to what is essential.

THE QUESTION OF GOD

From the beginning, one of the major questions facing Heidegger's philosophy was his attitude to God. Some argued that his definition of man as
'being-in-the-world' implied an atheist position. But Heidegger rejected all
interpretation of his thought as either theist or atheist—to define man as a
'being in the world' is not to suggest that in a theological or metaphysical
sense, man is merely a being of 'this world' (*bh*, 101). For Heidegger, 'world'
is neither a particular being, nor realm of beings, but much more the 'openness of Being' (*BH*, 100). Man *is*, he claims, in so far as he 'ex-sists' or stands
exposed to the openness of Being. The definition of man as 'ex-sistence',
therefore, gives no decision about the existence or non-existence of God.

Heidegger wrote in 1929: 'The ontological interpretation of *Dasein*
[(human) existence] as Being-in-the-world tells neither for nor against the
possible existence of God. One must first gain an adequate concept of *Dasein*
by illuminating transcendence. Then, by considering *Dasein*, one can ask
how the relationship of *Dasein* to God is ontologically constituted.'[22] For
Heidegger, transcendence is man's relation of openness to the entirety of
Being. Only when the truth of Being has been explored, and man's relation
to Being made clear, does even the *question* of God have significance. The
aspect under which God is meaningful, however, is not Being itself, but 'the
Holy', which stands, nevertheless, in relation with Being: 'Only from the
truth of Being can the essence of the Holy—the domain or presence of
divinity—be thought. Only in the light of the essence of divinity, can it be
thought and said what the word 'God' signifies' (*BH*, 102, 85–6).

---

will pervade the author's entire analysis of poetry, appears when with Hölderlin
   Heidegger calls it the "Holy"'. William Richardson, S. J., *Heidegger Through Phenomenology to Thought* (The Hague, 1963), p. 426.
21 Ibid., 544.
22 *Vom Wesen des Grundes* (Frankfurt, 1965), p. 39; trans. *The Essence of Reasons*, Terrence
   Malick (Evanston, 1969), p. 91.

What are Heidegger's objections to the philosophical arguments for God's existence? From the beginning, Heidegger rejected all efforts to affirm God by metaphysical reflection. In an early course of lectures on 'Augustine and Neoplatonism', we are told, 'Heidegger followed Luther in taking up an extreme anti-metaphysical position', claiming that original religious experience is perverted when conceptualized by metaphysical ideas.[23] According to Heidegger, thought can respond neither negatively nor affirmatively to the question of God's existence. It can no more be theist than atheist. This, however, is not because of any attitude of indifference, but 'out of respect for the limits which have been set upon thought as thought, precisely by what is to be thought, namely, the truth of Being' (*BH*, 103). Heidegger's conclusion is that the task of thought is to seek the meaning of Being. The region of the divine is quite distinct, and cannot be attained by reflection, although any approach is possible only from a nearness of human thought to Being.[24]

In order to gain a full understanding of what the 'Holy' signifies for Heidegger, we would have to include a detailed account of the Hölderlin commentaries. This, although fascinating in itself, would take us too far afield. Moreover, the matter is by no means clear; all we are offered are indications. Furthermore, we may only proceed on a presumption that Heidegger shares Hölderlin's conception of the Holy. Yet it cannot be expected that Hölderlin's view be altogether philosophical. His poetry is bound up with a unique mythology and constellation of images which have little in common with the thought of Heidegger. The way of interpretation, therefore, is fraught with difficulty.

In the commentary on the poem 'As when upon a day of rest . . . ' (*Wie wenn am Feiertage . . .*),[25] Heidegger meditates upon the Holy as revealed in Nature and mediated by 'the gods'. In the poem 'Homecoming' (*Heimkunft/An die Verwandten*),[26] there is an advance towards a single God, 'the High One' who dwells within the Holy. He is 'the Joyous One', who illumines the spirit of men and opens all things to their proper joy. On his homecoming, the atmosphere of people and things greeting the poet is 'joyous' and 'serene'. Nearer, however, than the joyful serenity of beings 'is

23 J. L. Mehta, *The Philosophy of Martin Heidegger* (New York, 1971), p. 14.
24 Cornelio Fabro summarizes Heidegger's approach to the question of God: 'Heidegger aims at the most radical position beyond all problematic, which may be reduced to the following conditional formula: "Granted that the truth of Being consists in an openness to the self-presentation of the Being of beings, the problem whether or not God exists can only be solved on the basis of the self-presentation of Being itself." It is from an experience therefore that the question must be decided, and not by any conceptual reflection. Is there such an experience? Heidegger accuses the modern age precisely of having forgotten this experience, and declares this to be its greatest error and original evil. It is the experience of the Holy.' *Introduzione all' ateismo moderno* (Rome, 1969), pp. 951–2. See Fabro's *Dall' essere all' esistente* (Brescia, 1957), p. 402.
25 *HD*, 49–77.
26 *HD*, 9–31.

the Serene itself (*das Heitere*), wherein both men and things first appear'. It is in this quality of 'joy and serenity' that the Holy is revealed. 'The Serene', says Heidegger, 'preserves and holds everything in tranquillity and wholeness. The Serene is fundamentally salutary. It is the Holy. For the poet, "the Highest" and the "Holy" are one and the same: the Serene.' (*HD*, 18) The High One 'who inhabits the Serene of the holy' draws near but, says the poet: 'To grasp him, our joy is scarcely large enough.' Hölderlin laments: 'We must often remain silent. Holy names are lacking.' The poet's song thus remains, comments Heidegger, a 'song without words' (*HD*, 27). He gazes into the Serene but cannot find the High One. Hölderlin declares: 'God is near and hard to grasp.' The poet is faced with mystery, and homecoming is precisely to learn to know this—not by unveiling or analysing, but by guarding it as mystery. He exclaims: 'Foolish is my speech. It is joy.' The poet's calling, says Heidegger, 'is to exist in that joy which preserves in word the mystery of proximity to the most Joyous' (*HD*, 24–5).

Although God remains hidden, we may ask: 'What is the nature of God as understood by Heidegger?' The God of Heidegger is clearly not the God of traditional philosophy, i.e. transcendent to beings and identical with Being itself: ' "Being"—that is neither God nor a world-ground. Being is beyond every being, yet nearer to man than each being, be it a rock, an animal, work of art or machine, be it an angel or God' (*BH*, 76). Heidegger seems to favour the divinity of a pagan mythology rather than theism in the traditional sense. God is simply one being within the world and merits no more than any other the full signification of Being. Heidegger does not consider God as transcendent to beings, but as a power immanent in the world.[27]

Heidegger's quest, we saw, is for the meaning of Being. Accusing the western tradition of neglecting Being, Heidegger seeks to recover its significance by recalling the earliest seeds of Greek thought and by urging a meditative thinking which will be open to the mystery of Being. What,

27 J. B. Lotz claims that Heidegger does not in fact even discuss the basic problem of atheism. For him, it is a question, not whether there is a divinity, but whether the divinity which exists approaches man or withdraws from him. The divine appears, therefore, in a mythological form which recalls that of Hölderlin. 'These gods are for Heidegger, as they were once for Hölderlin, not merely human projections but actual powers which as heavenly beings rule over mortals. In them is distilled the Numinous or Holy which belongs essentially to the world-phenomenon. They are the appearance within the world of the divinity, or the divine in so far as it can be attained through phenomenological analysis. All this functions primarily as a pagan substitute for christian theism' (*Sein und Existenz*, p. 109). Cornelio Fabro claims that the appeal to the Holy— which appears with more insistence in the later writings—constitutes perhaps the final word, but also the least concrete, on the foundation of Being.' With an explicit appeal to this 'cosmic and mystical theory of the sacred', Fabro remarks, Heidegger has defended himself against the charge of atheism which had followed that of nihilism: 'A purely formal defence, from which it is difficult to draw any original significance' (*Dall' essere all' esistente*, pp. 381–2). The god of Heidegger, it seems, is the god of poetry and myth rather than of philosophy.

ultimately, for Heidegger is Being?—Being is Itself.[28] Close to the path of thought, and attentive also to what is essential in things, lies, according to Heidegger, that of poetry which, following the trace of the 'Holy', seeks the track of divine being. Heidegger claims that with man's oblivion of Being there occurred also a loss of the divine. Reflecting upon the poetry of Hölderlin he seeks to discover the nature of the Holy, the realm in which the Being of God may be discerned.

AQUINAS AND THE QUESTION OF BEING

In the remaining pages I wish to reflect upon the method and fruits of Heidegger's approach, in the light of Aquinas' attitude to the question of being. Let us return to their common starting point—the primitive notion of being and its significance. For Heidegger, one of the reasons why the question of Being has fallen into oblivion is because it is presumed to be the most universal and emptiest of concepts and as such neither yields to, nor requires definition. According to Heidegger, however, although Being is the most universal concept, it is neither the clearest, nor one which requires no further discussion. It is rather—for this very reason—the most obscure of all. The fact that Being cannot be defined simply signifies that it cannot be grasped by the logic of traditional thinking. This does not relieve us of the search for Being, but calls all the more urgently for it. Being is in some way 'self-evident': in every relation towards beings we have already an understanding of 'Being'. This average understanding, however, remains obscure and reveals that in every relation or way of Being toward beings there lies *a priori* an enigma. The fact that we already dwell within an understanding of Being, and that the meaning of Being is still veiled in darkness, proves that it is necessary in principle to raise again the question of Being.

With much of this Aquinas could only agree; it is implicit in the very phrase cited by Heidegger as one of the prejudices against an adequate inquiry into Being: 'That which first falls within the understanding is being, the notion of which is included in all things, whatsoever anyone apprehends.'[29] Aquinas would concur that, even if 'Being' is the most universal concept, this cannot mean it is the clearest, or that it does not need any further discussion. However, for him it is by no means the most obscure, as

---

28 BH, 76: 'Doch das Sein—was ist das Sein? Es ist Es selbst.'

29 *Summa Theologiae ST*, I–II, 94, 2: Nam illud quod primo cadit in apprehensione, est ens, cuius intellectus includitur in omnibus quaecumque quis apprehendit. As Heidegger notes, being was designated a transcendental concept in medieval ontology. It surpasses the divisions of class and genus. From the point of view of knowledge, this is indicated in the agreement of being with the human spirit; the soul is the unique being whose nature it is to relate to all that is (*De Veritate*, 1, 1: ...aliquid quod natum sit convenire cum omni ente. Hoc autem est anima, quae quodammodo est omnia, sicut dicitur in III de Anima.). The ontological priority of human existence is here suggested but not clarified, according to Heidegger (*SZ*, 14).

Heidegger suggests it is. It is necessary to examine more closely how this concept is attained and what it signifies.

According to Aquinas, the concept of being is born through the first, spontaneous judgment of existence, namely, 'this is', 'something is': *'aliquid est'*. Being is the first known (*primum notum*), precisely because the first evidence is that things are; Being is the first and proper intelligible object, as sound is the first audible object (*ST*, I, 5, 2). The first assertion that can—and must—be made of anything is that it exists. This is for the most part done naturally and unreflectively; implicit in all our assertions is a recognition and acceptance of the existence of that to which we refer. This is the self-evidence of the notion of being of which Heidegger rightly speaks.[30] We must, however, make a distinction between this 'average intelligibility' or clarity of being and the obscurity Heidegger refers to. Even in the experience of something which is dimly perceived, we recognize it as 'something'; we are of necessity compelled to respond: 'it is'. Simultaneously there is brought into play a notion of what it is to be: a concept of being; not a diaphanous insight into the plenitude of reality, but a luminosity or clarity consonant with reality, whereby we grasp something of what it means to be; we recognize the demands of existence. It is the self-evidence of a concept which to us is obscure and confused but has nonetheless the power to illuminate certain fundamental aspects of the world—such as are expressed in the basic and universal laws of reality: if a thing is, then it is itself (principle of identity); in so far as something is, it is impossible for it not to be (non-contradiction);[31] a thing either is or it is not (excluded middle). Fundamentally laws of reality, these principles permeate all our thought, inquiry, discourse, indeed each of our actions. They make explicit the fundamental intelligibility of all things and the coherence and consistency of the universe. They are a guarantee that we can 'trust in being'.

This self-evidence, far from dispensing with the question of being, makes it more mysterious. The concept of being is not transparent in what is signifies. It denotes the sure reality of the thing or object affirmed, but as a subject in itself which transcends our awareness. Being is the primary datum, that which is first given; but it is given as something which is unfathomable in itself—indeed unattainable, since it surpasses all we can ever discover. This perplexity surrounding the elusive nature of what we know but do not comprehend is overwhelmingly greater when we seek to grasp the very existence of things. Indeed as Aquinas remarks, *esse* or 'to be' does not itself exist but is that in virtue of which things are.

Although the judgment 'this exists'—the first assertion that can be made of any thing—may seem banal, even superfluous, it is upon reflection rich in what it discloses regarding the nature of our knowledge and the status of its

30 *SZ*, 4: Das 'Sein' ist der selbstverständliche Begriff.
31 See again *ST*, I-II, 94, 2: Et ideo primum principium indemonstrabile est quod non est simul affirmare et negare, quod fundatur supra rationem entis et non entis.

object. In effect it comports two concepts of being. 'This' denotes the object as a reality given here and now as an individual to the senses in time and space. On the other hand, the verb 'is' expresses the individual in its most universal aspect or dimension, according to the ultimate meaning or intelligibility of being. The judgment of existence expresses, deficiently, unsatisfactorily but faithfully, all there is to be said about the individual existing thing. There is no detail of its being which is not implicit in its connotation. The judgment expresses the individual totally, but places it moreover in the universal context of all being and lays open the question why it exists.

The question of being—'What does it mean to be?', 'Why does something exist rather than not?'—arises when we recognize and reflect upon the difference between the two aspects of the real whose identity is affirmed in the judgment. Existence is affirmed of the sensible concrete given, but the individual sensible datum cannot be identified with existence *simpliciter*. The individual is not the totality of the real but has in some way a share of being. Implicit in the duality of 'it is' is the distinction between the essence and existence of the object affirmed. That which a being is, the source of its individuation, distinguishing it from all else, is other than the principle whereby it exists, and through which it belongs with all other beings to a common universe.

Aquinas stresses that all knowledge is rooted in the senses: 'The first object of our intellect in the present life is not being and the true indiscriminately, but being and the true considered in material things' (*ST*, I, 87, 3, ad 1). Simultaneously, however, the concrete sensible is grasped by the intellect in the light of the universal intelligibility of being. Aquinas, therefore, will agree with Heidegger that all knowledge occurs within an understanding of being; but for Aquinas it is more than something 'average'. The awareness or *habitus* of being illuminates the universe of beings, expressing each in the light of its ultimate intelligibility, at the same time reveals each and all as profoundly and inexhaustibly mysterious. Taken as a whole, Being is absolute, infinite, universal (this is the overwhelming intuition of Parmenides); each thing which is, regardless how minute, harbours an infinite dimension. What is being, that it can be partaken of or apportioned in this way? What does it mean to be—a fundamental, universal presence which cannot in itself be restricted (since it is opposed to nothing)—yet to be according to a definite mode or measure of being? What can measure the absolute, immense fullness of being? This is the very mystery of being as revealed in our experience: how is limited being possible? Is it not indeed a contradiction?

The concept of being provides the illumination which enables us to pursue the enquiry; it is also, more basically, the foundation which demands and inspires metaphysical reflection. It gives to all inquiry its compelling impulse and dynamism. The philosophic wonder of being is rooted in the very structure of the judgment of existence and what it discloses. The wonder at being is the twofold response to the positive and negative aspects of knowledge revealed in the judgment. I know that 'something is'; my affirmation is securely rooted in the evidence of existence, but I do not fully comprehend what is given me. I cannot account for it, since it does not reveal why it is, or explain of itself how it is that it should be.

In his commentary on Aristotle's *Metaphysics*,[32] Aquinas gives the radical reason for the tendency orienting the *desiderium sciendi*, by which 'all men desire to know.' The desire to know is a dynamic movement which orients man out of his unknowing towards the goal of complete knowledge; it is rooted in the very nature of man. Each thing, Aquinas remarks, naturally desires its own perfection. 'Since the intellect—by which man is what he is—considered in itself is all things potentially, but becomes them actually only through knowledge (because the intellect is none of the things that exist before it understands them) so each man naturally desires knowledge.' Furthermore, each thing has a natural inclination to perform its proper operation. Man's proper operation is to understand—through this he differs from everything else—hence the desire of man is naturally inclined to understand, and therefore to know.

Through his intellect, man is by nature related to all being. In potency, he is all things intentionally. This occurs in an indeterminate way through the universal openness of the soul to all reality ('the soul is somehow all things') and is fulfilled in the judgment of existence. In affirming 'it is', I also implicitly affirm: 'everything that is, exists'. I can generalize from an individual affirmation of existence to the affirmation of universal existence: from 'this is' to 'all of reality is'; even though I am certain that I will never apprehend everything—not even a single individual—in its fullness. (Aquinas notes: 'Our knowledge is so weak that no philosopher was ever able to investigate perfectly the nature of a single fly. Hence we read that one philosopher passed thirty years in solitude in order that he might know the nature of the bee.')[33] Nevertheless, in asserting of anything 'this is', I comprehensively express every aspect of its being, its plenitude and individuality. This knowledge while real and well-grounded, however, is vague and implicit. By the tendency to self-perfection intrinsic to all things, the intellect (in accordance with the discursive nature of human understanding) is dynamically oriented towards a more perfect knowledge. The intellect seeks actual knowledge of all things; this alone will adequately satisfy its intentional potency and need—thus the native tendency of the intellect to understand reality.

Implicit in my assertion of the existence of the individual is the affirmation that 'whatever is, is'; the mind recognizes that 'this' is not all-that-is. As a value or presence, being is not restricted or confined to the

32 *In I Met.* 1, 1-2.
33 *In Symbolum Apostolorum Expositio*, Prol. Opuscula Theologica II, ed. R. M. Spiazzi (Turin, 1972), p. 194: Cognitio nostra est adeo debilis quod nullus philosophus potuit unquam perfecte investigare naturam unius muscae: unde legitur, quod unus philosophus fuit triginta annis in solitudine, ut cognosceret naturam apis.

individual, but is universal: it extends to all that is. Being is the fundamental value common to all things; in affirming one, I somehow affirm the being of all. An incipient knowledge of all things is contained in my grasp of the individual. A knowledge of all is virtually present in the intellect, unbounded, unrestricted, confused. It is the distance between the certain but limited knowledge given in the individual and the equally certain and virtual but confused and inadequate knowledge which provides the tension impelling the dynamism of wonder, the desire to know. Its point of departure is a knowing which is aware of its own limitation.

For Aquinas, wonder is the admiration of something which falls within our experience but whose causes are hidden. The philosopher is inspired by an encounter with the marvellous. The philosopher, Aquinas remarks, resembles the poet in that both are moved by the marvellous. The mysterious is given to us; it presents itself as an indubitable phenomenon; its origin or ground, however, is undisclosed and it is precisely this origin which for Aquinas as for Aristotle is the goal of discovery. For both, philosophy is the search for the reason of the phenomenon. It could be described as a radical or vertical phenomenology, a search for the logos of the phenomenon. The ideal of knowledge is a knowledge through causes. Only when its cause is disclosed can the given object be properly said to be known. The *desiderium sciendi* is fulfilled in a discovery of causes.

TRUTH AND THE DISCLOSURE OF BEING

For Heidegger, truth is primarily a disclosure of Being. This was already grasped by the Greeks in their notion of truth as *ἀλήθεια* or 'unhiddenness'. According to Heidegger, therefore, thought is essentially an openness to the revelation of Being. Truth is granted by Being; all man can do is wait for its mystery to be revealed. Truth is not attained in human judgment and reasoning, or by any active effort to disclose the mystery of Being; it is given only in attentive waiting. Being is for Heidegger primarily a 'Presence', although man is necessary for the truth of Being—that Being may come to presence.

Traditionally, truth is defined as *adaequatio intellectus et rei*, agreement between intellect and thing. A judgment or proposition is true if it expresses being as it actually is. According to Heidegger, however, agreement is a superficial or derived consequence of a more original truth—the unfolding of beings themselves. The truth of predication, he claims, is based upon the pre-predicative revelation of Being within beings. Truth is primarily the unhiddenness or *ἀ-λήθεια* of Being. The only authentic response of thought is a releasement towards beings, an openness to the mystery of Being, and not the will to represent it correctly.

In his view of truth as unconcealment or *ἀλήθεια*, Heidegger indeed points to the origin of truth. Truth is grounded in the 'openness' of Being to man and man's corresponding openness to Being. Being reveals itself in beings. Man's spirit is marked by a capacity for the totality of being. Between being and spirit there is total correspondence.[34] However truth as such, it could be argued, is attained only when being is affirmed in an objective judgment of existence. Ἀλήθεια is the beginning of truth; judgment is its completion. Judgment is not a psychic or mental process within the mind to which there corresponds something in reality. It is the full, final and freely conscious realization of man's openness to beings. Judgment is not merely a derivation of ἀλήθεια but rather its perfection. Ἀλήθεια is the revelation of beings to man. Judgment is man's assent to Being. In judgment alone is the reality of existence attained; the disclosure of Being to man and man's openness for Being are united. In the proposition 'this is,' we consent and commit ourselves without condition to the revelation of Being; this assent of course is possible only on the basis of ἀλήθεια. Heidegger has admirably exposed this ground for the thinking of Being. The pre-predicative is brought to fruition, however, only in predication. This is neglected by Heidegger. He remains, thus, at the beginning of the process and does not reach its completion. As one author puts it: 'The pre-predicative revelation is the unreflected truth; the predicative truth is reflected revelation.'[35] Both are complementary and inseparable poles in man's relation with Being and in the revelation of Being to man. There is no disagreement but continuity between *adaequatio* and ἀλήθεια.

The pre-predicative revelation of Being makes possible the agreement of predication with reality. The truth of being is attained in judgment. This is more adequately understood in the light of Aquinas' notion of being. The classical definition of truth as *adequatio intellectus et rei* is correct as far as it goes. *Res* refers, however, simply to the quiddity or essence of a being. Primary in being is *esse* or the act by which it exists. Aquinas writes therefore, 'Since a thing includes both its quiddity and its act of being (*esse*), truth is grounded in the *esse* of a thing more than in the quiddity itself . . . The very act of being (*esse*) of a thing is the cause of truth.'[36] Aquinas distinguishes, therefore, between two operations of the intellect: the apprehension of essences, and judgment. The first perceives the quiddity of a thing, the second its act of being.

Judgment attains the actual reality of being. It affirms that a particular being exercises *esse* or its own act of being. It is an assent to actual existence: the final step in the revelation of being to man and the first in a reflection which will discover the inner structure of being. In affirming 'it is', I declare that the thing before me is more than an object of my knowledge; it exists in itself, and in virtue of its existence it belongs to the universe of beings. It is more in itself than I can ever know, yet I am certain of its existence. This is

34 Aristotle, *De Anima* III, 8, 431 b 21: ἡ ψυχὴ τὰ ὄντα πώς ἐστιν.
35 J. B. Lotz, *Das Urteil und das Sein* (Pullach, 1957), p. 189.
36 *In I Sent.*, 19, 5, 1; See ibid. ad 7; also *In Boethium de Trinitate* 5, 3.

beyond doubt. The judgment of existence is the fulfilment of a phenomenology, and the germ of a metaphysical reflection on reality. It perfects the openness of consciousness to being and man's reflective assent to the independent presence of what is given.

Now, because Heidegger fails to see the role of judgment in truth, he is unable to embark upon this reflection which would have borne fruit in his search for Being. There is, it can be argued, a more radical reason for Heidegger's failure to elucidate in an ultimate way the question of Being which he has so graphically raised. While he claims that the primacy of thought lies with Being, it is nevertheless clear that there is an element of dependence upon man for the presence of Being. It appears that Heidegger has to some degree espoused a position of immanentism. Is this not a paradox?—Heidegger rejects judgment, a human contribution to the lighting process of truth, in favour of an immanentist theory, while Aquinas emphasizes judgment without claiming that man is the measure of Being. For Heidegger, man is needed in order that Being may reveal itself.[37] 'Thrown' into the open he guards the truth of Being, so that beings may appear in the light of Being (*BH*, 75). Man is the 'shepherd' or guardian of Being. 'The essence of man is essential for the truth of Being' (*BH*, 94). This need for man in the presencing of Being is most explicit in Heidegger's lecture *Der Satz der Identität* (1957):

> Let us think of Being according to its original meaning, as presence. Being is present to man neither incidentally nor only on rare occasions. Being is present and abides only as it concerns man through the claim it makes on him. For it is man, open toward Being, who alone lets Being arrive as presence. Such becoming present needs the openness of a clearing, and by this need remains appropriated to human being . . . Being itself belongs to us; for only with us can Being be present as Being, that is, become present.[38]

It is indeed true that among beings, Being is only disclosed through the unique being which is man. Man is the only being who reveals Being. This is due to his spiritual nature. Aquinas remarks that 'every other being takes only a limited part in being,' whereas spiritual being is 'capable of grasping the whole of being.'[39] Because the soul is 'in some manner all things', since its nature is to know all things, 'it is possible for the perfection of the entire universe to exist in one thing.' As spiritual, man has a relation to all of reality. Thus the ultimate perfection which the soul can attain is to have

---

37 See note 8 above.
38 *ID*, 19–20. How is this to be reconciled with Heidegger's refutation of the charge of 'existentialist humanism' in *Letter on Humanism* ten years earlier?
39 *Contra Gentiles* (*CG*) 2, 112, 2860: Naturae autem intellectuales maiorem habent affinitatem ad totum quam aliae naturae: nam unaquaeque intellectualis substantia est quodammodo omnia, inquantum totius entis comprehensiva est suo intellectu: quaelibet autem alia substantia particularem solam entis participationem habet.

delineated in it the entire order of the universe.[40] So far, Aquinas agrees with
Heidegger. For St Thomas, however, human spirit is not required in order
that being may be. Being is not simply presence to spirit. Furthermore, only
in its relation with being is the human spirit discovered.[41] For Aquinas reality
is primary, both in the logical and ontological orders.

A crucial point of difference between Heidegger and Aquinas concerns
the status of being as given to us and the mode in which it is given. This is
the divergence between Heidegger's phenomenology and the realism of
Aquinas. For Aquinas, being is given to the senses and becomes present in
our consciousness as an object, i.e. as something first abiding in its own
existence, prior to all cognition, which can be so affirmed as ontologically
independent. For Heidegger, Being gives itself as temporal presence to human
Dasein and cannot be thought of beyond this revelation. This does not of
course necessarily mean that the Being of things resides simply in their being
for us, i.e. in their appearance to us; but that their Being, as far as man is
concerned, has no significance beyond its revelation to *Dasein*.

The objectivity espoused by Aquinas does not imply that things are
formally present as such to our knowledge in the same manner as they exist
in themselves. The ideal of objective knowledge is not to eliminate all intervention of the subject. According to Aquinas, what is known is of necessity
present to consciousness according to the mode of the receiving subject, the
individual knower. It should be emphasized, however, that the distinction of
subject and object does not introduce a duality within being. Being lies
before and beyond this distinction; both subject and object pertain to being.
Being is not opposed to human consciousness; rather, man who existentially
has a limited share in being, is by his consciousness intentionally open
without restriction to the totality of being. All beings are potentially objects
for the human conscious subject. To be is always to be more than to be an
object; however to be known in some way adds a notional richness to that
which is. Through such an intentional relation, being is brought to light; its
intelligibility is actualized. Before it becomes an object for knowledge, its
intelligibility is latent or dormant. Just as without the human eye the beauty
of the visible world has no meaning—in a sense it does not exist—it can be
said that the intelligibility of the universe is awakened as it is reflected
through human awareness. It becomes manifest in a fullness which it lacked
before. In this sense being needs man to come to presence; interpreting his
thought in this way, we can see an agreement between Heidegger and
Aquinas. For Aquinas, Being is independent of knowledge—a point of

40 *De Veritate* 2, 2: Dicitur animam esse quodammodo omnia, quia nata est omnia
cognoscere. Et secundum hunc modum possibile est ut in una re totius universi perfectio
existat. Unde haec est ultima perfectio ad quam anima potest pervenire, secundum
philosophos, ut in ea describatur totus ordo universi, et causarum eius; in quo etiam
finem ultimum hominis posuerunt, qui secundum nos erit in visione Dei.
41 *De Veritate*, 1, 1; see *ST*, I, 87, 3 ad 1.

difference with Heidegger—but is received according to the mode of the subject. How is this possible, without agreeing with Heidegger that beings in their manifestation are always appropriated to human *Dasein*? Is this not to make the object of knowledge exclusively relative to human being?

We must clarify. Knowledge without any relativity is an impossibility, a contradiction in terms, since cognition is of its very essence a relation between consciousness, embodied in and possessed by the individual, and a concrete given reality. However, as the object is viewed more and more in its universal and fundamental aspects, the certainty of its grasp is compromised less by individuating circumstances; there is a greater guarantee of objectivity. So, for example, whereas there may be differences of interpretation regarding the taste or colour of an apple, there can be no danger that the given object will be classified as a lemon or an orange. This grasp of its essential, universal, nature follows an abstraction from the individuating sensible qualities. Considering the apple further, from the most universal and fundamental perspective possible, I can view it simply as a being, as something which is. Concerning it I may pronounce the first and fundamental judgment of existence: 'it is'. With this judgment, knowledge acquires a universal and absolute viewpoint. In the assertion 'this is', I pronounce the anterior, primitive datum of what I perceive through my senses as subsisting in itself and as belonging within the universal ensemble of being which is relative to nothing. I recognize that its existential presence before my cognition is independent of my being and of my cognition.

For Heidegger, however, there appears to be a necessary dependence upon human being for the presence of Being. Being is Presence to man. Being needs man! This position has a number of consequences. Being becomes limited and finite; man has what certainly appears to be an excessive role in its disclosure.[42] Heidegger is enclosed within an immanentist circle of thought. Although he cannot simply be termed an idealist,[43] there is an ambiguity in his position which compels us to interpret it as one of immanentism: an essential and reciprocal relationship of Being with beings and of Being with consciousness.[44]

Enclosed within the horizon of immanentist thought, Heidegger cannot pronounce the 'objective' judgment of existence. He cannot go beyond that which immediately appears in order to affirm beings in themselves, indepen-

---

42 See for example *WM*, 40: '...weil das Sein selbst im Wesen endlich ist und sich nur in der Transzendenz des in das Nichts hinausgehaltenen Daseins offenbart... Im Nichts des Daseins kommt erst das Seiende im Ganzen seiner eigensten Möglichkeit nach, d. h. in endlicher Weise, zu sich selbst.'

43 *WM*, 47: Aber das Sein ist kein Erzeugnis des Denkens.

44 Laszlo Versenyi writes: 'In spite of all verbal emphasis on Being rather than man, Being remains man-related and man-bound... For all its supposed primacy in the relation (of man and Being), its disclosure is inevitably tied up with Dasein's self and world-disclosure, so that truth and Being still could not be but for the existence of man.' *Heidegger, Being, and Truth* (New Haven, 1965), p. 160.

dently of their presence to man. Nothing can be affirmed 'beyond' or 'outside' of human *Dasein*. Being is essentially a presence or appearance to man. Heidegger is not justified in asserting as an 'objective' statement: 'This being is.' He may only say: 'This being appears in its presence to me.' Unable to affirm beings through a judgment which affirms their independent existence, Heidegger is furthermore unable to advance in reflection upon the intelligible content of such judgment. He does not attain, therefore, to what does not reveal itself directly or is not immediately present to man. These limitations explain why Heidegger does not reach a final answer in his quest for Being.

PHENOMENOLOGY OR METAPHYSICS?

We may recall that there are two stages in the inquiry of philosophy. Firstly, an analysis of the phenomena given immediately in experience: a 'phenomenological description'; and secondly, a 'metaphysical' reflection upon these data to discover their inner principles and underlying ground. Such reflection seeks to answer the questions raised by phenomenological description. These stages in philosophic thought correspond to two primary characteristics of the human spirit: openness to the totality of being, and a capacity to reflect. Heidegger has analysed with striking richness the openness of man for Being—although it is necessary to question the role of man in the unfolding of Being—but has neglected the second step of disclosure: that of metaphysical reflection, in which being is disclosed in its inner principles. Only through judgment could he have entered the second, i.e. reflective level of thought, where Being reveals itself to man, not directly but by 'demonstration'. The latter is a mediated rather than immediate experience of Being; it is nonetheless valid and necessary, since it is the properly human discovery.

By emphasizing the nature of truth in its origin, Heidegger has not attained its fulfilment. This makes it further impossible for Heidegger to grant any value to 'discursive' thought—reasoning from one judgment to another to discover through reflection the inner nature of the being expressed in judgments. Such an 'active' effort to disclose Being is necessary if the question is to be elucidated. Heidegger's failure to recognize the need for a 'demonstrative' reasoning, and his adherence merely to an analysis of what reveals itself directly, is perhaps the reason for his failure to arrive at any conclusion to the question of Being. It explains moreover his subsequent reliance on the poets.

In the conclusion of his monumental work on Heidegger, Richardson writes: 'Heidegger's perspective from beginning to end remains phenomenological. By this we mean that he is concerned only with the process by which beings are lit up and reveal themselves as what they are for and to man.'[45] Being reveals itself as 'Presence'. Furthermore, this is understood

45 *Heidegger Through Phenomenology to Thought*, p. 627.

from the perspective of a temporal horizon. Phenomenology thus affirms a temporal and finite mode of Being. Whether or not this presupposes something more, a suprahistorical or infinite Being, namely Subsisting Being, cannot be answered by phenomenology itself. Phenomenology needs a deepening of method, a thinking which goes beyond its limits to answer the questions it itself has raised. The disclosure of phenomenology must be perfected by reflection upon the reality which is revealed. This is possible by virtue of the capacity of human spirit to return in reflection on its contents, to discover the inner nature of their being. Because of its agreement with being, the human spirit discovers in reflection the underlying principles of what it knows. Spirit itself is discovered only in its encounter with being, and truth is known when the intellect reflects upon itself. Man does not have, however, a pure intellect which would let him apprehend being immediately. The kind of knowledge characteristic of man is that of reason or discursive thinking. This is necessary if man is to pass beyond immediate sense experience in order to discover the inner nature of being, to know reality in its metaphysical structure.

Such reasoning lies beyond the scope of Heidegger's phenomenological description of man's immediate experience of beings. His analysis is rich in language and insight but remains a description. It narrates things within our experience but fails to seek the hidden, though positive, reality it contains. Finite reality, as revealed in immediate experience, does not present a sufficient explanation of its own existence. Description thus calls for a metaphysical reflection upon what is revealed so as to discover its inner, unrevealed constituent principles and underlying ground.[46]

Because he does not enter into reflection upon the immediate content of human experience, Heidegger stops at the initial significance of being as temporal, phenomenological presence. What is apparent is the presence of beings—in the language of St Thomas *existentia* or the fact of existence—although he is unable to affirm this objectively. Aquinas also begins with a 'phenomenology' or description of things, and observes the finite nature of their existence. However, he passes beyond phenomenology to a reflection upon the inner structure of beings and discovers the primary principle in virtue of which they exist, i.e. their *esse* or intrinsic act of being. Metaphysically, being is understood by penetrating to the primary and perfective principle by which things are: the radical act of being or *actus essendi* through which they exist. In recognizing this primary perfection and actuality we reach the inner structure of what has been offered to phenomenology as

---

46 James Collins writes: 'Description finds its proper realistic supplement in the method of causal implication and the discovery of principles of real being. Phenomenological description is a valid phase in the metaphysical enterprise but it cannot be followed exclusively without converting the study of being as being into a study of consciousness and its acts. Metaphysics is transformed into philosophical anthropology, unless description of human experience is supplemented by an attempt to draw out the existential implications of that experiential situation.' *The Existentialists* (Chicago, 1968), p. 226.

'presence'. Aquinas discloses metaphysically what Heidegger has described. He discerns in every being the limitation of *esse* by essence and is thus able to discern its participated nature, i.e. that being does not exist in itself of its own essence, but is caused or created. Aquinas proceeds, therefore, from the *esse* of finite being to *Ipsum Esse Subsistens*, who is divine or Absolute Being.[47]

According to Heidegger, the question of God lies beyond the limit of thought. There is, he grants, something 'divine' in things, which he calls the 'Holy' and assigns to the realm of poetry. Let us consider Heidegger's view regarding the role of philosophical reflection on God's existence, and his turn to poetry in his search for God.

HEIDEGGER AND THE QUESTION OF GOD

Heidegger does not deny the existence of God but simply states that God cannot be known by human thought. Every effort to prove his existence, he believes, leads only to blasphemy, since a god whose existence needs to be shown is ultimately 'a very undivine God'.[48] Philosophy, Heidegger declares, has lowered God to the status of a causal function, considering him simply as the highest value among beings. This is to diminish his essence; God is defined as *causa sui*: 'This is the proper name for the god of philosophy.' But, says Heidegger: 'Man can neither pray nor sacrifice to this god. Before the *causa sui*, man can neither fall to his knees in awe nor can he play music and dance before this god. The god-less thinking which must abandon the god of philosophy, god as *causa sui* is thus perhaps closer to the divine God.' It is preferable therefore 'to remain silent about God in the realm of thinking' (*ID*, 64).

It seems that Heidegger misunderstands both the purpose of reflection upon God's existence and the nature of the God who is available to philosophy. A demonstration of God's existence is not a proof, constructed (as Heidegger suggests) 'with all the means of the strictest formal logic' (*N*, 366). Nor is the aim to discover the God of religious experience. Furthermore, the notion of *causa sui* is rejected by Aquinas as impossible.[49] The 'uncaused cause of creation' is altogether distinct from a *causa sui* or 'self-causing cause'. (The former is revealed in philosophy as the ultimate source of intelligibility

---

47 Fabro states the radical difference between the views of Heidegger and Aquinas: 'While the Being of Heidegger is posited in the flow of time by human consciousness, the Being of St Thomas expresses either the fullness of the act of Being by essence (God) or that which reposes in the depth and root of every entity as the primordial and participated energy which constitutes it as distinct from nothing.' 'Santo Tomas de Aquino: Ayer, Hoy, Mañana', *Palabra* 103 (1974).

48 *Nietzsche* (Pfullingen, 1961), Vol. I, p. 366 (*N*).

49 *De Ente et Essentia* V. On the notion of *causa sui*, especially as relevant to Spinoza, see Rudolf Allers, *Thomas von Aquin, Über das Sein und das Wesen* (Frankfurt, 1959), p. 141.

in finite being; the latter is an impossible contradiction.) Heidegger mis-represents the Thomist conception of *ens creatum* as a unity of *materia* and *forma*.[50] For Aquinas, the fundamental composition in beings is not that of matter and form, but of essence and *esse*; the unity of matter and form constitutes the essence of a material being. St Thomas held that spiritual natures are absolutely free of all matter whatsoever and are therefore simple substances, composed only of essence and the act of *esse*.

For Aquinas, creation is not a kind of fabrication like that of human craftsmanship. The distinction is between creation out of nothing and an activity upon an already existing material. To create is properly to cause the *esse* or act by which beings are. Creation is the radical giving of being by HE WHO IS, by *Ipsum Esse Subsistens*, and the holding in existence of finite beings. The causality involved in creation is altogether different, therefore, from that effected by one being upon another. Likewise, the reflection which proceeds from beings to Absolute Subsisting Being is radically different from that by which we know cause from effect in the world of finite beings. Our knowledge of finite causality is confined to the intra-mundane, horizontal plane; reflection upon the origin of being leads us in a vertical direction, seeking that dimension which gives depth and density to finite being. It is not a logical process of proof, as Heidegger believes, but a 'foundational' or 'original' thinking in the proper sense. It seeks the ground and origin which is glimpsed obscurely in finite being. It requires all the 'releasement to things' and 'openness to the mystery' which Heidegger demands of authentic thought. In its wondrous 'releasement' to beings it recognizes the radical insufficiency of being and its absolute ontological dependence upon God, the Transcendent Being. Deepening the initial wonder at being, it unveils in the end the mystery of Infinite Being which is its origin. Reflection guides and purifies the wonder of the beginning, leading it to the mystery of the end. Here it truly 'releases' itself, 'opens' out, and comes to rest in a mystery which goes beyond its limits.

The god of philosophy is far from the God known through revelation. In this Heidegger is correct. About the God of religious experience, philosophy must remain silent: the God, says Aquinas, whom we know as the Unknown. Like Heidegger, St Thomas preferred to remain silent about God within the realm of thought: 'We do not see of God what he is, but what he is not.'[51] The silent mystery enshrouding God, Aquinas emphasizes, derives from his pre-eminent intelligibility. Each thing, Aquinas explains, is intelligible in so far as it is actual, i.e. possesses being; God therefore, whose Being is infinite, is infinitely knowable but cannot as such be known by the created intellect (*ST*, I, 12, 7). God is to our intellect as the sun is to the eyes of a bat—invisible by an excess of light (*ST*, I, 12, 1). Divine Being is unknown, not by virtue

50 See *Holzwege* (Frankfurt, 1963), p. 19.
51 *De Veritate* 8, 1, ad 8.

of his obscurity, but through an abundance of clarity.[52] God is honoured by our silence, not because we can say nothing about him, or are ignorant of him, but because we know our understanding of him to be deficient.[53] God is in himself eminently knowable, but to us remains sublimely unknown. 'At the end of our knowledge we know God as unknown (*tamquam ignotum*), since the mind has most progressed in knowledge when it knows his essence to be beyond all that it can apprehend in this life; but although it remains unknown what he is, it is nevertheless known that he is.'[54]

Aquinas' attitude is indeed refined and rooted in the inherently mysterious character of being as such; even finite being is in itself intelligible but cannot be fully grasped through human cognition. A fortiori, Absolute Being is in itself infinitely and pre-eminently intelligible; we can affirm that it is so but cannot in any way grasp or understand the full meaning of this. God is unknowable, simply because he is supra-intelligible; he is intelligible because he is Being, likewise he is unknowable because he is Being.

The silence of St. Thomas, however, comes at the end of his metaphysics, not before it begins. The silence of Heidegger is that of agnosticism. He does not treat the question of God, he claims, 'out of respect for the limits which have been set upon thought as thought, precisely by what is to be thought, namely the truth of Being' (*bh*, 103). These limits, I have argued, are the limits which Heidegger imposes, those of his phenomenology, which make it impossible to discover the inner principle or act of being which transcends the limits of finite thought, and affirm divine *Ipsum Esse Subsistens*.

Refusing to transcend the finite experience of being, Heidegger does not attain the Absolute and fails to answer his own question, 'Why are there beings rather than nothing?' He does not consider sufficiently what we may call the 'ontological indifference' of beings—that they might not have been, and do not contain within themselves a sufficient reason for their own being. Being is infinite (as Parmenides intuited), but with Heidegger is reduced to what is finite and related to man, in spite of all his efforts to guard its primacy. Inspired, nevertheless, in some way by a sense of the transcendent, unattainable by thought, he looks for guidance to the poet whose calling it is to seek the God who has 'withrawn' from the world. Here it appears there is hope of an encounter with the Divine.

How are we to understand the role of the poet and the nature of the Holy? The poet is the one who names the realm of the Holy in which man encounters God. The relation of Being and the Holy remains obscure. The question arises: if the Holy is a dimension of beings, or 'something' which

---

52 *In de Div. Nom.* I, iii, 82: Non enim est ignota propter obscuritatem, sed propter abundantiam claritatis.

53 *In Boethii de Trinitate*, II, 1,ad 6: Deus honoratur silentio, non quod nihil de ipso dicatur vel inquiratur, sed quia quidquid de ipso dicamus vel inquiramus, intelligimus nos ab eius comprehensione defecisse.

54 *In Boeth de Trin.*, I, 2 ad 1.

exists, is it not an element of Being, and thus accessible to thought? Or are there beings (the gods) which cannot be known in the thought of Being? Is thought confined within the sphere of Being itself? What is the place of privilege appointed to the gods that their being may not be grasped in thought? Yet 'only from the truth of Being can the essence of the Holy be thought' (*BH*, 102), in the light of which the significance of God is grasped. Does this God stand beyond Being or apart from it? He is named as one being along with others: is he not to be thought, therefore, within the thinking of Being? And, in the end, the poet laments: 'To grasp him, our joy is almost too small . . . We must often remain silent. Holy names are lacking.' There is only one thing to do: 'Without fear of the appearance of godlessness, to remain near to God's absence, and endure long enough in ready nearness to his absence, until out of proximity to the absent God the original word is granted which names the High One' (*HD*, 28).

Heidegger's search for a final response to the question of Being in the realm of poetry appears to be without issue. Predictably, his endeavour was imperilled from the start, once it left the fruitful bounds of thought which could have guided it to fulfilment in the affirmation of absolute being. Thus, it would appear, Heidegger's abandonment of thought is unphilosophical, and his search in poetry without success. Briefly, what Heidegger seeks is attainable by thought; but he has chosen the path of poetry.

AQUINAS AND THE GIFT OF BEING

For Aquinas, the key to the wonder of the world is the mystery of the superabounding love of God who freely chooses to endow the gift of being upon creatures. Divine love is the principle of the universe in its origin, its internal order and immanent dynamism, and its ultimate finality. The profound reason for the existence of things is the mysterious desire of God, who is the unbounded fullness and perfection of Being to freely share his existence and goodness with beings other than himself.[55] God's essence is to be (*esse*); properly speaking, he is not a being (*ens*), i.e. a *habens esse*, but *ipsum esse per se subsistens*, the pure and unlimited act of Being.[56] God is not only his essence, but also his own being. He alone is pure and infinite act.[57] In the simplicity of the act by which he is, he possesses infinitely all the perfections of Being.[58] Thus he alone can cause others in the radical manner of giving existence. The *esse* of beings can be caused by God alone, who is

55 For a more extensive treatment of this theme, see Fran O'Rourke, *Pseudo-Dionysius and the Metaphysics of Aquinas* (Leiden, 1992), chap. 9.
56 See *ST*, I, 4, 2, ad 3; *ST*, I, 7, 1; *ST*, I, 11, 4; *ST*, I, 12, 4; *ST*, I, 44, 1; *CG*, 2, 52; *De Ente et Essentia* 5.
57 *ST*, I, 3, 4: Deus non solum est sua essentia, sed etiam suum esse; *ST*, I, 75, 5, ad 4: Solus Deus, qui est ipsum suum esse, est actus purus, et infinitus.
58 *ST*, I, 4, 2.

esse per essentiam. The act by which things exist is created immediately by God. 'To create is, properly speaking, to cause or to produce the *esse* of things . . . to create, therefore, belongs to God according to his being, which is his essence.'[59] Creation is the gift of *esse*, the act of being; this is the first of created things.[60] As cause of the act at the very core of beings, God is present in all things: not only when they first begin, but as long as they are preserved in being. And since *esse* is what is innermost in beings, he is intimately present to them.[61]

Beings are finite because their essence is distinct from the act by which they exist. They do not exist essentially, i.e. are not the source of their own existence by virtue of their own resources—as a result of *what* they are. It is remarkable that the first and most fundamental of perfections should be none of those which beings themselves can produce or control by their own activity, but a perfection and actuality without which they could unfold no activity whatsoever, since it is the ground of their acting. Existence is 'the act of all acts and the perfection of all perfections'[62] and yet, as Aquinas remarks, 'no thing has power over its own being.'[63] Nothing we do can merit us existence, it can only be received. This is, perhaps, what Hölderlin fundamentally expresses in the line cited by Heidegger: 'Full of merit, yet poetically dwells man upon this earth.'[64] Being is a gratuitous gift, to which the poet is thoughtfully and thankfully attuned.

Why does God, absolute and perfect in himself, call into existence a universe of finite beings which cannot reciprocate the love which is their origin? Can there indeed be any reason for creation? If the universe adds nothing to God's perfection is it not superfluous? Is it not absurd that God should act for an end from which, it seems, he has no gain? Aquinas would reject such a conclusion. It does not follow, he declares, that since God is fully content with his own goodness he may not will anything else. What imposes itself is that whatever God wills, he can will only for the sake of his own goodness.[65] While God necessarily loves his goodness, he does not will by necessity the things he desires on account of his goodness.[66] While it is for his own sake that he creates the universe, he is not necessitated to do so.

---

59 *ST*, I, 45, 6: Creare est proprie causare, sive producere esse rerum... Et ideo creare convenit Deo secundum suum esse, quod est eius essentia. See *ST*, I, 8, 1: Cum autem Deus sit ipsum esse per suam essentiam, oportet, quod esse creatum sit proprius effectus eius.
60 *In I Sent.*, 38, 1, 1: Creare autem est dare esse. See *Liber de Causis*, Prop. 4: Prima rerum creatarum est esse.
61 *ST*, I, 8, 1.
62 *De Potentia* 7, 2 ad 9: Unde patet quod hoc quod dico esse est actualitas omnium actuum, et propter hoc est perfectio omnium perfectionum.
63 *De Potentia* 6, 7, 4: Nulla res habet potestatem supra suum esse.
64 See note 19 above.
65 *ST*, I, 19, 2 ad 2-3.
66 *ST*, I, 19, 3 ad 2.

That God loves his goodness is necessary; it is not necessary that this love be communicated to creatures. God is not obliged to will other things, but if he wills them it is for his own end. There is indeed a reason for creation— God's action cannot be futile—but there is neither need nor cause; and the only sufficient reason can be God's love for his own goodness.

While God is not in any way obliged, nevertheless, Aquinas suggests, it befits his goodness that he give existence to the universe. It is, he says, appropriate for God who is infinitely Good to share his goodness.[67] And since he acquires no gain from creation his motive is sheer generosity. Through the love which he has for himself, God freely calls into existence creatures which may reflect and share that love. Rejoicing in his own perfection, God freely chooses to share with creatures the love which he has for his own perfect Being, Beauty and Goodness. Aquinas declares that of all affections only joy and love can exist in God—though not as passions as they are in us (*CG*, 1, 91). God properly delights in himself, but he takes joy both in himself and in other things (*CG*, 1, 90). 'Love and joy, which are properly in God, are the principles of the other affections, love in the manner of a moving principle and joy in the manner of an end' (*CG*, 1, 91). Gilson comments: 'Because God loves his own perfection, he wants to have, so to speak, co-lovers of it; hence his will to create.'[68] Through an utter and total act of love, from which he himself merits no gain, God bestows the ultimate and fundamental endowment of existence itself. In a gratuitous celebration of the love which he has for his own goodness, God departs from the transcendence of his eternal and endless unity and draws into the intimacy of his infinite self-love creatures receiving a share of his goodness. Thus although he gains nothing through creation, it is nonetheless for his own sake that he creates.

Aquinas applies to creation the definition of love as a unitive power (*virtus unitiva*).[69] As most radical, God's love is originative and creative: the human will loves something because it is beautiful and good; the beautiful, however, exists because it is first loved by God. Our will is not the cause of things but is moved by them. Man is exterior to things; God, notwithstanding his transcendence, is intimately interior. Through a 'movement' of his will God is himself the cause of things and thus his love causes them to be and to be good, not vice versa.[70]

It is God's love of himself, of his own beauty and goodness, which moves him to lead beings out of nothingness and to raise creatures into union with himself. Divine love, therefore, is distinct from human love: for God to love is to cause the beloved to be. Divine love operates in the profound manner of a production (*habet efficaciam ad producendum*).[71] Beings are wrought from

---

67 *CG*, 2, 28, 7056: per modum cuiusdam condecentiae. See *CG*, 1, 86, 721; *ST*, I, 21, 3.
68 Etienne Gilson, *The Elements of Christian Philosophy* (New York, 1963), p. 187.
69 *ST*, I–II, 26, 2 ad 2.
70 *In de Div. Nom.*, IV, x, 439; *ST*, I, 20, 4; *ST*, I, 20, 4 ad 5.

nothingness, the vast, unimagined void of total and overwhelming absence, and elevated into union with eternal and transcendent love.[72] God's love infuses and creates goodness within beings; God's goodness is his reason for willing that other things be. It is by his will that he produces things in being. Thus the love by which he loves his own goodness is the cause of the creation of things.[73]

Aquinas also exploits the definition of love as an ecstatic virtue. In creating the world, God 'goes out' from himself in an ecstatic profusion of power.[74] Creation represents, as it were, an outward movement within the transcendent cycle of divine love, leading from itself to itself in perfect union. In an ecstatic and loving gesture, God departs from his transcendence and establishes in autonomous, nevertheless dependent, existence a universe which reflects in an outward way his own intimate dialogue of love. The multitude of creatures proceeds from divine unity as through an 'effusion', an outpouring as when many rivers arise from a single source, or water from a spring spills out (*diffundit*) into many streams.[75] In the division and multiplicity of gifts from divine goodness there is no lessening of the original, for the divine goodness remains undivided in its essence, unspent and simple. In a striking reversal of this image, Aquinas notes that, meditating on the works of God, the mind is kindled into a love for God's goodness. All the perfections scattered throughout the universe flow together in him who is the spring of all goodness: 'If, therefore, the goodness, beauty, and sweetness of creatures so capture the minds of men, the fountainhead of the goodness of God himself—in comparison with the rivulets of goodness which we find in creatures—will draw the inflamed minds of men wholly to itself' (*CG*, 2, 2).

Out of love for his goodness, God desires to share his perfection and bestow it as a gift. This is summed up in the principle: *bonum diffusivum sui et communicativum*,[76] which expresses the finality or purposiveness of divine causality. This principle must not be seen as a law governing the self-communication of God's goodness but is itself an expression of the fathomless freedom of the ultimate ground of Being, which gratuitously invites all finite things to being and goodness. It is God's free decision to radiate his goodness which inscribes the diffusive tendency as a universal character of the created world. *Bonum diffusivum* is not itself a universal and necessary principle flowing from the nature of existence, as are, for example, the laws of non-contradiction and sufficient reason. It is through reflection on the world, disclosed as a gift of God's generosity, that we can conclude that it is consonant with

71 *In de Div. Nom.*, IX, xii, 455.
72 *ST*, I, 20, 2: Amor Dei est infundens et creans bonitatem in rebus; *ST*, I, 20, 3: Amor Dei causa bonitatis rerum.
73 *CG*, 4, 20, 3570: Bonitas Dei est eius ratio volendi quod alia sint, et per suam voluntatem res in esse producit. Amor igitur quo suam bonitatem amat, est causa creationis rerum.
74 *In de Div. Nom.*, IV, x, 437.
75 *In de Div. Nom.*, II, vi, 214–5; VIII, iii, 770.
76 *De Reg. Princip.*, 4, 1040.

God's goodness to communicate his love. God's goodness is necessarily diffusive only in the love which he inspires within himself.

We can, reflecting a posteriori upon creatures, observe many examples of the diffusive and expansive character of goodness in act: the sun sheds its illumination, life propagates itself, chemical substances irradiate a determinate influence upon one another. The fecundity of goodness is reflected also at the human level: the learned person shares his knowledge, the lover seeks the good of the beloved, joy is infective—when we are sad we withdraw, when happy we feel the urge to spread our gladness. These are examples of a creaturely tendency, but creation itself is not governed by this principle. The diffusive, dynamic tendency of finite goodness is a reflection of divine generosity; experiencing its limited instances within the universe we can understand how fitting or appropriate it is that God creates. God creates neither out of need, i.e. to acquire any perfection which he is lacking, nor because of any intrinsic necessity to bestow his goodness. He alone is *maxime liberalis* (*ST*, I, 44, 4 ad 1).

The greatest difficulty in affirming the reality of God lies in the very greatness of its truth. The great unknown is an unknown greatness. It is almost too difficult for the mind to accept that there should exist a person, infinite in being and unceasing in love, whose nature is simply to be—to be absolutely—such that it is impossible for him not to exist; whose goodness is so generous as to generate the entire universe. As Maritain remarks, the universe is the only truly gratuitous work of art. It is almost natural for our intellect to balk before a truth so wonderful and sublime, since it is at ease only with what it can dominate and calculate. The alternative to mystery, however, is absurdity or contradiction: to claim that the world of our experience, which is insufficient in each of its aspects, is in need of nothing beyond itself. 'By accepting the freedom of the first cause, we make the contradiction disappear, but in its stead we find an ineffable and inscrutable mystery. Yet despite its obscurity this mystery is the light in which the whole of all finite beings, the world, becomes to some extent intelligible.'[77] The greatest mystery of all and in which we are ourselves involved is that God, who is infinite and in need of nothing, should have created the world.

The created universe is an outpouring of God's excessive goodness. In its most proper and positive sense, the created universe is in reality superfluous to God's being. Without God, the world would be indeed *de trop*: the most extreme absurdity imaginable. For Sartre, reality is indeed 'superfluous', because it does not fall within the dominion of human freedom. For Aquinas, creation is indeed superfluous—an outpouring of the goodness of God; without need he freely causes it to overflow from the superabundance of his infinite bounty. It is divinely superfluous in its origin and this is infinite mystery rather than absurdity. The universe of finite beings flows as a total

---

77 John A. Peters, *Metaphysics. A Systematic Survey*, p. 466, n. 157.

gift from the sheer generosity of divine goodness. To borrow the words of Robert Frost, creation is the 'gift outright'; beings add nothing to the perfection of God; God would be none the lesser had he not created. I can add no more to God's being than the very nothingness from which I have come. I am entirely a gift to myself bestowed by God. I add nothing to his perfection, yet I must be of eternal value to him; otherwise he would not have freely created me. Ultimately, God is his own gift to man; man is in a sense the reason for creation and his purpose is, for his own sake, to enjoy the gift of divine goodness.

The question of being, which awakens in wonder at the most insignificant reality, is only refined and purified, restored to its source, when we answer that it is a gift of goodness from the unlimited source of uncaused and infinite being. With this response the question is not simply somehow answered; it has been enlarged and imbued with an infinite dimension. it has become absorbed into a mystery which no longer has need of an answer. There has not only occured a change in the question but with it must take place a change in the enquirer and in our relation to what is now in question: the mystery of infinite Being. We cannot now place the question before us, but stand ourselves before the immensity of its mystery. The initial wonder at the mystery of being must now give way to a love of the goodness of Being which has given creation to us for the sake of our own fulfilment. The only appropriate thinking is now a thanking, the appropriate response is not one of question but of gratitude. 'In wonder all philosophy began; in wonder it ends: and admiration fills up the interspace. But the first wonder is the offspring of ignorance: the last is the parent of adoration.'[78]

---

78 S. T. Coleridge, *Aids to Reflection* (London: Ward, Lock, & Co, n.d.), p. 185.

Understanding the Human Mystery

Human Origins in Palaeoanthropology and Philosophy

BRENDAN PURCELL

The Greek odyssey of spirit, from Homeric epic to the insights of the Presocratic mystic-philosophers, gave rise to Plato's and Aristotle's articulation of a systematic philosophical anthropology. The experience of Jewish and Christian revelation, augmented by patristic writings and those of Neoplatonic and Arabic philosophers, led to the enormous expansion of that classic philosophic anthropology in the light of the understanding of created and uncreated freedom which can be found in Aquinas' *Summa*. The last century has seen a huge accumulation of palaeontological and archaeological information regarding the earliest human beings, some 40,000 years ago. This vast extension of the human time-horizon, with its accompanying questions about human origins and nature, would seem to require a further expansion in contemporary philosophical anthropology.

We shall be content in this essay to map out some of the directions we believe this further expansion should take. Our first two sections will simply indicate the palaeontological data confronting a contemporary philosophical anthropology, and the phenomenalistic framework within which those data are normally presented. We then proceed to discuss some of the difficulties which that evolutionist ideology has encountered in the palaeontological data. Fourthly, we will suggest how Aristotle's structural and dynamic understanding of human nature can order the range of new data on man. And finally we will sketch a context within which the issues underlying a philosophical palaeoanthropology may be resolved in terms of a philosophy of created and uncreated being.

I: THE PALAEONTOLOGICAL DATA: THE HOMINIDS

Palaeontologists have developed the category of *hominoids* as the superfamily to which belong the two families of *hominids* (of which man is the only survivor), and *pongids* (gorilla, chimpanzee, orang utan). The Latin word '*homo*', the root of this classification, betrays perhaps that their primary concern is to understand the extinct hominids and the apes through their relationship to man.

The first group of hominids, the *australopithecines*, have been classified into some five species, all located in Eastern and Southern Africa. All walk on two feet, their brain-sizes range from 400cc to 530cc, roughly three to four times the average for mammals of their size, and the second australopithecine species, *Africanus*, appears to have used, but not made tools. The various species span a period from 4m (= million) years to 1.25m years ago. The controversial East African species, *Homo habilis*, with a brain-size of *c.*700cc, 4.2 times the mammal average, which lived from 2m-1.5m years ago, also used tools, but is now regarded as belonging to the australopithecine group.

The second group of hominids includes the longest-surviving hominid, *Homo erectus*, which spread from Africa to Asia and Europe from 1.7m to 200,000 years ago. Erectines have a brain of *c.*1000cc, some 6.5 times the mammal average, and not only used, but made tools, with earlier claims that they used fire now strongly questioned. *Homo neanderthalensis*, the most complicated of all the hominid species, with a range of classic and derived types, is also to be found in Europe, Asia and Africa, from 200,000 to *c.*35,000 years ago. Neanderthals' brain-size is *c.*1500cc, 8 times the mammal average. They made a wider range of tools than *Homo erectus*, used fire for heat—although apparently not for cooking—and left what seems to be some evidence of burying their dead.

Homo sapiens constitutes the third and final hominid group. (The eighteenth century Linnaean classification of man as a species within the genus *Homo*, with its zoological implications, invited the range of nineteenth and twentieth century misclassifications of non-humans as falling under *Homo* that we have just listed.) Whether the first humans originated in Africa or the Middle East, they quickly spread to Europe, Asia and Australia, from about 40,000 years ago, probably reaching the Americas some 20,000 years ago. Human brains average about 1450cc, and as with Neanderthals', are some 8 times the mammal average or 3 times that of the chimpanzee or the first australopithecine.

Given that the foregoing hominid data are almost always presented within an evolutionary sequence, it will be necessary to disengage them from any ideological presuppositions before ascertaining their relevance for philosophical anthropology.

II: PHENOMENALISM IN SCIENCE

Some years ago, Desmond Connell pointed out that 'The gradual elimination of substance in the course of the development of modern thought is one of the most fundamental implications of the rejection of the tradition of metaphysics deriving from Aristotle.'[1] For our purposes, we shall touch on two related consequences of this loss of awareness of substance since the mid-sixteenth century. One result, at the level of theory, has been the emergence of what von Hayek has diagnosed as scientism. In his essay on

1   Desmond Connell, 'Substance and Subject', *Philosophical Studies* 26 (1979), 7.

'The Origins of Scientism', Eric Voegelin defines the basic dogma of scientism as 'the assumption that the mathematized science of natural phenomena is a model science to which all other sciences ought to conform.' This implies 'two great denials: it denies the dignity of science to the quest for substance in nature, in man and society, as well as in transcendental reality; and, in the more radical form, it denies the reality of substance.'[2] The issue then is not simply between the natural sciences and their understanding of the accidental (in the Aristotelian and Thomist sense—what Lonergan terms 'conjugate forms') and the philosophical science of substance, but the claim of the sciences of phenomena that their understanding of phenomenal relationships amounts to an understanding of the substantial order of reality.

Accompanying, and in part occasioning the preoccupation with the phenomenal aspect of reality as investigated by the natural sciences from the seventeenth century onwards, was the atrophy of Christian faith and spirituality. Replacing that faith were the various intellectualist or scientistic mass movements such as progressivism, positivism, Marxism, psychoanalysis, communism, fascism and national socialism.[3] These movements had in common that they invoked the prestige of the natural sciences to assert their own scientific nature. As Voegelin remarks, 'Without the prestige effect of scientism, such major intellectual scandals as the social success of positivism, or Darwinian evolutionism, or Marxism would be unthinkable.'[4] Keeping in mind both the theoretical deformation of phenomenalism and the social field of public unconsciousness in which the unseen reality of substance has been eliminated, we shall refer to a series of recent failures in palaeontological theory insofar as it has relied upon Darwinian evolutionism.

III. SOME DIFFICULTIES OF EVOLUTIONISM IN PALAEONTOLOGY

In his most recent book, *Wonderful Life*,[5] on the Burgess Shale, Stephen Gould berates what he calls 'the false iconography of the march of progress' (p. 31). He criticizes not only what he calls 'the great warhorse of tradition' (p. 36)—the familiar illustration of the various stages in the evolution of the horse—as quite fallacious, but the even more widespread iconography of human evolution, from monkey through apes through hominids to man (pp. 27–36). As Eldredge and Tattersall put it in their *The Myths of Human Evolution*:

---

2 Eric Voegelin, 'The Origins of Scientism', *Social Research*, 15 (1948), 462-3.
3 Eric Voegelin, *Science, Politics and Gnosticism* (Chicago, 1968), p. 83.
4 Eric Voegelin, 'The Origins of Scientism', *Social Research*, 15 (1948), 493.
5 Stephen Gould, *Wonderful Life: The Burgess Shale and the Nature of History* (London, 1989) (*WL*).

What could be simpler and more satisfying than an evolutionary sequence leading from gracile *Australopithecus* through robust *Australopithecus* to *Homo erectus* and thence via the Neanderthals to modern man? . . . The problem with schemes of this sort is that they assume that each stage is a direct descendant of the one before it and the ancestor of the one following . . . Approaching things in this way involves allowing data to determine relationships, whereas . . . there is actually no necessary connection between the two.[6]

As with the critics of Darwinian gradualism, those who criticize the familiar evolutionary context for the hominids, leading inexorably to the evolution of man, rarely advert to the limits of phenomenalism in biology, but are aware that the theory is breaking down under the weight of the facts. We shall mention four significant breaks in the hominid record.

The gap between hominids and all other hominoids

While the first hominid fossils go back only 4m years, evolutionary palaeontologists drew some comfort from *Ramapithecus*, an Asian hominoid that appeared, for example, to have dentition that indicated it should be placed in the hominid rather than in the pongid family of hominoids, some 15m years ago. Due to the discovery of more complete fossils of *Sivapithecus*, a species closely related to *Ramapithecus*, in Turkey and Pakistan, *Ramapithecus* is now regarded as belonging to the orang utan genus.[7] This leaves the first hominids, on the basis of the fossil evidence, abruptly appearing at 4m years ago, with no time for the gradual evolution of bipedalism, the unapelike opposable thumb, reduced canine dentition, and brain size proportionately larger than that of apes.

The gap between homo erectus and australopithecines

With the discovery of the most recent and complete *Homo habilis* fossil at Olduvai, Tanzania, only three and a half feet high, and with very long apelike arms, dangling to the knees, *Homo habilis* is regarded as no longer providing a clear transitional type between australopithecines and *Homo erectus*. Johanson et al., in their article 'New Partial Skeleton of *Homo Habilis*', note that 'views of human evolution positing incremental body size increase through time may be rooted in gradualistic preconceptions rather than in fact,' and that the new grouping of *Homo habilis* with australopithecines 'may imply an abrupt transition between these taxa [i.e., *Homo habilis* and *Homo erectus*] in East Africa.'[8] So that the gap between both species increases—as Johanson remarked in an interview in *Time* (1 June 1987): 'The new

6   Niles Eldredge and Ian Tattersall, *The Myths of Human Evolution* (New York, 1982), p. 121.
7   Roger Lewin, *Bones of Contention* (New York, 1987), chap. 6 (*BC*).
8   Donald Johanson et al., 'New Partial Skeleton of *Homo habilis* from Olduvai Gorge, Tanzania', *Nature*, 327 (1987), 209.

specimen suggests that the body pattern we call modern did not appear until *Homo erectus* and that it happened fairly rapidly.'

The gap between homo sapiens and all other hominids

Mellars and Stringer remark that the recent discovery of Neanderthal remains dated as late as 33-35,000 years ago at Saint-Césaire 'effectively precludes any hypothesis of a gradual evolution from Neanderthal to anatomically modern populations within Western Europe.'[9] And Gould writes that:

> Our closest ancestors and cousins, *Homo erectus*, the Neanderthals, and others, possessed mental abilities of a high order, as indicated by their range of tools and other artifacts. But only *Homo sapiens* shows direct evidence for the kind of abstract reasoning, including numerical and aesthetic modes, that we identify as distinctively human. All indications of ice-age reckoning—the calendar sticks and counting blades—belong to *Homo sapiens*. And all the ice-age art—the cave paintings, the Venus figures, the horse-head carvings, the reindeer bas-reliefs—was done by our species. By evidence now available, Neanderthal knew nothing of representational art (*WL*, 319).

Humans have a quite distinct skull-shape, with thinner walls, small or non-existent browridge, lighter face and jaws, with small teeth, and generally much lighter skeleton. There is clear evidence of what Mellars and Stringer call 'populations of essentially anatomically modern form' in the Middle East going back as far as 90-100,00 years ago, which we cannot discuss here, but such evidence they regard as confirming 'the idea of a largely independent development of "archaic" and "modern" populations' rather than 'the alternative of a gradual, linear pattern of evolution throughout this time range' (*HR*, 7).

The biochemical gap: the children of Eve

In the last decade, indications of human uniqueness have come to light at a molecular level also. According to neo-Darwinian theory, humans evolved in the various different regions where *Homo erectus* was distributed. However, research on mitochondrial DNA (mtDNA) in humans would seem to contradict this. Mitochondria are substructures within the cell with their own genetic machinery, information, and rate of change in a given species. Unlike ordinary, or nuclear DNA, which is inherited from both parents, mtDNA is inherited only from the mother in all species studied, from toads to human beings. When Rebecca Cann and her associates at the Dept. of Human Biology at Berkeley studied the variation in mtDNA in different

---

9 'Introduction' to *The Human Revolution: Behavioural and Biological Perspectives on the Origins of Modern Humans*, eds. Paul Mellars and Chris Stringer, (Edinburgh, 1989), p. 8 (*HR*).

species, they discovered a 5% variation between the two slightly different orang utan species (in Borneo and Sumatra), a 0.6% variation among gorillas, and an astonishingly low 0.3% variation among humans of all races. Because mtDNA inheritance seems to imply a single mother, Cann, Stringer and others support what has been called the 'Noah's Ark' theory—the emergence of the human race from a single origin. As D. Wallace, a U.S. biologist remarked, 'I think one of the things that I found most personally exciting about our discovery of a single female lineage of mtDNA is that it showed how closely related all the different people on our globe are to each other, and that in fact we are really part of one human family.'[10]

To conclude our account of the palaeontological applications of evolutionary theory in terms of the phenomena themselves, it is instructive to consider Niles Eldredge's comment on the behaviour of palaeontologists since the late 1940s:

> We have proferred a collective tacit acceptance of the story of gradual adaptive change, a story that strengthened and became even more entrenched as the [neo-Darwinian] synthesis took hold. We palaeontologists have said that the history of life supports this interpretation, all the while really knowing it does not.

Augros and Stanciu, who have quoted Eldredge, add that 'Something is gravely wrong with a theory that forces us to deny or ignore the data of an entire science.'[11]

IV: ARISTOTELIAN ANTHROPOLOGY AS PROXIMATE CONTEXT FOR PALAEOANTHROPOLOGY

We have listed above the various species of hominids, where that term itself is derived from the word '*homo*'. Palaeontologists are quite aware of the inappositeness of many of their terms. '*Australopithecus*' literally means 'Southern ape', although australopithecines have subsequently been found in East as well as South Africa, and they are certainly not apes. More to the point, the categories which—along with brain-size—were used as criteria for membership of the genus *Homo*: bipedalism (*Homo erectus*) and tool-usage (*Homo habilis*), have been overtaken by the discovery of australopithecine bipedalism and tool-usage. What then is the criterion for the classification of *Homo*, for being human in a technical sense? At this point I would like to consider,

10   In *Children of Eve*, transcript of WGBH/NOVA Broadcast (Boston, 1987), p. 25. Cf. Rebecca Cann et al., 'Mitochondrial DNA and Human Evolution', *Nature*, 325 (1987), 31-6; Chris Stringer and P. J. Andrews, 'Genetic and Fossil Evidence for the Origin of Modern Humans', *Science*, 239 (1988), 1263-8. In a letter, *Nature*, 329 (1987), 112, Cann et al. admit the need to recalibrate their previous estimate of 200,000 years ago for the first human 'mitochondrial mother', 'towards a more recent time'.
11   Robert Augros and George Stanciu, *The New Biology* (Boston, 1987), p. 175 (*TNB*).

firstly, some of the main palaeoanthropological standards for judging when a species is human. Then I shall refer to the criteria determining human nature in classic philosophical anthropology, using those criteria to assess the palaeo-anthropological standards. Finally, we shall see how the classical criteria are clearly instantiated in the morphology and activities of what palaeontologists refer to as 'Modern Humans'.

Palaeoanthropological criteria of humanity

In the last chapter of his *Bones of Contention: Controversies in the Search for Human Origins*, Roger Lewin lists the various criteria employed in palaeoan-thropology for judging what makes a hominid human. In the late nineteenth and early twentieth centuries the 'survival of the fittest' was a notion derived from economic and political utilitarianism. Applied to the evolution of man it was given strong racist connotations, resulting in 'a graded series of races' from Australian aborigines up to Caucasians. 'So it was that several threads of argument were woven together to form a theoretical fabric, whose pattern matched closely the ethos of the Edwardian world. If the white races were economically and territorially dominant in the world, it was surely the natural outcome of natural processes' (p. 308).

With the australopithecine discoveries of the 1930s and '40s, which 'showed that human forbears stood upright and were equipped with small brains as well as small canine teeth, the Darwinian structure began to come apart.' Against the notion of a gradual development at all levels, the australopithecines exhibited major physical change compared to the apes, yet with only slightly larger brains, which prompted palaeoanthropologists to look for a new criterion for human evolution. 'Tool use now emerged as the focus of human advancement, especially tools used as weapons' (p. 314). However, as Gribbin and Cherfass remark, 'now that we have the records of observers who have spent many patient hours watching animals in the wild, tool-use has faded somewhat from the forefront of exclusive characteristics. A whole host of animals, including even snails, has been seen using tools, and quite a few species modify objects in the environment and so can be said to manufacture tools.'[12]

Lewin sums up the dominant classification of the sixties in the words of an anthropologist: 'Hunting is the master behavior pattern of the human species' (p. 316). Or as Elwyn Simons put it in his textbook on *Primate Evolution: An Introduction to Man's Place in Nature*, 'For me, what it is to be human is to be more than just a tool-maker. It is to be a perfected, large-brained hunter.'[13]

However, once again the data outstripped the ideology, and with the dis-covery in the mid 1970s that 'the first stone tools in the archeological record did not begin to appear until at least a million years after the earliest hominids

---

12 John Gribbin and Jeremy Cherfass, *The Monkey Puzzle* (London, 1982, p. 228 (*MP*).
13 Elwyn Simons, *Primate Evolution* (New York, 1972), p. 276.

had already evolved a fully bipedal gait', 'the hunting hypothesis . . . began to fall apart' (Lewin, p. 316).

In more recent years, sharing and cooperation have been proposed as 'the key behavioral ingredients in hominid origins and human success' (p. 317). There has even been a feminist palaeoanthropological interpretative context: 'As a counterpart to the male-oriented hunting hypothesis, Adrienne Zhilman and Nancy Tanner suggested that the mother/infant bond and food-sharing among mature females were at the core of hominid origins' (p. 317–18).

In the light of such a range of opinions, it is hardly surprising that Lewin finds that the question regarding 'the role and status of our own species, *Homo sapiens*, in nature and in the cosmos' is 'by its very nature, simply unsolvable—even, or maybe particularly not, by the methodology of objective scientific investigation.' (p. 301) However, the palaeoanthropologists discussing what one writer has entitled 'The Myth of Human Evolution', do not seem prepared to go beyond exercises in scientistic mythmaking. According to another author whom Lewin quotes, responding to the comparison of theories of human evolution to 'primitive myths', 'What paleoanthropologists do is more, not less than scientific . . . The mythic dimension is plus, not instead of. The theories still have to resist attempts to prove them false; but they don't *mean* as much without those extensions into the extra-scientific' (p. 312). Perhaps it is at this point—when the phenomenal science of palaeoanthropology seems in danger of lacking all ultimate significance, due to its failure to focus on the substance of the human—that we should turn to the classic discovery of human nature which was carried out as a conscious advance beyond myth. As Voegelin has put it, 'The Greek differentiation of reason in existence has set critical standards for the exploration of consciousness behind which nobody is permitted to fall back.'[14]

Aristotelian criteria of humanity

For our purposes, we shall draw on two related ways in which Aristotle considered human nature, which we may here label respectively, dynamic and structural.

Voegelin translates the opening statement of Aristotle's *Metaphysics*: 'All men by nature reach out for knowledge,' where that reaching out is exemplified as the active raising of questions rising from a range of minor matters to the ground of the cosmos (981a13–982a20). Further, when Aristotle says that all philosophy begins in wonder (982b12f), he has in mind a 'wondering why things should be as they are' (983a14f), thus implying the quest for the ground. This quest is undertaken because of man's consciousness of being ignorant of what he should know (982b18), with the consequent dynamic

---

14   Eric Voegelin, 'On Classical Studies', *The Collected Works of Eric Voegelin* (*CW*), 12, ed. Ellis Sandoz (Baton Rouge, 1990), p. 264.

tension to reach beyond that state. So, for Voegelin, the first line of the *Metaphysics* could be paraphrased: 'All men are by nature in quest of the ground,' where this would be the classic meaning of human reason—for Aristotle, the core of human nature.[15] What is important to notice is that for Aristotle, as for Plato, the defining characteristic of human nature is its capacity to reach out towards and be drawn by the transcendent ground or Prime Mover of the cosmos.

Along with this dynamic understanding of man, there is also what we may call Aristotle's structural articulation of human nature. Voegelin speaks of this as 'the synthetic nature of man, in Aristotle's sense, with its realms of human-psychic, animalic, vegetative, and inanimate being'. He continues:

> These tiers of the hierarchy of being are related to each other in: (a) the material dependence of the higher on the lower and (b) the organization of the lower by the higher ones. The relations are not reversible. On the one hand, there is no *eu zen*, no good life in Aristotle's meaning, without the basis of *zen*; on the other hand, the order of the good life does not emerge from the corporeal foundation but originates only from the center of the existential tension [towards the ground of existence.][16]

In the light of these criteria—dynamic and structural—of human nature, we may now return to the more or less explicit presuppositions regarding the substance of humanity operative in palaeoanthropology.

Historically, the philosophic differentiation of a transcendent divinity and of man as the embodied being who is defined by his conscious orientation towards that transcendent ground, was correlative. It was accompanied by the definition of the cosmos or world as what was common to all reality other than human and divine. Each of these three realities was defined in relation to the others. However when, as in the modern period the experience of divine reality is eclipsed, the idea of man or of the world is hypostasized into an absolute, even though, as radically immanentized, such a Man or such a World does not exist, nor have they any meaning in the technical sense in which they were originally differentiated. Both Man and World were absolutized in eighteenth and nineteenth century French and German culture. However, it could be said that English-speaking culture showed its similar loss of the classical balance of the correlation between man, God and world by absolutizing the world or Nature, rather than man.[17] On this loss of balance in general, Voegelin remarks that 'if instead of the original reality, one part of the reality is erected into an absolute, all other

15 Eric Voegelin, 'Anxiety and Reason', *CW*, 28, eds. Paul Caringella and Thomas Hollweck (Baton Rouge, 1990), pp. 103-4.

16 Eric Voegelin, *Anamnesis*, trans. Gerhart Niemeyer (Notre Dame, 1978), p. 209.

17 See Basil Willey, *The Eighteenth Century Background: Studies on the Idea of Nature in the Thought of the Period* (London, 1940).

parts of reality must be construed as a function of the one absolute reality, which is only a part of reality.'[18] So that the relativizing of man as a function of the world can be diagnosed as an incomprehension of the classic understanding of man. What it does is to dissociate the already differentiated notion of man as intrinsically related to his divine ground from that divine pole of his existence, and posit a non-existent world-immanent Man. This approach 'reduces man to the hitherto last outgrowth of a natural evolution, beginning from some [material] origins and ultimately culminating, through a chain of organic beings, in man. So man is a function of that nature which is evolution, its last product' (*DH*, 44). We may regard this fundamental loss of ontological balance as a radical truncation of Aristotle's dynamic notion of human nature.

What of the vicissitudes befalling this structural understanding of man? This involved seeing man as a multilevelled reality, in which each level, from the most basic, metaphysical level of being, through physical, biological, sentient, intellectual levels, to participation in divine reality, interlocked with all others in the concrete unity of a human substance. Two related errors seem to underlie the heterogeneous series of classificatory standards (of the sort mentioned in Roger Lewin's useful listing) employed by palaeoanthropologists. On the one hand there is the fallacy of misplaced concreteness, in which each of the levels investigated by the sciences of phenomena is hypostasized in more or less unmixed ways. On the other hand, since everyone is aware that human reality involves a plurality of levels of some sort or another, these hypostasizations are often accompanied by reversals of the relationship of material dependence and formal organization, in which the higher levels are construed as constituted in being what they are by whatever lower level is considered decisive in classifying membership of the genus *Homo*.

Briefly moving downwards through the various hypostasized levels, we could begin with the dominant paradigm for palaeoanthropological classification in the later nineteenth and early twentieth centuries. Lewin has indicated that the criterion was drawn, via Darwin, from the competitive and utilitarian rationality of the imperialist ruling establishment of the period, whose success proved that the dominant white race was the fittest exemplification of humanity. Possibly the various palaeoanthropological theories which focus on tool usage and pragmatic or survival-oriented technological progress as their primary criterion also belong to this level of world-immanent rationality. Hypostasization of the next highest level, by a psychology of the emotions, whose origins may be found in seventeenth and eighteenth century notions of *libido dominandi* and *amour propre*, is extremely common among palaeoanthropologists. We have already referred to Lewin's listing of classificatory theories based on male aggressivity or female nurturance, while Lewin and Leakey have their own theory which combines both of these quasi-instinctual

---

18   Eric Voegelin, The Drama of Humanity. Transcript of Candler Lectures, Emory College, Georgia, 1967, by Edmund Carroll, p. 44 (*DH*).

characteristics.[19] At the purely biological level belongs the enormous palaeo-anthropological literature based on what Jacques Barzun referred to as the 'modern superstition' of race.[20]

At the biochemical level, the work of Sarich and Wilson, and Goodman, indicated a mere 1-2% genetic difference between humans, gorillas and apes, with orang utans significantly divergent from all three.[21] Gribbin and Cherfass, in their popularization of Sarich and Wilson's work, convey rather clearly their hypostasization of this level. They name their opening chapter 'One Per Cent Human', and enliven their account with statements like: 'What are people? People are apes genetically speaking, as closely related to our brothers the chimp and gorilla as they are to each other' (*MP*, p.31); 'The further from the DNA, the further from the truth' (p. 83); 'Our genes are, for 99 per cent of their length, the same as those of the apes. Our bodies are the bodies of infant apes. Our minds, however, which do set us a little way apart from the apes, seem unable to accept this information' (p. 246). A philosopher will have no difficulty in recognizing, behind the popularizing rhetoric, the gross technical error in metaphysics, by which the material dependence of the human intellectual capacity on imaginative presentations and indirectly on their neural and biochemical bases is misconstrued as implying that human nature is determined by its biochemical base. However, even regarding the lower anatomical level, the contributor to the entry on Molecular Anthropology in the recent *Encyclopedia of Human Evolution and Prehistory*, would find such biochemical reductionism inadequate:

> It is impossible at present to associate any adaptive anatomical special-ization of humans with any particular DNA change . . . we have never located a gene for bipedalism or cranial expansion, and it is likely that there are no genes 'for' these traits in the sense that there is a gene 'for' cytochrome or beta-hemoglobin. (*EHE*, 354)

This must conclude our brief indication of the phenomenalist limits of palaeoanthropology's central interpretative category, *Homo*, in the light of Aristotle's dynamic and structural understanding of human nature. We can turn now to the magnificent array of new data on human beings which have been provided by palaeoanthropology and related disciplines such as palaeoarchaeology and human biology.

The palaeoanthropological data in an Aristotelian context

These new data may be presented as enriching philosophical anthropology viewed both structurally and dynamically in the Aristotelian sense we have suggested.

19 Richard Leakey and Roger Lewin, *People of the Lake* (Harmondsworth, 1978).
20 See Jacques Barzun, *Race: A Study in Modern Superstition* (London, 1938); Eric Voegelin, *Die Rassenidee in der Geistesgeschichte von Ray bis Carus* (Berlin, 1933).
21 Ian Tatersall, Eric Delson and John Van Couvering, eds., *Encyclopedia of Human Evolution and Prehistory* (New York, 1988), entries on 'Hominoids' and 'Molecular Anthropology' (*EHE*).

The criticism of the hypostasization of various levels of human existence is in no way intended to invalidate the range of data on those various levels. We shall indicate the significance of such data from the biochemical, physiological, neurological, perceptual and intellectual levels, for an understanding of human nature considered structurally.

Biochemical level: We have already mentioned the 'Noah's Ark' model for understanding the human race, which proposes that 'all mtDNAs in modern human populations are descended from a single common ancestor who lived in Africa some 200,000 years ago . . . It is not biologically feasible to have multiple lines of descent without a common ancestor'.[22] What is of obvious human relevance in this hypothesis is that it would eliminate at one stroke any biological basis for a racist ideology. The hypothesis is supported by the fossil evidence for all human races, going back 40,000 years. Palaeoanthropologists also point out that the various racially different modern human populations 'show a fundamental similarity in anatomy, and it is difficult to believe that such a large number of characters in common could have evolved independently . . . in various parts of the world' (*EHE*, 270). Given the biological definition of species as 'communities of reproductively interacting organisms' (*EHE*, 538), the so-called Noah's Ark hypothesis provides a strong indication of the biological uniqueness of the human race.

Physiological level: At the physiological level, human beings have both a long childhood and a long period of post-reproductive survival, which have no counterpart either among apes or, according to new techniques for dating the age at death of fossil remains, among any hominids, including Neanderthals or what are called 'archaic *sapiens*' populations (*EHE*, 269). Adolf Portmann contrasts the highly specialized young animal's body-structure with the extremely unspecialized human infant body. Its very lack of specialization allows it unlimited adaptability in relation to what Portmann calls the 'social womb' of its human, including linguistic, environment.[23] The long ageing period would seem to ensure that the accumulated and radically non-instinctual experience and tradition of the human community is passed on by the older to the younger generation. What is of interest in both of these growth patterns is that they do not confer any merely biological advantage, and are meaningful only in terms of the human intellectual and spiritual culture they are aimed at serving.

Along with this inbuilt time-factor of the human organism, there is, uniquely in humans, a vocal tract capable of producing rapid, articulated sounds. The vocal tract includes the larynx which produces the sounds in its

22   Mark Stoneking and Rebecca Cann, 'African Origin of Human Mitochondrial DNA', in *HR*, p. 17.
23   Adolf Portmann, 'Anthropologische Deutung der menschlichen Entwicklungsperiode', in *Vom Lebendigen* (Frankfurt, 1973), pp. 75-92.

vocal folds or cords; the pharynx above it, in which the sounds receive major modification; the wide throat, tongue, high palate and smaller tooth area, all unique to humans. Even the shape of human teeth, which are not comparable to hominid or ape teeth, with their great evenness in height and width, means that they form 'an unbroken palisade around the oral cavity', a structural peculiarity essential for the production of spirant sounds such as *f, v, s, sh, th,* and others.[24] In all other mammals, the larynx is positioned very high in the neck, severely limiting their sound repertoire—as is the case with the human infant until about eighteen months. Australopithecine crania, at the base of the skull, indicate a larynx position similar to apes. Some scientists consider that the crania of late *Homo erectus* and archaic *Homo sapiens* 'indicate the presence of a vocal tract similar to our own' (*EHE*, 540), while Lieberman maintains that Neanderthals have a high larynx and would have ben incapable of articulate speech.[25]

Neuropsycholological level: In close correspondence to both these indications of a unique human physiology, are the data at the neuropsychological level, data which again do not make sense considered at their own level, but only in function of the higher level of human intelligence. I still remember a comment made by Luria, probably the greatest Russian neuropsychologist, during a laboratory demonstration in Louvain in the early 1970s, when he remarked that 'the brain is dumb': that considered on its own, without the conscious activities of the patient, no merely neurological examination of the human brain would yield an understanding of its characteristic features.

We have already mentioned the quantitative difference in the size of the human brain in relation to mammals, although this is hardly a decisive difference, given that our brains can be smaller than Neanderthals', and can vary from 1100cc to 2100cc with no noticeable difference in intelligence. The most striking differences are in the human brain's qualitative structure. The three most distinctive features are in the frontal lobes, and in those parts of the brain dealing with the reception and production of speech.

The frontal area of the brain is where development is most noticeable between australopithecines and erectines. In humans it provides the material basis for decision-making and future planning. In smaller monkeys the frontal area occupies 11% of the total neocortex (the topmost part of the brain), in chimpanzees, 17%, and in humans, 29%. Its integrative function is clear even neurologically, since it has two-way connections with almost all levels of the brain.

What makes the human frontal area unique is its connection with Wernicke's area (for speech-reception) and Broca's area (for speech-production)—since all of our decision-making and specifically human action involves

---

24   Eric Lenneberg, *Biological Foundations of Language* (New York, 1967), p. 42.
25   Philip Lieberman, 'The Origins of Some Aspects of Human Language and Cognition', in *HR*, pp. 391, 402-9.

verbal communication. Wernicke's area, close to our left ear, analyses heard speech, identifying its significant elements and integrating them into a meaningful sequence. Eccles points out that the area corresponding to it is proportionately very small in the orang utan brain, for example, while area 37, adjoining Wernicke's area and regarded as instrumental in understanding language, seems to have no equivalent, for example, in macaque or orang utan brains.[26]

Broca's area, concerned with what Luria calls expressive speech, deals with the synthesis of individual sounds into complex, successive units. The area is in direct contact with the lower parts of area 6, which control the movements of lips, tongue and larynx, essential for articulation. Again Broca's area is far less developed in smaller monkey and ape brains. There is evidence for a well-developed Broca's area (only slightly developed in small monkey and ape brains) in a *Homo habilis* skull [ER, 1470], and in erectine and later hominid skulls, but Holloway, a leading expert in the examination of endocasts from these skulls remarks that, 'Unfortunately, the posterior portion of the endocast, which contains Wernicke's region . . . seldom if ever shows convolutional details that would permit one to conclude that these hominids possessed language' (*EHE*, 99).

Imaginative/Symbolic level: The parts of the brain dealing with words and their meaning, Wernicke's area and area 37, overlap with area 19, considered to deal with the visual aspect of language, which in turn overlaps with areas 17 and 18, which process visual information. These overlapping areas perhaps constitute the neural basis for the human use of visual symbols. Hans Jonas' essay, 'Image-Making and the Freedom of Man' is an excellent meditation on the specifically human significance of phenomena at the perceptual level.[27] He puts himself in the position of an explorer from another planet seeking evidence of a specifically human presence. He rules out tools, hearths and tombs, focusing on images. Entering a cave, he notices on its walls lines or shapes which must have been produced artificially and which suggest a likeness to some living forms of types seen outside the cave.

He takes these as sufficient evidence of man. Why?

First of all, he points out that animal artefacts are directly connected with biological ends, such as nutrition, reproduction and hibernation, while a visual representation does not change the animal's condition, and must have another purpose. Then he lists the properties of an image: it is a likeness; it is produced with intent; the likeness is incomplete (i.e., if something were copied in all respects, say a hammer, you would have another hammer, not its image). This incompleteness involves selective omission—the first deliberate omission is for the image-maker to select what is relevant or significant in

26   John Eccles, *The Human Mystery* (Berlin, 1979), pp. 88–93.
27   Hans Jonas, *The Phenomenon of Life: Towards a Philosophical Biology* (New York, 1968), pp. 157–82.

the object represented; a second omission is to leave out all the senses except the visual; a third, to limit the representation to two dimensions, permitting greater expressive freedom in emphasizing what matters most. 'Thus a "less" of completeness can mean a more of essential likeness' (p. 161). Incompleteness and selective omission can lead to positive difference—as well as dissimilarity due to selective omission there can be alteration of the selected features themselves. 'With the rise of symbolic convention an increasing range of substitutions and graphical abbreviations becomes available—and it is in the exercise of this freedom, that the norm of the given object can be abandoned entirely for the creation of shapes never seen' (p. 162).

Finally Jonas gives his interpretation of the act of grasping the significance of the image:

> The principle here involved on the part of the subject is the mental separation of form from matter. It is this that makes possible the vicarious presence of the physically absent at once with the self-effacement of the physically present. Here we have a specifically human fact, and the reason why we can expect neither making nor understanding of images from animals. The animal deals with the present object itself. (p. 167)

What exactly would Jonas' visitor from another planet find? 'The evidence . . . points to a relatively abrupt and sudden florescence of many forms of symbolism . . . an "explosion" in symbolic behaviour . . . coinciding fairly closely with the first appearance of anatomically modern humans throughout western Eurasia.'[28] Mellars notes that this symbolic explosion occurs in Europe within 'a relatively short time (broadly, *c*.40-30,000 BP [i.e. Before Present])' (*MI*, p.356). Perhaps the earliest examples are the 'pseudomorphs' (outlines of bodies) at the Cueva Morin gravesite in NW Spain, dating from 36-40,000 B.P. (*MI*, 363). In his entry on Paleolithic Images, Marshack discusses a wide range of nonutilitarian symbolic artefacts in addition to the personal decorations found already with the Cro-Magnon remains (30,000 BP).[29] He lists a range of animal, human, and fantastic elaborations of animal and human figures, beginning with the beautiful Vogelherd horse figurines in Germany, from 32,000 BP. Marshack notes that it is now realized that there are 'dozens of symbol systems, each with its own iconography or set of images', representing 'different, often complex concepts and mythologized referential systems' (*EHE*, 424).

Beginning with the 'prewriting, prearithmethic forms of notation that first appear in the Dordogne area of France, ca. 30,000 BP', Marshack also discusses 'nonrepresentational symbol systems consisting of geometrical signs and motifs and accumulations of sets of marks' (*EHE*, 426, 423). Apart from

28 Paul Mellars, 'Major Issues in the Emergence of Modern Humans', *Current Anthropology*, 30 (1989), 363 (*MI*).
29 Alexander Marshack, 'Paleolithic Images', in *EHE*, pp. 421–8. See his *The Roots of Civilization: The Cognitive Beginnings of Man's First Art, Symbol and Notation* (London, 1972) (*RC*).

their possible function within mythic narrative, they may also have had pragmatic uses such as counting and calendar calculation.

Mellars also notes the 'degree of innovation in tool technology which is unparalleled during the earlier stages of the Paleolithic sequence', and 'the widespread appearance of fully anatomically modern hominids throughout large areas of Eurasia [and Australia]' (*MI*, 365, 371), as, along with the symbolic explosion, equivalently remarkable expressions of human inventiveness and the capacity to survive in almost all environments.

Since these forms of expression all involve what Jonas called 'the mental separation of form from matter', and cannot be understood without the capacity to carry out such an intelligent operation, we must finally turn to the defining level of human nature as it was understood by Aristotle.

Intellectual level: There is no need to treat the highest, intellectual, level of human nature considered as structure separately from human nature considered as dynamic, since both perspectives regard exactly the same reality.

After his masterly summary of the range of data characterizing the human revolution, Mellars, in seeking a cognitive or other reason for the clear difference between humans and all preceding hominids, suggests that such a reason 'can hardly be ascertainable from the archaeological record . . . My own impression . . . is that this question is ultimately unanswerable from the available archaeological evidence' (*MI*, 371, 378). He adds: 'Nevertheless, it is clear that explaining the complex of developments reflected in the biological and archaeological records of Eurasia from around 45,000 through 35,000 BP is one of the most significant challenges facing Palaeolithic archaeology today' (*MI*, 372).

It is here, perhaps most evidently, that a complementarity of the palaeoanthropological investigations and philosophic quest of the same human nature and its origins can be justified.

We have already summarized Aristotle's view in the *Metaphysics*, of the dynamic thrust of human nature as: 'all men are by nature in quest of the ground.' However, as Voegelin points out, Aristotle's 'all' is by no means a conventional flourish. For Aristotle, all men are aroused by the same *thaumazein*, but they can express their wondering about the ground of things either by myth or by philosophy. So, 'the *philomythos* [the lover of myth] is in a sense a *philosophos* [the lover of wisdom], for myth is composed of wonders' (982b18-19). Aristotle in these lines laid the foundation for a philosophy of man in historical existence, in which he could formulate what Voegelin has later called the equivalence of various levels of symbolization from the compactness of myth to the differentiation of philosophy, since these equivalent symbolizations originate in the same loving quest and arrive at the same wonders (*CW* 28, 105–6).

While we are quite aware of what Eliade calls the 'opaqueness of prehistoric documents', I would suggest that the proximate answer to the

question Mellars found 'ultimately unanswerable from the available archaeological evidence' may be found by interpreting such evidence in the light of
Aristotle's understanding of the constant of human nature throughout time,
that it is in search of the ground, of the mystery of existence. Before
attempting an analysis of an example of palaeolithic symbolization, it may be
useful to remind ourselves of Marshack's warning against the use of a
category such as 'primitive' when dealing with the first humans (*EHE*, 424),
and Eliade's comment that 'Consciousness of this unity of the spiritual
history of humanity is a recent discovery, which has not yet been sufficiently
assimilated.'[30]

Drawing on the interpretations of Marshack (*RC*, 277ff), Eliade (*HRI*,
17ff.), König and Voegelin,[31] we shall attempt an understanding of the painted
composition on the wall of the 16ft. deep shaft which appears to have been
the cultic centre of the Lascaux caves.

The composition, perhaps going back as far as 20,000 BP, portrays a life
and death struggle between two figures. On the right is a bison, whose head
is turning back, either to attack with its horns, or to gaze at its terrible
stomach wound, from which its entrails are hanging out. The wound seems
to have been inflicted by a long spear, which is lying across its body over the
wound. Facing the bison on its left is a figure of what could be a man, with a
bird's head, a long narrow rectangle for a body, four fingers on each hand,
and an erect phallus. Since the bison's horns are aimed menacingly in his
direction, and the male figure is falling backwards, it looks as if he has been
gored by the bison. Underneath the man is a complete painting of a bird,
facing left, in the opposite direction to the scene of conflict. The bird is
perched on a vertical line. What the bird is looking towards is the partly
completed figure of a powerful rhinoceros, striding further leftwards. Three
vertical sets of two dots are painted, in a horizontal direction, two sets under
the rhinoceros' tail and one in the direction of the man.

König has found bull, mammoth, and other horns frequently used to
represent moon-phases, and is inclined to see the dying bison as symbolizing
the waning moon. Since the earth is often represented by symbolizations of
its four directions—four lines, squares, etc.—she interprets the rectangular-
bodied male figure with its four-fingered hands, as symbolizing the dying
earth. The long vertical line on which the bird is perched could represent
the sun, moving in a line from east to west across the sky, while the bird
often represents a messenger from the heavens. The rhinoceros, the only one
in Lascaux, by contrast with the two dying figures, would seem to be a
representation of vigorous life, while the six dots might well indicate the six

30   Mircea Eliade, *A History of Religious Ideas, I, From the Stone Age to the Eleusinian Mysteries*
     (London, 1979), p. xvi (*HRI*).

31   Marie König, *Am Anfang der Kultur: Die Zeichensprache des frühen Menschen* (Berlin, 1973),
     pp. 236–7 (*AK*); *Unsere Vergangenheit ist älter* (Frankfurt, 1980), pp. 106–12; Eric Voegelin,
     Order and History, I, Israel and Revelation (Baton Rouge, 1969), pp. 1–15.

moons/months of the new year. The choice of the natural shaft could indicate its functioning as a symbol of the underworld, contrasting with the painted cave ceilings which could represent the heavens. While, due to the opaqueness of these prehistoric documents, all such possible significances must remain hypothetical, there is a remarkable and well-documented continuity of symbols from the palaeolithic through to neolithic and historical times, shown, for example, by Anati's and Priuli's work on the mesolithic and neolithic Alpine symbolizations, König's on the Île-de-France cave incisions, or Eliade's encyclopaedic survey of a huge range of neolithic symbols.[32]

We may presume that palaeolithic, as all other human societies, were burdened with the task of wresting the order of their existence from ever-threatening disorder. All known archaic societies experienced themselves as achieving this order by attuning themselves to the more ordered and lasting elements of the cosmos, in particular to its most unchanging elements, the constant order of the earth and of the celestial recurrences of the lunar and solar periodicities. Beginning with the rightmost tableau of the Lascaux 'triptych', it may be understood as representing an experience of cosmic defeat, with Earth and Heaven, Space and Time, locked in mutual destruction. We may imagine this ritualized coming to an end of the normal cooperation between the basic elements of the cosmos as linked with the depths of midwinter, when cosmic life and light are at their weakest. The 'central' tableau may be understood as the linking of a message of hope from the heavens with the promise of a renewed solar passage across the sky. The tableau to the left of the triptych could represent what that message presages: a renewal of life and strength throughout the first six moons of the new year. Taken along with the many other magnificent iconographic meditations that make Lascaux a huge palaeolithic cathedral, the story of the shaft may be understood as the account of a participatory event in which the human quest for truth, in response to the assuring movements of divine reality in the cosmos, achieved renewal in the experience of a re-ordering reality beyond the tensions of cosmic disorder.

It would unduly prolong our reflection on the harmony between the palaeolithic data and the classic understanding of human nature to do more than note the significance of what Marshack refers to as 'sanctuary caves'. The title of König's last book, *Unsere Vergangenheit ist Älter: Höhlenkult Alt-Europas*, conveys its intent to be a well-sustained interpretation of the religious meaning of palaeolithic symbolisms. There is also the significance of ritual burial of the dead, associated, it would seem, only with humans. (Mellars finds the various claims for Neanderthal ritual burials to be unsubstantiated: *MI*, 362, 378; cf. also, *EHE*, 370). Van Gennep, in *The Rites of*

32   Emmanuel Anati, *Camonica Valley* (London, 1965); *I Camuni: Alle radici della civiltà europea* (Milan, 1979); Ausilio Priuli, *Incisioni rupestre nelle Alpi* (Ivrea, 1983); Marie König, *AK*; Mircea Eliade, *Patterns in Comparative Religion* (London, 1971).

Passage, lists various funerary rites. What they invariably show is man's consciousness of participating in a reality outlasting the mere fact of passing away. This consciousness is amply documented by the discovery in palaeolithic graves, of grave goods, and of buried bones daubed with blood-red ochre as a sign or hope of continuing life.[33] What the first humans convey, within the compactness of the primary experience of the cosmos, is a quest for and responsiveness to the mystery of existence equivalent to the much later philosophic and revelatory experiences. They have left behind in funerary and cultic remains powerful indices of their awareness of the bipolar nature of existence as an 'intersection of the timeless with time', an awareness evoked through a range of symbolizations at times as awesomely beautiful as any later intimations of immortality and of the holy.

V: CREATIVE FINALITY AS ULTIMATE CONTEXT FOR PALAEOANTHROPOLOGY

We have suggested some pages ago that the classic understanding of human intellectual and spiritual nature might serve as the proximate explanation for the range of uniquely human palaeolithic activities. A theory of the nature of man rests on a theory of being; thus in what remains I will seek to advance from proximate to ultimate explanation. This can be attempted in three steps. I will first propose four principles as constituting all materially-based beings—matter, form, existence, and finality. In the ensuing discussion, 'finality' will serve as a summary of all four principles. A second step will indicate the ground of these principles in divine, creative providence. Taken together, both steps suggest the elements of a theory of creative finality; they will, in the third step, be applied to the data of palaeoanthropology, explanation of which Mellars sees as 'the most significant challenge facing Palaeolithic archaeology today'.

Four metaphysical principles: matter, form, existence, finality

One of the more obvious differences in our understanding of the material universe since classic and medieval times is the knowledge of the chronological sequence in which the various levels of being occur: physical, chemical, biological, botanical, zoological, and human. Darwin's own theory, purified of evolutionist extrapolations, was an attempt to understand the relationships between the various sequences of living beings, dated on the basis of the geological record. Not only has that record required the elimination of Darwin's gradualist interpretation and its replacement, for example, by the notion of 'punctuated equilibria' (Eldredge and Gould), which attempts to deal with the fossil data of sudden appearance and the

---

33 Arnold van Gennep, *The Rites of Passage* (London, 1977), chap. 8; Mircea Eliade, *HRI*, pp. 8-16.

long, unchanging persistence of new species.[34] This new formulation has been accompanied by the notion of *directed* change, occurring both at levels higher than the organism (unlike Darwin), and in relation to the ecological environment (coevolution). As Eldredge puts it, 'Nothing—literally no thing, no entity—exists in isolation from other entities in either of the two [i.e., genealogical and ecological] hierarchical process systems.'[35]

This dynamic perspective which evolutionary biology had already adopted for the biosphere, became requisite for physical cosmology with Hubble's and Lemaître's discovery, in the twenties and thirties, of the isotropic expansion of the universe.

What this unfolding sequence of levels of being exhibits is a series in which the earlier levels can function without the later ones, but the later levels depend on the earlier; for example, most animals depend on the photosynthetic activity of the blue-green algae and later of the green plants, for their oxygen and nourishment.

Pursuing our earlier discussion of matter and form (material dependence and formal organization), we must add a principle effecting the existence of any conjunction of material dependence and formal organization. The Thomist metaphysical context for materially-based being, of potency or matter, form, and act of existence, may be applied to what the sciences of phenomena have discovered as the many-levelled and interrelated reality of the dynamic universe.[36]

Let us term the operation by which a lower level provides the materials which can collaborate in making possible a higher level of existence, the *principle of emergence*. The operation by which the higher level gives in turn a generically superior context to such materials, integrating them into a higher system of laws, may be called the *principle of transformation*. And, since there is no intrinsic reason why that new level, with the things and activities which occur within it, must exist, a third constituting force is required by which that new level comes into being, which we may call the *principle of existence*.

As a ready-made and beautiful example, we can give the process of nucleosynthesis. The only place hot enough to 'cook' the light element helium into the heavier element carbon, apparently, is the heart of a dying star. Some 10 to 5 billion years ago, the first generation of stars, when their hydrogen cores burnt up at a heat of $100m°K$, in an incredibly finely tuned process, released carbon and the other heavier elements into the universe.[37]

a) By what we are calling the *principle of emergence*, these elements, particularly the trio of carbon, nitrogen and oxygen, along with hydrogen, became available to make up the basic building blocks at the biochemical level.

---

34   Niles Eldredge, *Time Frames: The Rethinking of Darwinian Evolution and the Theory of Punctuated Equilibria* (London, 1986), pp. 15, 190 (*TF*).
35   Niles Eldredge, *Unfinished Synthesis: Biological Hierarchies and Modern Evolutionary Thought* (New York, 1985), p. 214 (*US*).
36   See Bernard Lonergan, *Insight* (London, 1961), pp. 115-28, 454-8 (*IN*).
37   John Barrow and Frank Tipler, *The Anthropological Cosmological Principle* (Oxford, 1986), pp. 252-3.

b) We can understand what happened to those elements (in the extremely apt compounds of amino acids) in which they were swept up into at least one hundred proteins arranged in highly-ordered three-dimensional shapes, which constitute a living cell with its unique property of reproducing itself every twenty minutes, as occurring by means of the *principle of transformation*.

c) For biologists (who are no longer inclined to accept chemical evolution) there is nothing inevitable or deductive in the emergence of living from non-living matter. Monod saw it as 'a veritable enigma', and Crick remarks that 'the origin of life appears at the moment to be almost a miracle, so many are the conditions which would have had to have been satisfied to get it going.'[38] For our purposes, we can say that the principle by which life actually occurs is the *principle of existence*.

d) We may advance our use of traditional metaphysical elements to account for the chronological and conditioned series of levels of being— where the higher levels cannot function without the lower, and yet in their functioning achieve more and more freedom from the lower. Then we may see all the levels of being and their activities as constituting a linked sequence of dynamic and increasingly higher integrations resulting from the continual application of the principles of emergence, transformation and existence.[39]

Precisely because of the finely balanced and in themselves highly improbable conditioned series of levels of existence, Barrow and Tipler note that:

> The present Universe possesses features which are of infinitesimal probability amongst the entire range of possibilities. However, if one restricts this range by the stipulation that [human] observers should be able to exist, then the probability of the present dynamic configuration may become finite. (*ACP*, 250)

Without accepting any possible reductionism, which Jaki warns against in this formulation of the anthropic principle,[40] what seems to emerge from physical cosmology, and possibly from the life sciences up to palaeoanthropology, is a directionality in the universe. That directionality may be caught by the metaphor which sees each lower level of being offering to the possible next higher level the gift of its most highly elaborated material. Such offering requires a painful exodus of material from the simpler and less demanding existence at the lower level in order for it to be adopted and transformed by the next level, and so on up to man, who himself experiences an inner tension to transcendence. We may refer to this immanent, contingent, directed dynamism in the universe as the *principle of finality* (see *IN*, 444–51).

---

38 Jacques Monod, *Chance and Necessity* (London, 1979), p. 135 (*CN*); Francis Crick, *Life Itself: Its Origin and Nature* (London, 1982), p. 88.

39 For an adequate discussion of emergent probability, cf. Philip McShane, *Randomness, Statistics and Emergence* (Dublin, 1970).

40 Stanley Jaki, *God and the Cosmologists* (Edinburgh, 1989), pp. 189–92.

Divine creative providence as ground of metaphysical principles

But if the universe and all its components can be understood in terms of its constitutive principles of emergence, transformation, existence and immanent finality, the further question arises, whence these co-principles of being? Perhaps our strongest criticism of phenomenalism in science has related to what may be called the fallacy of answering the unasked question about existence. As Philip Rieff puts it: 'Modern scientific myths are not myths of transcendence but myths of revolt against transcendence.'[41] An example of such a revolt is Hawking's attempt at resolving an aporia of existence arising within astrophysics with an answer from the phenomenal level.[42] Another well-known attempt to evade the question of existence can be found in Crick's revival of the theory of 'panspermia' which resolves the question of the origin of life by transposing the issue to outer space, whence it is suggested the earth was seeded.

The concluding statement of Hawking's much more serious work, *The Large Scale Structure of Space-Time*, which he co-authored with George Ellis, showed a greater awareness, from within a scientific perspective, of the question of existence:

> The creation of the Universe has been argued, indecisively, from early times . . . The results we have obtained support the idea that the universe began a finite time ago. However, the actual point of creation, the singularity, is outside the scope of presently known laws of physics.[43]

Similarly, Eldredge notes that 'the origin of life is beyond the purview of standard evolutionary theory' (*US*, 216). Whatever the current hypothesis regarding the physical universe, physicists can never prove by science that the universe exists but must, rather, presuppose it. And whatever phenomenal explanation may be offered as to how life came to be, the existence of living beings is the underlying presupposition of the biological sciences. The fact of existence at all levels of being cannot be due to any particular cause, since existence itself is too universal an effect to be explicable in terms of a particular cause. For Aquinas, its cause must be the most universal cause of all. Since God is *ipsum esse per suam essentiam*, that is existence itself, then created existence is his proper effect, just as to burn is the proper effect of fire (cf. *ST*, I, 8,11).

In their own discussion of a metaphysical context for the biological sciences, Augros and Stanciu (*TNB*, 229) refer to *Contra Gentiles* 3, 70, where

41 Philip Rieff, *Freud: The Mind of the Moralist* (Chicago, 1979), p. 204.
42 Stephen Hawking, in his *A Brief History of Time* (London, 1988) (*BHT*), states that 'if the universe is really completely self-contained, having no boundary or edge, it would have neither beginning nor end: it would simply be. What place then for a creator?' And, more emphatically, on the same hypothesis of a materially boundless universe, 'It would neither be created nor destroyed. It would just BE' (pp. 141, 136).
43 Stephen Hawking and George Ellis, *The Large Scale Structure of Space-Time* (Cambridge, 1973), p. 364.

Aquinas speaks of the causation of created causes—which would have been his answer to our question, whence the co-principles of being:

> For this is not a result of the inadequacy of divine power, but of the immensity of his goodness, whereby he has willed to communicate his likeness to things, not only that they might exist, but also that they might be causes for other things. Indeed all creatures generally attain the divine likeness in these two ways. By this, in fact, the beauty of order in created things is evident.

The sciences of phenomena, as we have seen, provide us with a systematic understanding of the physical through to the anthropological levels of the universe—a universe whose potentiality, forms and sequence of forms, existence, and finality, scientific methodologies take for granted. A philo-sophical cosmology and biology can articulate these basic metaphysical elements in the context of a philosophy of world-immanent and created being. From the viewpoint of a philosophical theology, these metaphysical elements, principles or causes, are themselves caused by providence. And not just discretely: rather the created causes are caused 'in a simultaneous unity' whose effect is 'the colossal multiplicity of all the operations of all the creatures in the whole of the universe throughout the whole of time'.[44] Lonergan summarizes Aquinas' understanding of providence when, in 'On God and Secondary Causes', he writes of the

> master-plan that envisages all finite causes at all instants throughout all time, that so orders all that each in due course has the conditions of its operation fulfilled and so fulfils the conditions of the operations of others. But since the only subject of such a master-plan is the divine mind, the principal agent of its execution has to be God. Demonstrably, then, God not only gives being to, and conserves in being, every created cause, but also he uses the universe of causes as his instruments in applying each cause to its operation and so is the principal cause of each and every event as event.[45]

If 'finality' may be considered to indicate summarily Aquinas' philosophy of the created beings of our universe, and 'creative' his understanding of uncreated being in their regard, then the contextual approach we are suggesting here may be called 'creative finality'.

Such a philosophical context can resolve intellectually the aporias of the sciences of phenomena. While there is perhaps an unwitting gnosticism in the final lines of his *A Brief History of Time*, what Hawking is seeking appears to dovetail with Aquinas. With reference to 'the question of why it is that we and the universe exist', he concludes, 'If we find the answer to that, it

---

44 Joseph McCarroll, *The Development of Bernard Lonergan's Understanding of Divine Providence* (unpub. PhD thesis, Belfast, 1988), p. 146.
45 Bernard Lonergan, *Collection*, ed. F. E. Crowe, (New York, 1967), p. 58.

would be the ultimate triumph of human reason—for then we would know the mind of God' (*BHT*, 146). Aquinas would add: 'analogically'.

How creative finality may clarify the specific problem of palaeoanthropology will now be addressed.

The palaeoanthropological data within the ultimate context of creative finality

Palaeoanthropology and its related sciences have provided a range of new data for which we can try to provide a philosophical framework—in terms of the principles of emergence, transformation, existence, and finality, with their underlying ground of creative providence.

The principle of human emergence: There is the range of characteristics, mitochondrial, genetic, anatomical (human bipedalism, hands with opposable thumbs, facial expressivity, developmental cycles of childhood and ageing), and neural—including the vocal tract. While there are obvious similarities— genetic, anatomical and neural—between humans and primates such as chimpanzees and gorillas, there remains an enormous depth of difference written into the approximately 10^{13} DNA bases in the human cell. Difference in what? What marks off the hominoids and those species most closely related to them (lemurs, tarses and lorises) from other mammals is their greater reliance on the higher sense of sight over smell, with the associated development of stereoscopic vision and reduction of olfactory apparatus and its neural correlate. Accompanying this greater visual capacity there is an improvement in grasping and manipulative abilities, including hands and feet with nails rather than the more specialized claws of the more powerful large carnivorous mammals. Comparative zoologists speak of the hominoids' and lower primates' greater adaptability rather than their greater, and less flexible, adaptation. So that hominoids and lower primates have an advantage of greater sensori-motor and perceptual capacities (also indicated by their greater average brain-size) over their generally larger, carnivorous mammal cousins.

The hominids' larger brains, and skills in tool-using and tool-making, would seem to indicate an increased development in sensori-motor and perceptual capacities.

However, the human capacity for speech, already written into the first human cell, seems to indicate not simply a shift from the perceptual primacy of sound over sight—since that might occur in animals lower than hominoids—but a shift to a different order, that of significant communication. Stravinsky remarked: 'Nothing is likely about masterpieces, least of all whether there will be any. Nevertheless a masterpiece is more likely to happen to a composer with the most highly developed language.'[46] While the breakdown of Darwinian theory (by no means overcome with the some-

---

46   Quoted by Philip McShane, *Process: Introducing Themselves to Young (Christian) Minders* (Halifax, N.S., 1989), p. 304.

what descriptive replacement of punctuated equilibria) leaves us without any convincing explanation of developmental transitions at the phenomenal level, the following statement seems permissible: If the sudden emergence of new species has a developmental relationship to earlier ones, then the pre-human hominids, with the up to then most highly developed neural-perceptual-sensory-motor capacities, are intelligible as the material basis drawn on by the Composer in his creation of the human 'masterpiece'. Along with what may be an evolutionary instance of the principle of human emergence, in this case of hominid development, there are the specifically human elaborations in the human body we have mentioned, inexplicable at the level of perceptual laws, which we may see as constituted by the principle of human emergence.

The principle of human transformation: There is the question, what the material elaboration of the human body—its neural, perceptual and linguistic capacities, along with its inbuilt rhythms of childhood and ageing—is *for*. The more than million-year span of many hominid species would seem to have more than exhausted the possibilities of merely sensori-motor and perceptual skills, no matter how advanced. Augros and Stanciu quote the biologist Dobzhansky:

> Man's structural peculiarities only suffice to place him in a monotypic zoological family, with a single living species. His mental capacities are far more distinctive. If the zoological classification were based on psychological instead of mainly morphological traits, man would have to be considered a separate phylum or even kingdom. (*TNB*, 222)

In his *De Anima* (431b2), Aristotle characterized the psychological trait that specifies man as essentially different from all other animals with the remark that 'the mind grasps the forms in images'. The principle of human trans-formation, what palaeoanthropologists speak of as the human revolution, is expressed primarily in the human quest for the mystery of existence, a quest expressed in the earliest symbolizations of *Homo sapiens*. There is nothing in the hominid development of perceptual capacity, or in the specifically human bodily morphology, which entails that the human mind must exist—or which determines its contents. Yet specifically human morphology cannot be understood by itself except as providing the material basis for human intelligence and freedom. What the palaeolithic record shows are beings with a symbolically expressed consciousness of reality equivalent to our own. That consciousness ranges from orientation towards the pragmatic and everyday to orientation towards participation in the mysterious source of cosmic order and existence.[47] Earlier we have touched on the equivalence

---

47 See Brendan Purcell, 'In Search of Newgrange: Long Night's Journey into Day', in Richard Kearney, ed., *The Irish Mind* (Dublin, 1985), pp. 39-55.

of the human mythic and philosophic quests. The psychological basis for these quests, we are suggesting here, is the human mind or intellect that transforms the finite symbols of the cosmos made available by its emergent perceptual and imaginative base, rendering them transparent for transfinite reality.

The principle of human existence: What of the principle of human existence? While our understanding of a human being, palaeolithic or otherwise, includes a material element through the principle of emergence, and an intellectual or spiritual element through the principle of transformation, we have to ask how such a material-spiritual being can come into existence. There is a basic mystery and wonderfulness about each existent thing, in so far as there is nothing in its essence which excludes the possibility of its non-existence. There is nothing about the singularity of the Big Bang that implies it had to occur. Nor did life have to emerge on earth alone, and possibly, nowhere else in the universe. Nor did conscious life, at the sentient and perceptual levels, necessarily arise from bacterial, protist and plant life. However, there is something about the existence of each human being that exceeds in wonderfulness and mystery the actual occurrence of the Big Bang or of life.

The probability of the human cell occurring by chance has been calculated as 1/256 followed by 2.4b zeros, and Barrow and Tipler write that the probability of the random occurrence of the human genome is between $10^{-12,000,000}$ and $10^{-24,000,000}$. They continue: 'These numbers give some feel for the unlikelihood of the species *Homo sapiens*' (*ACP*, 565). Jérôme Lejeune, a human geneticist, would hold, against any dualism, that this improbability is the improbability of the coming into existence of the human being, and not just of the cell or genome: 'In the very first instants of life, the genetic code and the ovum's molecular structure, spirit and matter, body and soul require this extreme complexity because what is happening is the beginning of this new wonder which we call "a human being".'[48] From the geneticist's viewpoint, the first human cell can only be of a being belonging to the human species. From the philosopher's viewpoint, the up to 10,000b bits of information contained in the DNA of the human cell can only be understood in view of the human spirit. As Lejeune remarks with regard to the 98% genetic similarity between humans and chimpanzees, 'what does a 98% similarity of words matter in two different texts? The meanings could be completely different, depending on how the phrases are constructed. It is that which makes the difference between the species' (*EC*, 47).

But the biological improbability of the coming into existence of the human being is only an outward expression of the far greater improbability of the human being's intellectual and spiritual existence. Aristotle who, as a philosopher, was aware of the specific difficulty posed by a human nature

48   Jérôme Lejeune, *L'Enceinte concentrationnaire* (Paris, 1990), p. 140 (*EC*).

intrinsically intellectual yet materially dependent on the human body, expressed his difficulty in *The Generation of Animals*:

> That is why it is a very great puzzle to answer another question, concerning Reason. At what moment, and in what manner, do those creatures which have this principle of Reason acquire their share in it, and where does it come from? This is a very difficult problem which we must endeavour to solve, so far as it may be solved, to the best of our power. (735b5)

No doubt, we would speak somewhat differently to Aristotle, of the unique human person, 'who determines his own being through his free action, [thereby] becoming good or evil, that is, self-determining himself in an absolutely fundamental manner.'[49] It is when one reflects on what a human person is and does as a person that the radical discontinuity of human personal existence from all other beings in the universe comes clearly into focus. In his review of John Eccles' *Evolution of the Brain: Creation of the Self*, J. Z. Young admits that how conscious self-awareness arose is 'a mystery'. He goes on to quote Eccles' attempt at resolving it, in which Eccles argues that as all 'materialist solutions fail to account for our experienced uniqueness, I am constrained to attribute the uniqueness of the Self or Soul to a supernatural spiritual creation.'[50] (Eccles does not intend 'supernatural' in the technical sense, as involving, e.g., grace, since Young quotes his immediately following phrase, 'each Soul is a new Divine creation'). Young asks at what stage of human evolution does Eccles believe this intervention began. He finds the answer in Eccles' quoting of the biologist Lack, who considers that 'a supernatural event took place at the time of man's first appearance, before which our ancestors were protohuman mammals, and after which, through the divine gift of a soul, they were truly human' (Ibid., 118). While Young does not accept Eccles' answer, he does agree that 'these are serious and difficult problems of science and philosophy.'

A brief analysis of the act of procreation for any human being may help our understanding of the origin of the first human(s). I would suggest that in the light of our earlier discussion, the reproduction of, say, non-human mammals by their parents occurs because the latter are caused by divine causation to be 'causes for other things'—in this case for their offspring. Human parents, unlike animals, can choose to procreate, yet their freely chosen acts of procreation, as Aristotle was aware, cannot produce a rational soul but only the living body or living material structure of a human person. Employing Aquinas' development of Aristotle's metaphysical elements, we can say that the human person is constituted as materially-based by his body, as of a rational nature by his soul, and as existent by his act of existence. On this basis, we would have to disagree with Eccles,[51] when he maintains that

49 Josef Seifert, *Essere e Persona* (Milan, 1989), p. 359 (*EP*).
50 J. Z. Young, 'A Change of Mind', *Nature* 344 (1990), 117-18.
51 John Eccles, *Evolution of the Brain: Creation of the Self* (London, 1989), p. 237.

the divinely created soul 'is implanted into the growing foetus at some time between conception and birth'. Lonergan approaches the issue with this question: 'Are electrons things within atoms, atoms things within compounds, compounds things within cells, cells things within animals, animals things within men?' (*IN*, 258). The answer is in the negative—the fact that the laws of chemistry can be verified in cellular activity does not mean that chemical elements exist as things within the cell; the fact that the laws of biology can be verified in a human cell does not mean that cells exist as things within the human person. It is precisely the reverse, both in knowledge and in existence. The reason why geneticists designate a human cell as human, biologically continuous from the very first cell to the mature human organism, is not primarily biological at all. Rather, the technical classification of any data as human derives from the Greek differentiation of reason we have already discussed. And in that differentiation, the human body is understood as the materially necessary correlate to human reason. From the viewpoint of existence, there cannot exist a human foetus which is not a human being, nor is the first human cell a biological thing or a zoological thing. The only existent human thing that can be classified as human, therefore, is the human person.[52]

This means that the parents, as caused causes of the new human body, and God as the only possible, and direct cause of the human soul, co-operate in the procreation/creation of a new human person, since neither the living human body, nor the human soul of that living body, exists separately.

The relevance of this digression is to suggest an analogous approach to the coming into existence of the first human(s). The co-operative acts of procreation and creation together constitute the principle of existence of the human person. In the context of the universe considered as dynamic, it could be suggested that the caused causation of hominid development could have functioned in a manner analogous to human procreation, in providing at its highest level of elaboration the living matter suitable for transformation by the first divinely created human soul(s). (We should acknowledge the formulation in Genesis 2, 7: 'Then the Lord God formed man of dust from the earth, and breathed into his nostrils the breath of life; and man became a living being.') In this case, the principle of existence of the first human(s) would be the co-operative acts of a late hominid co-creation and the divine creation of the first human soul(s). Lest these dry words somehow empty out what Eccles speaks of as 'the human mystery', a more imaginative writer has caught that mystery better: 'There may be a broken trail of stones and bones faintly suggesting the development of the human body. There is nothing even faintly suggesting such a development of this human mind. It was not and it was; we know not in what instant or in what infinity of years. Something happened; and it has all the appearance of a transaction outside time . . . We can accept man as a fact, if we are content with an unexplained

52   See Kevin Doran, 'Person—A Key Concept for Ethics', *Linacre Quarterly* 56, 4 (1989).

fact. We can accept him as an animal, if we can live with a fabulous animal. But if we must needs have sequence and necessity, then indeed we must provide a prelude and crescendo of mounting miracles, that ushered in [man] with unthinkable thunders in all the seven heavens of another order . . . [53]'

The correlative principles of human finality and creative providence: There are the issues of human finality and creative providence in relation to man. That these realities were experienced as intertwined from the very beginning may be adduced from the frequency with which symbolizations of rituals of renewal occur. Along with imaginatively dense evocations of the recovery of cosmic-divine order such as we have seen in the Lascaux shaft, there are repeated palaeolithic motifs celebrating new year rebirth over winter death both in the rejuvenation of celestial and of earthly (animal) life. Such renewal of the more lasting partners in the cosmic-divine drama was longed for by humans, whose frequent burial sites—from the first Cueva Morin burials through the Cro Magnon site to the explicit linkages of cosmic-divine and human rituals of renewal in neolithic sites like Newgrange and Maes Howe— attest to the human hope of outlasting death as final disorder through participation in the annual resurrection of the heavens and the earth.

In the more differentiated symbols of philosophy, we have distinguished between human finality and the divine creation of man. We shall now return briefly to this distinction, and explore it with reference to the three dimensions of human existence, personal, social and historical finality, each in relation to divine creation.

Having explored an enormous range of mythic, philosophic, revelational, mystical and ideological symbolizations, Voegelin has articulated the constant structure in consciousness which renders them equivalent in terms of Question and Mystery.[54] His 'order of foundation from the depth' and 'order of creation from the height' (*OH*, 335) correspond to what we have spoken of as finality and creation. He points out the utter inadequacy of attempting, as have, for example, Hawking and Crick, 'to find an answer by developing a doctrine concerning spatio-temporal events' (*OH*, 330). Rather, 'There is no answer to the Question other than the Mystery as it becomes luminous in the acts of questioning' (Ibid.). Finality, from the depth of its first existence perhaps some 15b years ago, first becomes aware in its incarnate human consciousness of its eschatological movement beyond the structure of the universe—at what Aquinas called the horizon and frontier between time and eternity.[55] In human consciousness the universe 'becomes luminous for the creative constitution of all reality from the height of the divine ground'

53 Gilbert Chesterton, *The Everlasting Man* (London, 1925), pp. 37-8.
54 Eric Voegelin, *Order and History* IV, (Baton Rouge, 1974), pp. 316-30 (*OH*), and cf. Noreen O'Carroll, The Equivalence of Symbolic Forms (unpub. PhD thesis, Dublin, 1990) for a full development of this issue.
55 *CG*, 2, 68: quasi quidam horizon et confinium corporeorum et incorporeorum; see *CG*, 3, 61.

(*OH*, 334). In the light of this realization, there is a fundamental shift in the balance from the universe becoming consciously self-transcendent in man, to the creative ground of which he is in search: 'Things do not happen in the astrophysical universe; the universe, together with all things founded in it, happens in God' (*OH*, 334).

Regarding personal finality in relation to divine creation, most readers will be familiar with Steven Weinberg's comment at the end of his brilliant account of the Big Bang, that 'The more the universe seems comprehensible, the more it also seems pointless.'[56] Contingency at the biological level, profoundly misunderstood as mere randomness, has provoked in Monod a reaction as passionate as Sartre's *La Nausée* to an apparent utter opacity of meaning:

> It offends our very human tendency to believe that everything real in the world is necessary . . . The universe was not pregnant with life nor the biosphere with man. Our number came up in the Monte Carlo game . . . [Man] must realize that, like a gypsy, he lives on the boundary of an alien world; a world that is deaf to his music, and as indifferent to his hopes as it is to his suffering or his crimes. (*CN*, 137,160)

Gould confronts the collapse of a phenomenalistic and determinist biology with more Anglo-Saxon phlegm, yet draws the same conclusion as Monod.For Gould, 'human nature' must be seen as 'the embodiment of contingency' (*WL*, 320). This is particularly so since the survival of *Pikaia* (perhaps the first chordate, and therefore at the head of the phylum to which all vertebrates, including humans, belong) 'was a contingency of "just history".' Gould continues:

> I do not think that any 'higher' answer can be given . . . We are the offspring of history, and must establish our own paths in this most diverse and interesting of conceivable universes—one indifferent to our suffering, and therefore offering us maximal freedom to thrive, or to fail, in our own chosen way. (*WL*, 323)

Since the universe, and the human beings it contains, is contingent in being, it must be grounded in its existence by necessary being. And, as Seifert points out, 'necessarily existing being can give origin to contingent beings only if it possesses freedom . . . only if it can *freely choose* to create contingent beings' (*EP*, 483). Rather than, as for Monod, Weinberg and Gould, contingent existence implying ultimate absurdity—the factual existence of non-necessary being can occur only if grounded by free, transcendent existence. If we apply this to the human context, keeping in mind Aristotle's affirmation of the ethical priority of the intrinsically human good over material or emotional values—or Kant on humans as never means, but ends in themselves—we may say that unlike all the things in the non-human

56   Steven Weinberg, *The First Three Minutes* (London, 1978), p. 149.

universe, each human being is freely and creatively chosen into existence by Absolute Freedom, for his or her own sake. Nor, since human intellectual and spiritual existence is personal, can its creative ground itself be less than personal. Drawing on the language of the Decalogue and of the thornbush episode in Exodus, we may say that each human person is a you-for-God, a God who is himself the personal depth of existence as I AM. Edith Stein sums up well our personal finality towards union with our creative source:

> So the riddle of the I remains. For the I must receive its being from Someone else—not from itself. I do not exist of myself, and of myself I am nothing. Every moment I stand before nothingness, so every moment I must be dowered anew with being . . . This nothinged being of mine, this frail received being, is being. It thirsts not only for endless continuation of its being but for full possession of being.[57]

What of social and historical finality in relation to creation? Anthropology and history confront us with an immense range of data on the scattering of societies whose members throughout space and time belonged and belong to the same biological human type. While we are aware that there is no particular mystery attaching to all the members of an animal species, since that species can be explained in terms of genetics and zoology, in what sense can we speak of a universal humanity or humankind? Certainly, the work of Rebecca Cann and others indicates a genetic basis for one humankind, but that genetic unity is not specifically different to the genetic unity of other species. However, if we understand the finality of each human person in relationship to his creative ground as Question to Mystery, then that same dynamic orientation towards participation in divine being can be grasped as the finality of humanity in history. Aquinas' statement of this issue is his well-known proposition that, '*secundum totum tempus mundi, Christus est caput omnium hominum*' (*ST*, III, 8, 3). Voegelin's statement in *The Ecumenic Age* I would regard as the best philosophical elaboration:

> The divine-human flux of presence is a given only as far as it is founded in man's biophysical existence on earth; the divine presence itself, though experienced by man who exists in time and space, is not a spatio-temporal given . . . Universal mankind is not a society existing in the world, but a symbol which indicates man's consciousness of participating, in his earthly existence, in the mystery of a reality that moves toward its transfiguration. Universal humanity is an eschato-logical index . . .
>
> Without universality, there would be no mankind other than the aggregate of members of a biological species; there would be no more a history of mankind than there is a history of catkind or horsekind. If mankind is to have history, its members must be able to respond to the

---

57   Edith Stein, *L'Être fini et l'être éternel* (Louvain, 1972), pp. 60-1.

movement of divine presence in their souls. But if that is the condition, then the mankind who has history is constituted by the God to whom man responds. A scattering of societies, belonging to the same biological type, thus, is discovered to be one mankind with one history, by virtue of participation in the same flux of divine presence. (*OH*, 305)

VI: CONCLUSION

In the Prologue to *Joseph and His Brothers*, Thomas Mann wrote of the quest for human origins demanded by the new data of palaeontology and palaeoarchaeology, a quest which was unresolvable at the phenomenal level:

> Deep is the well of the past. Should we not call it unfathomable? That indeed may be so, if and perhaps only if, it is the past of that human essence that is being spoken of and questioned; that enigmatic essence . . . whose mystery very understandably forms the Alpha and Omega of all our speaking and questioning, bestowing stress and fire to all speech, on all questioning its urgency.
>
> For the deeper we sound, the further down into the underworld of the past we grope towards and arrive at, the more the beginnings of the human, its history, its culture, prove to be completely beyond our grasp, and no matter what agelengths we unspool our plumbline to, they always recede again and further into fathomlessness.[58]

The title of our essay suggested a shared exploration of the human mystery. The set of unresolvable issues that confront us in palaeoanthropology and palaeoarchaeology would seem to require a specific philosophic discipline, much as the aporias of astrophysics and of biology require a philosophical cosmology and a philosophical biology. This discipline may be called philosophical palaeoanthropology.

As Mann has indicated, such a discipline would itself be an act of participation in the same quest for truth that motivated the first humans. The philosophical palaeoanthropologist must have the radical empiricism that demands of himself the same openness to the question regarding the beginning (a question which is, as we have suggested, the specifically human expression of the finality of the universe), and to the experience of the answering mystery from beyond (what we have spoken of as divine creativity), that characterized the *dramatis personae* of the First Act of the drama of humankind in history. To appreciate those first humans adequately, he must feel himself united with them in what Voegelin has called 'a communion of existential concern'.

Philosophical palaeoanthropology is an integral part of a philosophy of humanity in history. Whoever practises it will be conscious of the later giant steps in the unfinished story of humanity, of the range of mesolithic and

58   Thomas Mann, *Joseph und seine Brüder* (Frankfurt, 1964), p. 7.

neolithic symbolizations, of the ancient near-eastern civilizations, of the astounding field of spiritual outbursts from the Pacific to the eastern Mediterranean that go by the names of Confucius and Lao Tzu, the Upanishadic mystics and the Buddha, Zoroaster, Moses, Isaiah, Jeremiah and Ezechiel, the Greek philosophers, Jesus, St Paul and St John, Mohammed and the later Sufi mystics. Within that wider context, all the key experiences and symbolizations of the human quest for truth, including the palaeolithic, along with the equivalently profound disorientations of this quest, are grasped in their empirical historical interrelations and grounded in their common experience or rejection of absolute Being.

Each step in that Pilgrim's Progress of humankind has its own beauty, its own mark of tragic suffering and painful exodus. But the very first words uttered on that journey, still speaking to us across thirty-five millennia, can have the evocative power to encourage us on our own pilgrim's way, through what at times can appear as a collective dark night of the spirit, to the luminosity of fuller *participatio creata lucis increatae.*

Liberty, Finitude and Transcendence
An Augustinian Hypothesis

JAMES McEVOY

In his admirable preface to his own widely admired play, *A Man for All Seasons*,[1] Robert Bolt develops an apologia for his secular appropriation of St Thomas More:

> I am not a Catholic nor even in the meaningful sense of the word a Christian. So by what right do I appropriate a Christian Saint to my purposes? Or to put it the other way, why do I take as my hero a man who brings about his own death because he can't put his hand on an old black book and tell an ordinary lie? (xiii)

The play turns about the human and philosophical question, 'What is man?':

> When we ask ourselves, 'what am I?', we may answer 'I am a Man', but are conscious that it's a silly answer because we don't know what kind of being that might be; and feeling the answer silly we feel it's probably a silly question—though we cannot help asking it all the same. (x)

The question 'What is man?' brings us to the idea of the self:

> We no longer have, as past societies have had, any picture of individual Man (Stoic Philosopher, Christian Religious, Rational Gentleman) by which to recognise ourselves and against which to measure ourselves; we are anything. But if anything, then nothing, and it is not everyone who can live with that, though it is our true present position. (ix)

If in turn we go to society for an answer to the question we

> find no fixed points, but only the vaunted absence of them, 'freedom' and 'opportunity'; freedom for what, opportunity to do what, is nowhere indicated. (ix)

For Bolt, the human sciences of sociology and psychology are powerless to answer this most universal and yet most intimate of questions. In order to counter nihilism Bolt writes, brilliantly, uneasily, searchingly, honestly, in an endeavour to discover 'a sense of the self' which could help with the riddle of freedom. As a secular contemporary, he eschews in his quest all recourse to 'magic'—though he has in fact made a very remarkable return to a 'religious' subject in his more recent book, *The Mission*.[2]

---

1 Robert Bolt, *A Man for All Seasons* (London, 1960).

A Man for All Seasons is about More's use of his own freedom in the face of the threat of death: his extraordinarily clear sense of his selfhood led him with admirable lucidity—albeit not without pain—to die, rather than swear a false oath:

> More was a very orthodox Catholic and for him an oath was something perfectly specific; it was an invitation to God, an invitation God would not refuse, to act as a witness, and to judge; the consequence of perjury was damnation, for More another perfectly specific concept. (xiii)

In his own secular idiom, Bolt reflects upon More's devotion to his deep sense of God:

> It may be that a clear sense of the self can *only* crystallize round something transcendental, in which case our prospects look poor for we are rightly committed to the rational. I think the paramount gift our thinkers, artists, and for all I know, our men of science, should labour to get for us is a sense of selfhood without resort to magic. Albert Camus is a writer I admire in this connection. (xiv)

Thomas More's liberty led him in and through his sense of finitude, in the very focused shape of the threat of a traitor's death, to the deeper and deeper appreciation of divine providence in creation and history. Bolt, that admirable writer, seeks to discover the truth of human liberty in a climate neither religious nor metaphysical, but he disdains both the prosaic liberalism of the do-as-you-please kind and the banal consumerism of the get-and-spend variety (in which, as he clearly sees, the self ends by becoming a commodity—even though still an equivocal one). He wishes for a positive conception of spiritual liberty, one which will have no rationally unacceptable (or 'magic') presuppositions or overtones. His attempt raises in a very personal and yet very accessible way the question as to whether and to what extent a lived realization of liberty (including a mature consciousness of the contingency and finitude of life) can be sustained beyond nihlism and without any foundation *sub specie aeternitatis*.

It is, I think, of value to return in the present context to the example of a thinker whose spiritual itinerary led him through profound pessimism concerning both truth and freedom, to a motivated ratification of his own

----

2   *The Mission* (London, 1986). The first part of *The Mission* is set in early eighteenth-century Ireland, in Kerry and Tipperary. The hero (or rather, one of the two heroes), Gabriel O'Donnell, a scion of the dispossessed people, becomes a Jesuit priest, is ordained in Italy, returns to Ireland and is imprisoned by a landlord because of his support for the landless natives, Gabriel's own people. His experience of the degradation and brutality of imprisonment it is which forms him interiorly for his heroic and sacrificial resistance to the colonial exploitation of the S. American Guarani Indians. The film amputates this first part of the story.

finitude and a conception of human liberty as an experience which, taken at its spiritual height and in its fragile grandeur, can only be founded upon the freedom of God. I mean St Augustine, who in his *Confessions* reveals his own transition from the experience of the nothingness of human life in the face of death, to the hard-won conviction that reflection upon death and finitude is the beginning of wisdom—and with that, of freedom.

In Book VI of the *Confessions*[3] Augustine narrates the loss he experienced at the age of nineteen or twenty of an unnamed friend of similar age, who died of a sudden fever. Here, as throughout the 'biographical' part of the work (Books I-IX), two layers of experience constantly intertwine—the account of what he was at each significant point in his early life (up to thirty-two years), and the reflection and judgment of the writer, now aged forty-six. The first level consists of a vivid account of the experience of grief and loss and speaks to us movingly, across the interval of centuries, of the pain of final separation felt so acutely in the early part of life; the second layer of meaning offers Augustine's reflections upon that early and overwhelming pain, but does so from all the temporal distance of twenty-six years.

The absolute darkness of grief is the predominant motif of the description of the pain of loss:

> My heart was black with grief. Whatever I looked upon had the air of death. My native place was a prison-house and my home a strange unhappiness. The things we had done together became sheer torment without him. My eyes were restless looking for him, but he was not there. I hated all places because he was not in them. They could not say 'he will soon come', as they would in his life when he was absent. I became a great enigma to myself and I was forever asking my soul why it was sad and why it disquieted me so sorely. And my soul knew not what to answer me.[4]

Misery and torment invaded the young Augustine, and he was 'at once utterly weary of life and yet in great fear of death', 'the cruellest enemy'. His fear extended to the future, with the abrupt realization that any human being could be snatched away from his love with the same shocking finality and suddenness as his friend had just been (trans., p. 51). How and why should he ever expose his heart again to the tragic vulnerability of friendship and love—since all love unites what death will inexorably divide, new love being merely the seed of new grief? Augustine knew, all at once, rebellion against the human condition of mortality—rebellion that was futile and lacking in all measure or sense of reality, since it was rebellion against the very order of things, rebellion vanquished before armed. Those dark emo-

3 *Confessiones* IV, iv, 7 – ix, 14.
4 Trans. Frank Sheed (London, 1944), p. 49.

tions so unaccountably typical of profound grief, namely, anger and resentment at the loss, and guilt at being oneself still there while the loved one is no longer, pushed him towards flight, the solaceless refuge of the bereaved: he left Thagaste for Carthage to escape grief (as a widow might sell the marriage home and move); but it was unavailing flight, for he brought his grief with him; it had become part of him, and life was changed for good. Augustine describes how he hated the advent of the morning light, which returned him to his grieving and desolate state of alienation. His only solace lay in the tears, 'which had taken the place my friend had held in the love of my heart' (p. 50).

The account Augustine gives of his experience has more than a hint of nihilism about it. The blackness he felt around him was unrelieved by any light of hope. All value seemed to have departed from his customary delights. His notional faith had as yet no anchorage in experience and was useless to him; he found nowhere to rest his burden, which fell back again and again heavily upon him. He felt that death, in destroying life, destroys at the same time the values that life has built and leaves nothing behind, save aching memories in the hearts of the ones who are soon to follow those already dead.

But winding through this remembrance of unrelieved pain in meaninglessness is the perspective of the writer who has come to accept and to affirm the order of things, and of experience, as the expression of the divine wisdom and love: finitude can indeed be affirmed as finitude, can be loved as finite, but only on condition that it is loved in its transcendent dimension, in God himself: 'O madness that knows not how to love men as men!' (p. 51). The English version cannot convey the particular sense of the Latin, *amare homines humaniter* for we have here no simple reduplication of meaning but an assertion of essential physical mortality. *Homines* are born and die; not to love them *humaniter* that is to say, according to the mode of their existential fragility, is *dementia* and *stultitia*, madness and folly. This meaning is a far cry from the *humaniter* of Ciceronian friendship, which inculcates affective empathy—the ability and disposition to feel the same joy and the same pain as one's friend—but which makes no reference to the essential and innate precariousness of all and every human love.

The Augustinian injunction, the fruit of his own experience, will not be to cease loving humans but rather to order one's love upon the pattern of reality, rather than upon wish, will, whimsy or illusion: it will enjoin upon human beings to love each other, not as though we will never die but precisely as beings who must die, and who cannot therefore sustain (on either side of a reciprocal relationship) the unconditional weight of a love that is unmeasured, absolute and (ontologically speaking) absurdly and destructively directed, if it is given to mortals 'as though they were never to die'. The injunction will indeed be, to love *homines humaniter*—but to love them in God, who is never lost and in whom all that is real, true and good subsists and will be preserved everlastingly.

> If material things please you then praise God for them, but turn back your love upon him who made them lest in the things that please you, you displease him. If souls please you, then love them in God, because they are mutable in themselves but in him firmly established; without him they would pass and perish. Love them, I say, in him, and draw as many souls with you to him as you can. (p. 55)

The rule of love that is no longer self-indulgent and illusion-bound, love that faces death but holds in faith to the conviction that *Vita mutatur non tollitur*, can only be this:

> Blessed is the man that loves thee, O God, and his friend in thee, and his enemy for thee. For he alone loses no-one that is dear to him, if all are dear in God, who is never lost. (p. 53)

Thus it was that Augustine lost the immortality of youth, that carelessness regarding death, that subterranean feeling that so much was still to come in life—that death was still far-off and for others rather than for himself.

About ten years later (probably) we find him locked in earnest discussion with his friends Alypius and Nebridius over the subject of death.[5] This is far from being the last word of Augustine on the matter, for it was one to which he returned throughout his life and his writings; but it fixes a particular moment in his own evolution, and, moreover, it brings up a hypothesis which deserves to be developed philosophically, even though Augustine himself does not pursue it.

But first for the discussion among the three friends. During all the fluctuations he underwent in his twenties some elements of that faith which he had imbibed 'with his mother's milk' kept recurring, or were relative constants within, so to speak, the whirlpool of his experience. One of those was the love of Christ as the great teacher of wisdom. Another, as it turns out, was belief in the immortality of the soul and in the judgment after death.

> I discussed with my friends Alypius and Nebridius concerning the nature of good and evil, and Epicurus would certainly have won the palm in my judgement if I had not believed that after death there remained life for the soul and treatment according to its deserts, which Epicurus did not hold. And I put the question, supposing we were immortals and could live in perpetual enjoyment of the body without any fear of loss, why we should not then be happy, or what else should we seek? I did not realise that it belonged to the very heart of my wretchedness to be so drowned and blinded in it that I could not conceive the light of real good and of beauty loved for its own sake, which the eye of the flesh does not see but only the innermost soul. I

5 VI, xvi, 26.

was so blind that I never came to ask myself what was the source of the pleasure I found in discussing these ideas, worthless as they were, with friends, and of my inability to be happy without friends, even in the sense of happiness which I then held, no matter how great the abundance of carnal pleasure. For truly I loved my friends for their own sake, and I knew that I was in turn so loved by them. (p. 99, amended).

In other words, Augustine, according to his own mature view, had sunk so deep in the habits of pleasure that he was close to becoming an Epicurean by conviction, and only the remnant of his Christian faith deterred him from capitulating to that philosophy. Still the thought is with him, that mortality alone restrains us from holding and practising a carnal notion of the good life, according to which pleasure is to be sought and pain to be avoided, and that is all there is to it. The thought of death brings pain . . . so, suppose we were immortals, would we not then have a life without any pain? Augustine passes immediately to a criticism of himself as he was at that point in his life, for even admitting this idea: he was foolish and blind not to recognize wherein lay the true origin of his love of the very conversation with friends, which had seen this absurd hypothesis thrown up; for deeper reflection upon the origin of friendship and love, he feels, would have terminated his wandering impulses at that point and would have brought him to reflect that 'to love friends for their own sake' and to know that love to be reciprocal, re-introduces at once the dialectic of love (or friendship) and death. Loving people *for their own sake* (and not just to pass futile time) raises the questions of death, of nihilism and of immortality; of how to love *for their own sake*, yet *humaniter*, in the face of our death, beings that are going to die.

Si essemus immortales . . . If we were immortal, why should we not be happy, or what would we still seek over and above that?
    Reflecting upon the death of his friend Augustine had said:

> That first grief had pierced so easily and so deeply only because I had spilt out my soul upon the sand, in loving a mortal man as if he were never to die. (p. 52)

Diligendo moriturum acsi non moriturum; ten years or so later we find Augustine making a kind of thought experiment involving the hypothesis of physical immortality, to test out ideas about happiness, with the results we have seen already. At this point I wish to leave Augustine's book and to reflect upon the relationship between death and value, using this intriguing Augustinian method of testing by means of an unreal hypothesis, that of physical but deathless life.

Does death remove all value from life and require rebellion in the style of Camus, as a consequence of which man may learn to 'love, to create, in the midst of the desert', that is, within a meaningless, unintelligible and absurd world?[6]

'*Si essemus immortales*': let us suppose the dream of Faust realized in ourselves—but without the unutterable price exacted of Faust, that of death and damnation. We have the perpetual and assured enjoyment of all physical goods and pleasures. Since corporeal integrity (Augustine's *in perpetua corporis voluptate sine ullo amissionis terrore viveremus*) goes hand in hand with our hypothetical deathlessness, we enjoy youth unending and perfect health, and no accident can ever harm us; even if we fall over a cliff we break no bones. Since no harm can touch us we are spared all fear, and we enjoy besides the ever-renewed realization of all possible satisfactions, in an existence without temporal limits. Would we be happy, because not subject to contingency and temporal finitude; or what would we still want to have over and beyond all that we had already?

Is it not clear at once that in the hypothetical state of physical integrity and deathlessness no recognition of our humanity, either in oneself or in others, would any longer be possible? Since we would know neither need nor desire, no help would ever be offered, no sacrifice ever be required in favour of others. And regarding our use of time: no choice, no alternative would ever be imposed, since in endless time we could do endless things endlessly, and all possibilities of enjoyment would necessarily be realized. The result would be utter boredom accompanied by a total indifference with regard to others, a complete exteriority of hearts—the inevitable product of perfect autonomy and autarky. No reciprocity or mutual friendship would ever matter, for no relationship could ever make a decisive difference to our lives, or involve our liberty by placing us before a turning-point. There would not even remain the requirement to reproduce, for there is no point in reproducing within an immortal species. What would take the place of friendship if not the boredom of unending repetition, or else perpetually changing associations, granted that the gift of an 'I' to a 'You' would lack all coherent structure and the other individual would be indefinitely replaceable, just like oneself?

This surrealist hypothesis has only one point and purpose, which is to show that death is not in truth the destroyer of all human value and good—as Augustine in his nihilistic moment thought and as Camus was always strongly tempted to think—but in fact their revealer; indeed, no value could

6 Albert Camus begins the chapter 'Nihilisme et Histoire' of *L'homme révolté*: 'L'insurrec-tion humaine, dans ses formes élevées et tragiques, n'est et ne peut être qu'une longue protestation contre la mort, une accusation enragé de cette condition régie par la peine de mort géneralisée. Dans tous les cas que nous avons rencontrés, la protestation, chaque fois, s'adresse a tout ce qui, dans la création, est dissonance, opacité, solution de continuité. . . . Au monde des condamnés à mort, à la mortelle opacité de la condition, le révolté oppose inlassablement son exigence de vie et de transparence définitives.'

be recognized, if we were otherwise than physically mortal. Furthermore, no true recognition of good as good is possible without a profound consciousness of death. A perfectly banal example will serve to illustrate this truth.

The student who faces examinations but needs help with the immediate preparation will, one supposes, be grateful to a fellow student who volunteers to spend, say, two evenings with the one in need of help. Now, what exactly will the other be grateful for? (I have tried this out in class and found that it does in fact, perhaps surprisingly, take a little time for the penny to drop!) It might be said, 'for the fellow student's grasp of the course and ability to coach'; but then there might be many students who knew the course but who would not have been willing to help. Gratitude is evoked in this case by the sacrifice of the fellow-student's time as well as by his expertise, but more fundamentally by the former than by the latter. But why, then, is time of value—if not because it is always necessarily limited, and limited by death? The student, in short, whether he realizes it or not, is grateful to his fellow student principally and ultimately because the latter is going to die. It is our natural, temporal finitude alone which imposes choices upon us and thereby invokes our liberty, since we cannot realize all possibilities in our lifetime, not even one after the other: we must choose for a given evening to work, to play or to do nothing, or perhaps a little of all three; but the deliberate choice of one of these will rule out the other two, at least for that evening.

Liberty, once it is truly conscious of its own finitude, becomes ever more aware of the unique value offered by each and every instant of mutual help and friendship, since no moment of experience can ever be repeated, any more than a moment of time can be made to recur. We are on the way towards ever truer freedom, when we attempt to incarnate in our experience and action the realization that each and every human being (including those whom we may not like, or who are our enemies) is irreplaceable, and that every relationship with another person is capable by our very nature as mortals—but as mortals made by love for love—of touching another in the depths of the spirit; and for good or for evil—for death and finitude, after all, do not create the good but only reveal it to our reflection. Our liberty cannot be true unless it comes creatively to terms with the commitments we have made and with the impossibility of living several lives in one. Faithfulness is difficult for human beings to sustain right to the end, or in the hardest parts of life, and it is only to be expected that it ceases to be valued (or even understood) within a purely secular and terrestrial perspective. Only upon the divine liberty can spiritual freedom be based, and only in reliance upon the divine wisdom can we hope to be wise, or at least to love wisdom as we should and to grow in it.

But the Psalmist said it with eloquent brevity:

> 'Teach us, Lord, the shortness of our life, that we may learn wisdom of heart.'

Philosophy, Art, Creativity

LIBERATO SANTORO

Philosophy, conceived in its original emergence as the 'archaic' and 'cosmic' unification of 'all in one', is the map-of-totality.[1] If this statement qualifies the Greek and Classical understanding of philosophy as the search for the ἀρχή of the κόσμος, in modern times the metalanguage of philosophy is practised rather as the continuous process of re-modelling the ever-changing landscape of reality. Hence, for us, even the most complete and systematic map cannot but be open to further expansions and renewed outlines. This is so because, if nothing else, every map as every model needs to be read, decoded, transmitted, interpreted, hence understood and misunderstood in the spirit of faithful infidelity and responsible violence.[2]

Totality, for me here in time, can only be grasped and defined asymptotically; it can only be experienced by approximation. The resulting design or blueprint, the penultimate probable map, the most adequate hypothetical model would then exhibit, in its minutest details, the essential features of openness, novelty, change, order and disorder. The map-of-philosophy may well reveal totality to be a totality of fragments. Reality may be revealed to be the continuous re-ordering of its parts and elements, as in the galactic interaction of constellations: not a static, closed and fixed order, but a living, changing organism preserving its ordered complexity precisely in its striving towards a more serene simplicity.[3] Following and remodelling the order of the universe, the open order of totality, philosophy—as experience—is the exercise of transcending: it is the foretaste of Paradise.

The fragment that follows is only a trace and an indication, a suggestion and a seminal attempt at articulating a discourse on totality. The main intention of the discourse is the search for the meaning of quality. The leading key-word is creativity. The context is language. The guiding co-

---

1   I also refer to Heraclitus, Fr. B 50, where the philosopher announces that the ultimate intelligibility consists in the unification of totality: ἓν πάντα. See Martin Heidegger's interpretation of Heraclitus' fragment in *Vorträge und Aufsätze* (Pfullingen, 1954); and in *Was ist das—die Philosophie?* (Pfullingen, 1956).

2   'In order to extract from what the words say, what those words want to say, every interpretation must necessarily employ some violence.' Martin Heidegger, *Kant und das Problem der Metaphysik* (Bonn, 1929), p. 192. See also E. Betti, *Teoria generale della interpretazione* (Milano, 1955), Cap. III: 'Metodologia ermeneutica'; and G. Mounin, *Teoria e storia della traduzione* (Torino, 1965), pp. 13-26.

3   The idea of 'constellation', with its link to the idea of 'utopia' and the understanding of philosophical discourse as 'fragment', is convincingly presented in T. W. Adorno's *Negative Dialektik* (Frankfurt am Main, 1966), (Part II).

ordinates for the mapping are derived from reflection on art and its inbuilt poetic logic of transcendence.

It is seemingly easy to argue for the generally accepted, almost obvious, quasi tautological coincidence or even identity of art and creativity. The words are often used as if they were semantically interchangeable and co-extensive, if only at the level of their connotative functions. The tacit acceptance of the identity and co-relation between the two terms—embedded as it is in our quotidian experience and practice of language—can be partly explained by means of reference to the history of Western thought. We may recollect Plato's image of the demiurge toying with mirrors[4] and Aristotle's poetic/genetic conception of art[5] as the exercise of 'bringing something into being'. The Medievals understood the craftsman's and artist's activity as analogously participating in and imitating the very act of divine creation. The idea of art as specifically definable in terms of creativity is, finally, central to Romantic artistic and literary theories, grounded as they are upon the corollary idea of *genius*. It ought to be stressed that the Romantic and Idealistic understanding of creativity rests theoretically on the thematized principle of subjectivity. Creativity is the very essence of subjectivity conceived as the agent and the active process of self-alienation, self-unfolding, self-realization, self-expression. Art itself is, hence, seen as the objectified manifestation of the subject. It should also be noticed that the Romantic/Idealistic suggestions are, by and large, simplistically adopted or superficially rejected as foregone conclusions totally divorced from their speculative and theoretical presuppositions.

While postponing the discussion of the identity between art and creativity, which I shall articulate in the terms of contemporary philosophical preoccupations, I will begin by suggesting that even the metalanguages of aesthetics ought to unfold according to the logic of creativity, and in some cases they do so. The advanced suggestion, however, is tenable only if aesthetics, as a philosophical endeavour, transcends the closures of normative and dogmatic models, and if the problematic separation between aesthetics and poetics, by and large sustained throughout the Western tradition, is finally abandoned.

Most, if not all, aesthetic theories since Baumgarten in modern times are articulated as normative doctrines. In this they have, I suggest, suffered the fascinating influence of Plato's Idealism. Aesthetic discourse, in the West, has inherited the Platonic and Neoplatonic prejudice according to which art is understood as the realm of participated form and beauty, where the idea of form and beauty is conceived as a metaphysically transcendent and hypostatically divine paradigm. From this follows the somewhat negativizing absorption of art by a polarized psychology or metaphysics of beauty, dangerously

4   Plato, *Rep.* 596d-e.
5   *Metaph.* 1032b 1; *Nic. Eth.* 1140a 9; *Poet.* 1451b 27; *Phys.* 190a 5. See Liberato Santoro, 'Some Remarks on Aristotle's Concept of Mimesis', *Revue des Études Anciennes* 82 (1980), 31-40; and 'Aristotle and Contemporary Aesthetics', *Diotima* 10 (1982), 112-21.

bordering on one-sidedness or perilously abstract generalization. From this—
particularly so with Plato—also follows the corollary that poetry, far from
being an autonomous and autarchic articulation of experience, should rather
be in function of moral and political education. Art can, on the one hand, be
a serious and responsible playing with memories, images and shadows of
ideas, in order to perfect attunement to the order of pure and spiritual ideas.
In this case art would absolve its prescribed educational, political and moral
function, thus surrendering any claim to autonomy. On the other hand, art
could be a frivolous and dangerous—though quite gratifying—playing with
images, for the purpose of sensory pleasure. We would, in this case, indulge
in it by forgetfully betraying our vocation to metaphysical truth.

The Platonic and Neoplatonic tradition reached its maturity—though
translated into the language of subjectivity—in Hegel's philosophy where
aesthetics is articulated as the science of man-made beauty; and further
survived in all the projects that define themselves as theories of beauty.
Understood as the philosophy of beauty in opposition to the theory of art,
aesthetics preserves the characters of an a priori science, even when presented
as the systematization of results deductively obtained after historical and
critical analysis. Generally speaking aesthetic theories, grounded as they are
upon particular conceptual models, presuppose the prejudices endemic to
the adopted and pre-elaborated philosophical doctrine. Hence, aesthetics
tends to apply categories and concepts dealing with taste and beauty to the
experience of art, constraining both art in the making and the understanding/
fruition of art within the bounds of a priori and abstract theoretical models.
From such a closed and limited understanding of aesthetics, taken in separation
from poetics, derive its inability to adequately deal with contemporary artistic
phenomena, and the endless debates—particularly within the Anglo-American
positivist and analytical tradition—concerning the validity of judgments of
taste and the very possibility of defining art and beauty.[6] Philosophical
aesthetics, understood—in opposition to poetics—as a reflection on the
meaning of beauty, taste and the peculiarity of sensory experience we call
aesthetic, is, to quote Nicolai Hartmann, bound 'to delude and disappoint us'.
Otherwise, as a normative discipline which operates with pre-established
logical models and categories, aesthetics can never grasp and justify the very
essence of art as the activity which aims to produce works distinctively
characterized by some degree of novelty.

The idea of beauty, which in classical thought is conceived as an ontological—and therefore pre-subjective, pre-psychological—category and an
objective property of reality, implies the principle of transcendence: the
necessary existence of a supreme Being and a perfect Order, prior to and

6   Instances of these difficulties and unease at defining art and beauty are to be found,
    among numerous others, in C. K. Ogden and I. A. Richards, *The Meaning of Meaning*
    (London, 1972) [1923], pp. 139-59; and in a more recent book, rigidly within the
    analytic tradition and spellbound by the figure of Wittgenstein looming over-large: B.
    R. Tilghman, *But is it Art?* (Oxford, 1984).

beyond the realm of contingent beings. Aquinas' reflections on the nature of beauty—as a transcendental property of being[7]—are particularly eloquent and expressive of the classical and metaphysical (particularly Platonic) way of thinking.

Beside the enormous influence of Platonic Idealism—quite congenial to the Christian world-view—as the main source of inspiration for aesthetic theories as theories of beauty, Western thought has been informed by the philosophy of Aristotle. Unlike Plato's approach—inherited by the aesthetic tradition inspired by him—Aristotle's considerations on art initiated the articulation of a poetic theory and focused upon the close analysis of artistic/aesthetic artefacts, their internal structure and the processes of artistic production. While Plato gave priority to the concept of beauty—in order to ground a discourse on art—Aristotle 'at the beginning of his *Poetics* put aside the concept of beauty and launched upon the study of art.'[8] Aristotle is concerned with the specific nature of the activity that brings to light the particular type of artefacts we call poetic, artistic or aesthetic. In other words, unlike aesthetic theory mainly preoccupied with reflection on the meaning of beauty, Aristotle has grounded the possibility of a poetic theory primarily concerned with the reflection on the meaning of art as a particular way of making artefacts. Hence, his poetics can be read as a form of literate, reflective, theoretically responsible, internal or immanent criticism. Obviously the distinction between aesthetics and poetics, though indicative of mutually exclusive practices, is stressed here mainly for methodological reasons. They should be seen, by now, as complementary approaches which, in their synthesis, would vanquish many misleading confusions and preoccupations caused by mutually exclusive polarization of interest and stress. In more general terms, the interaction between Platonic and Aristotelian philosophy ought to be revisited in a similar spirit of synthetic reconstruction, in so far as philologically and theoretically possible. Equally so, and in the same spirit of dialectical revision, the complementary inter-dependance and co-habitation of the classical world and the contemporary mind is in need of attention. Failure to note and thematize the symbiosis of 'the ancient and the modern' would only revive the misguided preoccupations of the 17th century *querelle des anciennes et des modernes*. Even worse, it would lead to the nihilism, scepticism and cultural dualism which vitiates the strategies of Deconstructivism and the Derridian exclusive, un-dialectical difference of 'presence' and 'absence', heralding—with much noise—the penultimate void of pre-structured absence.

I shall, at this stage, suggest a viable, though abstract and schematic, qualification of the meaning of creativity. Creativity is the source, power and disposition to bring into existence or to produce something. That which

---

7   See Umberto Eco, *Il problema estetico in Tommaso d'Aquino* (Milano, 1970); and Joseph De Finance, *Connaissance de l'être* (Paris-Bruges, 1966), pp. 193-206.
8   Wladislaw Tatarkiewicz, *History of Aesthetics* (The Hague-Warsaw, 1970), Vol. 1, p. 139.

is brought into existence is, obviously, something new and constitutes a new event. Hence, we could argue that—in a very wide sense—any human action is creative, that any instance of making (τέχνη or ποίησις) is originative of something new. However, we categorize, in a more specific and restricted sense, the creative act as that which gives origin to something exceptional and beyond the norm, something more surprising, unexpected and unfamiliar, something improbable, rare and unique, something more ostensibly rich in quality, something unprecedented and novel. In this more specific and not easily definable sense,[9] creativity denotes the disposition to determine a quality-leap: the emergence of a totally unfamiliar epochal vision or world-view, the birth of new ways of understanding, the origin of a new episteme, the expression of a novel sensibility, the discovery rich of many meanings and capable of disclosing numerous, new and previously unsuspected paths and patterns of experience. In this more exclusive connotation creativity implies the attitude to assimilate, interpret and re-formulate past experiences while—at once—modelling projects for the future. Creativity is, then, understood in function of the past while—at once—determining the future. It is the activity of renewing the past: reading, interpreting and questioning the order and disorder of the past and of past codes, while—at once—positing new orders, new codes and uttering new messages. I suggest that creativity should be conceived as a function and instance of the hermeneutic experience and of experience seen as the cohabitation of past and future in the present. Thus understood, creativity could be adequately defined as the leap of imagination into the future, the projected anticipation and constitution of the future, the invention and recognition of something new: which presupposes the deep and competent assimilation of the past.[10]

In the light of the preceding suggestions, I can now attempt to articulate and justify the analogy and affinity between creativity and art. The clarification of the meaning of art will provide an exemplary instance of the meaning of creativity. Art, in its widest connotation, is a mode of action, more precisely a manner of making and the knowledge of how to proceed in the activity of making. Art is, in other words, the totality of actions and processes aimed at forming, informing and ordering reality: a *'transformation into form'*,[11] with the unavoidable result of inducing, inspiring and sustaining a disposition of contemplation, aesthetic gratification, aesthetic *'arrest'* as Joyce would put it. Art draws the horizon of human encounters with a previously alien reality, 'the earth' which, by the order-giving and formative

---

9 See C. R. Rogers, 'Towards a Theory of Creativity', *ETC: A Review of General Semantics* 11 (1954) 249-60.

10 See, in particular, H.-G. Gadamer, 'Die Universalität des hermeneutischen Problems', in *Kleine Schriften*, (Tübingen, 1967), Vol. 1, p. 106.

11 Gadamer, in his *Wahrheit und Methode* (Tübingen, 1965), speaks of art as 'Verwandlung ins Gebilde'. This felicitous expression could also be rendered as 'metamorphosis into image'.

power of artistic insight and craft, is spiritualized, humanized, thus being transformed into a 'world'.[12]

Simply, and assuming the most general meaning of the word, in art and through art we encounter nature and transform it into culture. If this is so, art is an existential modality and disposition which qualifies and specifies human existence as such.[13] It must be noted, furthermore, that the very first act and event of transformation of nature into culture—the primordial and dramatic event which marked the birth of humanity, history and culture—presupposed and, at once, coincided with the invention of the sign, the beginning of language, the establishment of codes: it meant seeing something as something else.[14] The first act of creativity—the invention of signs—defined, instanced and crystallized the very essence of hermeneutic experience and of experience as hermeneutics. The neutral and meaningless pebble is suddenly seen as the flint, the totality of nature is seen and interpreted as culture and is hence 'translated'—by the informing hand—into cultural tools and artefacts. The very first act of human creativity, and its first instance, is at once the beginning of the sign-making process, the 'linguistic constitution of the world' and the act of interpretation, or the beginning of the hermeneutical experience. The adequate understanding of nature allows the leap of imagination into culture as the constitution of the human world. The understanding of the past is the fundamental and unavoidable 'condition of possibility' for any human constructive project. Culture itself, as endless semiosis and as totality of 'project', can be none else but renewed revisitation, anamnesis, co-habitation and symbiosis of past experience seen as something else. The invention of the first sign implies the overcoming of previous codes—as it were—and the obsolescence of previous forms of reading/interpreting/understanding. To be precise, these are—in the invention of the first sign—neither codes nor forms of cognition or volition. What I have referred to as 'the previous codes', challenged and overcome by the invention of the first sign, are rather instances of purely natural, blindly pre-cultural, animal-like 'experience': quasi-codes of an unmediated raw complex of signals and physiological stimuli.

The first act of culturalization of nature, the birth of the human world, the transformation and transcendence from nature into culture—instanced as it is by the sign-differential-leap and understood as the origin of technical transformations, and hence of art in the strict sense of the word—constitutes a 'qualitative leap': an absolutely unprecedented, unfamiliar and new event. The novelty of that primordial experience is guarded, treasured and contained in what we call Art or Fine Art: the experience of reiterated epiphany, the presence and manifestation of the world seen/perceived/experienced/

12 See M. Heidegger, 'Der Ursprung des Kunstwerkes', in *Holzwege* (Frankfurt, 1952).
13 See U. Eco, *A Theory of Semiotics* (Bloomington, 1979), pp. 22-4; and L. Santoro, *Presupposti filosofici dell'arte moderna* (Urbino, 1978), p. 17.
14 See U. Eco, ibid.

beheld as if for the first time, in the innocent light of a pristine gaze. The irruption of the epiphanic event, which works of art imply and determine, produces in us a growth and refinement of experience, grounds and projects our future, activates the transcending transformation of reality into its own ideal form.

The consideration—even though brief—of the nature of the work of art as a semiotic phenomenon, could assist in clarifying the meaning of the preceding suggestions. Let us observe, to begin, that although every act of transformation of nature into culture fundamentally affirms itself as generative of existence and as productive of new meaning—hence as creative in the wide sense of the word—a large number of human acts falls prey to 'technical reproducibility', to use Walter Benjamin's pregnant and effective formulation. In these cases, the light of novelty is obscured and almost imperceptible. The artistic artefact, the aesthetic message on the contrary exhibits, more so than any other kind of artefact, the essential characters and the mark of creativity. The work of art violates the norm. It critically questions the previous codes. It constitutes itself as a message carrier of new meanings and generative of new possible and probable codes.[15] However, it must soon be added that the aesthetic message, while questioning and overcoming the previous structured codes of experience, does not totally and exclusively suspend, bracket, ignore and negate them. On the contrary, its very novelty is sustained, nourished and constituted by the dialectical/ hermeneutical dialogue and symbiosis with past re-interpreted, re-enacted, re-lived codes. Creativity could not be intelligible without reference to tradition. More so, it seems clear to me that novelty is always the fruit of insistence in tradition; and I am equally convinced that revolutions are real, productive and effective or meaningful, in so far as they are authentic fruits of tradition.

Ambiguous, polysemic and self-referential, the work of art as aesthetic message is open to a multiplicity of readings which incessantly and indefinitely re-formulate and re-invent new codes and, hence, further possibilities for the emergence of new messages. The entire art-universe is fundamentally the global experience of interpreting old codes, their partial violation perpetrated by new messages, finally the production of new codes, new dictions and new readings. For this reason it can be safely suggested that in art we find one of the most luminous expressions of what we call human creativity, and that art can be seen as expression, image and form of the very essence of human experience as inscribed in the dialectical and hermeneutical circle of cultural/historical rootedness in tradition and existential projection into an ideal future. For the same reason, art—not unlike philosophy, contemplation and prayer—instances the meaning of transcendence as 'going beyond' the given, and the need/desire/nostalgia for transcendence as 'ideal order'.

15 See U. Eco, 'Sémantique de la métaphore', *Tel Quel* 55 (1973).

It seems obvious that aesthetics, understood as the philosophical metalanguage concerning the meaning of beauty, the justification of judgments of taste and the explanation of the type of sensory/intellectual experience qualified as aesthetic, cannot but 'disappoint us' or encourage all kinds of subjectivist, nominalist and 'analytic' excesses and confusions, if not sustained by the metalanguages of poetics, understood as the reflection on art: the processes of making aesthetic artefacts and the internal, objective structure, language and logic of the same artefacts. Consequently, aesthetics—as philosophy of art and beauty—can fulfil its task only in so far as it articulates itself in an indefinite circularity of re-codification of its categories. By changing and re-structuring itself—following in this the dynamism and violence of new artistic messages—aesthetics can assist in the understanding of philosophy *simpliciter* and of the possible future paths and projects of philosophy. It would enable us to rethink the Platonic and Greek idea of ἔρως φιλοσοφός. The new aesthetics would dispose us to more readily perceive the essence of art as a creative, utopic and transcending energy.

The alchemy of art consists in expanding the horizons of human experience. It consists in refining our ways of relating to the world and of giving meaning to the world. Art makes us realize that the possible, the ideal, the not-yet-real world is as real as what we in our half-awake, everyday existence, commonly hold as real. It makes us conscious of the fact that reality is a dynamic process, a field of forces unfolding in ever new growths of meaning and new more pertinent projects. Art announces what could be dismissed as improbable and incredible in so far as ideal. Finally, art as a creative experience makes us understand the human world as a world of work, production, expression, transformation of nature, sign-process, language, action. Art enables us to redeem the deep significance of play, happiness, imagination, hidden and embedded as it is in the humblest act of making. Art helps us to re-discover the transcendent value, the absolute quality, the divine meaning of what we call life and perhaps do not quite yet understand.

The Challenge of Newman's Vision
of the University

DAVID WALSH

The appearance of Newman's *Idea of a University* and the subsequent establishment of the Catholic University of Ireland in 1854 called into question the entire historical drift of the modern world. At a time of increasing specialization, utilitarianism, rationalism and secularism, Newman took his stand on the side of integration, philosophy, intuition and faith. Without engaging in reactionary polemics he provided a reasoned demonstration of the necessity for a spiritual foundation within the educational process, which has subsequently become the classic modern statement on the subject. The aphoristic quality of many of Newman's pronouncements derives not merely from a masterful writing style, but much more from the ultimacy of intellectual penetration in many of the positions he had reached. Contrary to the image of comfortable Victorian urbanity that still attaches to him, Newman always had the spiritual courage to follow his convictions to their logical conclusion. It is for this reason that many of the (frequently overlooked) statements of the *Idea* strike us even today as startling in their unconventionality. As for instance when in Discourse IX he concludes that 'a University cannot exist externally to the Catholic pale, for it cannot teach universal knowledge if it does not teach Catholic theology.'[1] This moreover is a principle which he is anxious should not be misunderstood as merely requiring the provision of chairs of Catholic theology. He explains that

> a direct and active jurisdiction of the Church over it and in it is necessary, lest it should become the rival of the Church within the community at large in those theological matters which to the Church are exclusively committed,—acting as the representative of the intellect, as the Church is the representative of the religious principle.[2]

The notion that the intellectual disciplines require a spiritual foundation beyond themselves and that such a foundation is best preserved by the spiritual authority of the Church, is a suggestion sufficiently unfashionable to ensure it would be neglected by the majority of Newman's readers. He is universally regarded as the defender of the ideal of a liberal education in opposition to the pressures for utilitarian training. But whether liberal education can continue in the absence of a commitment to the life of the

---

1 John Henry Cardinal Newman, *The Idea of a University*, ed. Martin J. Svaglic (Notre Dame, 1982), p. 163.
2 Ibid. See also pp. xxxvii and 18.

spirit, is a question that few of his admirers have been prepared to openly confront. Can the great humanizing articulations of the past be sustained apart from the spiritual roots that gave them birth? David De Laura has revealed an ironic side to this issue in his study of how Newman's own literary Catholic humanism was in the following generation deflected into the 'fluid, relativistic, and "aesthetic" humanism of Pater'.[3] The prospects for avoiding such misinterpretations and returning anew to the spiritual foundations are, however, greater today because the secular humanist experiment has now run its course and the results have become fully apparent. Technology pursued apart from any reference to the ultimate ends of human existence has demonstrated its dehumanizing effect, and the shallowness of cultural aestheticism has proved its inability to restore the life of the spirit in man. Reality itself has compelled a rethinking of our intellectual and educational assumptions.

For this reason we can, I believe, be more sanguine about the possibility of reexamining the issues raised by Newman in an atmosphere free of ideological distortions and preconceptions. One might even hope that the radical nature of his proposal for a Catholic University would once again be appreciated and due recognition accorded to his principle of the necessity for a spiritual foundation to the *studium generale* that is the main business of a University. For the problems that Newman predicted are the very ones that have now come to fruition. All that has changed is the starting point. Newman's concern was with the atheistic or diluting effects of the secular disciplines on religion; our difficulty is the incoherence of such arts and sciences set adrift from the ordering reality of Spirit. From either direction one arrives at the same conclusion: that the proper functioning of the mind of man is impossible without an acknowledgement of the transcendent order within which it exists, that the attainment of man's full humanity is dependent on a love that lifts us up beyond the merely human level, that man cannot even be man without God. For the defence of faith against the subversion of rational critique is correlatively the defence of reason against the destructiveness of its own excesses.[4] In the present study we will focus on the latter half of the argument, the necessity for a spiritual foundation

---

3 David J. De Laura, *Hebrew and Hellene in Victorian England: Newman, Arnold and Pater* (Austin, 1969), p. xi. De Laura summarizes the problem as follows: 'To perpetuate the values that Arnold and Pater subsumed under the term "culture"—despite the absence of older sustaining religious and social beliefs and an increasing divorce from the actualities of modern society—remains, I believe, the tragically unfulfilled aspiration of twentieth century humanists . . . Far from comprising an "episode" of a past culture, the issues first raised with some clarity and penetration by Newman, Arnold and Pater are the issues defining the quality of our failure' (pp. xix–xx).

4 Neither the utilitarianism of Bentham nor the glorification of knowledge by Brougham raised man to anything higher. 'In morals, as in physics, the stream cannot rise higher than its source. Christianity raises man from earth, for it comes from heaven; but human morality creeps, struts, or frets upon the earth's level, without wings to rise. The Knowledge School does not contemplate raising man above himself.' Newman, 'The Tamworth Reading Room', *Essays and Sketches*, Vol. II (Westport, 1970), p. 188.

from the viewpoint of the secular disciplines themselves. This approach is recommended, not only because such problems are most in evidence today, but also because it presents the relevance of Newman's case for a religiously grounded education in the most widely accessible way. Our exploration will begin with his critique of the dominant intellectual trends of the modern world, paying particular attention to his predictions and what has actually happened; we can then turn to the solution he proposed, in the form of a Catholic University, and to how he sought to make it persuasive to those who did not share his presupposition of faith.

I

The great danger against which Newman worked all his life was the denigration of the importance of religion in human life, and the correlative error of expecting that its role could be replaced by intellectual enlightenment. As an issue it was manifested in his advocacy of a pastoral role for the tutor when he held that position at Oriel College.[5] But it was first brilliantly crystallized in his letters on the Tamworth Reading Room. Nothing better epitomized the new spirit of universal utilitarian education than the establishment of such public reading rooms. They were founded on the twin convictions that education was best served by prohibiting discussion of the fruitless controversies in religion and politics, and instead promoting the cultivation of 'Useful Knowledge [as] the great instrument of education' ('Tamworth', p. 174). Knowledge has the capacity to make us better, on the conception of Lord Brougham, because man 'by being accustomed to such contemplations will feel the *moral dignity* of his nature exalted' (p. 176). The essential weakness of this argument is deftly exposed by Newman through his insistence on asking '*how* these wonderful moral effects are to be wrought under the instrumentality of the physical sciences?' Under such closer scrutiny it emerges that no specific mechanism is envisaged beyond 'a mere preternatural excitement under the influence of some stimulating object, or the peace which is attained by there being nothing to quarrel with' (p. 182).

Newman then went on to show that the acquisition of knowledge without the ordering influence of Christianity is, on the contrary, likely to lead to an overweening pride in one's own accomplishments. Men are not moved by reason or, as he so paradoxically states it, 'man is *not* a reasoning animal' (p. 205). In the absence of a higher spiritual restraint the inevitable human tendency towards self-aggrandizement is given free rein. Moreover this is no merely accidental consequence but a virtual necessity of our nature, as Newman makes clear when he returns to this topic in the *Idea of a University*. The portrait drawn there of the gentleman's morality—'one who

---

5   A. Dwight Culler, *The Imperial Intellect: A Study of Newman's Educational Ideal* (New Haven, 1955), chap. 3 and *passim*.

never inflicts pain'—has the kind of intuitive accuracy that is immediately recognizable. The best that can be expected from such intellectual refinement is the 'mere human loveliness' of Oxford which, while it may prepare us for the true inner transformation of grace, if left to itself will degenerate into a shallowness barely concealing a well-bred hedonism. Its central heresy 'is the substitution of a moral sense or taste for conscience in the true meaning of the word'.[6] Because of the gentleman's concern with external appearances virtue becomes identified with what is pleasing and affords a convenient opportunity for socially tolerated vice. 'Thus at length we find, surprising as it may be', Newman concludes, 'that the very refinement of Intellectualism, which began by repelling sensuality, ends by excusing it' (p. 153).

What the intramundane perspective of the sciences lacks is a recognition of the height and depth of human existence, the seriousness of sin and the need for divine grace. Newman does not accept the suggestion that the study of nature will lead us to contemplate its Creator. It is just as likely, he contends, when religious feeling is absent 'to lead the mind to the atheistic theory, as the simplest and easiest'.[7] But even when natural investigations are given a religiously favourable interpretation they never arrive at the God of Christianity; at most they can reach 'the animated principle of a vast and complicated system' denominated by such terms as 'world soul', 'vital power' or 'Supreme Being'. It is emphatically 'not the Almighty God'. The essence of religion, which Newman identifies as 'the idea of a Moral Governor and a particular Providence', can only be apprehended through the moral intuition of sin and redemption in human conscience. It is this inner moral-religious experience that should form the centre of education in Newman's view:

> I consider, then, that intrinsically excellent and noble as are scientific pursuits, and worthy of a place in a liberal education, and fruitful in temporal benefits to the community, still they are not, and cannot be, *the instrument* of an ethical training; that physics do not supply a basis, but only materials for religious sentiment; that knowledge does but occupy, does not form the mind; that apprehension of the unseen is the only known principle capable of subduing moral evil, educating the

6 *Idea*, p. 146. For his remarks on Oxford see 'Site of a University' in *Essays and Sketches*, Vol. II, pp. 299f.

7 'Tamworth', p. 209. He includes literature in this critique in the *Idea*, p. 167: 'Here then are two injuries which Revelation is likely to sustain at the hands of the Masters of human reason unless the Church, as in duty bound, protects the sacred treasure which is in jeopardy. The first is a simple ignoring of Theological Truth altogether ... The second, which is of a more subtle character, is a recognition indeed of Catholicism, but (as if in pretended mercy to it) an adulteration of its spirit. ... while Science is made to subserve the former of the two injuries, which Revealed Truth sustains,—its exclusion, literature subserves the latter,—its corruption.' See also p. 28, and *An Essay in Aid of a Grammar of Assent* (London, 1931), p. 416 on the corruption of religion.

multitude, and organizing society; and that, whereas man is born for action, action flows not from inferences, but from impressions,—not from reasonings, but from Faith. ('Tamworth', p. 213)

The neglect of this spiritual foundation affects not only the prospect for order in individual and social existence, for it also has a deleterious impact on the autonomous intellectual disciplines themselves. Here Newman is at his most prescient. He recognized that the expansive new sciences which appeared so self-sufficient would very quickly lose their own coherence, without a reliable means of relating themselves to the ultimate context of life in which they exist. Separate modes of inquiry, without the restraining influence of an integrated viewpoint, would result in the aggressive claims of the various partial viewpoints to represent the totality—a phenomenon with which we are familiar in the rise of 'ideologies'. Indeed there is a remarkably contemporary ring to many of Newman's observations on how the devotees of a single science become 'bigots and quacks' in their insistence on their own discipline as the key to everything. We are unfortunately all too well acquainted with the 'man of one idea'.[8] So well acquainted in fact that we find even Newman's most outrageous examples somewhat commonplace today. As for example when he describes behaviourist psychology as the most bizarre abstraction imaginable;[9] or the claim of political economy that the drive to accumulate 'is, to the mass of mankind, the great source of *moral* improvement' far superior to Christianity; or the historian who maintains that certain doctrines cannot be true because they are not original to the apostolic documents.

The source of the problem, Newman diagnoses, is the exclusion of theology or more broadly of faith from the horizon of the sciences and from their setting in the University. Since learning is a circle or a whole, 'the systematic omission of any one science from the catalogue prejudices the accuracy and completeness of our knowledge altogether, and that, in proportion to its importance' (*Idea*, p. 39). Such is the case of those sciences and institutions that aim at a purely secular learning. Newman can hardly make his point more strongly:

> In a word, Religious Truth is not only a portion, but a condition of general knowledge. To blot it out is nothing short, if I may so speak, of unravelling the web of University Teaching. (pp. 52–3)

8 *Idea*, pp. 37, 44, 57.
9 What we now know as behaviourist social science, Newman introduces by asking us 'to imagine what cannot be. I say, let us imagine a project for organizing a system of scientific teaching, in which the agency of man in the material world cannot allowably be recognized, and may allowably be denied. Physical and mechanical causes are exclusively to be treated of; volition is a forbidden subject.' (*Idea*, p. 41. For the other illustrations cf. pp. 69, 72).

Without a spiritual context the other disciplines are incapable of resisting the temptation to provide a comprehensive explanation for the whole of reality. Left to themselves 'these foreign sciences will assume certain principles as true, and act upon them, which they neither have the authority to lay down themselves, nor appeal to any other higher science to lay down for them' (p. 73). The effect serves only to reinforce the isolation of the disciplines from one another and the incoherent superficial 'viewiness' which Newman saw as one of the most harmful effects of the new educational movement.

The results of this experiment with a purely secular and largely utilitarian education have subsequently confirmed his worst fears. For the decline of reason has now advanced far beyond the point that Newman could foresee, making his warning examples sound like descriptions of what we readily take for granted. We are no longer surprised when we are told that it is not the business of science to consider 'values', rather that its sole concern is an objective analysis of the 'facts'. The distinction is universally accepted as absolute. Nor are we shocked when under the focus of such a factual analysis man himself is quantified according to his physical, chemical, biological, psychological and social constituents.[10] The implication is that he is nothing more than the sum of his elements, and that even his highest moral-religious intuitions might ultimately be explainable as the result of certain neurotic maladjustments, social conditioning, class consciousness or other residual historical baggage.[11] Having swallowed everything thus far it is not much further to acquiescing glumly in the decline of man's freedom as the price that must be paid for exploiting fully the benefits of technology's control of human nature. We can give serious consideration to the paradox first noted by C. S. Lewis, that man's final conquest of human nature will mean the abolition of man.[12]

We are accustomed to acknowledging the moral vacuum in which science and technology operate, but much worse is the loss of spiritual substance that

10 As Leon Kass observes: 'The notion of the "distinctively human" has been seriously challenged by modern scientists . . . We are witnessing the erosion, perhaps the final erosion, of the idea of man as something splendid or divine, and its replacement with a view that sees man, no less than nature, as simply more raw material for manipulation and homogenization.' 'The New Biology: What Price Relieving Man's Estate', *Science* 174 (1971), 786.

11 Darwin, for example, acknowledged his 'innermost conviction' that 'the universe is not the result of chance. But then with me the horrid doubt always arises whether convictions of man's mind which has developed from the mind of the animals, are of any value or at all trustworthy. Would anyone trust in the conviction of a monkey's mind, if there are any convictions in such a mind?' Letter of 3 July, 1881. Quoted in Francis Darwin, *Charles Darwin: His Life* (London, 1983), p. 68.

12 C. S. Lewis, *The Abolition of Man* (New York, 1947). On the contemporary problems of science and technology see Hans Jonas, *Philosophical Essays: From Ancient Creed to Technological Man* (Englewood Cliffs, 1974); David Ehrenfeld, *The Arrogance of Humanism* (New York, 1978); Christopher Booker, *The Seventies. The Decade that Changed the Future* (New York, 1980).

has occurred in those very disciplines intended to preserve it. The dominance of the scientific-technological ethos is not entirely due to its pragmatic success; in far greater measure it results from the failure of the humanities to provide an adequate spiritual counterweight to the rationalist wasteland. Arts and letters have become victims of the same disease and we look in vain to them for healing help. A spiritual crisis means that the agencies responsible for the restoration of order are incapable of taking action. Having become so imbued with the prevailing climate of scepticism, relativism and hedonism the humane disciplines are scarcely capable of recovering our essential humanity through an openness toward transcendent truth. The best that can generally be expected is a refined aesthetic expression of man's modern state of alienation—albeit a critique that suffers from the same disorder in its inability to recognize the possibility of existence in right order.[13]

The phenomenon is by now quite familiar to us in the art, literature and philosophy of the closed self in all its diverse manifestations. In recent years literary criticism has joined in the process with its emphasis on deconstructing, reducing and generally disintegrating the meaning of texts.[14] Our only consolation in these bleak developments is that the preoccupation with emptiness is not an enduring theme; eventually it undermines the *raison d'être* for its own form of expression. It becomes simply too boring and we are ready to move on. The history of art from the Renaissance is a good illustration of the sequence for, beginning with a shift to secular treatments, we have a gradual narrowing of the range of subjects until, in the twentieth century, art itself becomes the main theme and the entire process reaches a virtual dead end.[15] The study of history is coming under a similar kind of pressure as the dramatic expansion of historical materials confronts us anew with the question of meaning, of what makes the past worth remembering in the first place. Even academic philosophy must surely be ready to abandon its more than fifty year sojourn in the desert of linguistic analysis, and some preliminary indications show a willingness by philosophers to once again take their stand on the only solid ground available: the human experience of existence. We might even hope that the traditional queen of the sciences, theology, can recover its role by sloughing off the residual effects of positivism and forthrightly insisting on the reality of its subject matter as grounded in the truth of man's spirit.

13 One of the earliest exemplars of this type of literature is probably Matthew Arnold's 'Dover Beach'. In our own century the form has been carried about as far as possible in the works of Franz Kafka and Samuel Beckett. See the observations of Eric Voegelin in 'Henry James' "The Turn of the Screw"', *Southern Review* (1971), 3–48.

14 See Gerald Graff, *Literature Against Itself* (Chicago, 1979); Harold Bloom, *The Breaking of the Vessels* (Chicago, 1982); Denis Donoghue, *Ferocious Alphabets* (Boston, 1981).

15 See Titus Burckhart, *Sacred Art in East and West* (London, 1967); Hans Sedlmayr, *Art in Crisis: The Lost Center*, trans. Brian Battershaw (Chicago, 1958); Booker, *The Seventies*, particularly his comments on the thinly disguised sense of disappointment in Kenneth Clark's TV series, 'Civilisation', when the 'progress' of art reaches our own time.

In every case the root of the problem lies, not so much in the autonomous functioning of the disciplines *per se*, but in their separation from the spiritual life of man which ultimately guarantees the meaning, rationality and goodness of their knowledge. Such a critical dissociation occurs, Newman recognized, when the force of transcendent truth has lost its ability to command assent. He understood the problem well and traced it to its source in Lord Brougham's conviction 'that man shall no more render account to man for his belief, over which he has himself no control' ('Tamworth', p. 177). It is the reduction of spiritual truth to the level of purely subjective emotion, where true and false, right and wrong, no longer have any application. Newman diagnosed it as the peculiarly 'modern form of infidelity' which is unwilling to outrightly reject the Christian faith, but instead insists 'that Religion is not the subject-matter of a science' (*Idea*, p. 290). It is on this ground that theology was to be excluded from the new universities and the secular disciplines to withdraw from the guiding influence of spirit. For without a principle or criterion of truth theological science can hardly sustain the claim to knowledge. Indeed it is difficult to avoid eventually reaching an atheistic conclusion since, as Newman observed, there is not 'much difference between avowing that there is no God and implying that nothing definite can for certain be known about Him' (*Idea*, p. 30).

It is against this liberalism, 'the anti-dogmatic principle', that he directed the battle of his life. He saw it as reducing the awesome mystery of God to the level of human understanding, human feeling and human convenience, as he explained at length in the note on 'Liberalism' appended to the *Apologia*. There we find his definition of the phenomenon which for theoretic accuracy can hardly be surpassed:

> Now by liberalism I mean false liberty of thought, or the exercise of thought upon matters, in which, from the constitution of the human mind, thought cannot be brought to any successful issue, and therefore is out of place.[16]

Having begun with the generous intention of making the transcendent reality of God more accessible to the finite capacity of man, it can only succeed in undermining the first principles of thought and action, the truths of revelation, and unfolding finally into a full admission of atheism. The beginning of this development Newman traced to the Reformation, especially its establishment of the principle of private judgment and the right of individual conscience. 'The spirit of lawlessness came in with the Reformation, and Liberalism is its offspring.'[17] Once this subjective viewpoint has become normative it did not take much more to conclude that 'no religious tenet is important unless reason shows it to be so', that 'no one can believe what he does not understand', that 'no theological doctrine is anything

16 *Apologia Pro Vita Sua*, ed. David J. De Laura (New York, 1968), p. 218.
17 Ibid., p. 152. See also p. 188 and *Idea*, p. 22.

more than an opinion', and so on. Newman regarded it as an inexorable philosophical sequence leading from Protestantism to Latitudinarianism, to Liberalism, and finally to atheism. In the last analysis no merely human judgment can 'withstand and baffle the fierce energy of passion and the all-corroding, all-dissolving scepticism of the intellect in religious inquiries' (*Apologia*, p. 187).

I I

What kind of force then is capable of checking this onslaught? Newman rejects the conventional enlightened approaches of relying on the progress of civilization, universal education, and even the Protestant trust in Scripture. His reason for dismissing the latter is most revealing of his position for, as he explains,

> a book, after all, cannot make a stand against the wild living intellect of man, and in this day it begins to testify, as regards its own structure and contents, to the power of that universal solvent, which is so successfully acting on religious establishment. (*Apologia*, p. 188)

The only effective way of countering the 'wild living intellect' must be an institution possessing 'a direct, immediate, active, and prompt means of withstanding the difficulty.'[18] It would have to be a divinely appointed power 'invested with the prerogative of infallibility in religious matters'. Knowing for certain the meaning of every portion of the divine Revelation, it would be capable of defining its own limits and of deciding when new developments are in accord or in conflict with the *Depositum* of faith. It would thereby preserve the foundational spiritual truth on which the whole structure of human knowledge and society is based. Such a description, Newman gradually came to conclude, applies to only one entity in the world today: the Catholic Church. For it is only a spiritually authoritative Church that is capable of protecting the authoritative source of transcendent truth, that it is revealed by God to man and can be apprehended in no other way. As a real organizational force the Church is ideally suited 'for smiting hard and throwing back the immense energy of the aggressive, capricious, untrustworthy intellect' (*Apologia*, p. 189).

Discounting for the moment the militant (even chauvinistic) tendency in Newman's thought, it is difficult to resist the logic of his position in general. For a religiously grounded university, whether Catholic or not, is surely the appropriate setting for intellectual exploration, being already in attunement with the spiritual truth from which all knowledge arises and towards which all knowledge leads. 'It is Religion, then, which suggests to Science its true conclusions; the facts come from Knowledge, but the principles come of

18 Ibid., p. 189, and pp. 89, 160.

Faith' ('Tamworth', p. 210). If we do not wish to break up the 'circle of secular knowledge' we cannot exclude the divine source, whose self-revelation within conscience and within history discloses the meaning of it all. 'How can we investigate any part of any order of Knowledge, and stop short of that which enters into every order? All true principles run over with it, all phenomena converge to it; it is truly the First and the Last' (*Idea*, p. 19). Newman takes it as axiomatic 'that all knowledge forms one whole, because its subject-matter is one' and draws the unequivocal conclusion 'that we cannot truly or fully contemplate [the universe] without in some main aspects contemplating Him' (*Idea*, p. 38). It is this integrating spiritual vision that is the key to his whole conception of a liberal or philosophic education. The *cognitio fidei* forms the 'illuminative reason' at the centre and thereby makes possible 'the clear, calm, accurate vision and comprehension of all things, as far as the finite mind can embrace them, each in its place, and with its own characteristics upon it' (*Idea*, p. 105). Christianity, where it has been made 'the element and principle of all education', provides a foundation to literature and science that perfects them in the service to highest spiritual truth. 'Where Revealed Truth has given the aim and direction to Knowledge, Knowledge of all kinds will minister to Revealed Truth.'[19] The rationality of the various autonomous disciplines is only assured when they are oriented towards the true spiritual end of existence and take their bearings in relation to it.

Once this context, of man's participation in the order of transcendent truth, has been acknowledged, then the secular arts and sciences can find a foundation for the assumptions on which they are based and which by themselves they are ever unable to justify. Our understanding of nature, for example, as an intelligible independent reality, which is the presupposition of all the natural sciences, can only be derived from our trust in the order of God's creation. For without assuming the intelligible ground of nature it would be impossible to place any reliance on the generalized results of our investigations. On the other hand if we adopt a purely exploitative, manipulative view of nature then it ceases to be a consistent coherent reality, and we very quickly lose sight of what it is we are studying.[20] Or even worse, we

---

19 'Tamworth', p. 190. 'If we attempt to effect a moral improvement by means of poetry, we shall but mature into a mawkish, frivolous, and fastidious sentimentalism;—if by means of argument, into a dry, unamiable longheadness;—if by good society, into a polished outside, with hollowness within, in which vice has lost its grossness, and perhaps increased its malignity;—if by experimental science, into an uppish, supercilious temper, much inclined to scepticism. But reverse the order of things: put Faith first and Knowledge second; let the University minister to the Church, and then classical poetry becomes the type of the Gospel truth, and physical science a comment on Genesis or Job, and Aristotle changes into Butler, and Arcesilas into Berkeley.' Ibid., pp. 190–1.

20 As our ability to create new forms of life advances, for example, it will become more difficult to distinguish between the natural and the unnatural and, in general, to prevent the different biological types from losing their identity in a common organic aggregation.

forget whom our actions were intended to benefit. The dehumanizing impact of technology arises chiefly because of a failure to consider the goals in relation to the ultimate ends of human existence.[21] Nor would we lack such moral guidance if we recognized that not everything about man can be explained away in terms of further factors. The truth of man's existence, far from being submerged forever in a morass of subjectivism, has already been apprehended by those gifted individuals whose spiritual advances have constituted the history of mankind. The great works of religion, philosophy, literature and art were not created as 'cultural masterpieces'; they are the symbolic forms in which such individuals elaborated the representative spiritual truth of their experiences. It is only by bringing a willingness to participate in the ethico-religious order created by them that their meaning will become transparent to us, and thereby provide the indispensable illumination for the problems of a scientific-technological society today.[22]

But to be convinced beyond a vague or general agreement on the need for a spiritual foundation to the secular disciplines of inquiry, we must be willing to follow Newman in his affirmation that spiritual truth is attainable and that its authoritative interpretation is possible, principally within the Church. He understood the difficulty well and recognized that he could have no impact on the modern world unless he was able to make his case persuasive to those who did not share his starting point. That is precisely the task he set himself in writing *An Essay in Aid of a Grammar of Assent*. It was to show how religious knowledge is possible, how we may distinguish between true and false varieties, and how the assent of faith is both eminently reasonable and beyond reason. He intended the work to be a demonstration of 'the *organum investigandi* given us for gaining religious truth, and which would lead the mind by an infallible succession from the rejection of atheism to theism, and from theism to Christianity, and from Christianity to Evangelical Religion, and from there to Catholicity' (*Grammar*, p. 499). It is therefore a key source to his views on the nature of spiritual truth and of the grounds for assenting to it. The ideas contained in the *Grammar* had been

'If truth be the power to change or to make the object studied, then of what do we have knowledge? If there are no fixed realities, but only material on which we may work our wills, will not "science" be merely the "knowledge" of the transient and the manipulable? We might indeed have knowledge of the laws by which things change and the rules for their manipulation, but no knowledge of the things themselves. Can such a view of "science" yield any knowledge about the nature of man, or indeed, about the nature of anything?' Kass, 'New Biology', p. 787. See also Eric Voegelin, 'The Origins of Scientism', *Social Research* 15 (1948), 462–94.

21 As a useful antidote we might consider Socrates' ironic remarks on how the navigator, who brings his passengers safely to port, will not feel he has done them any great service, 'aware as he is that he has put them ashore no better in either body or soul than when they embarked.' *Gorgias* 512a.

22 For a more extended discussion of this point see my 'Restoring the Lost Center of Education', *Thought* 58 (1983), 363–74.

part of Newman's thought for decades, but it was only in writing this work that they acquired a complete philosophical formulation. The result is a brilliant, and still underrated, resolution of the most perplexing epistemological objections to Christian faith, and an emphatic affirmation of the truth of Christianity that alone provides intellect with its foundation.

His argument begins be defining the nature of knowledge in general and then shows that religious knowledge is of essentially the same type. The first step was to prove that we do have knowledge of reality and that we are not confined solely to the results of probabilistic reasoning. This he was able to do through a psychological analysis of the nature of assent, the act that terminates the accumulation of evidence by affirming that a state of affairs exists. Unlike most modern philosophers Newman began by accepting the natural functioning of the human mind and insisted that it is illusory to think we can get behind it to any more fundamental mode of certainty. This freed him, as he explained, from the burden of 'devizing, what cannot be, some sufficient science of reasoning which may compel certitude in concrete conclusions, to confess that there is no ultimate truth besides the testimony born to truth by the mind itself' (p. 350). By this means he was able to expose the falsity of the dominant strands of modern empiricist and sceptical epistemology. For the testimony of our minds contradicts their conclusion of uncertain or merely probable knowledge: we are routinely certain of a great many truths and are only infrequently shown to be mistaken in them.

The unconditional nature of assent is the central discovery in Newman's analysis of human knowing. His recognition that 'there is no medium between assenting and not assenting', provided the basis for confidence in our common sense knowledge of truths 'which lie outside the narrow range of conclusions to which logic, formal or virtual, is tethered' (pp. 176, 179). Even when we assent only to the probable truth of a proposition it is not a certain degree of assent, but an absolute assent to the degree of its probability. What guides the giving or withholding of assent and thereby provides the criterion of truth is, on Newman's conception, the sense of certitude which he defines as 'a deliberate assent given expressly after reasoning' (p. 229). The sense of certitude is 'the bell of the intellect' although, like conscience which is the regulator of the will, it must be properly formed to do its function right. It is to this capacity of right judgment in reasoning that Newman gives the name 'Illative Sense' ('from good sense'). More fundamental than language or rules of inference, it is the ratiocinative mind itself for

> only under its penetrating and subtle action [does] the margin disappear, which I have described as intervening between verbal argumentation and conclusions in the concrete. It determines what science cannot determine, the limit of converging probabilities and the reasons sufficient for a proof. (p. 360)

In the final analysis it is not any principle of logic that enables us to make the leap of assent: it is the living mind determining itself for judgment.

Basically the same process occurs, Newman contends, in arriving at knowledge of transcendent reality. The combination and convergence of evidence for the existence of God and the truth of his revelation remains inconclusive, until a supervening act of assent brings the process of deliberation to a close. What is different about religious knowledge is that a divine formation of the will is an essential predisposition to the assent of faith. Reflecting on his own movement towards truth in the *Apologia*, Newman explained that God 'co-operates with us in our acting, and thereby enables us to do, and carries us on, if our will does but co-operate with His, to a certitude which rises higher than the logical force of our conclusions' (p. 157). This important restatement of the traditional *fides caritate formata* he attributes originally to Keble: 'It is faith and love which give to probability a force which it has not in itself.'[23] Indeed for Newman the preeminent source for our knowledge of God is conscience; the advance or decline in moral goodness is what provides the criterion of truth in religious matters. His 'general principle' is 'that no religion is from God which contradicts our sense of right and wrong' (*Grammar*, p. 419). Conscience is the connecting link between creature and Creator, for in its voice we recognize 'the One to whom we are responsible' and the living God in whom we move and breathe and have our being. The opening of the soul is required to lead us beyond rational deism to the full amplitude of Christian truth.

In contrast, the 'religion of civilization and of philosophy' is only a mockery because it is based on the autonomous self-confidence of closed human reason. It lacks the mark of authentic religion whose 'large and deep foundation is the sense of sin and guilt' (*Grammar*, p. 400). Only the latter puts us existentially in the presence of God, acknowledging the true offensiveness of our wrongdoing and preparing us to receive the redemptive divine revelation that alone can save. All genuine religion, Newman insists, originates in a self-revelation of the divine. 'The Religion of Nature has not been a deduction of reason … it has been a tradition or interposition vouchsafed to a people from above' (p. 404). There is no such thing as a religion of reason, although there is the natural religious experience of mankind that can provide a common starting point. It is universally characterized by the awareness of man's guilt and need of reconciliation as he stands before God. And while the sacrifices of natural religion do not fully answer this need, they are nevertheless indispensable in predisposing men to recognize the truth of God's ultimate redemptive action in Christ:

23 *Apologia*, p. 28. Newman considered this statement of the case to be insufficiently logical and preferred his own formulation that religious certitude was 'the result of an *assemblage* of concurring and converging possibilities' (p. 29). His fundamental agreement with Keble's conception is, however, emphasized in the motto of the *Grammar of Assent*: 'Non in dialectica complacuit Deo salvum facere populum suum.'

> Natural Religion is based upon the sense of sin; it recognizes the disease, but it cannot find, it does but look out for the remedy. That remedy, both for guilt and for moral impotence, is found in the central doctrine of Revelation, the Mediation of Christ. (p. 487)

The regenerating 'image of Christ' will be apprehended as the answer only by those whose questioning openness has already prepared them to receive it.

Having made the assent of faith, the love of God in Christ becomes the 'living truth' radiating its light over everything else. It provides us with an authoritative spiritual principle by means of which we may judge the rightness or wrongness, truth or falsity, of the multifarious intellectual developments that issue from the modern world. Convinced of the truth that endures, our spiritual and intellectual foundation remains unshaken in the face of apparent conflicts of science and religion or literature and faith. 'A thousand difficulties', Newman repeated, 'do not make a single doubt.' At the same time the light of faith enables us to recognize the presence of the Spirit in that Church whose fidelity to the original divine revelation calls forth our response of obedient submission to its wisdom. It is in the nature of revelation that 'an authoritative depositary of the things revealed will be found practically to be involved in that idea' (*Idea*, p. 335). From which it follows that the Church is the primary source for our understanding of revealed truth, and that 'reason rightly exercised leads the mind to the Catholic Faith, and plants it there, and teaches it in all its religious speculations to act under its guidance' (*Idea*, p. 137). This is, besides, consistent with the idea of a providential God who intervenes in human affairs and wishes to have the knowledge of himself authoritatively transmitted to every generation. What causes difficulty, as Newman recognized, was the claim of the Church to judge infallibly not only of religious matters but also 'to animadvert on opinions in secular matters which bear upon religion' (*Idea*, p. 197). He saw the danger of ecclesiastical encroachments on the independence of intellect and his response was simply to straightforwardly acknowledge it. He pointed out that such clashes do not issue in infallible pronouncements of doctrine, have generally turned out to be only pseudo-conflicts, and have neither within nor without the Church been sufficiently serious to diminish freedom of inquiry. Whatever the inconvenience of such occasional frictions may be in individual disciplines it is bound to be much less, in Newman's view, than the cost of spiritual disorientation in those many souls who 'in consequence of the confident tone of the schools of secular knowledge, are in danger of being led away into a bottomless liberalism of thought' (*Apologia*, p. 200).

The paradoxical conclusion is, therefore, that the free pursuit of truth, which conventionally presupposes liberation from the shackles of religious authority, is now recognized as best attained under such spiritual tutelage. In no other way can the spiritual first principles, which form the basis for all argument yet themselves are beyond argument, be preserved. The truth of spirit can only be intuited; it requires a voice that speaks with the transcendent authority of its source to win our unconditioned assent. But what, it will be objected, of those who do not or cannot make this assent? Newman's argument may be persuasive to those who share his own experience of faith; it is not clear how it can be regarded as normative for all inquirers alike in whatever field of study they pursue. How can he finally escape the charge of subjectivism, given his own admission that the assent of faith requires a divine cooperation of the will to bring the reasoning process to its conclusion? This is the difficulty involved in his defence of a spiritual oversight of the University and, in addition, explains why so many of the originally church related institutions have broken their connection with religion. There is no doubt that this is the fundamental objection which must be confronted if his project is to survive. Newman himself was willing to face it. It is largely due to his resolute honesty in struggling with it that he was able to make a convincing case for Catholic education at a time when the spiritual nature of education had already begun to be widely abandoned. If his achievement is to have continuing relevance today we must be willing to reflect anew on how the spiritual authority of the Church is commensurate with the intellectual authority of the academy.

As we have seen, part of Newman's response to this criticism has been a negative defence. The autonomous intellectual disciplines are incapable of grounding their own presuppositions, are perennially inclined to attach ultimate significance to their own perspective on reality, and frequently engage in the kind of sceptical analysis that undermines the foundations of morality and religion. Newman's predictions in this regard have been shown to be remarkably accurate, and this is clearly the part of his argument that is likely to evoke most widespread agreement. It is the positive expression of spiritual truth, of the Christian revelation, that is the source of greatest difficulty. There his strategy was to show that the assent of faith is not fundamentally different from the process of judging the truth or falsity of any statements about reality, although he acknowledged that the sufficiency of evidence was not to be attained through the accumulation of facts alone. It was necessary to appeal beyond them to the voice of God that is universal to human nature, the voice of conscience. In its imperious commands we can eventually discover the living presence of the One from whom its authority ultimately emanates. But this is not yet faith until the final component, of conversion wrought by divine grace, has brought about that definitive illumination by which we see all things differently.

Newman did not wish to go beyond this account into an exploration of spiritual experience because of his aversion to emotionalism within religion. He had seen how evangelical Christianity had played into the hands of atheism by admitting that knowledge of God was primarily to be obtained through feeling, and not through objective theological reflection. He wished to preserve dogmatic theology as a legitimate field of inquiry and indeed to emphasize it as the foremost science of reality. Yet how could this be if it rested on private experience of faith? Newman did not spell out concretely how this inner reality is related to the outer reality explored in the other modes of inquiry. What was required was an explanation of how spiritual knowledge is knowledge in the same sense as we have knowledge of the physical world or of social relationships. How can it be knowledge if its foundation is wholly within private experience? The answer of course is to deny the exclusively private status of faith, as Newman did in part by referring to the universal nature of conscience. The experience is not radically private if it is in fact a universal dimension of the human condition.

What Newman did not do was to explain how those modes of experience differ. The realities to which the symbols of spiritual experience refer, God, man, sin, grace and redemption, do not exist as self-contained entities in the external world. It is this non-objective status, in the sense of non-visible, non-tangible quality, that is often taken to indicate their unreality and hence their purely subjective source. But this is not so. Indeed, religious experience invariably leads to the opposite conclusion—that it is the solid material reality of the external world that is unreal compared to the preeminent reality of transcendent Being. The appropriate inference is that the conditions for experiencing transcendent reality are different from those for apprehending immanent existence. Divine reality becomes present only through our participation in its ordering force; it is only to the extent that we are already willing to carry out its commands that we are capable of hearing the voice of God. It is this participatory character of spiritual experience that makes its communication problematic, for the symbols are meaningless unless we have experienced the reality to which they refer or are sufficiently open to engage in an imaginative reenactment of the experience. Yet at the same time religious symbols are not wholly opaque even to those without the underpinning experience. The experiential participation in their reality is the result of a meditative unfolding of the questions that are constitutive of human nature in every time and place.[24]

An awareness of this relationship is indicated in Newman's remarks on natural religion which he adamantly refused to identify with any form of rational deism. However, he did not elaborate on the consequences of this recognition, of which the first is that his own insistence on moral and spiritual formation is shown to be, not only desirable, but an essential ingredient in any educational process that is to include an acquaintance with the divine. Without a personal relationship we have have no knowledge of that to which the symbols refer. The second consequence is that Christian faith is not the insular concern of a fraction of mankind within the course of history. It is one form of the divine-human encounter that can be placed on a continuum of equivalent experiences which embraces all of the religions of

24   See Eric Voegelin, 'Immortality: Experience and Symbol', *Harvard Theological Review* 60 (1967); also *Anamnesis*, trans. and ed. Gerhart Niemayer (Notre Dame, 1978).

the world, including atheism. For they are all more or less adequate unfoldings of the divine-human relationship that is already present with the question of the ground of all that is. The third consequence is a fuller explanation for Newman's own recognition of the need for an institutional interpreter of the truth of revelation. It is because the source of faith lies in this participatory experience that its content must be protected by dogmatic formulation within the Church; the continual danger of distortion through the over-reaching of those not willing to enter by way of divine submission makes such a defence essential. There is both a constant temptation to possess spiritual truth as external fact and an equally constant response of sceptical critique of the spiritually bankrupt symbolism that results. Authoritative judgment must be exercised and it can scarcely be effective without an institutional base.

Further explication is needed, in other words, if Newman's analysis is to make sense in the contemporary setting, although such elaboration is no more than following out the direction he has already indicated. For above all Newman stands as a leading example of the engagement of faith with the problems of the modern world. Secure in his conviction that all truths are reflections of the one Truth, he was tolerant of the multiplicity of apparent contradictions, and free to work for that spiritual regeneration through the power of 'Grace' or the 'Word' that 'by which ever name we call it, has been from the first a quickening, renovating, organizing principle' in the life of man ('Tamworth', p. 187). He was not afraid to 'swim in troubled waters', but neither did he underestimate the nature of the challenge before him. He knew the extent to which he was going against the impetus of modern civilization, that like St Philip Neri his best hope was 'to yield to the stream, and direct the current, which he could not stop, of science, literature, art and fashion, and to sweeten and to sanctify what God had made very good and man had spoilt' (*Idea*, p. 179). He was enough of a realist to recognize that the exposition of error cannot reverse the direction of an historical movement. And by any measure his practical accomplishments can only be classified as modest. They included such notable failures as his educational reforms at Oxford, his attempted reform of the Anglican Church, and the eventual demise of the Catholic University of Ireland. Yet he retained a philosopher's conviction that inefficacy does not in any way diminish his obligation to bear witness to the truth. He knew that the secular world must sooner or later come to recognize the spiritual need within itself that is its own deepest truth.

> People say to me, that it is but a dream to suppose that Christianity should regain the organic power in society which once it possessed. I cannot help that; I never said it could. I am not a politician; I am proposing no measures, but exposing a fallacy, and resisting a pretence. Let Benthamism reign, if men have no aspirations; but do not tell them

to be romantic, and then solace them with glory; do not attempt by philosophy what once was done by religion. The ascendency of Faith may be impracticable, but the reign of Knowledge is incomprehensible. The problem for statesmen of this age is how to educate the masses, and literature and science cannot give the solution. ('Tamworth', p. 203)

Hope and History*

JOSEF PIEPER

In the last decade of the eighteenth century—the decade of the French Revolution—someone asked the question: whether the Human Race is continually advancing towards the Better. This 'someone' was Immanuel Kant. Considered abstractly, there are, he says, three possible answers to this question; nothing is already decided, at least so it seems. First, Yes, we are advancing; second, No, we are declining; third, history takes its course more or less on the same level. Now one of these possible answers is immediately eliminated without discussion—the second: 'retrogression to the worse' (as he calls it). This is simply inconceivable for Kant. Why? Because this would imply that mankind might 'blot itself out'; and precisely this, for the man of the eighteenth century, is a manifestly unthinkable notion. Exactly the same idea, on the contrary, has become for the man of this modern epoch not only conceivable and arguable but immediately acute. 'Man's existence now, and for the first time, is threatened'—that is the first statement of a paper given at a symposium in London in 1962 on 'Man and his Future'. And of course, the most striking argument is the actual destructibility of man by his own weapons. This has been said many times in the historical or philosophical literature of recent years.

This knowledge gives us from the outset such a superiority over the man of the eighteenth century (according to Kierkegaard's grim remark: he who is deluded is wiser than he who is not deluded)—that it might not seem very fair to debate this matter with Kant. Is it not that he was simply unable to conceive the selfdestruction of man as even technically possible? True, but the nature of historical man has not changed since Adam—or should I say Cain. By the way, I have used the term 'modern epoch'; epoch sounds all too deceptively like long duration and it may give the likewise deceptive impression of academic neutral distance; it conceals somewhat the explosiveness of our situation which may suddenly change, from one moment to the next, into catastrophe. Nobody will—as Konrad Lorenz says—predict 'a long life' for man, when he looks at him as he is today: the hydrogen bomb in his hands, which he has received as a gift of his reason, and the instinct of agression which that same reason is unable to master. At the London symposium which I already mentioned, it was said repeatedly: 'These are not long-term problems, they are upon us now.'

It goes without saying, in this situation the question 'Hope and History' has got an unprecedented urgency. But what actually does this question

---

* Agnes Cuming Lecture, Department of Metaphysics, University College Dublin, 22 April 1986.

mean exactly? The problem 'Hope and History' indeed may be viewed under several different aspects. I should like to mention only two of them. Firstly, does it belong or not to the nature of human hope to possibly reach its fulfilment in the field of history? Can what man is hoping for possibly be realized in history? Secondly, does the course of human history actually foster and encourage the hope of man; in other words is it possible, without any intellectual dishonesty, not to despair, looking at human history?

But before we go into any further discussion, it has to be stated as clearly as possible what we shall understand by 'hope' and what by 'history'.

What then do people mean whenever they speak of hope and hoping? The first element is certainly expectation. But it is possible to expect something which I do not hope for. I can also expect something indifferent and irrelevant or even something terrible; but I speak of hope only if longing and desire are involved. I hope only for something good ('good' in a very wide sense: good weather; 'how good that you have come!'). Yet, longing and desire alone do not make hope. Possibly I may yearn after something which I know I shall never get, which means after something I am not really hoping for. Hope implies confidence and even a kind of certainty. Of course, there is also futile hope, and there are hopes that are disappointed in the end. But in the very moment in which I become sure of the fruitlessness of my hope, I cease hoping. This, by the way, is the reason why joy belongs— if not to the essence of hope—then to its permanent company. Hope aims at the attainment of what we love, therefore it cannot be without joy.

In a German philosophical dictionary I found as a first description of hope: *freudige Erwartung*, joyful expectation. This certainly is very much to the point, although it is far from a complete characterization of what everybody actually understands by hope. It may well be that I expect something desired, something wished-for with confidence and joy, and nevertheless nobody would speak of hope! There is a famous German poem which begins 'Come, peaceful night, world's comfort, come . . . ' I could possibly say this from the depth of my heart—but of course it would be nonsense to speak of hope here. Nobody hopes for nightfall. I cannot hope for anything that will happen anyway, with necessity.

Also, whatever may be reached easily and without much trouble cannot be really an object of human hope. The ancients spoke of the *bonum arduum*, the 'steep good', that is, something that does not lie within my grasp; something I may possibly fail to attain. At this point yet another element of the concept of hope comes into view: the object of hope is not at the disposal of the one who hopes. Nobody hopes for something which he is able to make or procure himself; and if so, we do not speak of hope. We need only take a look at everyday usage: I hope the train will arrive in time; let us hope the weather will be fine tomorrow; it is to be hoped that our friend will regain his health; we hope that there will be no World War III—and so on. One thing is completely clear in all of these expressions: what we are hoping for is not at our disposal. If an artist who is about to transform his idea into a material work of stone or wood, perhaps verses, says: I hope I shall succeed in doing so— then he is expressing, quite correctly, the fact that this does not depend on himself alone; or when a joiner tells me: I hope the desk or bookcase will be delivered within the agreed time—he expresses, again quite correctly, that he is depending on several circumstances and other people outside his range of influence. I should like to extend this example a little further; if this same joiner, after a long discussion on the very special shape of that desk or bookcase, were to say: I hope I shall succeed in making the desk exactly according to our outline—well, I think, I had better take on another joiner, since nobody speaks of hope at all if he really is able to make something by himself. A father may say to his high school son: I hope next year you will be much more diligent; but if the son were to answer: I hope so too—that would just be cheeky nonsense. All of which, taken together, signifies something rather serious; I quote Gabriel Marcel: 'The only genuine hope is directed towards something that does not depend on ourselves.'

Human language however, spoken and understood by everyone, has *in petto* some more, perhaps unexpected, insights. In Plato's *Symposium*, Diotima speaks of the strange phenomenon that although there are many makers, only one maker is called simply *the* maker, *poietes*, the poet. Similarly, she continues, with the linguistic scope of 'love': there are many kinds of love, love of parents, love of friends, love of one's native country and so on; but if you simply speak of lovers you do not mean those who love their country or their parents; you mean those who love in the sense of Eros. And I think that again something similar is verified in the case of hope. Countless different things, from fine weather for a vacation to peace in the world, can be objects of hope—and in fact they are. Nevertheless, there seems to be again only one object, the hope for which makes a man simply and so to speak absolutely hopeful. Perhaps the inverse viewpoint may make things clearer. There are a thousand hopes which man may give up and which may be dashed or buried—without man's becoming necessarily hopeless in the absolute sense. Apparently, there is again only *one* single hope, the hope for one thing, the loss of which would make a man plainly hopeless, purely destitute of hope. The question is: what sort of hope is this? For what must man have lost hope, so that it might be correctly said: he is simply without hope and plainly hopeless?

In order to be able to answer, or even to discuss this question adequately, we have to consider a distinction for which neither the English nor the German language has the terms, in contrast with French which distinguishes between *espoir* and *espérance*. One German philosopher suggests a distinction between 'hope' (singular) and 'hopes' (plural)—which does not seem bad. The enormous relevance of this fundamental distinction, however it may be named, comes to light as a result of the findings of modern medical psychology. I am speaking of the very exact phenomenological investigations which were made some years ago at the University Hospital of Heidelberg by Professor Herbert Plügge. For years Plügge concerned himself with the psychological situation of people for whom hope had become questionable in a very decisive way, namely with the situation of incurables, of people who had just learned that they were terminally ill; and also with the mental condition of people who had tried to commit suicide. In the course of this purely empirical investigation, Herbert Plügge caught sight—as he puts it—of a quite different hope; different from what he then called ordinary, common and everyday hopes (plural again!), this new hope is singular; Plügge calls it the 'fundamental' or 'genuine' hope. Ordinary hopes are directed towards objects that belong to the world, towards something which we are expecting from somewhere else, towards news, success or physical health—whereas fundamental hope has no object of this kind; you cannot point to it with your finger, and it is rather difficult to describe. Moreover, fundamental hope seems to come about only if ordinary hopes are disappointed. But of course, *the* hope (singular) also does have an object. Plügge says that this object does not belong to those things that man can *have*; it has to do with what man himself *is*; the object is self-realization in the future or personal wholeness.

One main point however—I am quoting Herbert Plügge—is that genuine hope comes into existence out of the loss of ordinary hopes. Disappointment means here: to become free from and to get rid of an illusion. The illusion which, perhaps from the beginning, nobody is able to avoid consists—or consisted—in the belief that the wholeness of existence implies the attainment of certain material goods, including bodily health; whereas disappointment all of a sudden enables us to realize what we perhaps already knew 'theoretically': namely, that not only does the true wholeness of man consist in something else but also, that we ourselves in fact hope for this 'something else' with a much more vital and even with an invincible power of soul. And yet, disappointment means far more than the correction of an error. Plügge speaks of 'liberation'. The definite experience of incurability, he says, makes possible a freedom from the captivity of illness, which could not possibly be attained before the breakdown. The relevance of these findings, I think, goes far beyond the immediate topic of Plügge's investigation: after all, as regards our final outcome in death we are all without exception in the same position. Every deep disappointment of a hope, which had been directed towards something within this world, possibly conceals within it the chance that *the* hope (singular) without any resignation—this is important—might turn to its true object and that, in an act of liberation, a larger breathing space within existence might be opened up and entered into. Precisely in disappointment, and perhaps in disappointment alone, do we receive the invitation, which we certainly are not bound to follow, to enter this greater area of existence, the realm of *the* hope.

The question may be raised, of course, whether *the* hope, fundamental hope, cannot perhaps be also disapointed, Surprisingly, it appears that the answer to this question must actually be: 'no', *the* hope cannot be disappointed! Man may lose it, he may give it up or put it aside—which should then properly be called, not disappointment but despair. Disappointment can never happen to *the* hope. And why not? Where is it written?—The answer I think should start from a clearer understanding of what 'disappointment' means. It means the positive experience of fruitlessness and of non-fulfilment. Now this experience can never be made in the case of *the* hope—because the time-span of waiting for the event of fulfilment (or non-fulfilment) is exactly identical with the time-span of life itself. Despair does not mean that hope actually has been disappointed, rather despair is the anticipation of such a disappointment; to despair means to anticipate non-fulfilment. The moment, in which the true result of human existence is revealed, remains imminent precisely as long as that same existence endures. There is not one moment in life in which a man, be he a hundred years old or at the threshold of death, would be allowed, or even able to say: now I am no longer 'on the way', fulfilment lies no longer in the future, I already possess whatever has been intended for me.

To put it another way: man's existence itself has the structure of 'not yet'; I could say also: it has the structure of hope.

Now, it is not hard to see that this hope-structure of man's existence has to do with his historicity, that is to say, with the quality by reason of which man is able to have history. History could even be called the field of man's hope (and hopes).

At this point we should clarify what we understand by history. The German word *Geschichte* is derived from *Geschehen*, which means 'to happen'; history is that which happens. But apparently not all that happens is history; there are also non-historical happenings. That water flows, that lightning strikes, the turn of the tide—all that is not history. It has been said that an event, even such a natural event, becomes a strictly historical one as soon as it comes into relation with man. This is true to some extent. But not even all that happens to man himself automatically makes his history. That we are born, grow up, age and die—this is not, strictly speaking, our history. And not even what we encounter in our life—be it a person (a teacher, a loved one, an adversary); be it loss or gain of fortune, health or beauty; what we possess by birth (talents, temper, strength or weakness)—all this is not our history either, not yet. Our history is what we make of all this; our history is the union of what happens and of what we ourselves do in response. An event becomes strictly historical whenever freedom, responsibility and decision come into play, also the possibility of guilt and error.

This again is the reason why historical events cannot be deduced or calculated; they cannot be derived from what is already known. This, among others, makes the difference between history and evolution. And I should say that this very difference is in danger of being obscured and forgotten in our contemporary discussions. But it is exactly this difference which is important with regard to hope. In a brief formula it could be said: with hope and evolution there is no problem at all; the problem is: hope and history.

I once had the honour of having Pierre Teilhard de Chardin among my listeners, at a lecture given in Paris in 1951. Unfortunately I did not know this at the time; I only learned it ten years later, when I also learned that Teilhard de Chardin passionately rejected my thesis. My topic was 'The Hope of the Martyrs', *l'Espérance des Martyrs*. And I was especially anxious to make one thing clear: that there is no point in speaking of human hope at all if there is no hope left for the martyr, that is, for him, whose innerworldly hopes have become totally and absolutely groundless and who, in the common meaning of the word, is in a hopeless situation—in the concentration camp, about to be executed, left alone, ridiculed—and so on. I did not suppress either that nowhere is it written, that the situation of the martyr has to be an exception which may only take place here and there, especially in remote times and countries. Teilhard, as I said, rejected vehemently as defeatism even the way of putting the whole question. The decisive point is quite a different one—as Teilhard says (in a letter published later in his biography); the decisive question is: whether there is, for man, biocosmically (*biocosmiquement*) a right to hope beyond all sentimentality, philosophy and mysticism; the decisive point is that, in terms of its evolutionary potential, mankind is objectively young and full of future.

Now this is exactly what I call confounding history and evolution. Of course there is evolution, that is, the development and unfolding of what was already there, still enveloped and enfolded both in the realm of the specifically human and also in the realm of the intellectual life! In the earliest clutch of pre-historic man at the powers of nature and in the very first use of any energy of the material cosmos there was something still undeveloped, which then consistently, and even to some degree automatically, over man's head, has been unfolded, up to the conquest of atomic energy. And there is no doubt at all that mankind will develop and immensely improve all its achievements in this field. Regarding this possibility of progress we certainly may look forward to the time to come with composure, confidence and hope. Also with hope? At this point we hesitate. In fact we are not at all confident or hopeful and calm—facing the growing perfection for instance of nuclear weapons. And this nervousness has its reason in something quite different from any disbelief in the evolutionary potentiality of human technological intelligence; it has its reason in the anxiety about what man, as a moral being, may actually do with this immeasurable power and for which purpose he may use it.

At this point, I think, the difference between history and evolution becomes absolutely obvious. In Teilhard's main work, *The Phenomenon of Man*, there is one sentence, in which both aspects are linked: 'If mankind takes advantage of the immense duration it has before it, it has enormous possibilites before it.' Now, the potential of immeasurable possibilities (mankind is still young!)—this is the aspect of *evolution*! On the other hand, the 'if' (if mankind makes use of its possibilities)—this is the aspect of *history*. But what actually happens and what will happen, that will be decided not in the field of evolution but in the field of history. And nothing but this is of immediate concern to us; this is a question of life and death. After all, the question of the biological potentiality of mankind does not prevent us from sleeping; but the question of our historical future does! We are always faced with this question.

At the same time, however, it is clear that there is an enormous difference with regard to the answerability of both questions. It might be quite possible to find out scientifically whether mankind, as a species, is still young; but how can we possibly find out, whether mankind, hoewever young, will one day erradicate itself? Here freedom and decision are at play; and that is why there will never be any calculable certainty about man's historical future, even if the methods of statistical prognosis may be perfected as much as possible. Certainly, it was possible to predict rather exactly, some years in advance, how many fatal traffic accidents there would be in the city of Danzig in April 1945—but that the very city of Danzig would scarcely exist at this time and that there would be no traffic at all there—this could not be predicted, at least not on the basis of statistics. There is in Pascal's *Pensées* a remarkable aphorism; it is decipherable only if you consider the year in which it was written. The aphorism runs: 'Could anyone, enjoying the friendship of the King of England, the King of Poland and the Queen of Sweden have believed that he might be without refuge and asylum in the whole world?' 1656! This was the year the King of Poland was deposed; two years before, the Queen of Sweden had abdicated; and the King of England had been executed seven years earlier. No refuge any more!

The truly historical event, concrete in every respect (when? where? who?)—but this is of interest only to the person concerned!—the historical event cannot be foreseen at all in prognosis. For this, a kind of prediction is necessary which would not depend on the knowledge of some 'footholds' in the past or in the present—as all prognostication does; for the art of prognosis consists in discovering in the fund of experience itself pointers to the future. With this I have already given a kind of negative definition of prophecy, which if there is such, is the only prediction which could possibly grasp a future historical event. As I said, it belongs to the essence of history that it cannot be deduced from what has been before; now prophecy, by its very nature, is a kind of prediction, which does not refer to anything that has been before.

The question is, whether there is strictly prophetic information about the historical future. If not, it is meaningless to make any conjectures on how history might go on or even how it might end.

This is the quite respectable reason for the deep mistrust with which we take notice of visions of the future, proclaimed with more or less certainty in the realm of science, philosophy, social religions etc. How are we to know that the human race is in fact continually advancing to the Better? How is anyone to know that man's effort to change the world, socialistically or not, will actually bring about the Golden Age, the *regnum humanum*, the kingdom of liberty—and so on. Who really knows anything about it?

But this is only one objection. The other doubt that comes to mind in considering all those visionary expectations is even more to the point; it has to do quite directly with the topic of hope. In all those visions of the future, not a single word is said about *death*. I am not speaking here of a metaphysical theory of death or such; no, I am speaking of the very simple fact that we shall be dead before the Golden Age will have come. At the London symposium of 1962 I already spoke of, Hilary Koprowski, Professor of Medical Research of the University of Pennsylvania (when you take a closer look at the biographical appendix, you will notice that he is a Polish immigrant, bearing on his shoulders the burden of the old Europe)— Professor Koprowski ironically called into question all the optimistic planning which thrived to excess in the climate of that convention; he reminds his listeners of the fact of death, quoting the poet E. E. Cummings: 'It is funny, you will be dead some day'; and he also quotes the old epitaph *Et in Arcadia Ego*, which does not mean 'I too have been in Arcadia' but: 'Even in Arcadia am I, Death!' And I think he intended to say: What about Arcadia and the Golden Age so long as there is such a thing called Death? 'Salvation is vain—unless it delivers us from death'; this is a sentence by Gabriel Marcel which I immediately understand and subscribe to—whereas I do not understand one single word of what Ernst Bloch has to say on this same topic: that the certainty of class consciousness is 'a herb against death'. Of course, there is no expectation that death could ever be put out of the world. And, of course, I do not say that it would be absurd to hope as long as the person hoping must die. By the way, death does not happen to the universe, to society, to evolution, but exclusively to the individual person. Hope also is not performed by any subject other than the individual person. I repeat: I do not say that hope is meaningless so long as there is death—no conception whatsoever of a future state of mankind, which simply leaves death out of account, that man's destiny is to die, can ever claim seriously to be an object of human hope at all. Of course, I may cultivate some prognostic ideas of what people will do on this planet, let us say, two hundred years from now (trips to the moon; pocket-sized electronic means of communication; raising the average lifespan by ten or twenty years etc.); and I may rightly become enthusiastic about these results of human intelligence and courage. But: how and in what sense could I place my hope in all that? It concerns me in so far as I am curious, interested in the future, eager for knowledge; but it does not concern me in so far as I hope. The hoping person is not one who wants to know something; he is one who wants to receive something that is good, to partake of *the* good.

Everybody knows the polemical phrase: 'to feed with hopes of the beyond' (*Jenseitsvertröstung*). This phrase occurs a hundred times in Marxist literature and is not very far from the famous 'opium of the people'—the phrase implies, as you know, the charge that one diverts the attention of the exploited from promoting their just interests by telling them of the glory of Heaven. I do not say that this never happened or that it may not happen again. But I insist on this: if those decidedly innerworldly pictures of the future simply leave death and the other side of death out of consideration— our own future, impending for all of us—they are themselves a merely abstract and deceptive consolation; and, in an exact inversion of the usual phrase, it is they which turn the people's attention to something which indeed is absolutely 'beyond' their real life. The only future which in fact has already begun, is the life on the other side of death (as Karl Rahner has said). This does not mean, not at all, that the earthly history of man and mankind do not concern the hoping individual; but it does mean that if earthly history is to possibly concern my hope (*the* hope of mine), it has to be thought of in connection with my own destiny on the other side of death.

How then are we to conceive of the historical future of man? I said, if there is no legitimate prophecy, nobody knows anything. Now, Christians are convinced that such strictly prophetic information on history exists indeed; among their sacred books there is, for instance, the Apocalypse. But it lies in the nature of a prophecy not to be just a plain description of what will happen in the future; a prophecy does not deprive the time to come of its character of being really future; it still remains unknown to us. John Henry Newman said: 'The event is the true key to prophecy.' On the other hand there certainly *is* something which we really get to know by accepting a legitimate prophecy as truth.

But what is it that we get to know? First of all we are confirmed in an insight, which our own thinking is able to reach: that man's history will not come to its fulfilment in the way of a continuous process of evolution. Even at the heart of universal history it is the frontier of death which separates mankind from its own perfection. Even Teilhard de Chardin, although enthusiastically convinced of the absolute future of the universe, speaks of a point of dissolution (*point de dissociation*), through which evolution must go in order to come to perfection. Immanuel Kant, in his last years, speaks much more realistically and more clearly to this point, in his pondering essay 'The End of All Things'. This end—the essay begins—apparently has to be thought in analogy to the death of the individual, which in devout language he says—far from ironically—is usually called a transition out of time into eternity. In this conception there is, Kant says, something horrible and at the same time inviting; this is the reason why man cannot cease turning his terrified eyes on it always anew. One thing is again, I think, altogether evident: this step out of time can never be imagined as a gradual continuous development, but rather as a kind of rupture and destruction—again in analogy to human dying which also looks more like destruction than progress and fulfilment. And if fulfilment and consummation are really attained through breakdown, and together with it, this happens not only in a hidden way, but against every appearance—this is indeed what we believe of the 'good' human death and also above all, of the paradigmatic death in the fullness of time: no observer could have found out what in truth has happened here.

Whoever considers this, may be prepared to accept a further and even more important message included in the Apocalyptic prophecy; and he will no longer be inclined to take it as something absurd, even if terrifying. The message is this: that human history within time (this is important!) will not end with the plain triumph of the true and the good nor with the clear victory of reason and justice, but with something, which again may be hardly distinguished from a catastrophe—not a cosmic one but a historical catastrophe, consisting in a gigantic pseudo-order, upheld and guaranteed by political power, a world tyranny of evil.

Although the modern mind, taking notice of this, may first be about to rebel, in fact such a gloomy expectation is quite familiar to the historical thinking of our epoch. Friedrich Nietzsche for instance, passionately interested in the topic of 'the future' (his major work, which was never completed, was to have been entitled: What is coming?)—Nietzsche copied in his (post-humously published) notebook a quotation from Baudelaire under the heading 'Further Evolution of Mankind'; Baudelaire for his part speaks of an imminent 'phantom of order', as he calls it, established by the political power with the help of violent measures which 'would make present-day humanity shudder, apathetic though it has become'. A modern politician, legitimated by an especially intimate knowledge of totalitarian regimes, Hermann Rauschning (formerly president of the Senate of Danzig, today farmer somewhere in the United States), thinks it altogether possible that there might emerge a world civilization of materialistic gratification based upon progressive dehumanization under the totalitarian monopoly of power, held by a World Grand Inquisitor. The term 'Grand Inquisitor' calls to mind the name of another great European, who likewise had a presentiment of what was to come: Dostoevsky. And indeed, in his 'Legend of the Grand Inquisitor' we read the bewildering statement: 'In the end they will lay their freedom at our feet and say to us: Make us your slaves, but feed us.' Perhaps I should also quote the fierce remark from the 'Ungarbled Thoughts' of the Polish intellectual Stanislaus Lec: 'I should have to laugh if they hadn't finished the destruction of the world—before the end of the world.'

But our objective is not to discuss modern visions of the historical future; we are still asking what prophetic information might be attainable about the end of history. Of course, there would be little sense in attempting a private interpretation of the Apocalypse; instead we should find out what the serious theology of today has to say on this point. It is true that modern theologians react rather laconically as soon as the question of the end of the world or even of the Antichrist comes up. There is little tangible truth at hand, remarks Karl Rahner. But if you look closer at the little they actually say, you get a rather clear answer. The answer goes like this (I am quoting modern theological handbooks and dictionaries, Catholic and Protestant): the antagonistic character of history will be intensified at the end; an extreme concentration of the energy of evil and a vehemence is to be expected, never known before in the fight against Christ and Christianity (and against all men of good will, Thomas Aquinas said in the thirteenth century); the *potentia saecularis* of the Antichrist is called 'the strongest world power in history', and so on. I think this alarming message cannot be easily ignored. Its implications certainly are manifold; but one thing again is made unmistakably clear: it is impossible to think of the end of history as the crowning and harmonious conclusion of an uninterrupted and continuous though perhaps difficult and dialectic advancement—although, as Teilhard de Chardin rightly says, this would be much more in harmony with 'theory' and certainly not only with the theory of evolutionism but also with Marxism and the idealistic philosophy of Progress.

The conception of history behind the Apocalypse is thoroughly different. Because in this conception not only human freedom, even freedom for evil, is taken seriously, but also 'the evil one' is considered to be a demonic power of history—therefore conflict, frustration, failure, irreconcilable discord and even catastrophe cannot be foreign to the essence of human history, not even in its normal course.

Nevertheless, this is not the last word of the Apocalypse; of course not. The last word and the decisive message is, in spite of all, a blissful ending beyond all expectation; triumph over evil, victory over death, quenching of thirst at the source of life, resurrection, God's dwelling with men, New Heaven and New Earth (all these terms and images are taken from the Apocalypse). In all of this something is also clearly said about hope; true hope cannot be touched or paralysed by Man's being prepared for an inner-worldly catastrophic end—whether this end is called dying, martyrdom, defeat of the good or world dominion of evil.

But now the two previous questions, both of them, are coming back in their full sharpness. Has it not come true, that human history is a matter of despair? Or what reasons for hope could possibly be furnished by history? Further, does it not really belong to the nature of human hope, of 'the' hope (singular) that it can never be satisfied within the field of history.

This last question indeed has been answered meanwhile. If this worldly human existence itself has the structure of 'not yet', and if man as a pilgrim is really 'on the way', up to the moment of his death—then this hope, identical with our existence itself, is either thoroughly absurd or it will find its final fulfillment on the other side of death, 'beyond' the here and now.

Nevertheless, the charge of a secluded 'beyondness' would absolutely miss the point—for several reasons. These reasons, however, can be made evident,

I am afraid, only to Christians. This does not mean that wrong ideas of hope do not also exist among Christians, especially wrong ideas of its 'beyondness'. But in this case Christians misunderstand themselves. However, it might possibly be expected that non-Christians may just take notice of the Christian arguments on this point.

First of all, it is not true—as Friedrich Engels and the Marxists maintain—that Christian hope aims at the perfection of a separate history of the Kingdom of God, beside 'real' history, which Christians allegedly declare to be meaningless. The opposite is true. It is precisely *this* worldly creation: the creation before our eyes—the perfection of which, however, we expect will be achieved through death and disaster; the kingdom of God will be realized nowhere but in the midst of historical mankind. It is true that nobody can know what in fact 'resurrection' and 'New Earth' mean concretely. But what else could they mean if not this: that not the least jot will ever be lost of anything that in the world's history is good, true, beautiful, genuine, and just.

Above all—this is the second point—Christians are convinced that the frontier of death between here and beyond has in a certain sense already been overcome, from the other side, namely by that event signified by the theological term 'incarnation'.

One of the recurring symbols in which men have tried to make clear to themselves the quintessence of what they are hoping for is: the Great Banquet. Plato, too, uses this metaphor; and I think this should not be forgotten. He reminds us not only of the *synousia*, the common life of God and man on the other side of death; he describes also the banquet in which the soul participates, outside of time and in a supercelestial place, as a guest of the gods, satisfied by the contemplation of the highest Being. Christians could not say it much better; indeed, they say it not very differently. But Plato, for his part, could not have the least inkling of that community around God's table, in which Christendom recognizes and celebrates the anticipation and the real beginning of the Great Banquet on the other side of death. From the earliest time this anticipation has been called *synaxis, communio,* communion—which not only means communion with God, but also mutual community among men—a community which is misunderstood and misused, if it is not conceived and realized as an alliance from which nobody must be excluded by any arbitrary restriction. I think a better and deeper foundation of human solidarity cannot be conceived. But it is also true that wherever the true solidarity of men is realized, or even longed for, this universal banquet, knowingly or not, is being prepared, no matter what the key-words: democracy, realm of freedom, classless society, provided— this is very important—that dictatorship and discrimination (even the liquidation of others) is not likewise on the programme; for in that case everything is corrupt from the beginning.

The connection with our topic 'hope' is closer than it might seem. Namely, wherever, and by whomever, the realization of fraternity among men is recognized and pursued as the essence of what we are hoping for, there is *eo ipso* an underlying connection to the elementary hope of Christendom.

The great tradition of Christian theology has always said: a non-Christian, who is convinced that God, in a manner that pleases Him, will be the deliverer of man, believes by an 'implicit faith' in Christ. I think we should also speak correspondingly of an implicit hope.

Thus, whoever summons all the energy of his hope for a perfect human community (to come?), in which man is man to his neighbour and no longer a wolf (as Ernst Bloch puts it) and the goods of life are justly distributed, is particpating in the hope of Christendom. And the implicitly faithful non-Christian, who often enough outrivals the declared Christian by his living and serious faith, may likewise surpass him by the ardour of his hope—whose 'religious' absoluteness (contrary, perhaps, to his own manifesto) seems to show how much the expectation is aimed at something that cannot be brought about by any human activity of changing the world.

On the other hand, such correspondences can only be perceived from the side of explicit faith and hope. To put it more agressively: if Christians do not perceive those underlying conformities and call them by their proper names, nobody in the world will perceive them; which means that they will remain mute and without any historical effect. Everybody knows how much there is still to do in this field.

But correspondences and conformities do not yet mean identity. And the distinction of Christianity is also an everlasting task. And in conclusion I should make a short remark on one of the points of difference, namely on the non-fixability of the object of hope (of *the* hope).

Gabriel Marcel several times formulates the profound insight that *the* hope always reaches beyond the objects which originally kindled it; and that *the* hope loses its finest quality as soon as man makes conditions, and even as soon as he tries to imagine concretely what he is hoping for.

True hope keeps itself open for a fulfilment which surmounts every thinkable human plan. Whoever is living in this true hope will direct the energy of his heart not so much towards the militant carrying through of defined plans, or eschatological visions of order (by which as everybody knows, the solidarity of mankind has too often been trampled upon); on the contrary, he will direct the energy of his heart towards the daily realization of what is 'now' good and just. I surmise that this might be the true and the most human form of all historical activity. This surmise has nothing to do with any reluctance regarding the radicalism of great political decisions and even less with any lack of confidence in the future of human history. But it does have to do with the mistrust of any limitation and fixation of the object of our hope.

The reason for this mistrust has been formulated very adequately by the great German poet Konrad Weiss. He says: every attempt to outline a fixed image of the future of mankind is burdened with the heavy paradox that 'it is not mankind which is the goal of the Incarnation.'

Index